100 Y[obscured]
Lo[obscured]
Twent[obscured] [obscured]tures

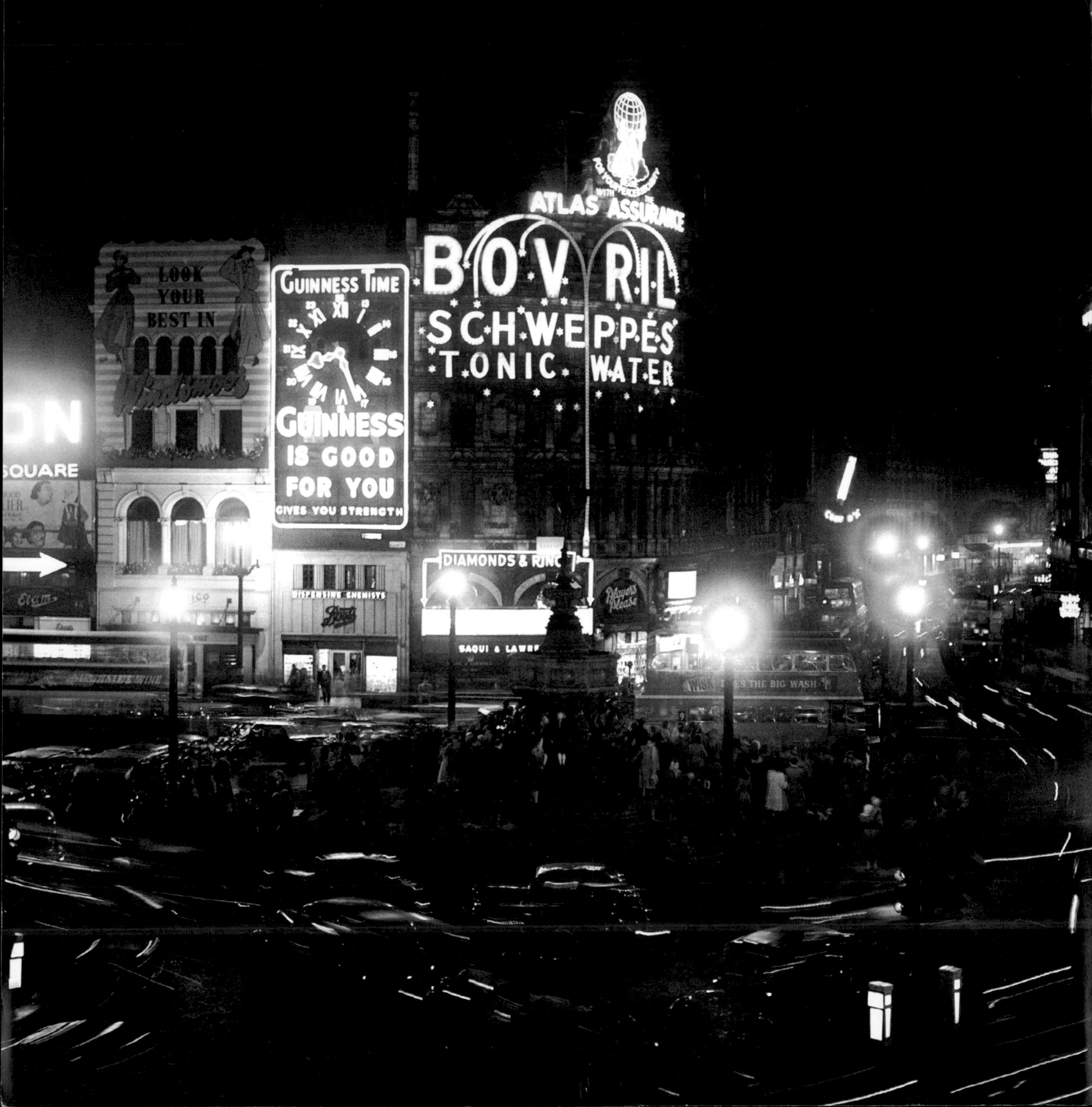

ATLAS ASSURANCE
BOVRIL
SCHWEPPES
TONIC WATER
GUINNESS TIME
GUINNESS
IS GOOD
FOR YOU
GIVES YOU STRENGTH
LOOK
YOUR
BEST IN
SQUARE
DIAMONDS & RINGS
DISPENSING CHEMISTS
Boots
SAQUI & LAWRENCE
Players Please
THE BIG WASH

100 Years of London
Twentieth Century in Pictures

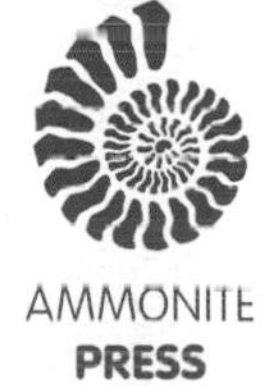
AMMONITE
PRESS

PRESS
ASSOCIATION
Images

First Published 2009 by
Ammonite Press
an imprint of AE Publications Ltd,
166 High Street, Lewes, East Sussex BN7 1XU

ISBN 978-1-906672-25-6

British Cataloguing in Publication Data. A catalogue
record of this book is available from the British Library.

Editor: Huw Pryce
Series Editor: Paul Richardson
Picture research: Press Association Images
Design: Gravemaker + Scott

Colour reproduction by GMC Reprographics
Printed and bound by Kyodo Nation Printing, Thailand

Page 2: Electric signs light up Piccadilly Circus for the first time since the war.
4th April, 1949

Page 5: St Paul's Cathedral from Bankside Power Station.
May, 1955

Page 6: Barclays and Citigroup offices at Canary Wharf.
6th August, 2004

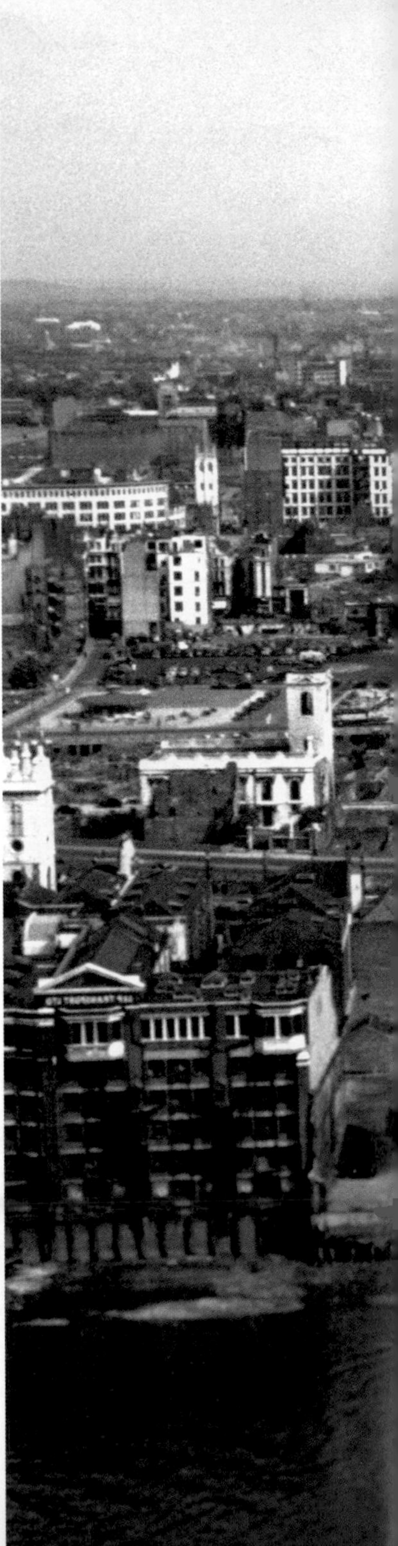

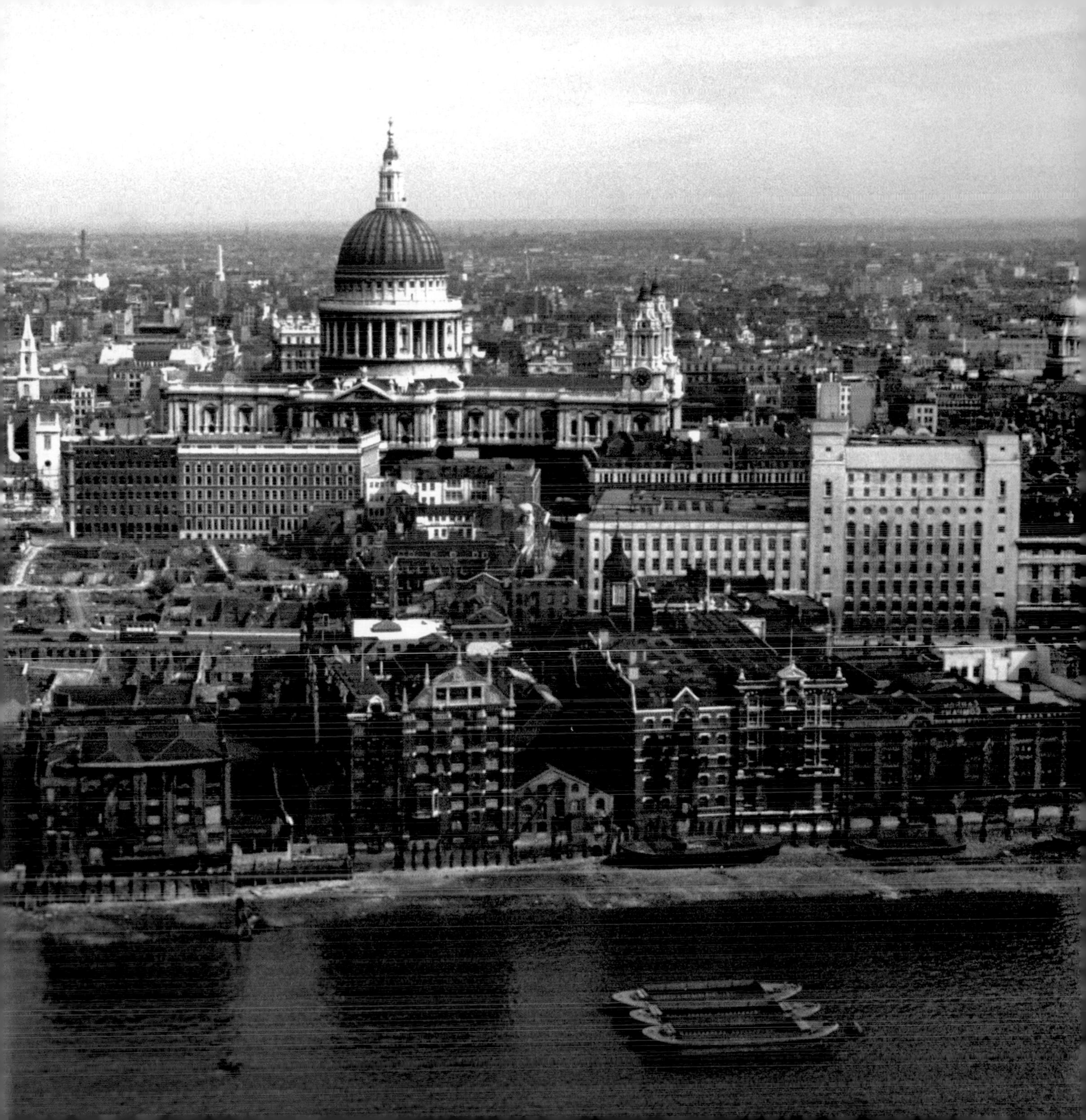

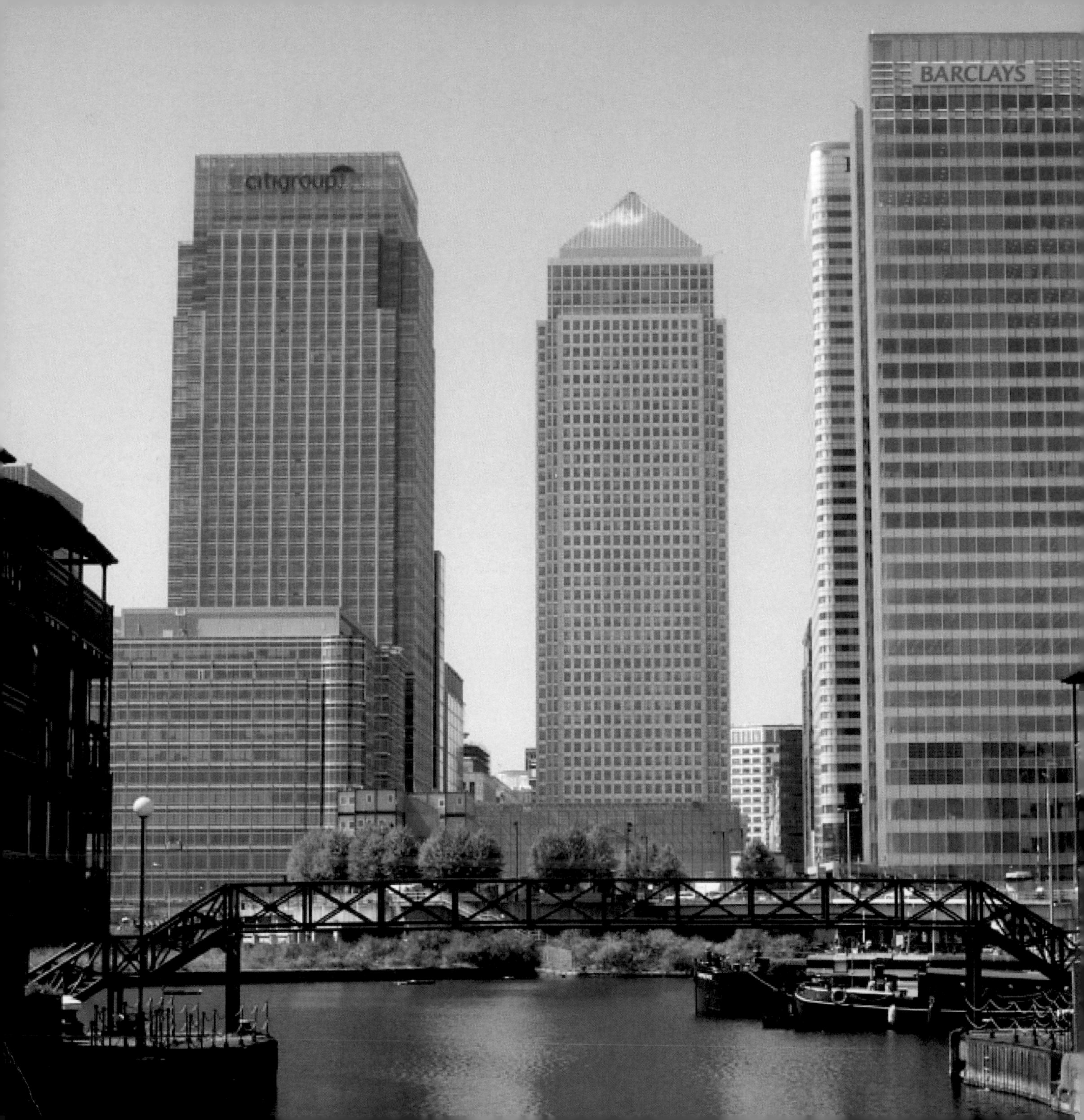
citigroup
BARCLAYS

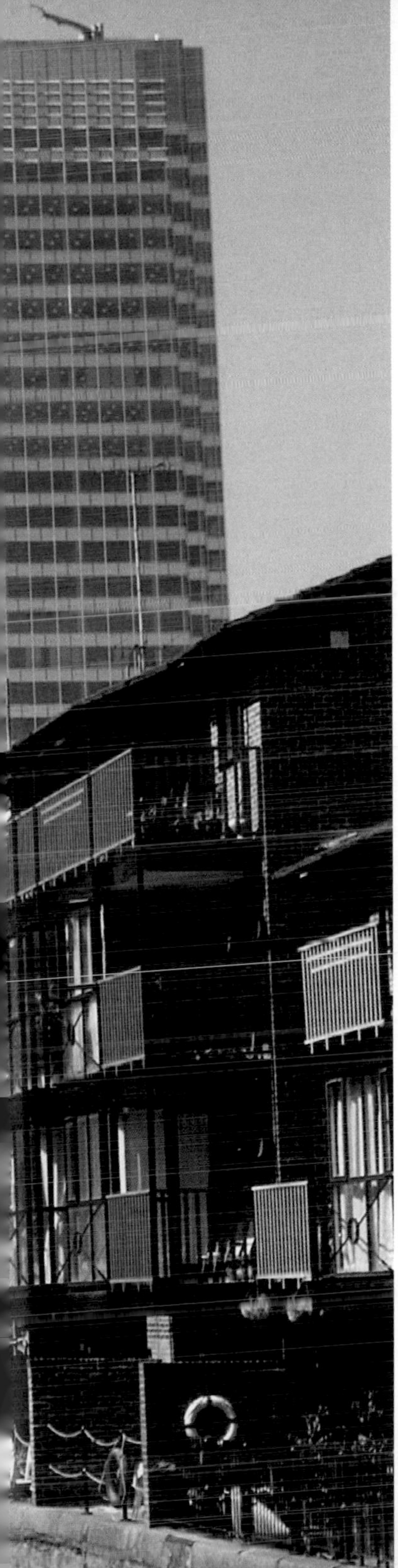

Introduction

One of the world's great capitals, London is steeped in history while being the home and workplace of some seven million people. When this book's first picture was taken the city was the hub of a great empire; now it is the cosmopolitan capital of a member country of the EU. During that tumultuous century the city has hosted two Olympic games and now prepares for its third; it suffered the bombs of two world wars and endured – endures still – generations of terrorism. London has ever been a stage on which great events unfold.

Yet amid the pageantry, demonstrations, sporting events, disasters, publicity stunts, riots and carnivals, booms and crashes, London's everyday life rolls on. And at every turn, a photographer of the Press Association has been there with his camera to make a record. Newspapers gained the ability to reproduce large numbers of half-tone images in 1897. However, the nature of photographic equipment of the time – bulky wooden cameras, flash powder and glass plates – meant that images were still difficult to obtain, requiring bright daylight or complete stillness for a clear picture.

It is a tribute to the early photographers whose work features here that their images display a spontaneity that belies the preparation behind them. Those hurdlers at the 1908 Olympic games weren't posing, but are captured clearly nonetheless. Who is the boy on the roof above a young Winston Churchill at the Sydney Street siege? What equipment was used to capture commuters clambering onto a moving tram in 1919? Themes emerge from these pictures and weave through the lives of the city's generations. How Londoners travel and work, how they buy food, celebrate, survive and mourn, how newcomers arrive and assimilate, how civilians and royalty fight wars, all remain burned onto glass plates, celluloid negatives and hard drives, waiting to be called back into existence here, each image as fresh as the day it was captured.

Although Britain's influence waned with the passing of its empire, London remains a world city and financial centre, a capital of the arts and home of the music industry. It swung in the 1960s, marched and demonstrated in the 1970s, gave in to rampant greed in the 1980s then re-emerged as a cultural powerhouse with Cool Britannia in the 1990s. As the old Roman river crossing moves into her third millennium, the cameras of the PA's photographers are there to bear witness to what comes next.

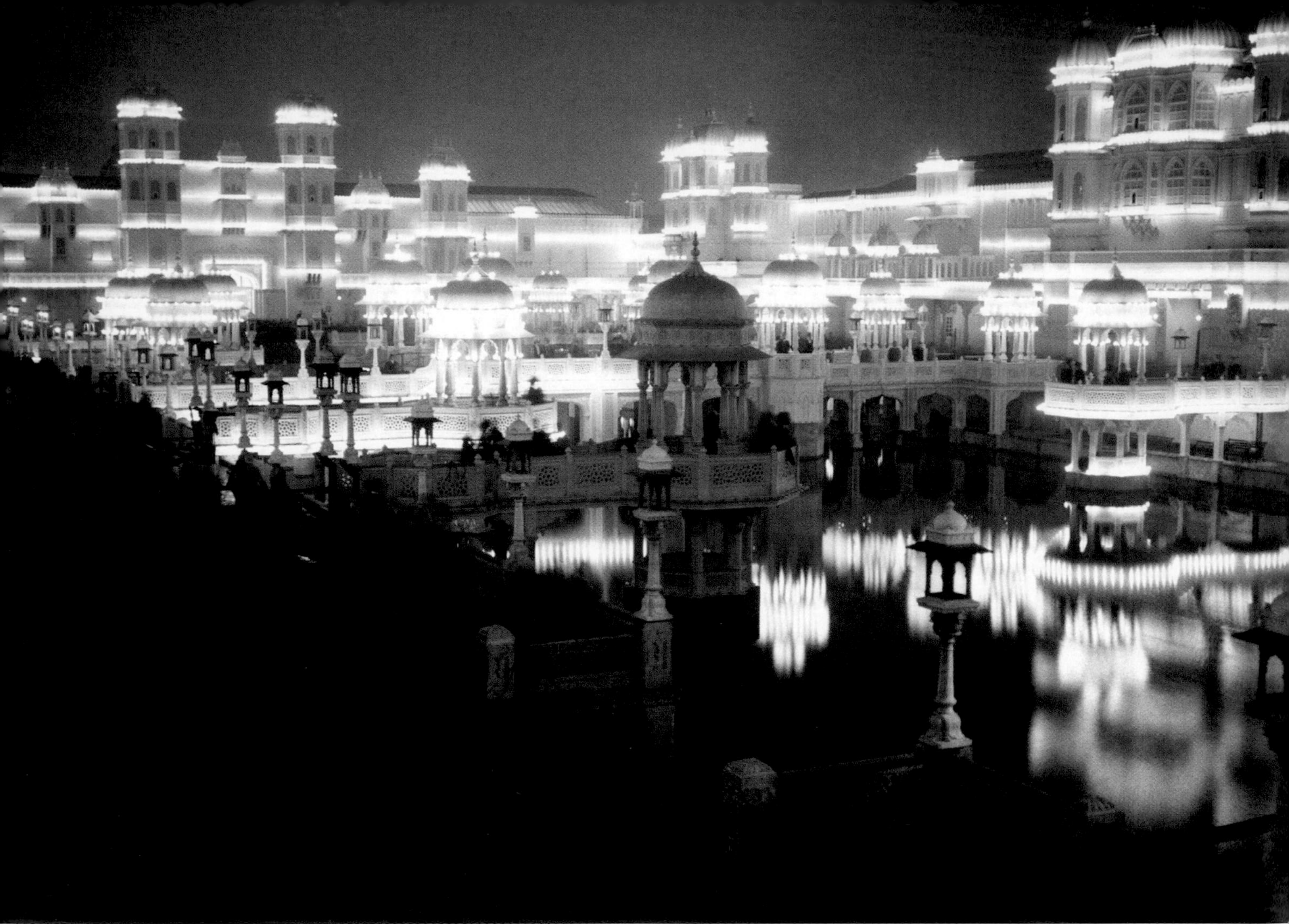

A night scene at the Indian exhibit, a Mughal-style palace complete with lake, at the Franco-British Exhibition, White City.
14th May, 1908

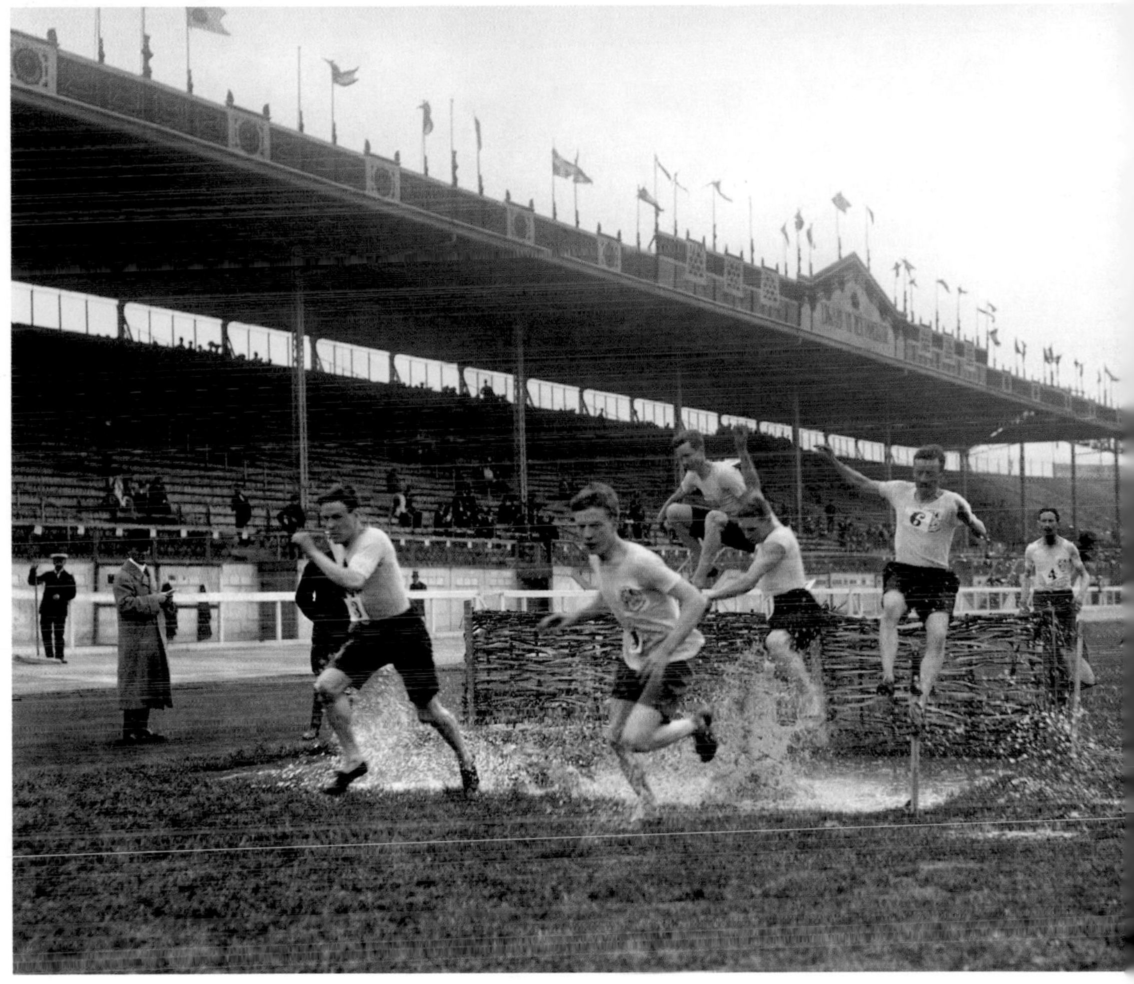

Athletes leap through the water jump in the 3200m steeplechase at the 1908 London Olympic Games, White City.
18th July, 1908

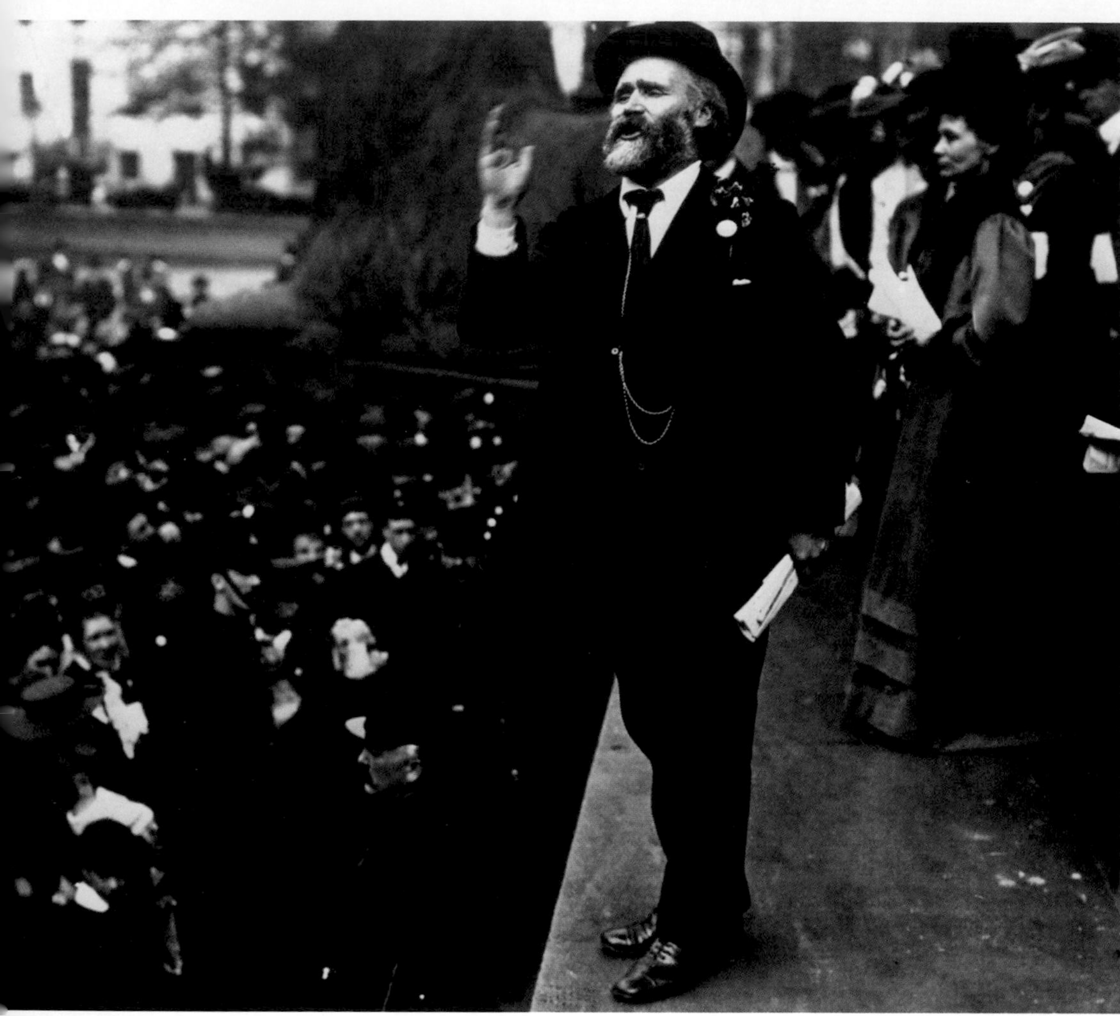

Labour Party leader Keir Hardie speaking at a Women's Suffrage demonstration in Trafalgar Square. Just behind is Emmeline Pankhurst, the founder of the Women's Social and Political Union.
1910

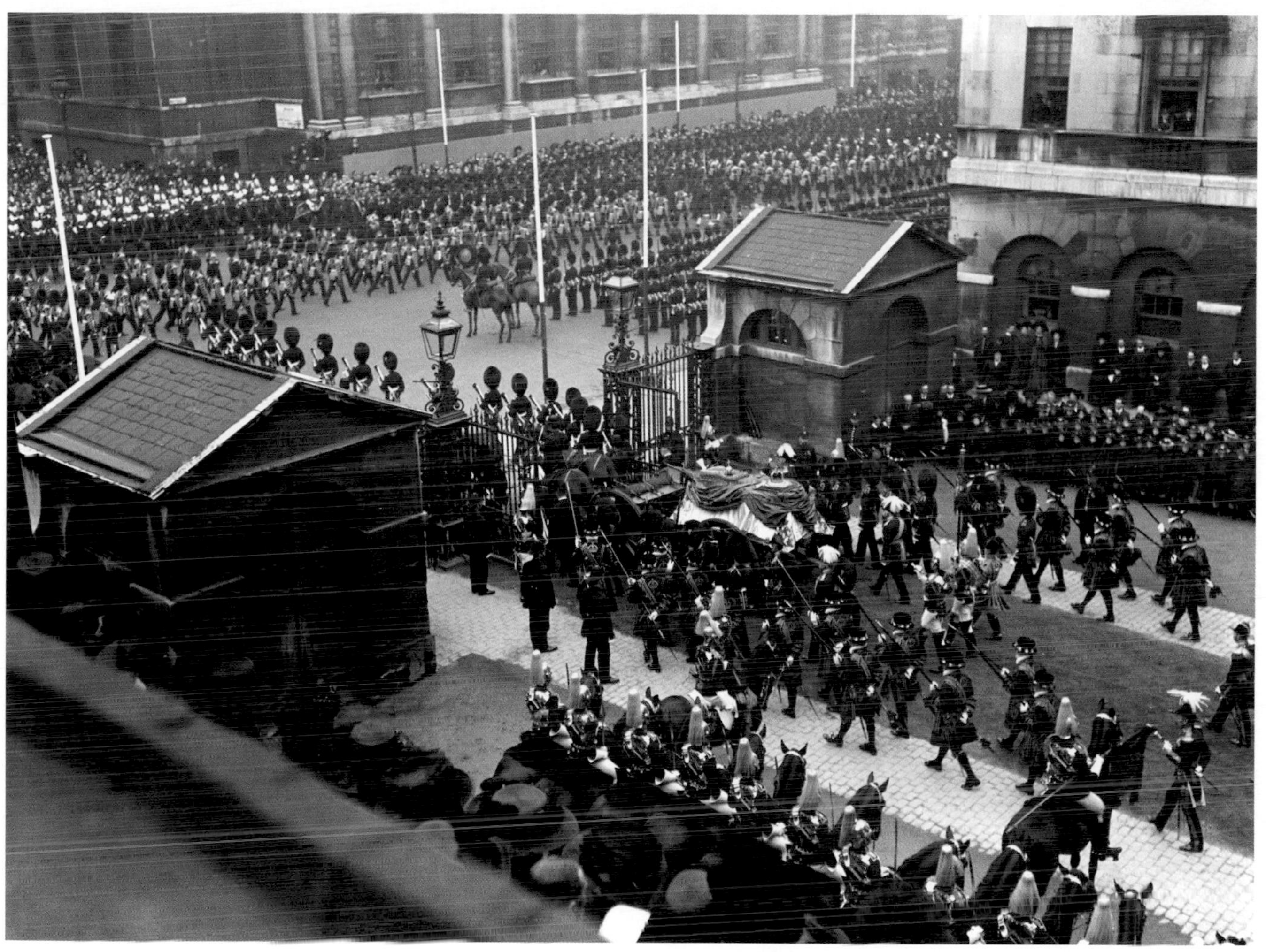

The funeral procession of King Edward VII on its way to Westminster Abbey. The King's coffin, followed by King George V (bottom R), is borne on a gun carriage through Horse Guards into Whitehall.

21st May, 1910

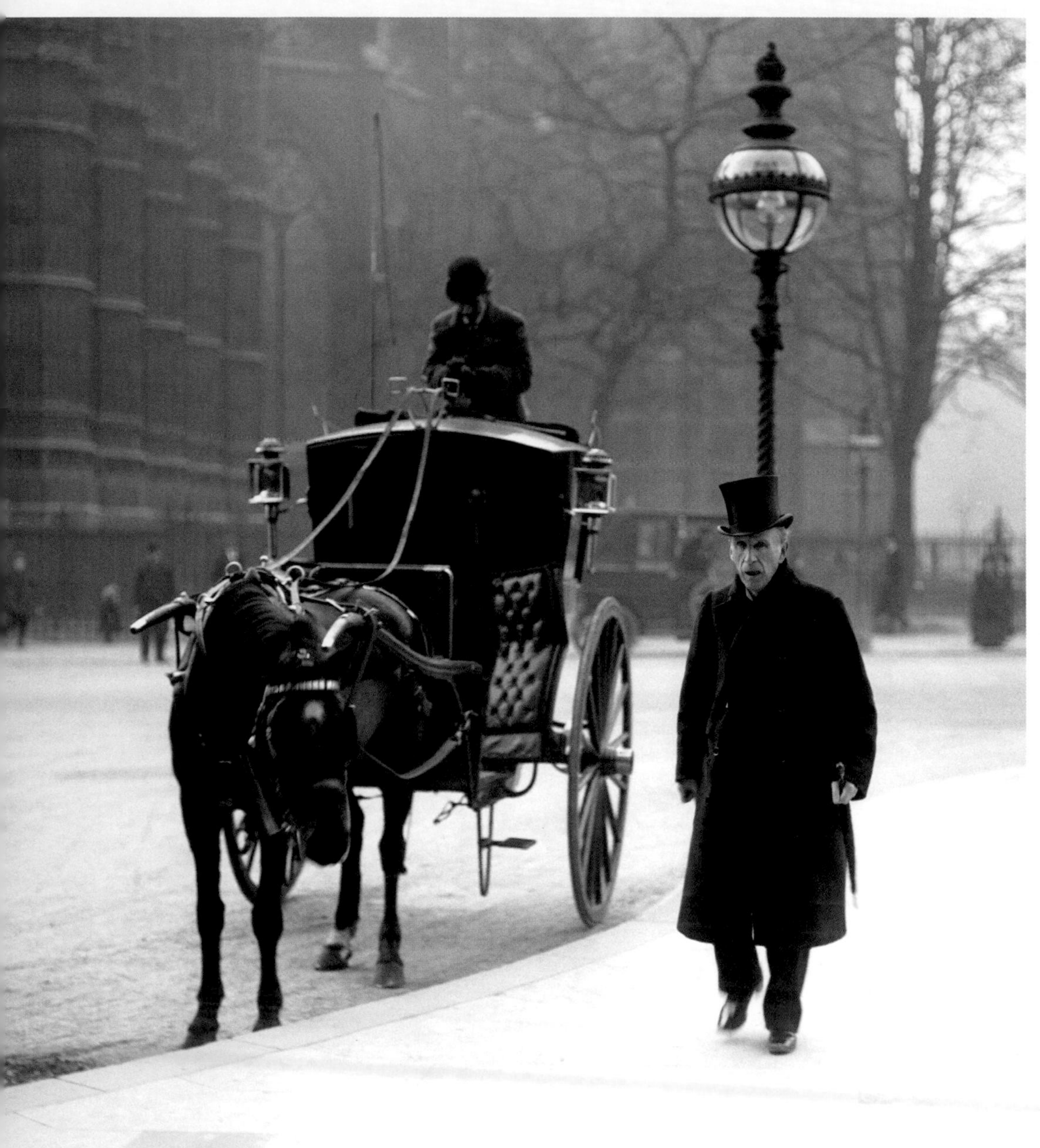

The newly appointed Lord President of the Council, Lord Morley, opposite the Palace of Westminster.
December, 1910

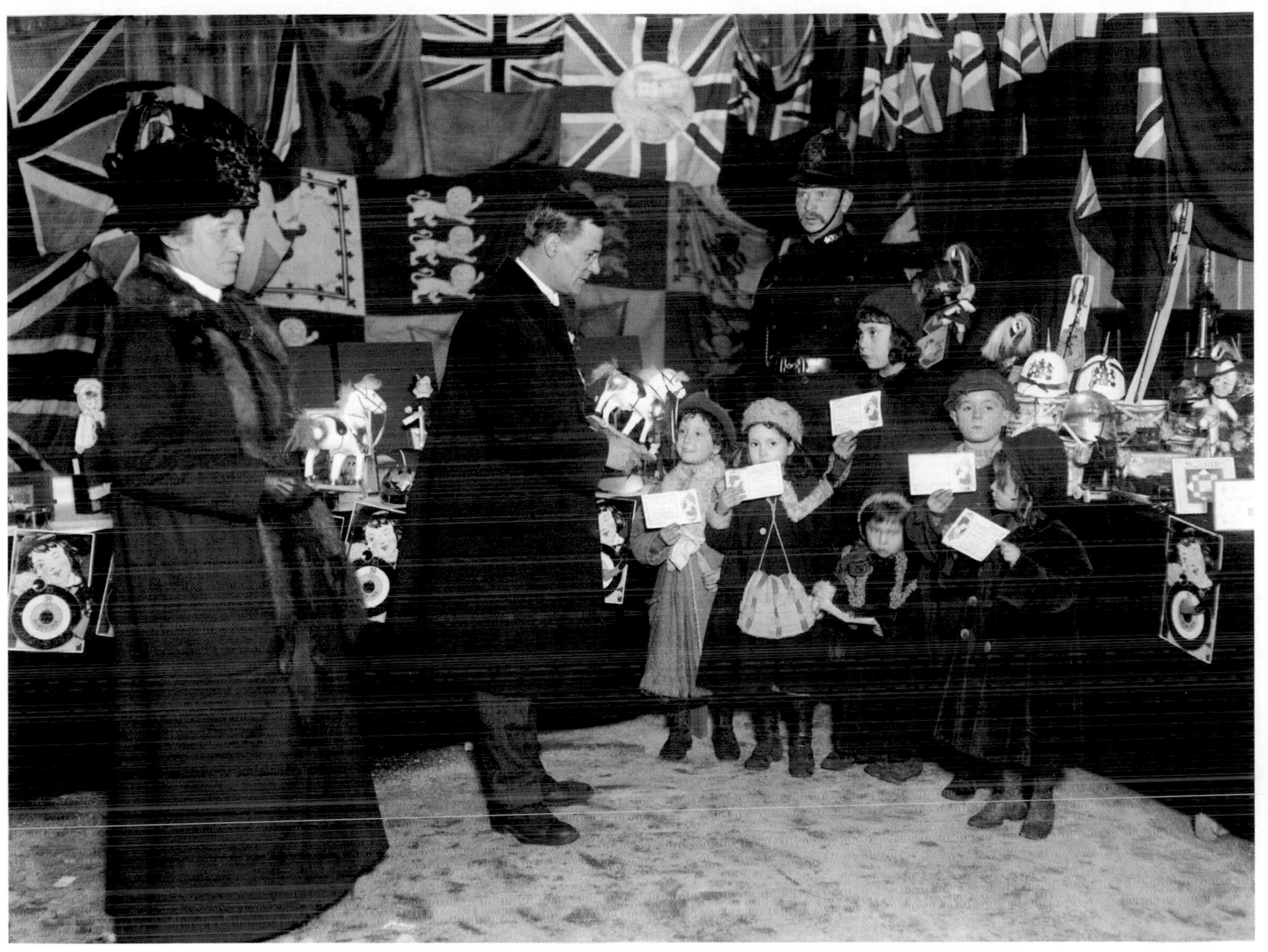

Music hall star, Coster Comedian Gus Elen, distributes toys at Christmas to children of Balham district.
December, 1910

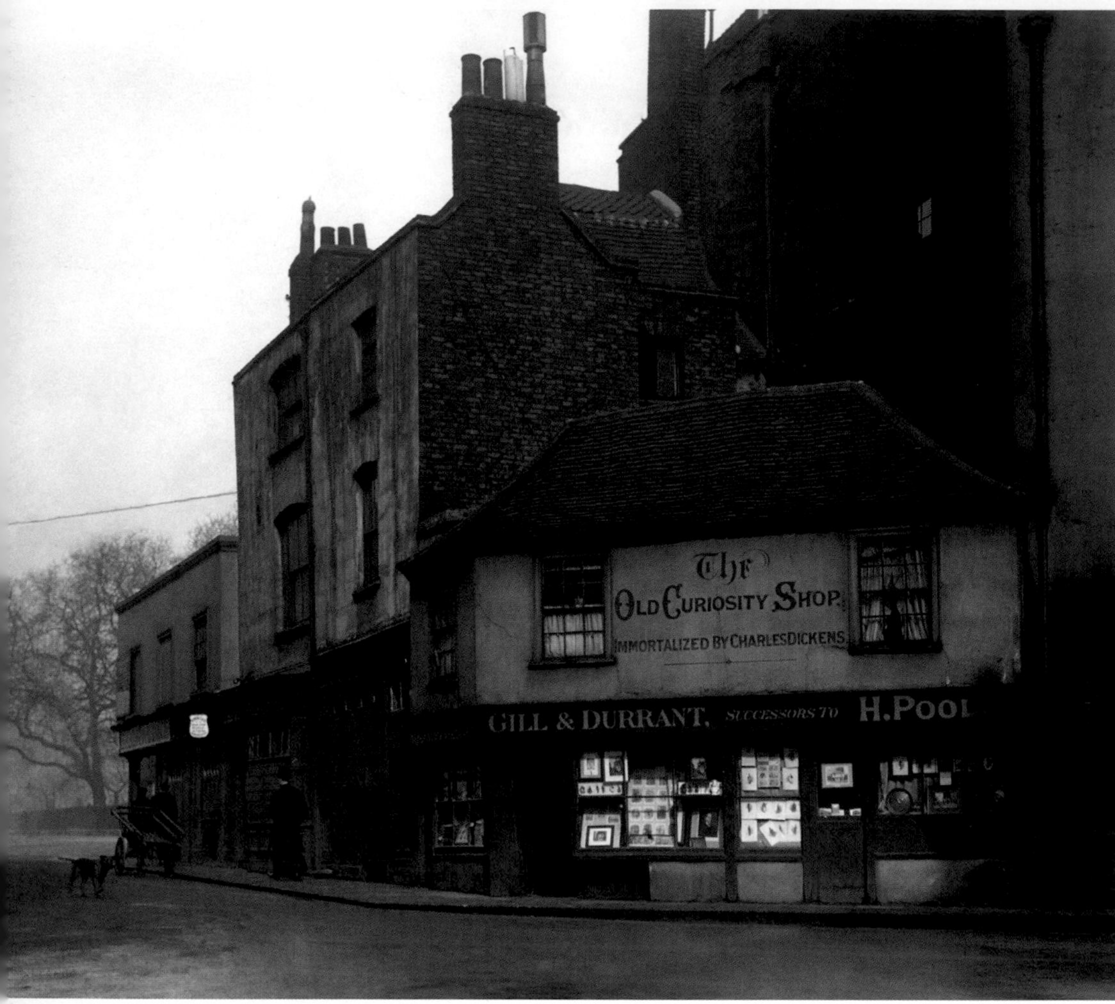

The Old Curiosity Shop, Portsmouth Street. Constructed using wood from old ships, the building survived both the flames of the Great Fire of 1666 and the bombs of the Second World War.
1911

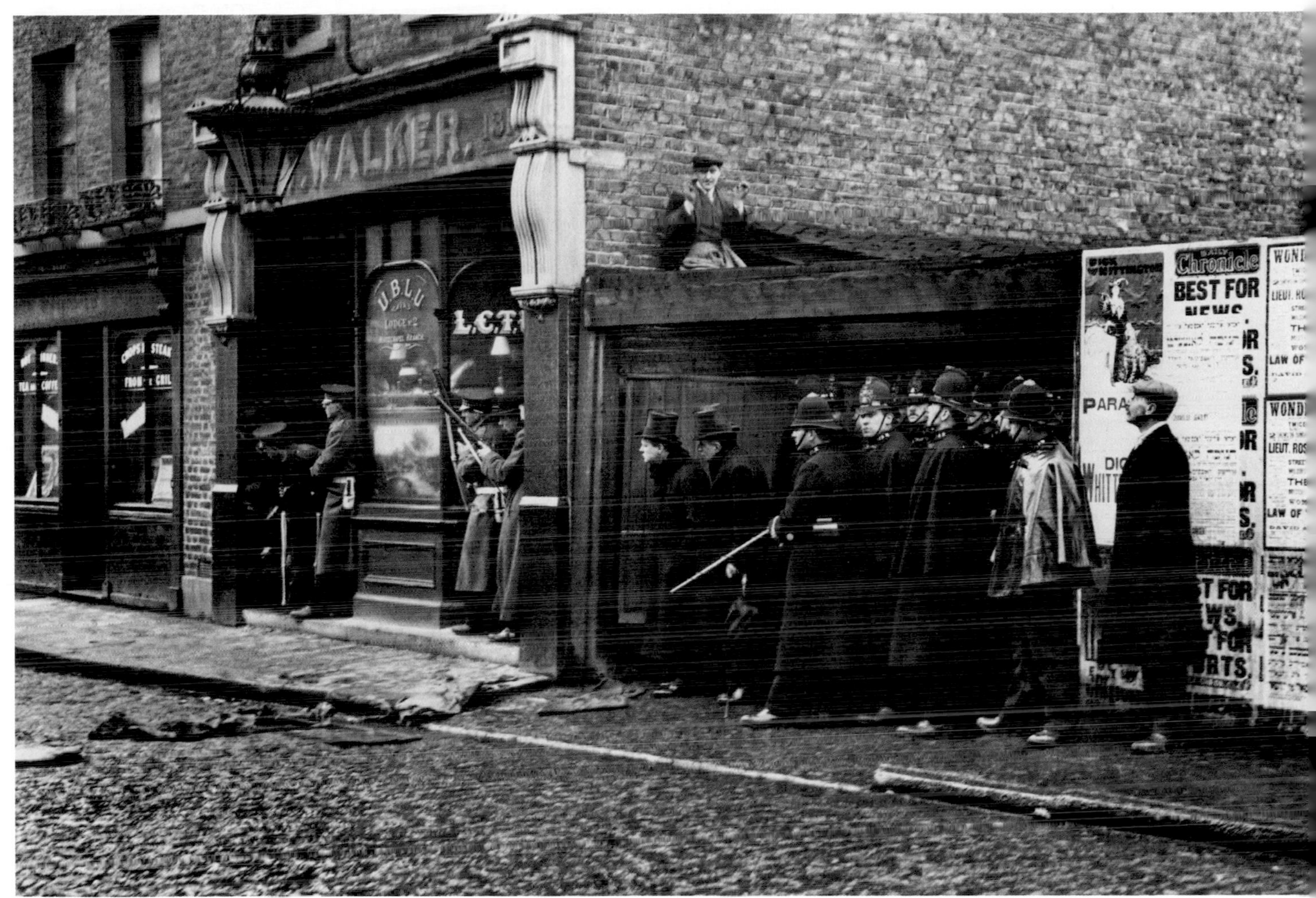

The Home Secretary Winston Churchill (L, in top hat), during the siege of Sidney Street in Stepney, when guardsmen and police fought with anarchists besieged in a terraced house.
3rd January, 1911

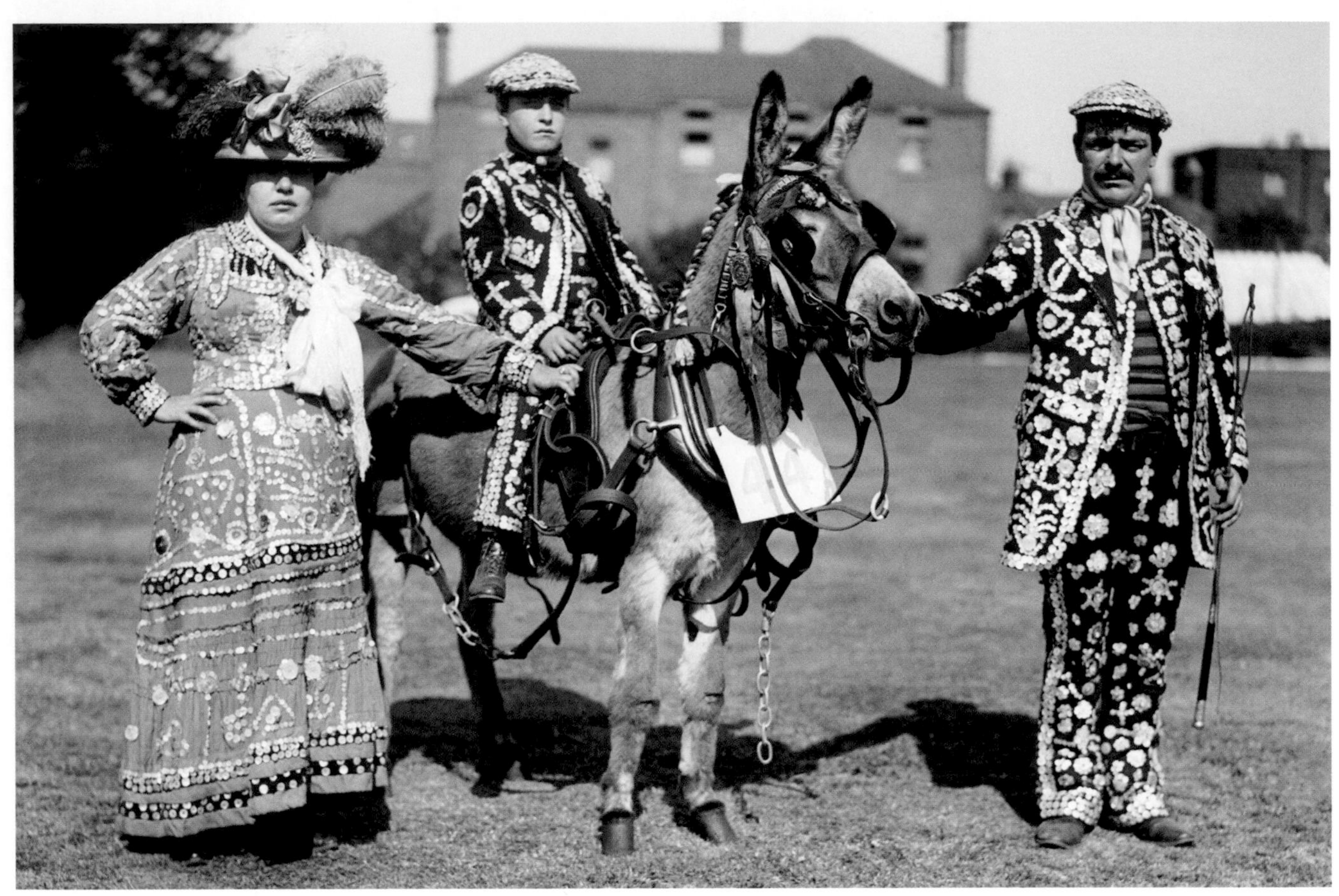

A family party of pearly royalty at Peckham Derby Show.
June, 1911

The Coronation procession of King George V passes down Fleet Street.
22nd June, 1911

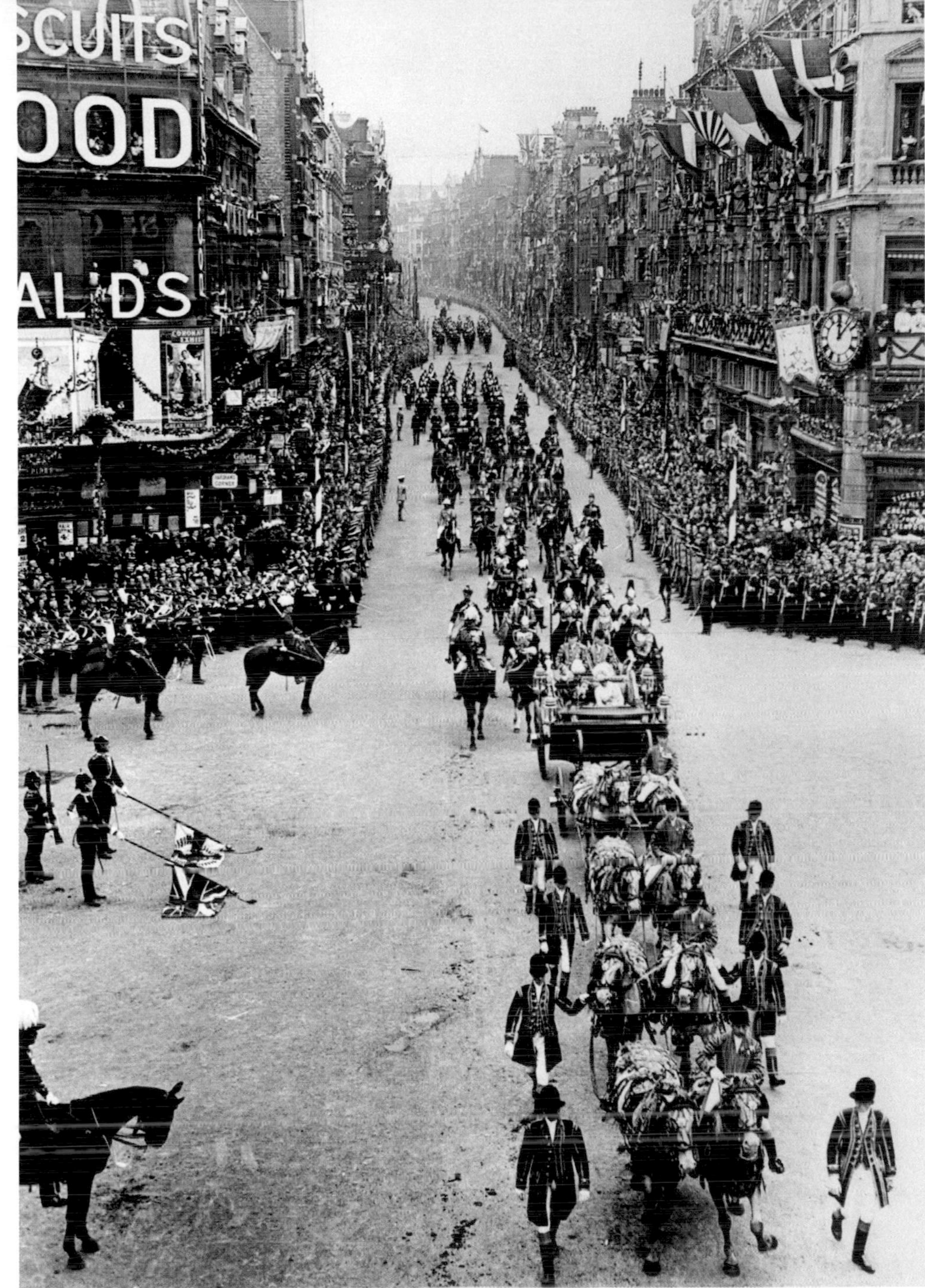

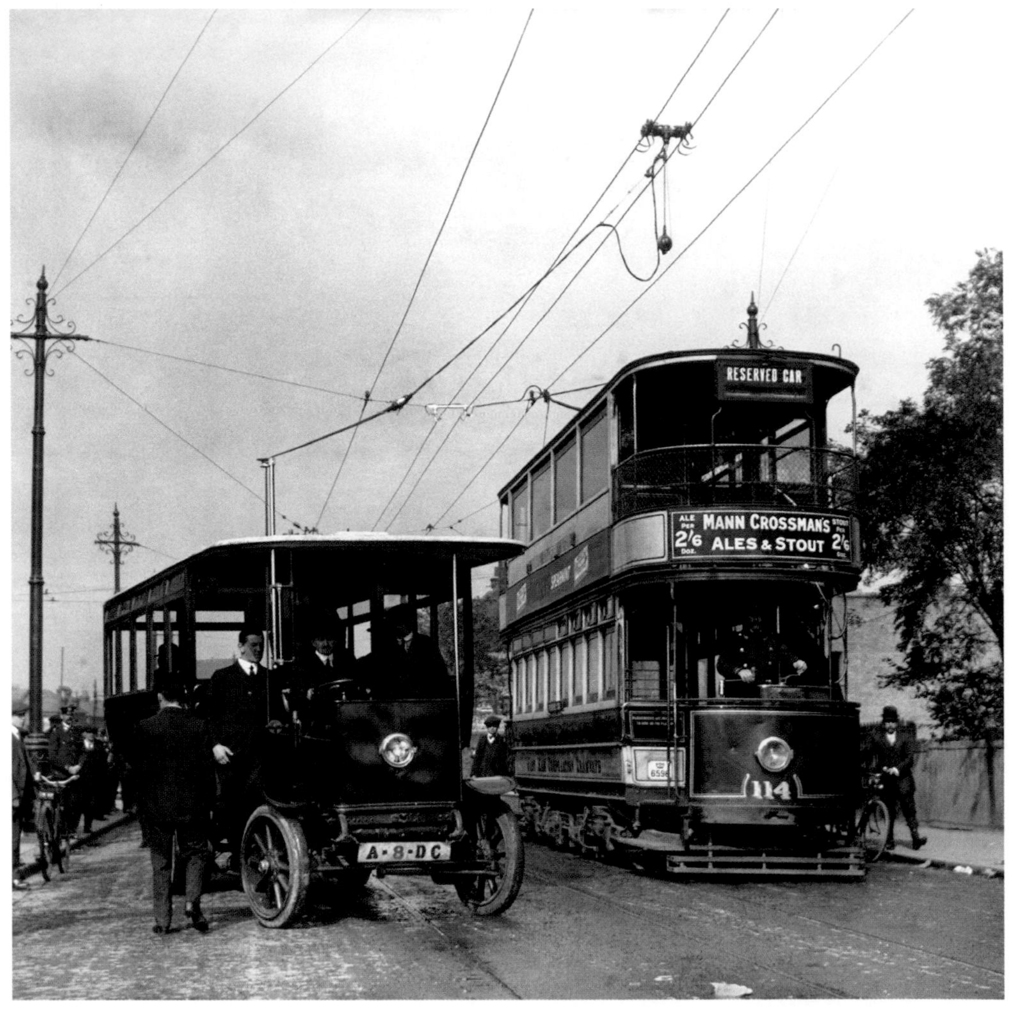

A trackless tram – an early trolley bus – together with a conventional tram on the East Ham Tramways.
1912

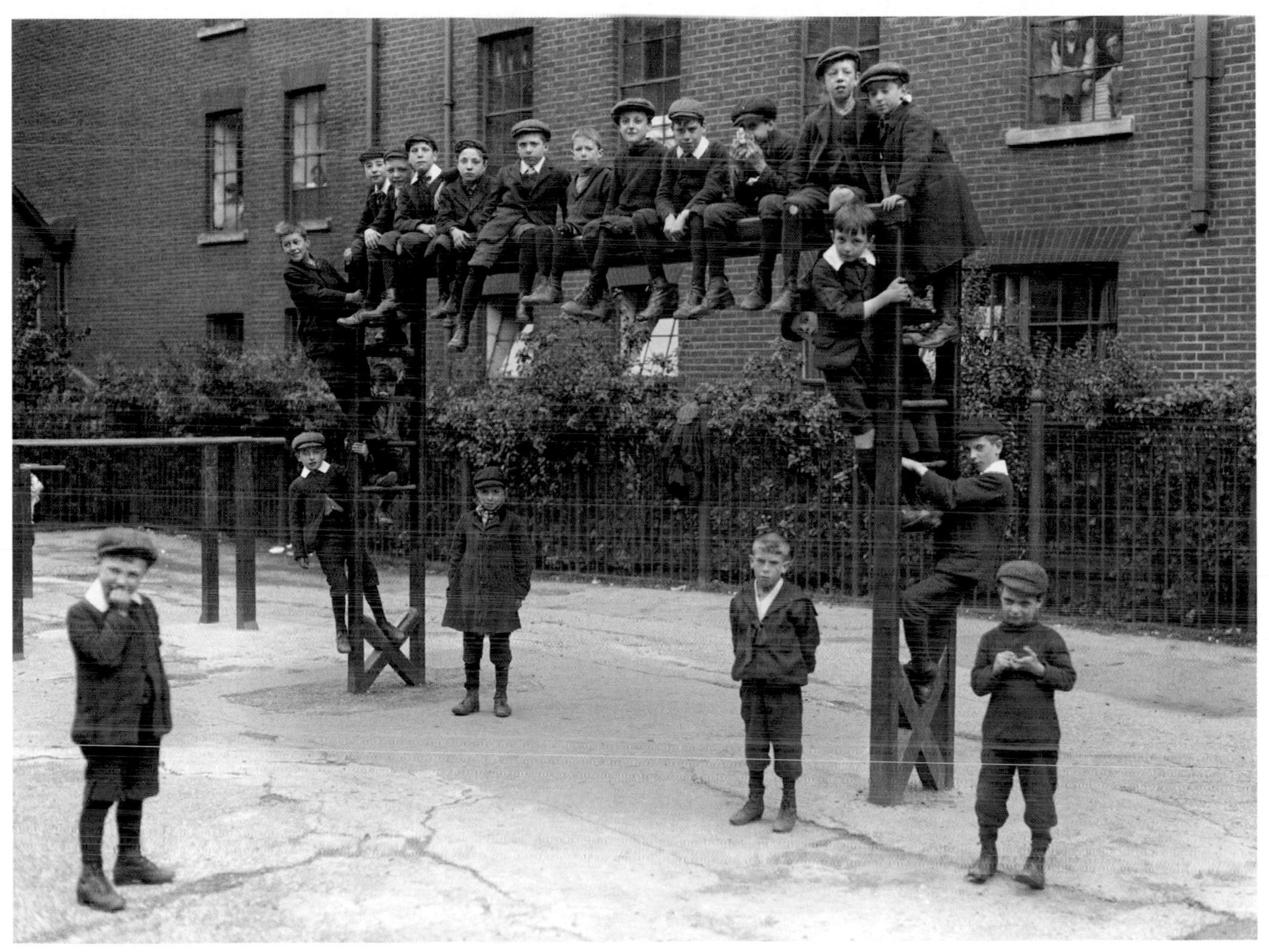

Drury Lane playground.
4th January, 1912

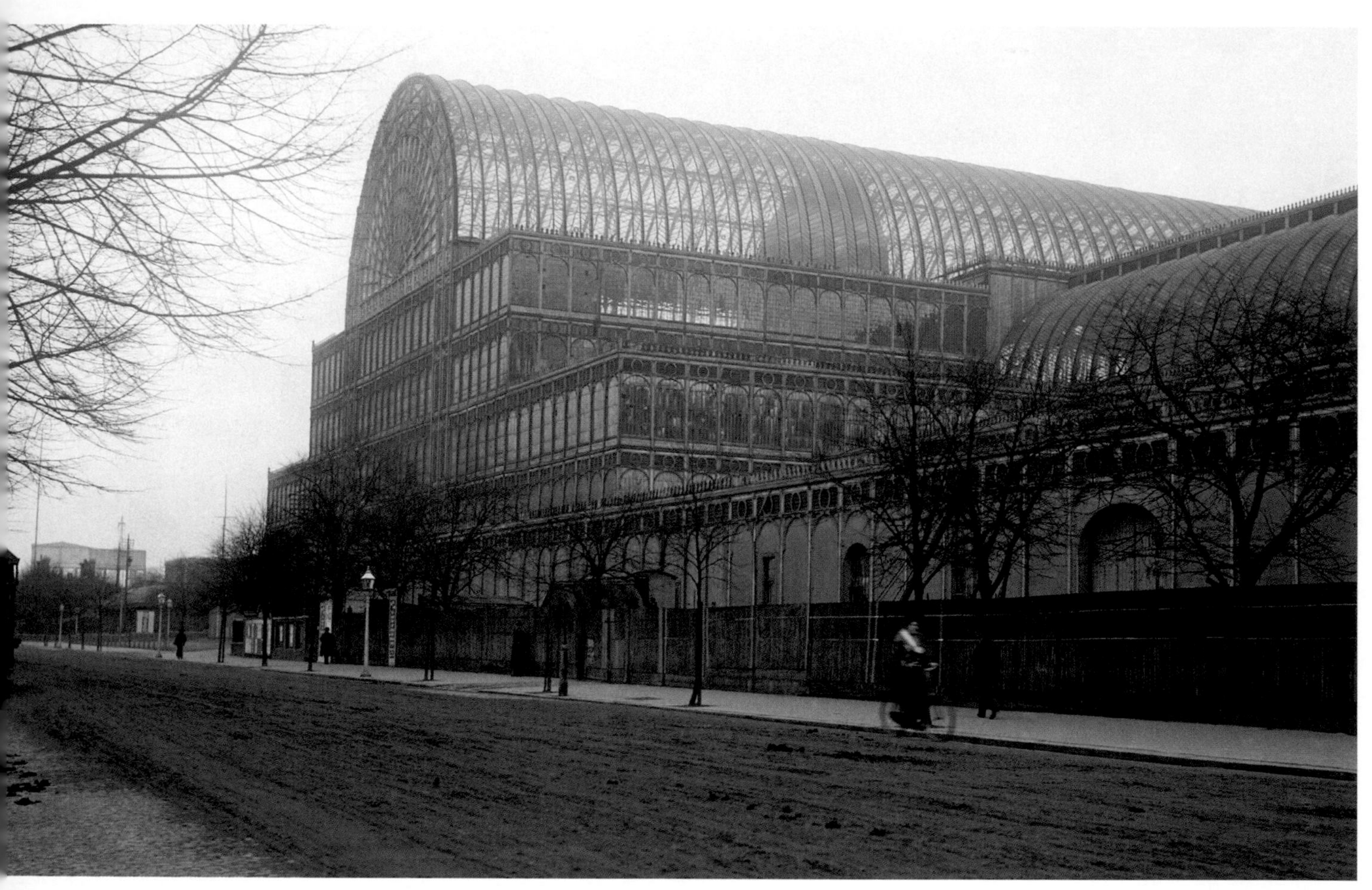

The Crystal Palace, Sydenham Hill. It was built originally in Hyde Park to house the Great Exhibition of 1851, after which the building's creator, Sir Joseph Paxton, raised over £500,000 to move it to the area now known as Crystal Palace.
1913

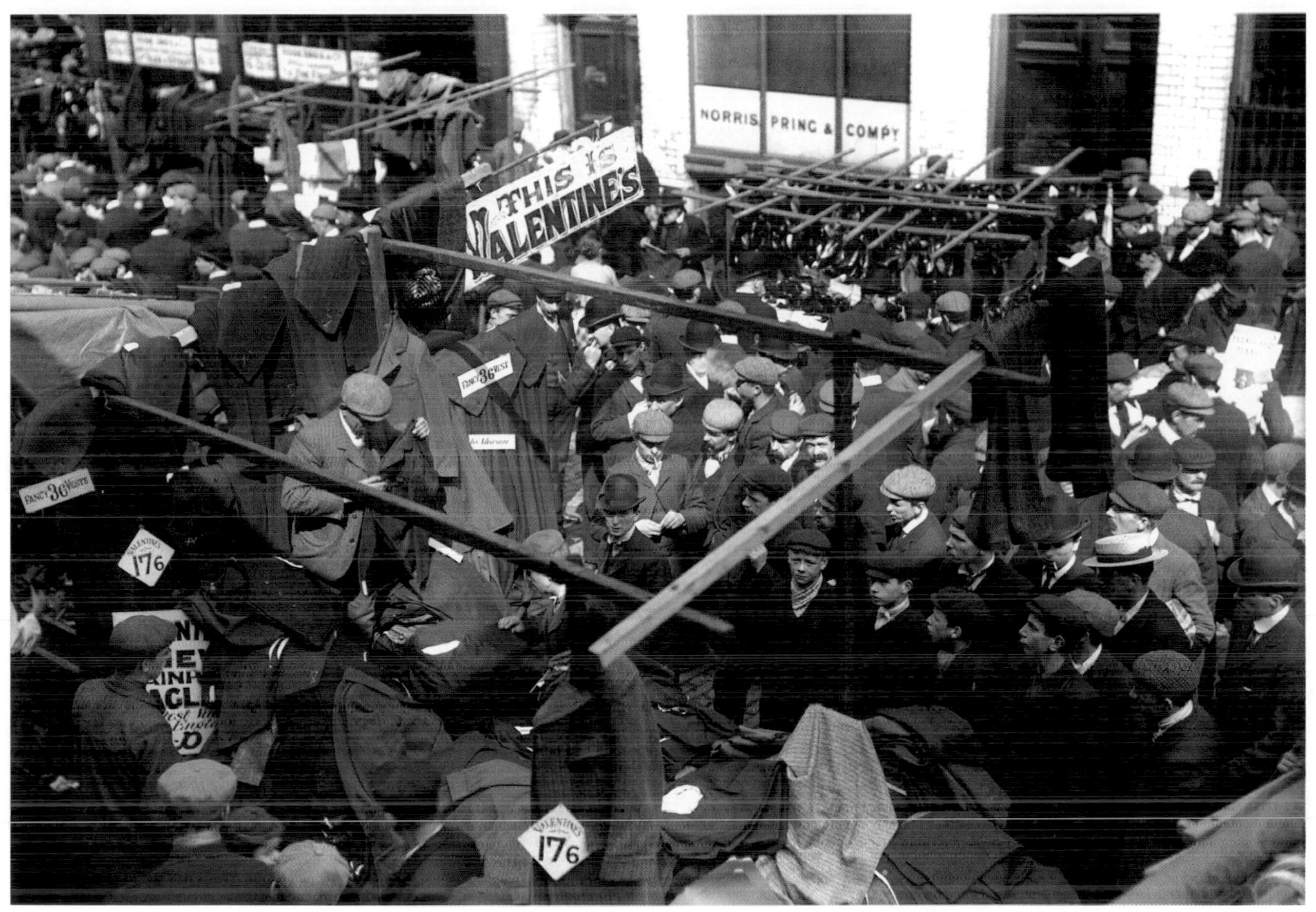

Petticoat Lane Market.
1913

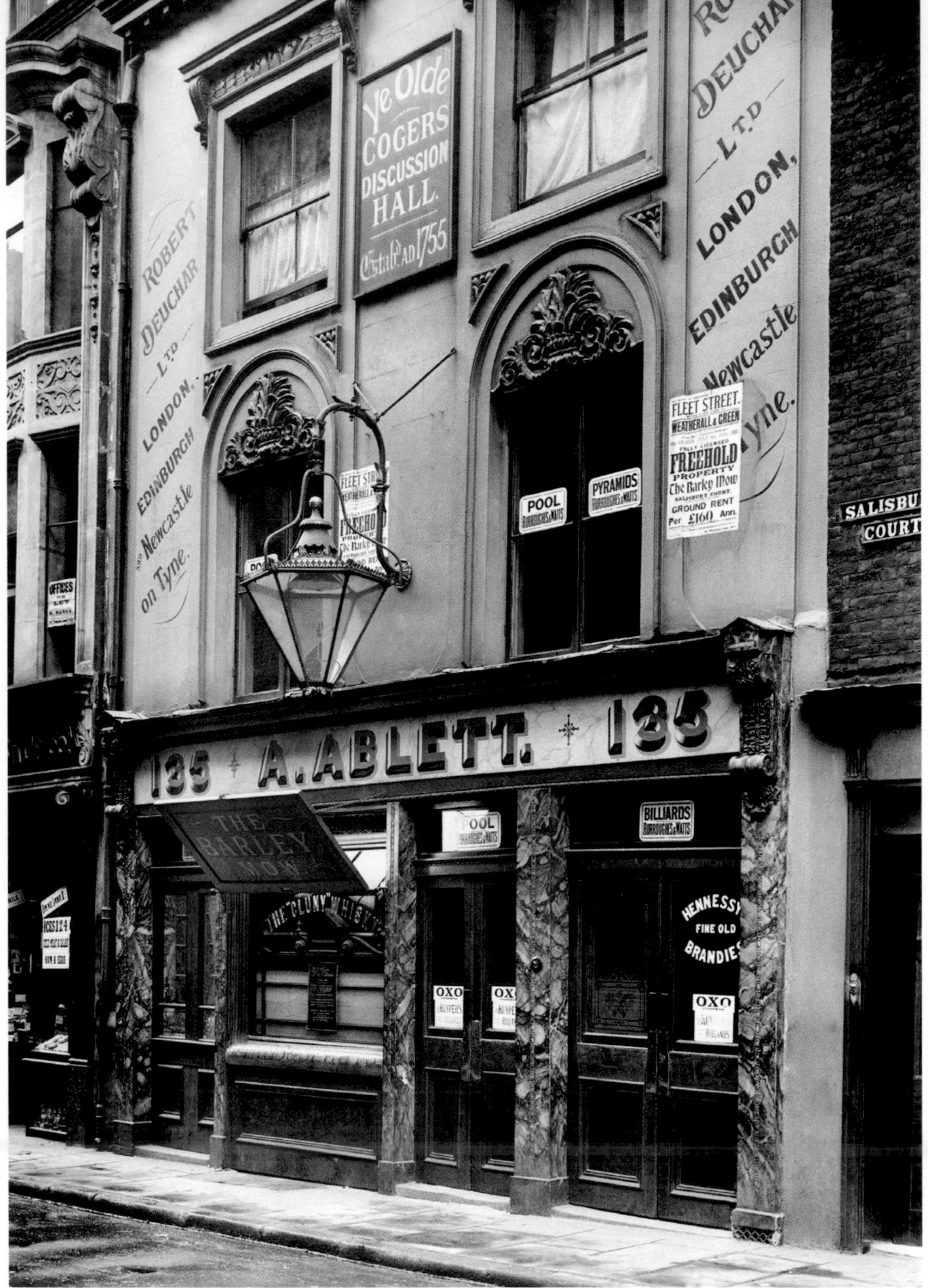

Ye Old Cogers' Discussion Hall at Salisbury Court.
The Society of Cogers was established in 1755. Still active today, it is the oldest debating society in the world.
1913

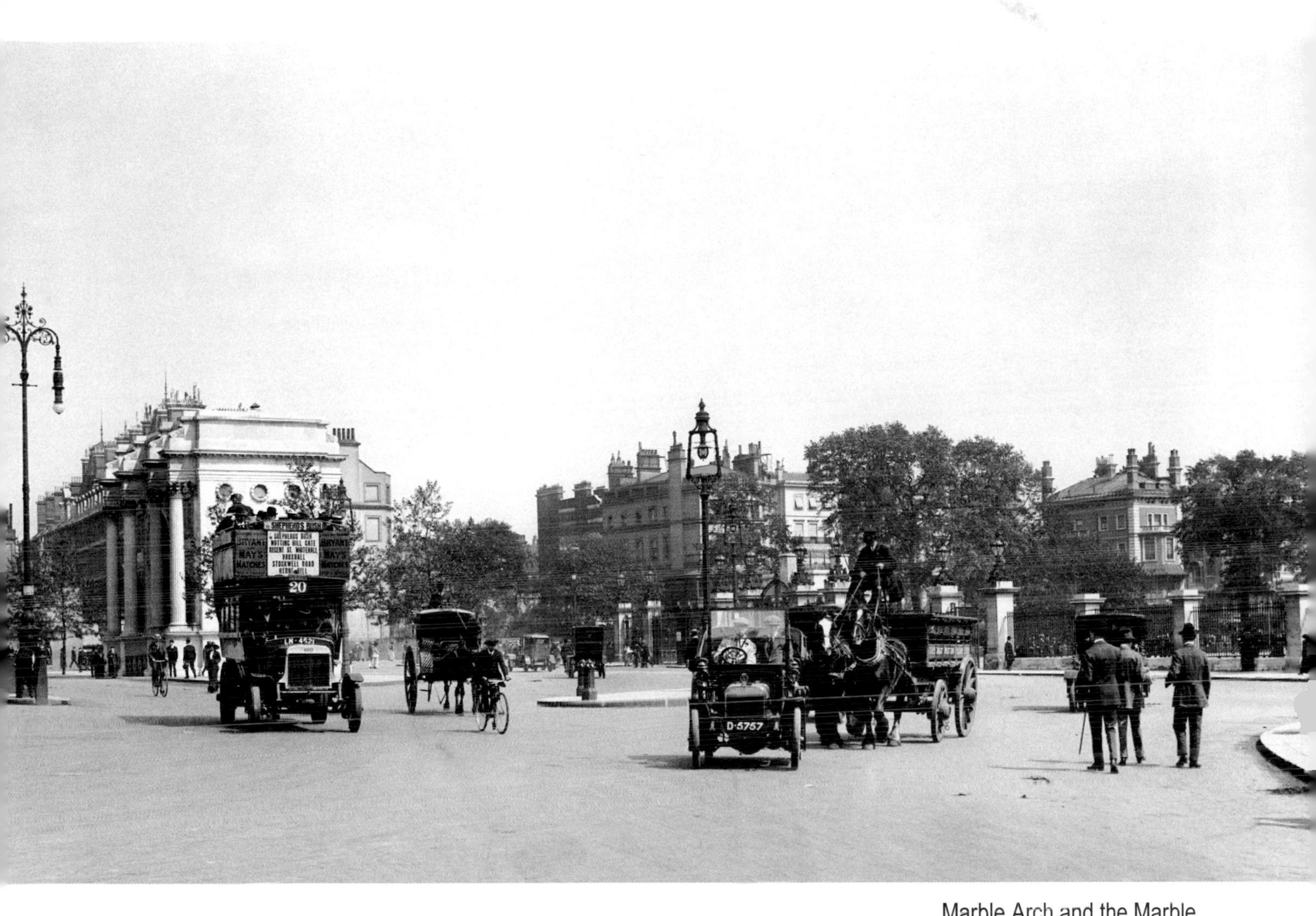

Marble Arch and the Marble Arch roundabout. The Arch housed a small police station until 1950.
May, 1913

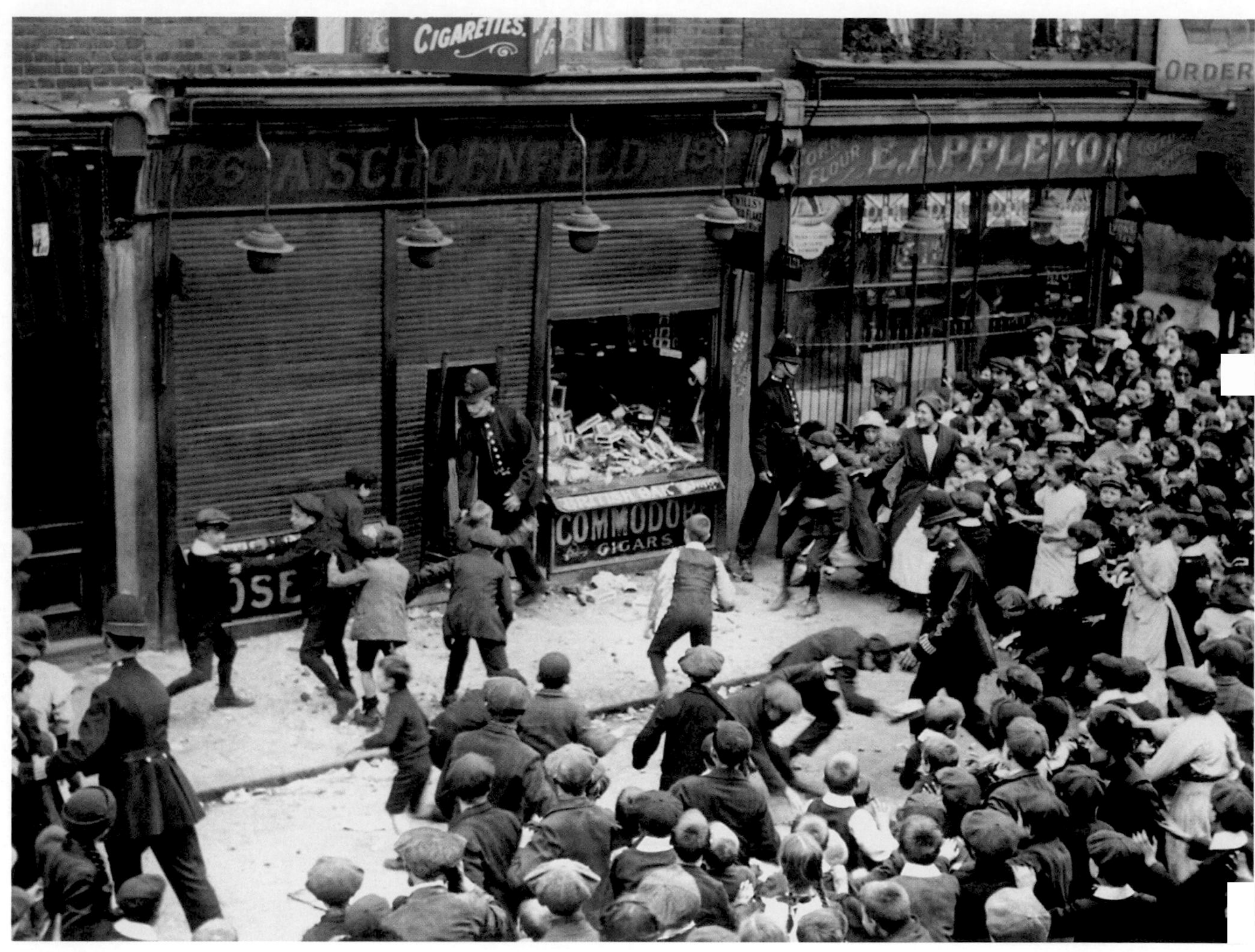

Anti-German demonstrators break Schoenfeld's window in Chrisp Street, Poplar, following the sinking a few days earlier of the passenger liner *RMS Lusitania* by a German submarine.
13th May, 1915

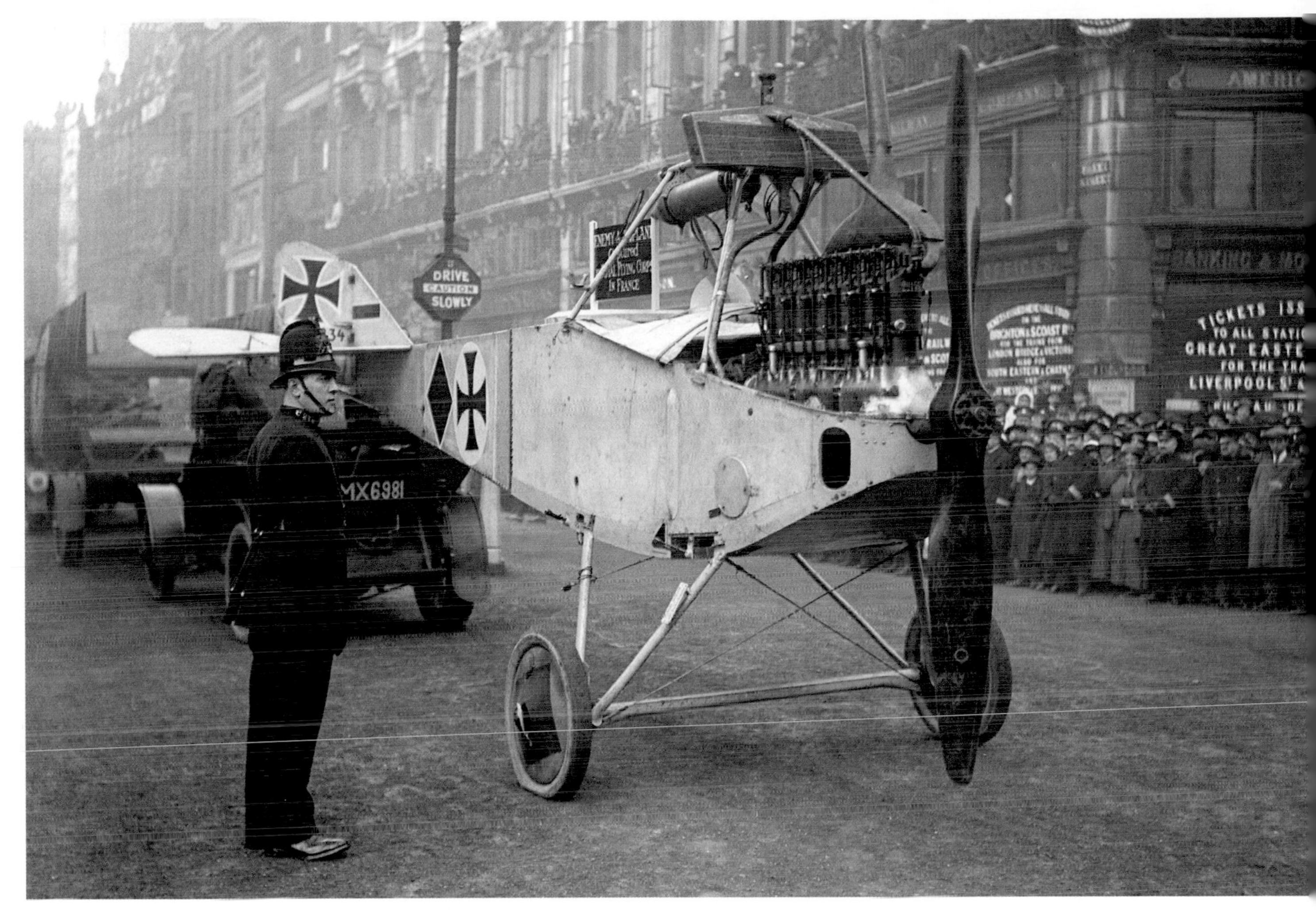

The fuselage of a German aircraft, captured in France, is paraded along Fleet Street as a trophy during the Lord Mayor's Show.
August, 1916

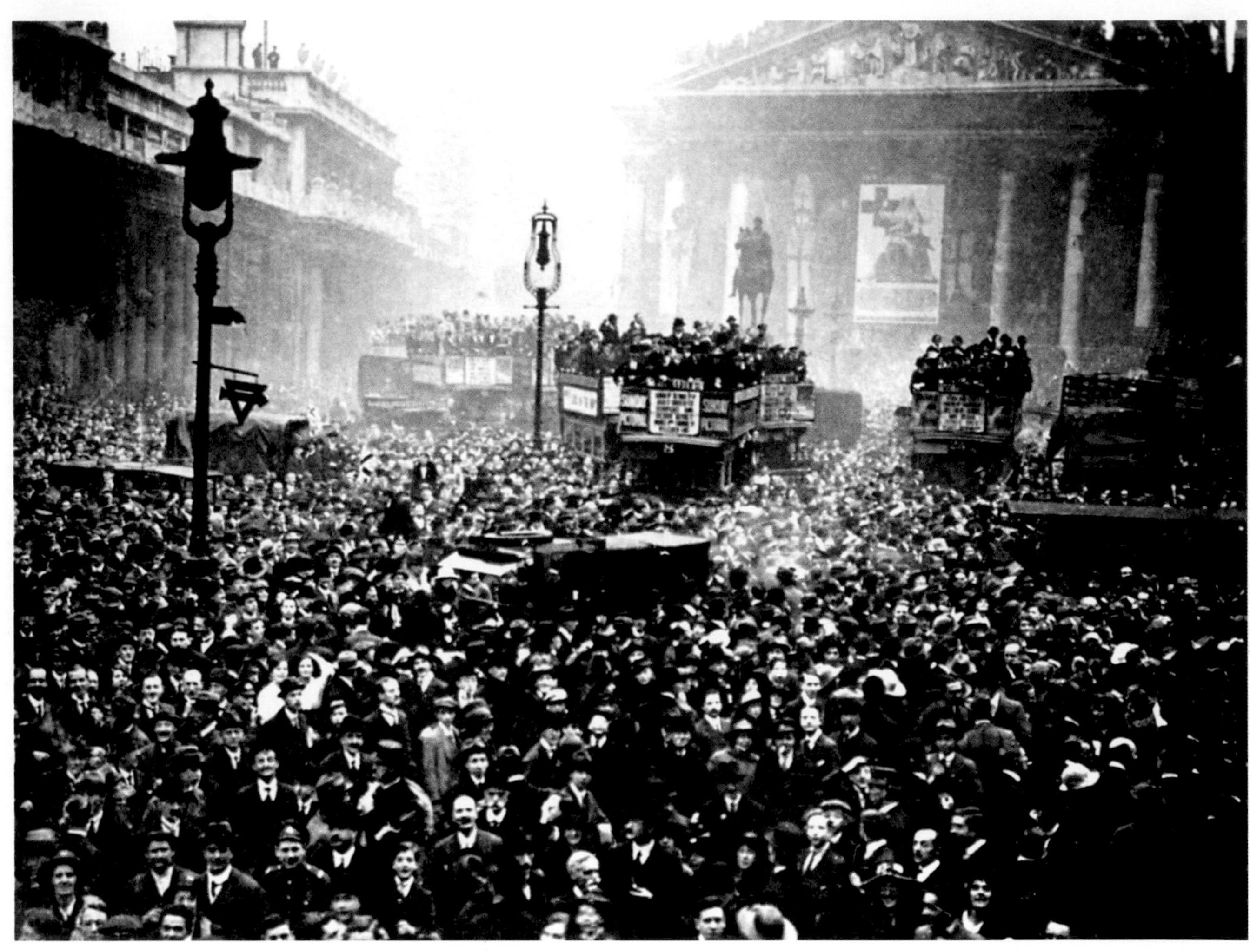

A huge crowd outside the Stock Exchange and the Bank of England after the announcement of the Armistice, which heralded the end of the First World War.
11th November, 1918

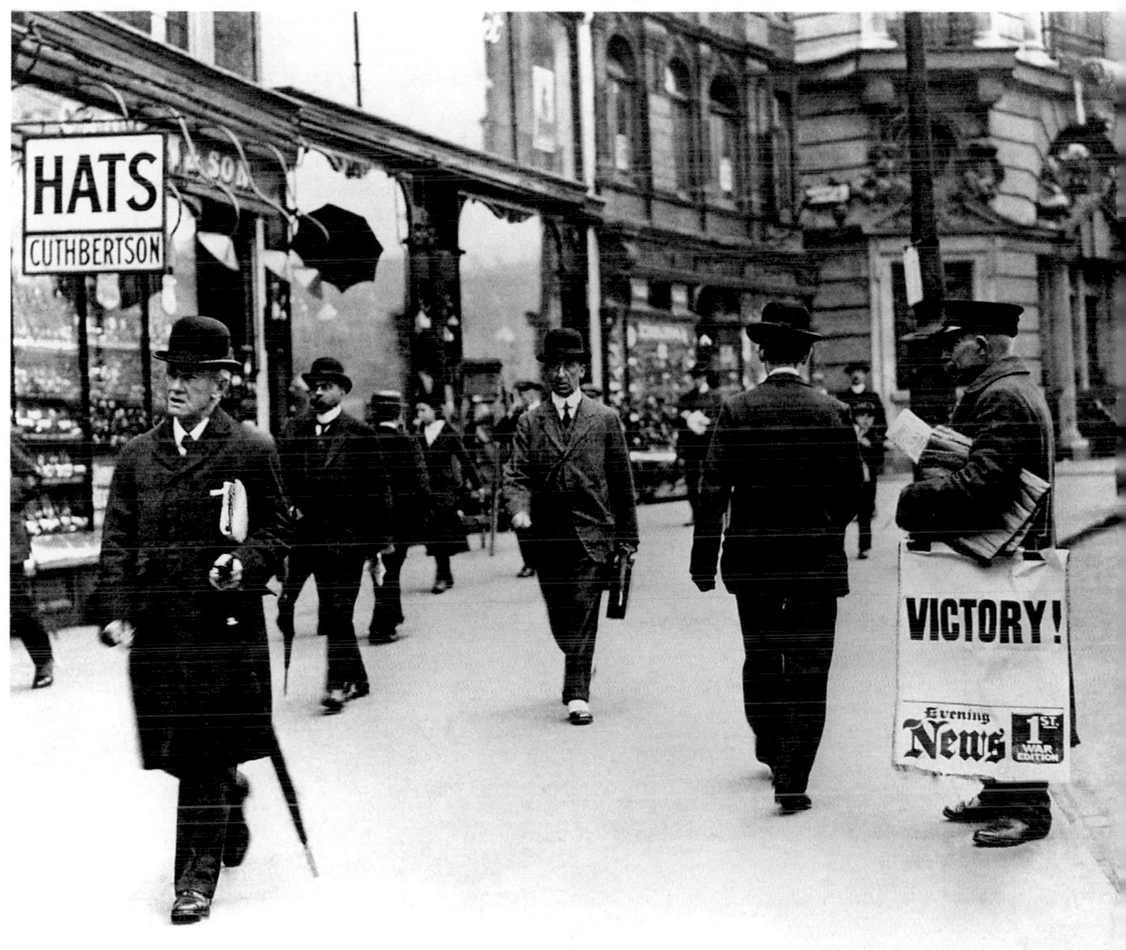

News of the Allied victory reaches the Aldwych.
11th November, 1918

Former Suffragette Christabel Pankhurst casts her vote in the 1918 General Election, the first in which women – albeit only those over 30 years of age – were permitted to vote.
14th December, 1918

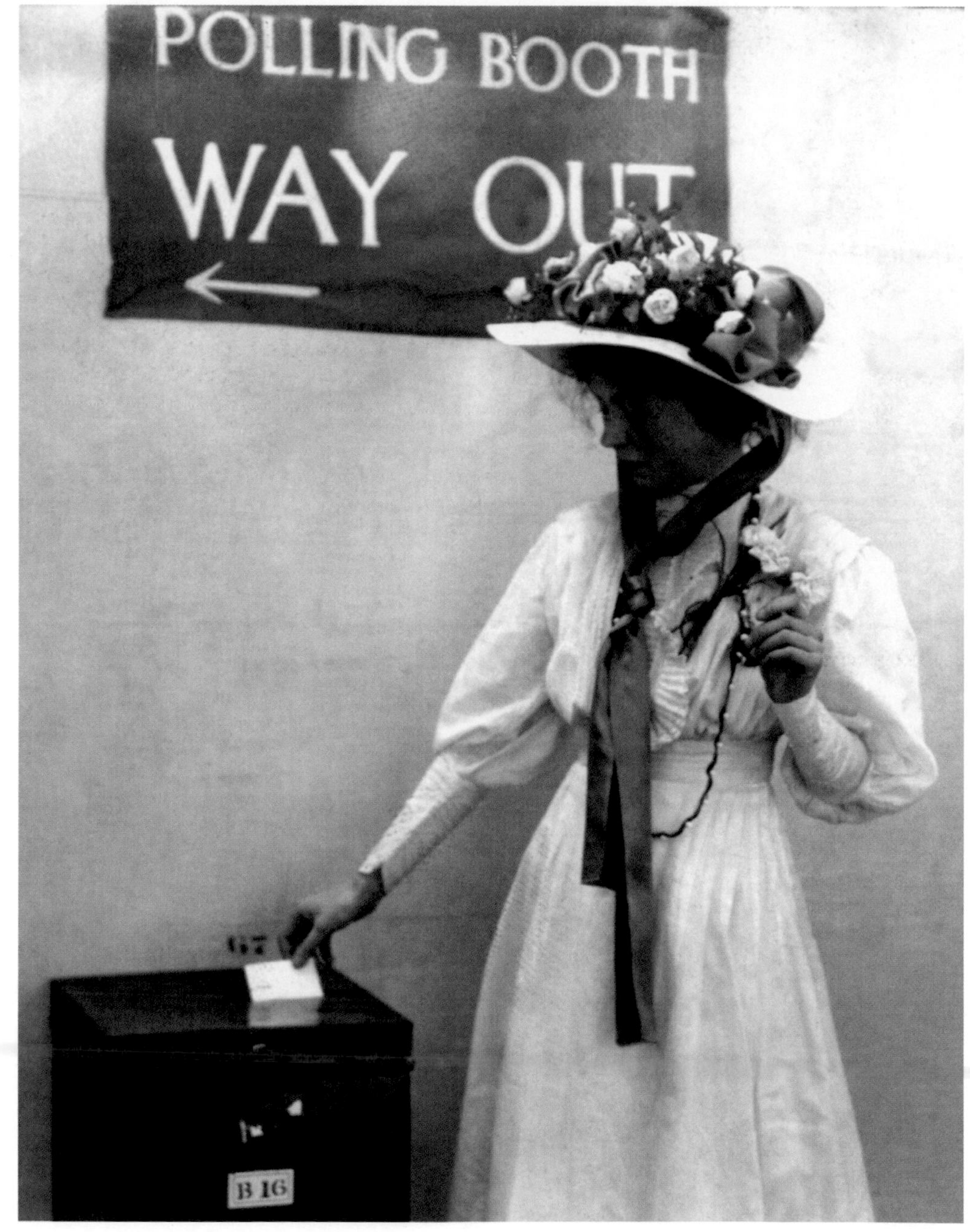

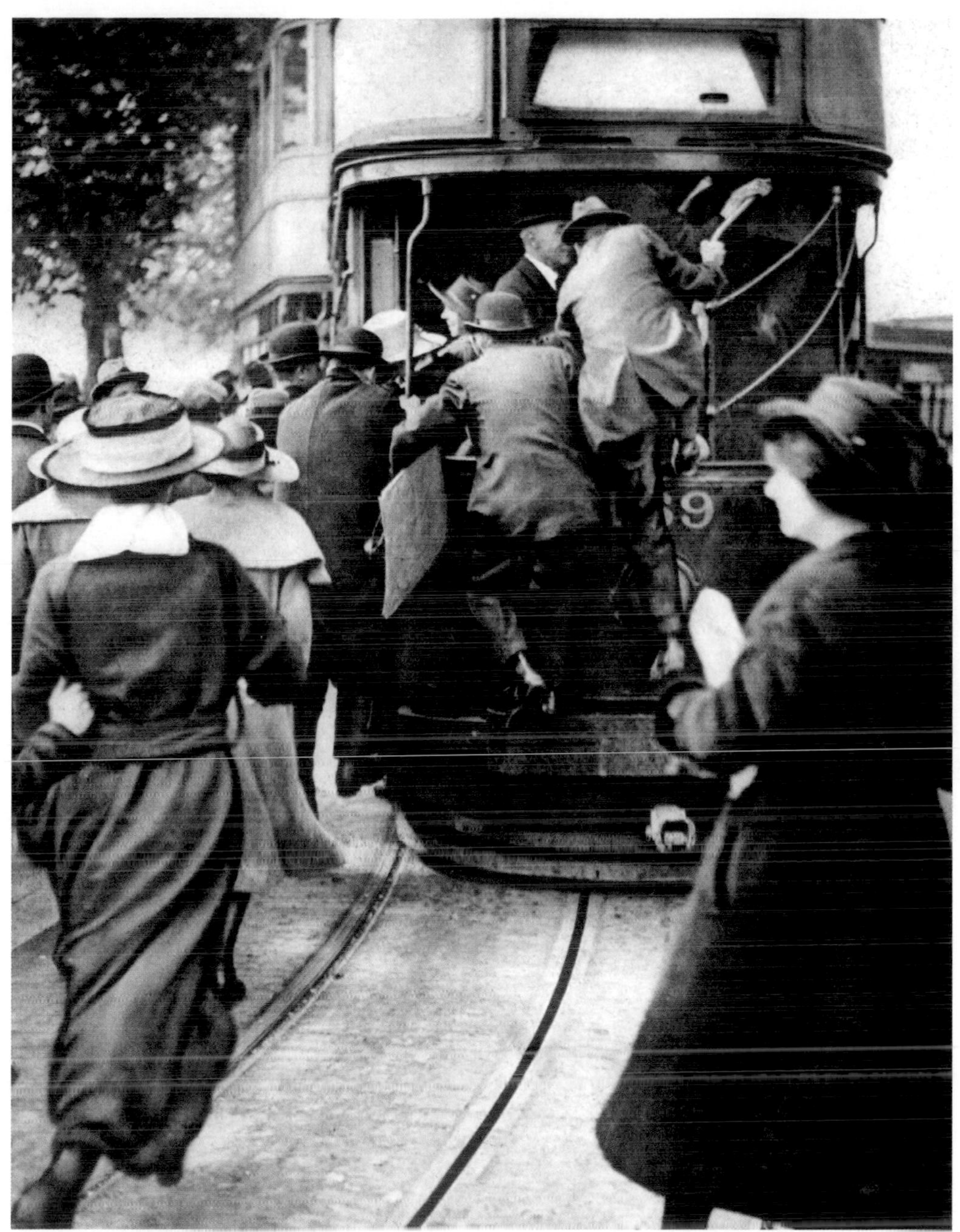

A rush for trams on the Victoria Embankment during a railway strike.
1919

Facing page: Slum dwellings in the East End.
May, 1919

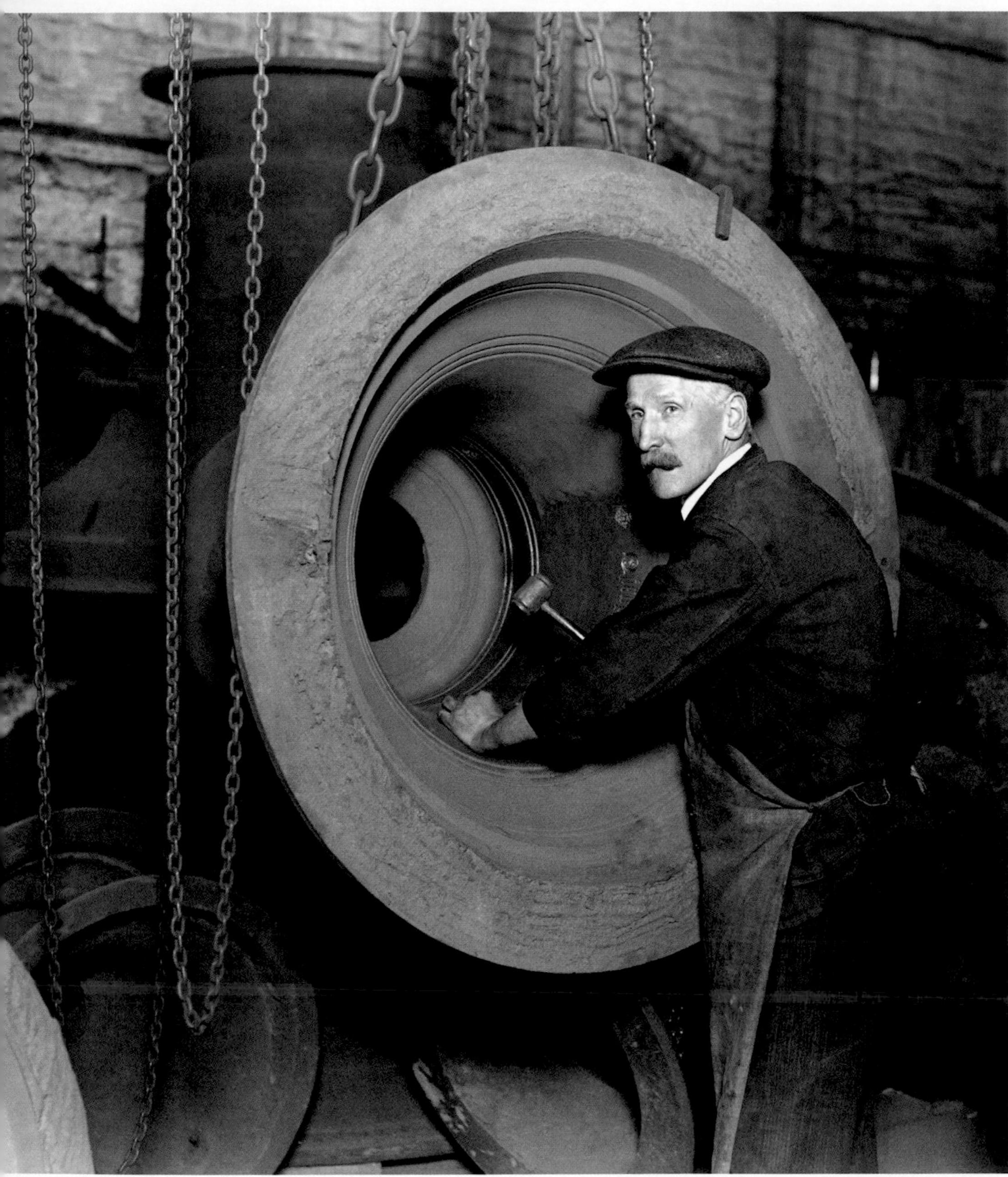

The Whitechapel Bell Foundry – the oldest manufacturing company in the world. Big Ben – the hour bell of the Great Clock of Westminster – and Philadelphia's Liberty Bell were both cast here.
1919

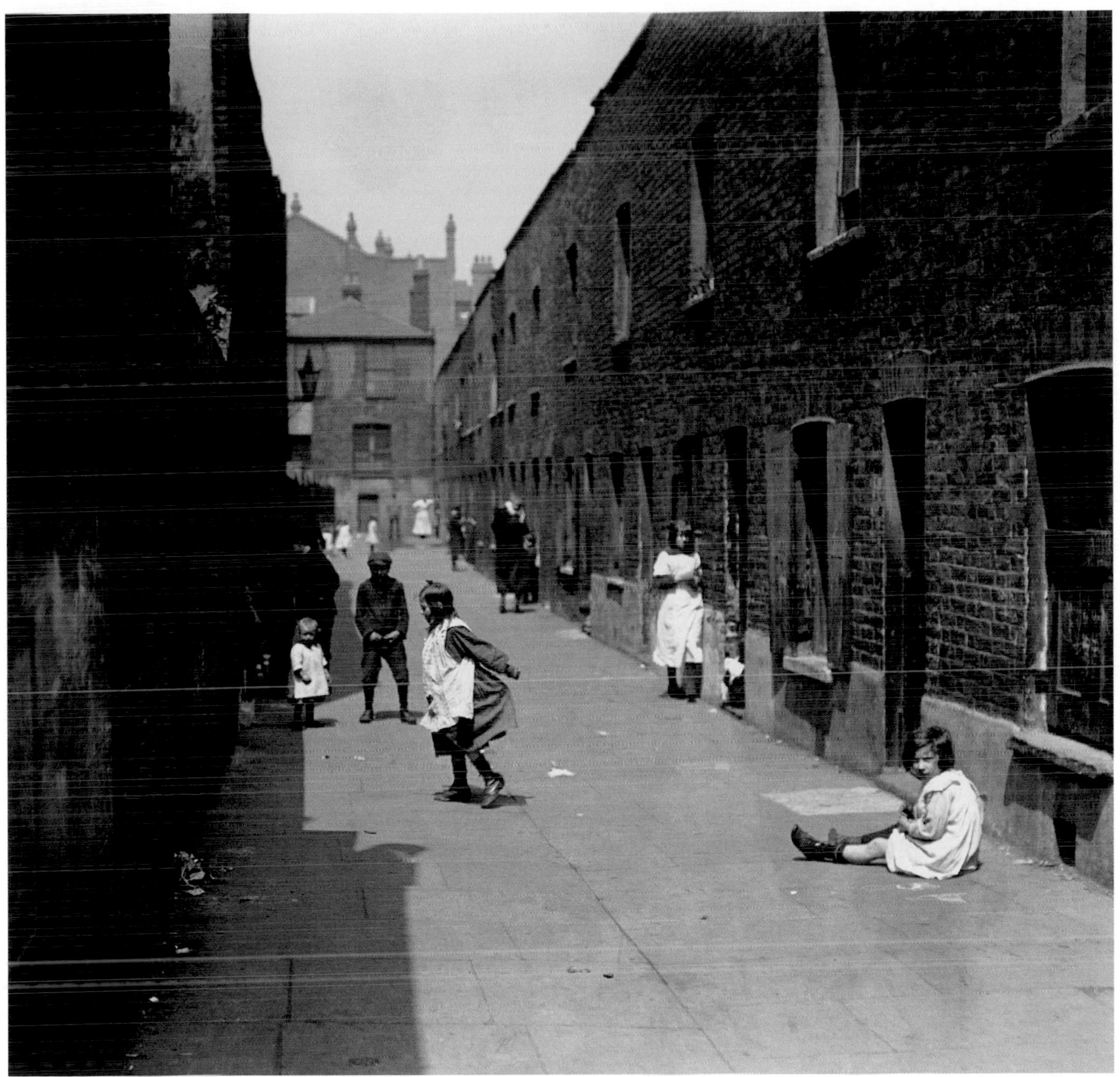

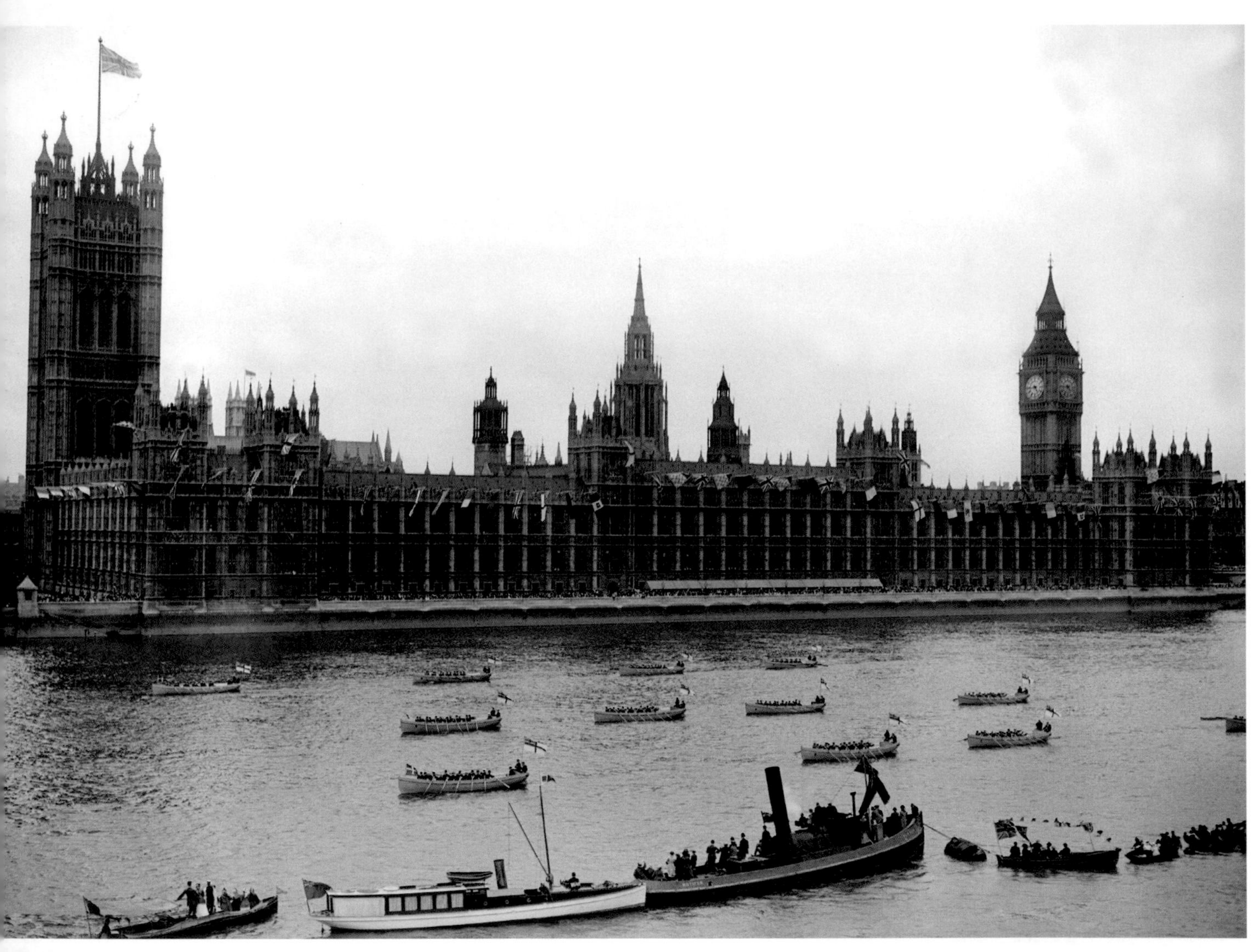

Royal Navy 12-oared cutters taking part in the River Thames Peace Pageant.
4th August, 1919

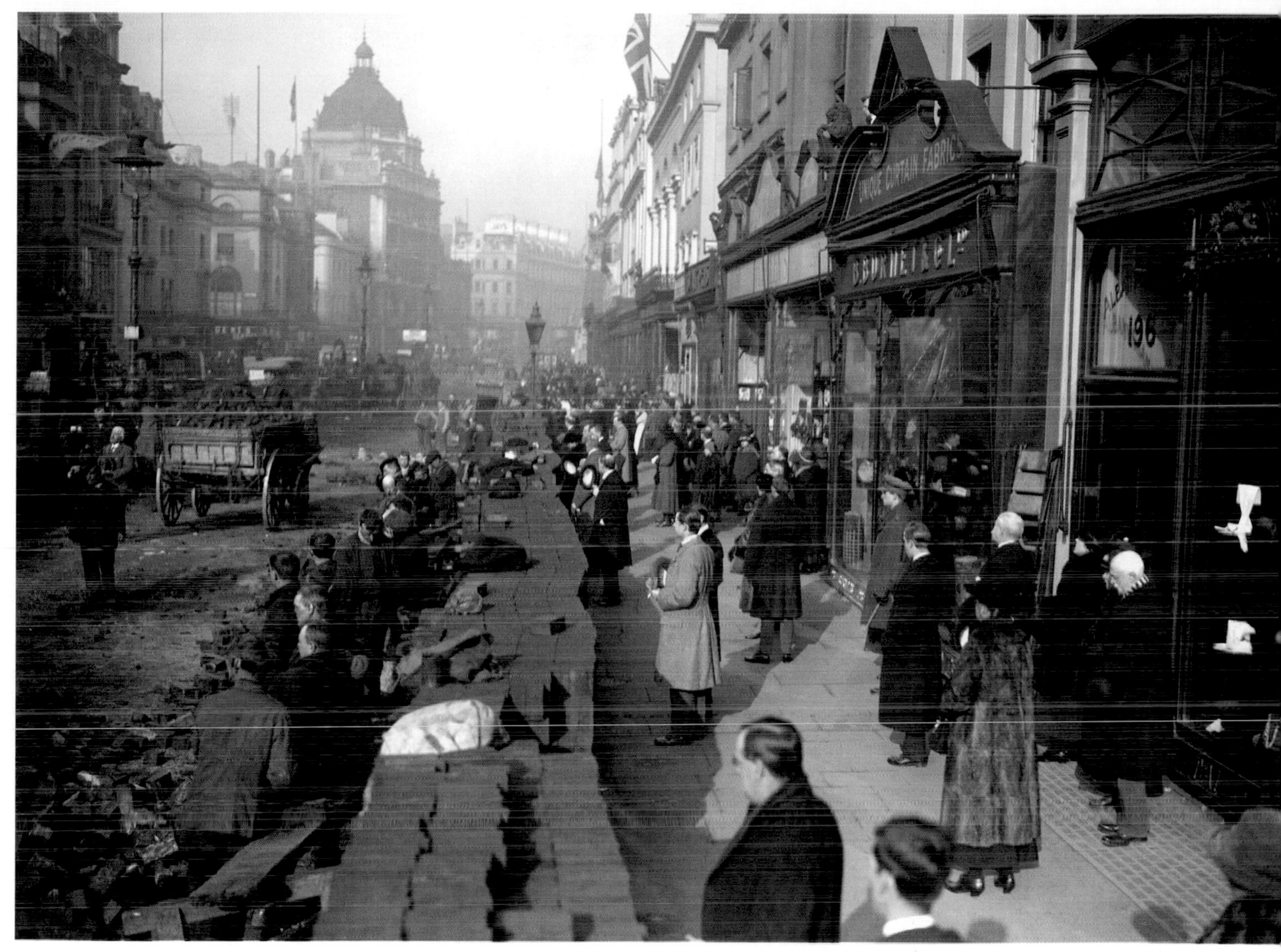

Road workers and pedestrians observe the two-minute silence on the first anniversary of the end of the First World War.

11th November, 1919

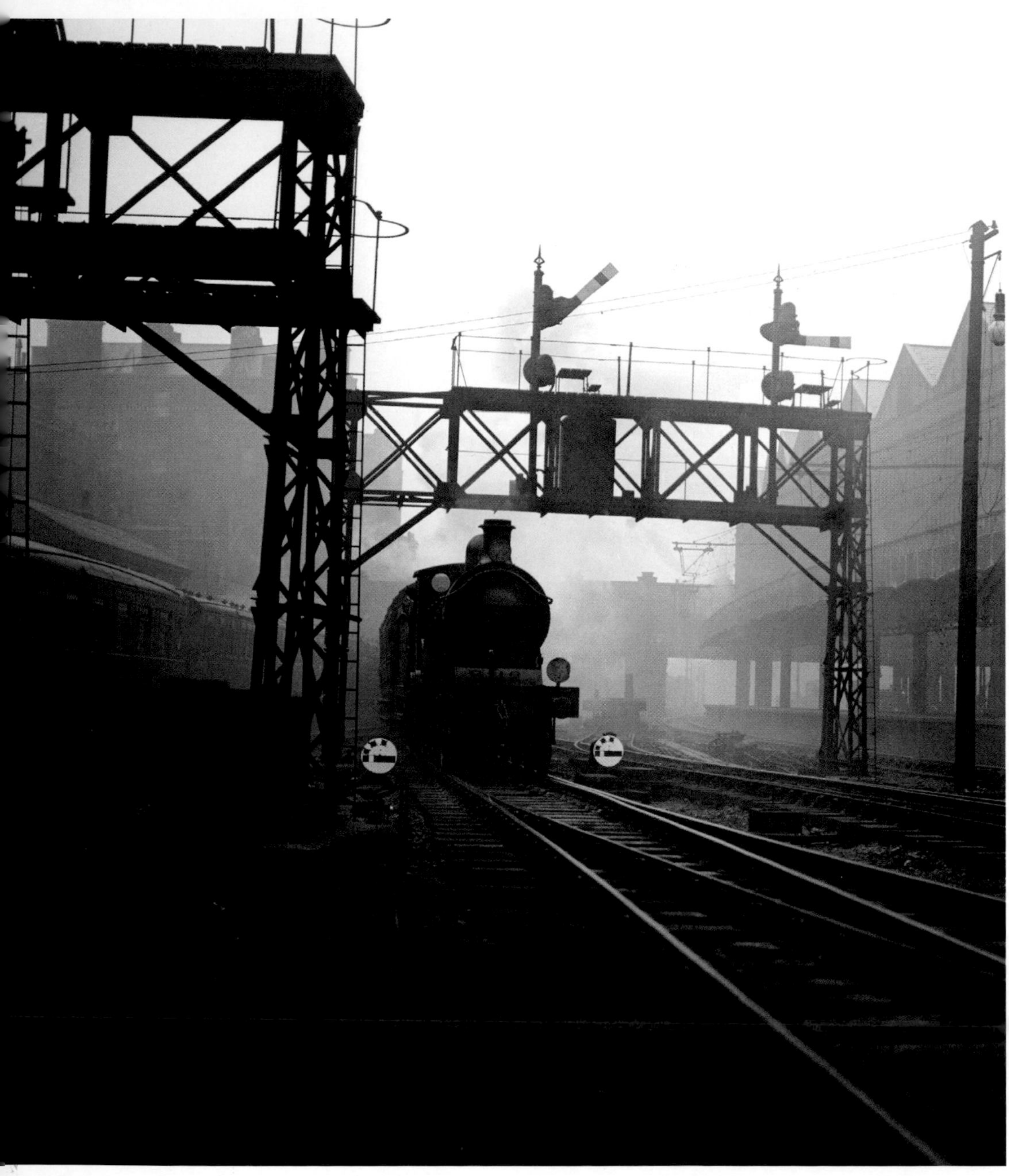

The Chatham express leaves Victoria Station with the new signalling apparatus in the raised position, indicating *All Clear*.
5th January, 1920

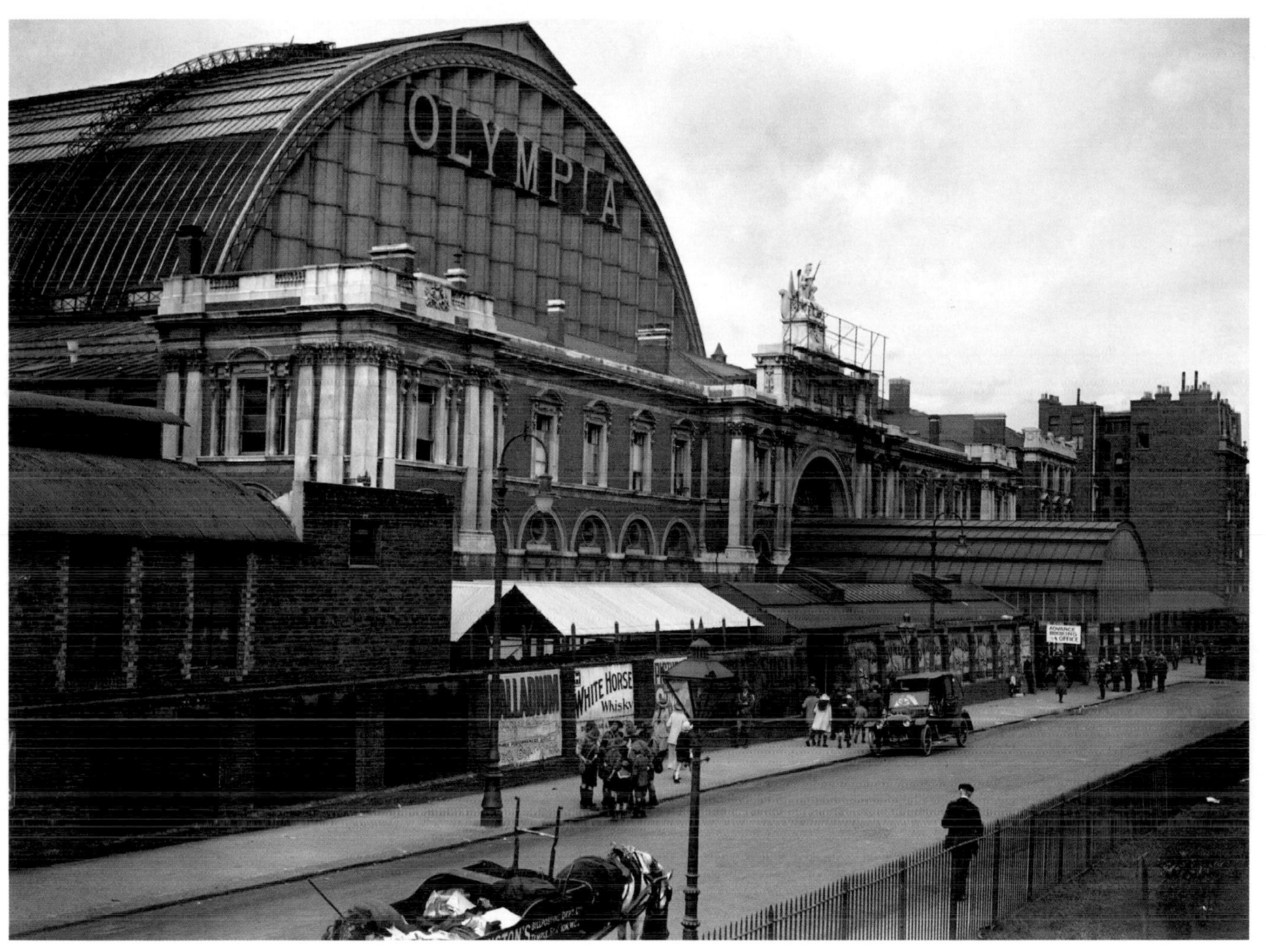

Scouts arrive at Olympia Exhibition Centre for the world's first Boy Scouts' *Jamboree.*
August, 1920

The coffin of the Unknown Warrior rests in the west end of the nave of Westminster Abbey.
11th November, 1920

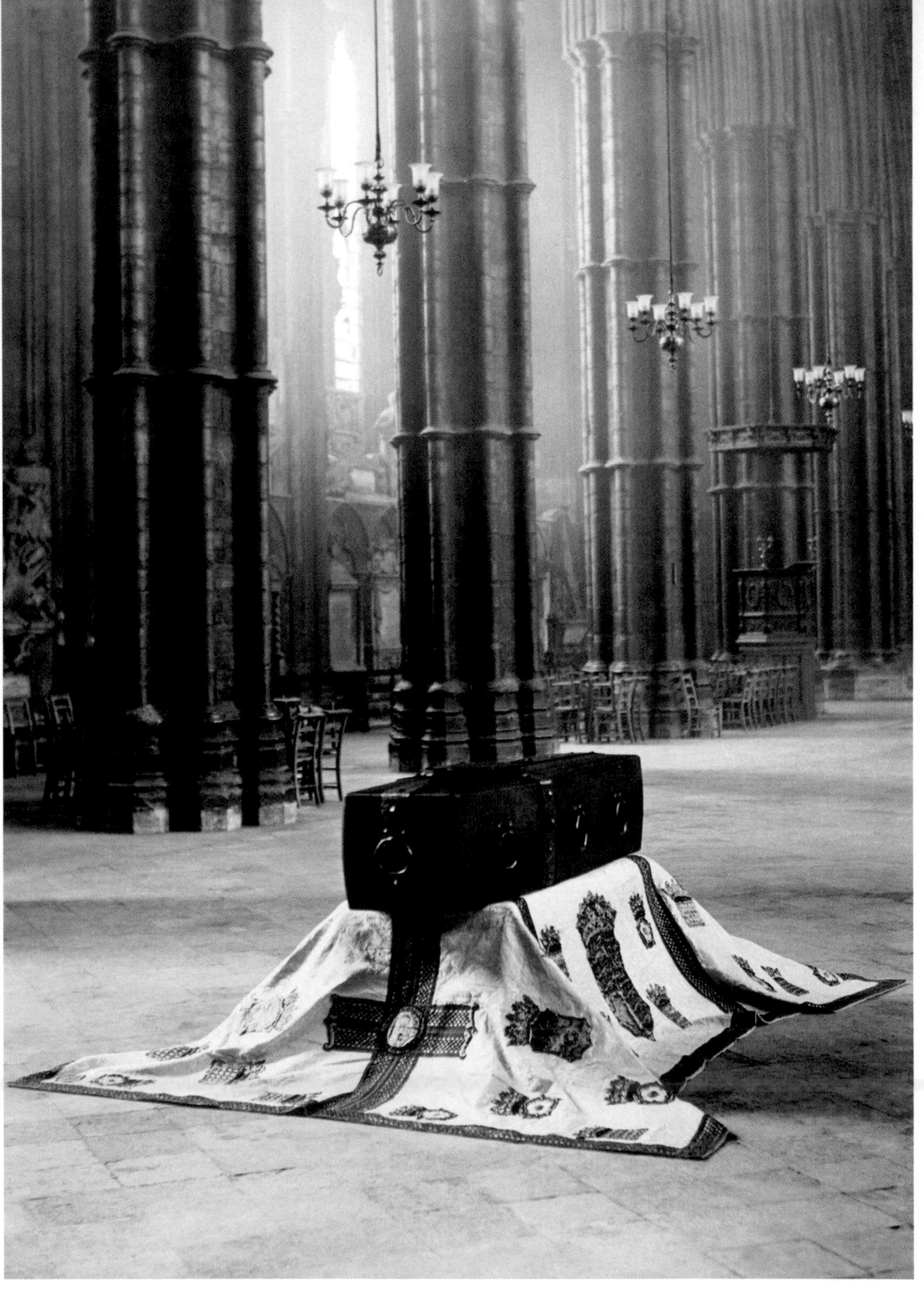

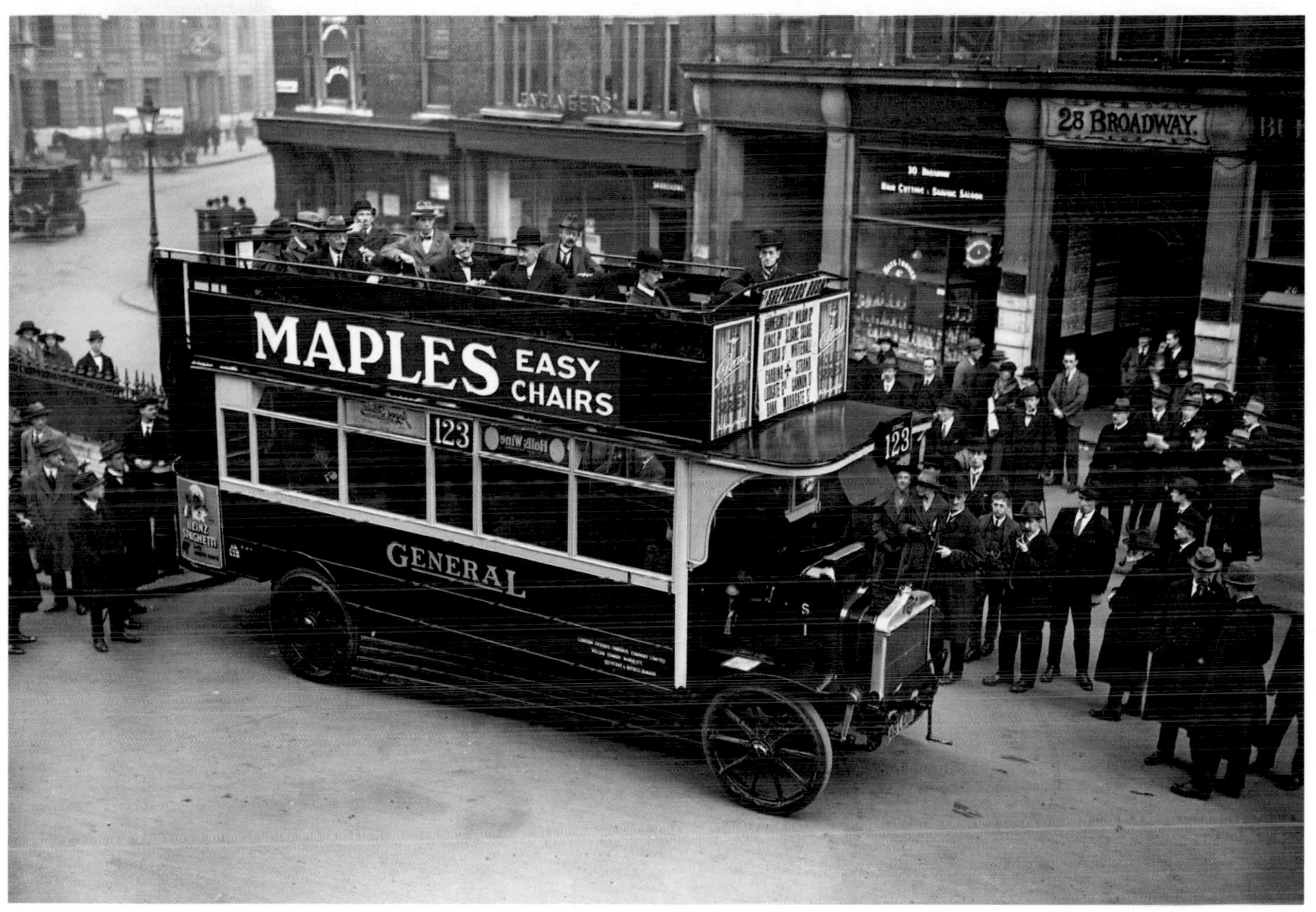

A *K* type motorbus, in The Broadway, Westminster.
16th November, 1920

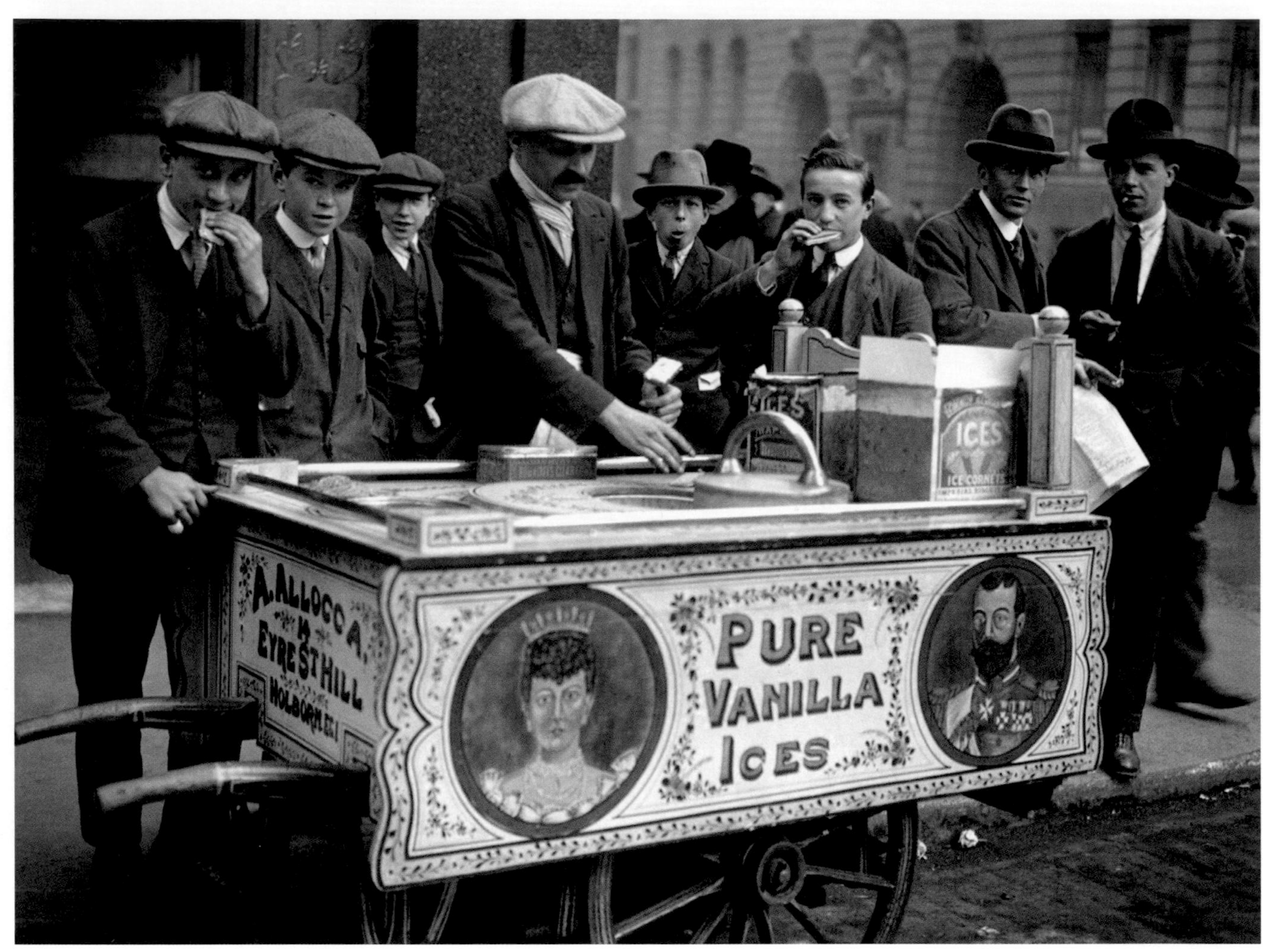

Mr Allocca, one of London's many Italian ice cream sellers, and his patriotically decorated cart.
3rd January, 1921

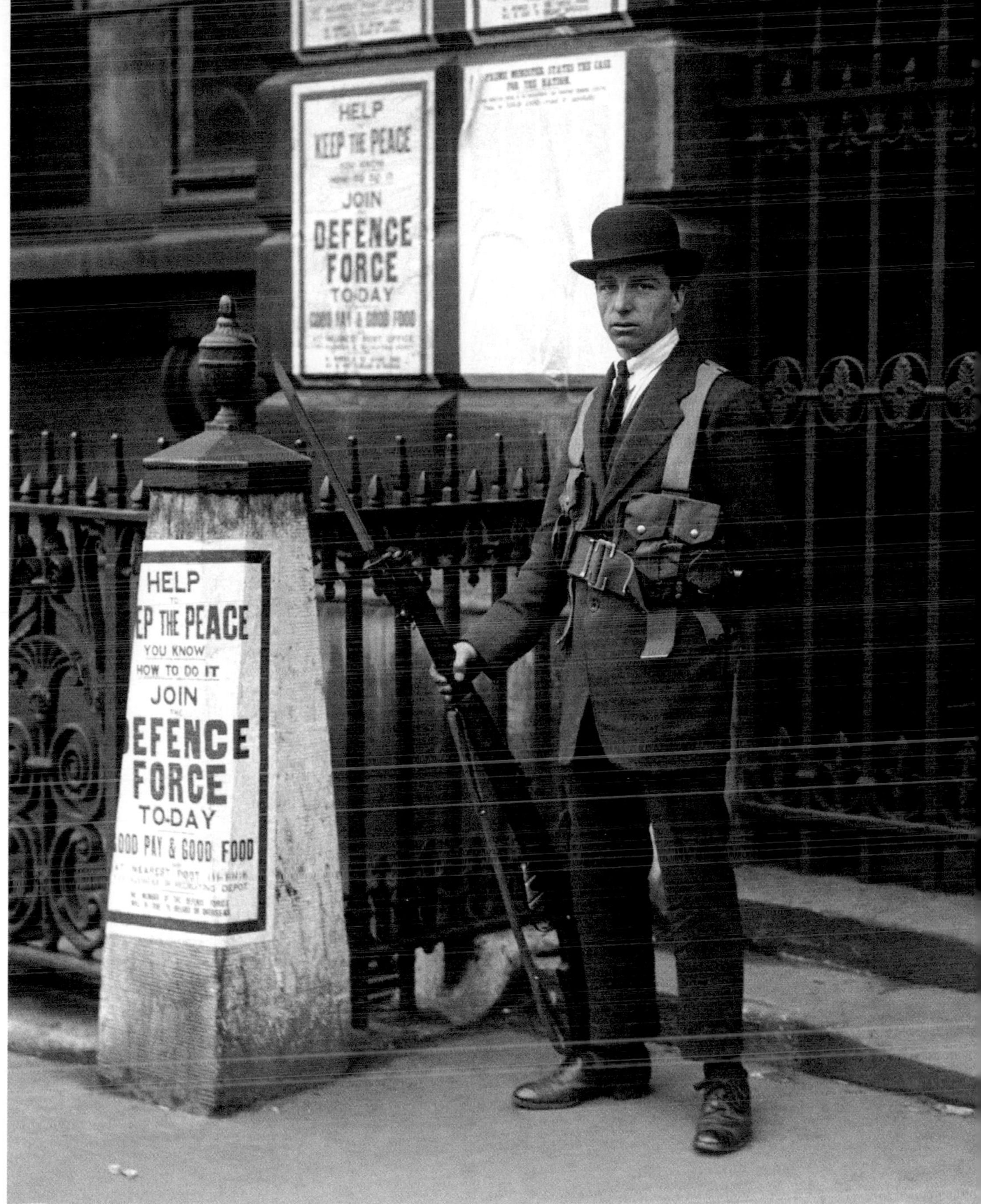

A Defence Force sentry at Somerset House, during the strike crisis of 1921. Defence Force members were taken from the Territorial Army but did not wear uniform, as the TA cannot be used to suppress civil disturbances.
1st April, 1921

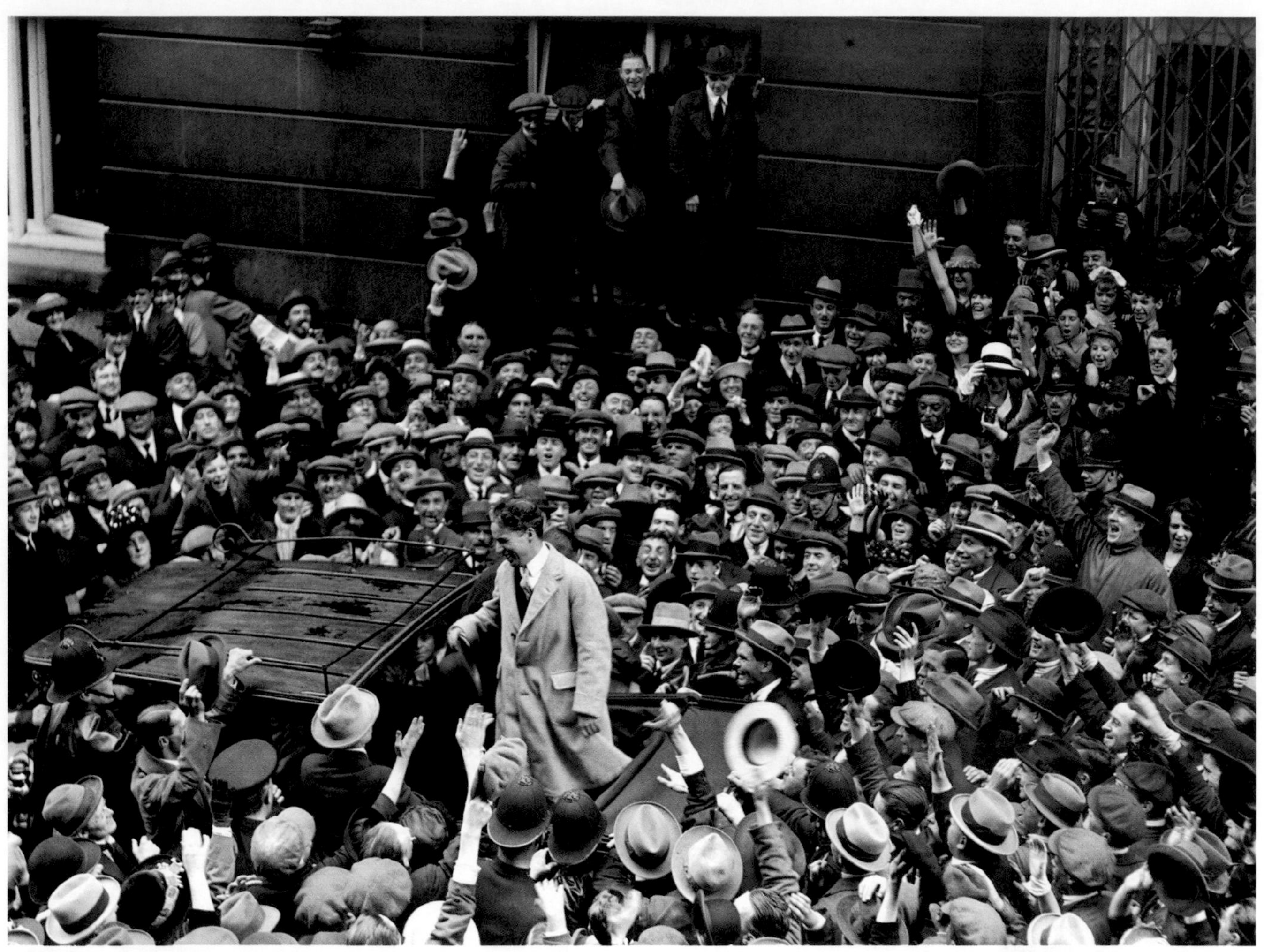

Charlie Chaplin returns to his native London to promote his new film *The Kid*.
10th September, 1921

Facing page:
Waterloo Station.
25th April, 1922

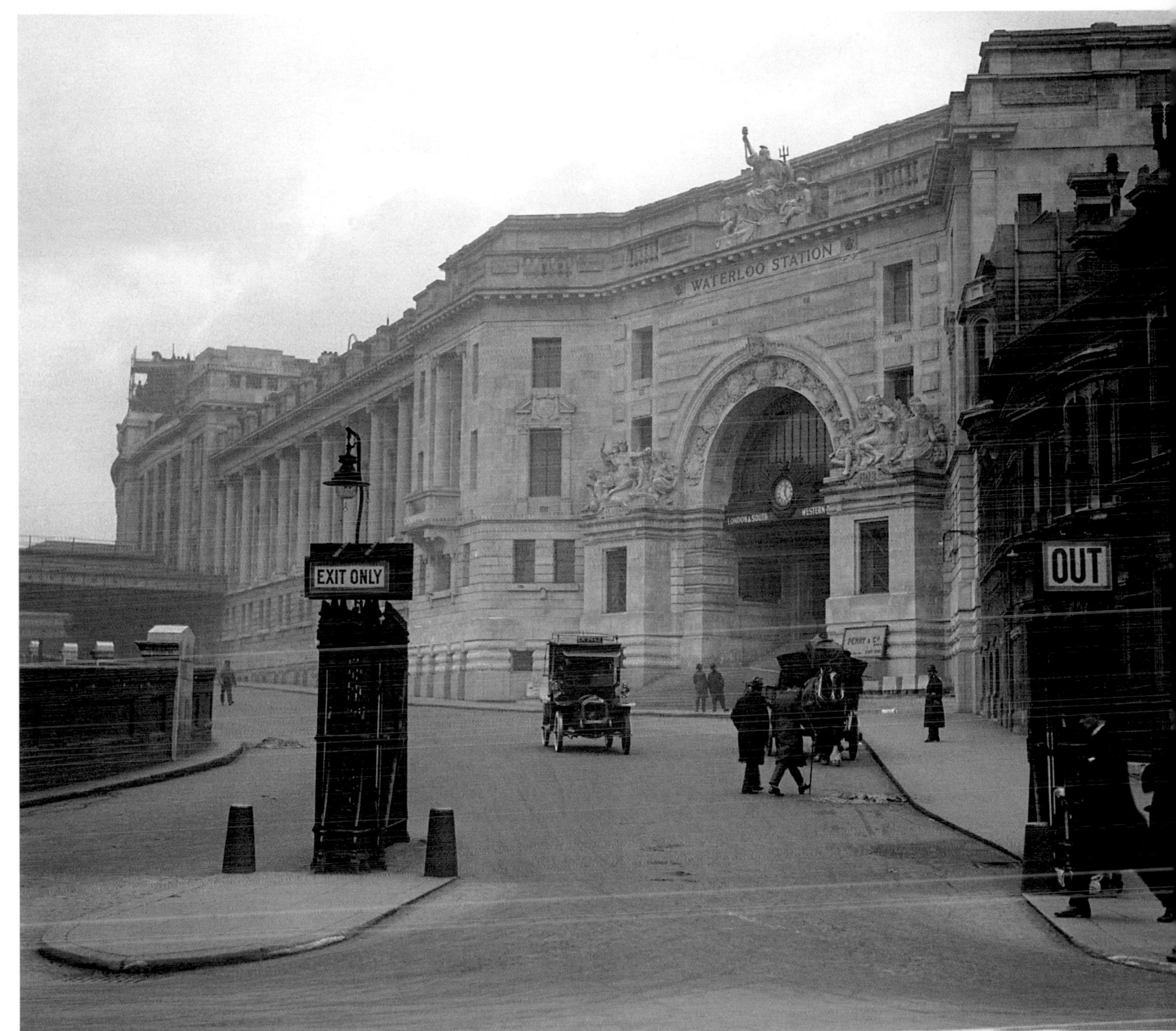
WATERLOO STATION
EXIT ONLY
OUT

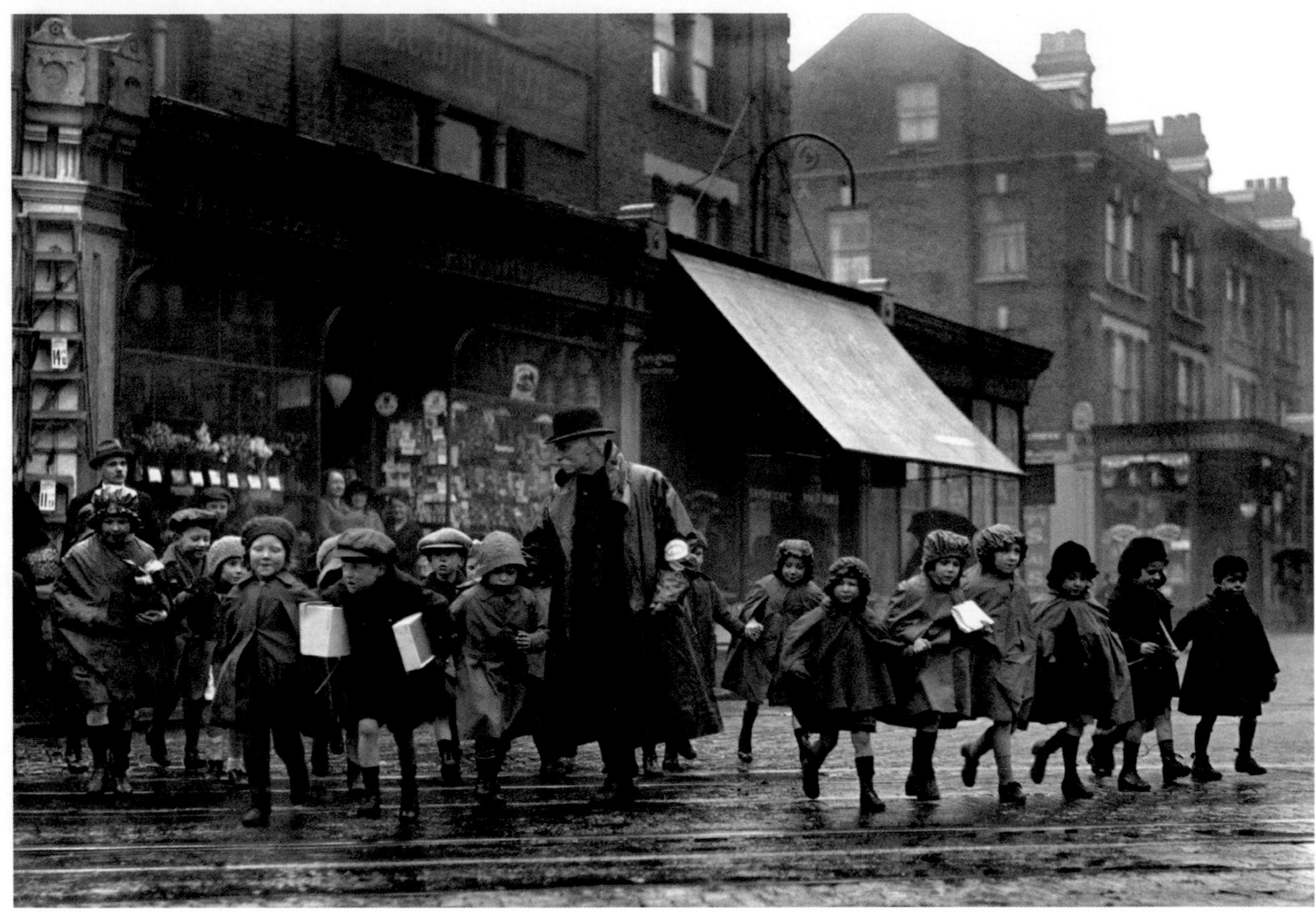

Volunteer crossing guard Mr Cannell shepherds children across the road at Tufnell Park. Many such volunteer guards were old soldiers.
6th November, 1922

Facing page: A dustman in Kentish Town. Motorised dustcarts first appeared on the streets of the capital in the 1920s.
13th July, 1925

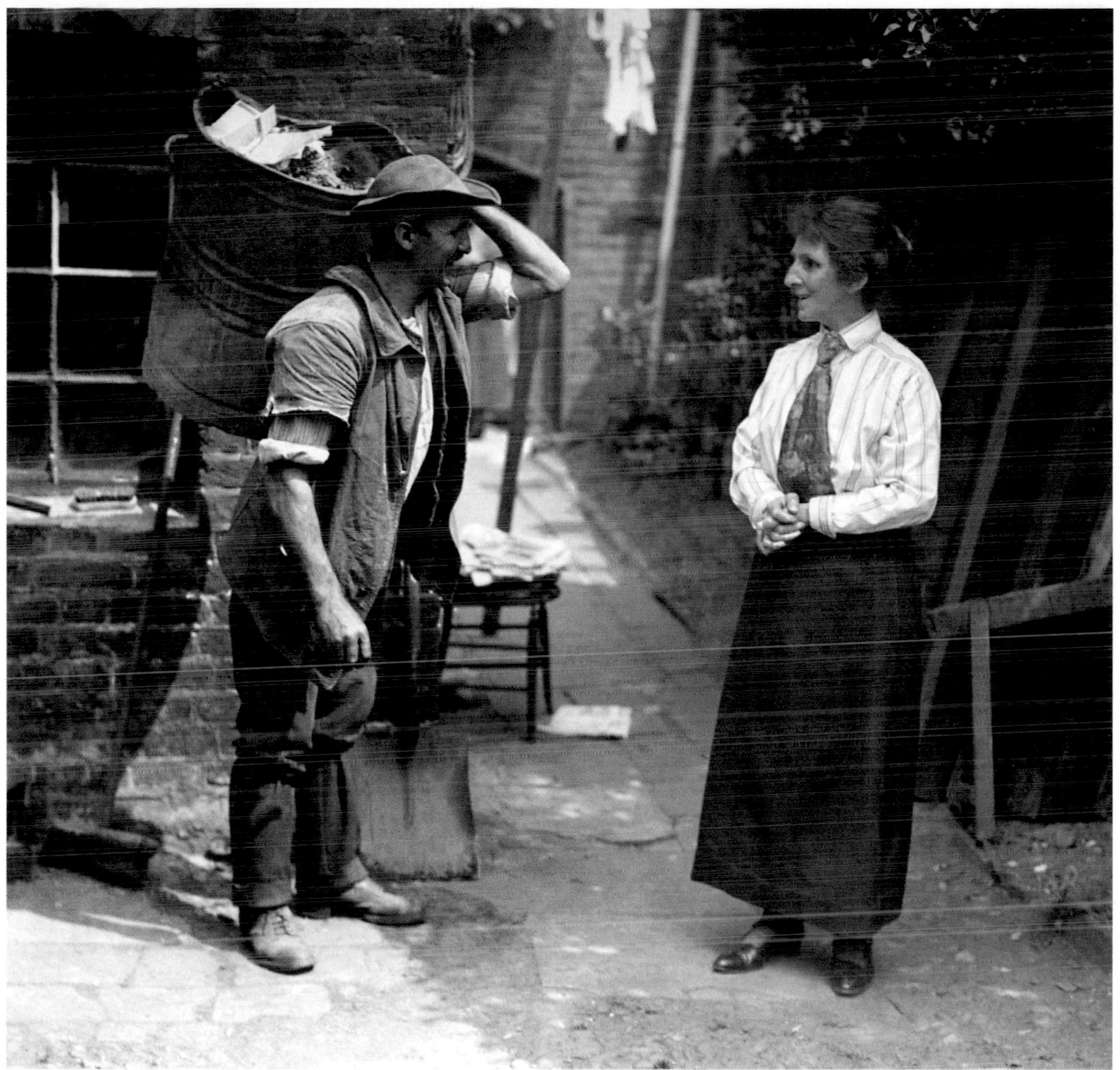

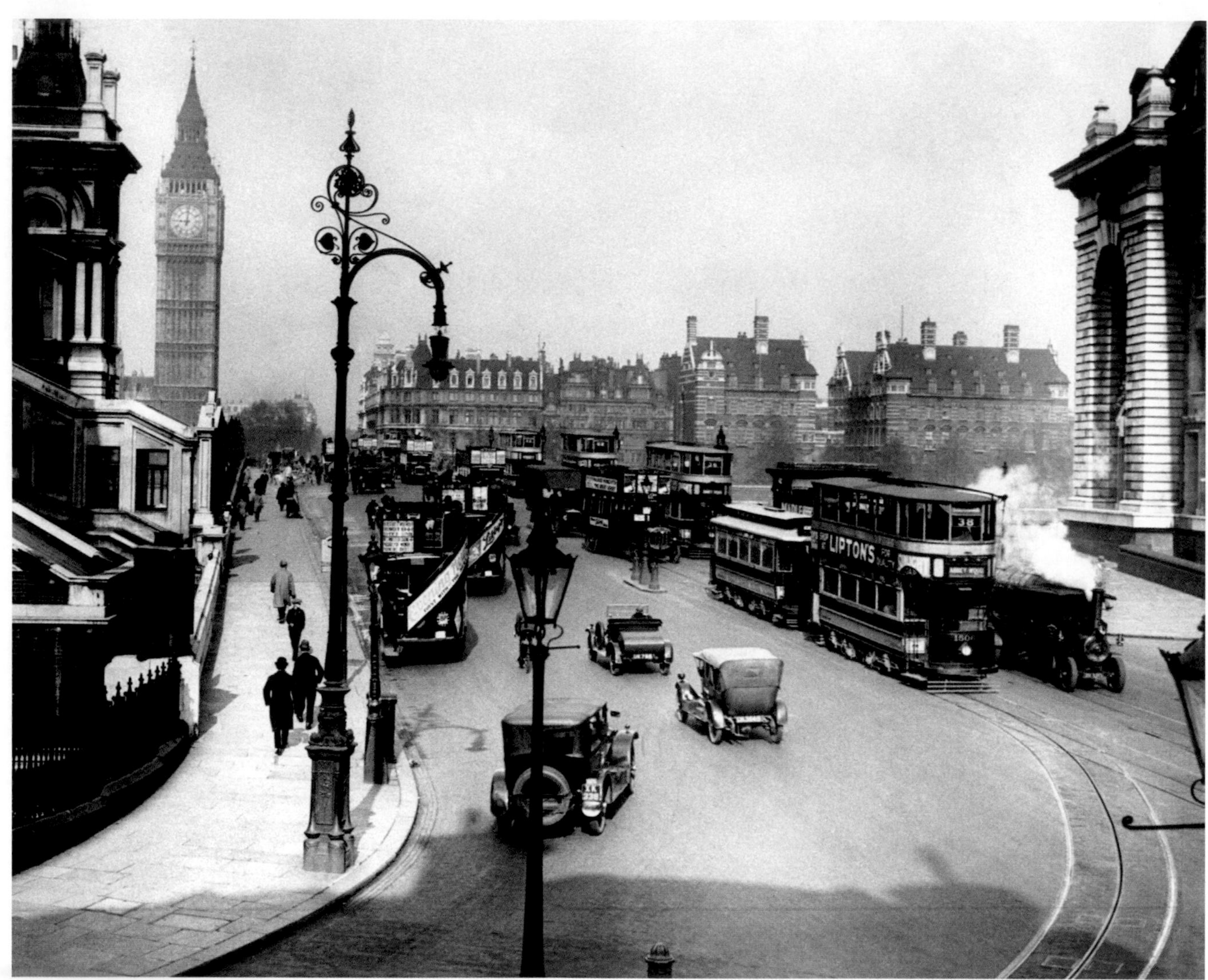

Traffic returns to normal across Westminster Bridge following the General Strike.
18th May, 1926

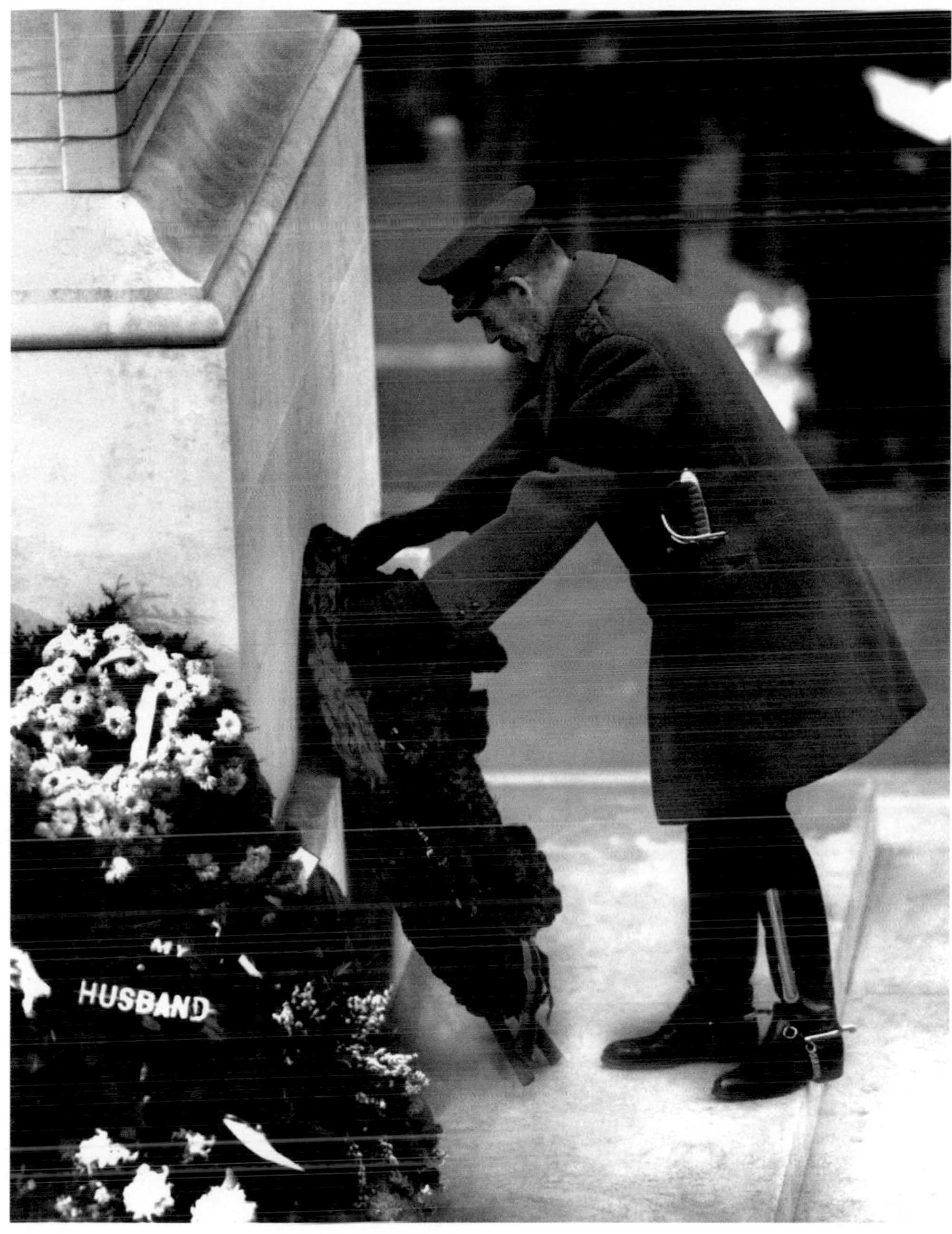

King George V places his wreath at the Cenotaph on Armistice Day.
11th November, 1927

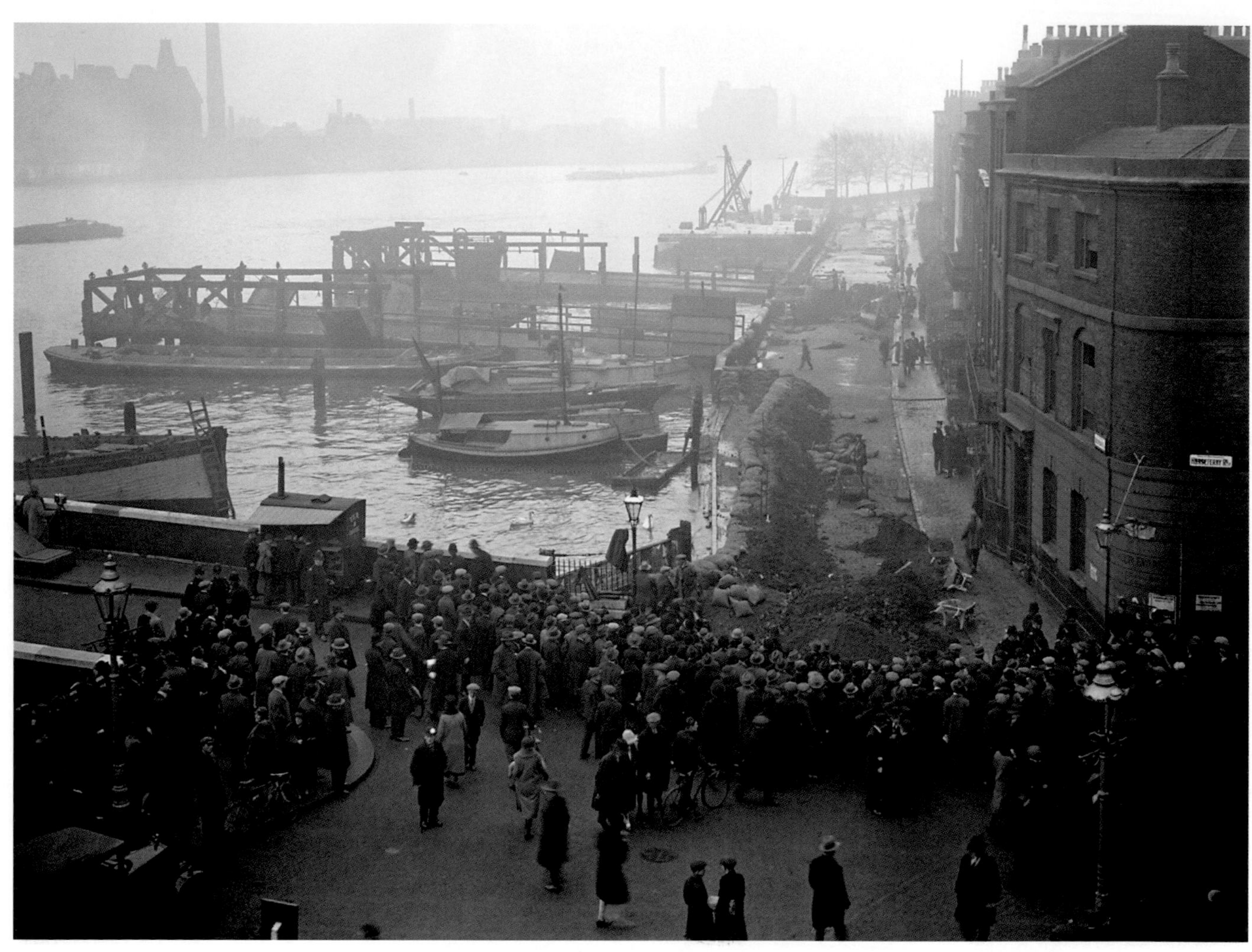

Floods at Grosvenor Road, Westminster. On 6th January 1928 the flood tide on the Thames turned out to be six feet above the predicted level. Many low-lying areas on the river flooded, including Battersea, Pimlico (where the first breach occurred, flooding the Tate Gallery) and Westminster. Further up the river, at Lambeth, the defences gave way and drowned 14 people in their basement flats.
7th January, 1928

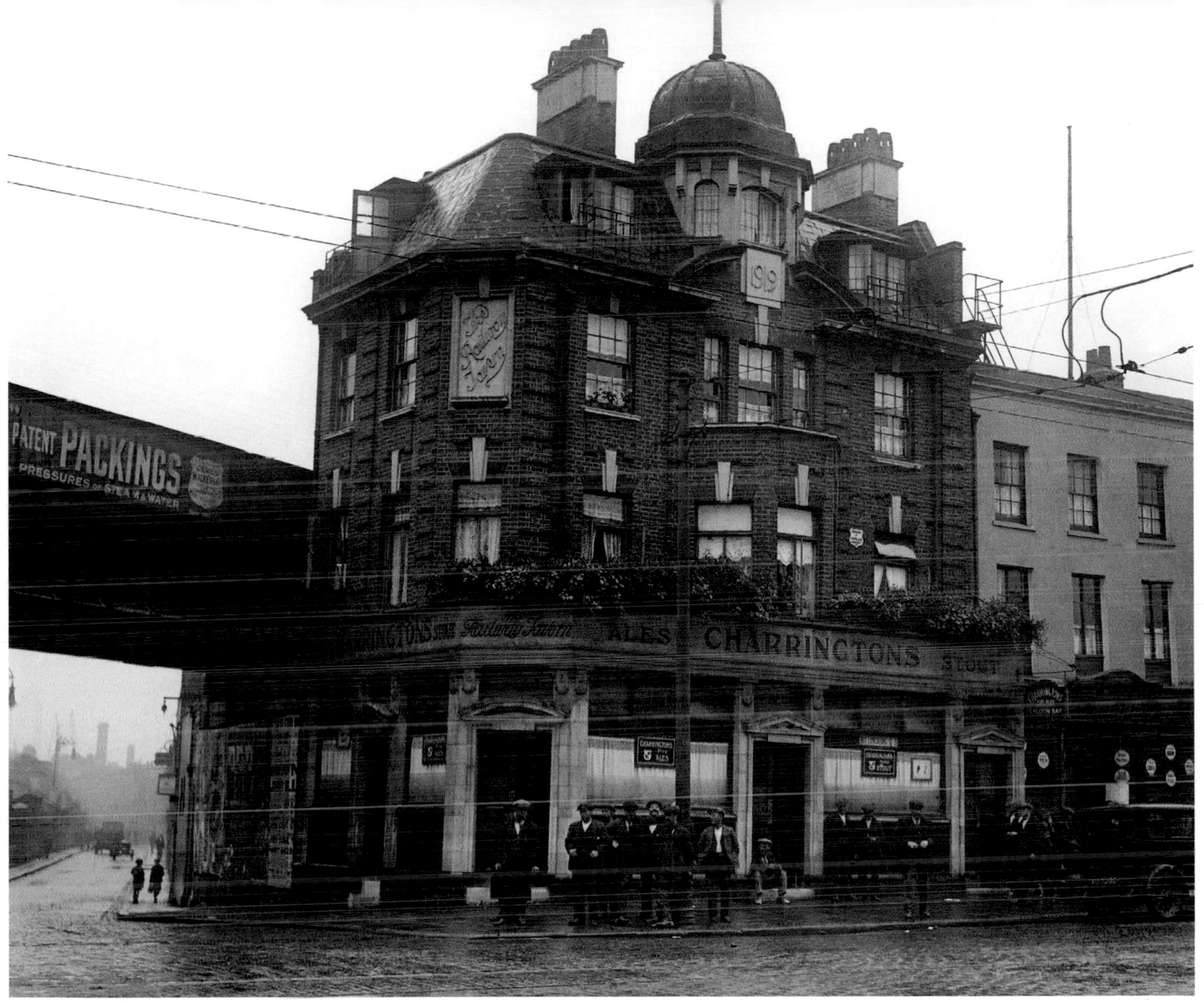

The Railway Tavern on West India Dock Road, Limehouse.
August, 1928

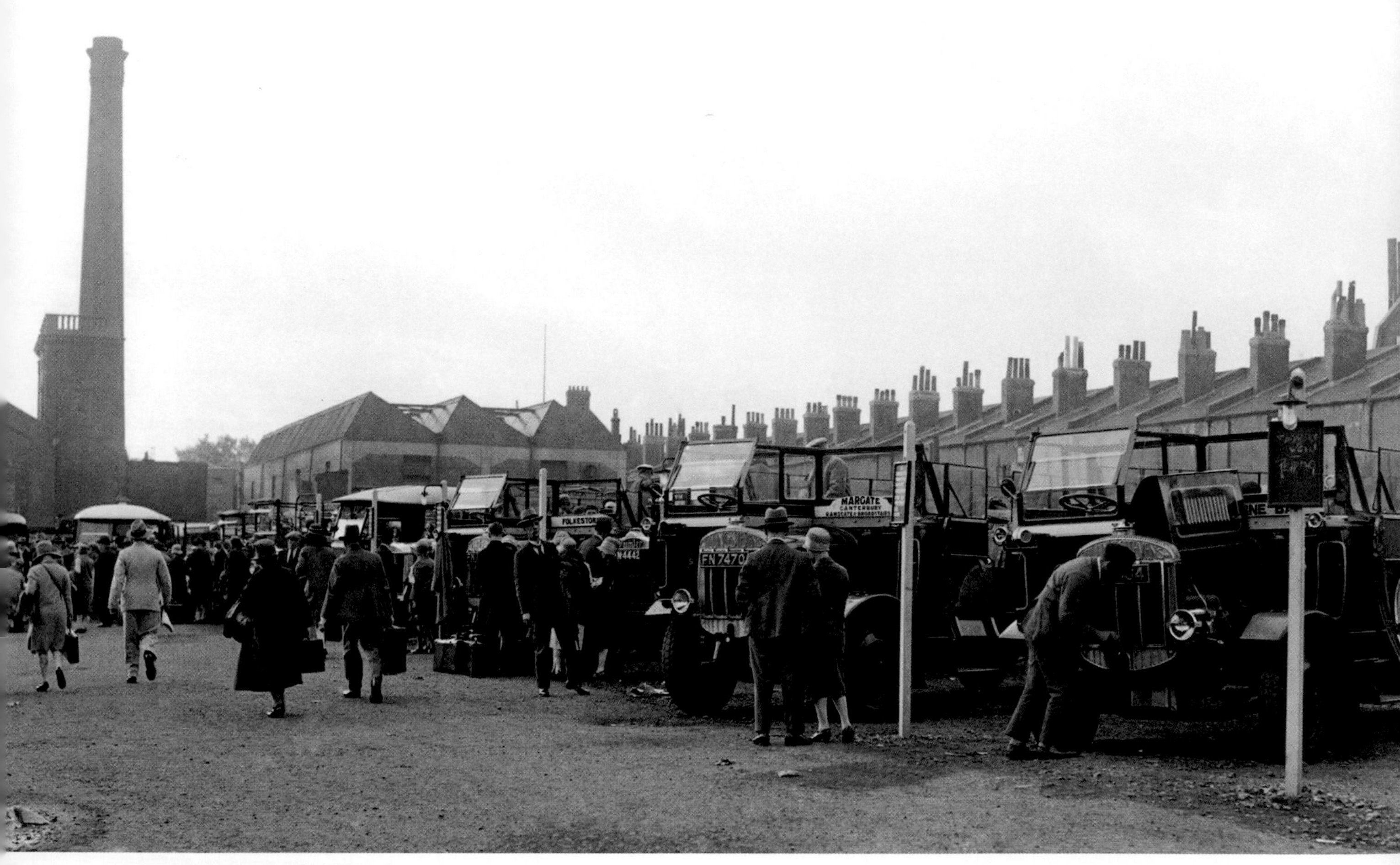

London Coastal Coaches' charabancs at the coach station on Lupus Road, Westminster, prepare for day trips to the coast.
August, 1928

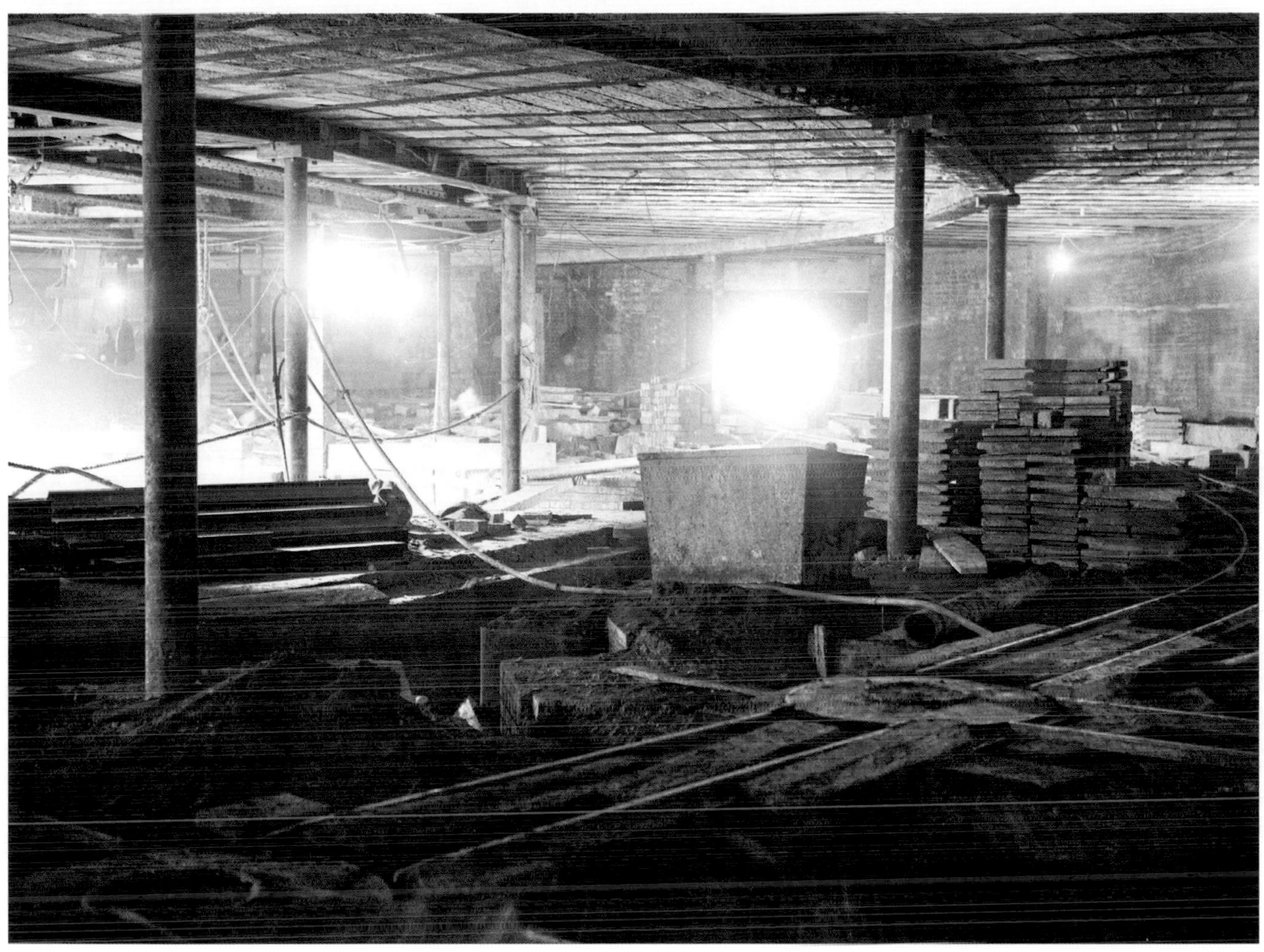

Upgrading work at Piccadilly Underground Station.
September, 1928

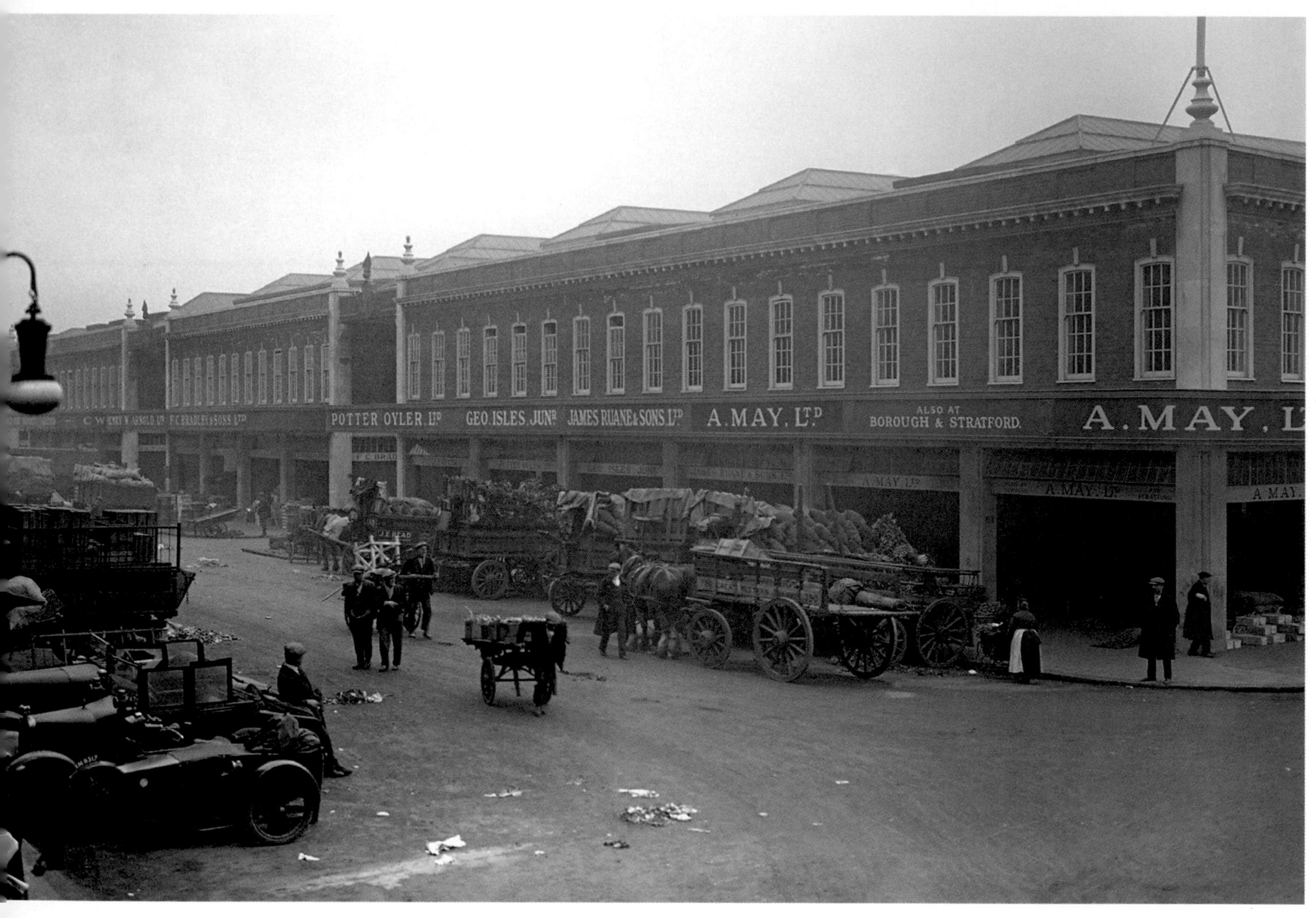

The new £2m Spitalfields Market stands ready to open. Claimed, at the time, to be Europe's finest market, the new development on the site of the original market took nine years to build.
2nd October, 1928

Facing page: A mobile greengrocer demonstrates an economical way to deliver.
February, 1929

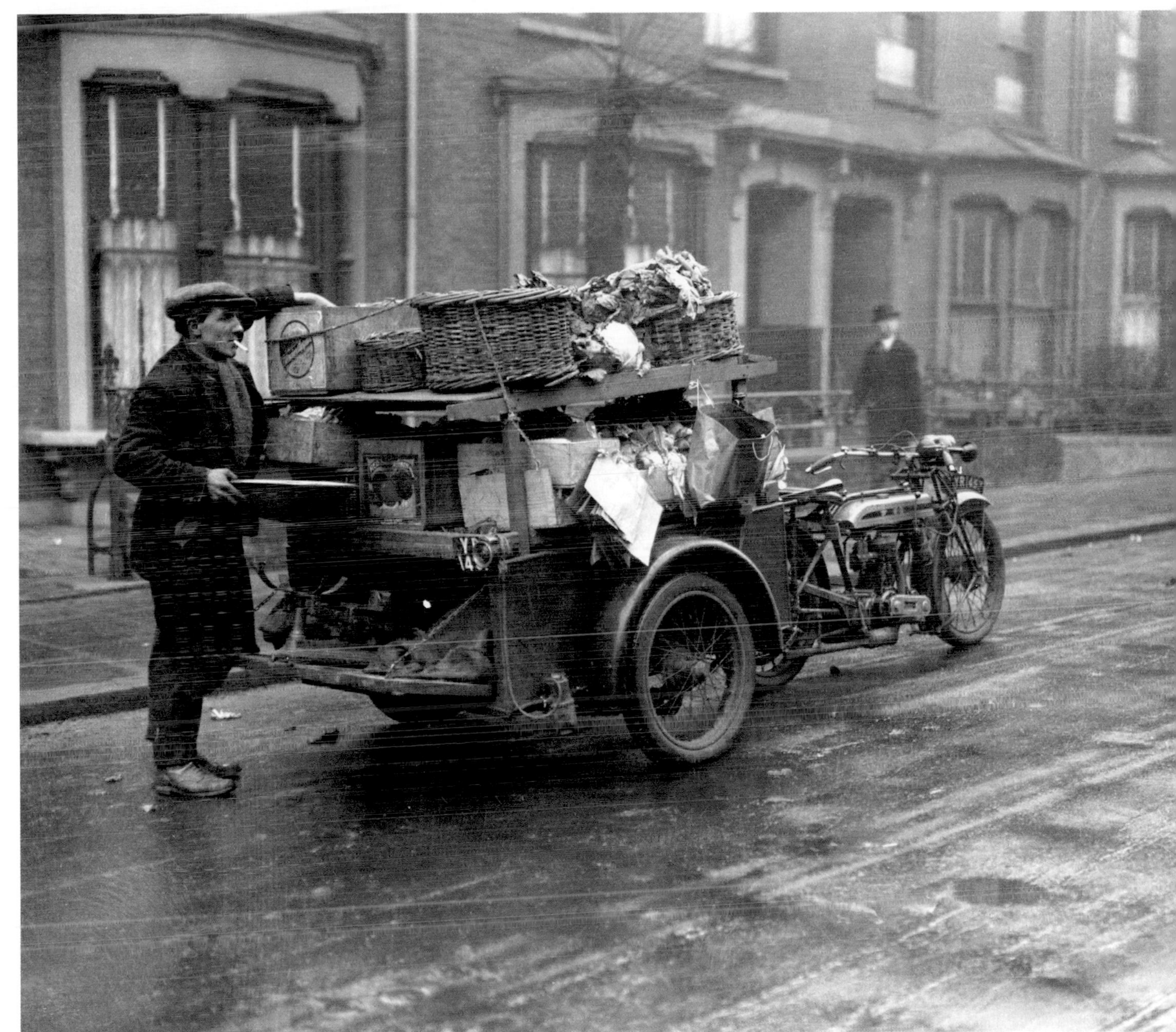

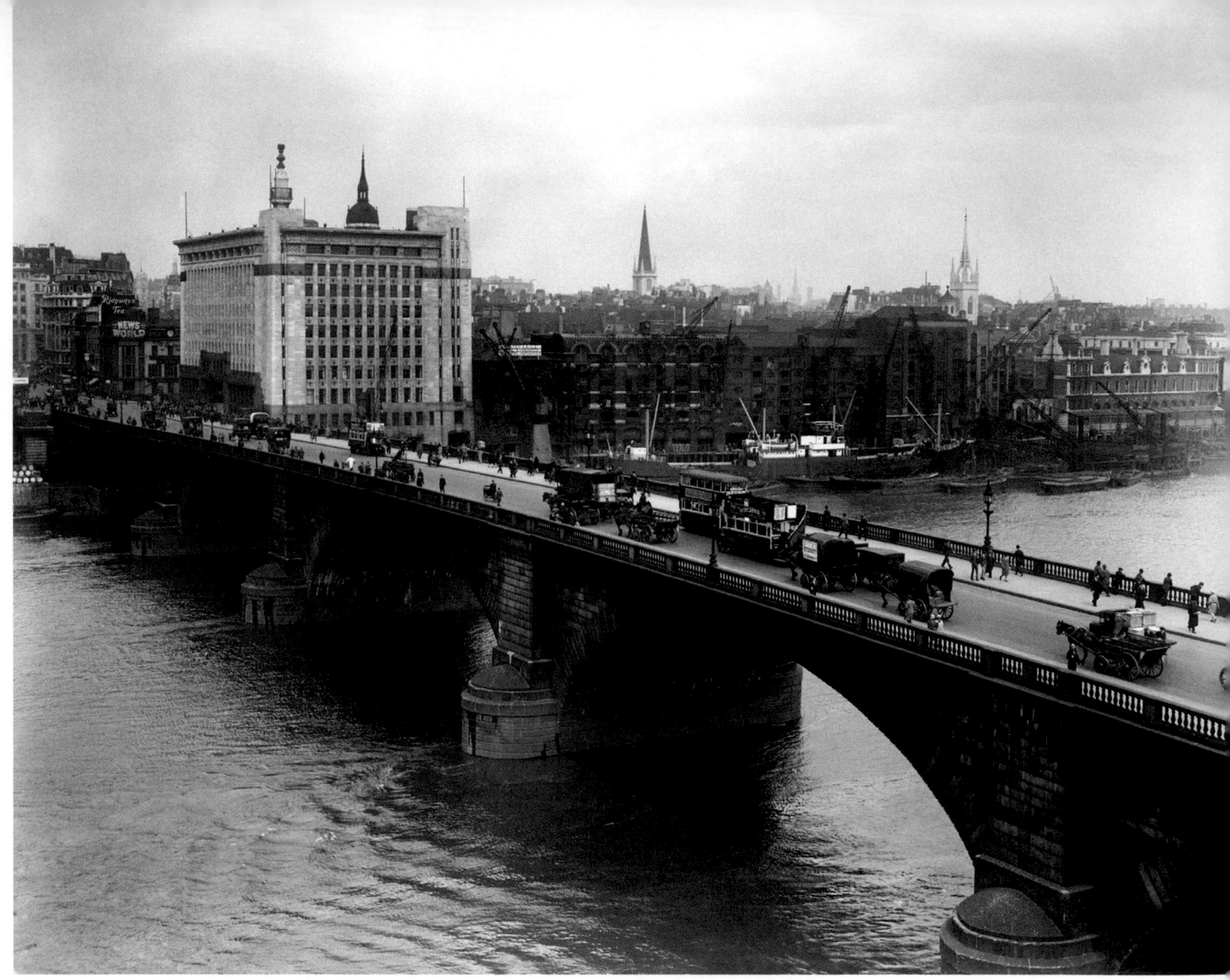

John Rennie's London Bridge, dismantled in 1972 and now a tourist attraction in Lake Havasu City, Arizona. Claims that the buyer, Robert P McCulloch, was expecting Tower Bridge were later denied by the Arizona businessman.
May, 1929

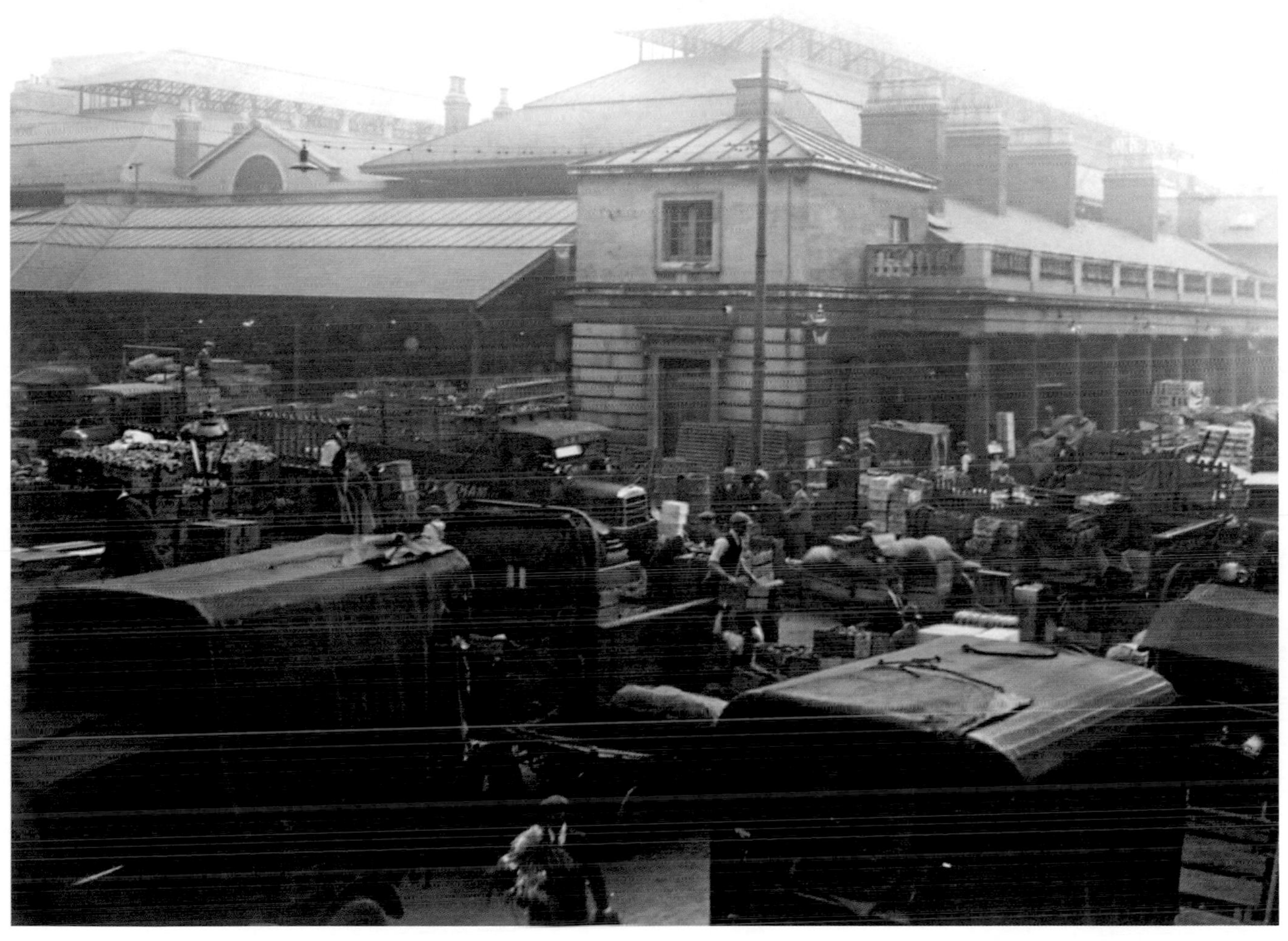

Covent Garden. The famous market was moved to Nine Elms in the 1960s.
10th May, 1929

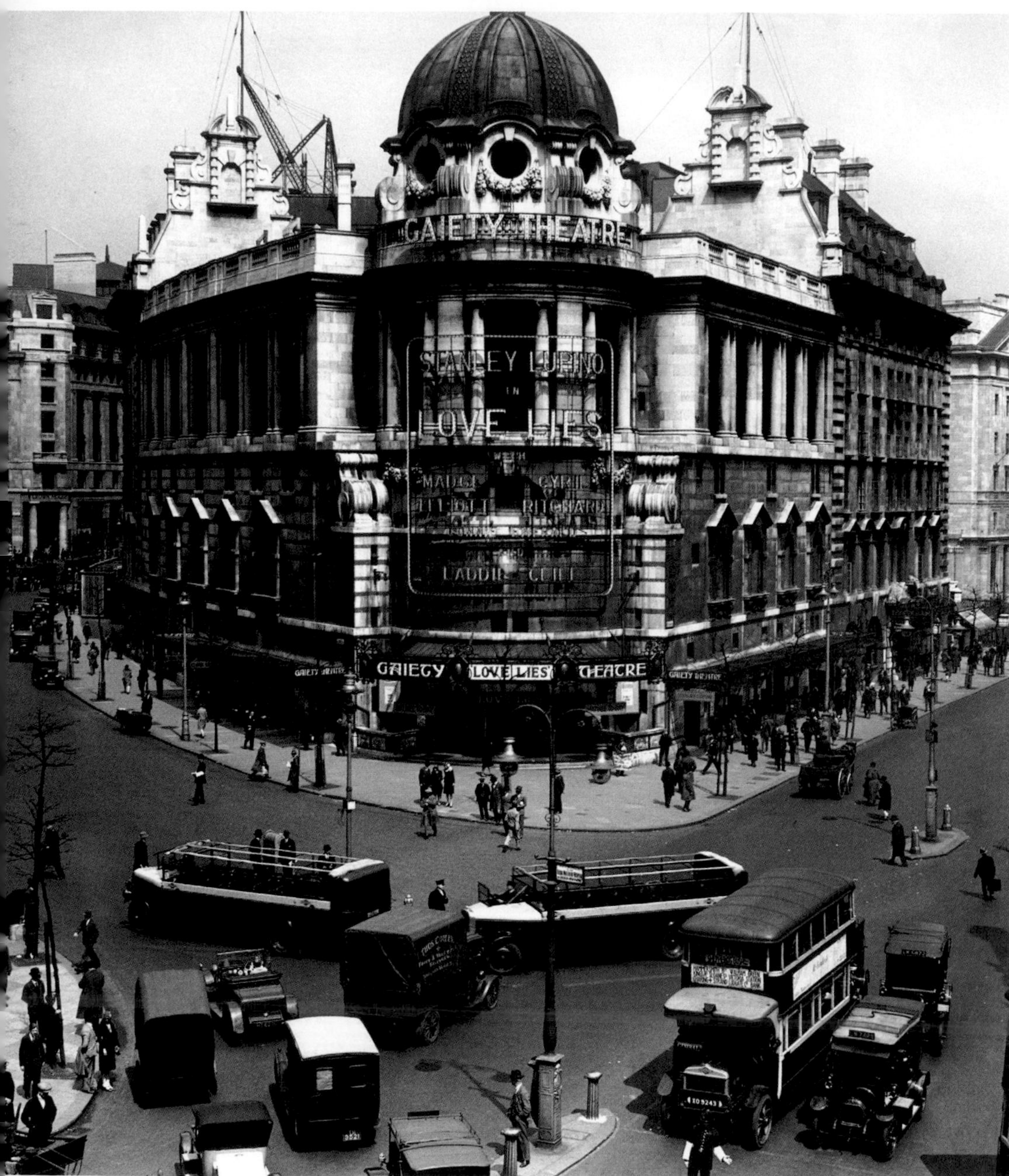

Facing page: Power returns to the Houses of Parliament after a lengthy failure during which government business was conducted by candlelight.
24th November, 1929

The *Gaiety Theatre* on the corner of The Strand and Aldwych.
11th October, 1929

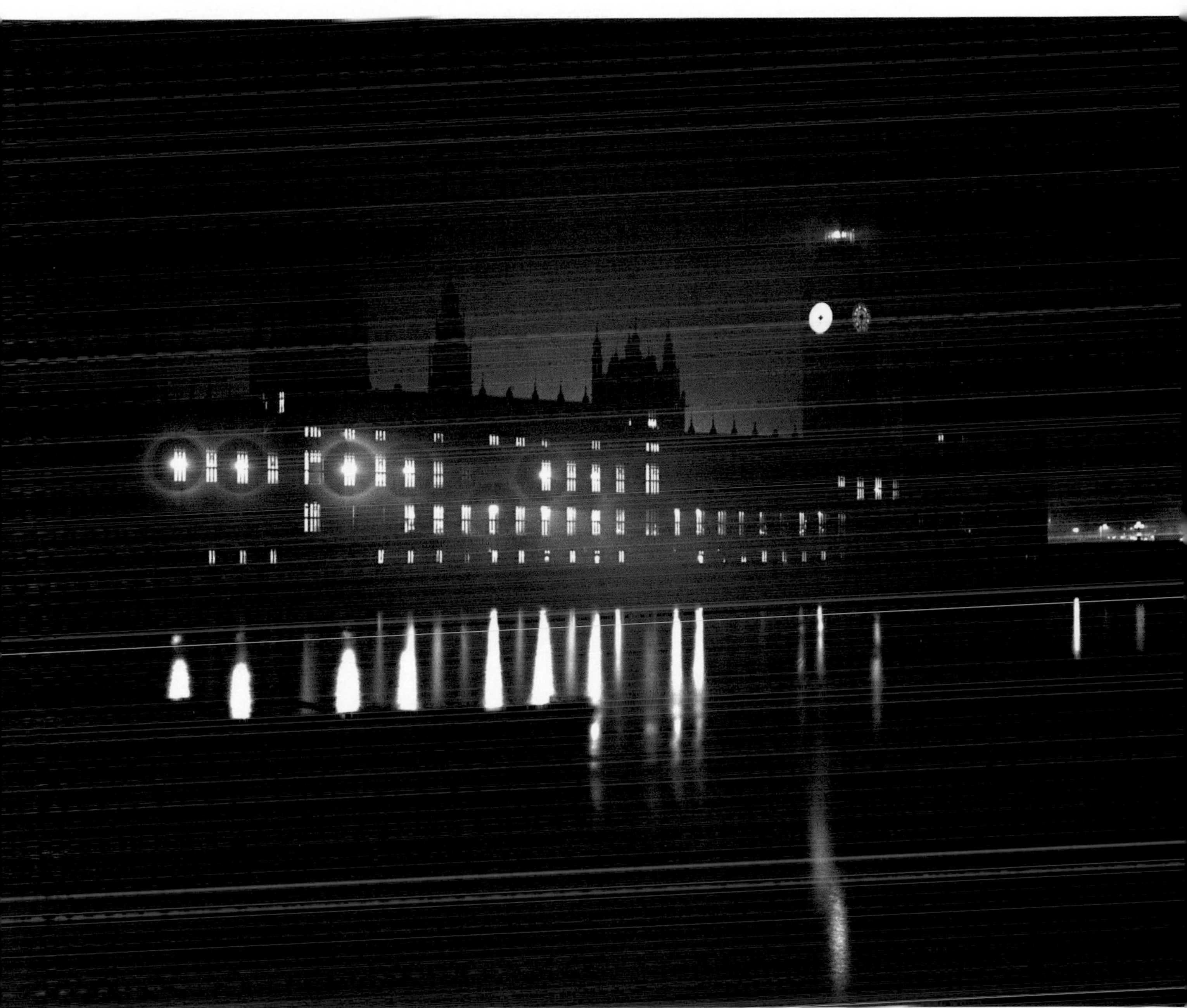

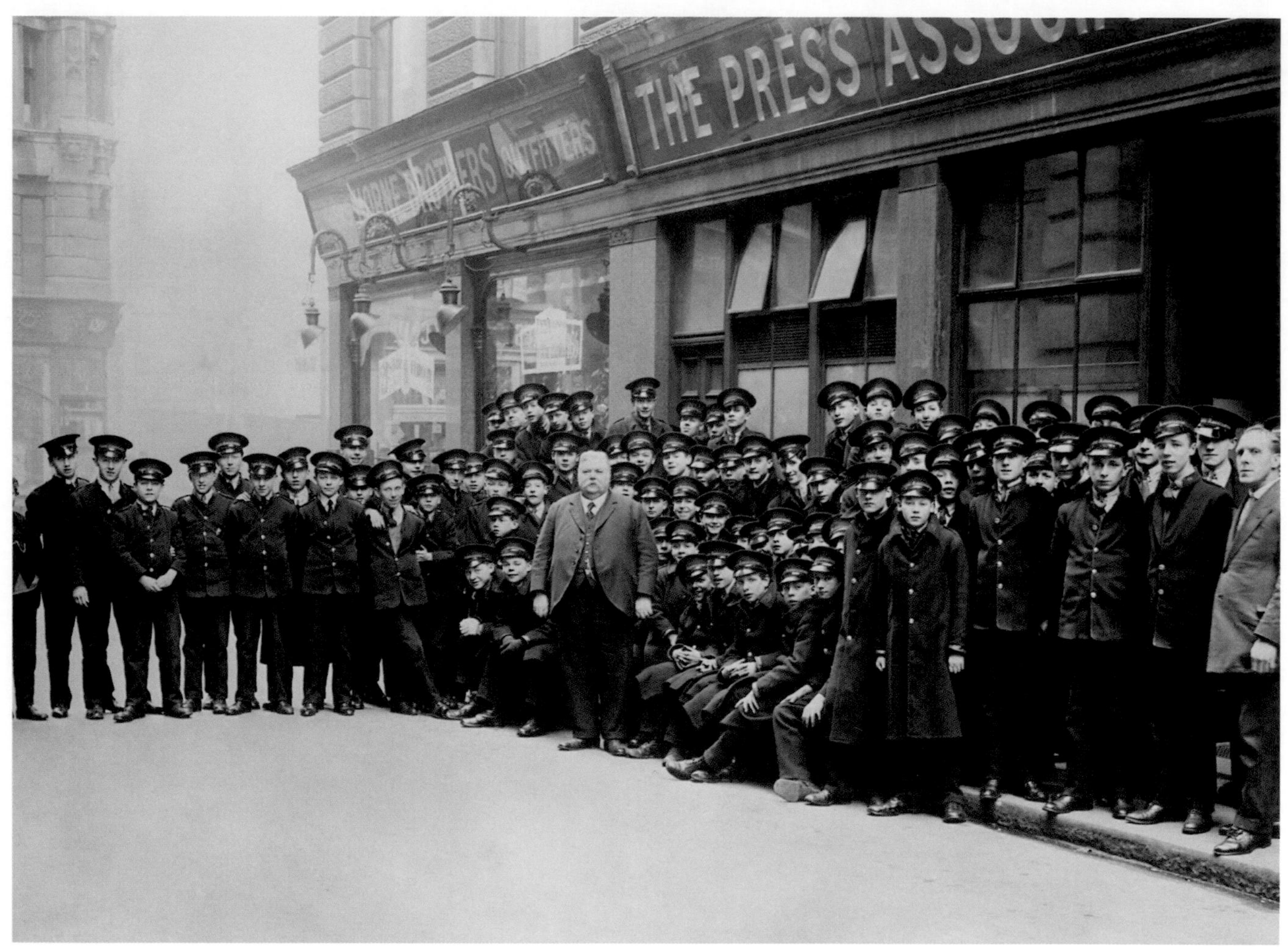

Dispatch Superintendent Walter Cattermole with Press Association messenger boys outside the PA in Fleet Street. Cattermole's small army, many of whom came from the poorest parts of London, were inspected daily. Their blue uniforms were often followed by cries of '*pick-a-narny*' (pig in harness), an old Cockney term for soldiers in the regular army. Although a disciplinarian, it would take a great deal for Cattermole to fire a messenger. A big man with a big heart.
1930

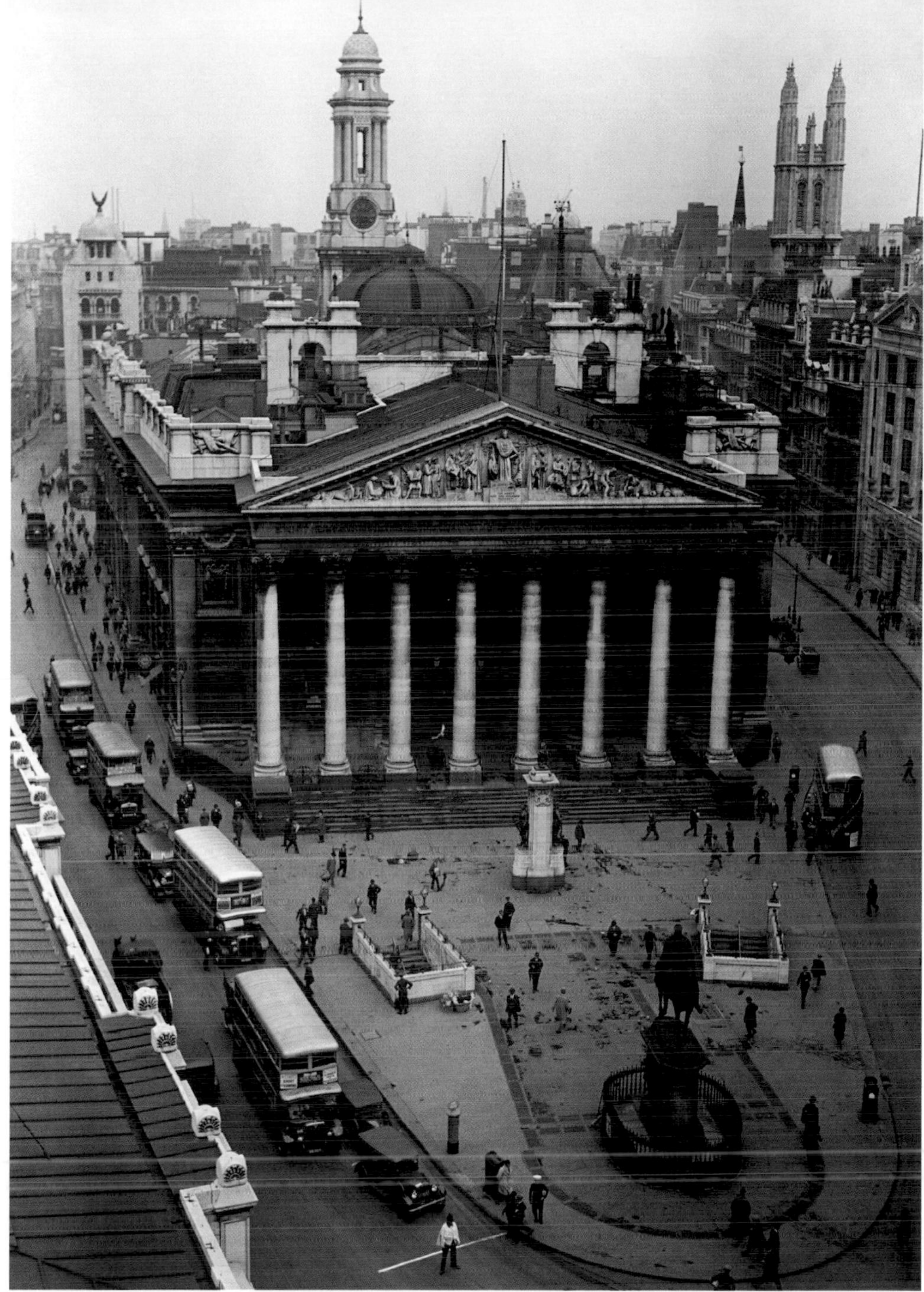

Building work in the City opens up a new view of The Royal Exchange on Threadneedle Street.
18th June, 1931

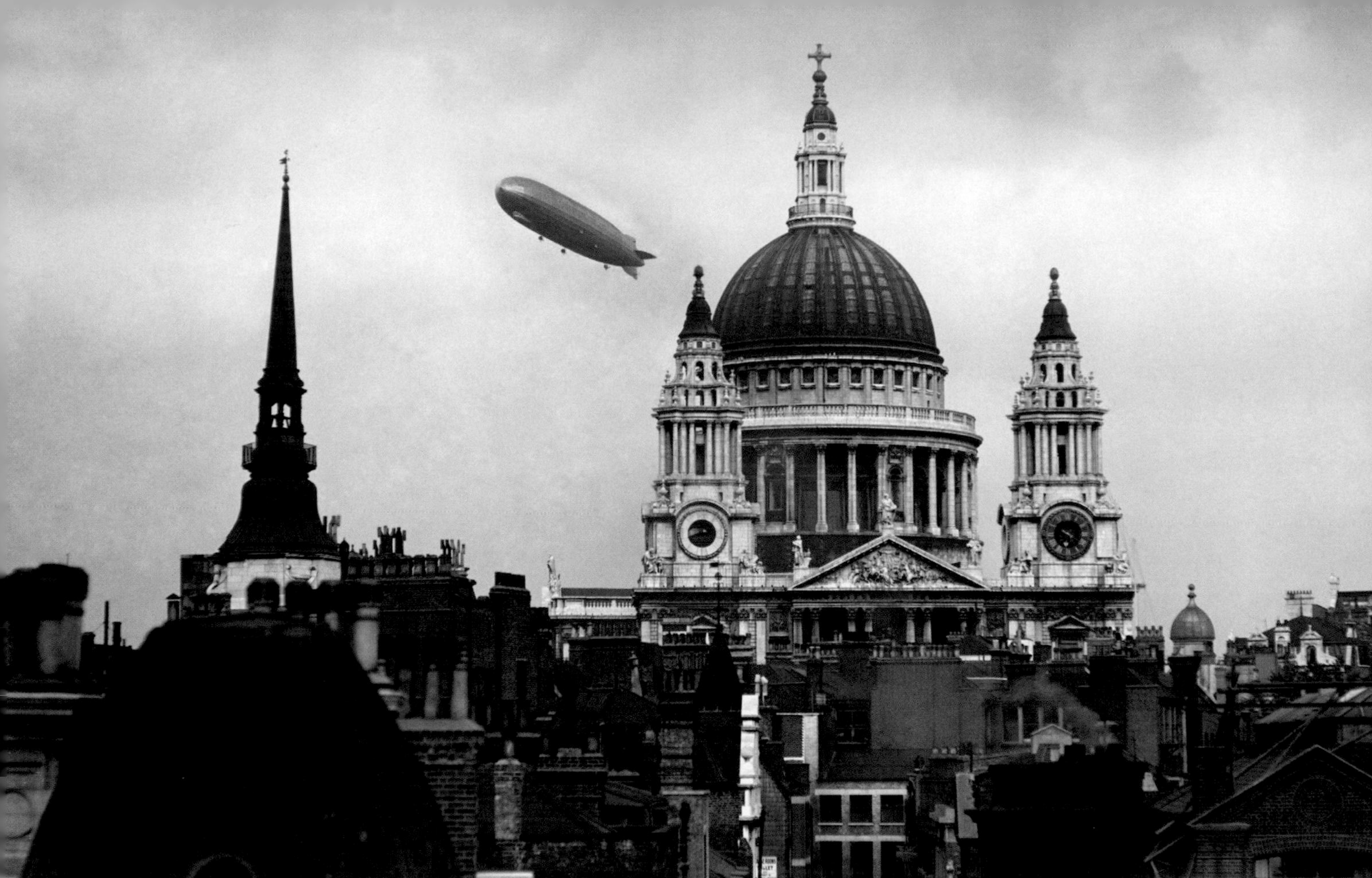

The *Graf Zeppelin* flies over St Paul's Cathedral in London on its 24-hour cruise around the British Isles.
18th August, 1931

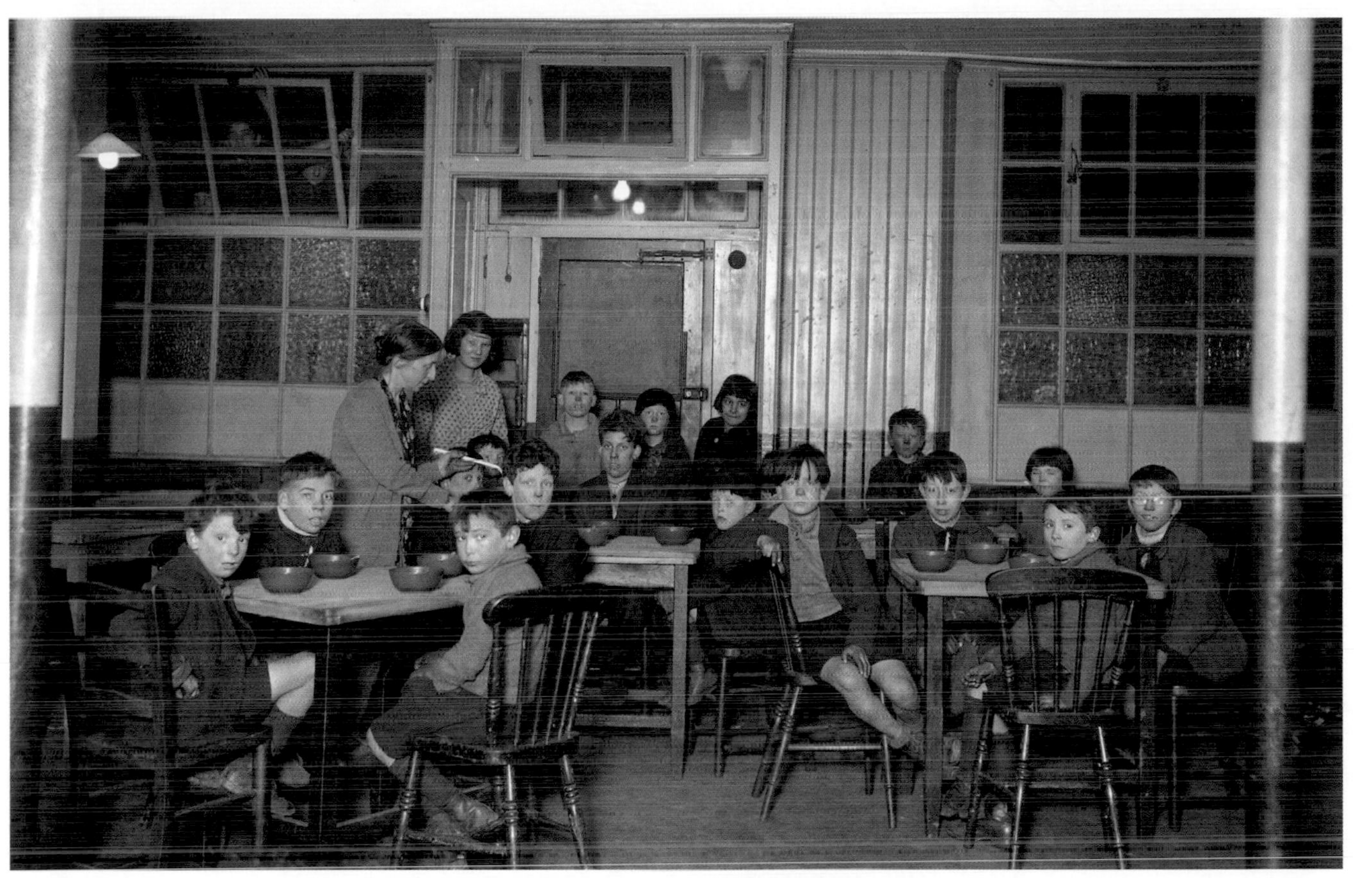

Poor children in Canning Town are fed soup to supplement their meagre diets.
25th November, 1931

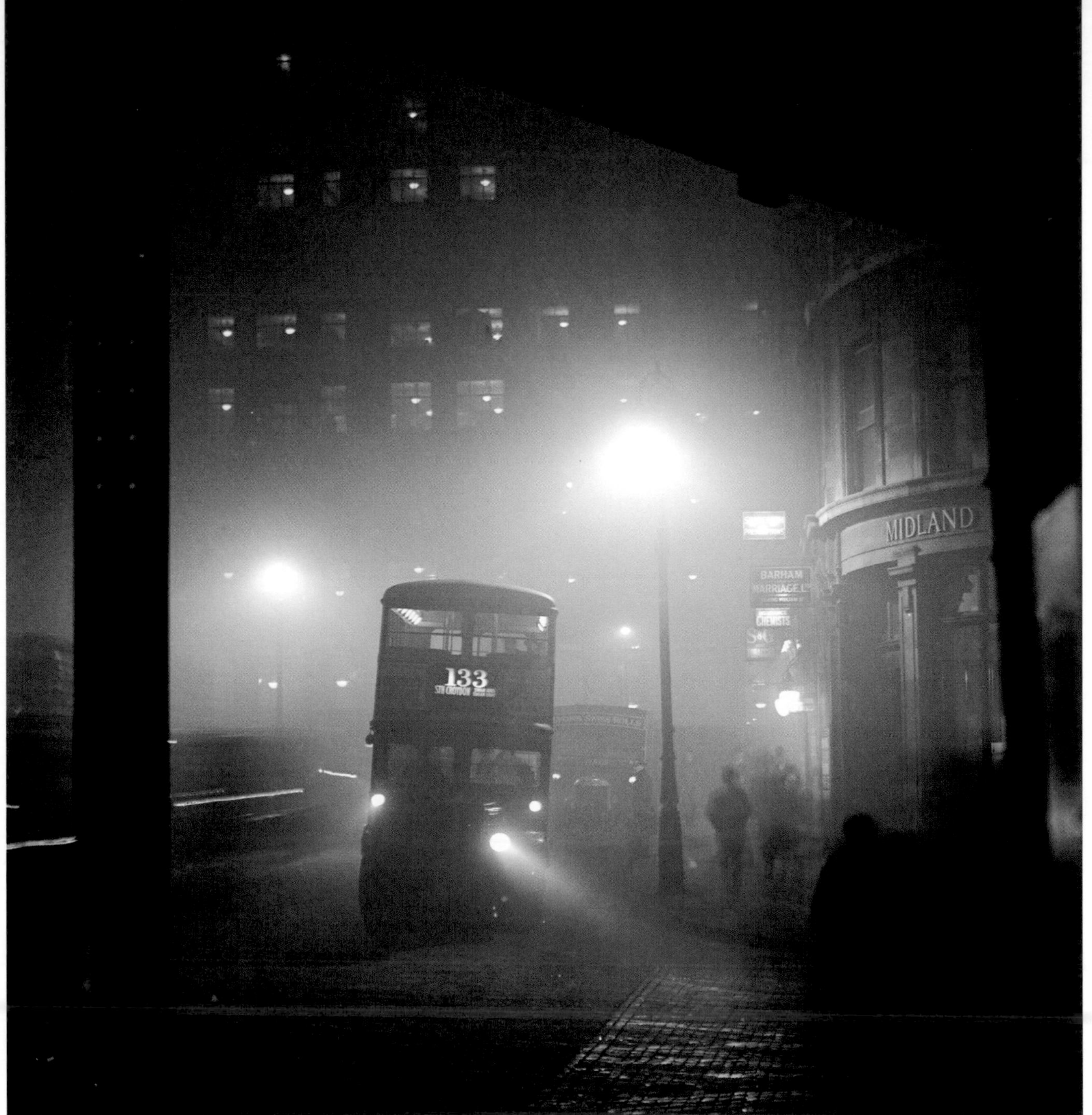
MIDLAND
BARHAM
CHEMISTS
133

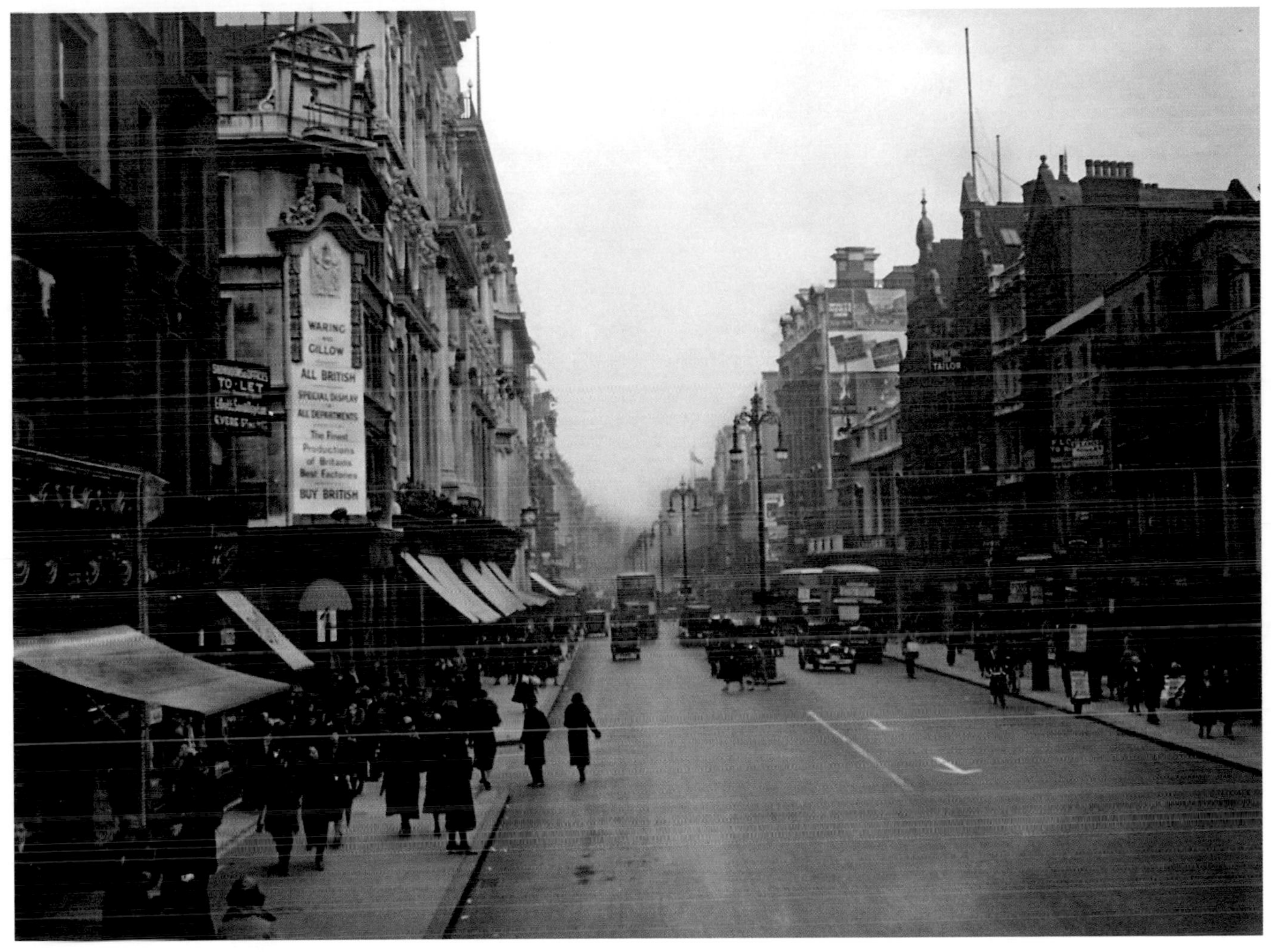

Oxford Street.
April, 1932

Facing page: Industrial activity and the use of coal fires to heat homes caused long bouts of thick fog known as '*pea-soupers*'. These fog-bound days see increases in road accidents, crime rates and in respiratory ailments in the poor, the old and the very young.
March, 1932

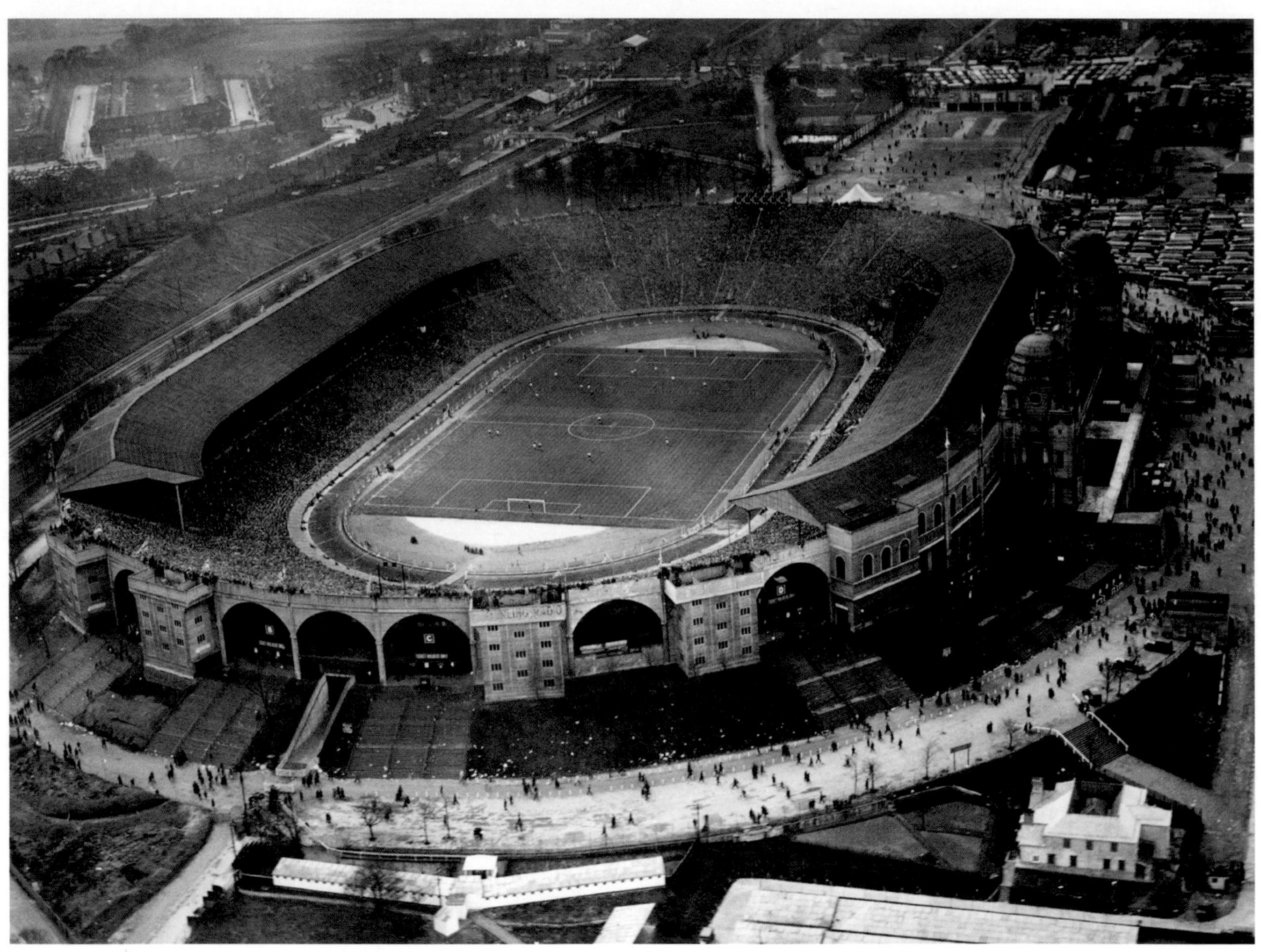

The FA Cup Final at Wembley Stadium. Arsenal v Newcastle United.
23rd April, 1932

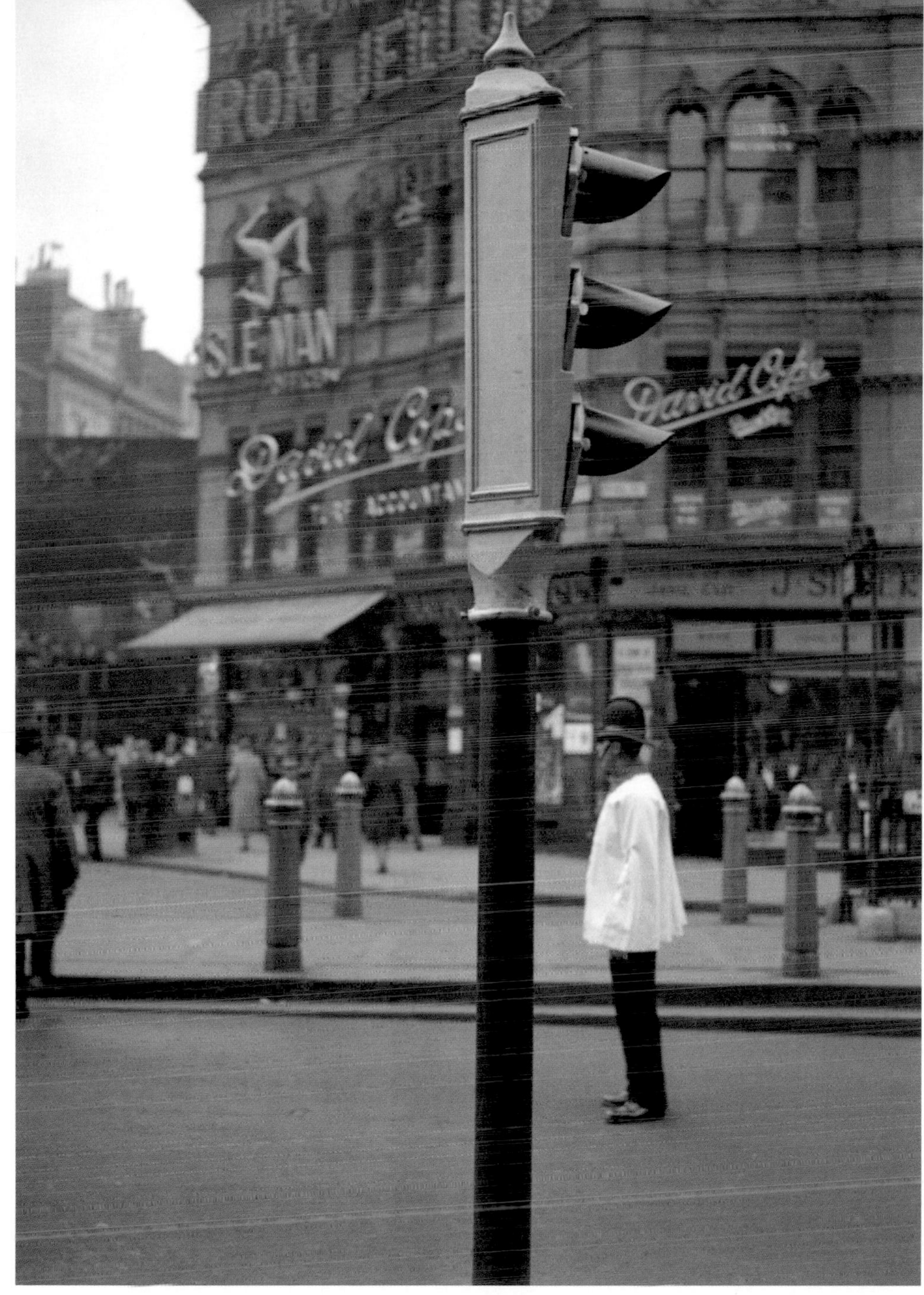

Britain's first modern traffic lights, at Ludgate Circus.
19th May, 1932

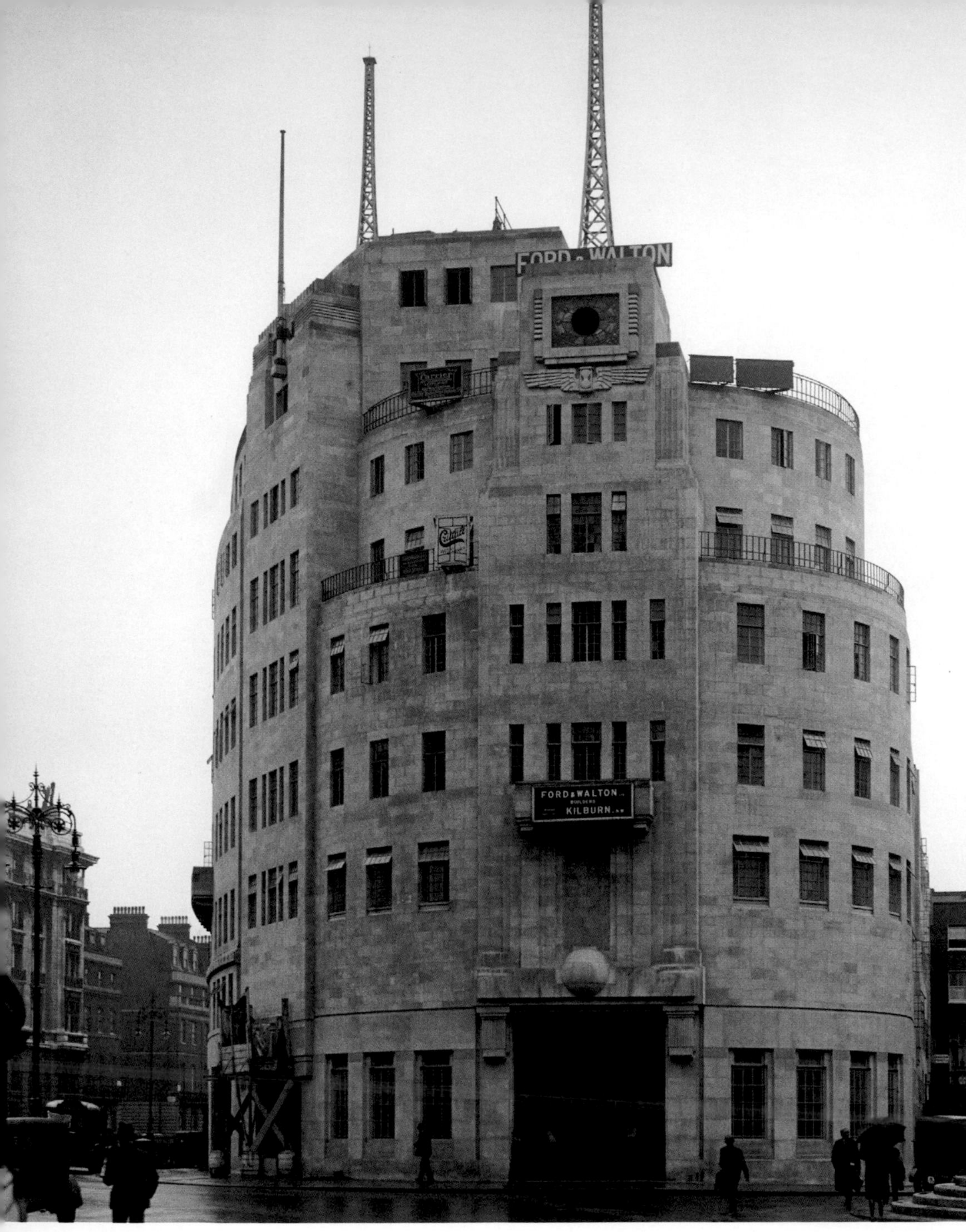

The newly built BBC Broadcasting House. Eric Gill's controversial statuary is still a work in progress; the major pieces, *Prospero* and *Ariel,* are absent from above the front door. Gill's scaffolding is set up to work on a smaller bas-relief (L).
13th August, 1932

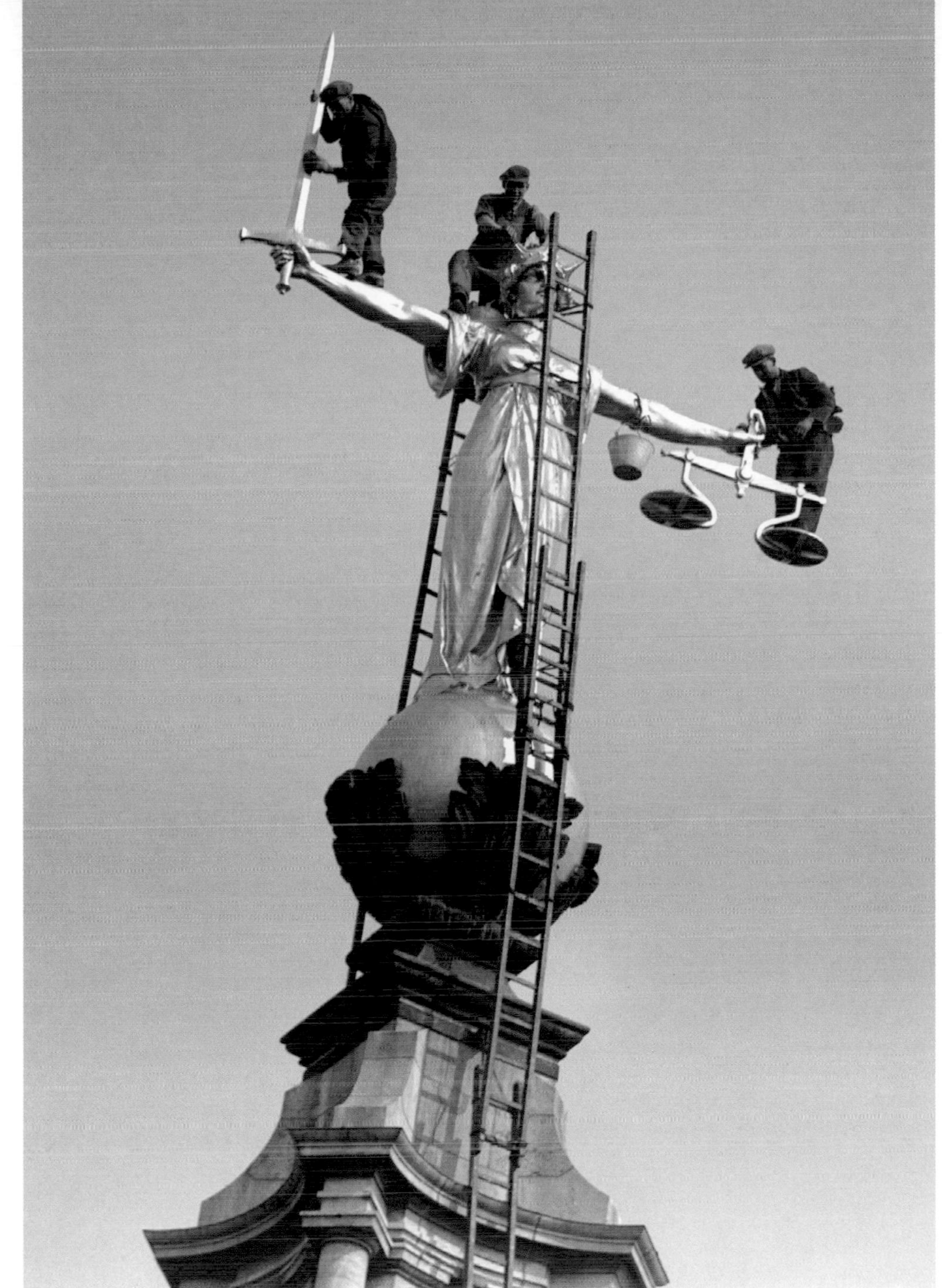

Cleaning the *Lady of Justice* atop the Old Bailey.
6th January, 1933

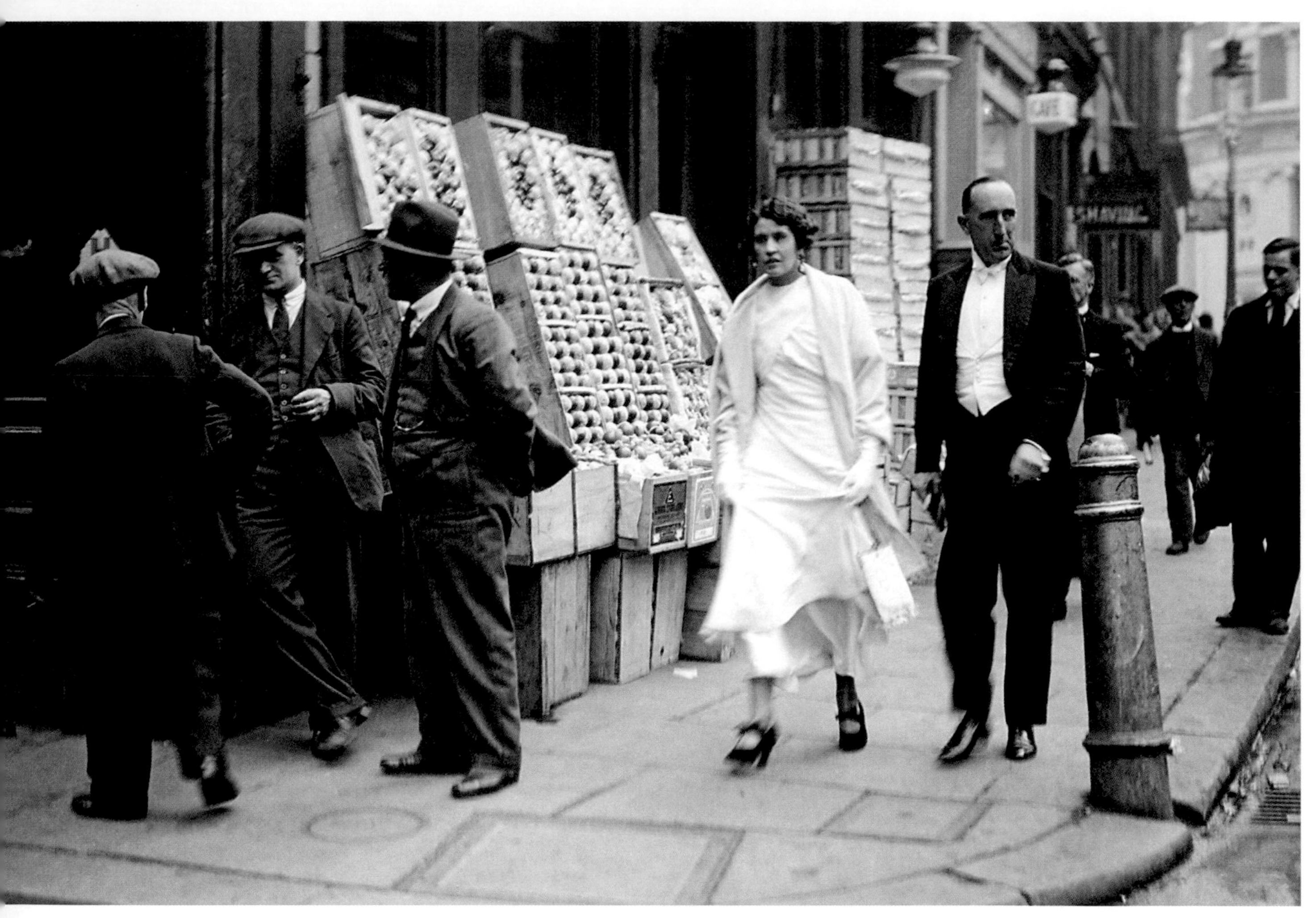

The proximity of many of London's theatres to Covent Garden market brought 'toffs' and the 'costers' into close proximity with each other. A situation used by George Bernard Shaw to set the scene for his play *Pygmalion*, an adaptation of which became the film *My Fair Lady*.
May, 1933

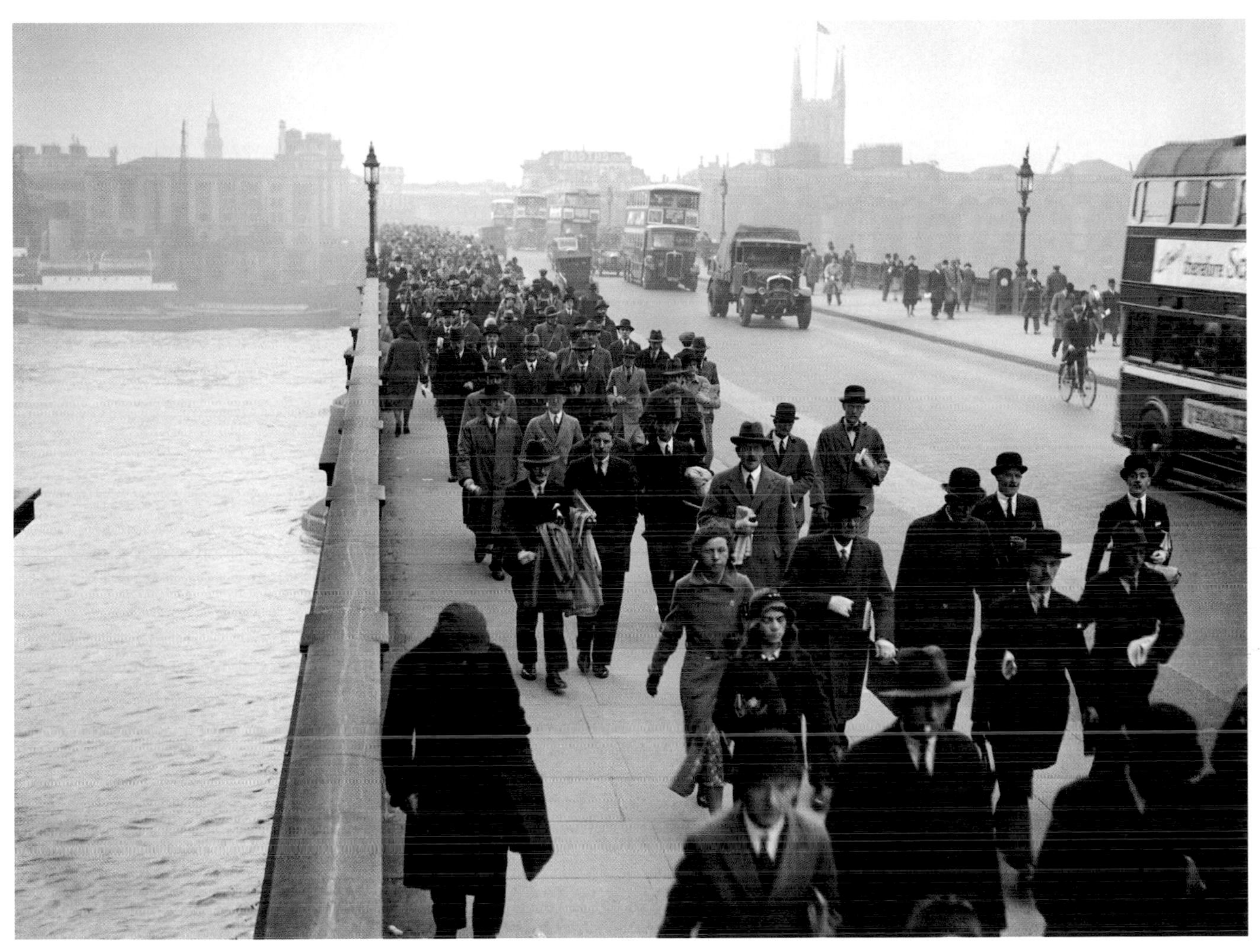

Morning rush hour on London Bridge.
May, 1933

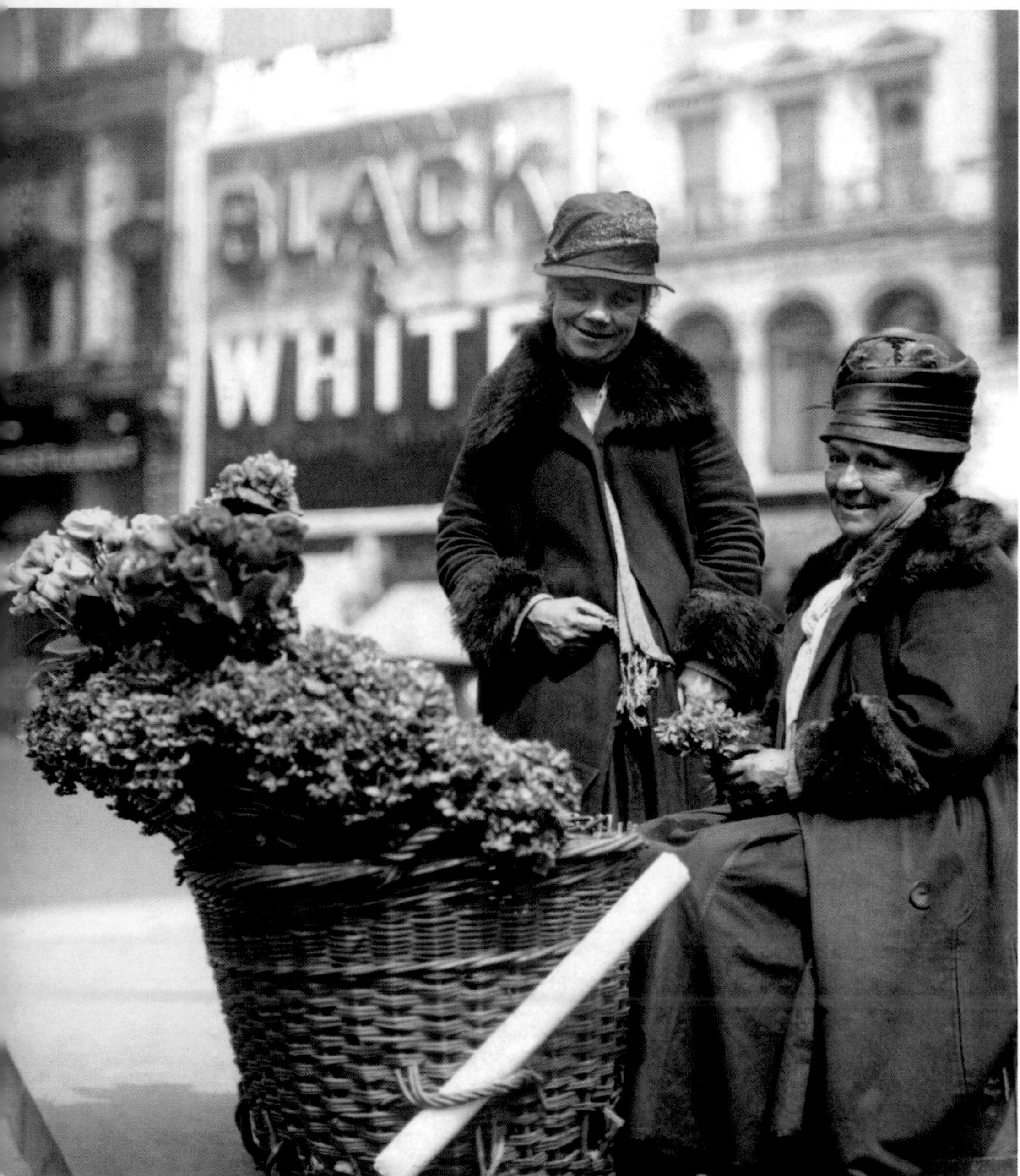

Real life Eliza Doolittles. Lizzie Sanger and Polly Beecham (R), Piccadilly flower sellers.
12th May, 1933

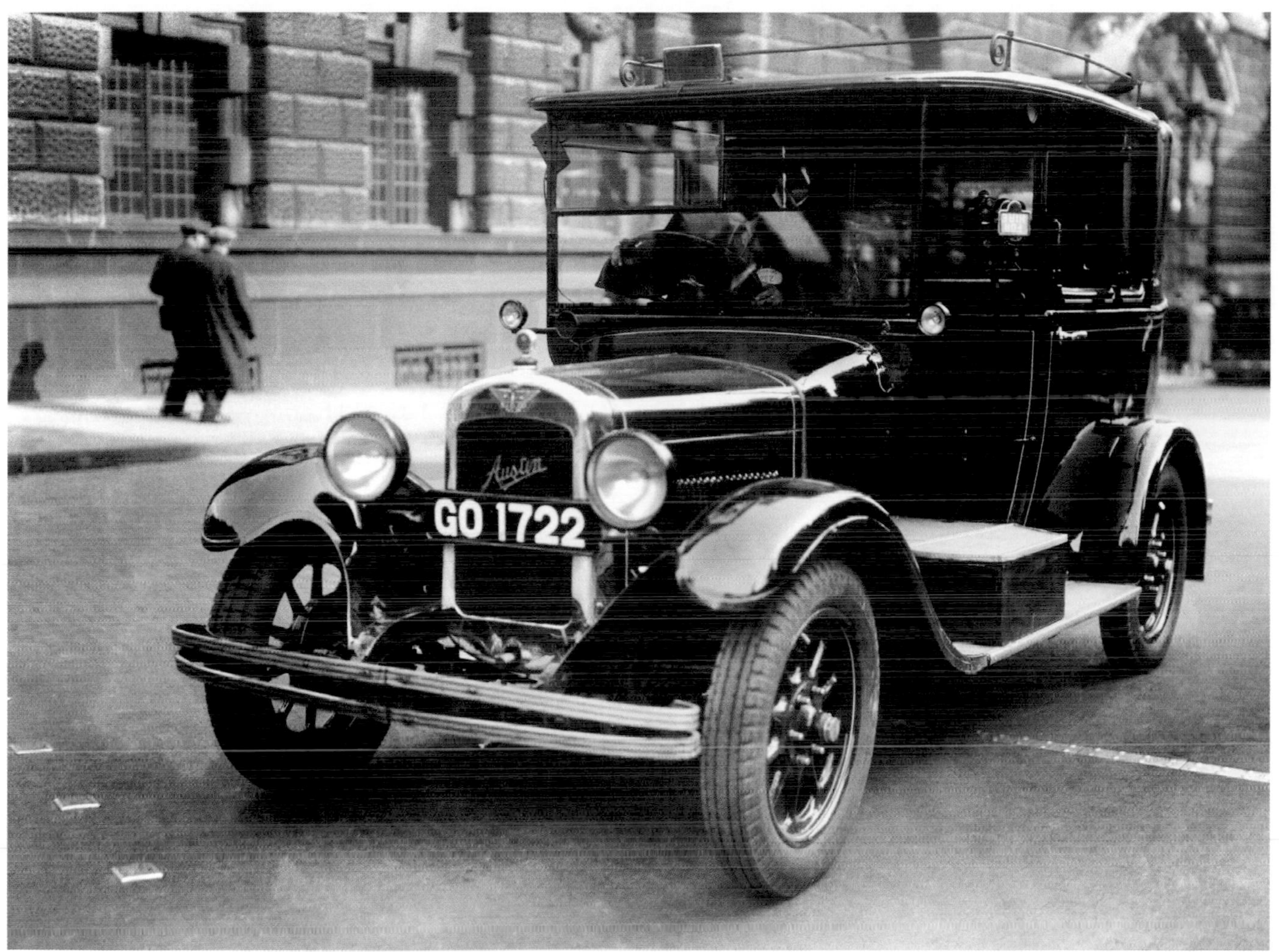

An Austin 7 taxi cab.
May, 1935

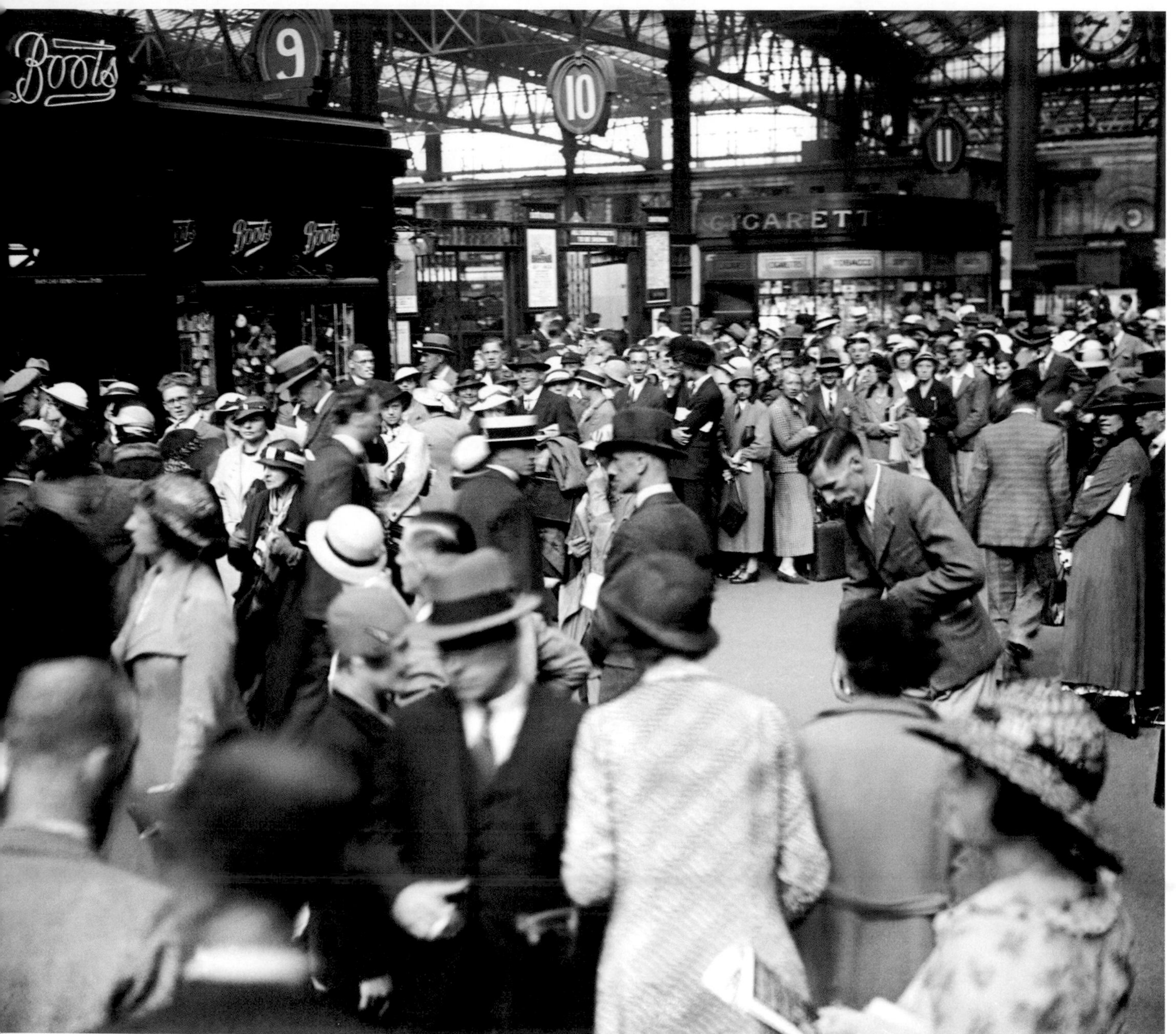
Boots
9
10
11
Boots
Boots

Facing page: Holiday crowds at Waterloo Station.
23rd July, 1935

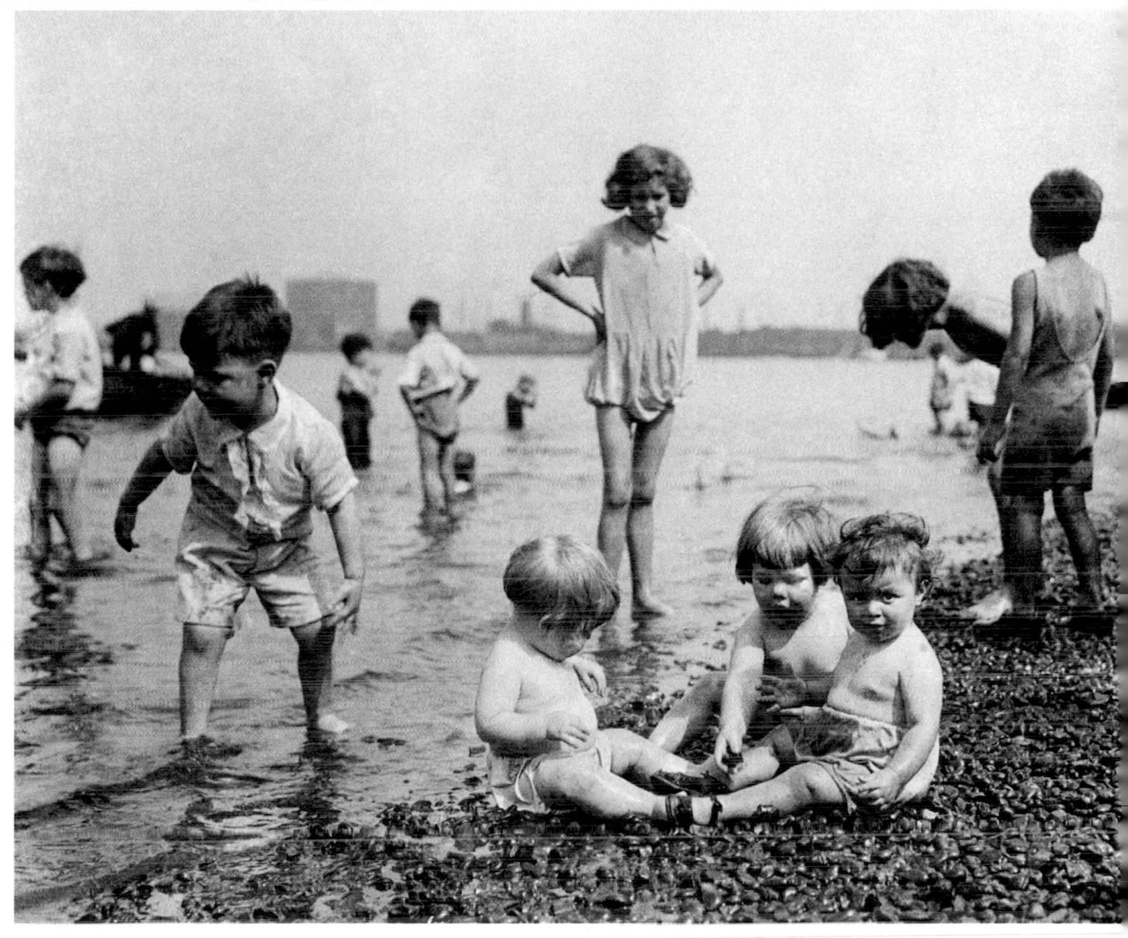

Paddling at Greenwich riverside.
26th September, 1935

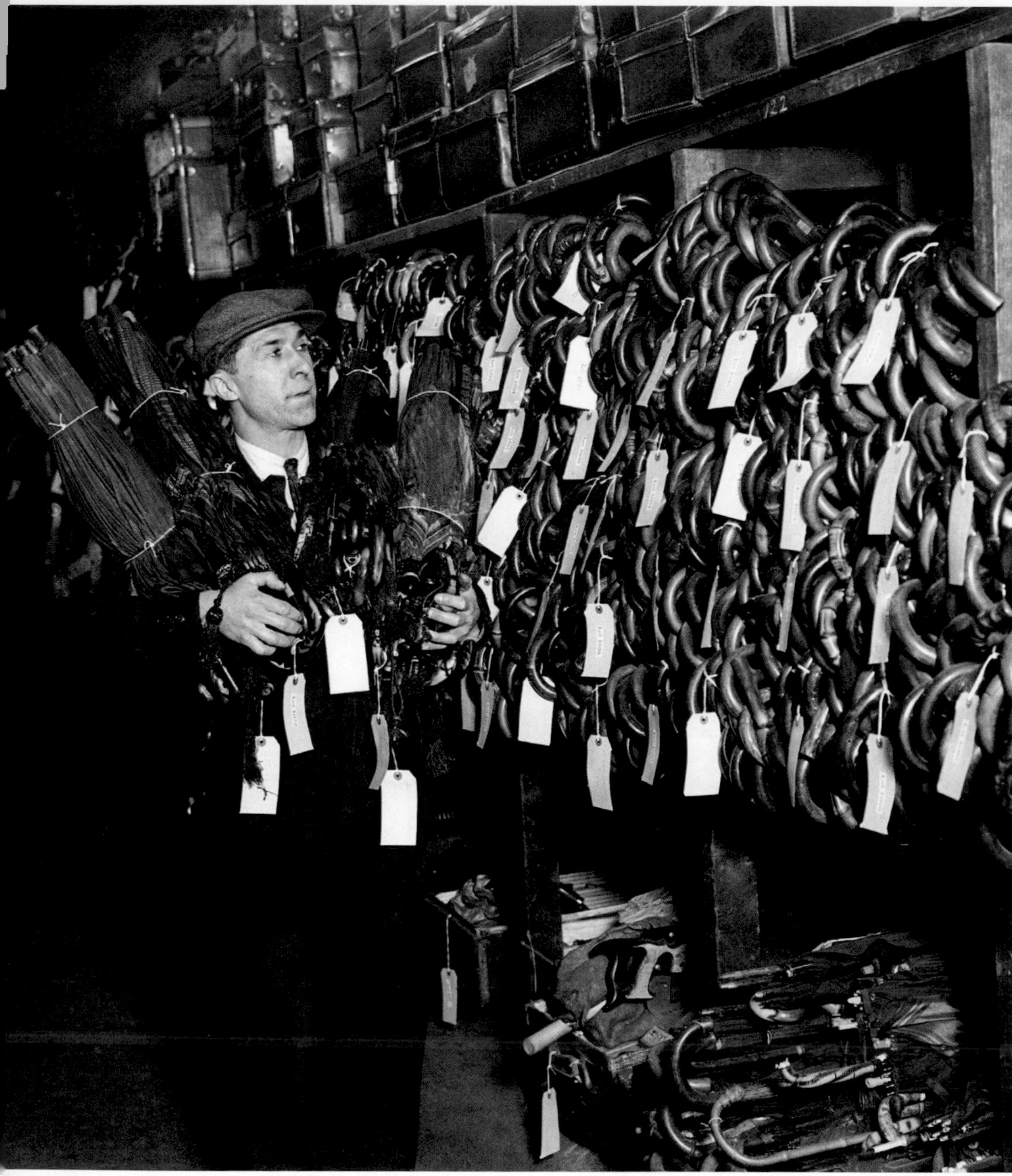

The Lost Property Department at Waterloo Station.
April, 1936

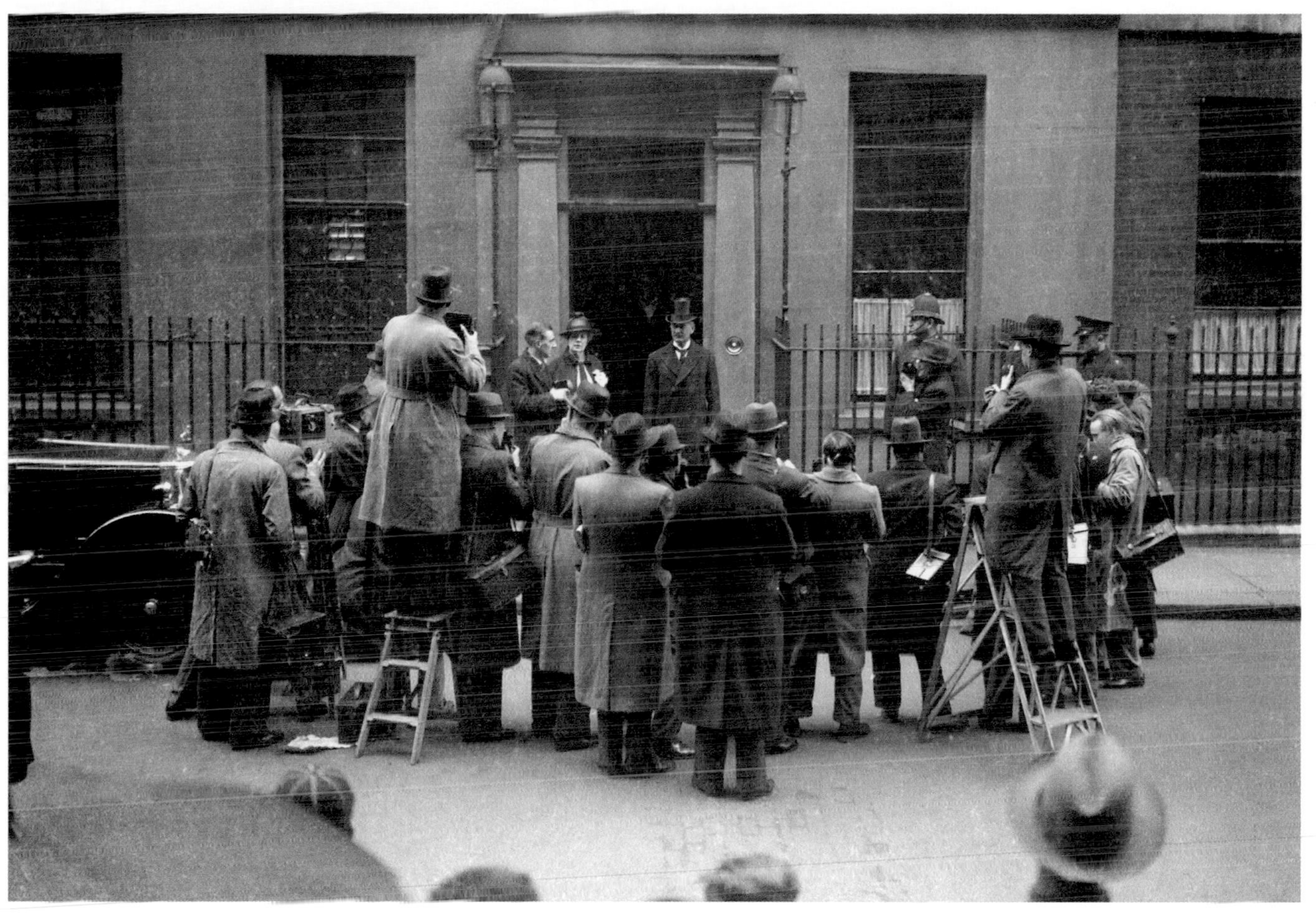

The Chancellor of the Exchequer, Neville Chamberlain, leaves 11 Downing Street on Budget Day.

10th April, 1936

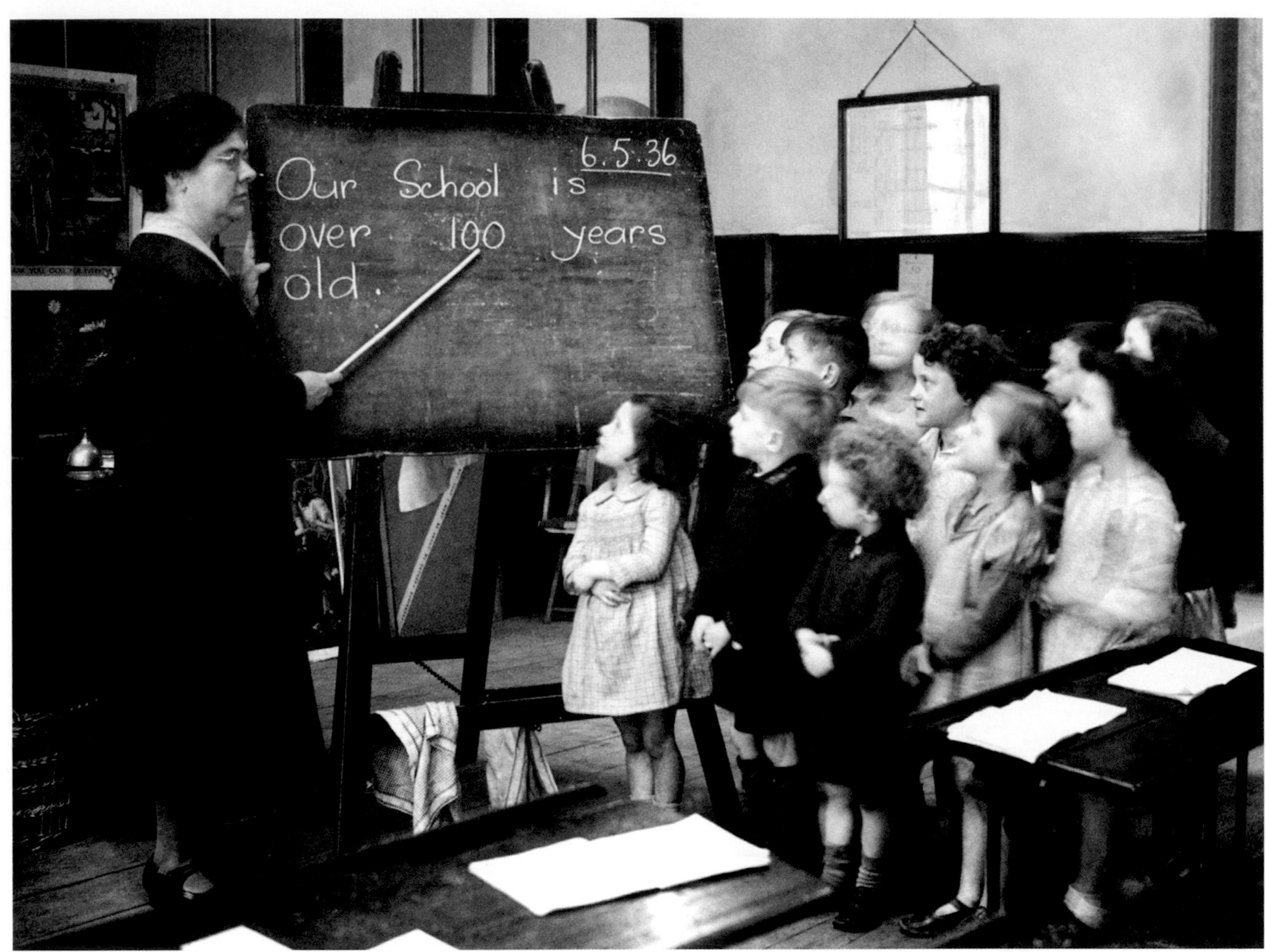

Fun and games at St Bride
and Bridewell Precinct
School.
6th May, 1936

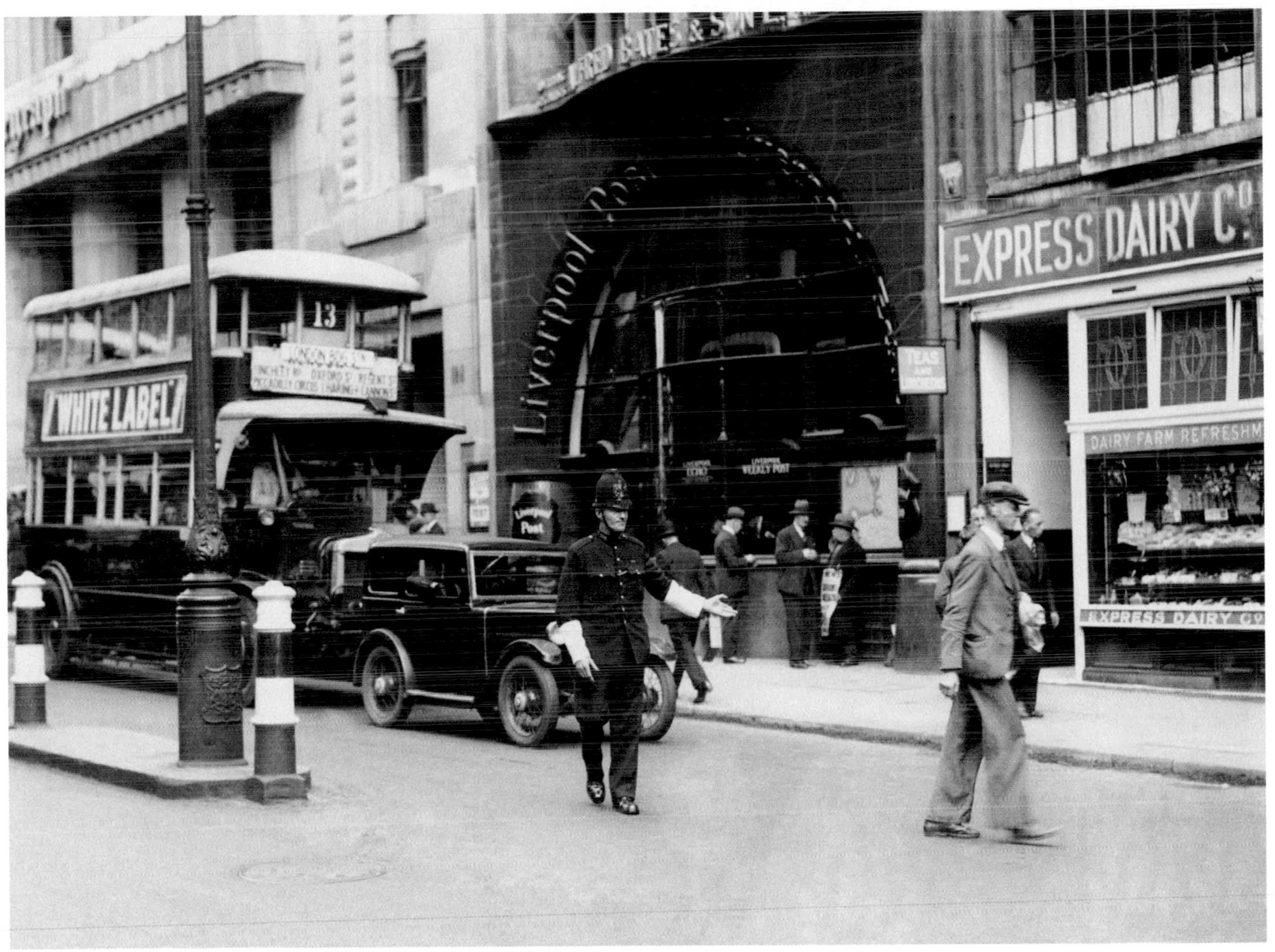

A policeman holds up traffic
in Fleet Street.
24th July, 1936

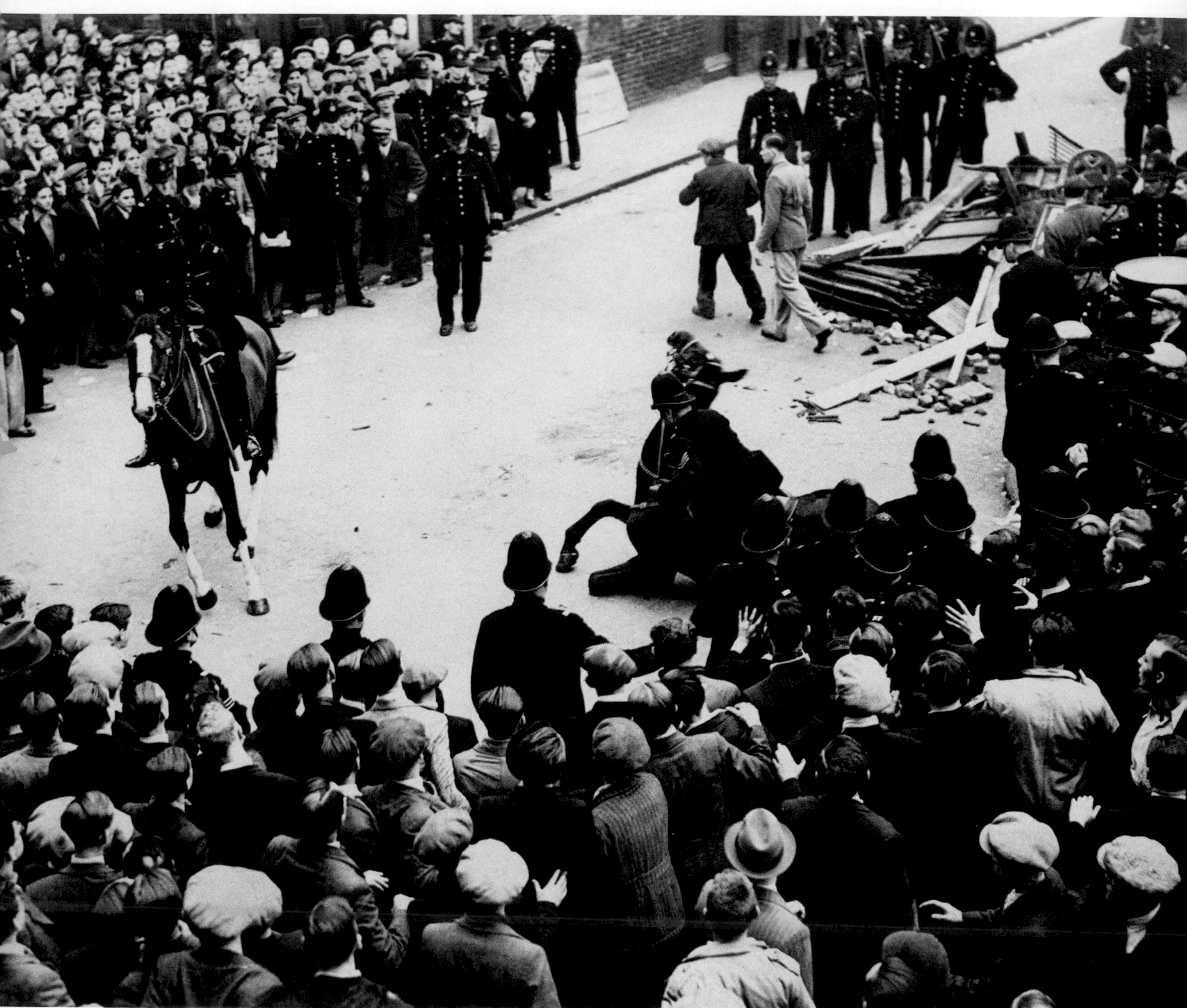

Facing page: A police horse falls during the Great Fascist March through East London to Bermondsey. Residents of the East End fought pitched battles with police and Moseley's Blackshirts, forcing the fascists to use a different route, in what became known as *The Battle of Cable Street*.
4th October, 1936

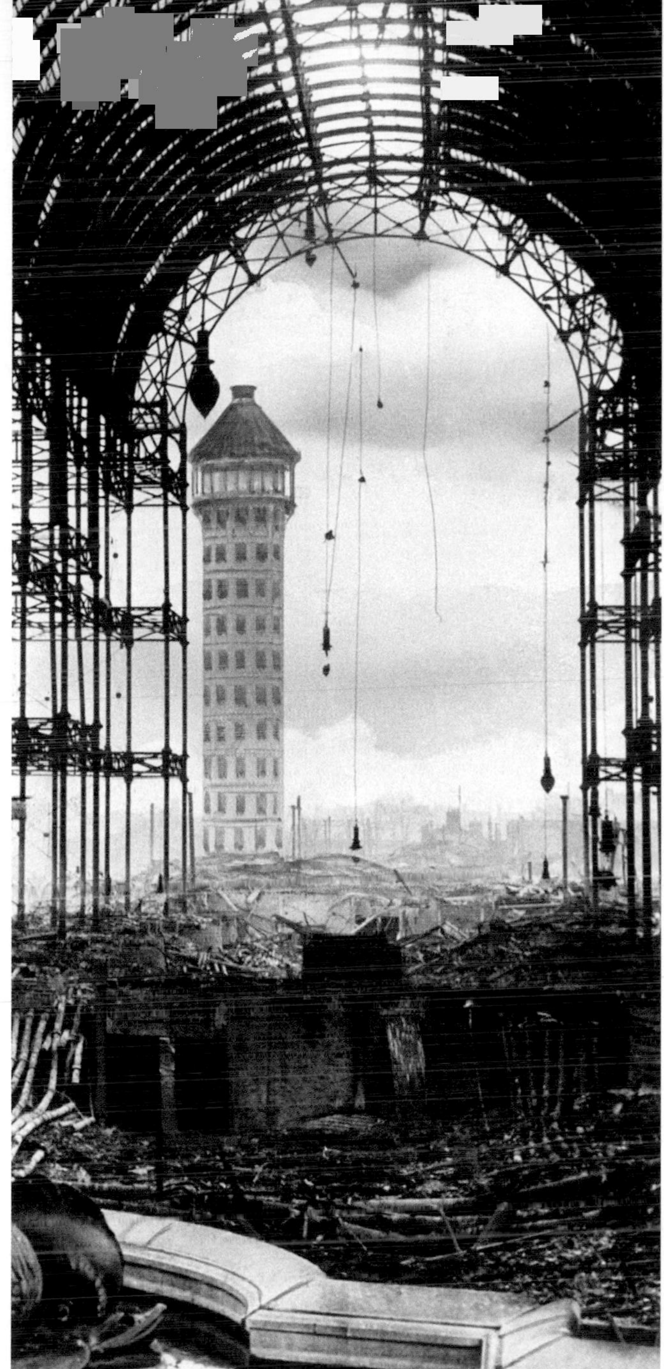

One of the two water towers, built by Isambard Kingdom Brunel, which were left standing after the first Crystal Palace fire in 1936. War Department occupation of the site during the Second World War, and a second fire in 1950, completed the destruction of the great landmark.
December, 1936

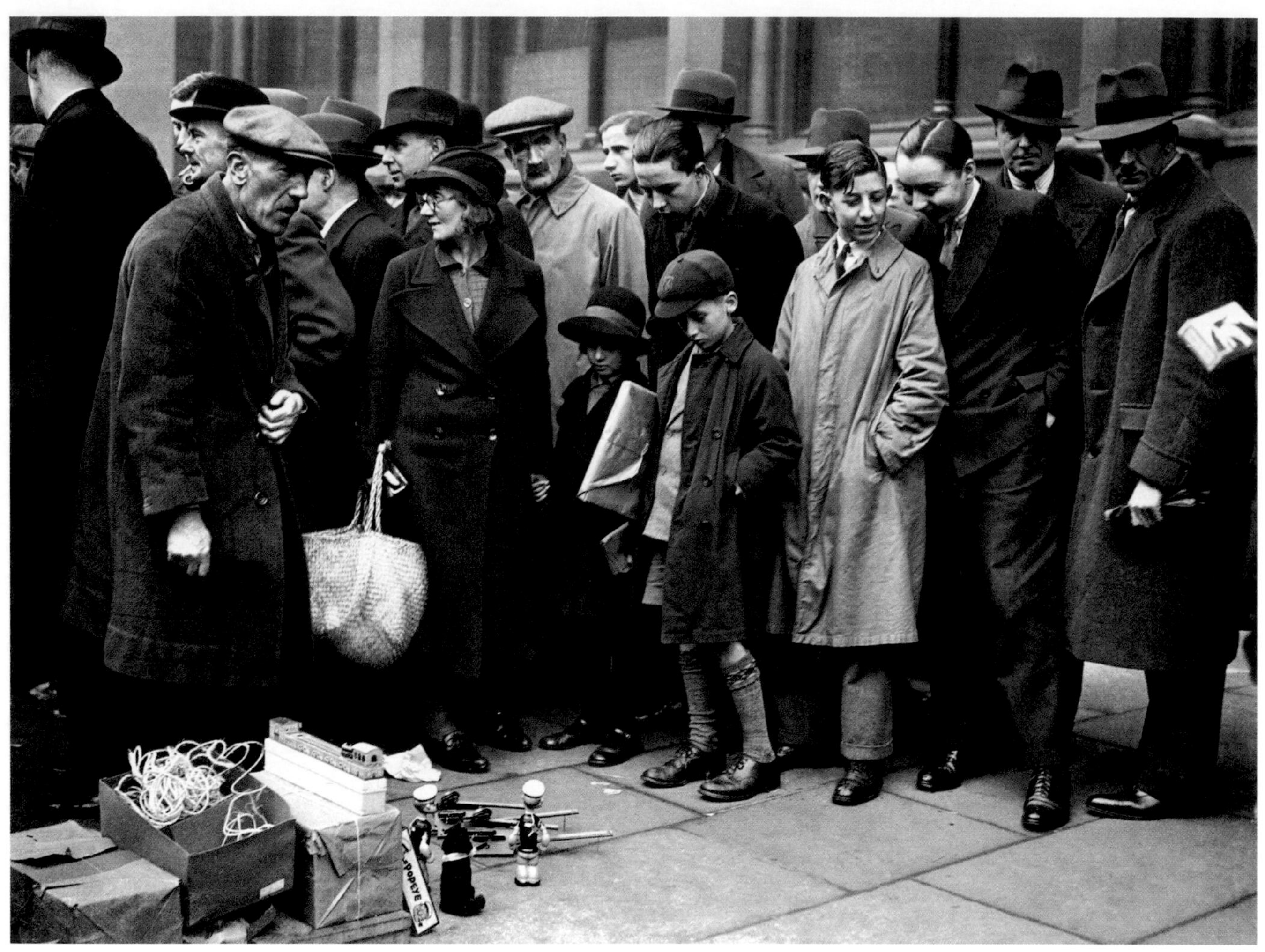

A hawker sells toys at Holborn.
14th January, 1937

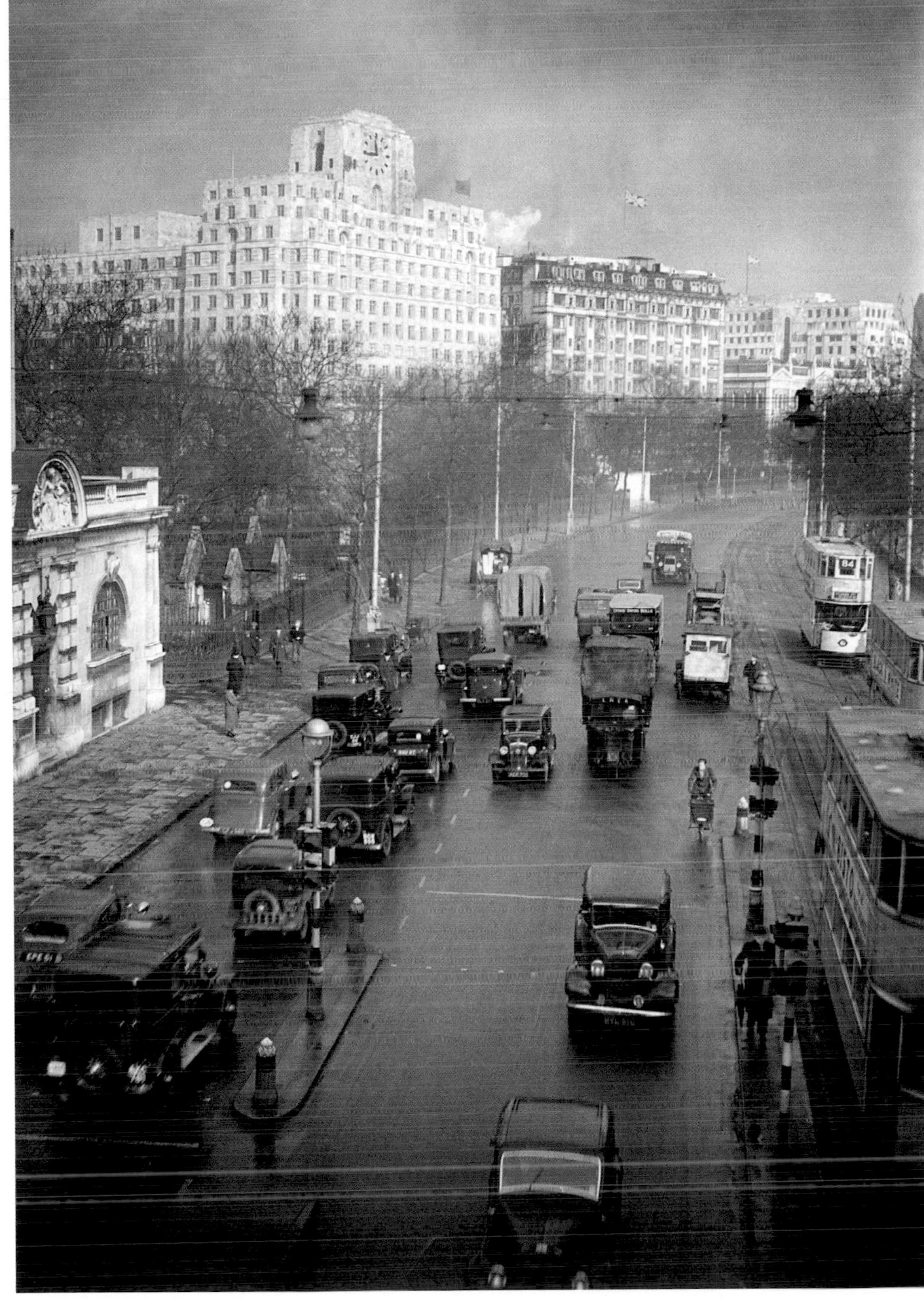

The Embankment from Hungerford Bridge.
February, 1937

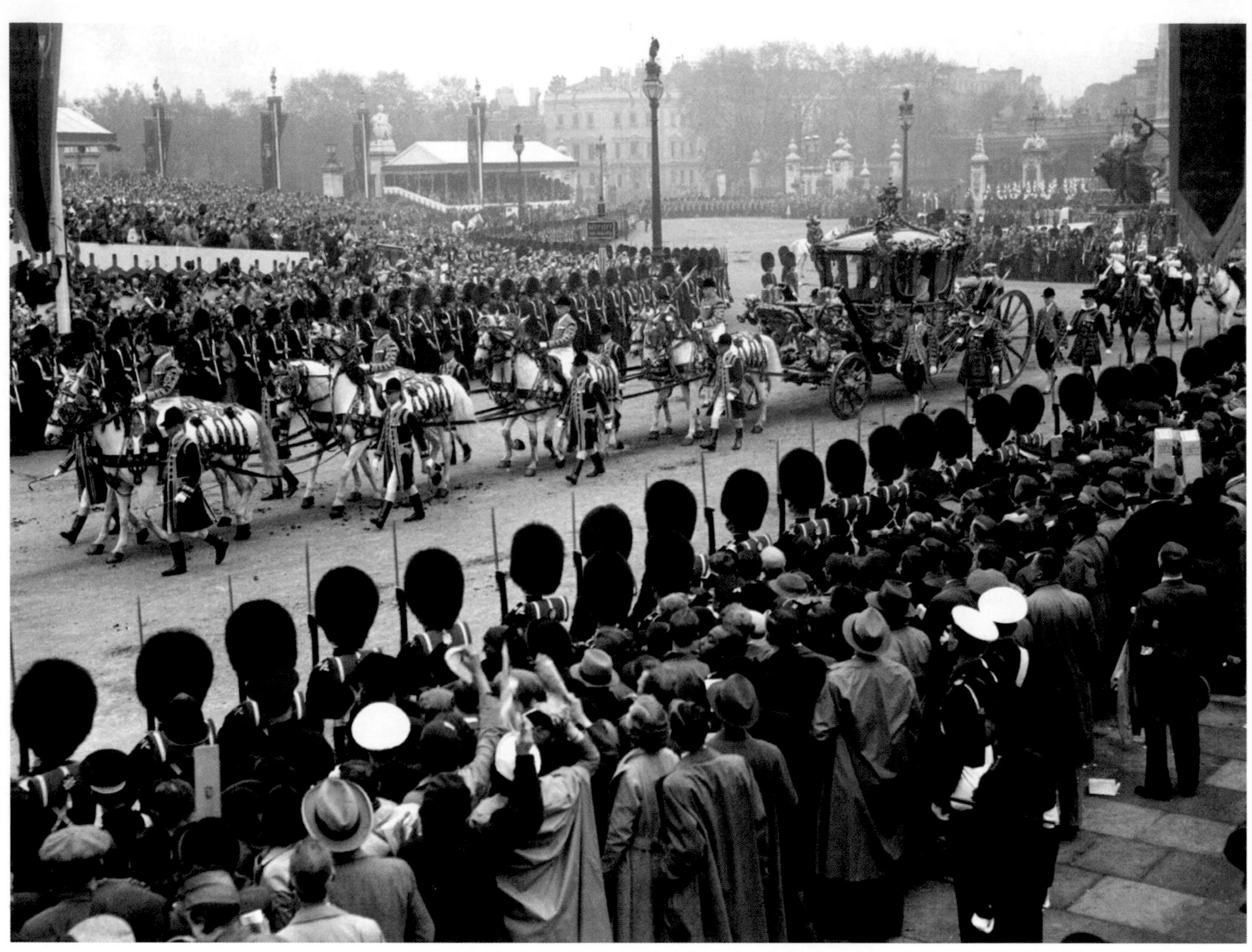

The Duke and Duchess of York leave Buckingham Palace for the Coronation at Westminster Abbey, after which they will be King George VI and Queen Elizabeth. The new Queen left her bouquet on the Tomb of the Unknown Warrior in honour of her brother Fergus, who was killed at Loos.
12th May, 1937

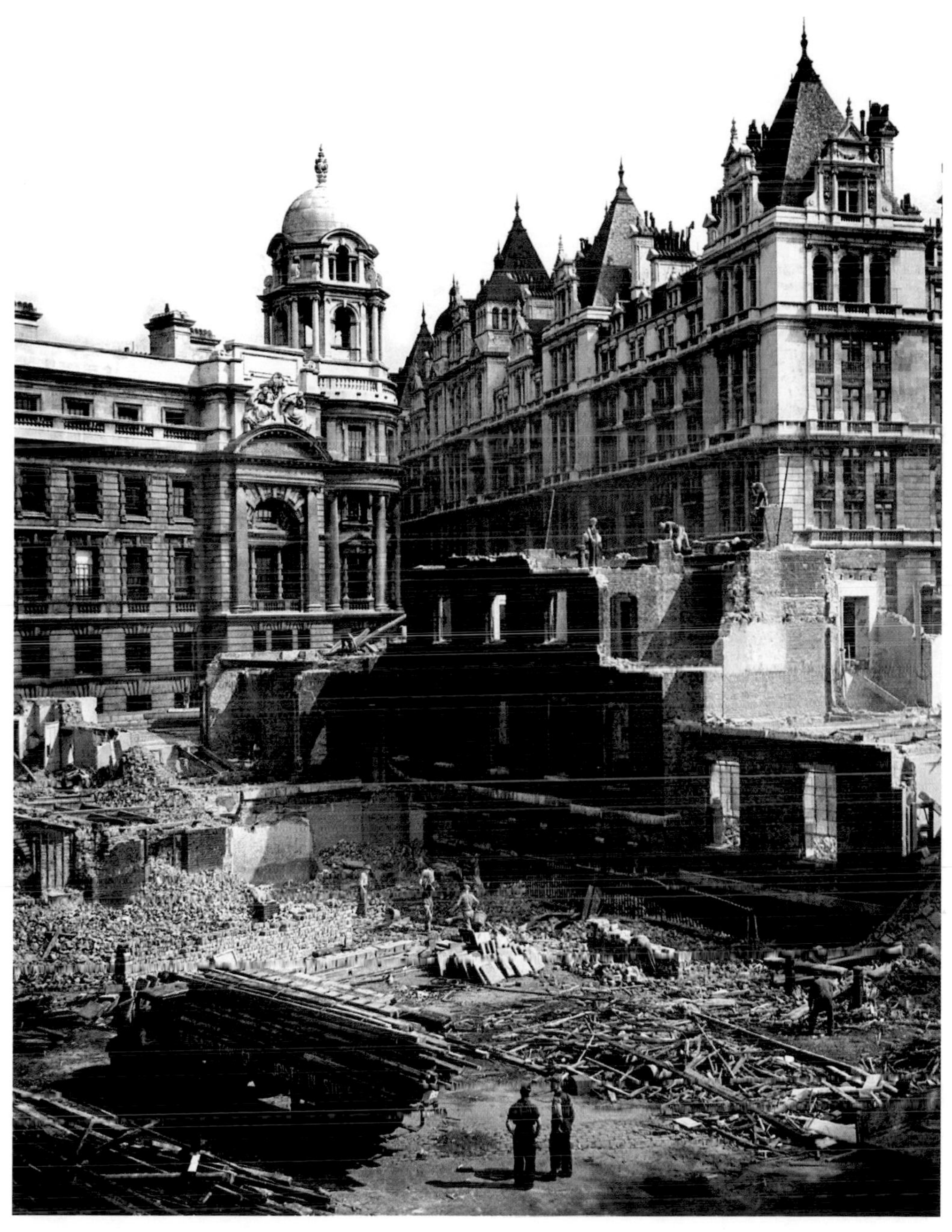

Demolishing the rear of Whitehall for re-building.
1938

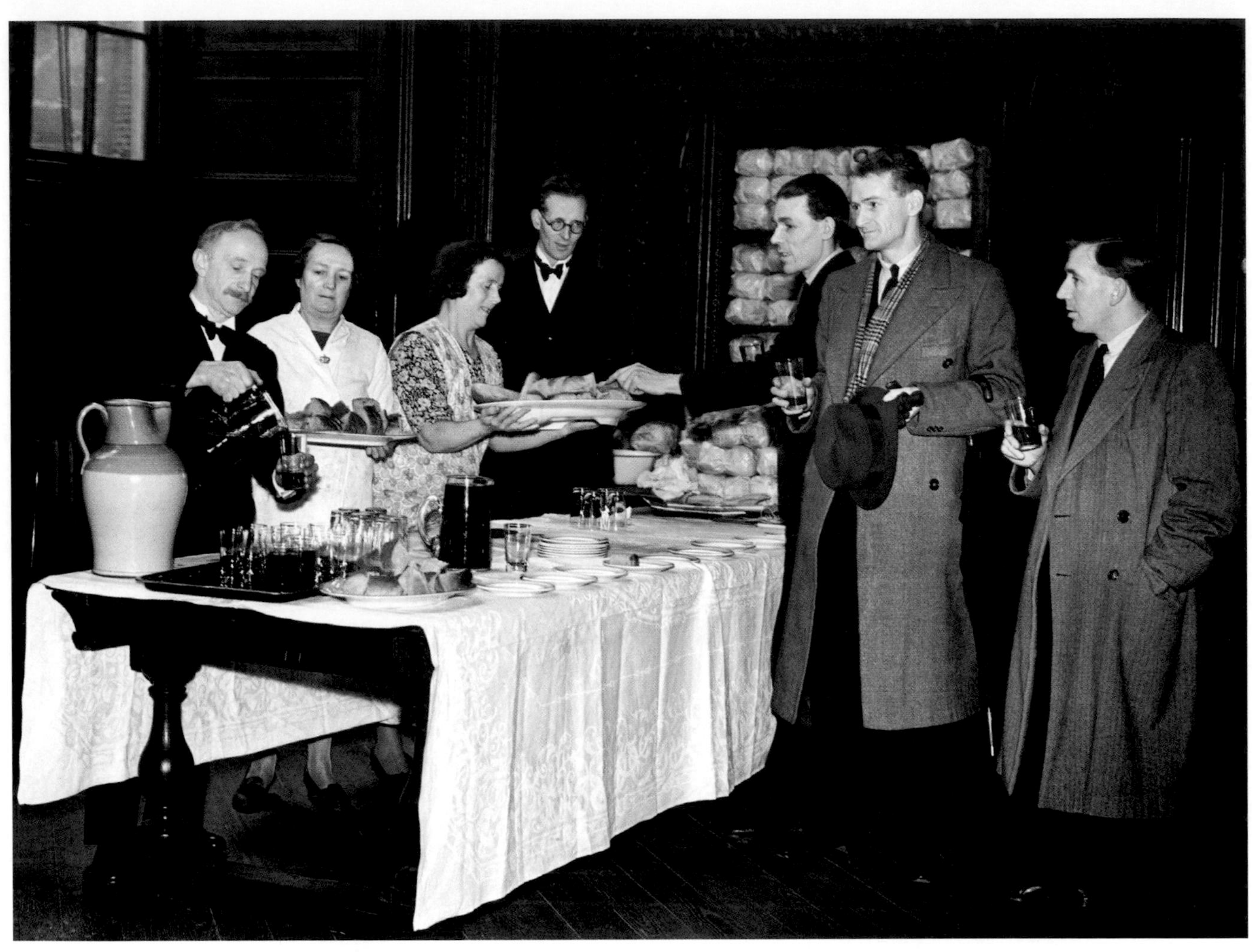

Ash Wednesday. Ale and cakes are traditionally distributed to members of the Stationers and Newspaper Makers Company at Stationers Hall.
4th February, 1938

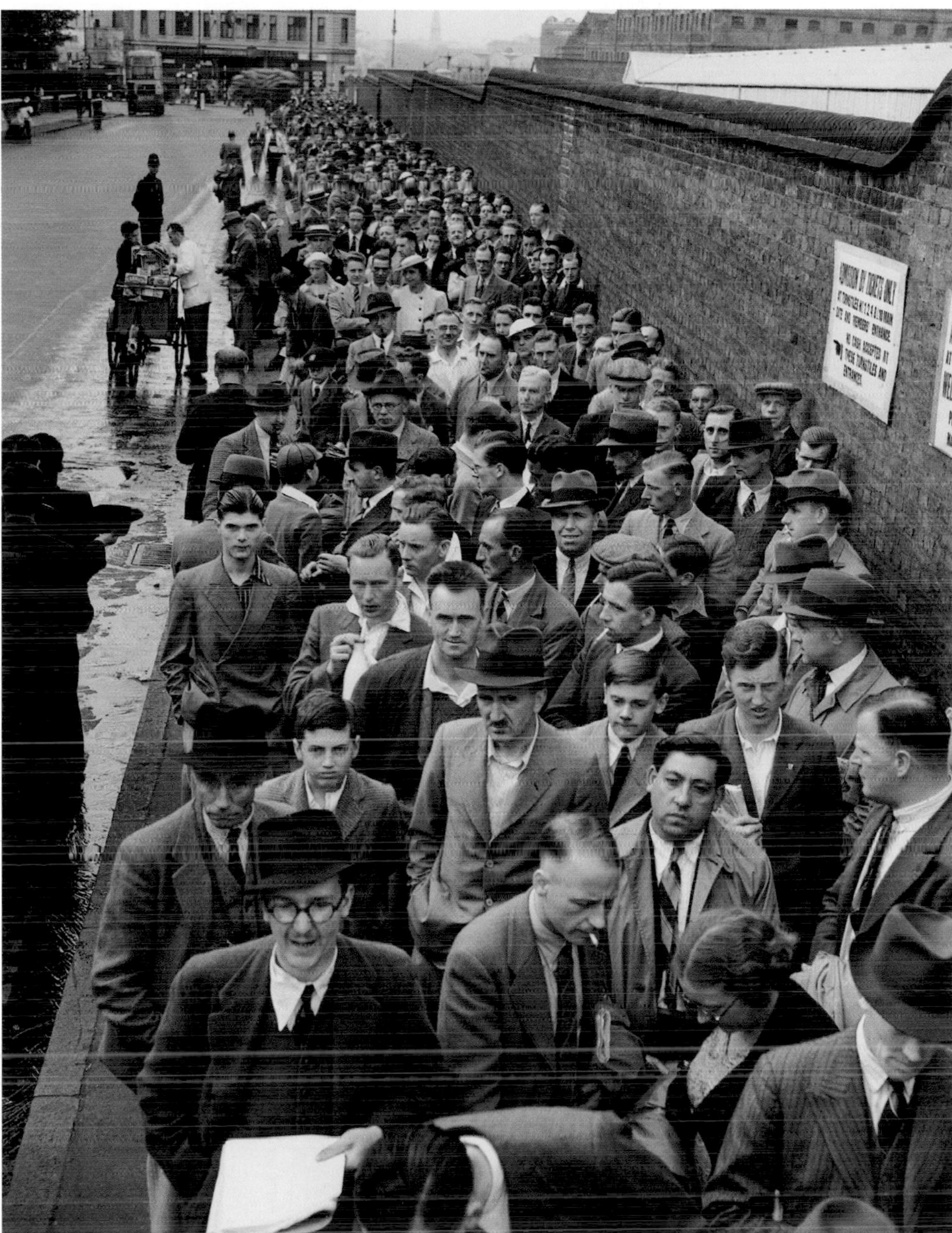

Queues outside Lord's on Saturday morning to see the continuation of the Wally Hammond/Les Ames fourth wicket partnership in the Ashes, Second Test, England v Australia.

25th June, 1938

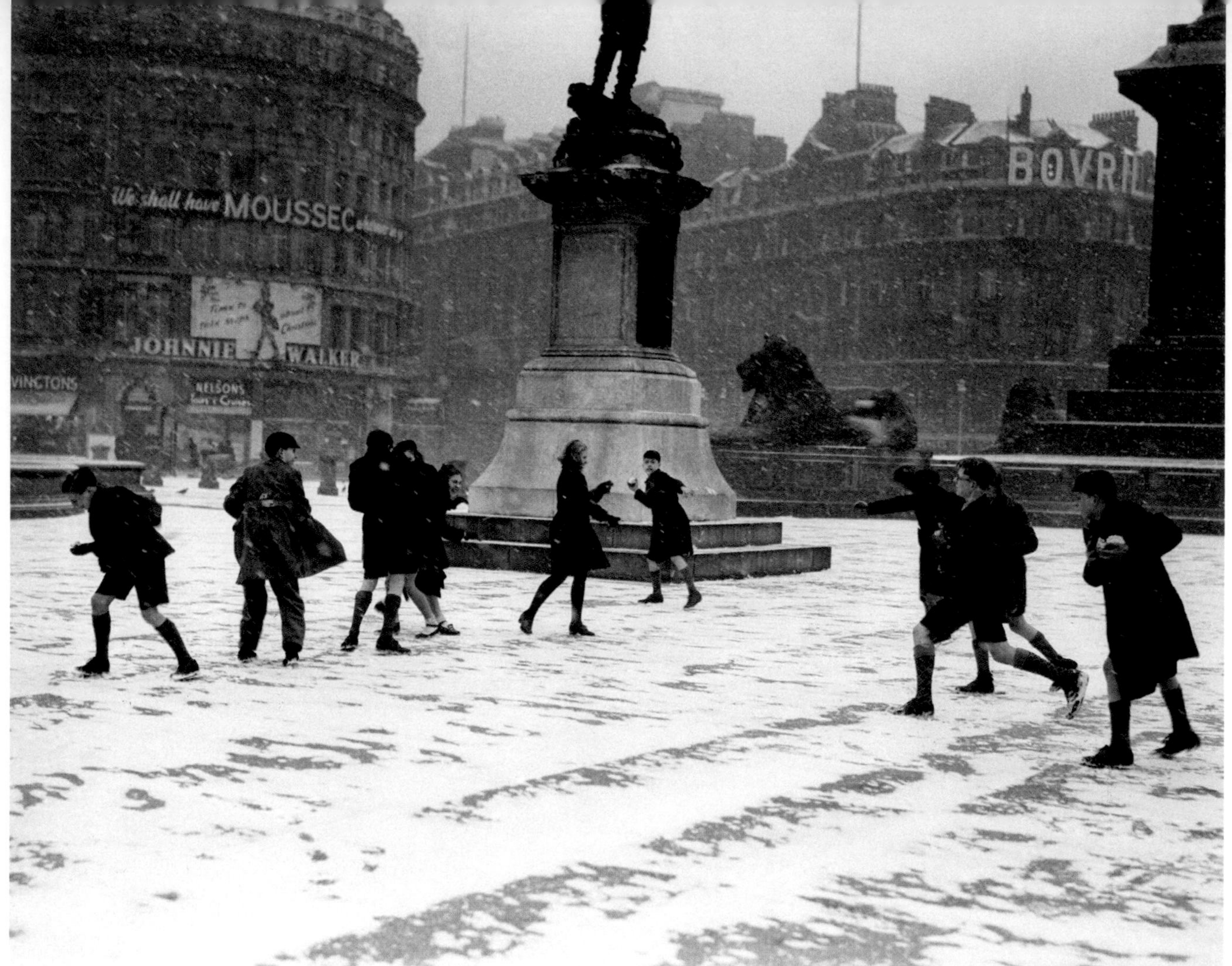

Snow in Trafalgar Square.
7th November, 1938

Piccadilly Circus just before the start of the Second World War. The famous *Shaftesbury Memorial* with its winged statue (not actually *Eros*, but his brother *Anteros*) has been covered prior to being removed for the duration of the conflict.
May, 1939

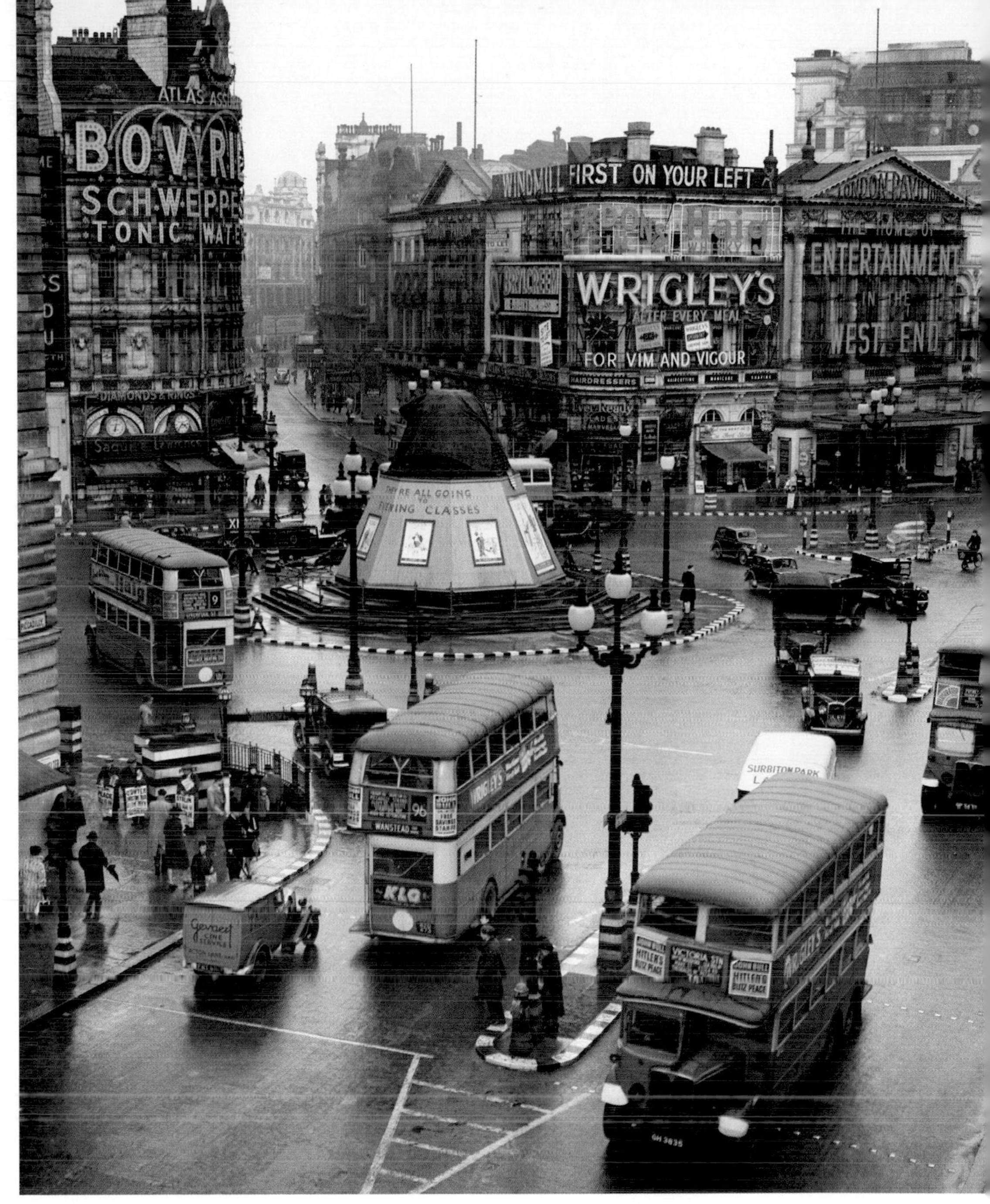

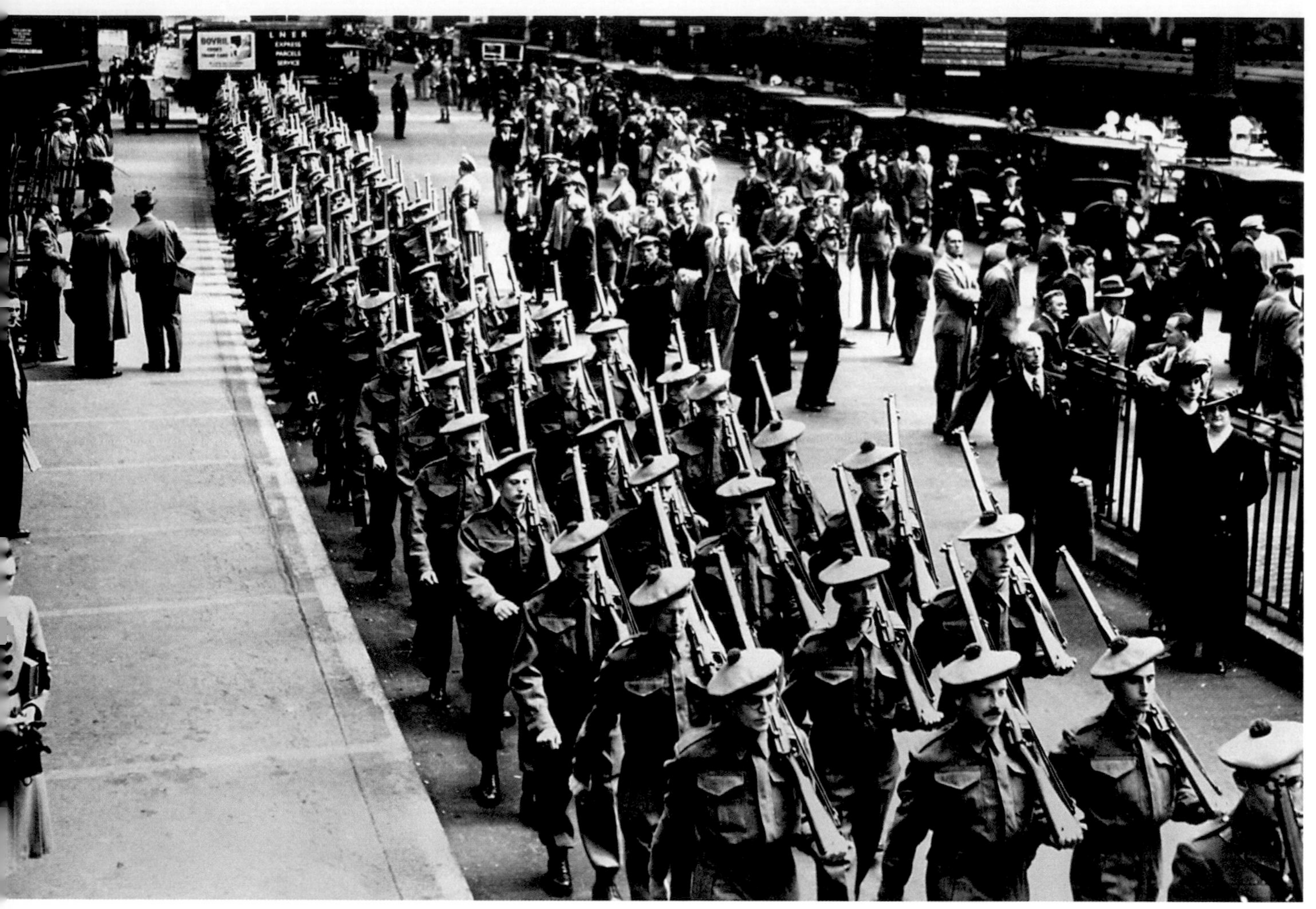

Scottish troops in transit
through London.
July, 1939

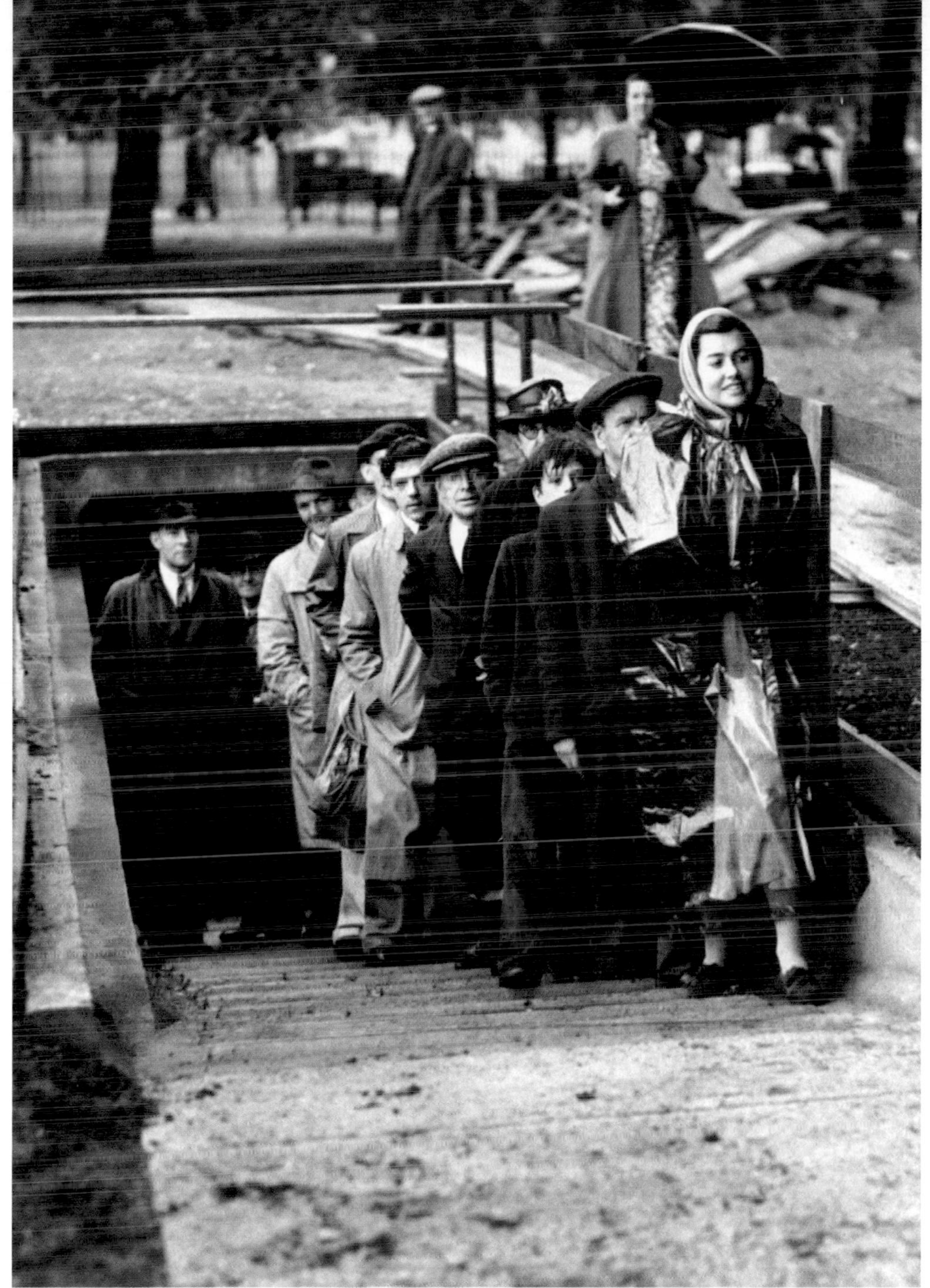

A four-mile long public air raid shelter opens into a London park. Training exercises are a daily occurrence as Londoners begin to realise that, should war break out, they are living in an attractive target area. Air raid drills, gas mask drills and evacuation drills become part of everyday life and the face of London takes on a grimmer aspect.
August, 1939

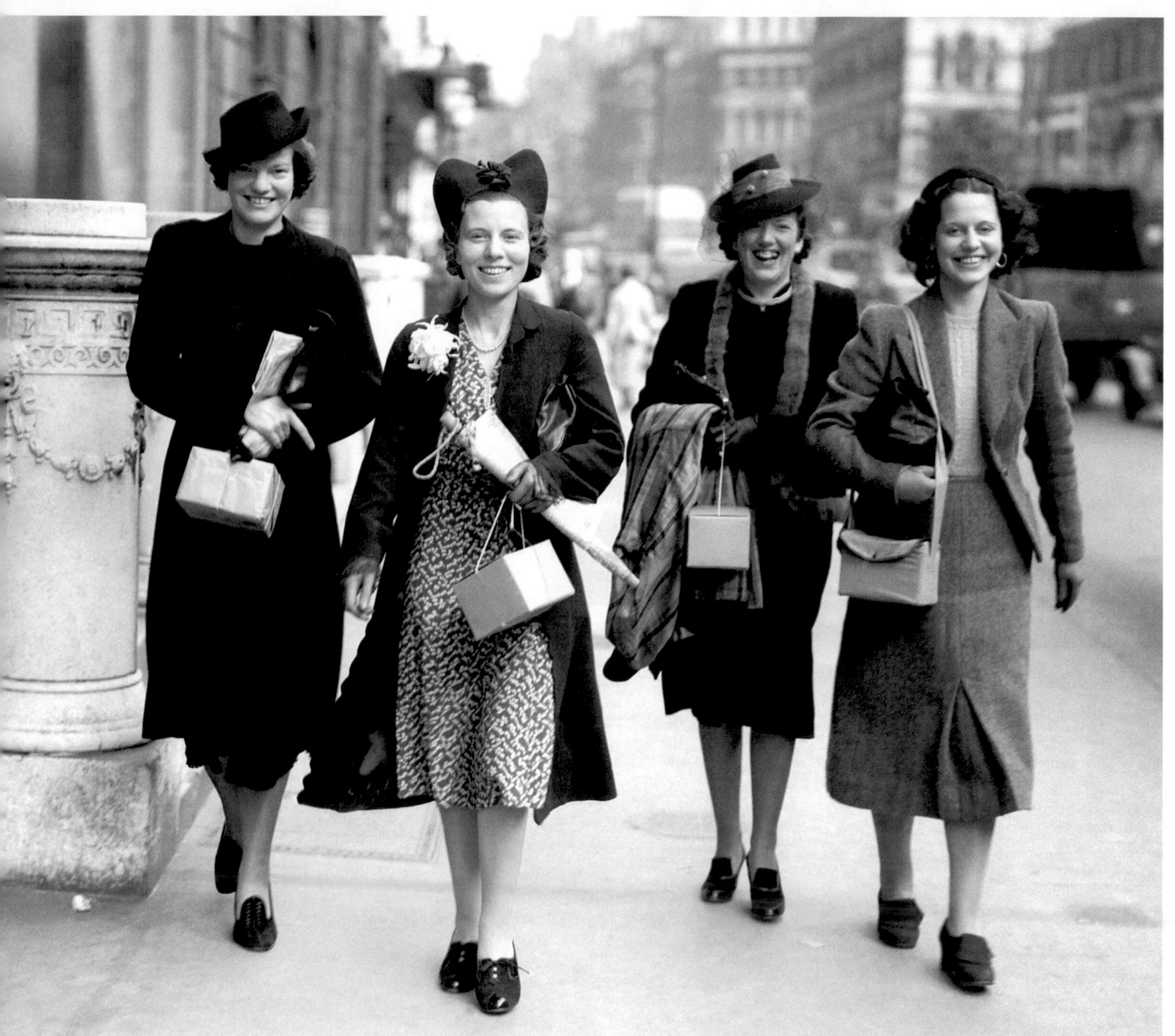

Facing page: Women on their way to work with gas masks in boxes.
August, 1939

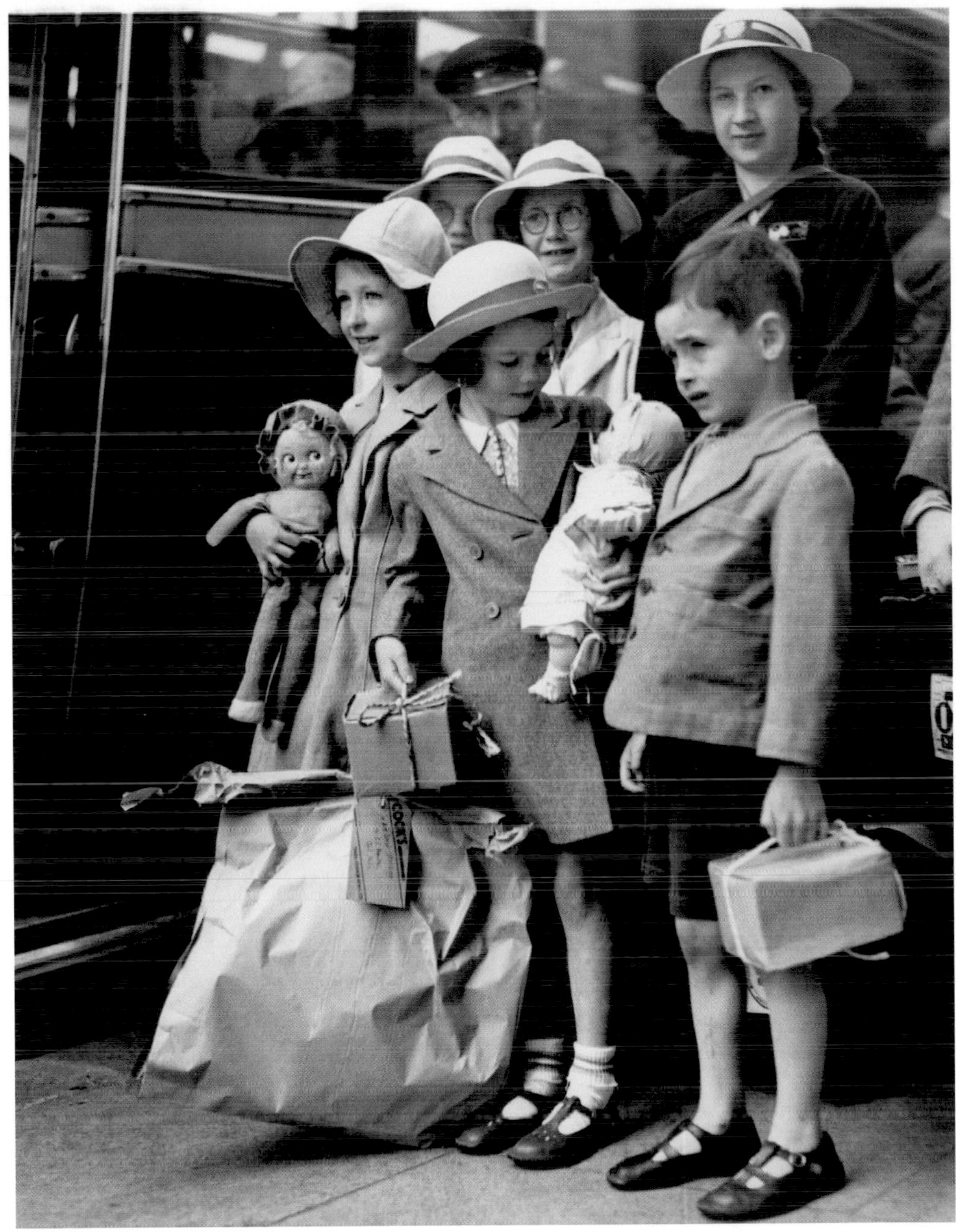

Operation Pied Piper: London evacuees with gas masks and luggage all set for evacuation to the country.
1st September, 1939

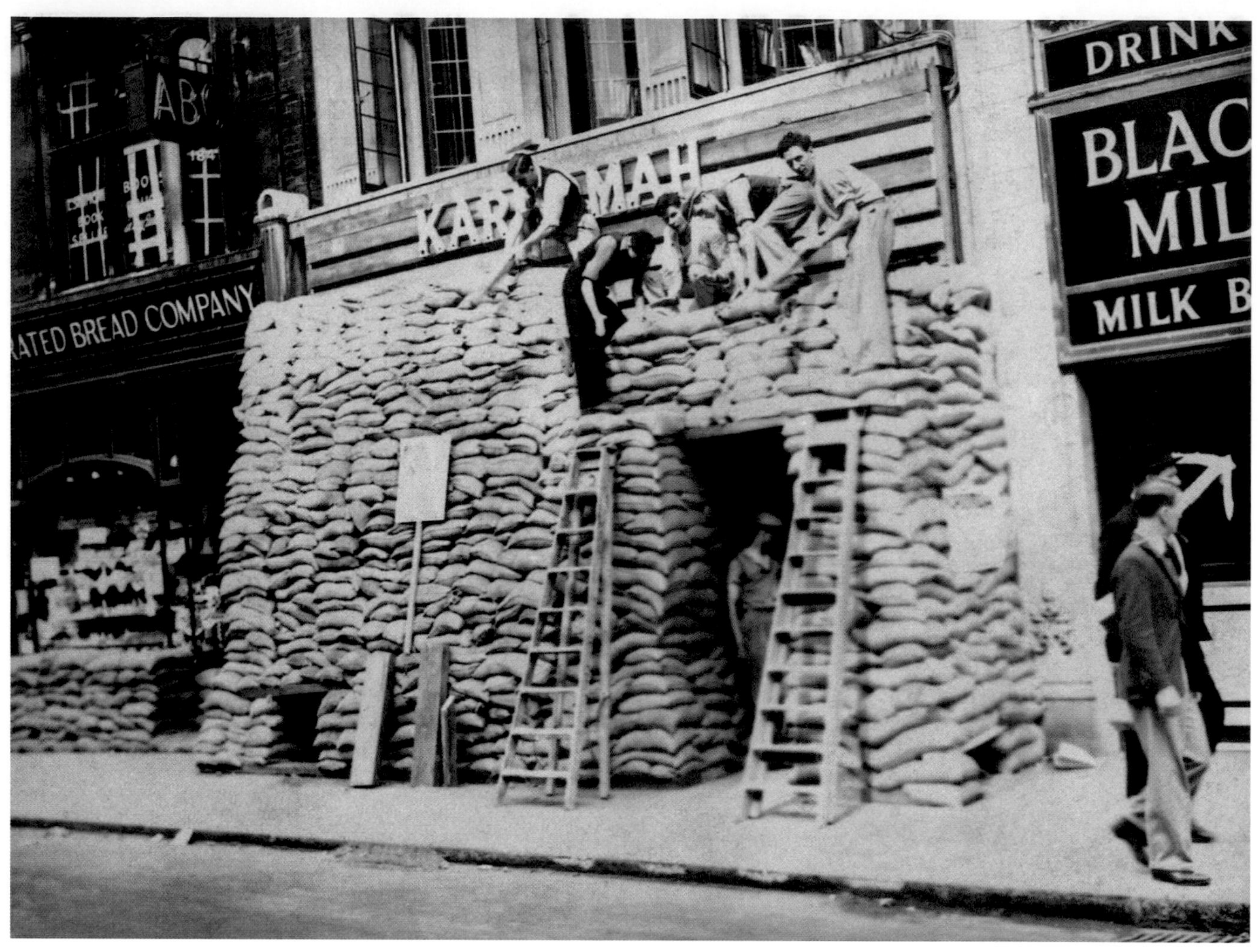

Workers fill shop fronts with sand bags for blast protection.
3rd September, 1939

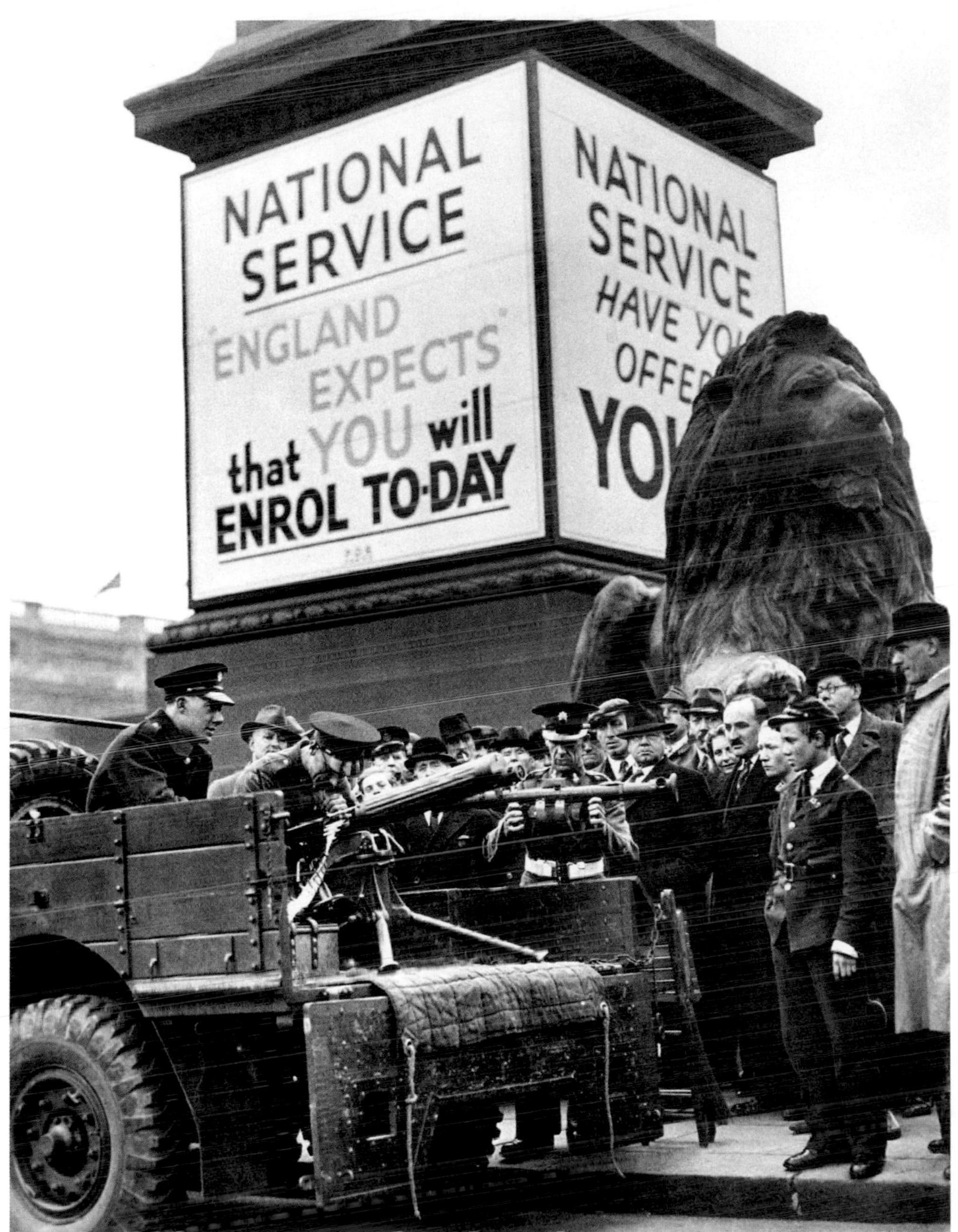

Soldiers demonstrate a Vickers machine gun and a rangefinder to onlookers in Trafalgar Square as part of a recruiting drive.
5th September, 1939

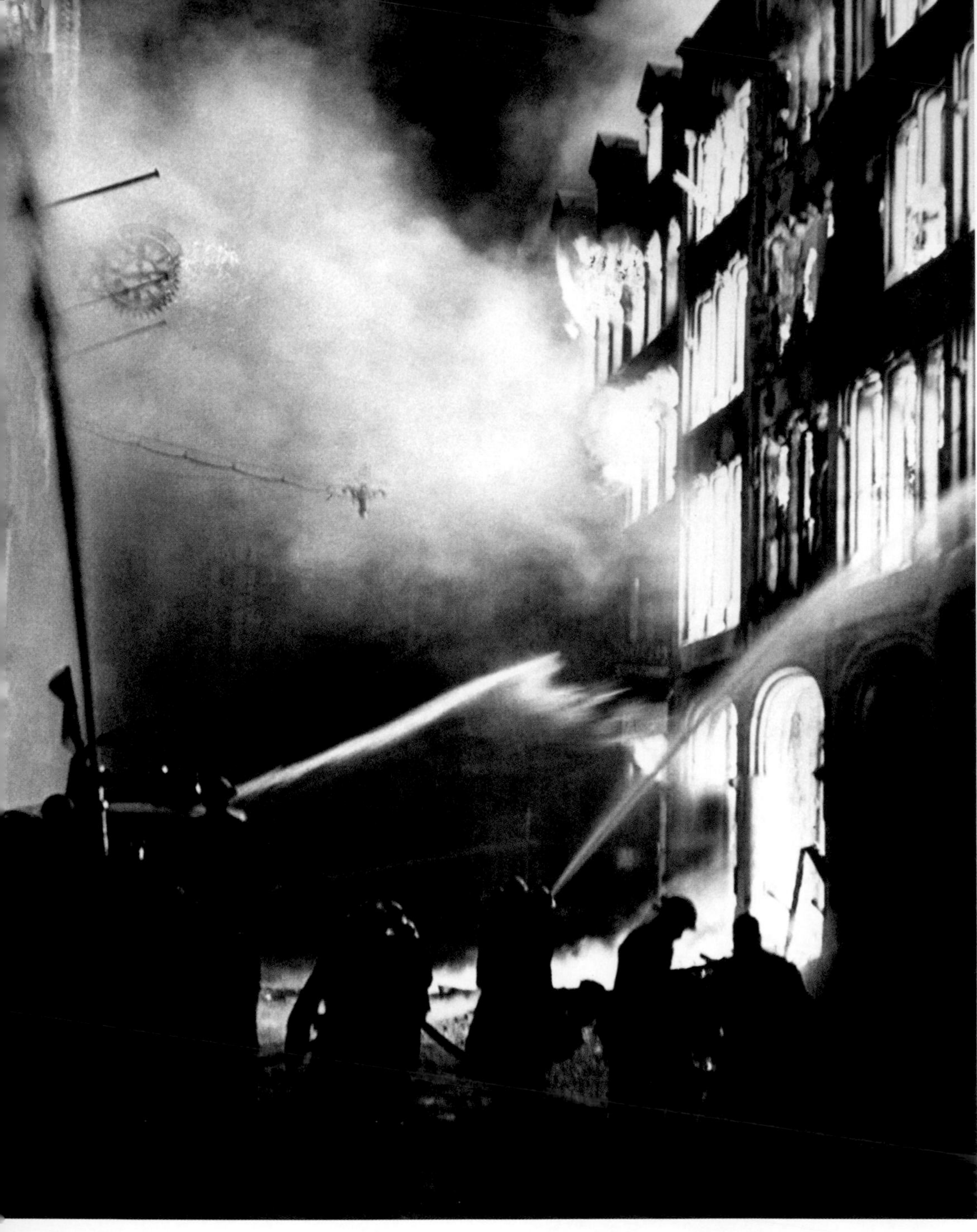

Firemen attempt to tackle a blaze caused by incendiary bombs during the Blitz.
24th August, 1940

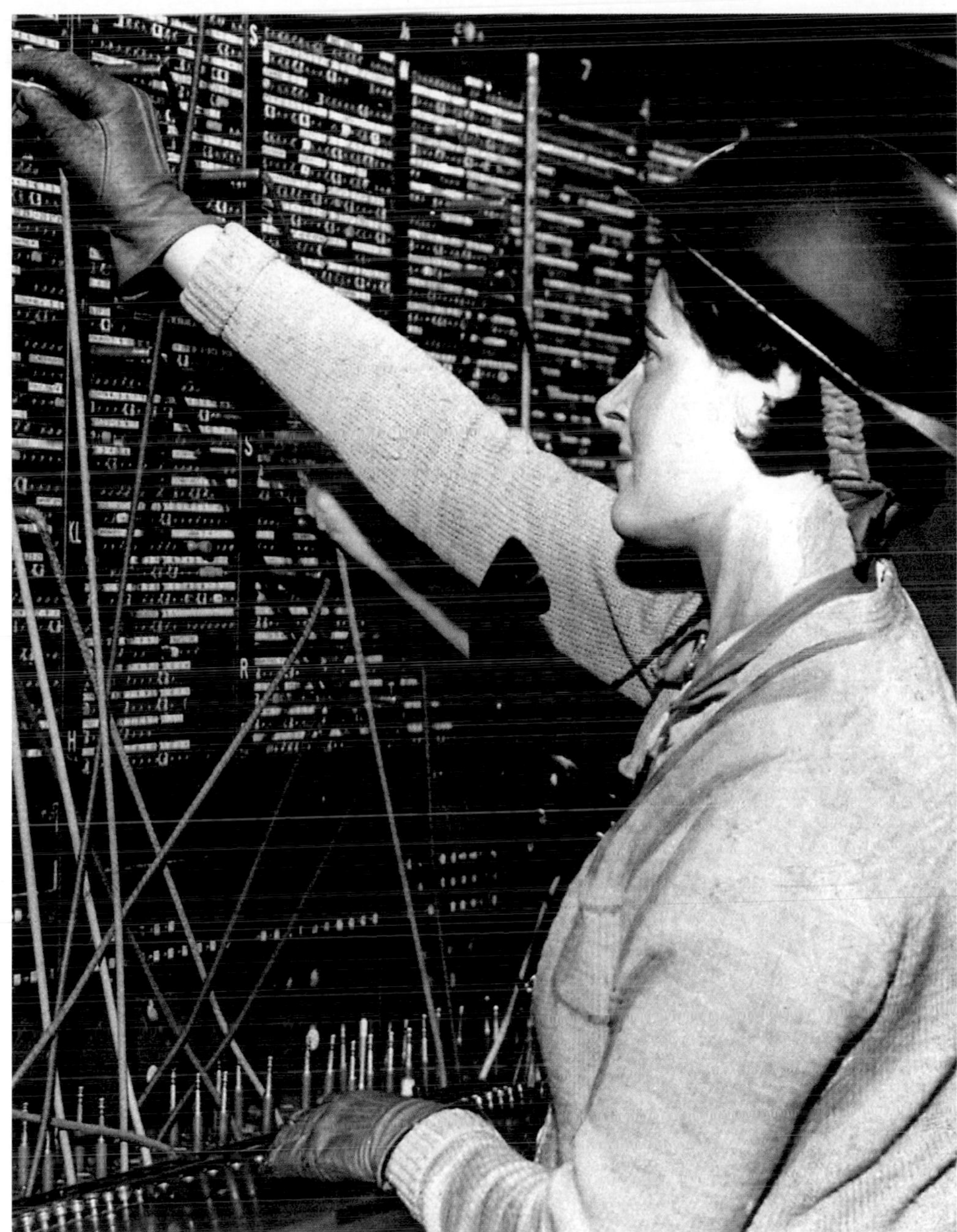

Hard hats must be worn: particularly by those who remain at their posts during air raids.
September, 1940

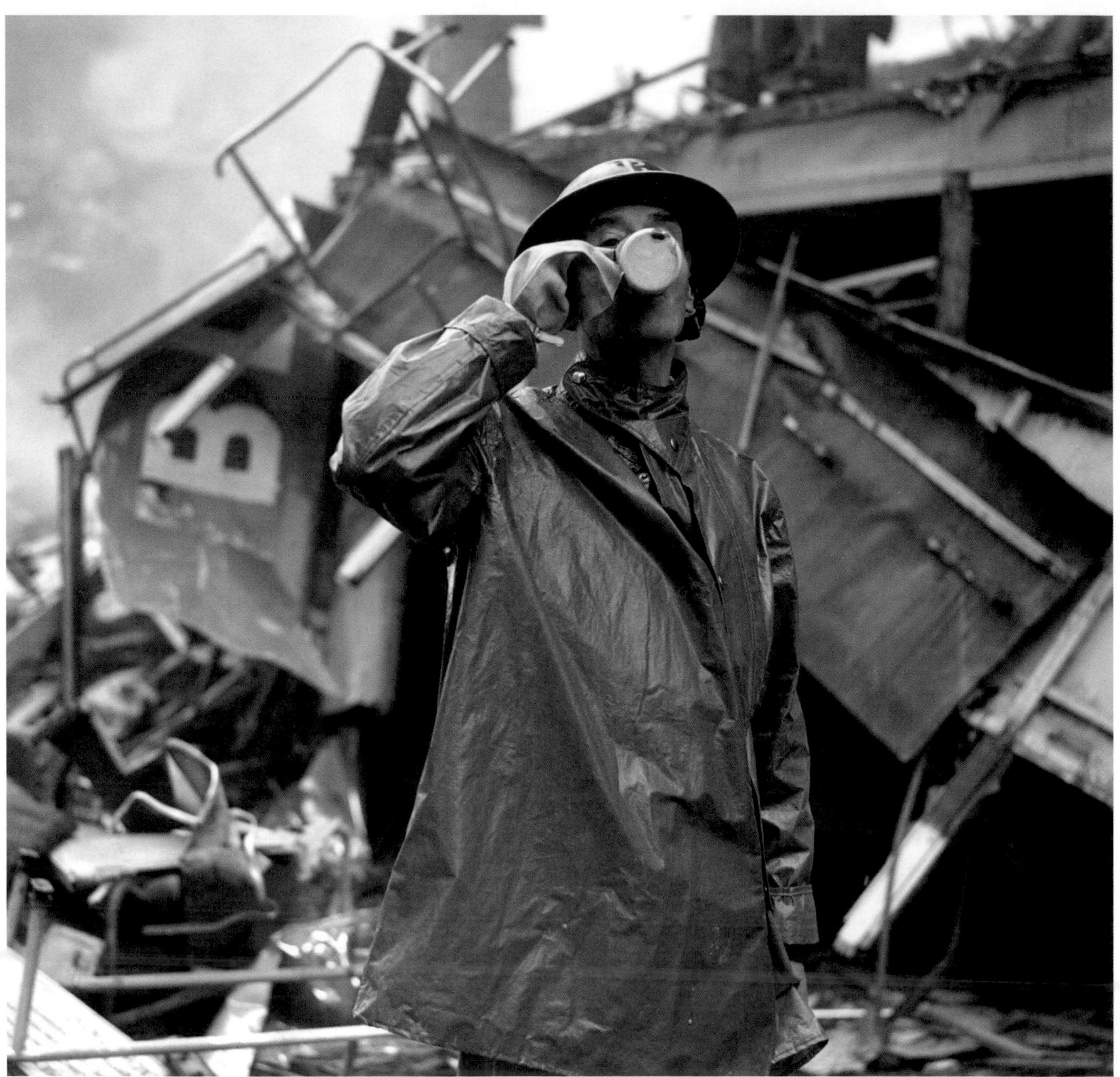

Facing page: A fireman enjoys a richly deserved cup of tea amid the destruction of the Blitz.
9th September, 1940

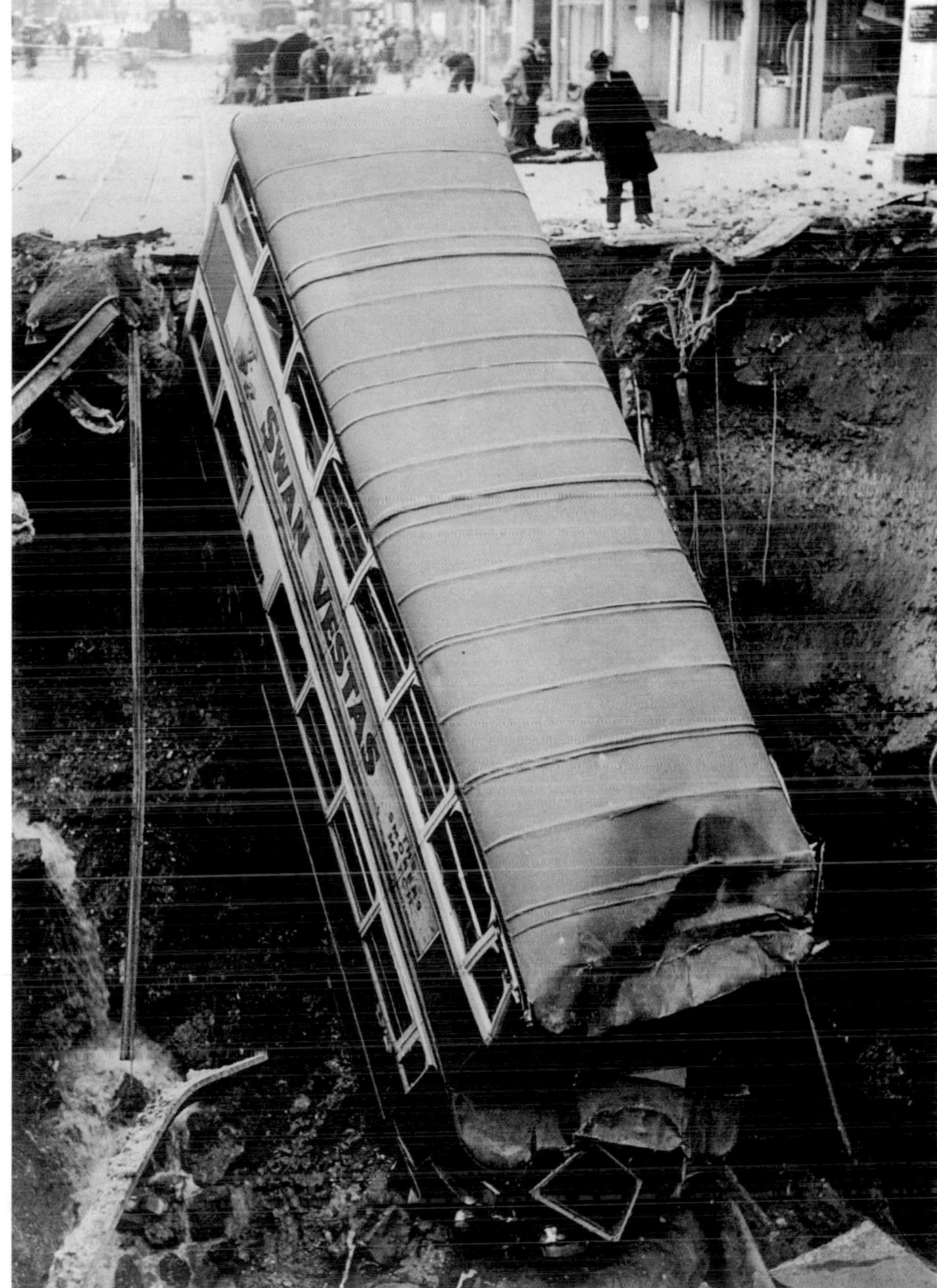

A crater literally big enough to park a bus in, in Balham.
14th October, 1940

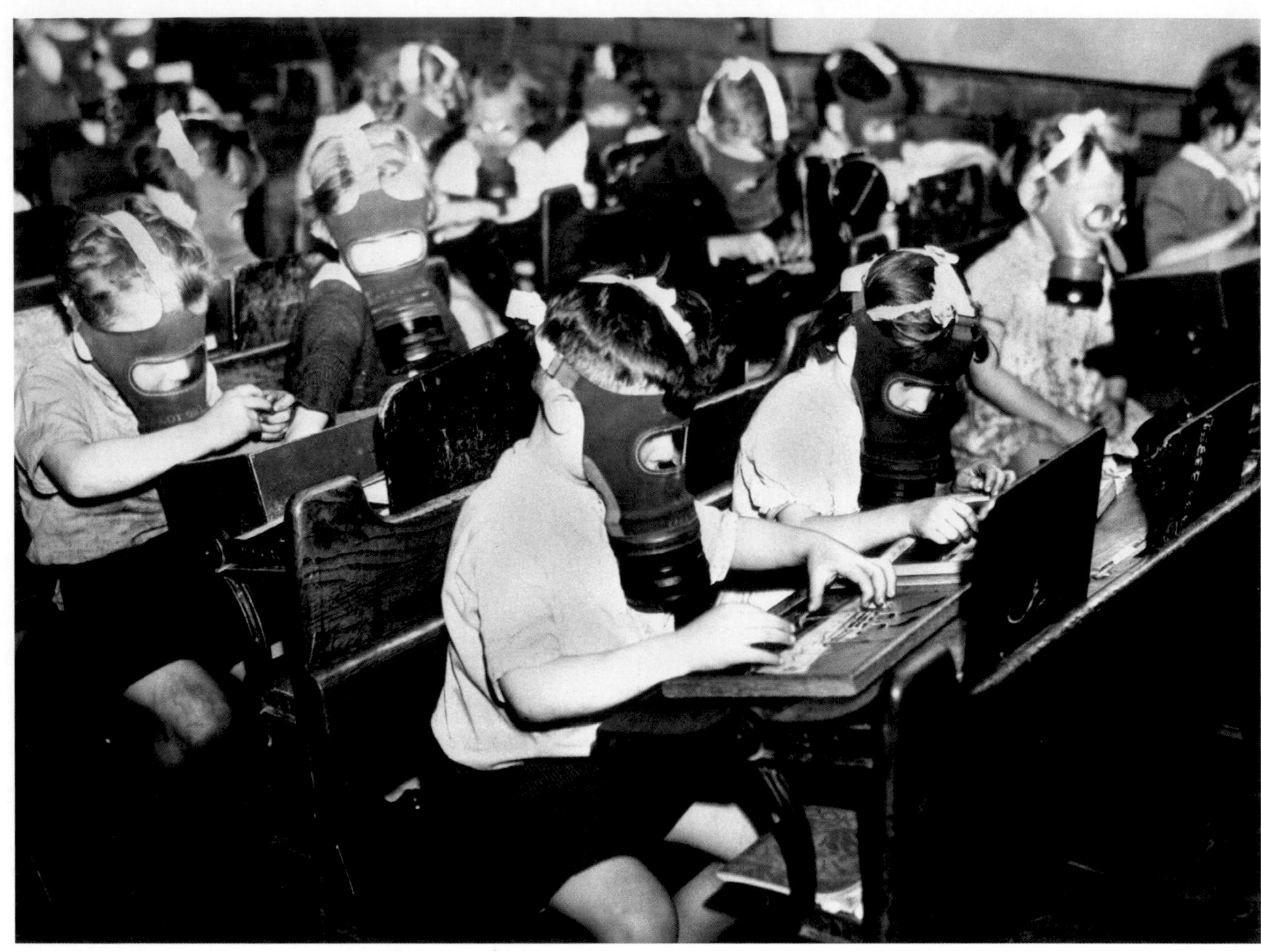

Children at a Clerkenwell school. Many of those evacuated came home before the bombing started.
1941

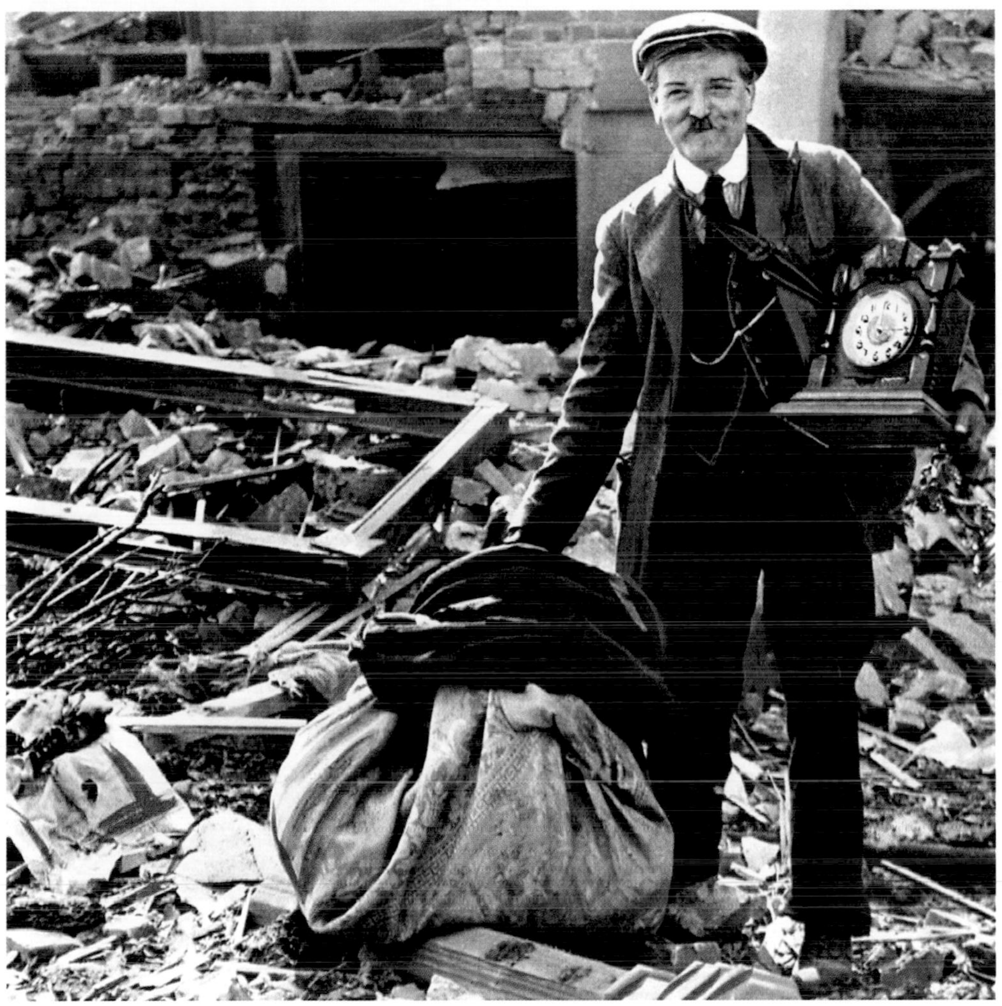

Putting a brave face on it: a Londoner recovers the remains of his belongings from the rubble of his bombed home.
1941

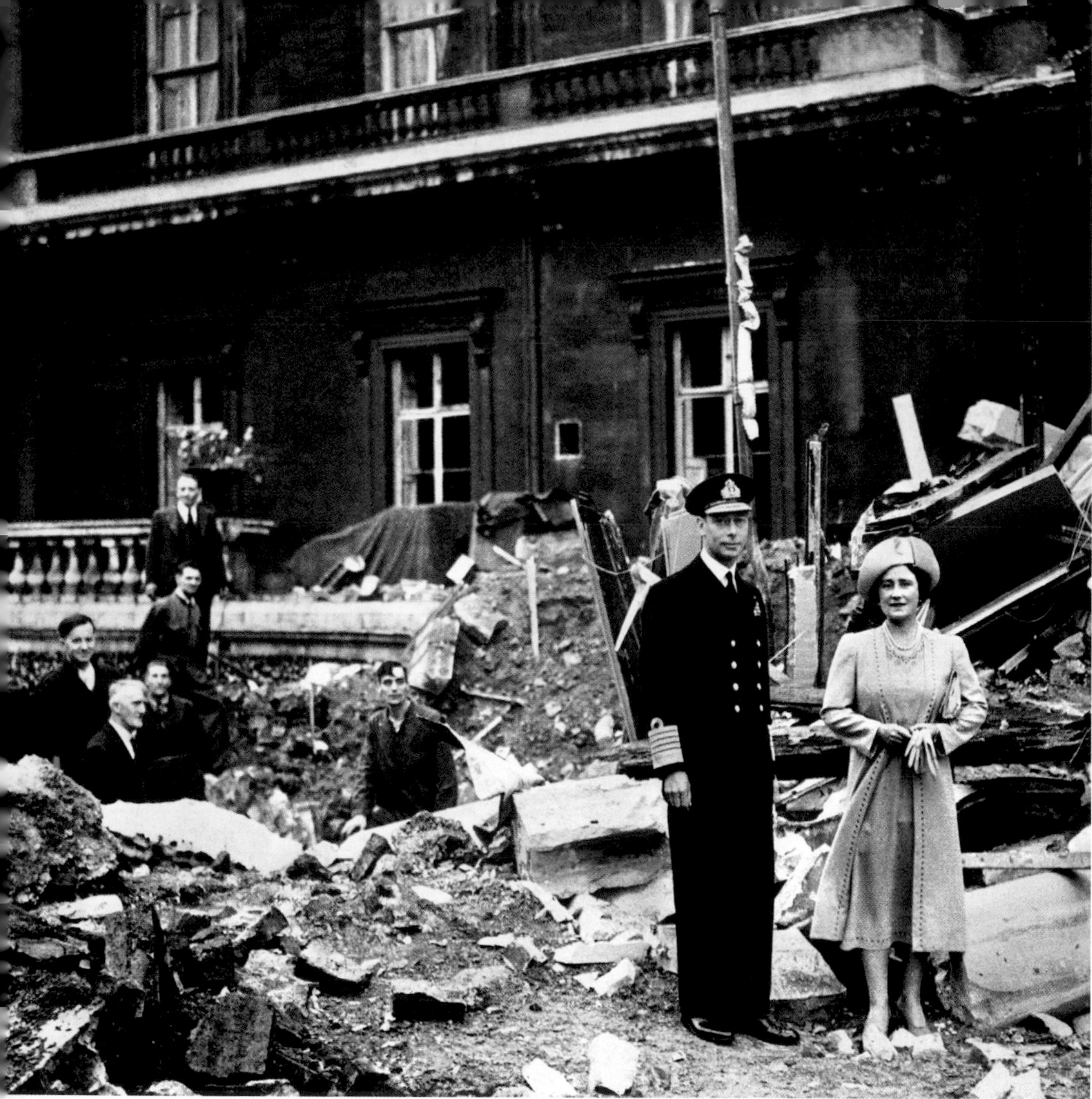

Bomb damage at Buckingham Palace. The palace was a priority target for the Luftwaffe. "*Now we can look the East End in the face*" said Queen Elizabeth.
1941

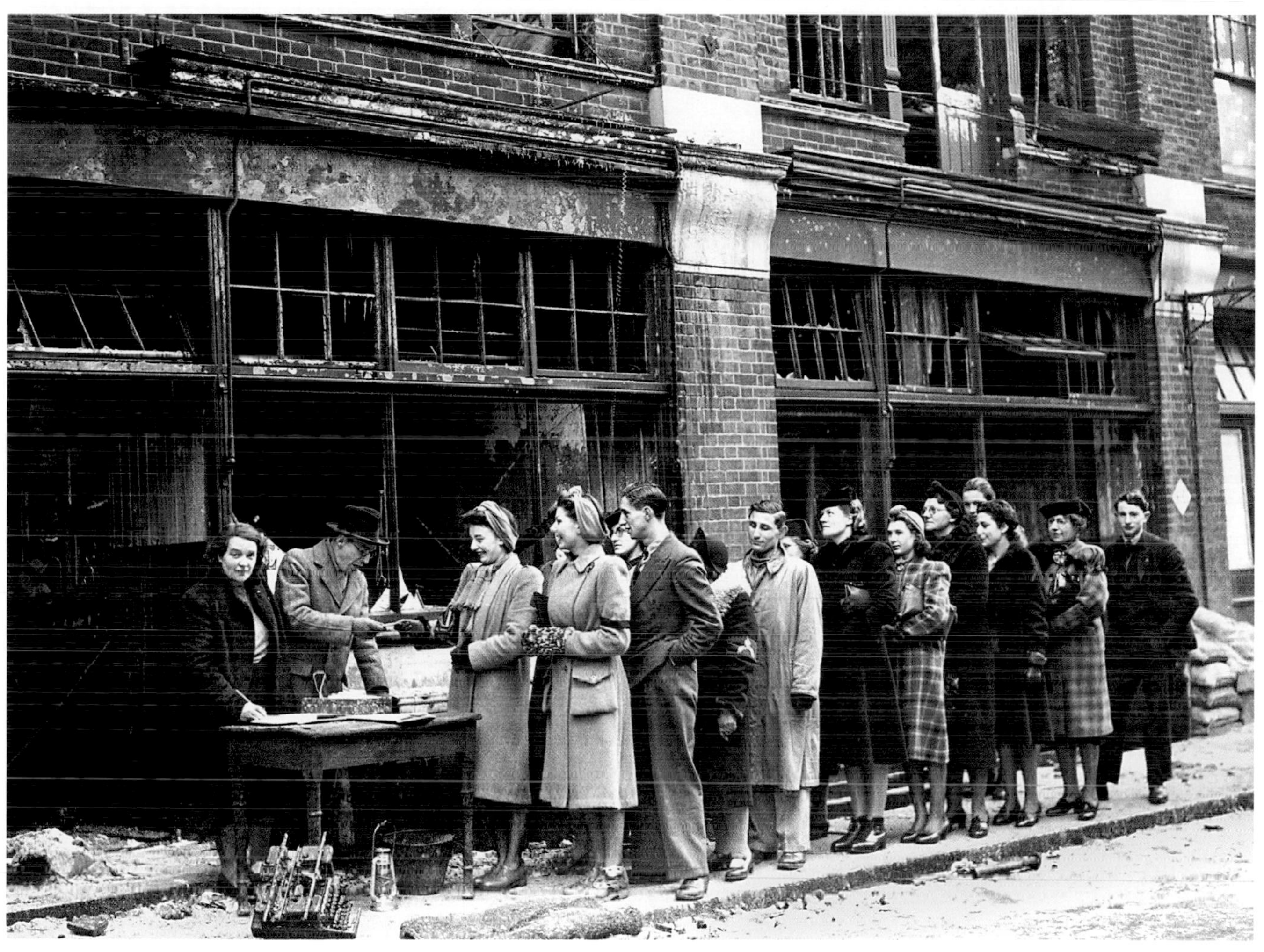

Staff of the Sport and General Press Agency are paid their wages outside their wrecked offices.
3rd January, 1941

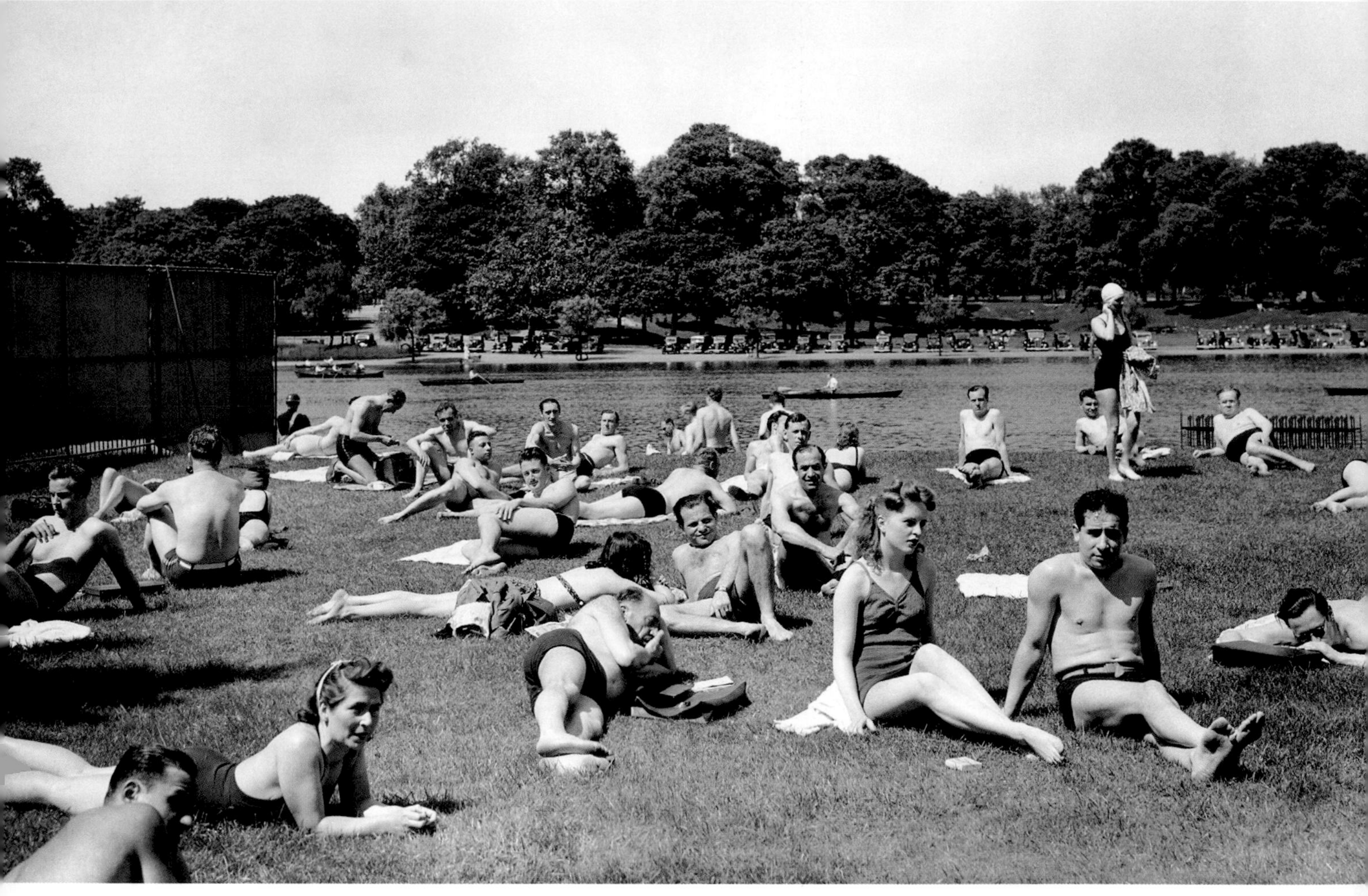

Sunbathing at the Hyde Park Lido.
16th June, 1941

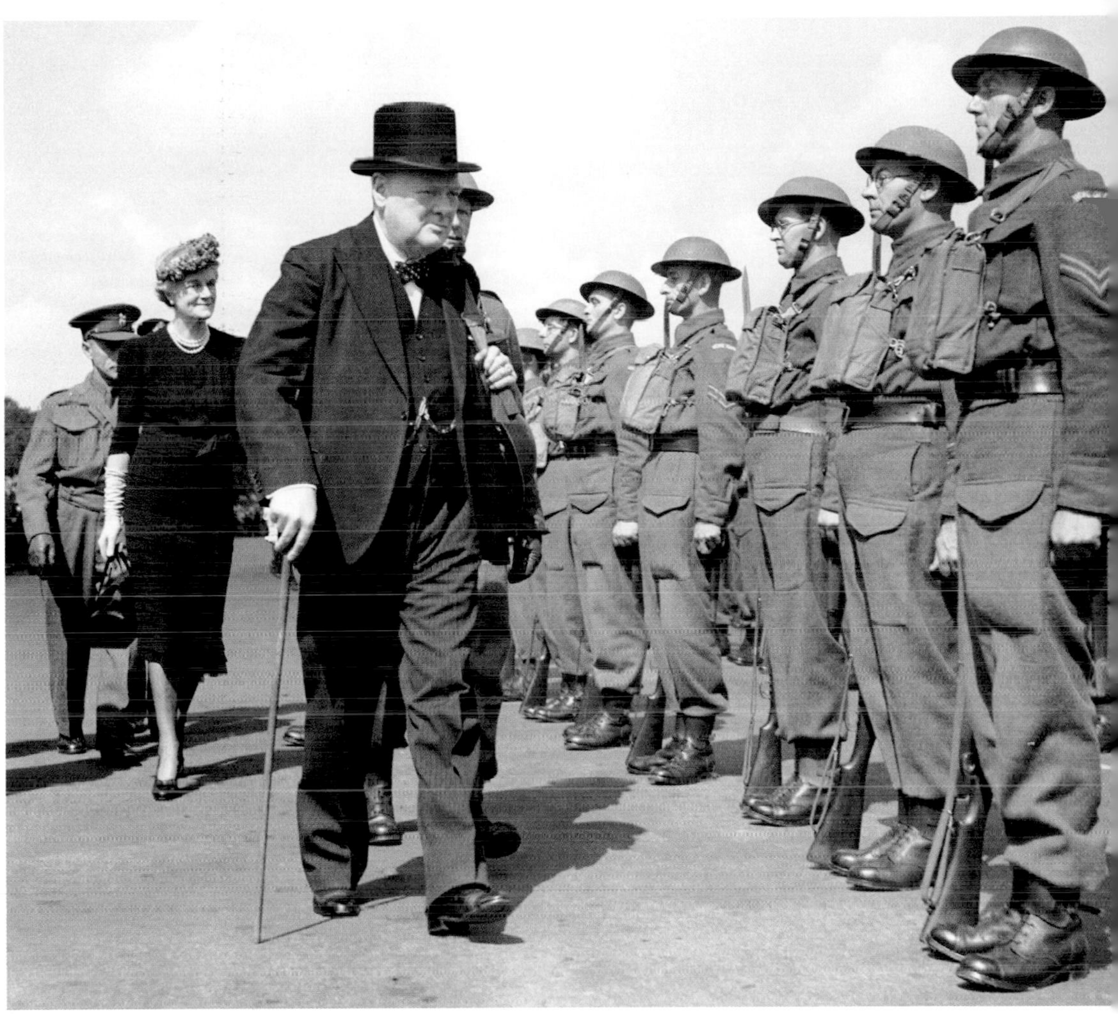

Prime Minister Winston Churchill inspects the Home Guard in Hyde Park.
14th July, 1941

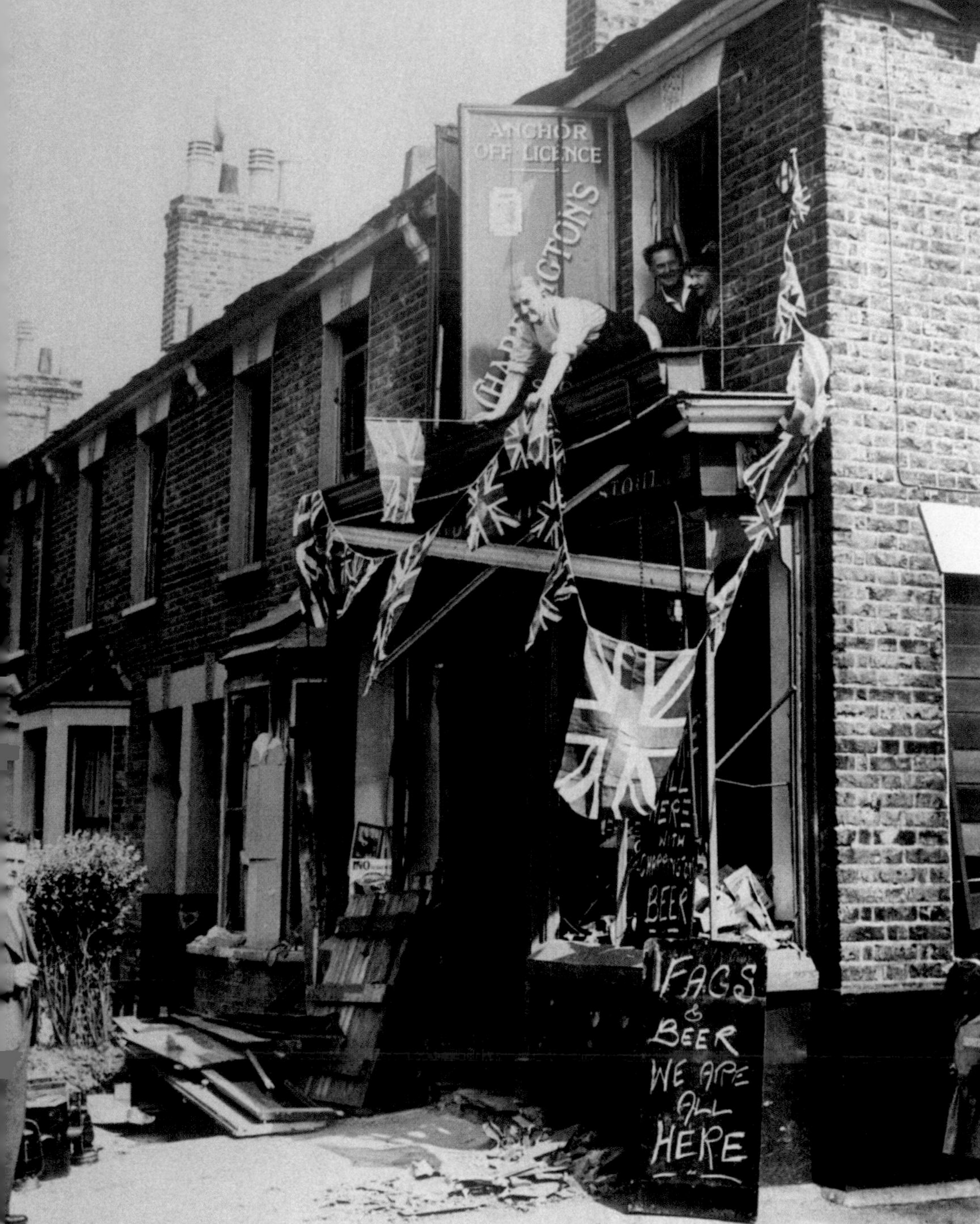

Business as usual, even though the shop has been bombed.
28th October, 1941

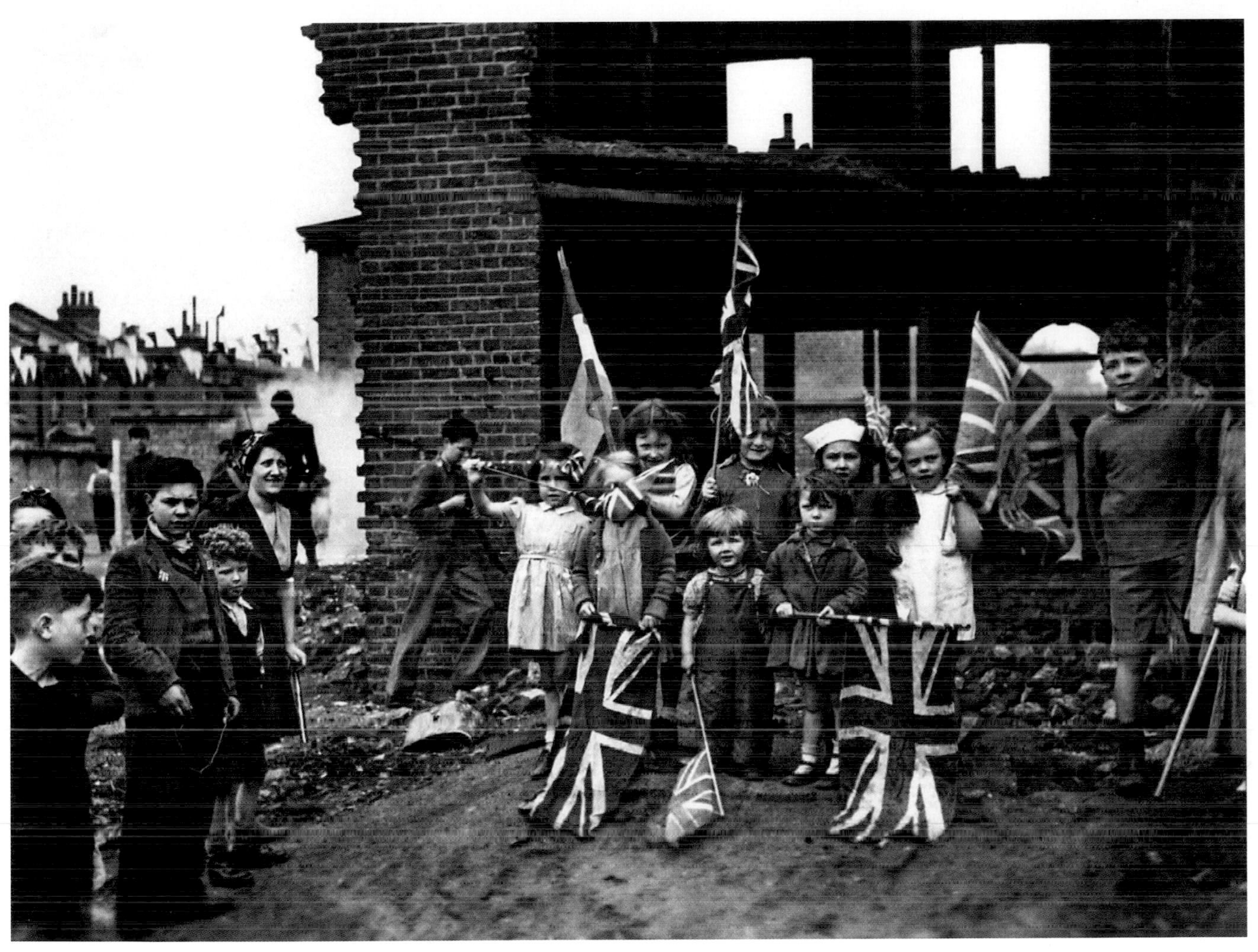

Young Londoners celebrate VE Day (Victory in Europe Day), amidst the ruins of their homes in Battersea.
8th May, 1945

Facing page: Work begins to repair the damage done by the Blitz and rocket attacks during the war.
June, 1945

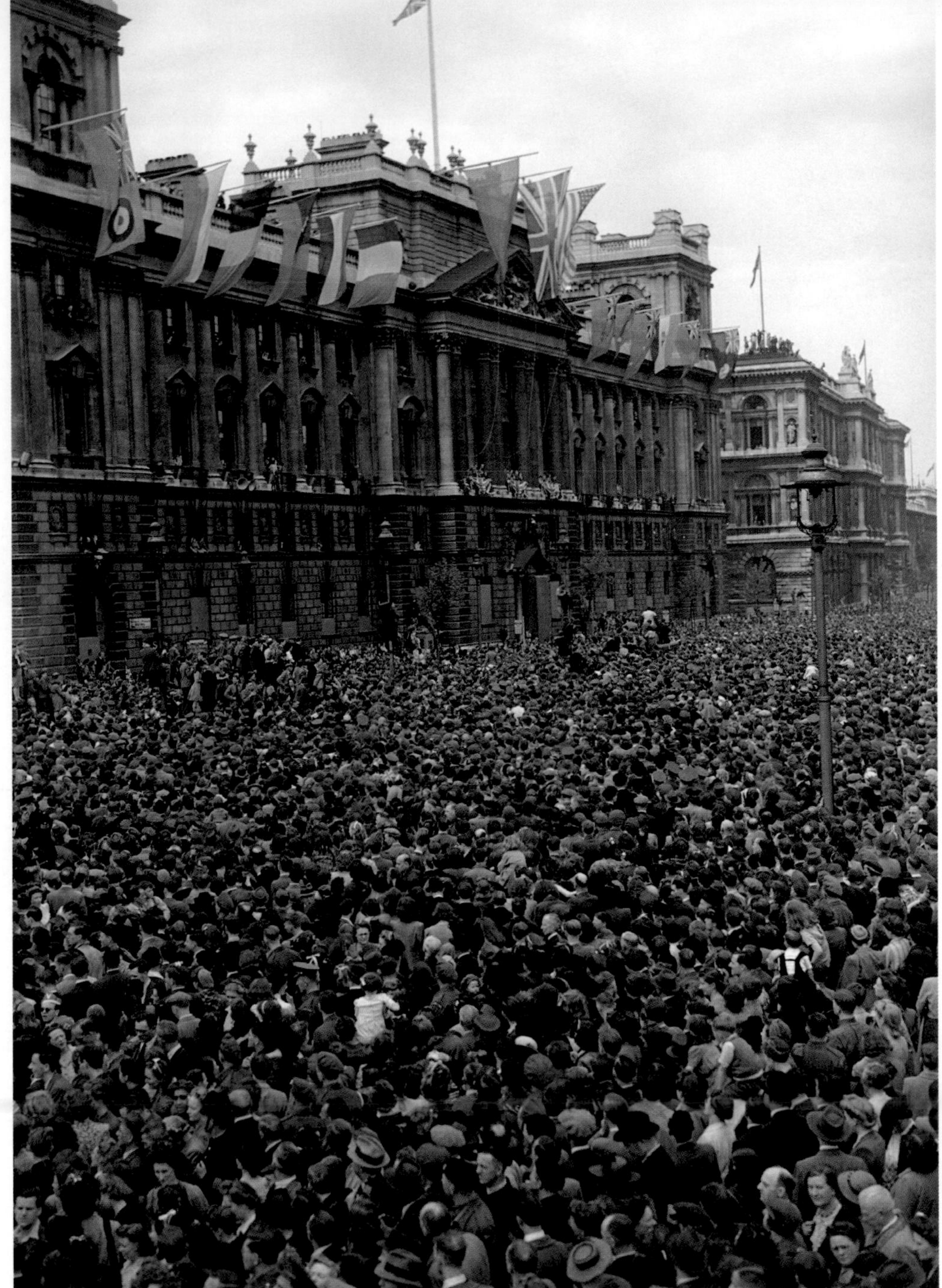

Crowds at Whitehall celebrate VE Day.
8th May, 1945

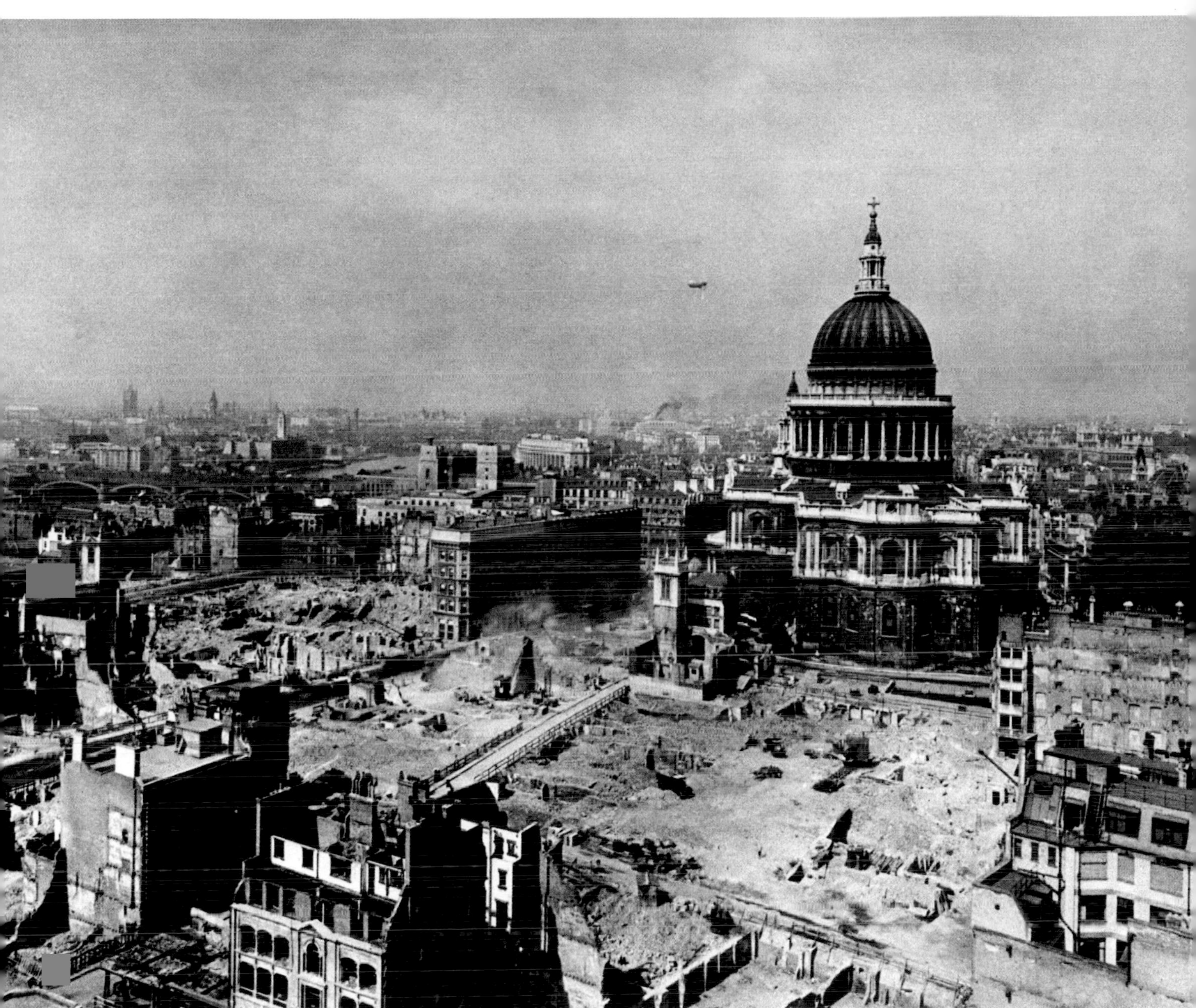

Facing page: St. Paul's Cathedral lit by searchlights, on VJ night.
15th August, 1945

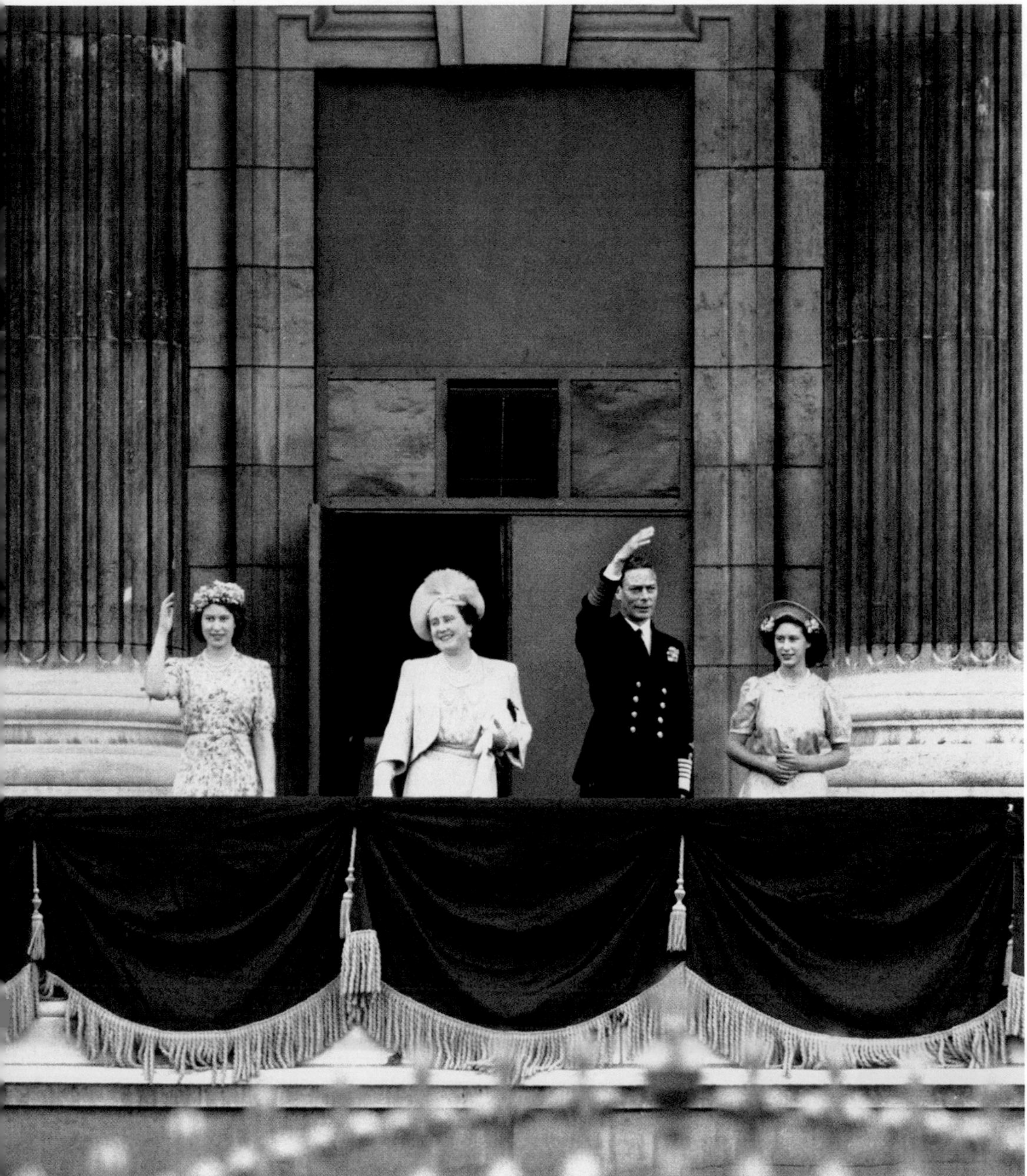

King George VI with the Queen, Princess Elizabeth and Princess Margaret on the balcony of Buckingham Palace on VJ (Victory over Japan) Day.
15th August, 1945

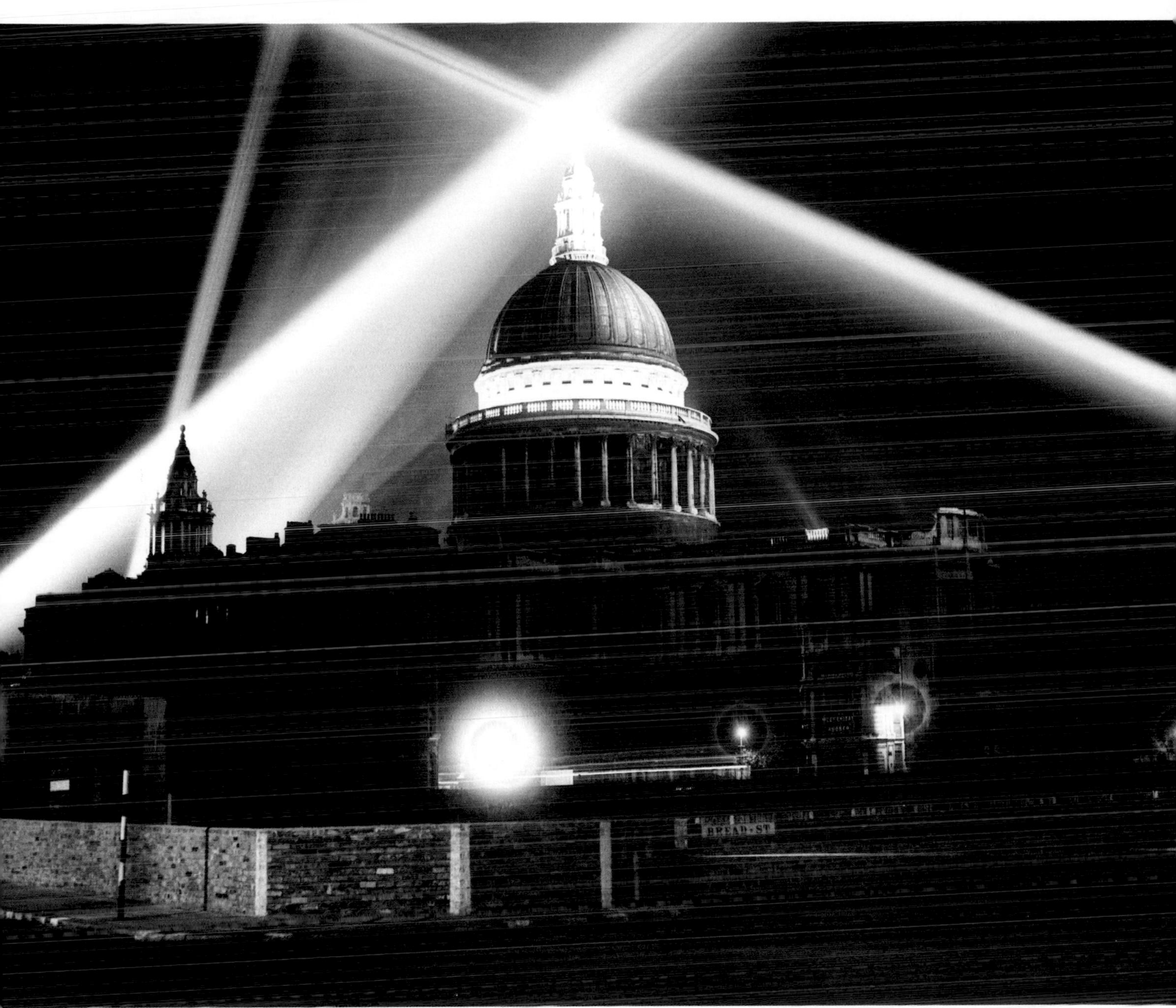
BREAD-ST

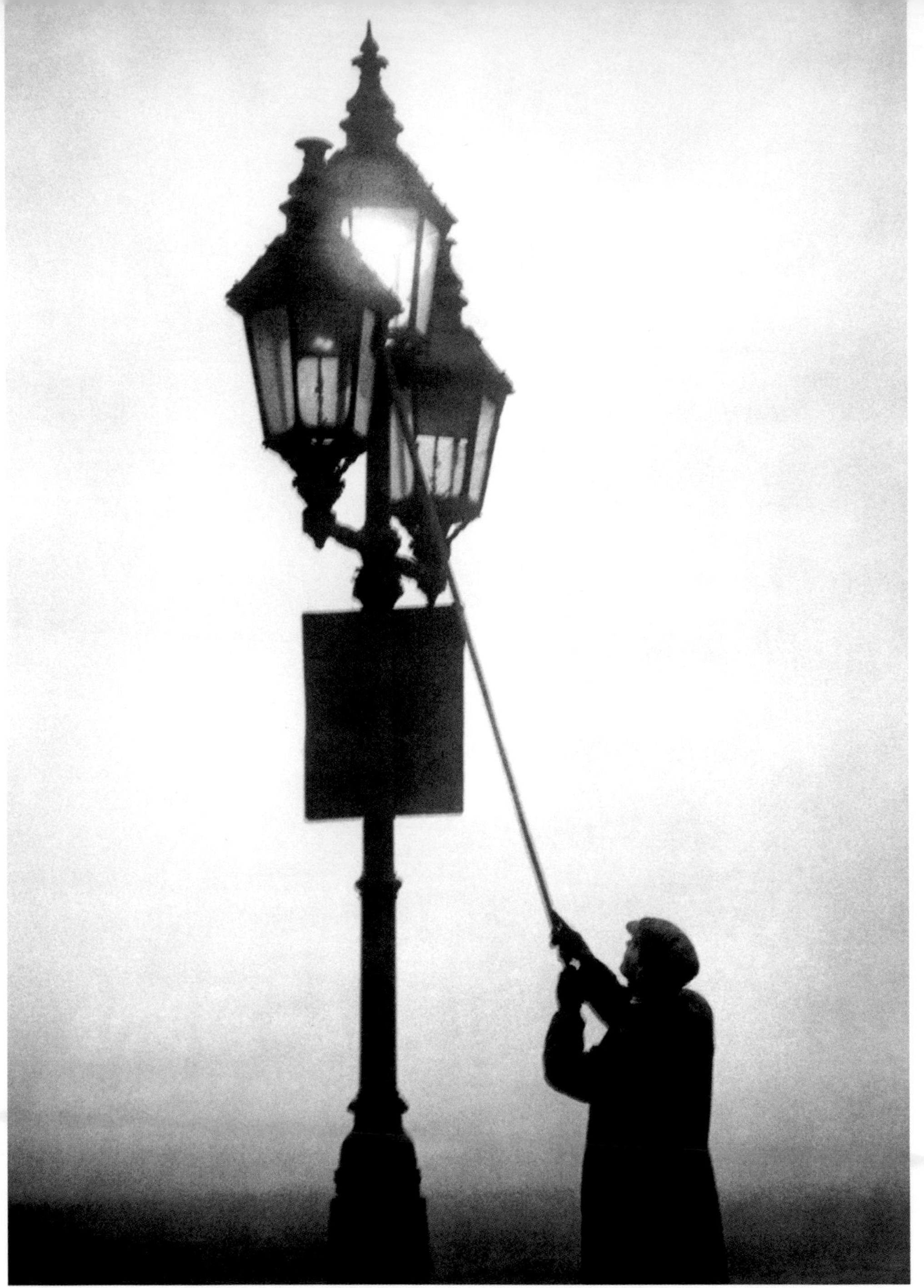

A lamplighter in
a *pea-souper* fog.
31st December, 1945

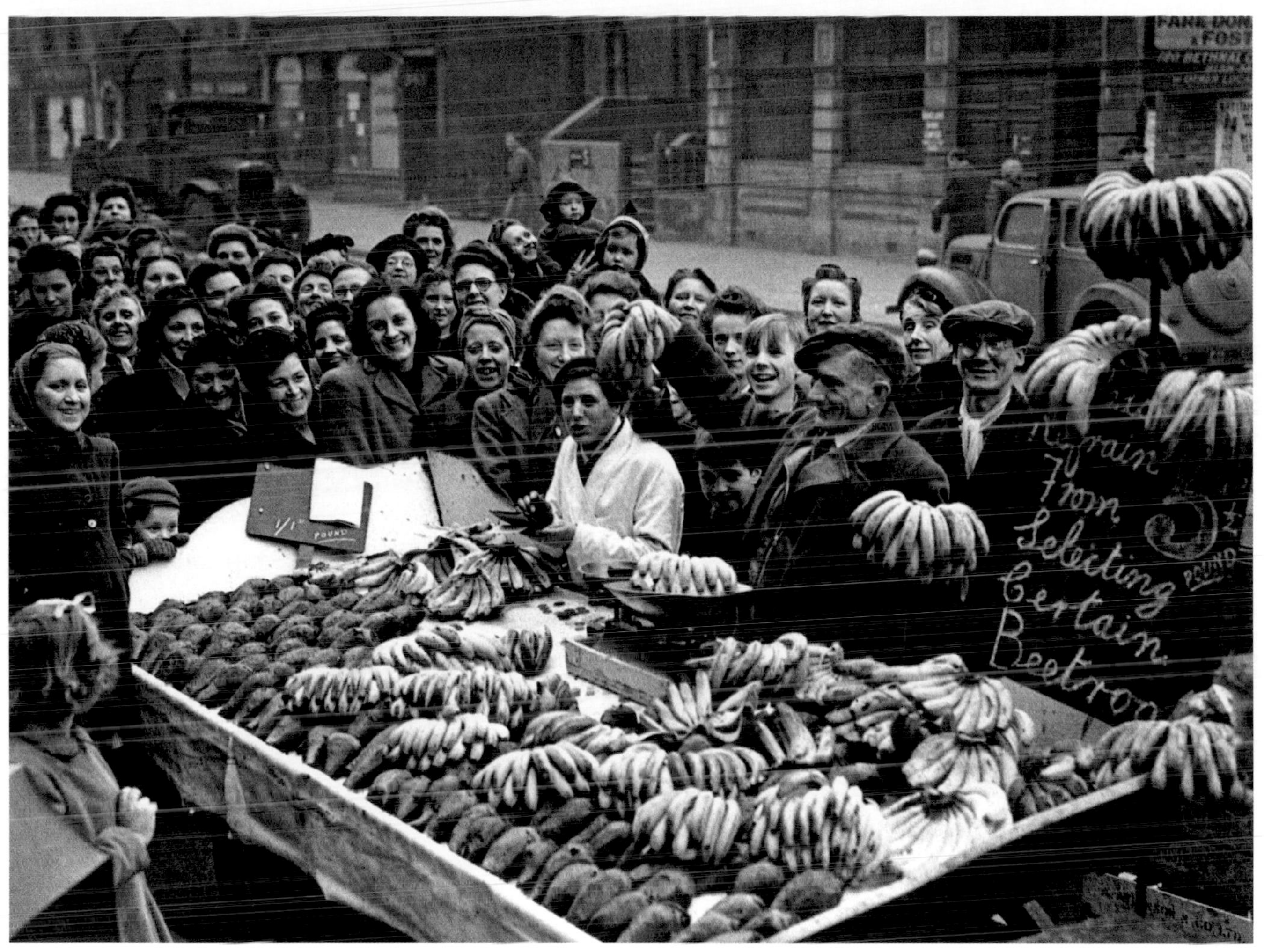

Bethnal Green women queuing for much awaited bananas that have been scarce since the beginning of the war. Rationing did not end in the United Kingdom until the 1950s.
1946

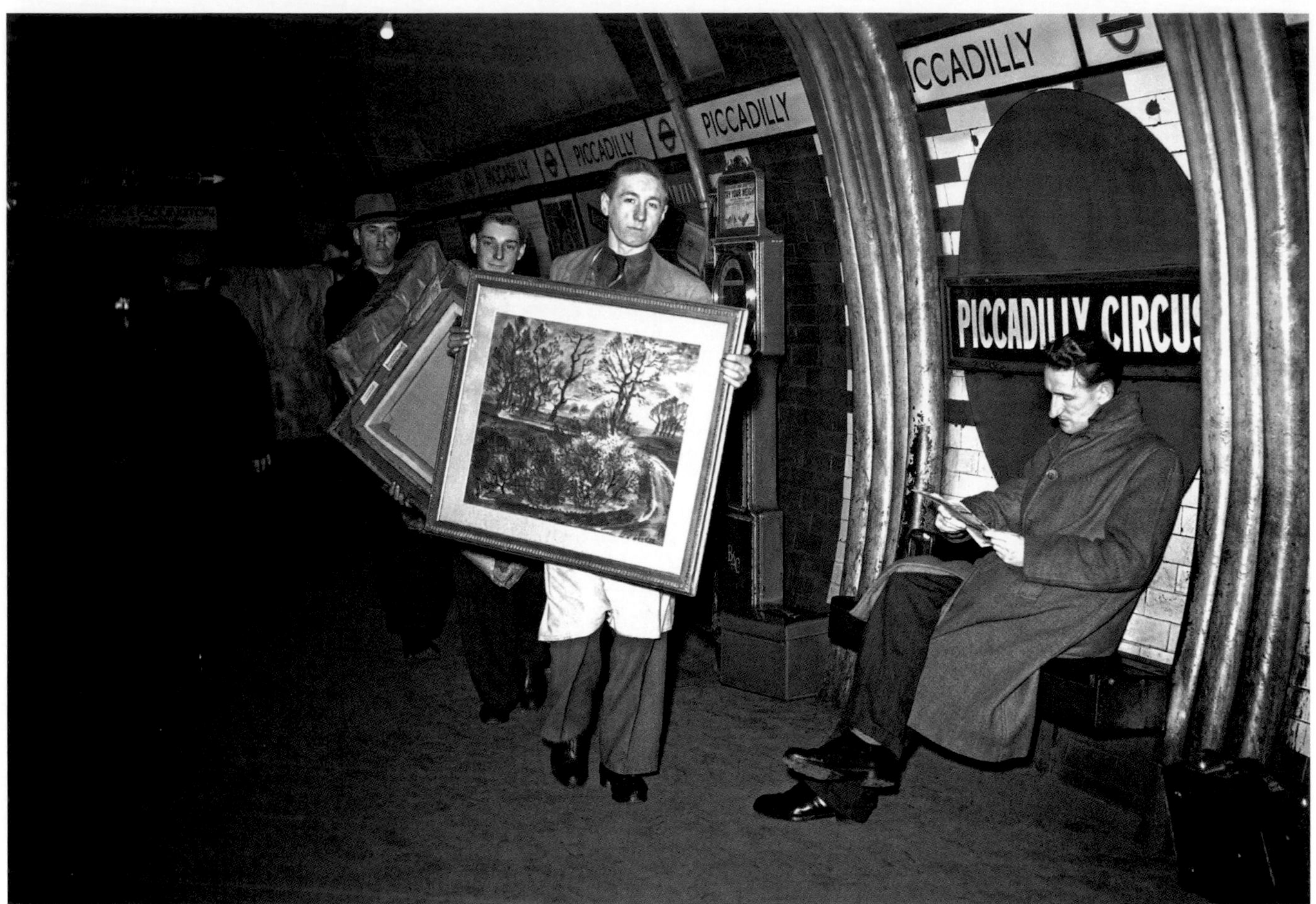

Eighty feet below Piccadilly Circus is a part of the underground station known as *Aladdin's Cave,* where national art treasures from the Tate Gallery and the London Museum were stored at the outbreak of war.
4th February, 1946

Facing page: Tanks and bulldozers leave Admiralty Arch in London.
8th June, 1946

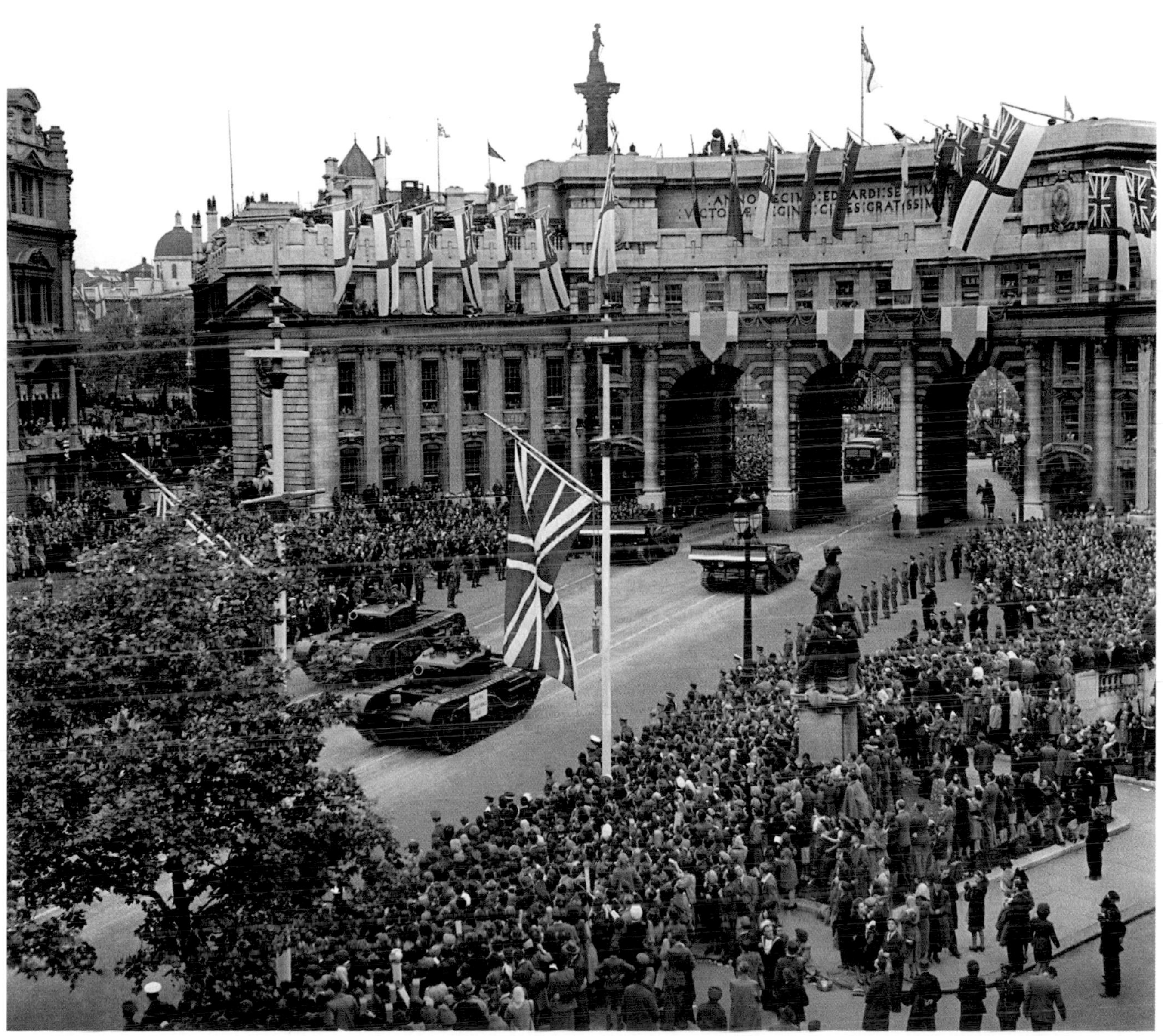

Facing page: Hoarding around a bombsite.
1947

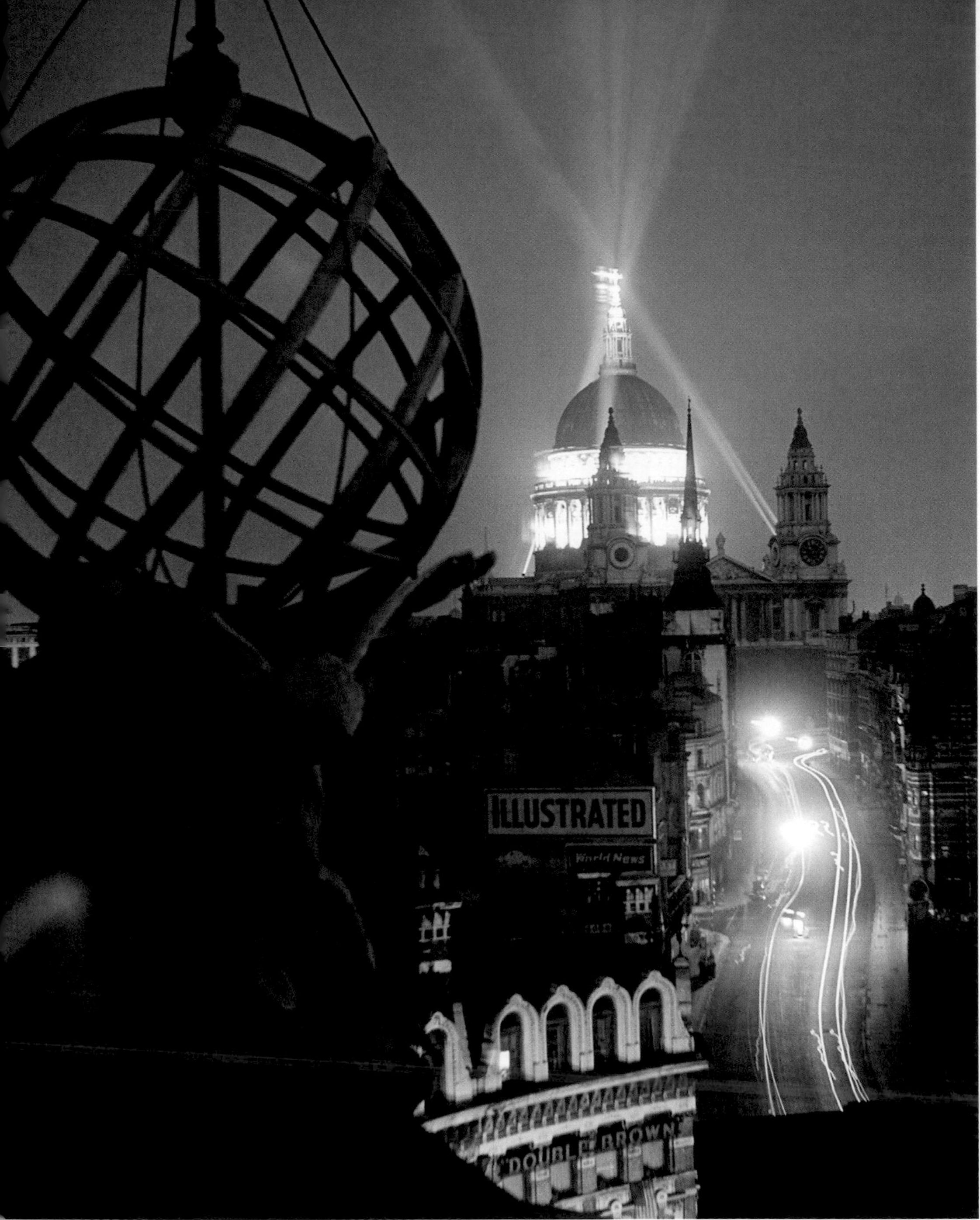

The view of St Paul's Cathedral on Victory night from Ludgate Circus.
8th June, 1946

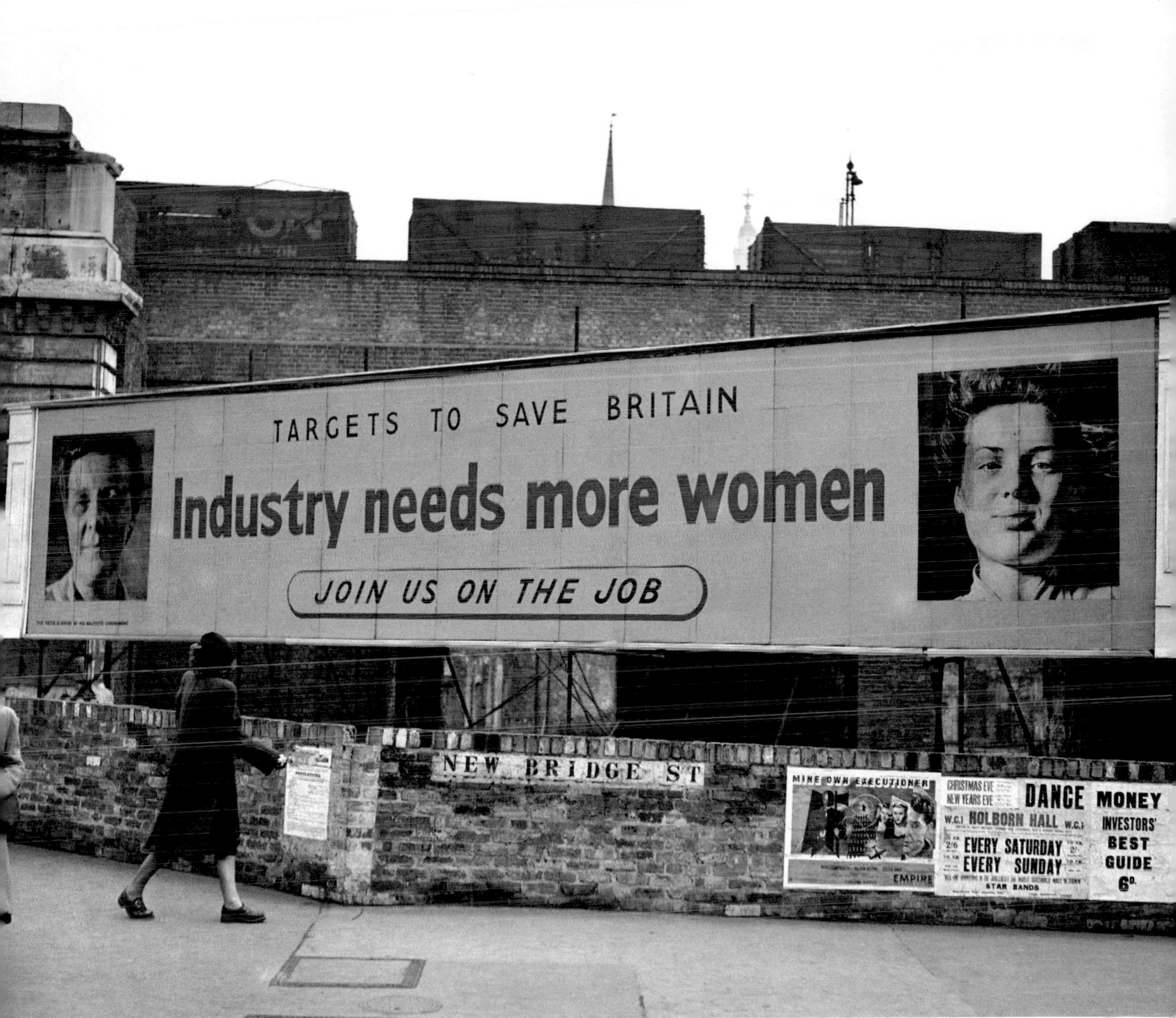
TARGETS TO SAVE BRITAIN
Industry needs more women
JOIN US ON THE JOB
NEW BRIDGE ST
MINE OWN EXECUTIONER
EMPIRE
CHRISTMAS EVE
NEW YEARS EVE
DANCE
W.C.1 HOLBORN HALL W.C.1
EVERY SATURDAY
EVERY SUNDAY
STAR BANDS
MONEY
INVESTORS' BEST GUIDE
6D.

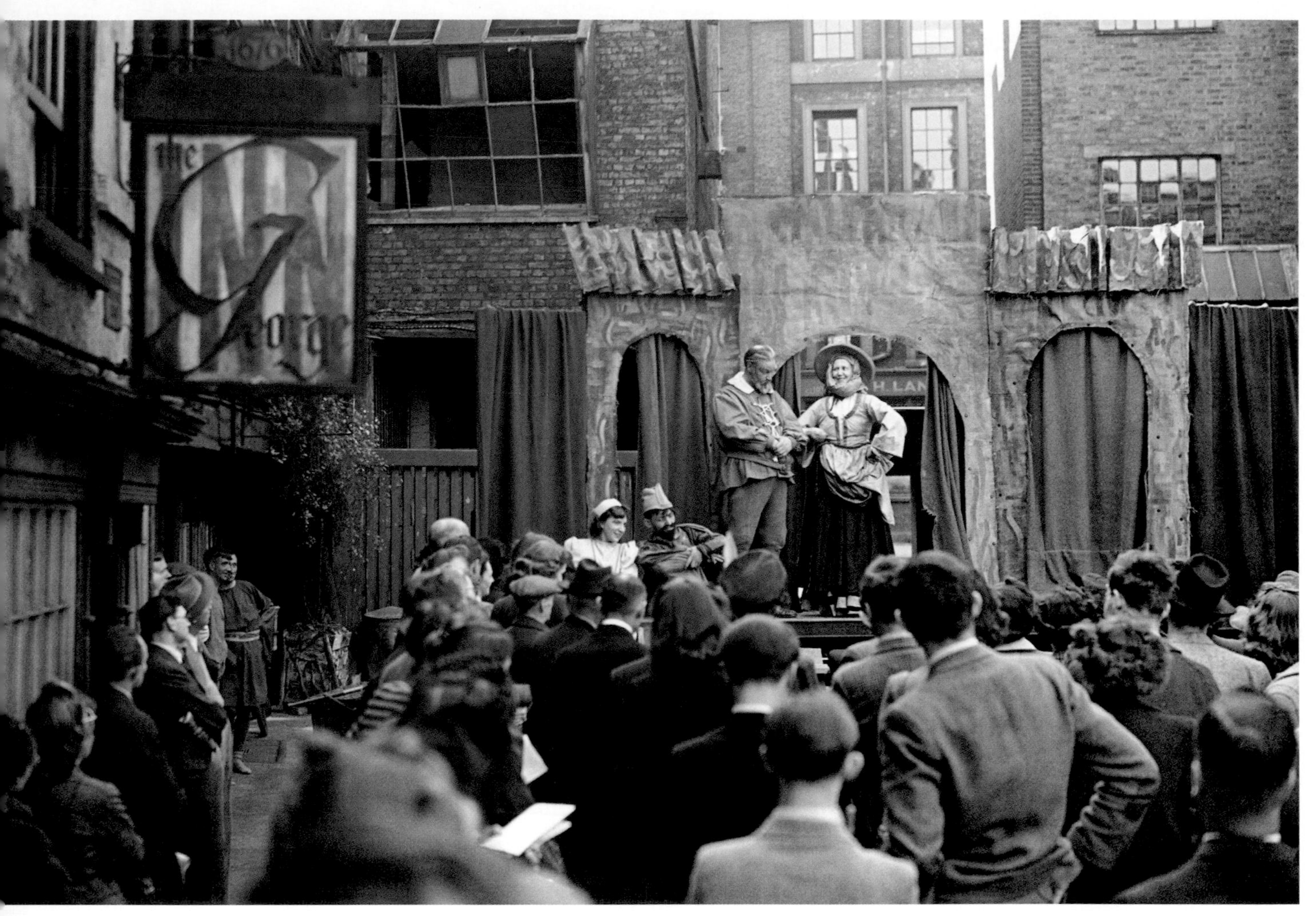

A presentation in the traditional Elizabethan manner of Shakespeare's *The Merry Wives of Windsor* in the courtyard of the George Inn, Southwark, near the site of the original *Globe* theatre.
26th April, 1947

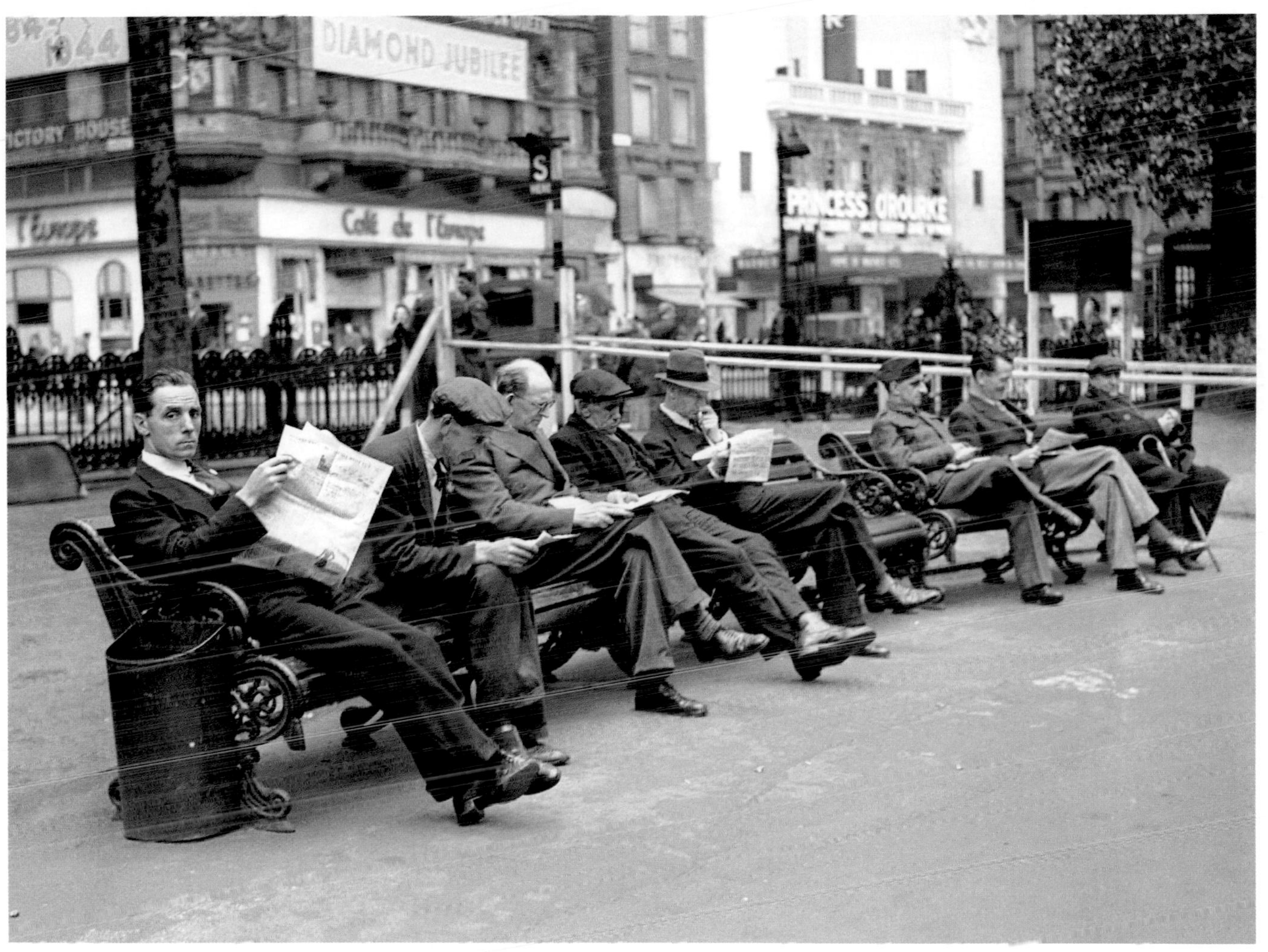

Leicester Square.
13th November, 1947

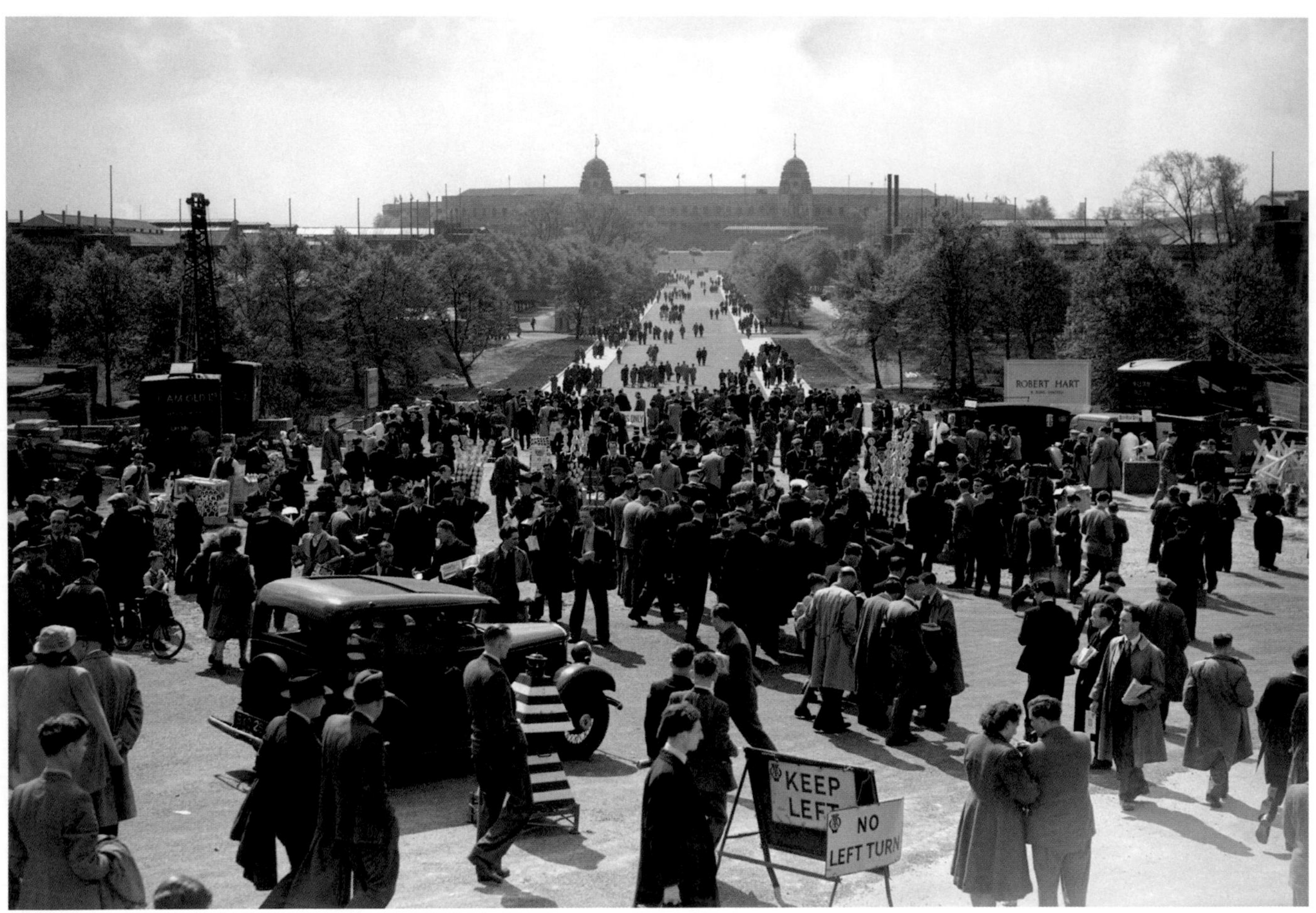

Blackpool and Manchester United supporters take the new Olympic Road on their way to Wembley Stadium for the FA Cup Final.
24th April, 1948

Facing page: The Pool of London looking west.
June, 1948

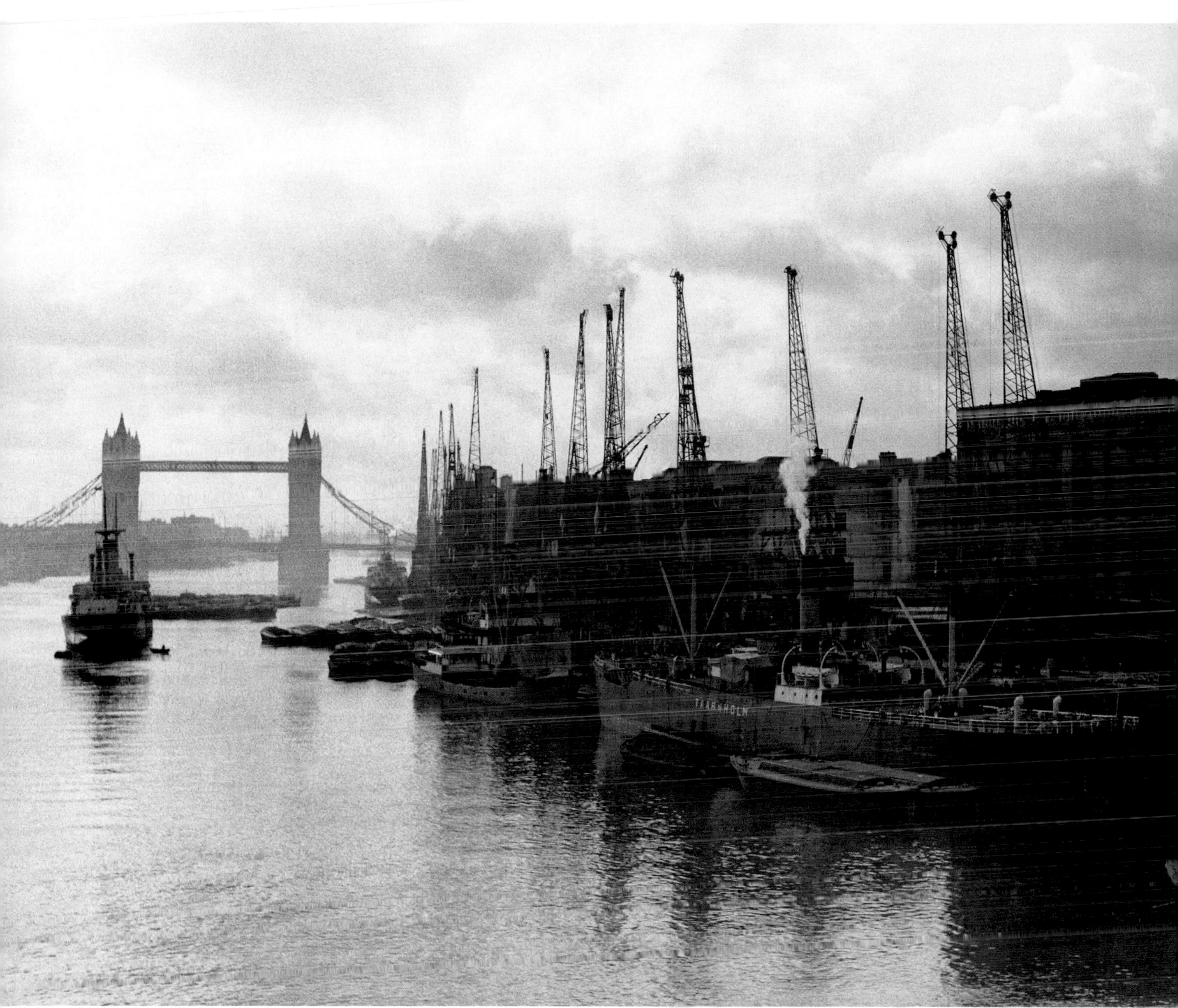

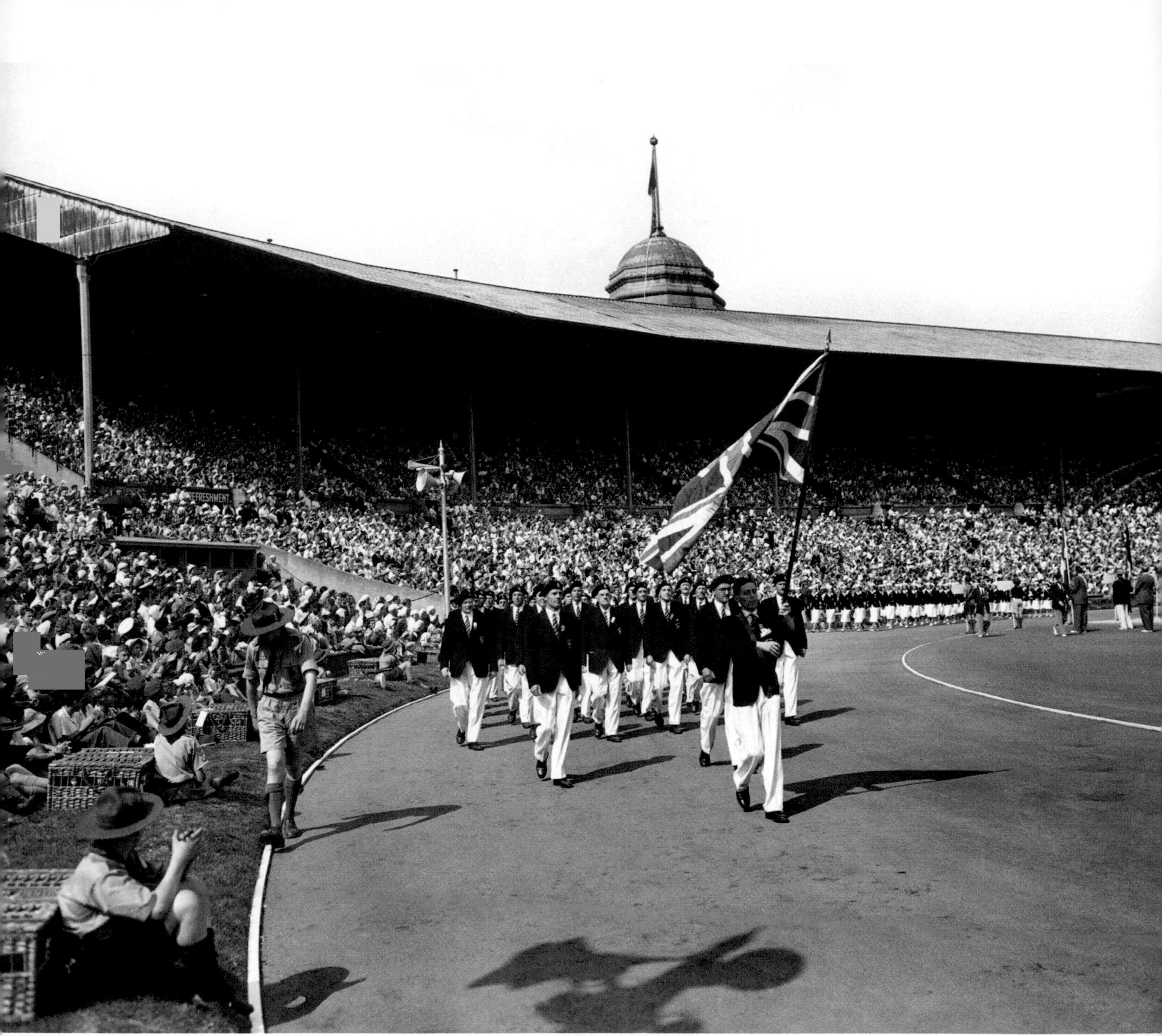
REFRESHMENT

Facing page: The Great Britain team marches around Wembley Stadium during the opening ceremony of the 1948 London Olympic Games.
29th July, 1948

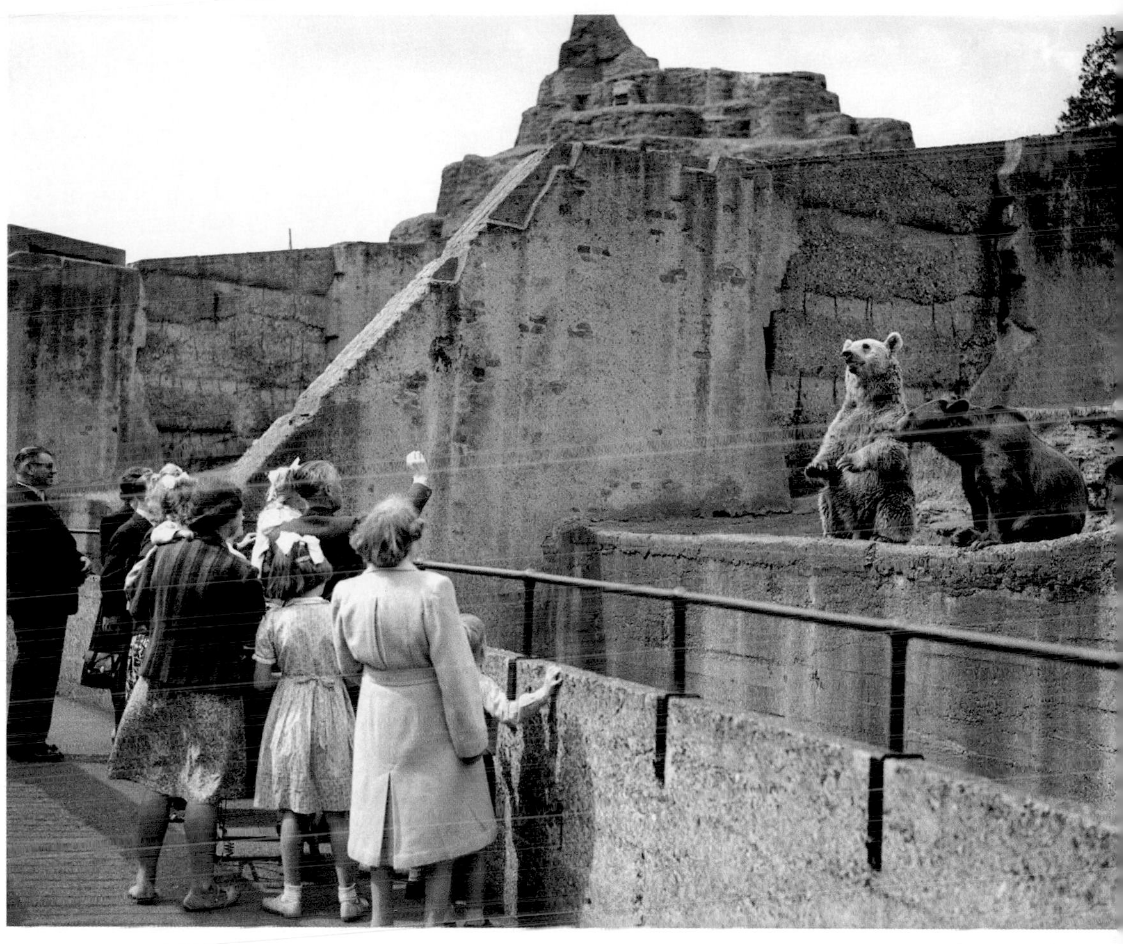

Bear Mountain, the main bear enclosure at London Zoo.
16th August, 1948

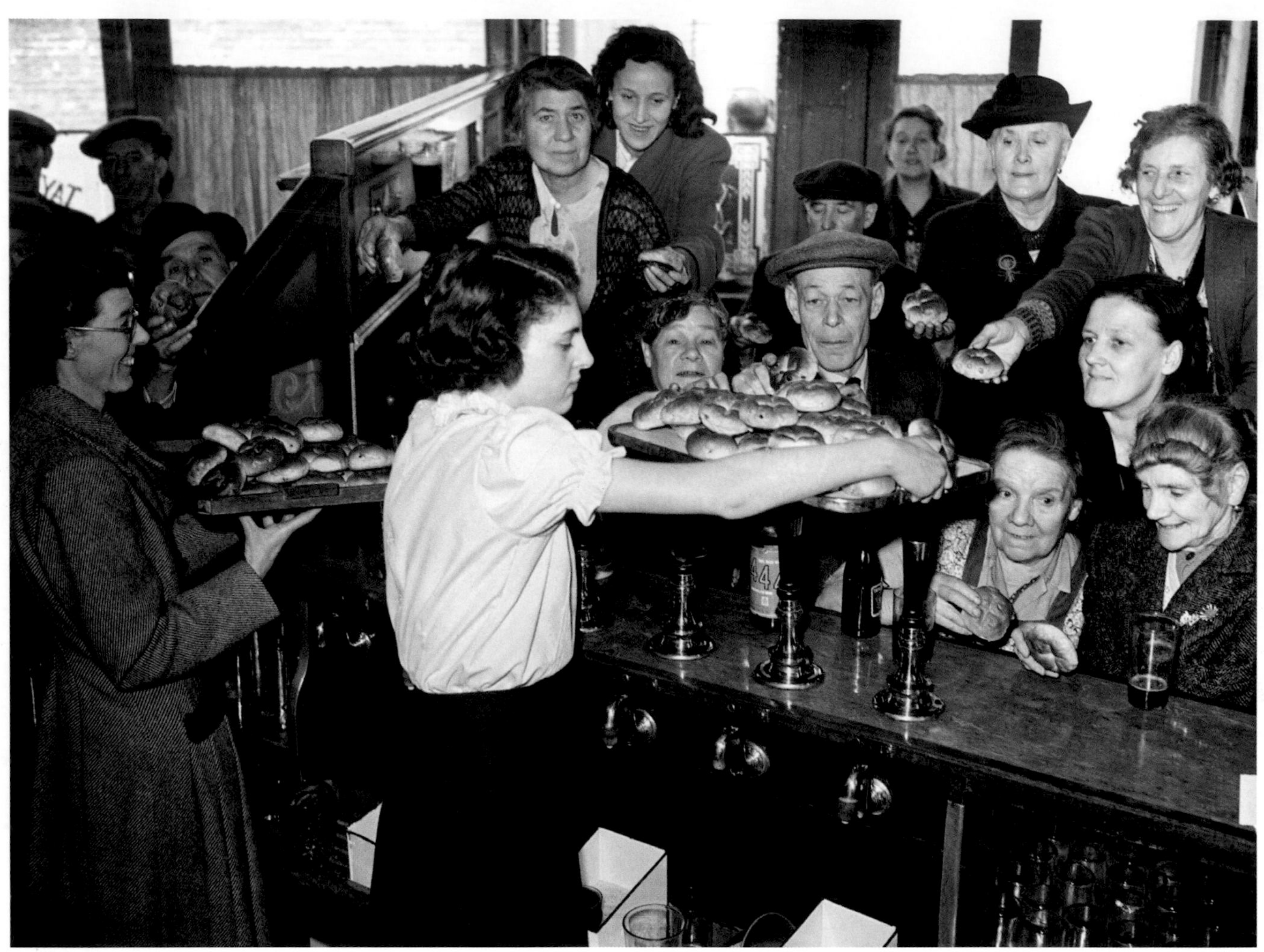

Free hot cross buns for customers according to 300 year old custom at St Bartholomew's the Great, Smithfield.
16th April, 1949

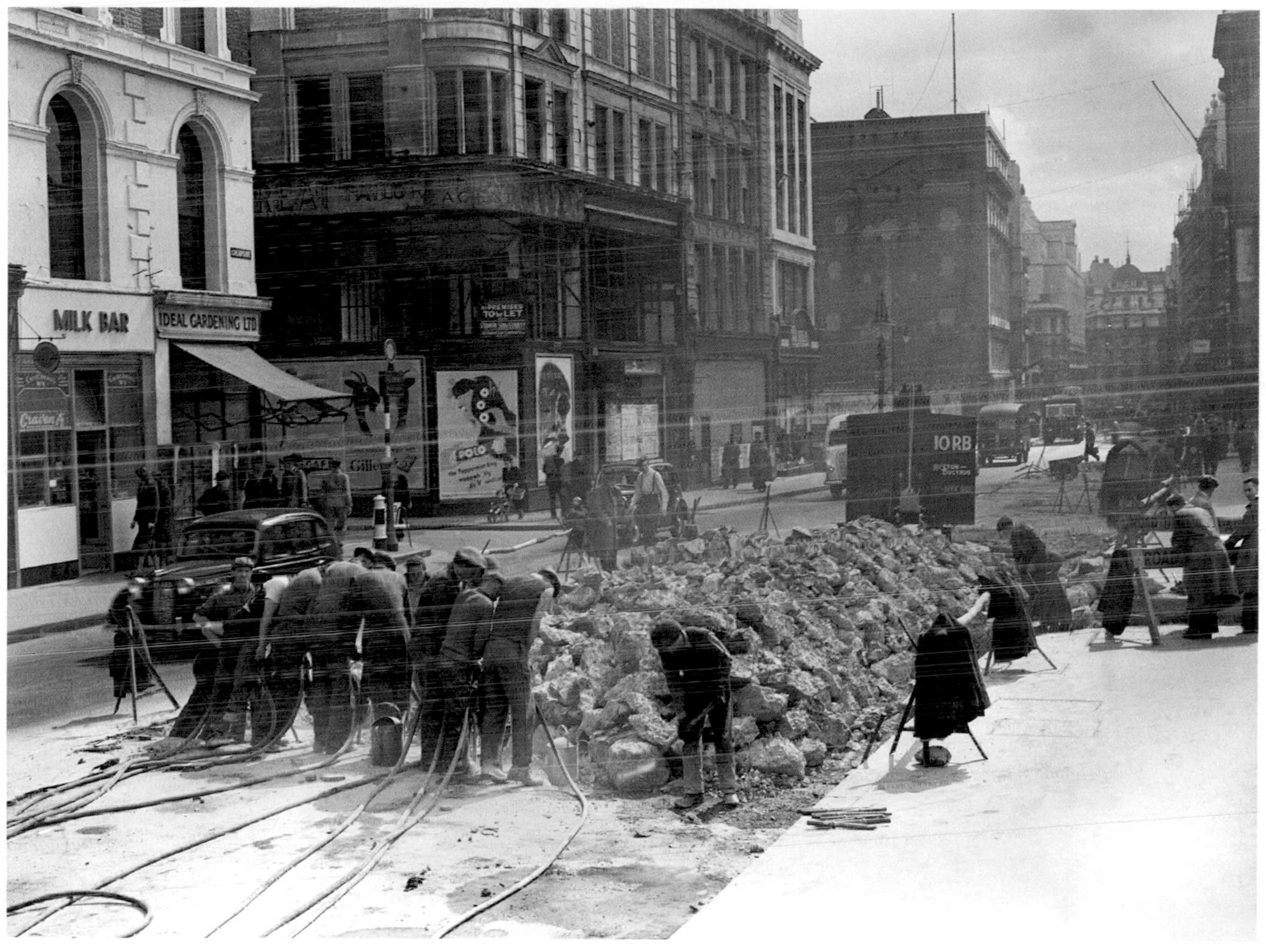

Cheapside was extensively damaged by the heat of incendiary attacks during the Blitz. Portions of the roadway had to be completely replaced.
25th May, 1949

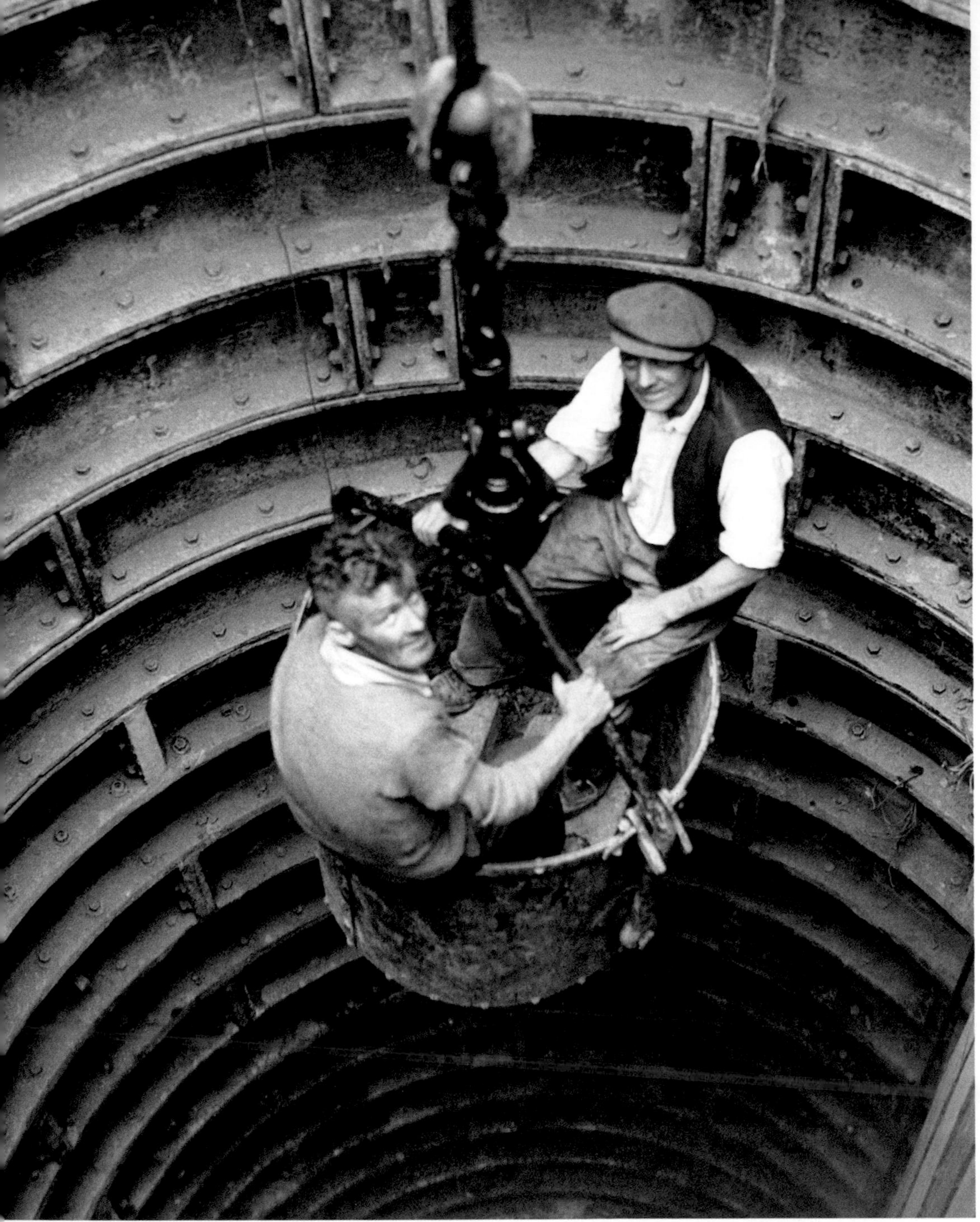

Facing page: Sweet rationing, to the horror of British children, is reintroduced and will not end until 1953.
12th August, 1949

A short commute for tunnel workers at Waterloo Station.
7th July, 1949

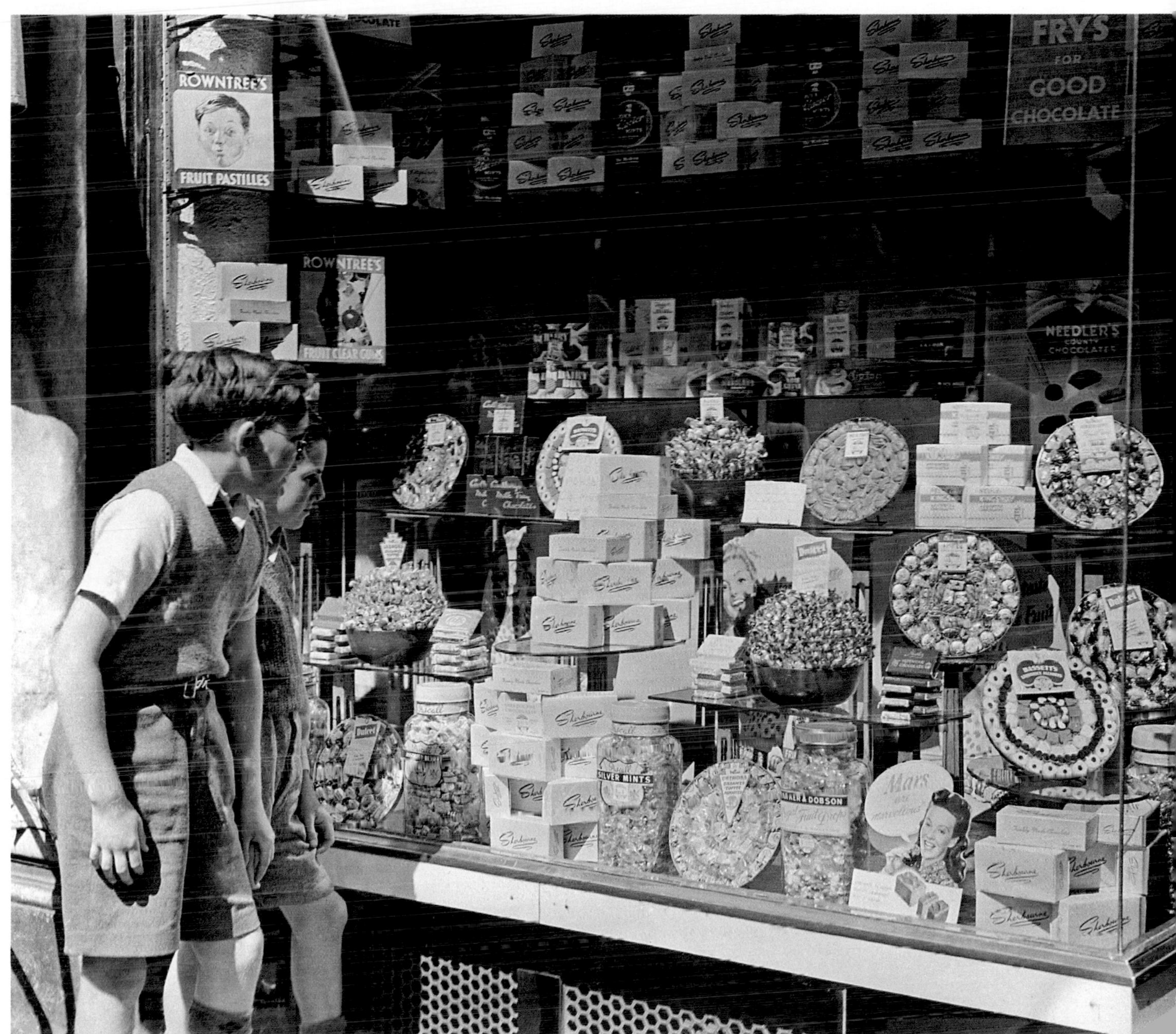
ROWNTREE'S
FRUIT PASTILLES
ROWNTREE'S
FRUIT CLEAR GUMS
FRY'S
FOR
GOOD
CHOCOLATE
NEEDLER'S
COUNTY
CHOCOLATES
SILVER MINTS
Mars
are
marvellous

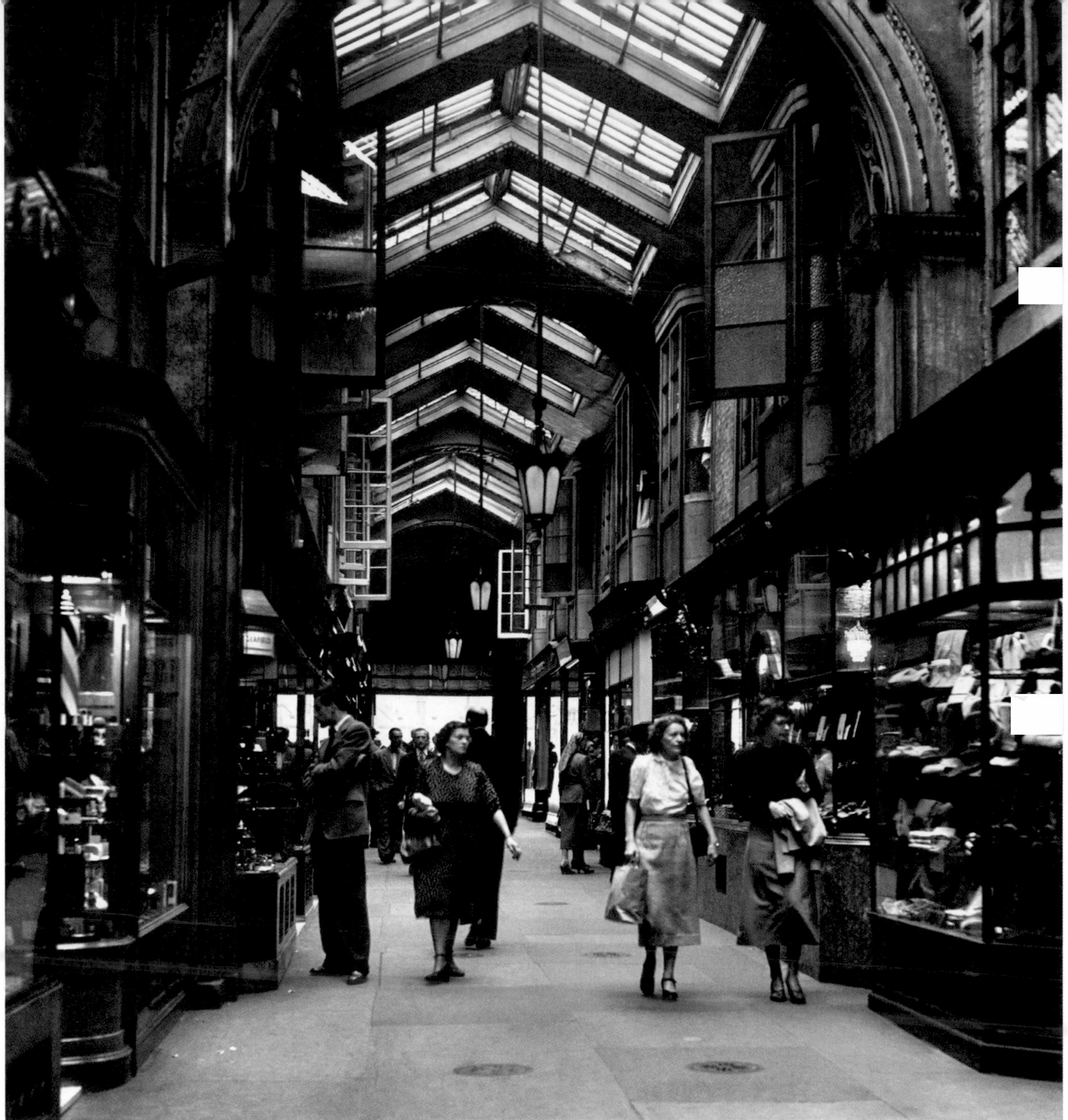

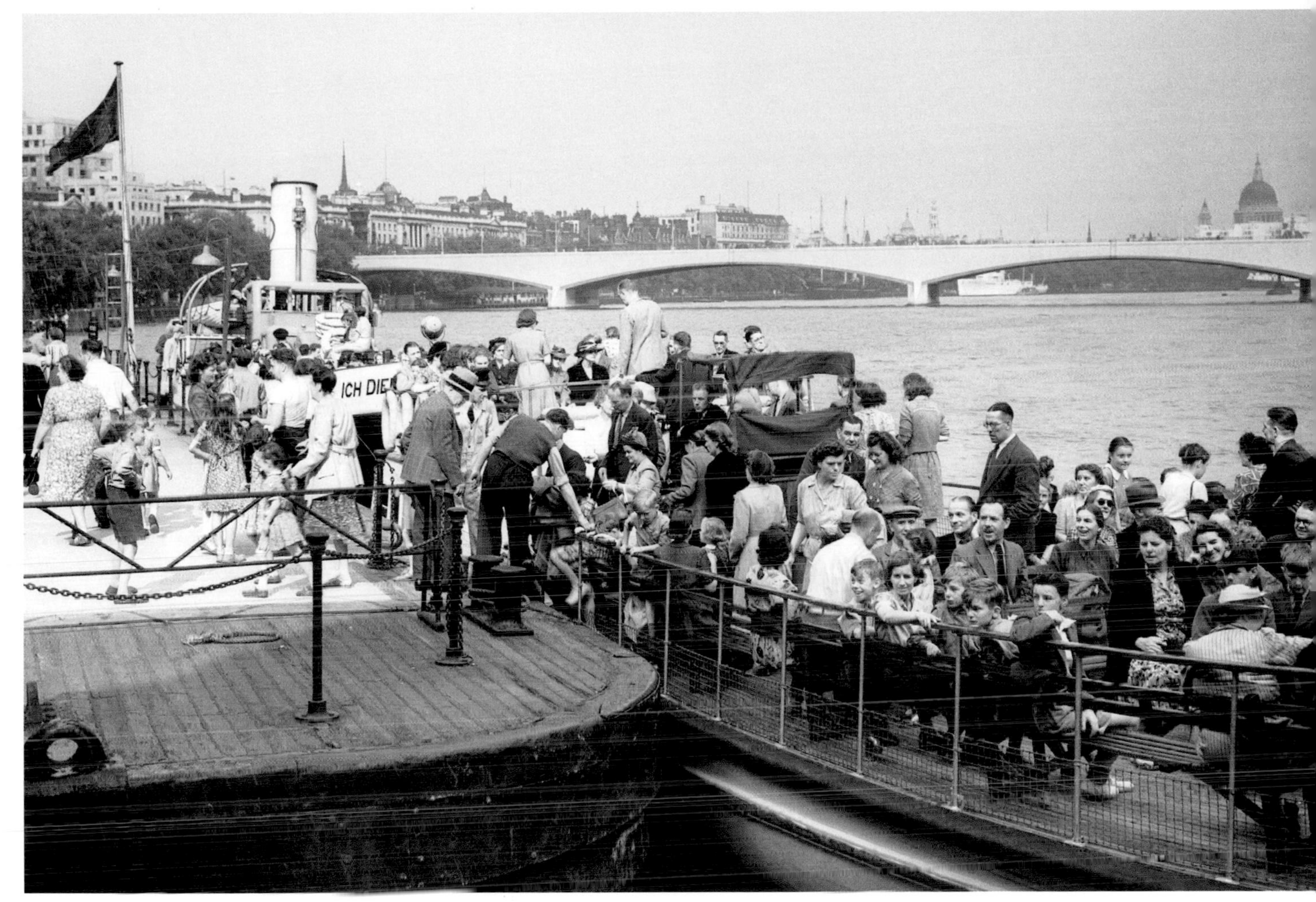

Passengers board the Thames waterbus at Charing Cross.
22nd August, 1949

Facing page: The Burlington Arcade, from the Piccadilly end.
22nd August, 1949

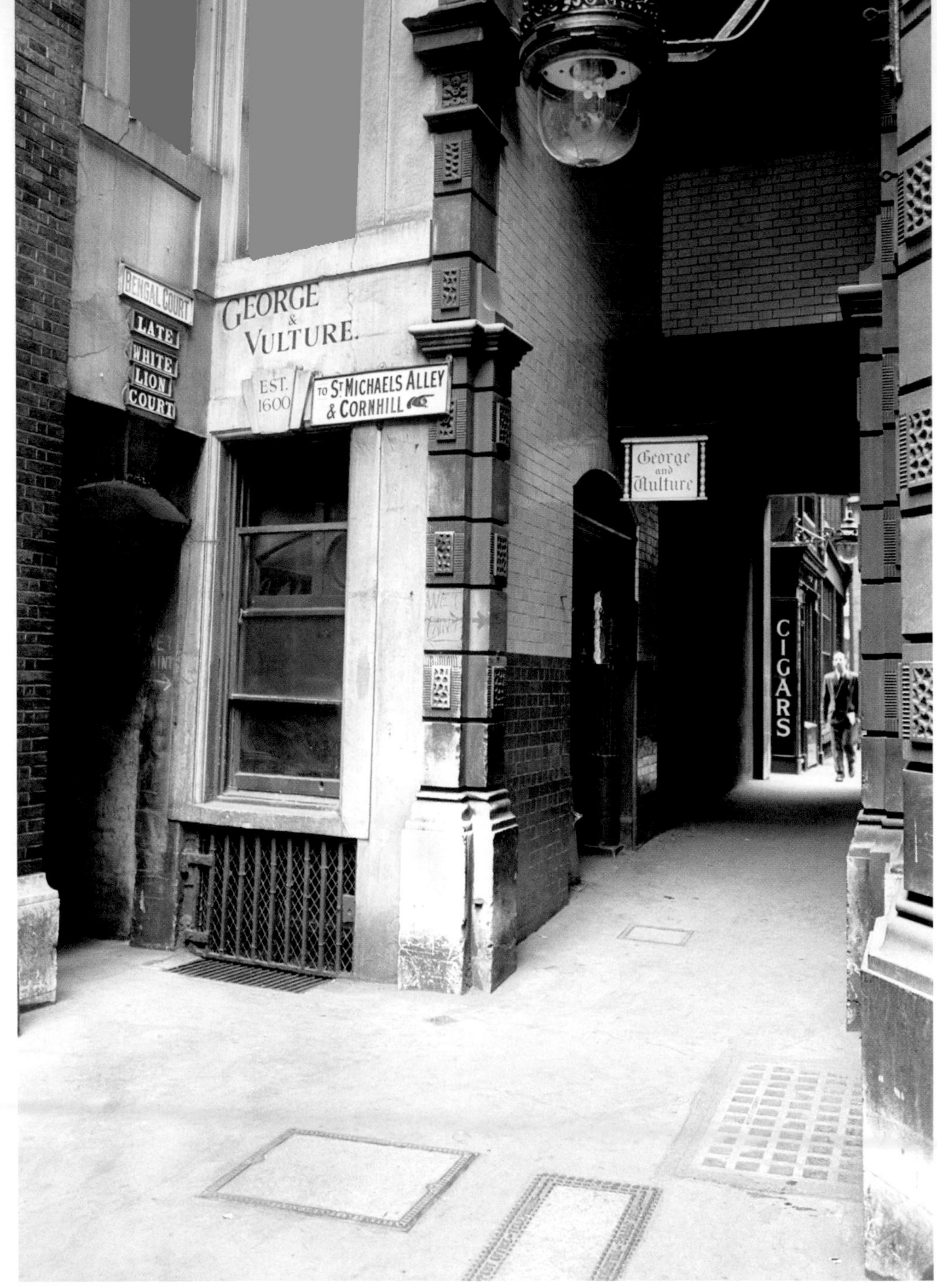

The rear of the George and Vulture Inn in Castle Court, near Lombard Street in the City. Dickens made this the base for the City Pickwick Club and the Dickens family gathered here at Christmas.
22nd August, 1949

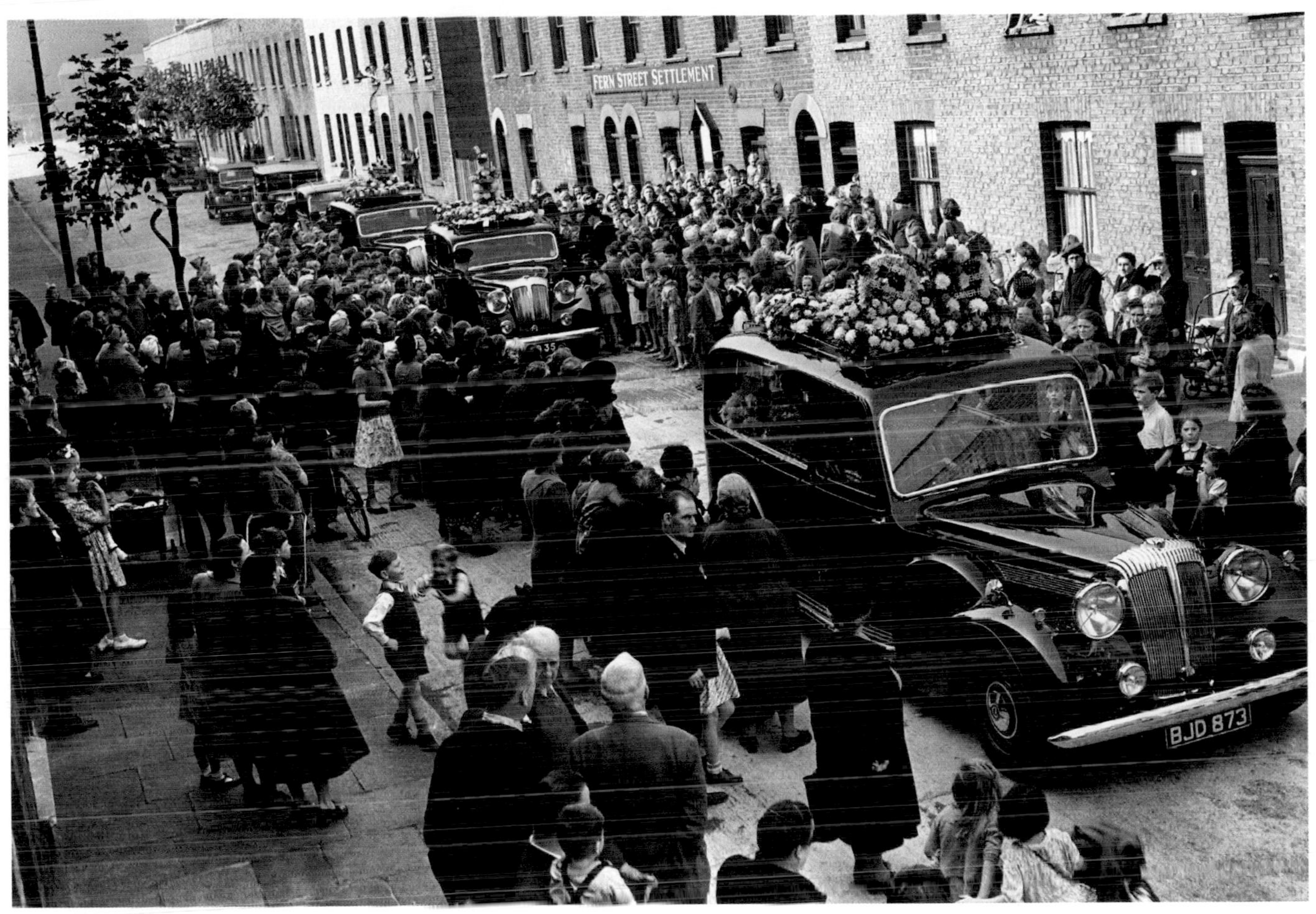

The funeral of Clara Grant, *The Bundle Woman of Bow,* passes the Fern Street Settlement, which she founded to give aid to deprived children.
13th October, 1949

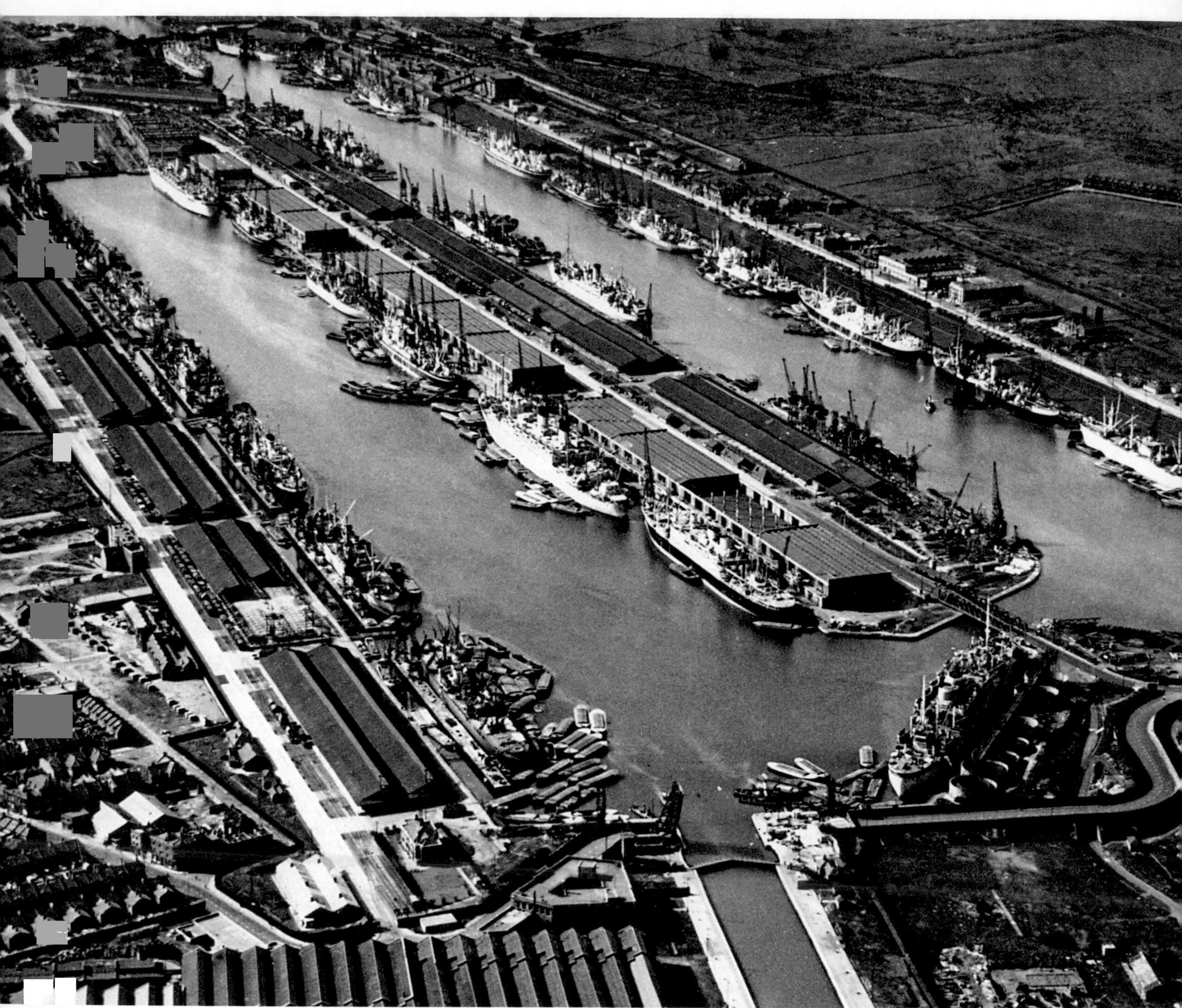

Facing page: The Port of London.
1950

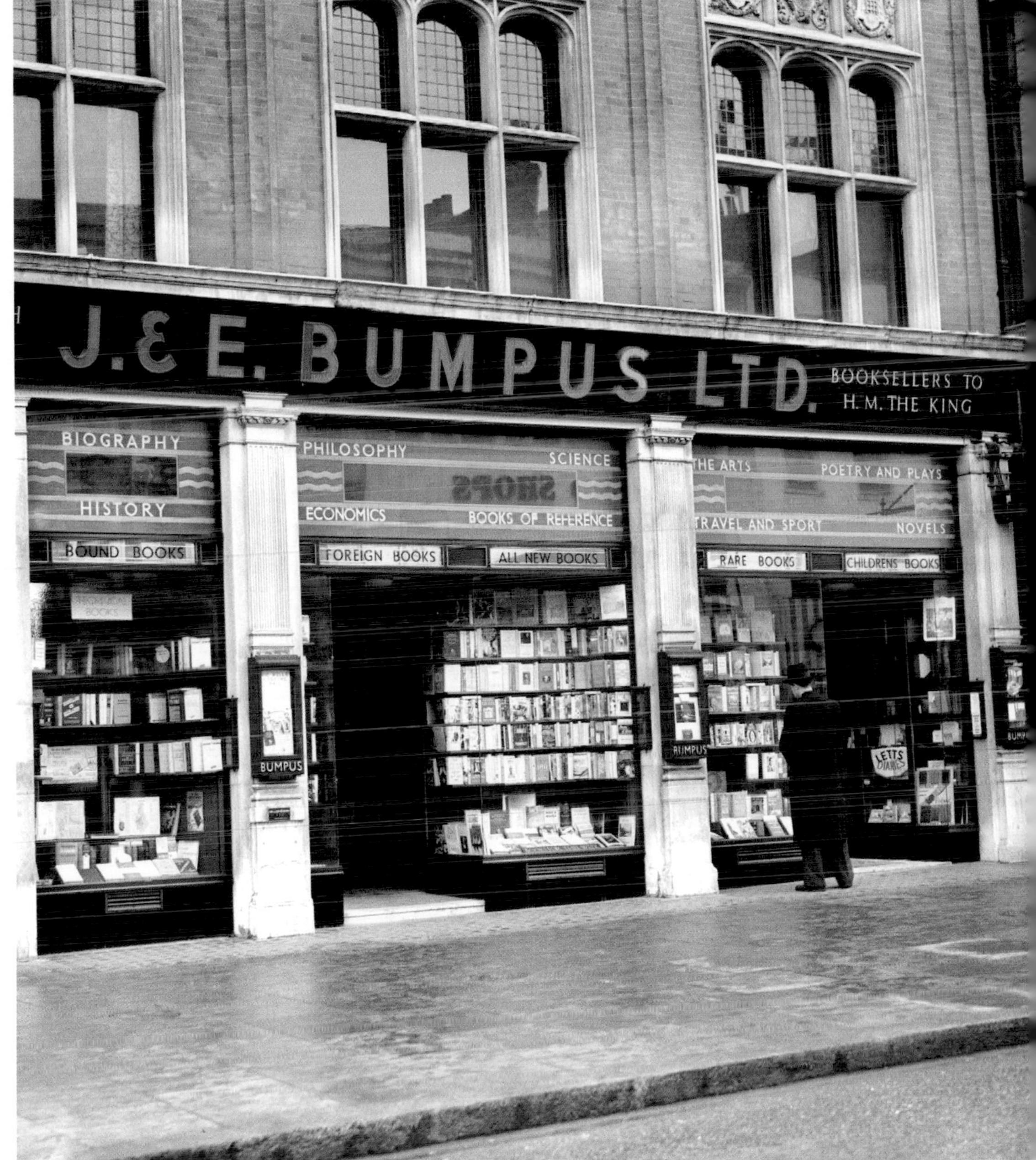

The front of the Bumpus Bookshop, bookseller to King George VI, on Oxford Street.
2nd January, 1950

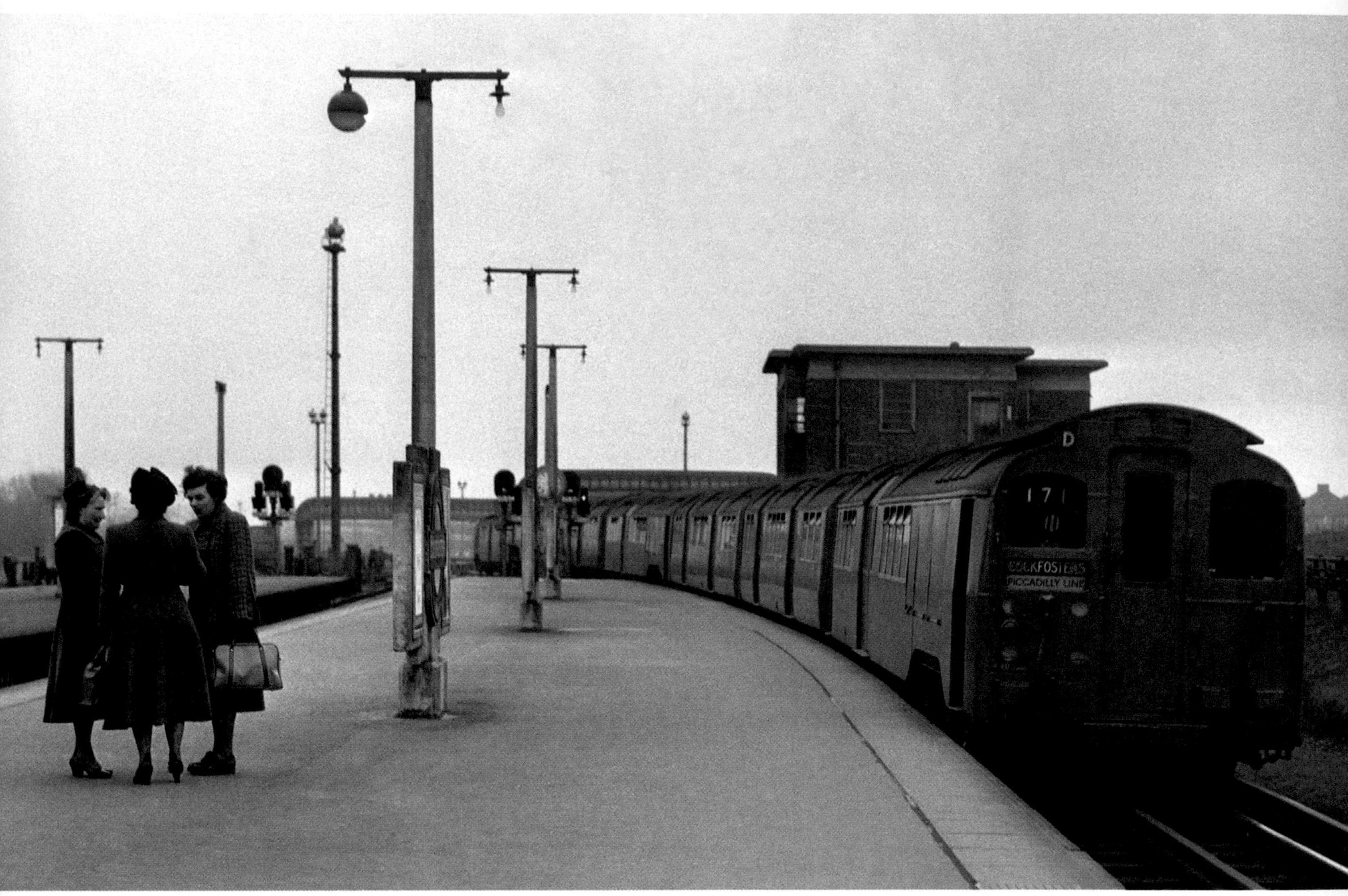

Cockfosters Station,
the northern end of the
Piccadilly Line.
25th February, 1950

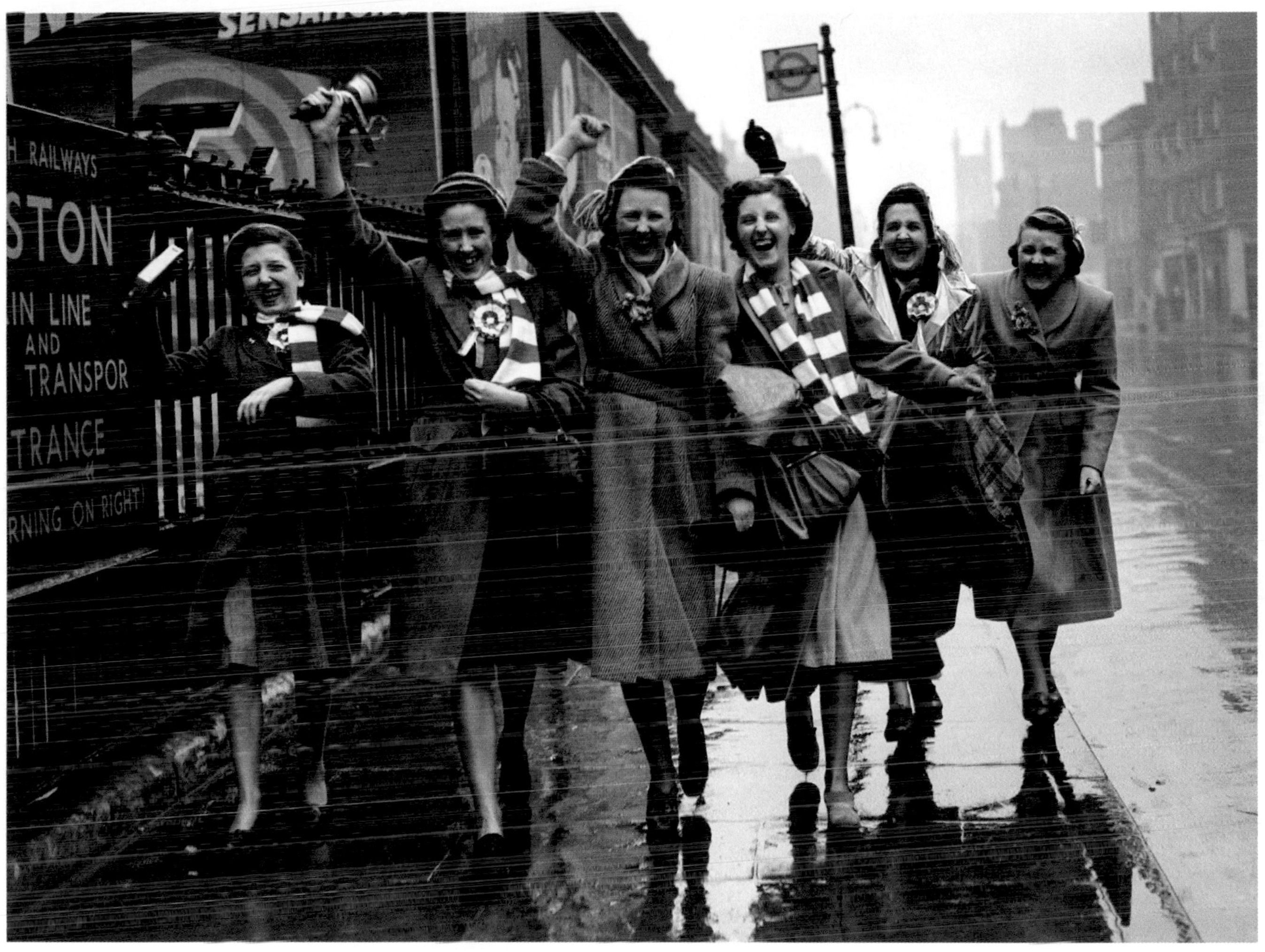

Liverpool girls head for Wembley Stadium for the FA Cup Final, Liverpool v Arsenal.
23rd April, 1950

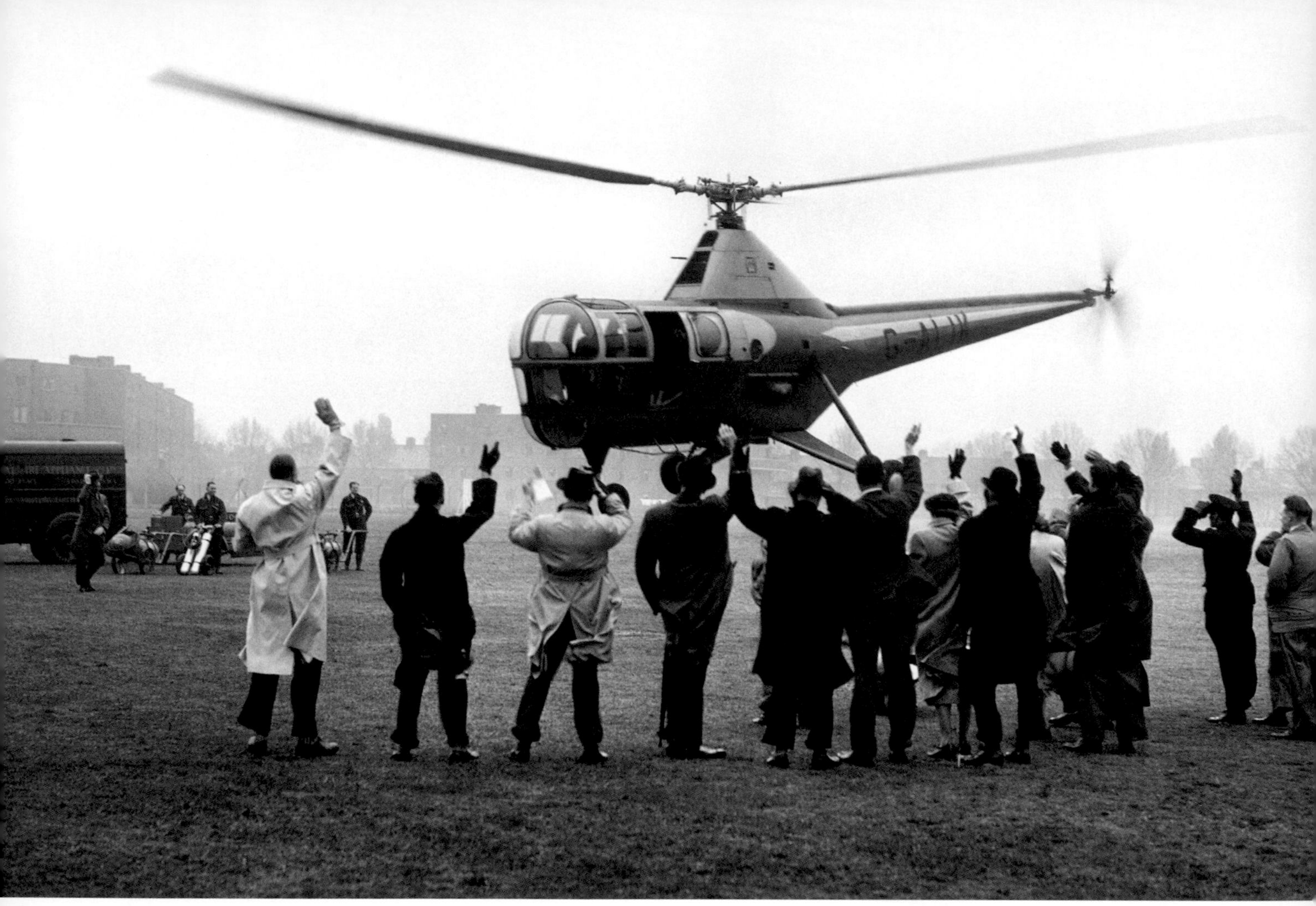

The world's first helicopter passenger service, from London to Birmingham, takes off from the Harrods' Sports Ground in Barnes.
5th May, 1950

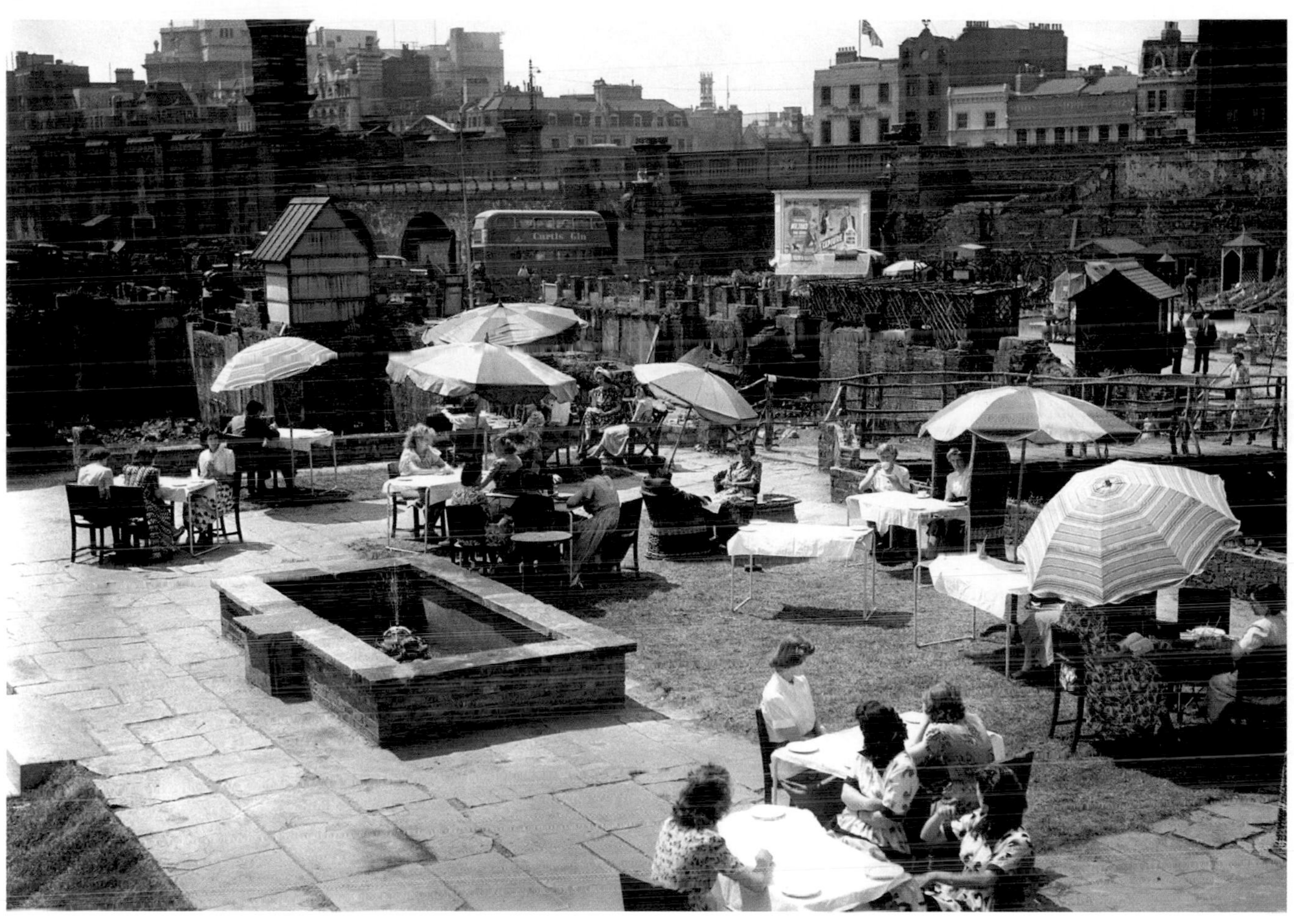

Ludgate Hill Gardens
open-air cafe.
26th May, 1950

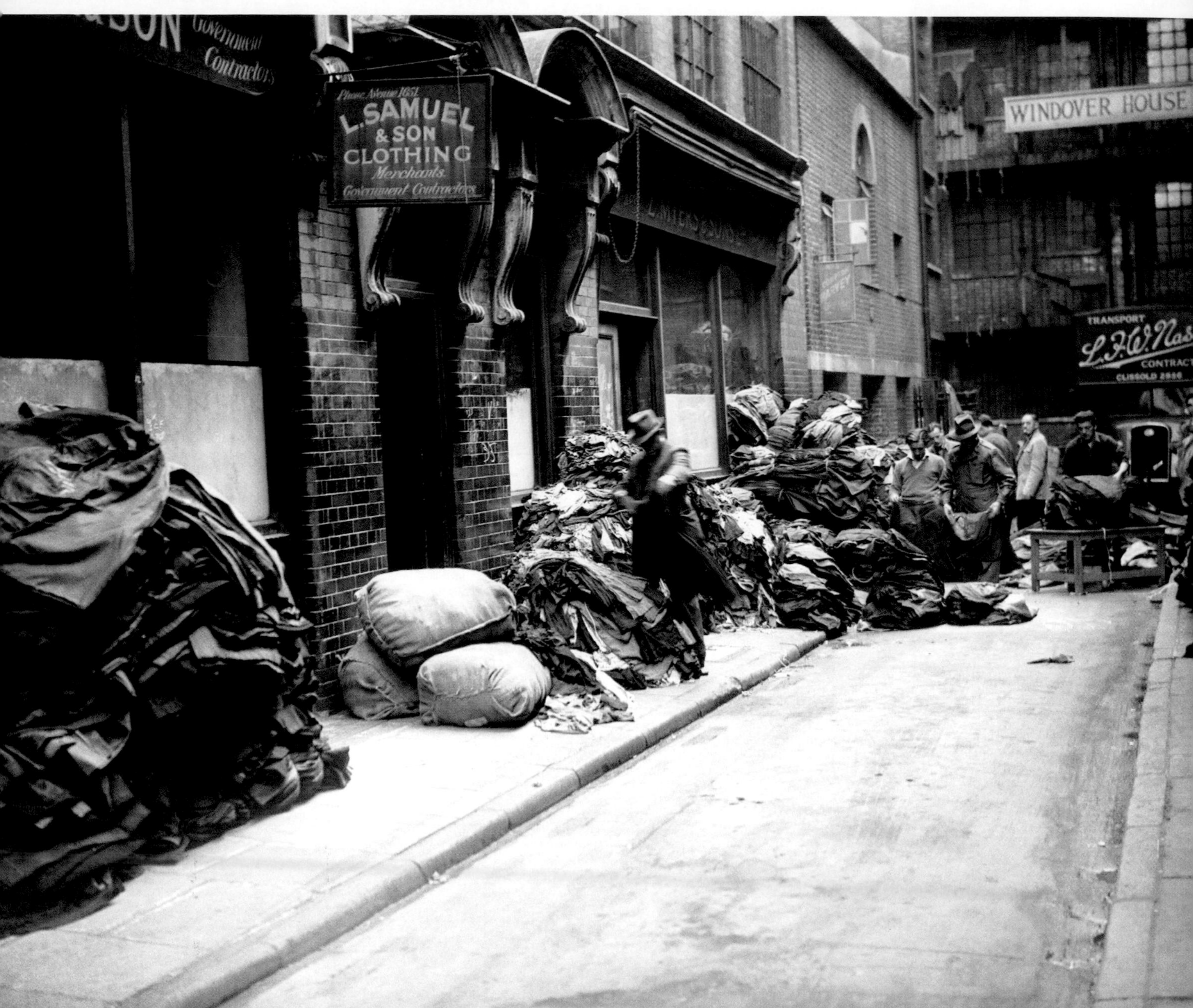
Government
Contractors
L. SAMUEL
& SON
CLOTHING
Merchants
Government Contractors
WINDOVER HOUSE
TRANSPORT

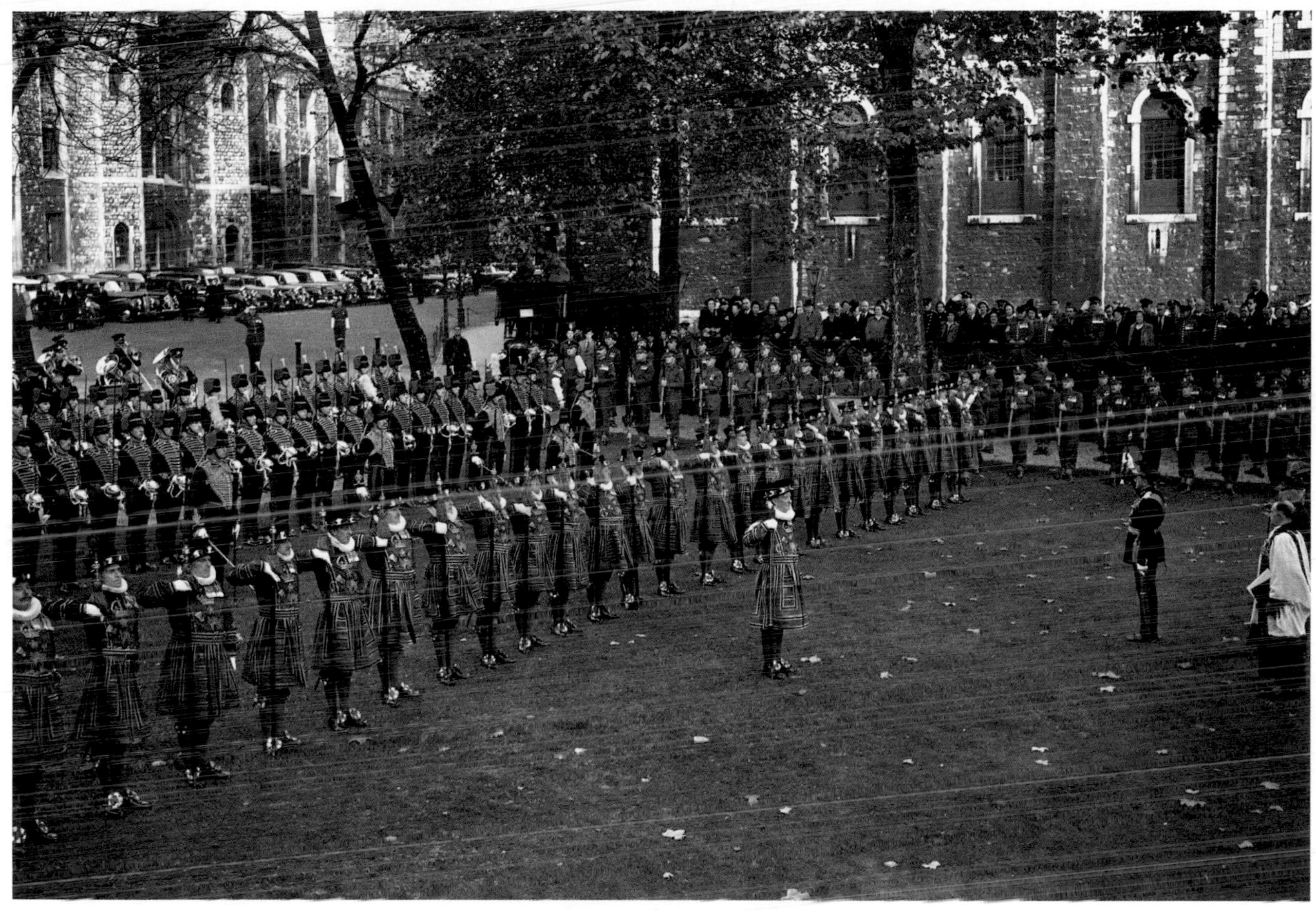

Yeoman Warders lined up for the swearing-in of the new Constable of the Tower of London.
19th October, 1950

Facing page: Clothier Street, Houndsditch. Old clothes are received for processing into such things as stuffing for furniture and toys, duffle for coats and rags for papermaking.
7th October, 1950

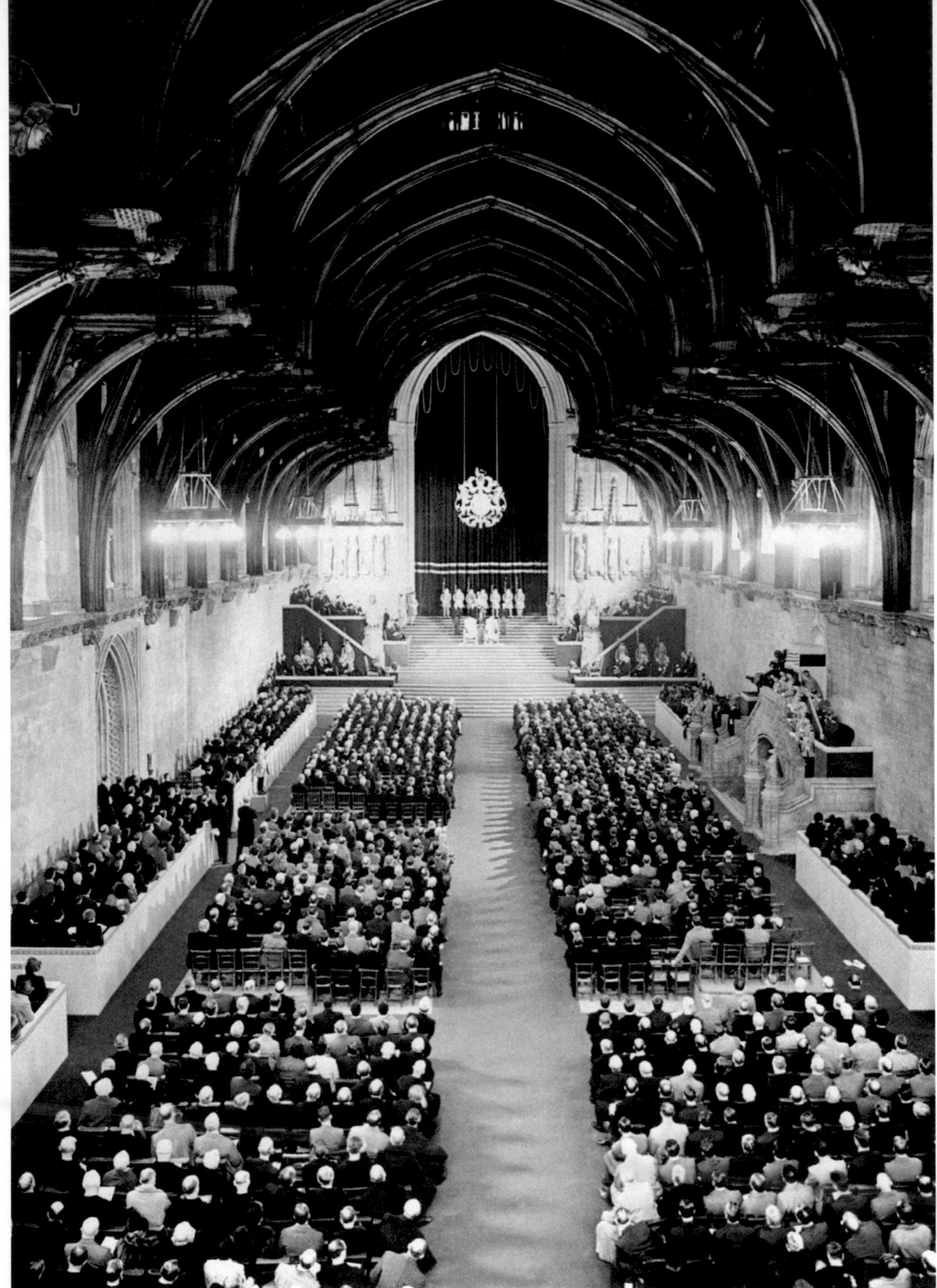

Facing page: Tim Healey and his fruit stall in the gateway of Lincoln's Inn.
13th November, 1950

Westminster Hall during the opening of the new chamber of the House of Commons.
25th October, 1950

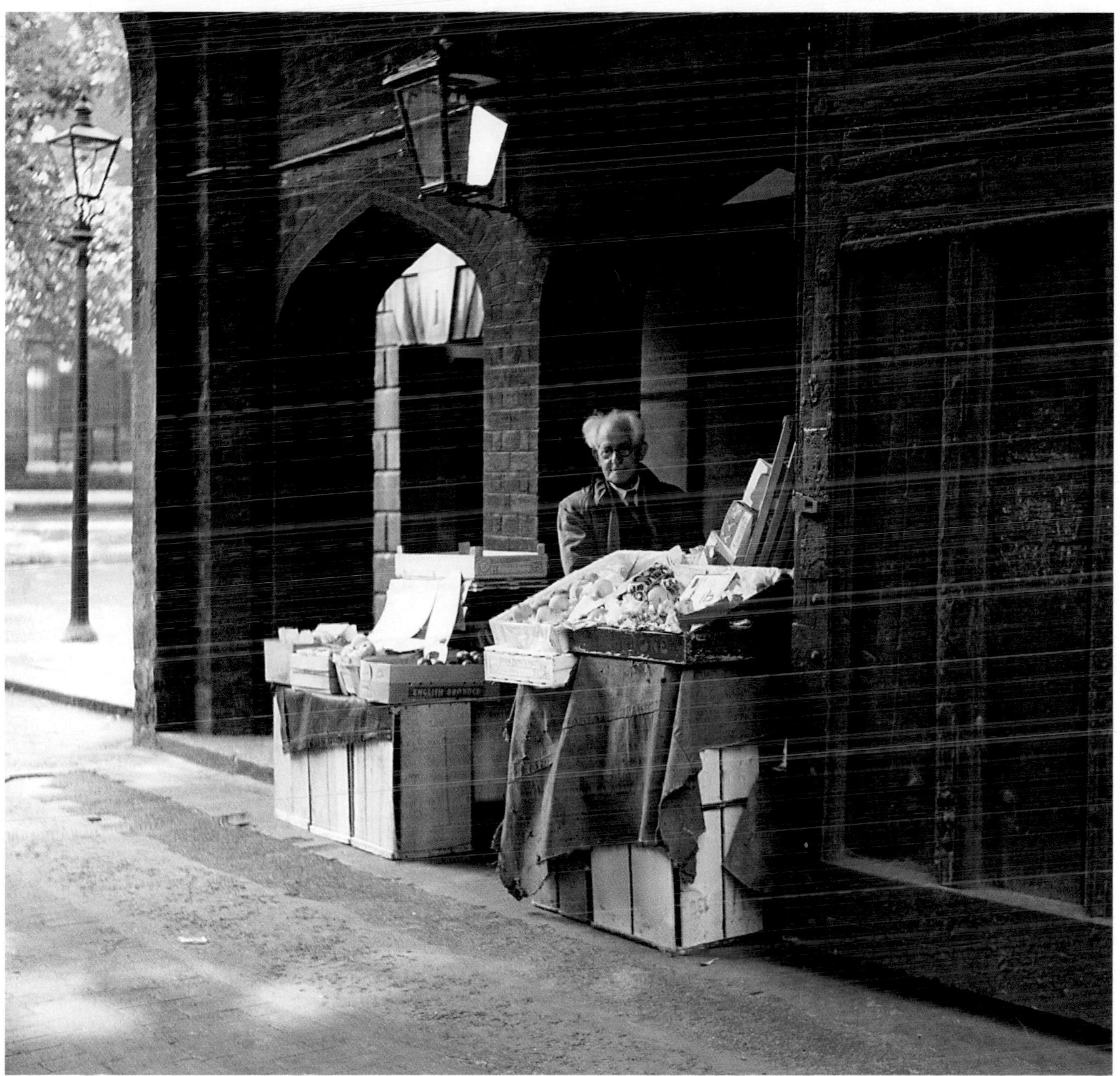

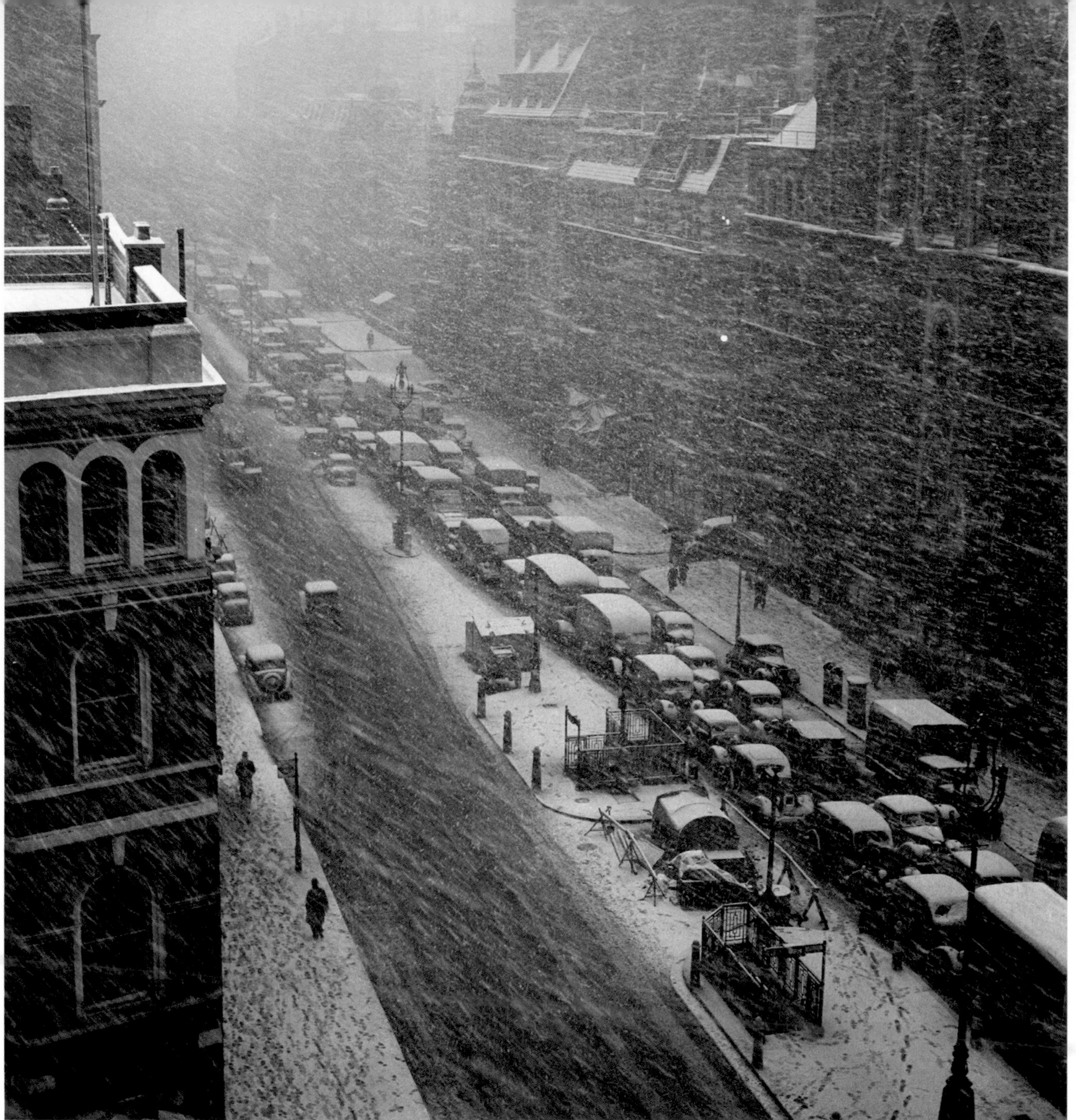

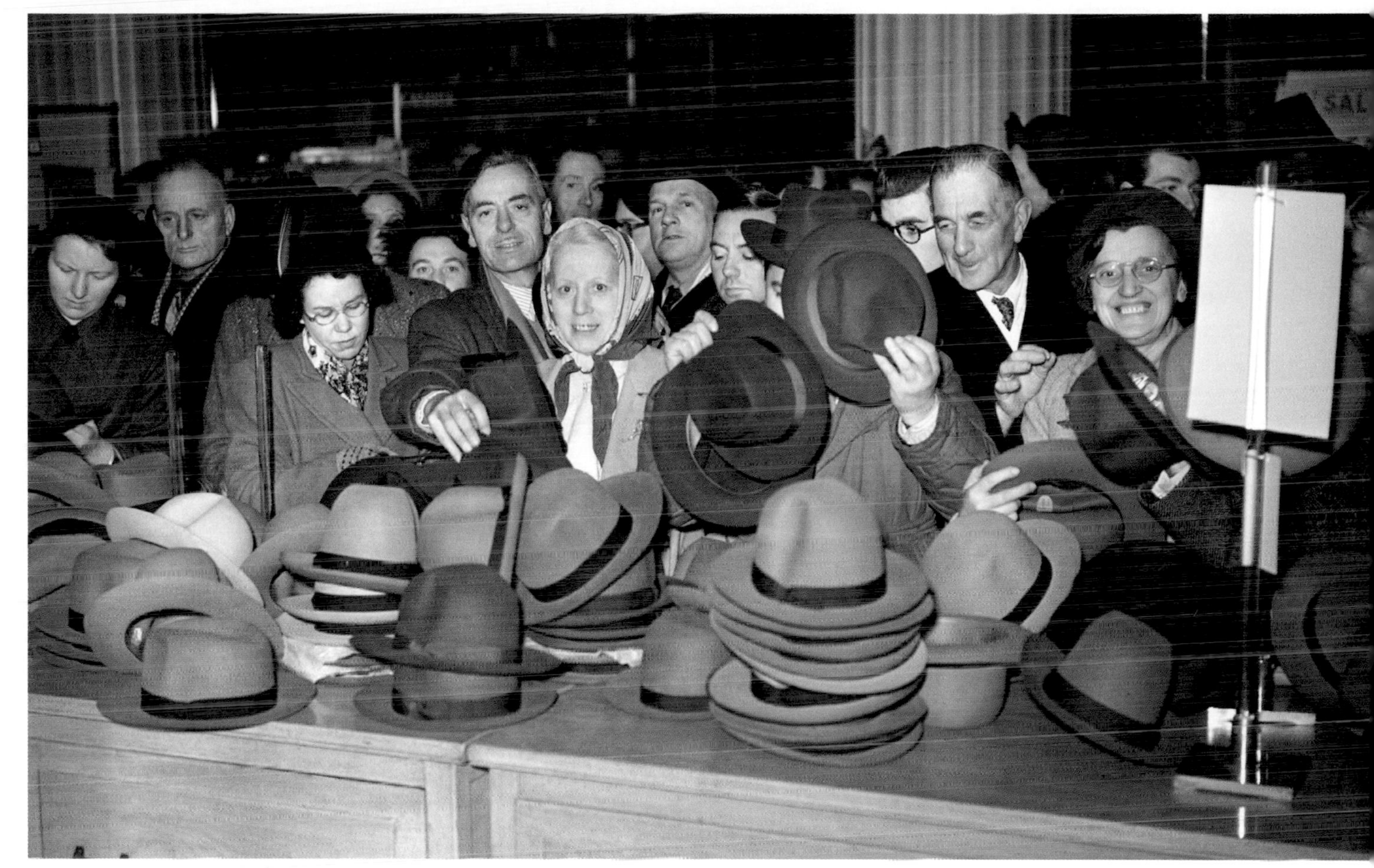

Selfridges during the winter sale.
1951

Facing page: Snow closes Farringdon Street.
1951

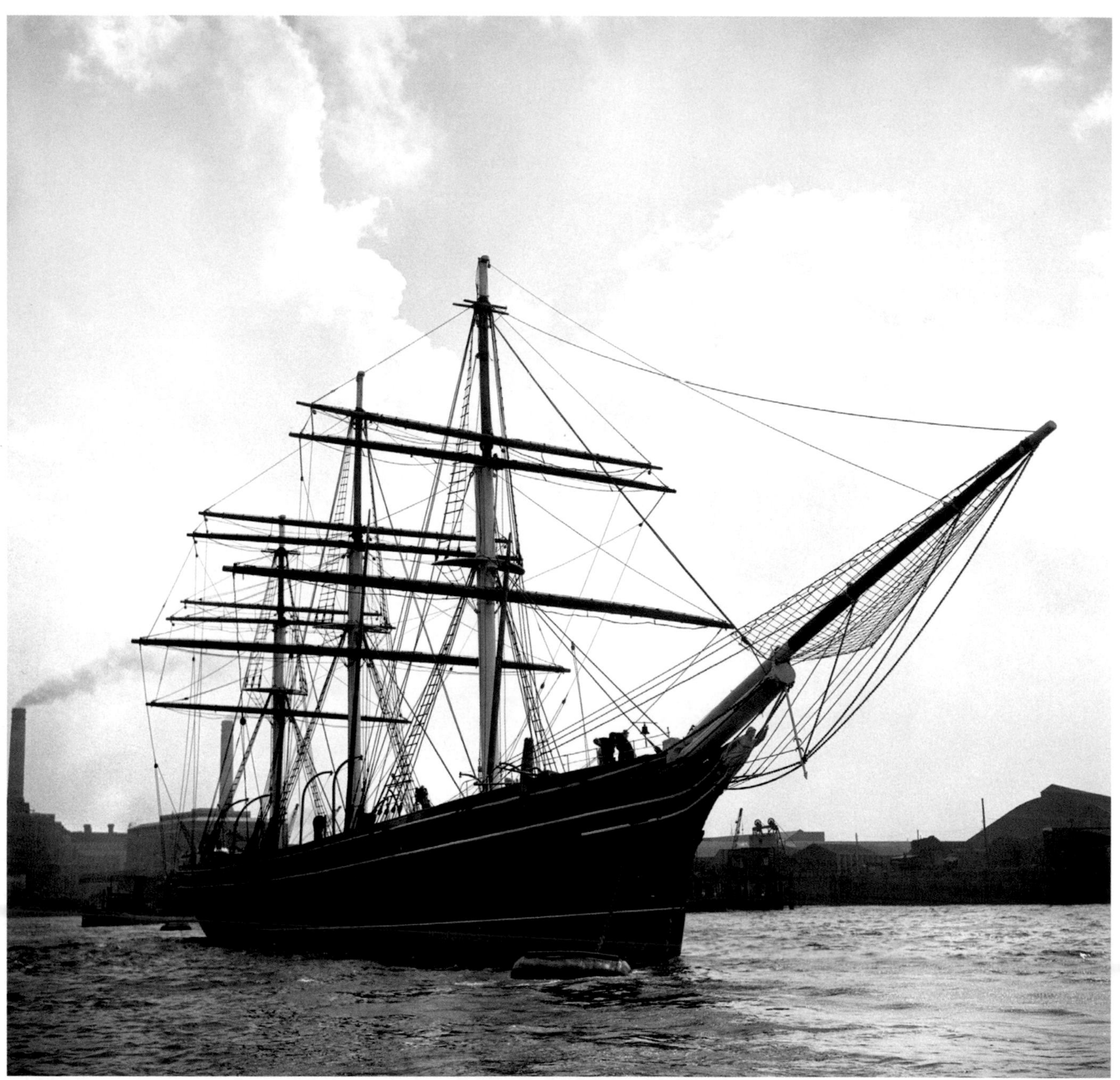

Facing page: The *Cutty Sark* moored off Rotherhithe in readiness for the Festival of Britain. The clipper, relic of the China tea trade and the wool races from Australia, was in regular service from 1870 to 1922. She was laid up for 16 years until being towed to the Thames in 1938 for presentation to the Thames Nautical Training College.
May, 1951

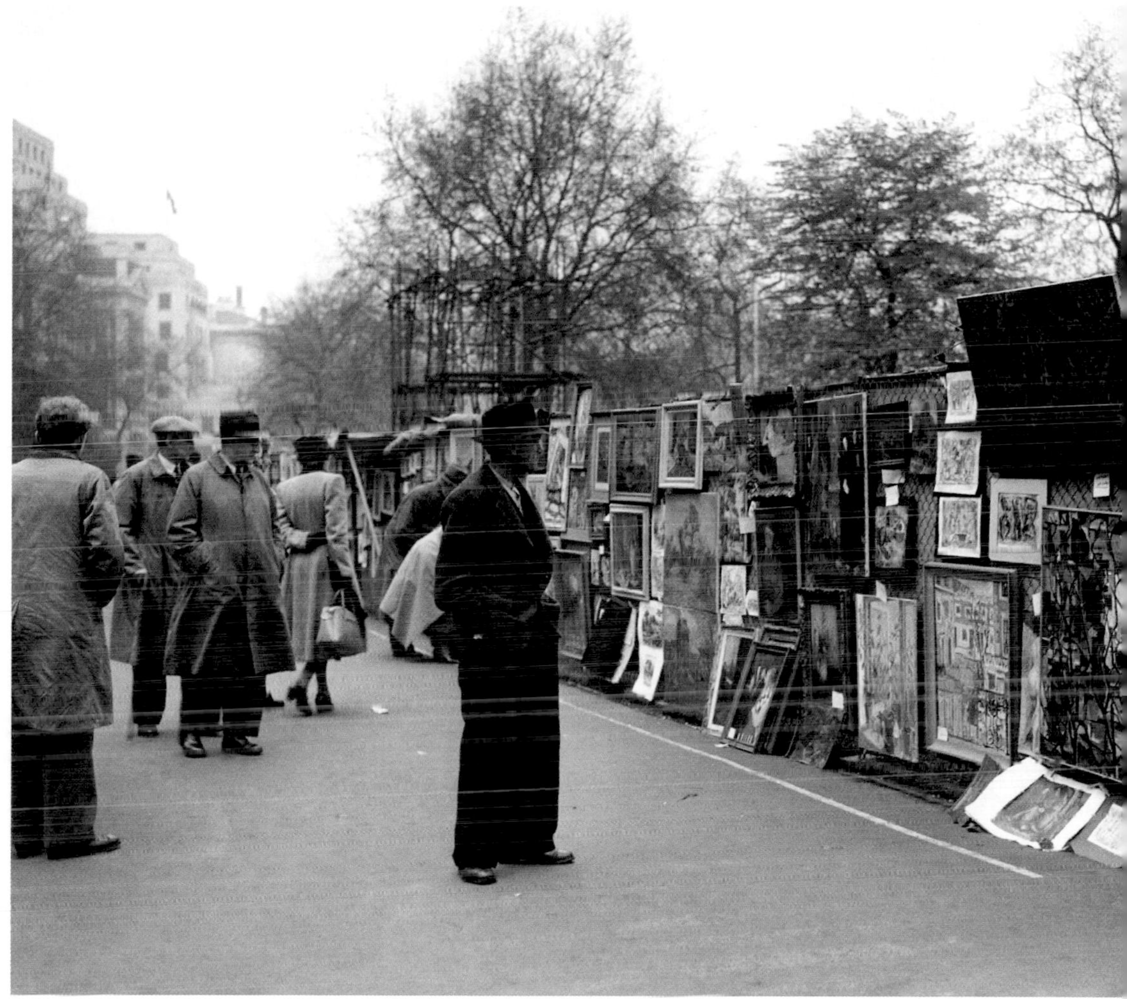

Open-air art exhibition at Victoria Embankment Gardens during the Festival of Britain.
7th May, 1951

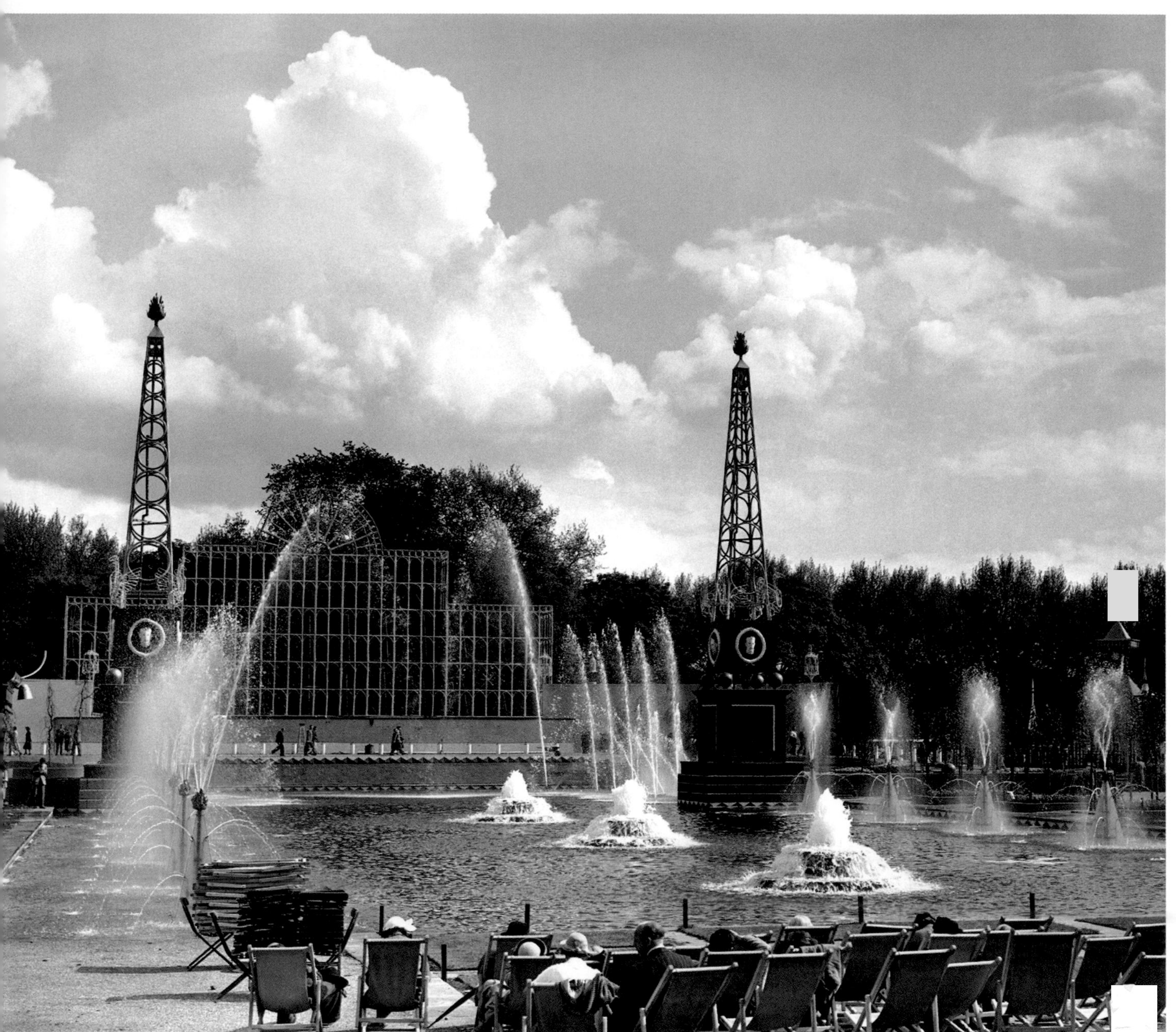

Facing page: The Festival Lake, in the pleasure gardens, Battersea Park.
25th May, 1951

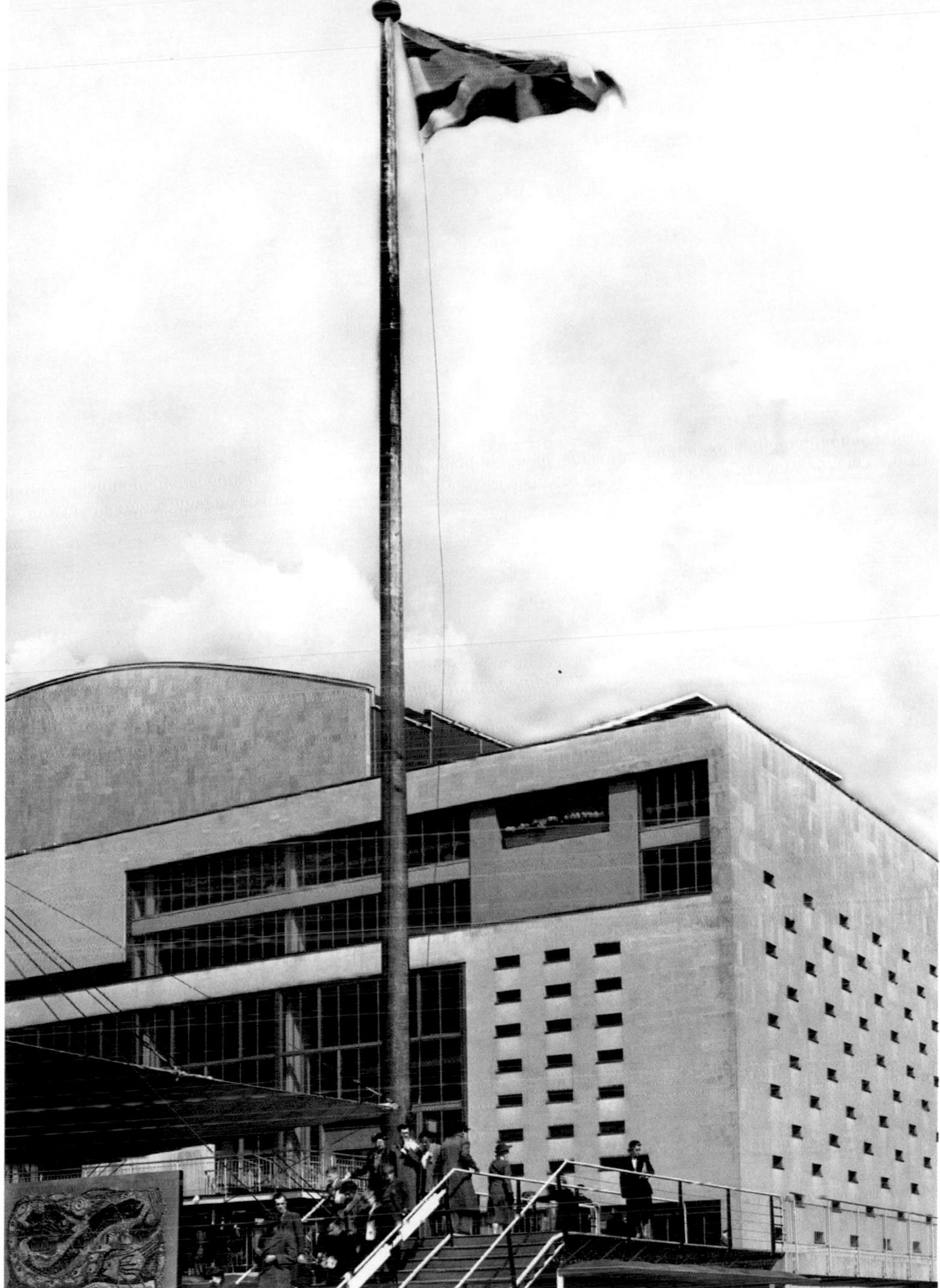

The world's tallest flagpole in front of the Royal Festival Hall during the Festival of Britain.
29th May, 1951

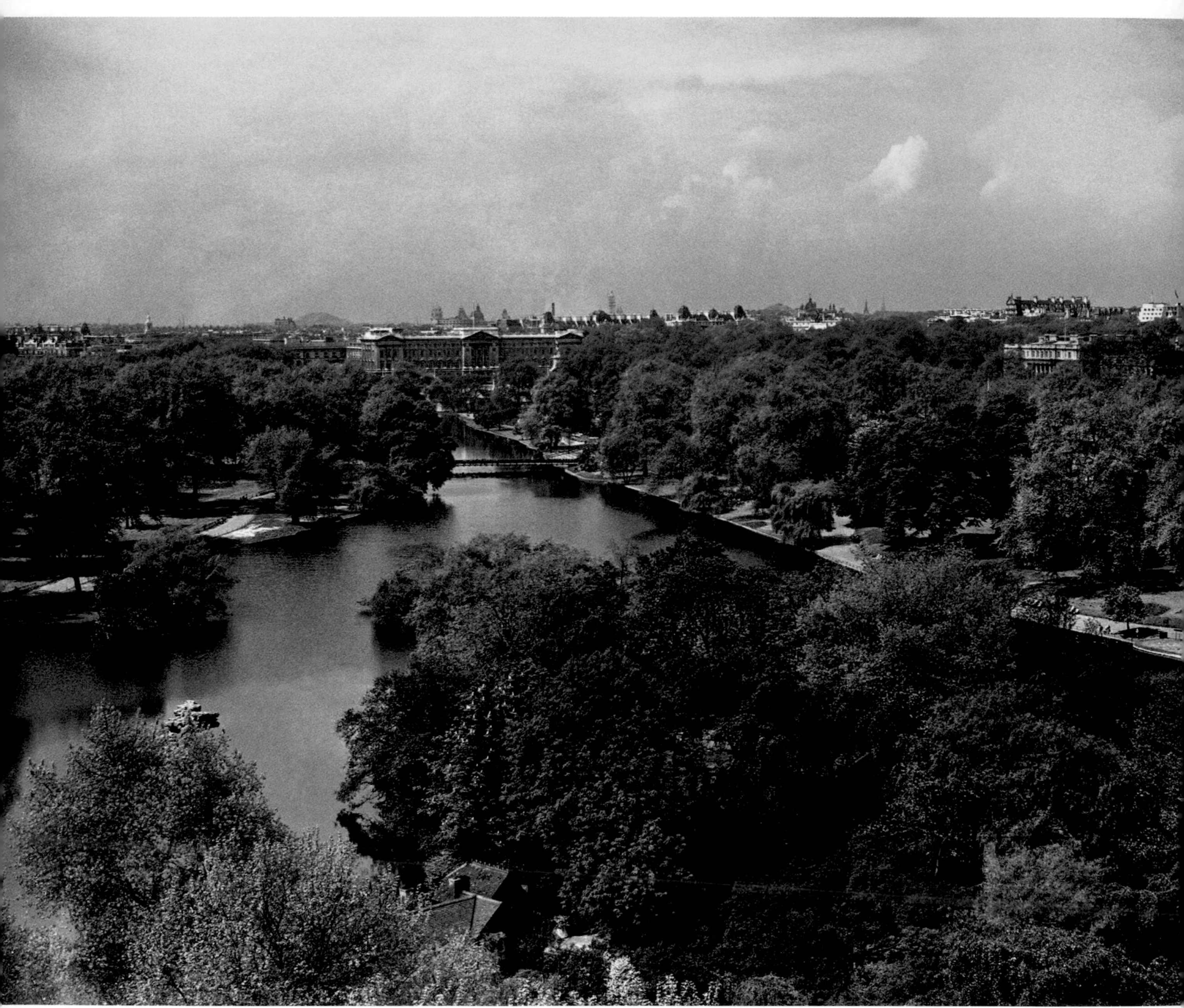

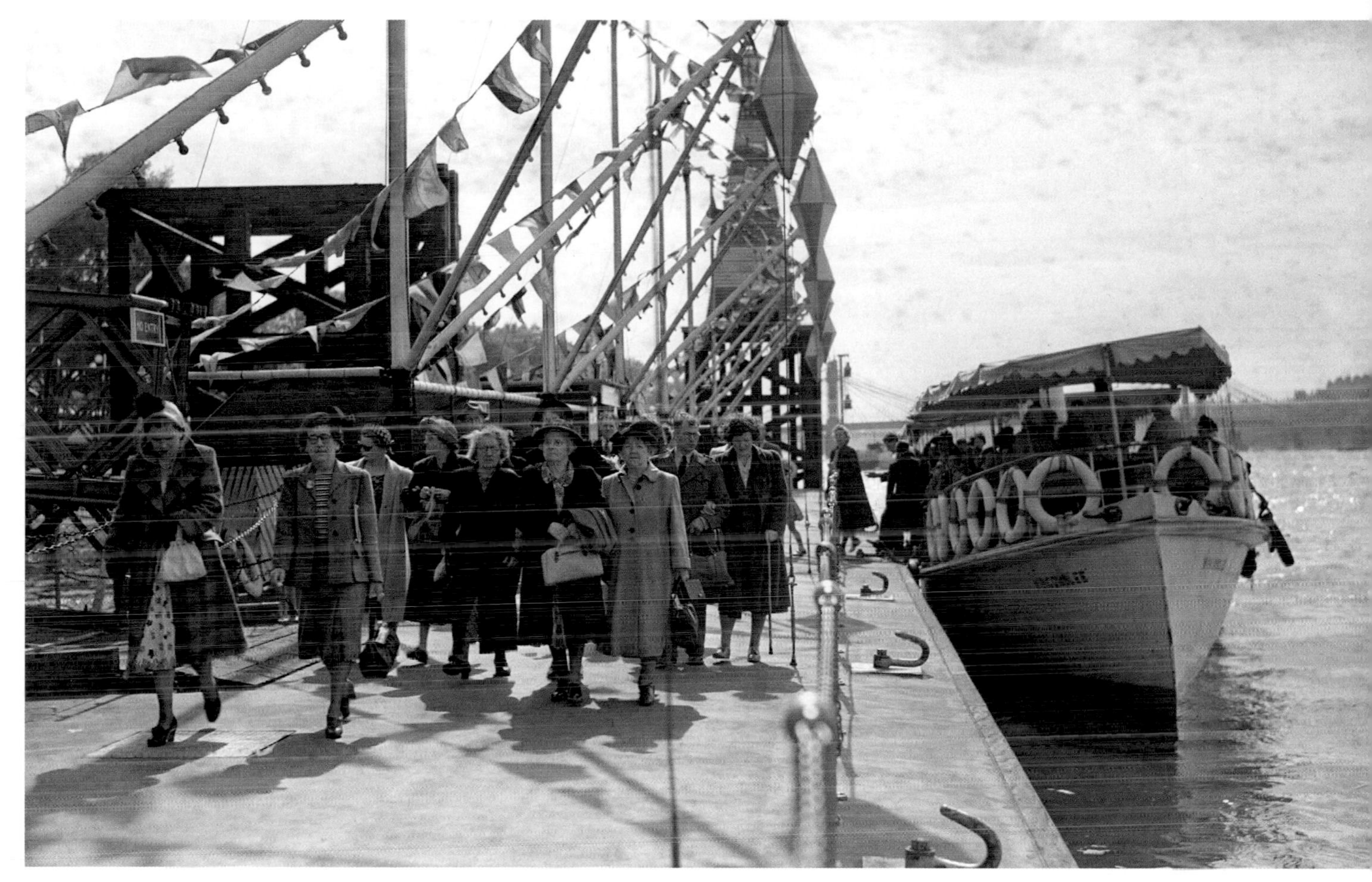

Thames Water Bus Service: passengers walk along the landing stage for the Festival in Battersea Park.
7th June, 1951

Facing page: Buckingham Palace and St James' Park from the roof of the Foreign Office.
2nd June, 1951

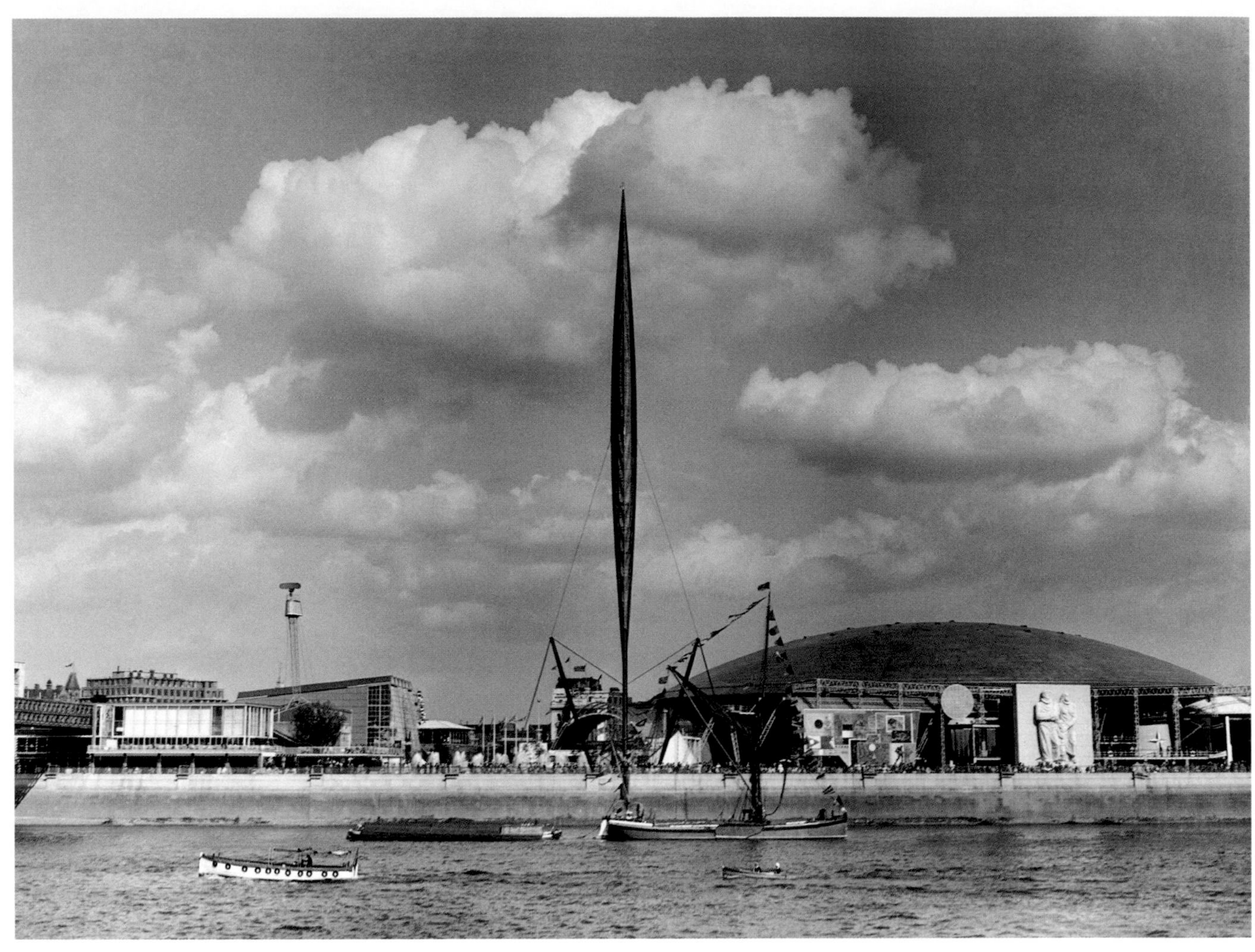

The South Bank seen from Victoria Embankment during the Festival of Britain. The *Skylon* (C) generated enormous interest. Controversially it and *The Dome of Discovery* (R) were demolished and sold for scrap when the Festival ended.
15th June, 1951

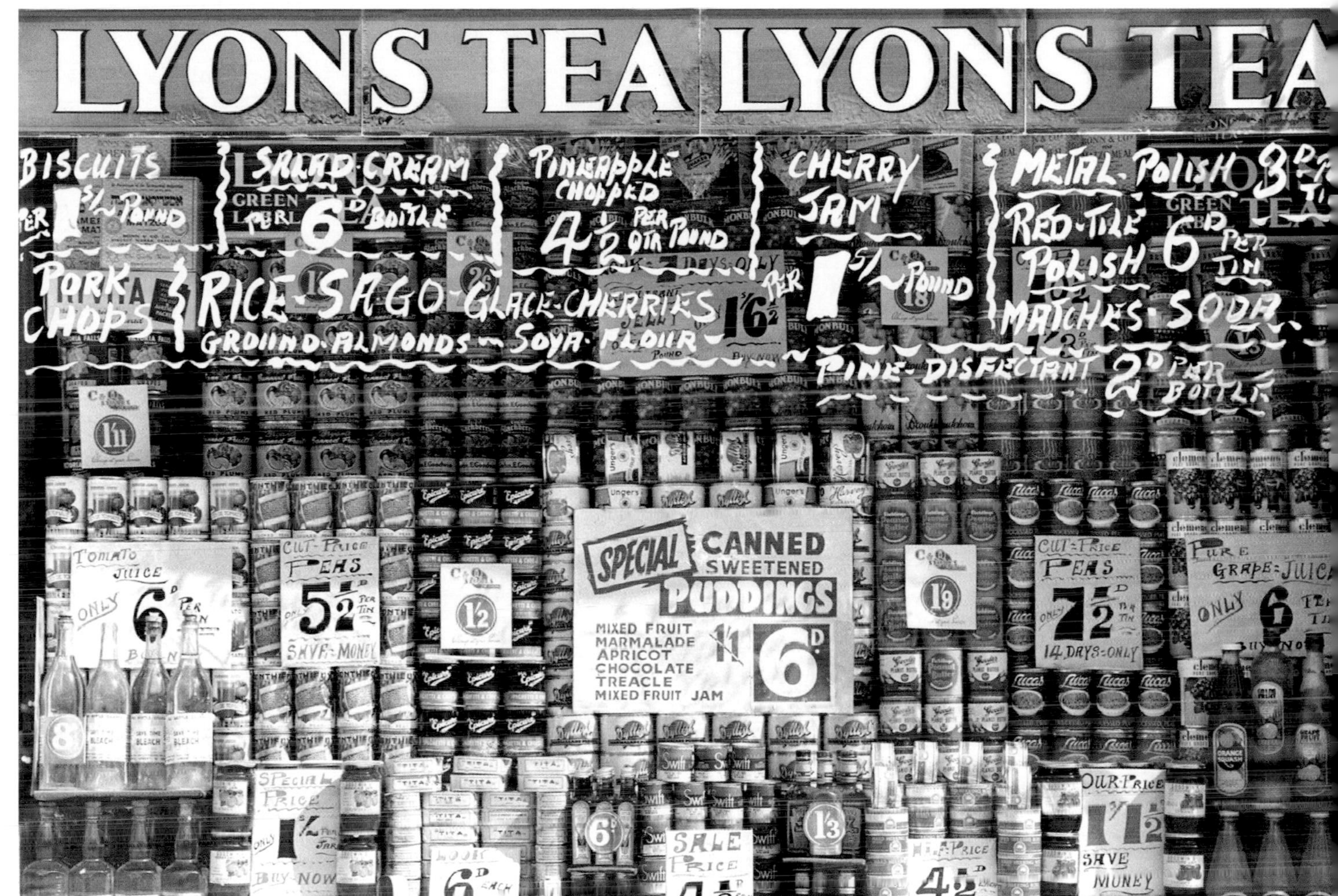

A grocer's window.
11th July, 1951

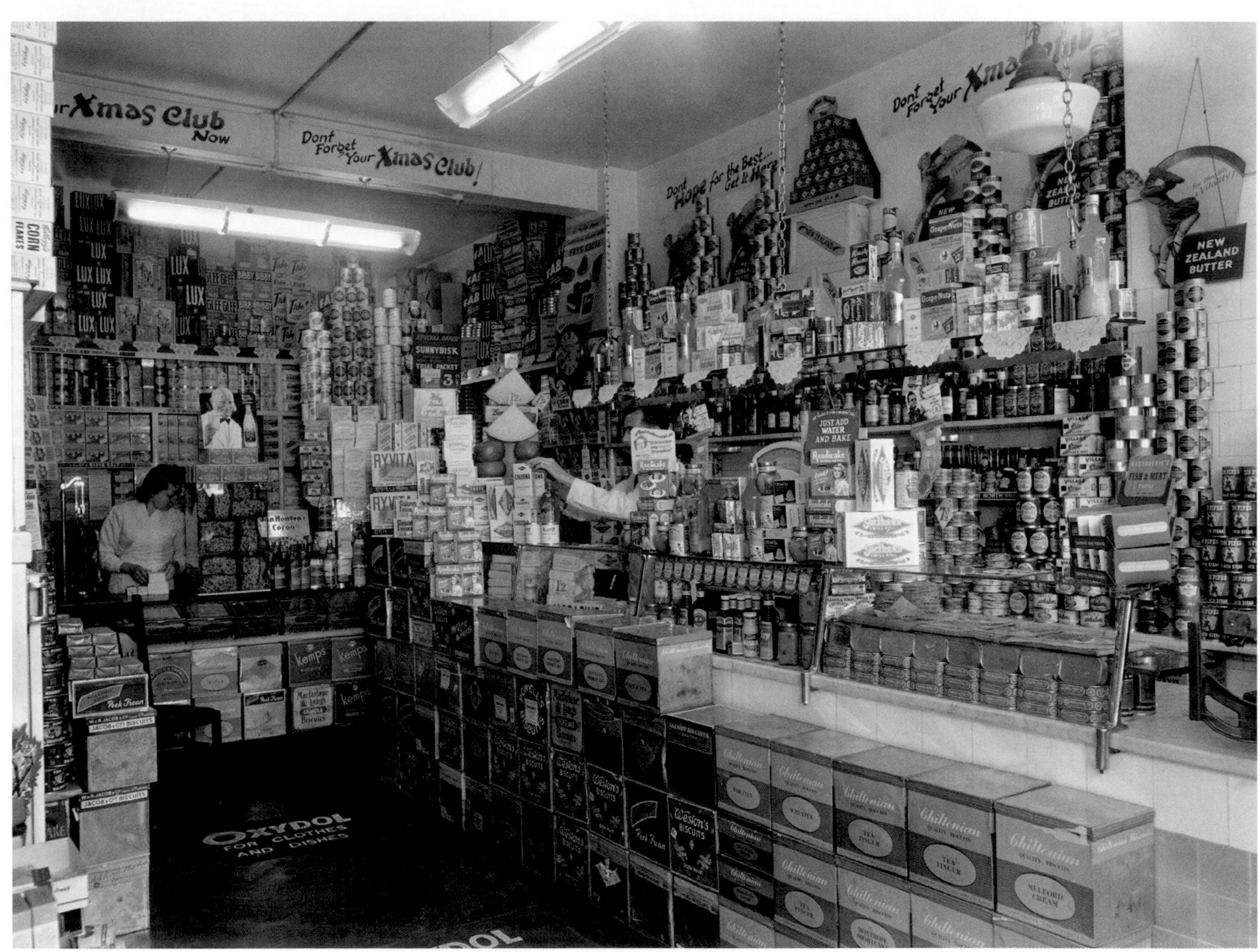

The interior of a grocer's shop before the rise of the supermarket. Marks & Spencer opened their first self-service shop in 1948, Sainsbury and Gateway (Somerfield) followed suit in 1950. Tesco opened its first supermarket in 1954.
11th July, 1951

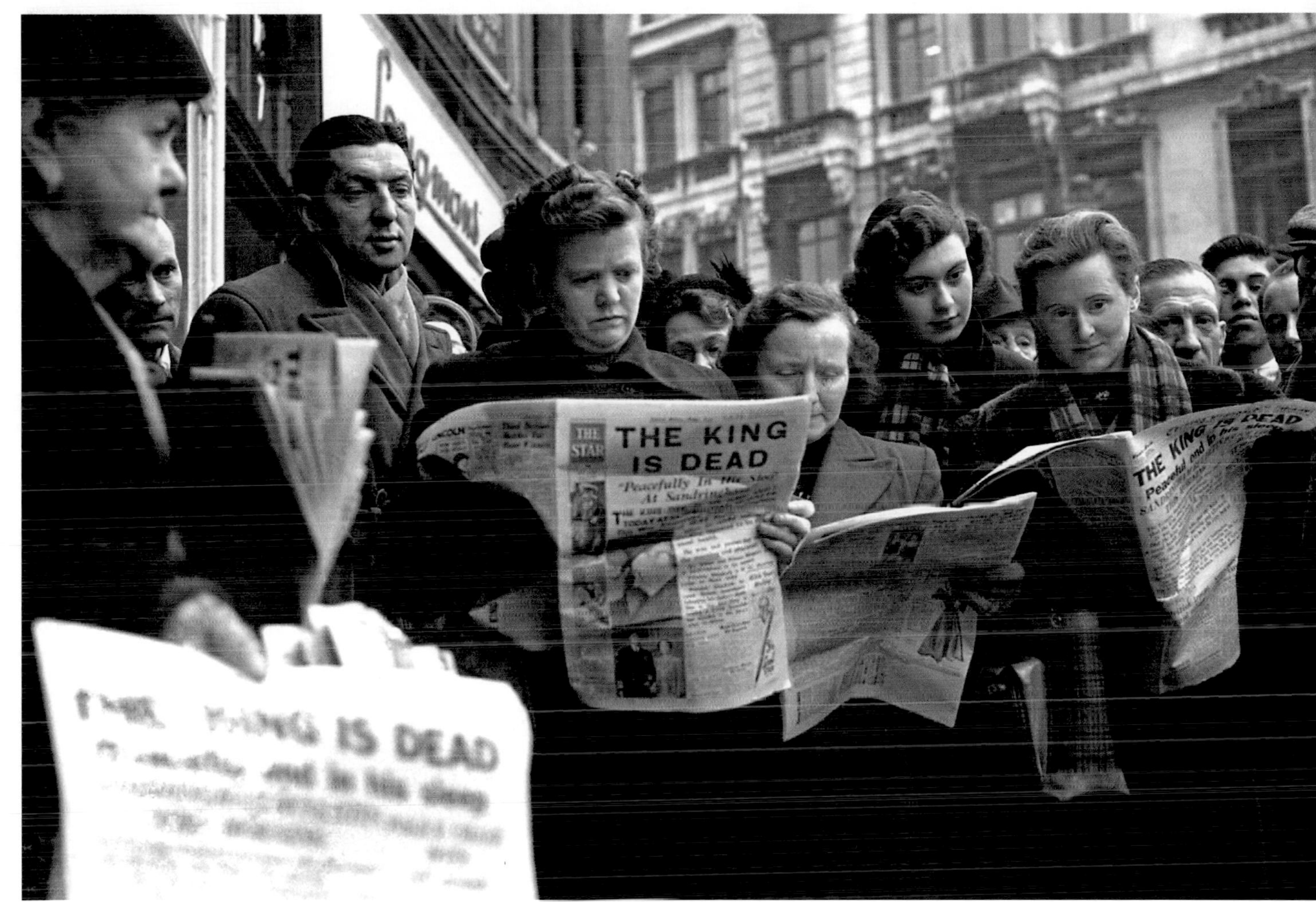

Lunchtime crowds at Ludgate Circus read news of the death of King George VI.
6th February, 1952

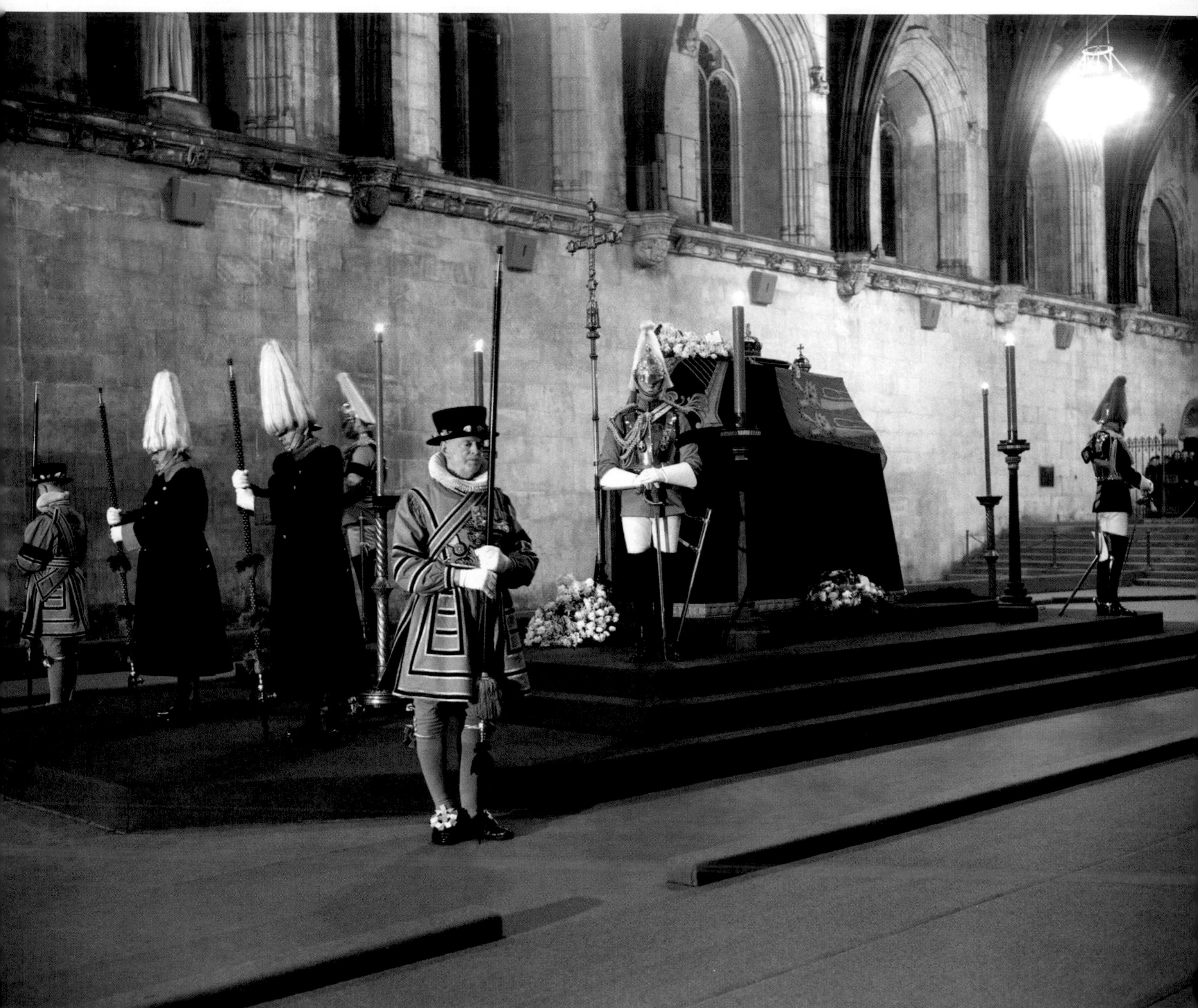

Facing page: The King's coffin lies in state at Westminster Hall.
11th February, 1952

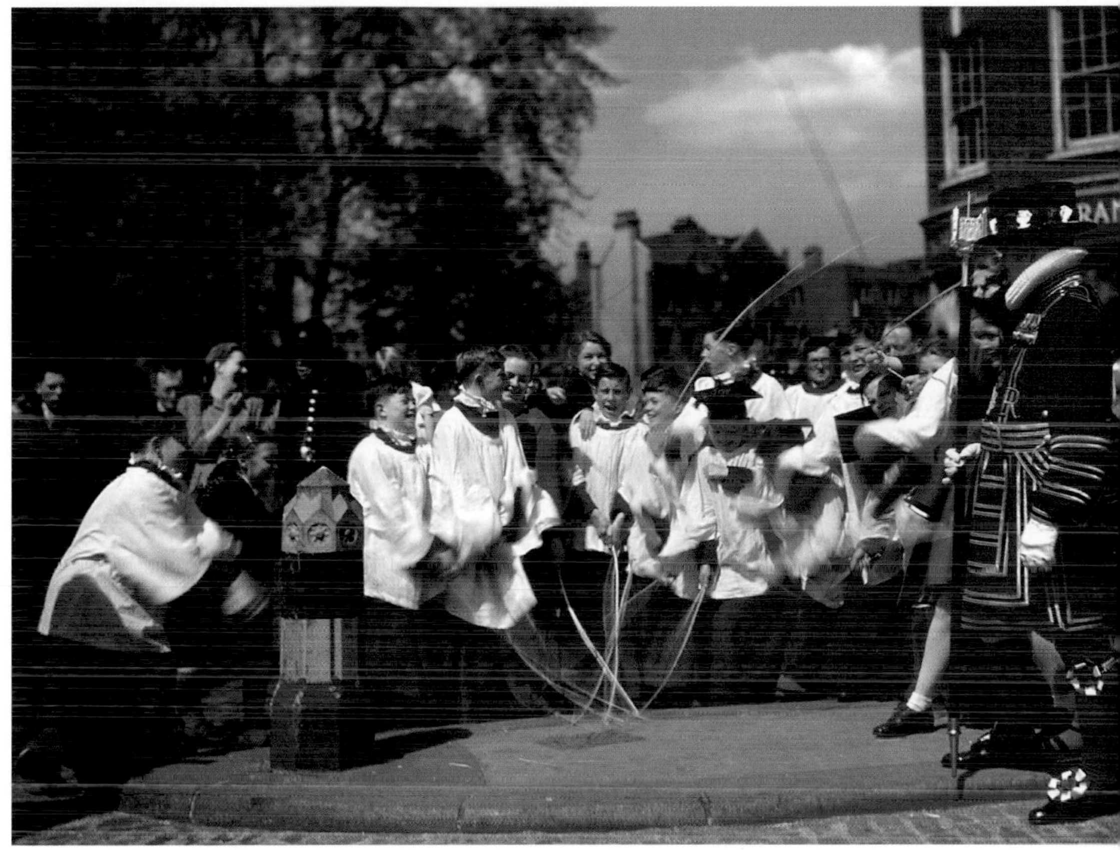

Choirboys Beating the Bounds at the Tower of London.
22nd February, 1952

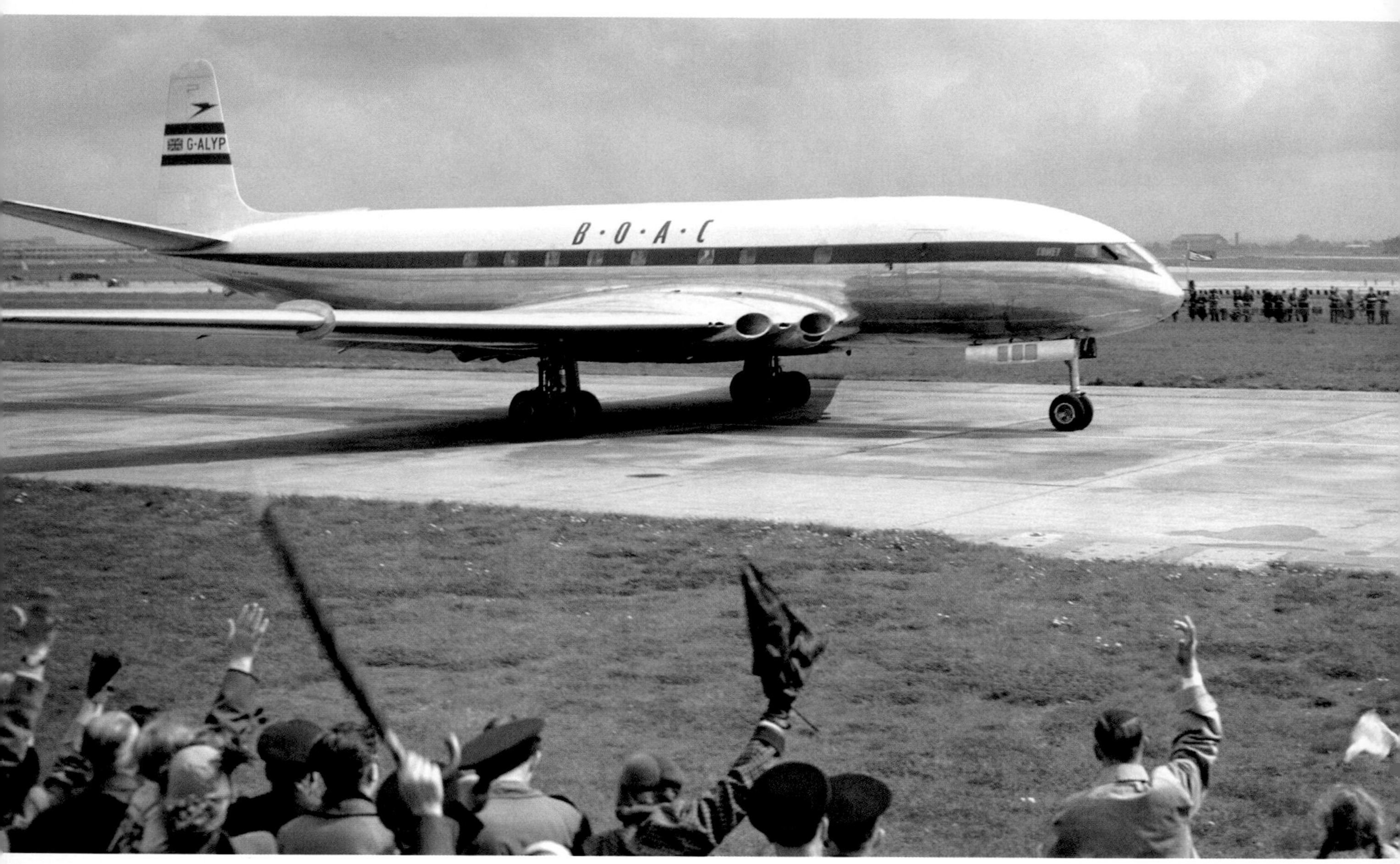

The world's first regular jetliner service. A 36-seater de Havilland *Comet,* G-ALYP of British Overseas Airways, takes off from London Airport on the inaugural passenger flight to Johannesburg, South Africa.
2nd May, 1952

Facing page: The last week of the London tram service.
30th June, 1952

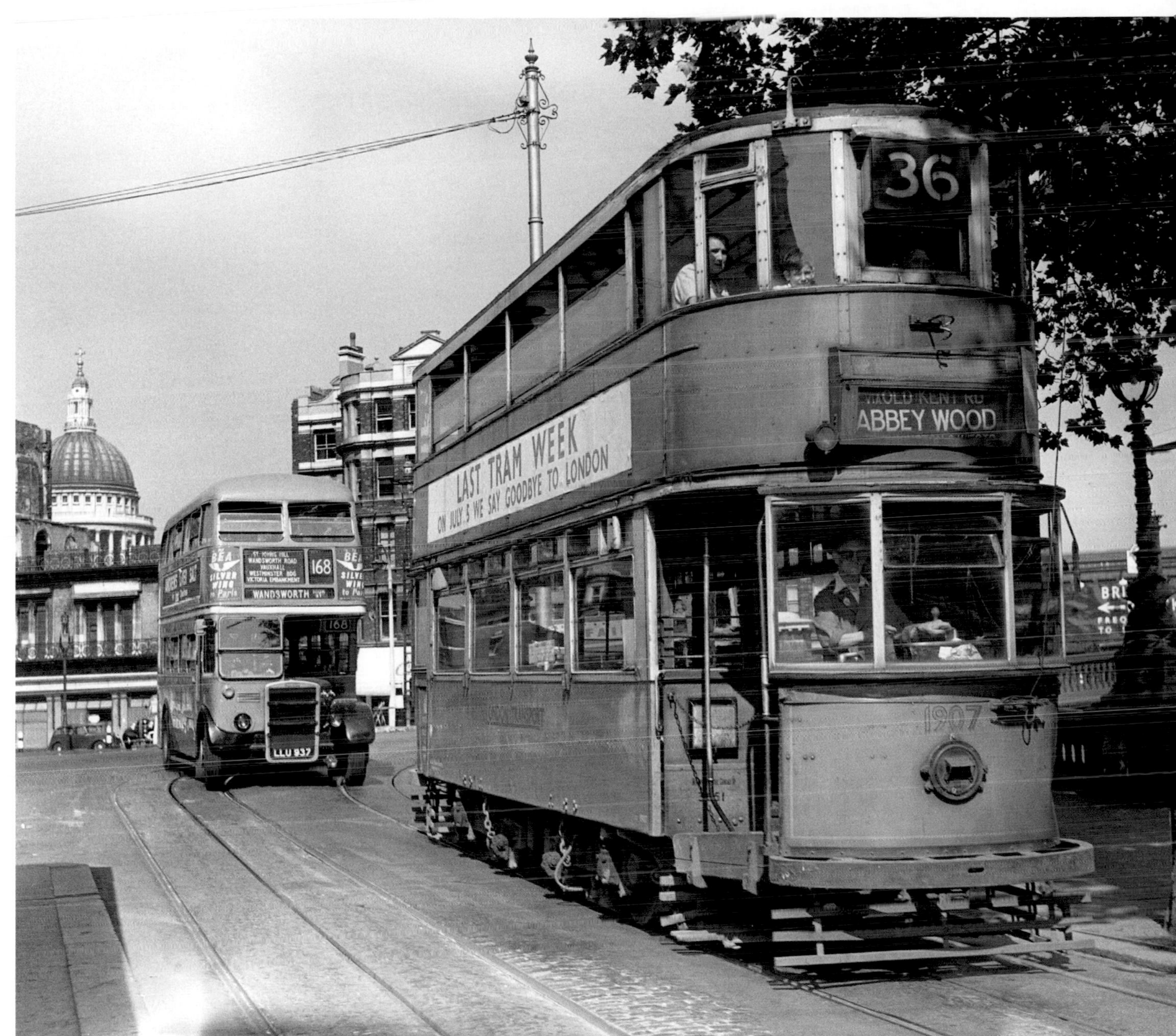
36
ABBEY WOOD
LAST TRAM WEEK
ON JULY 5 WE SAY GOODBYE TO LONDON
168
WANDSWORTH
LLU 937
1907

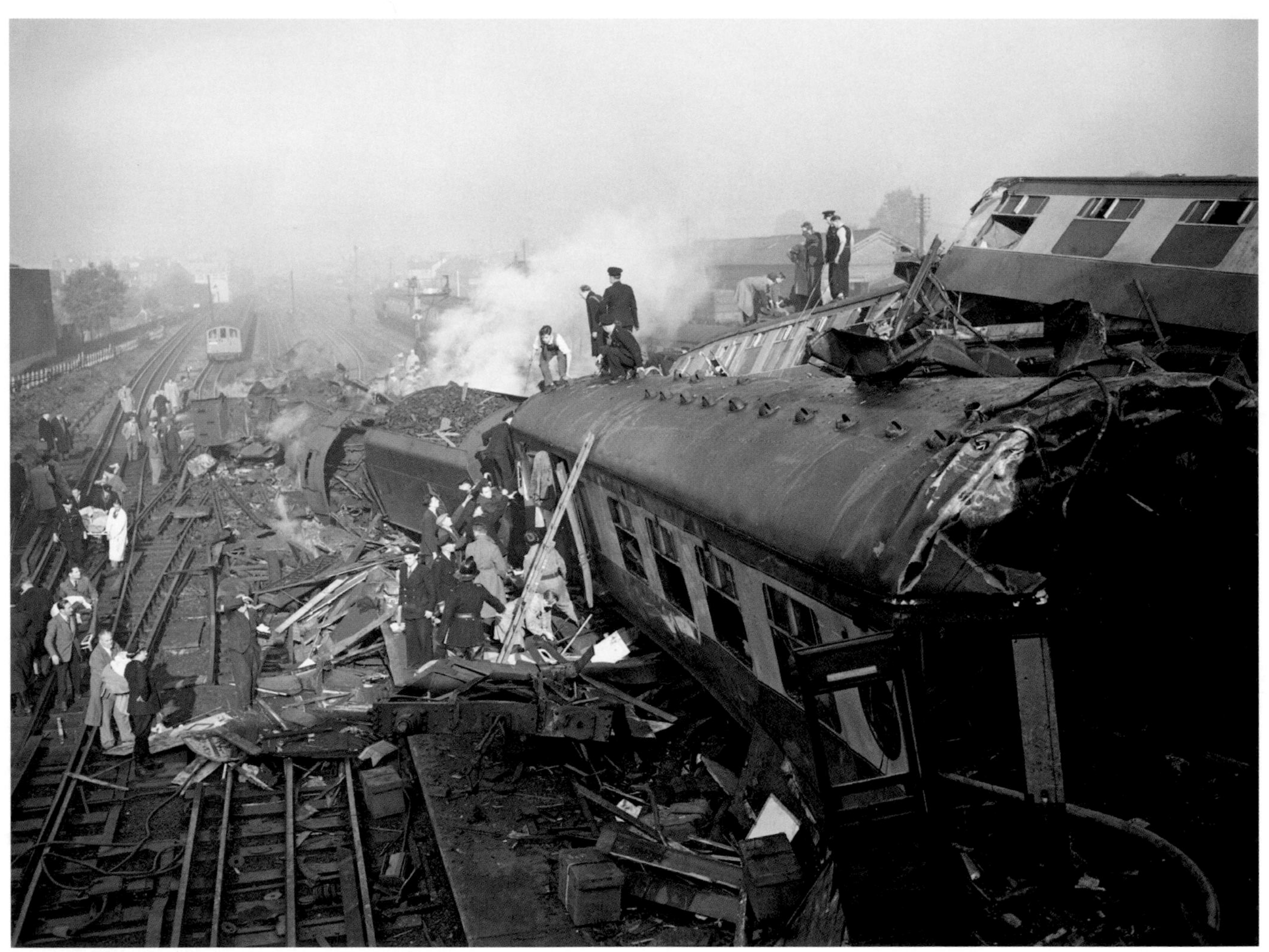

Britain's worst peacetime rail disaster. An express train from Perth struck a local train at Harrow and Wealdstone station and then an express going from Euston to Liverpool struck the derailed coaches. One hundred and twelve people were killed.
8th October, 1952

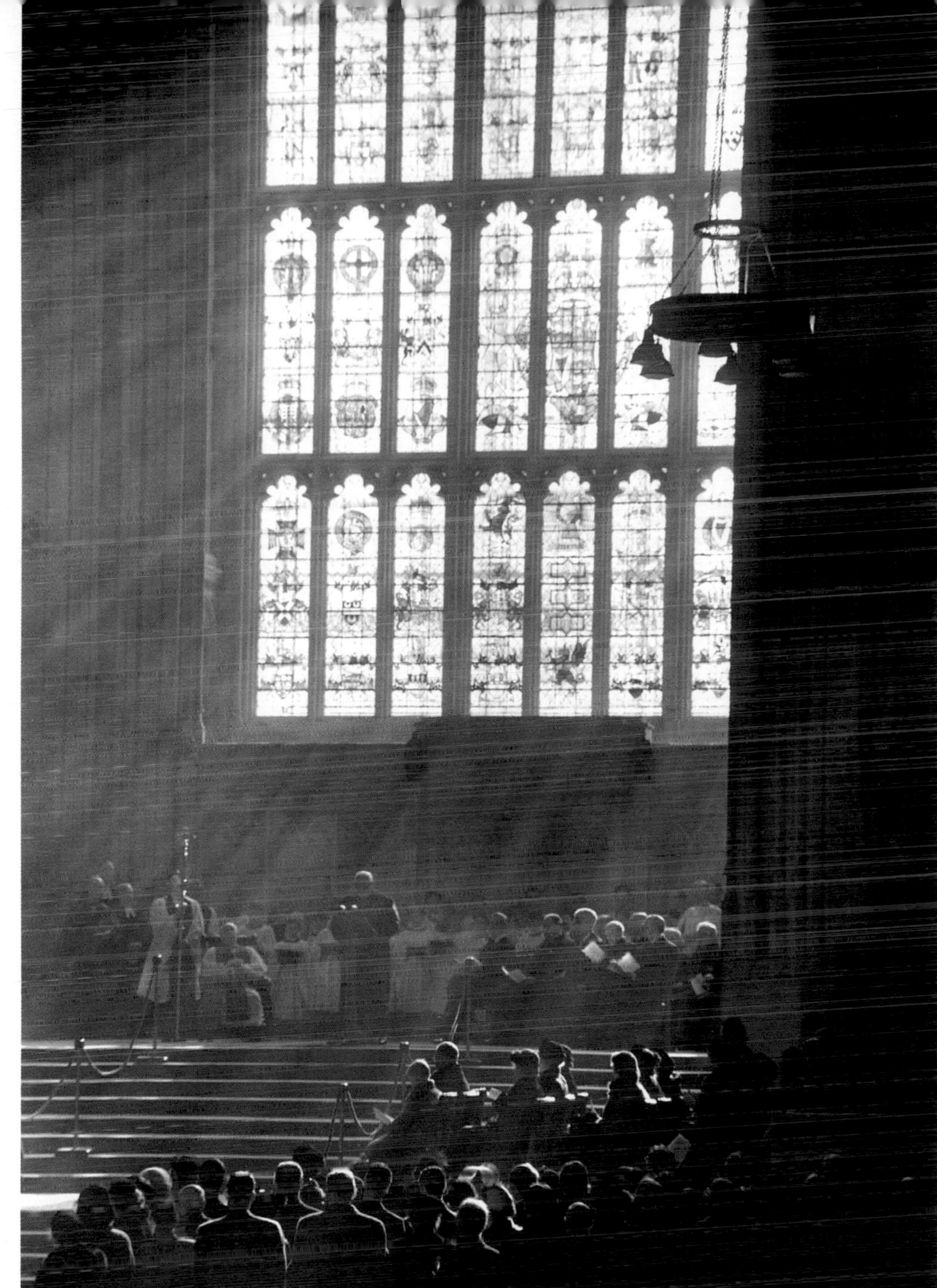

Prime Minister Winston Churchill speaks at a service for a memorial dedicated to Members of Parliament in Westminster Hall.
12th November, 1952

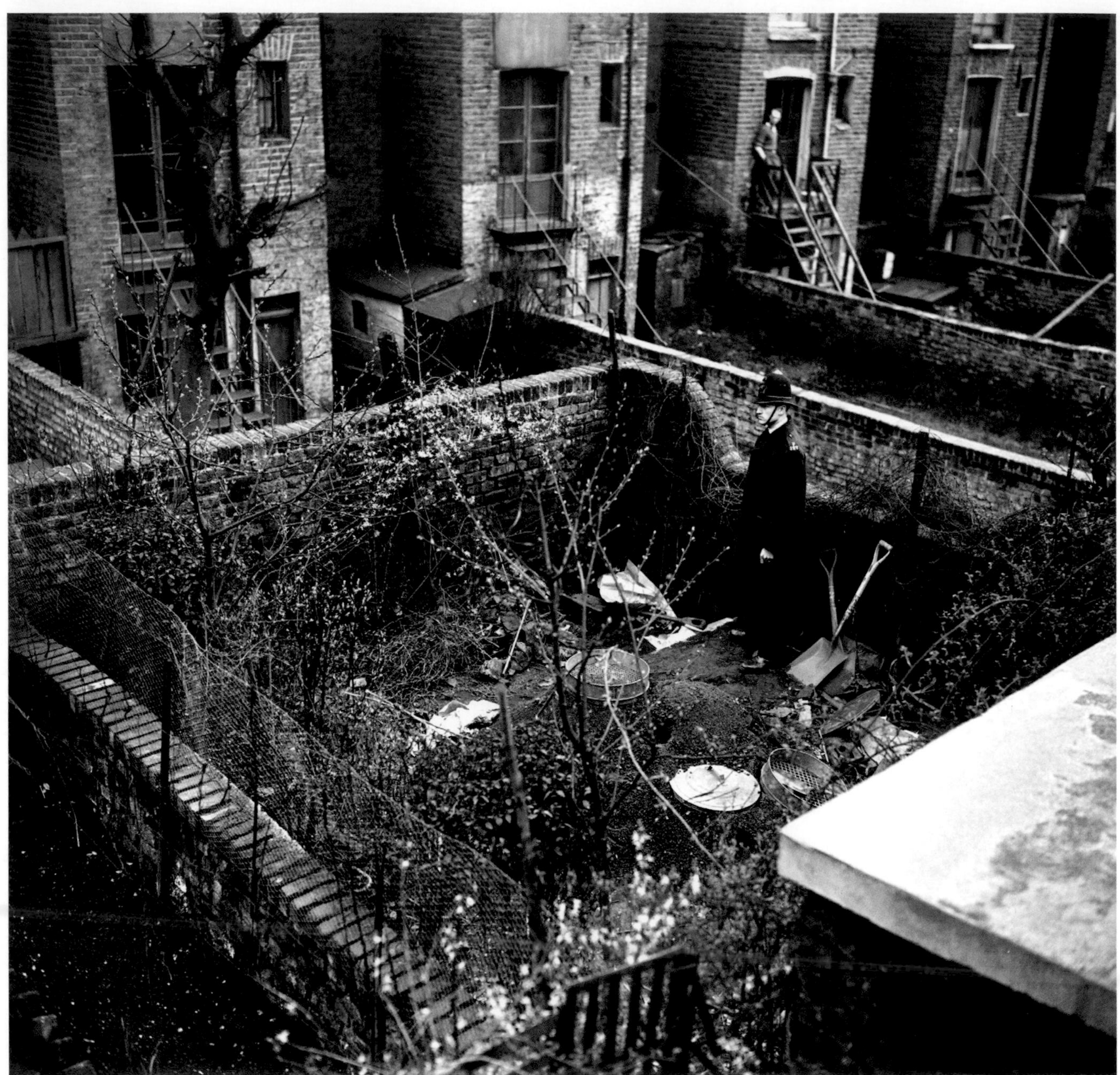

Facing page: A policeman in the garden of 10 Rillington Place in Notting Hill, where human bones were found buried a few inches under the soil. The bodies of four strangled women had already been discovered at the address and police were searching nationwide for suspect John Reginald Christie.
28th March, 1953

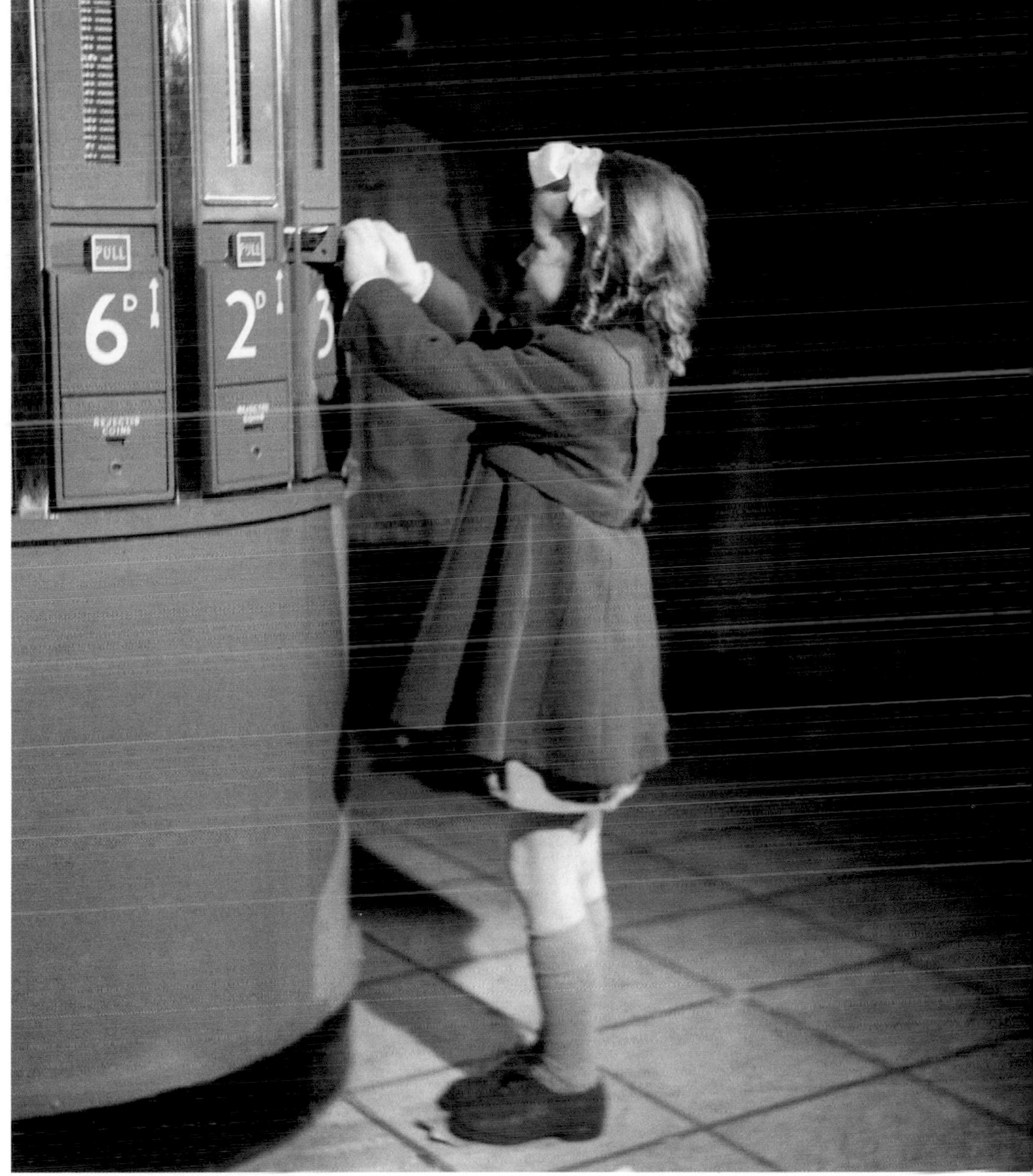

Sweet rationing comes to an end.
2nd April, 1953

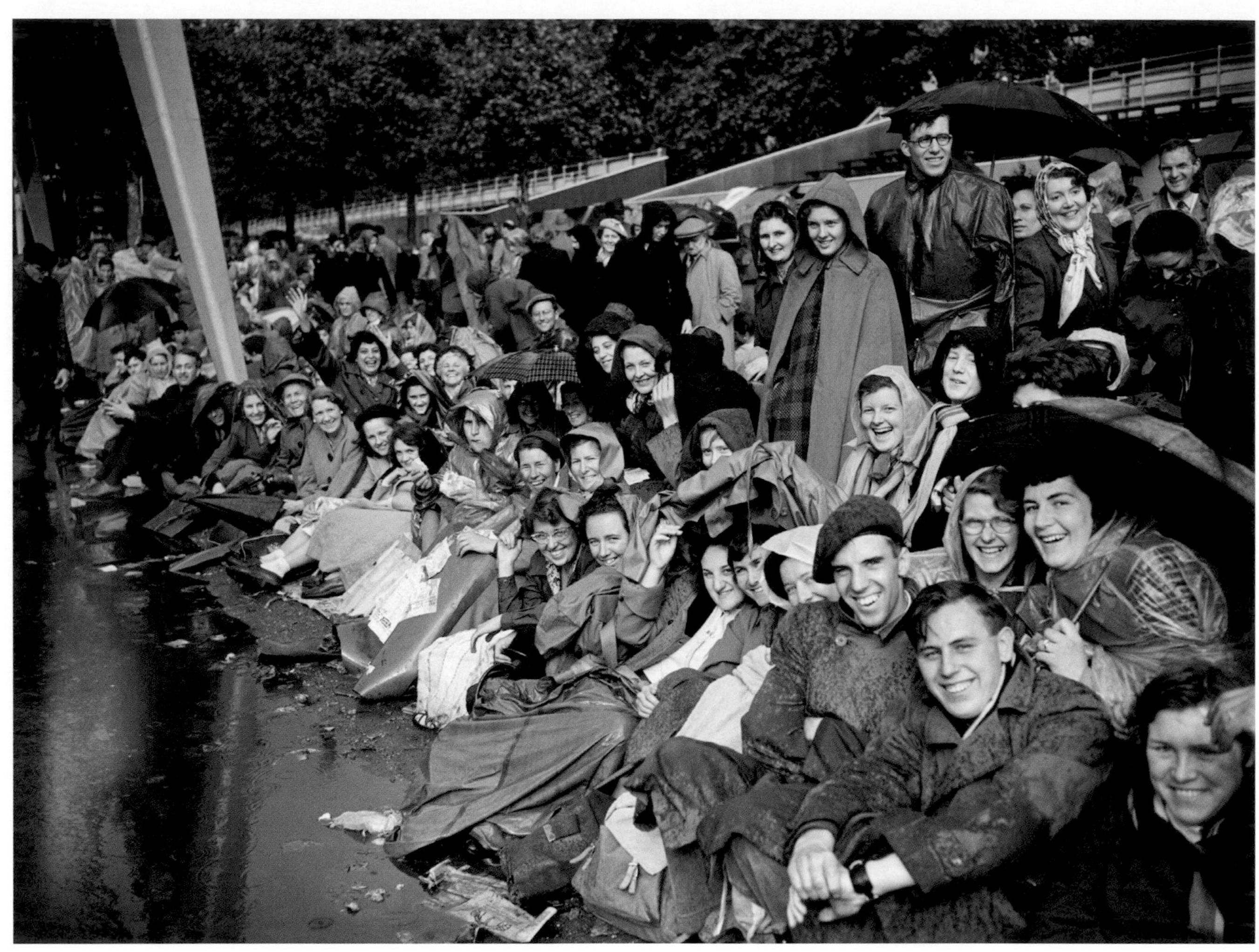

Crowds line The Mall for the Coronation of Queen Elizabeth II.
June, 1953

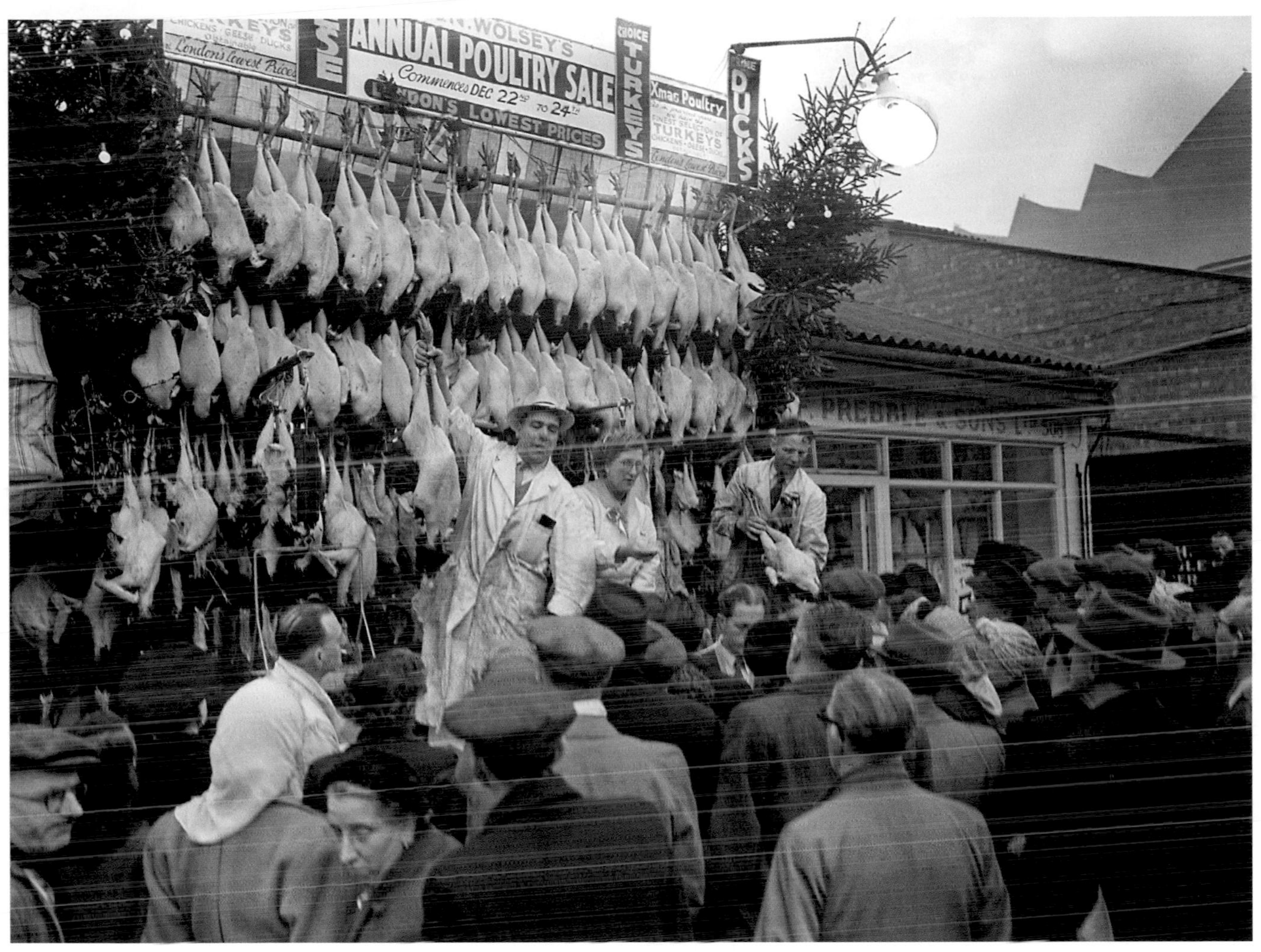

Turkey auction at Smithfield Market.
23rd December, 1953

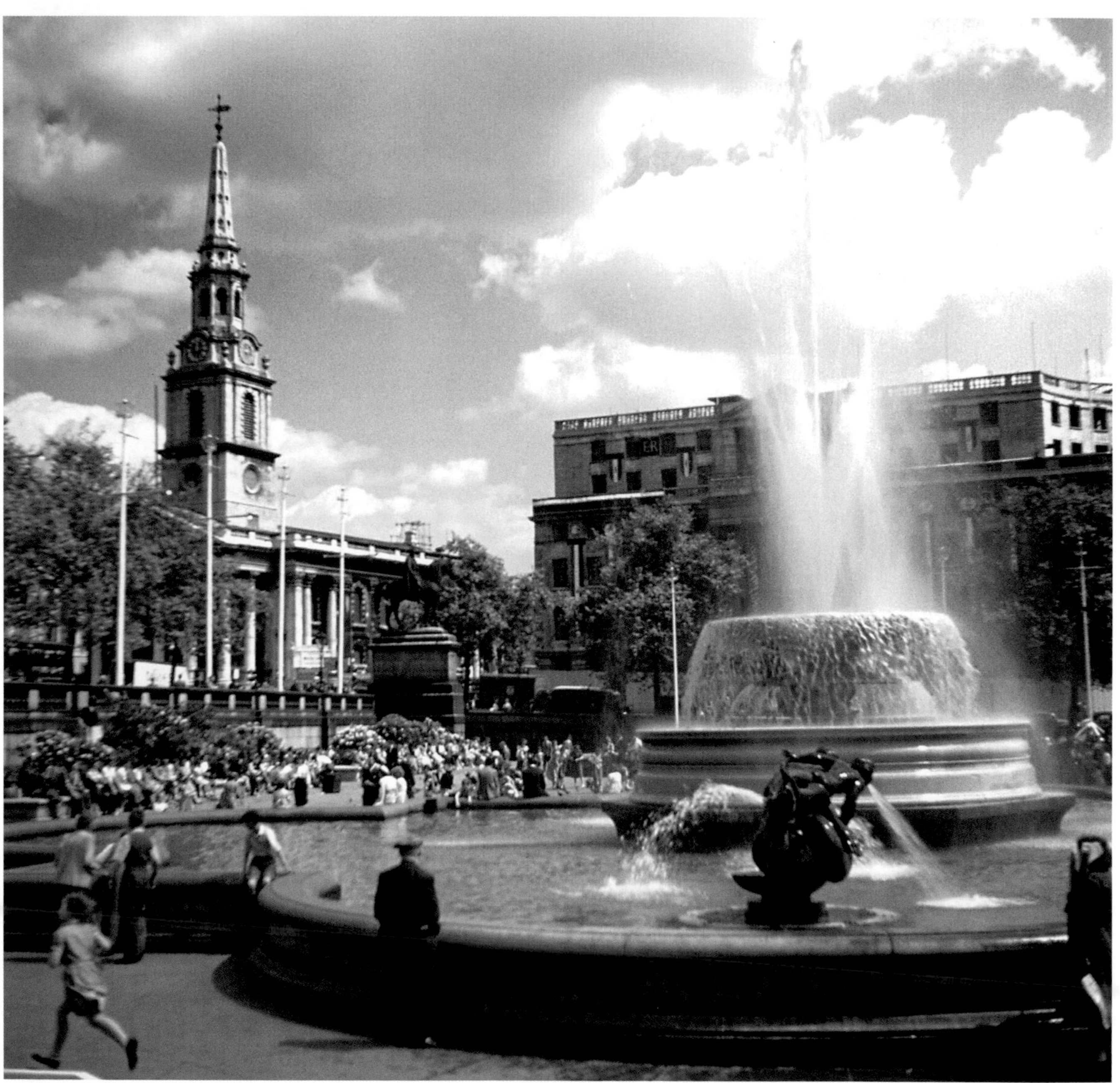

Facing page: Trafalgar Square in summer.
1954

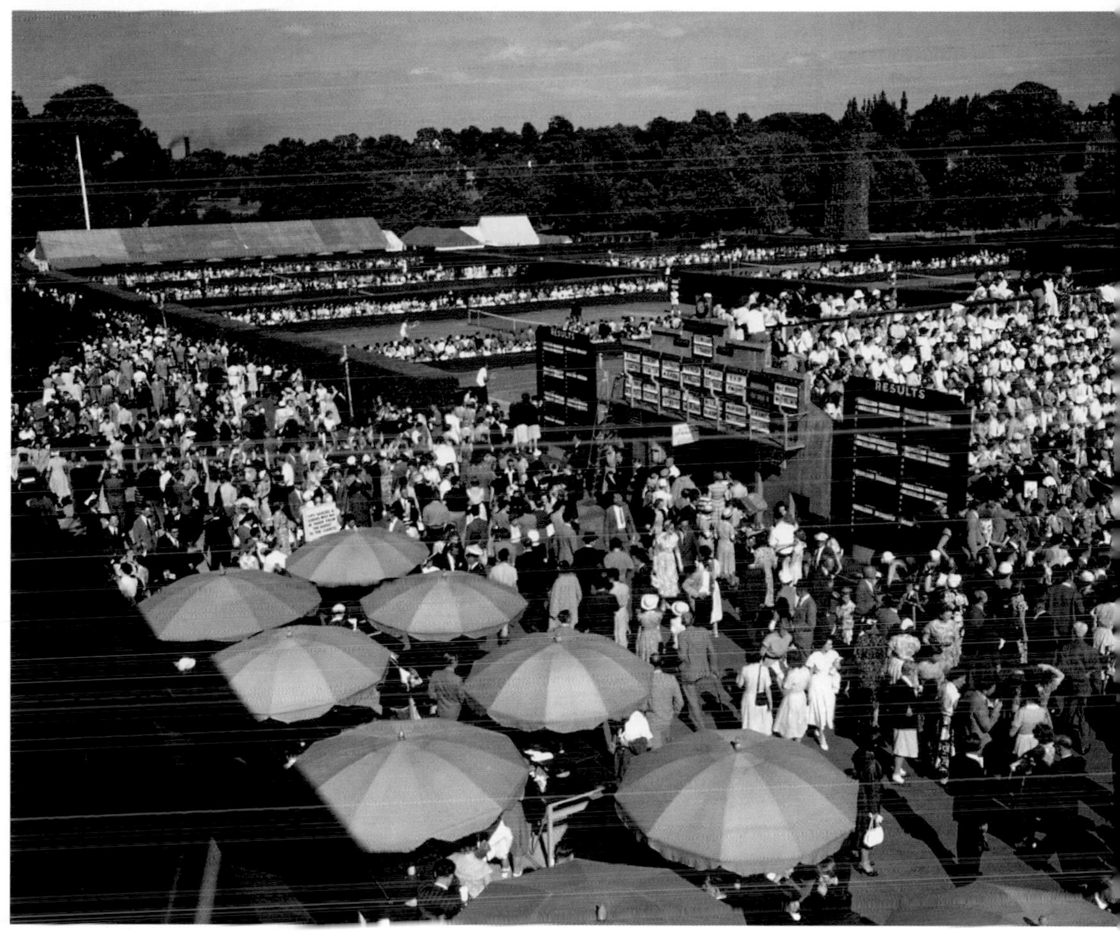

The All England Club, Wimbledon.
June, 1954

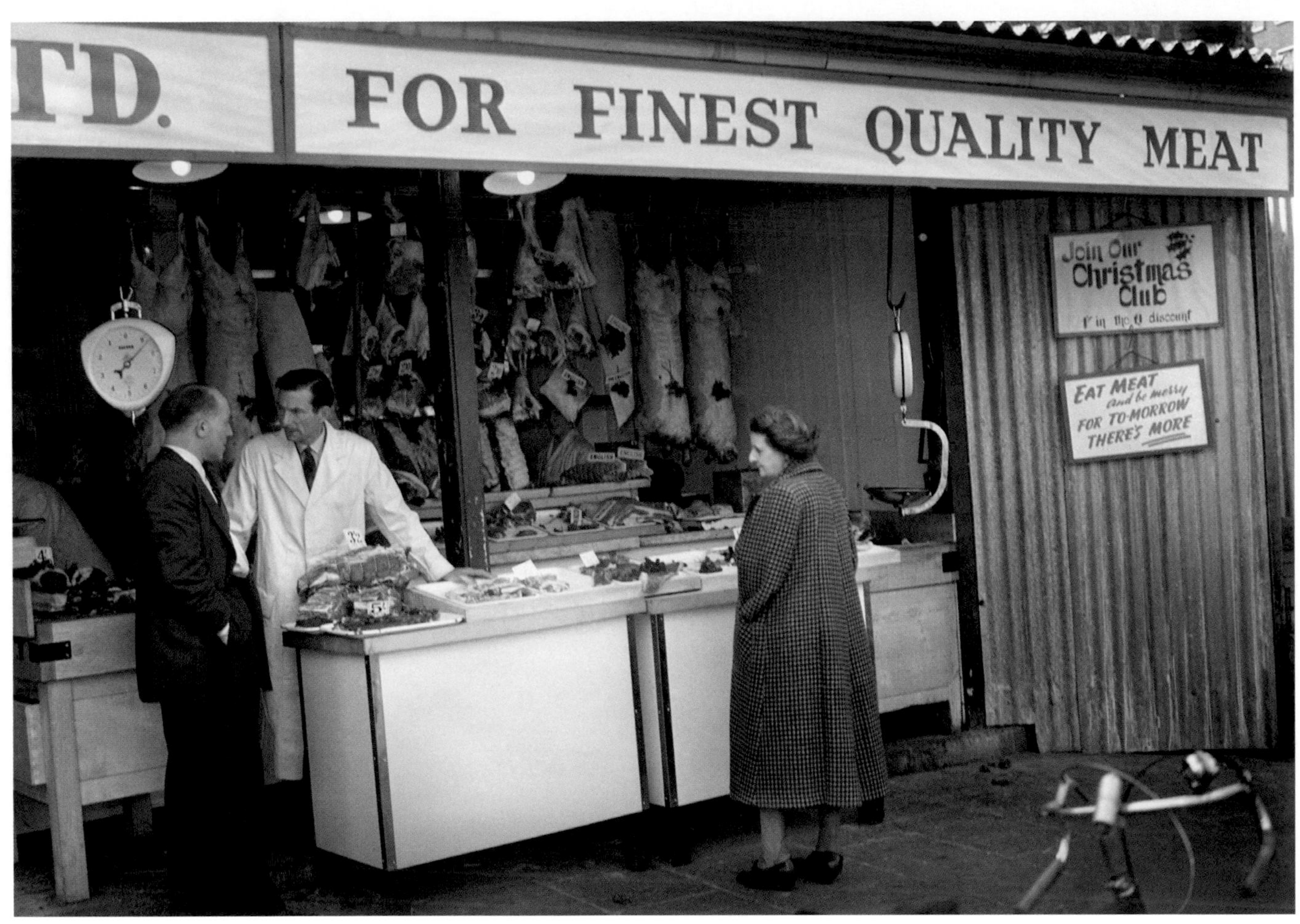

Smithfield Market, as rationing comes to an end.
7th July, 1954

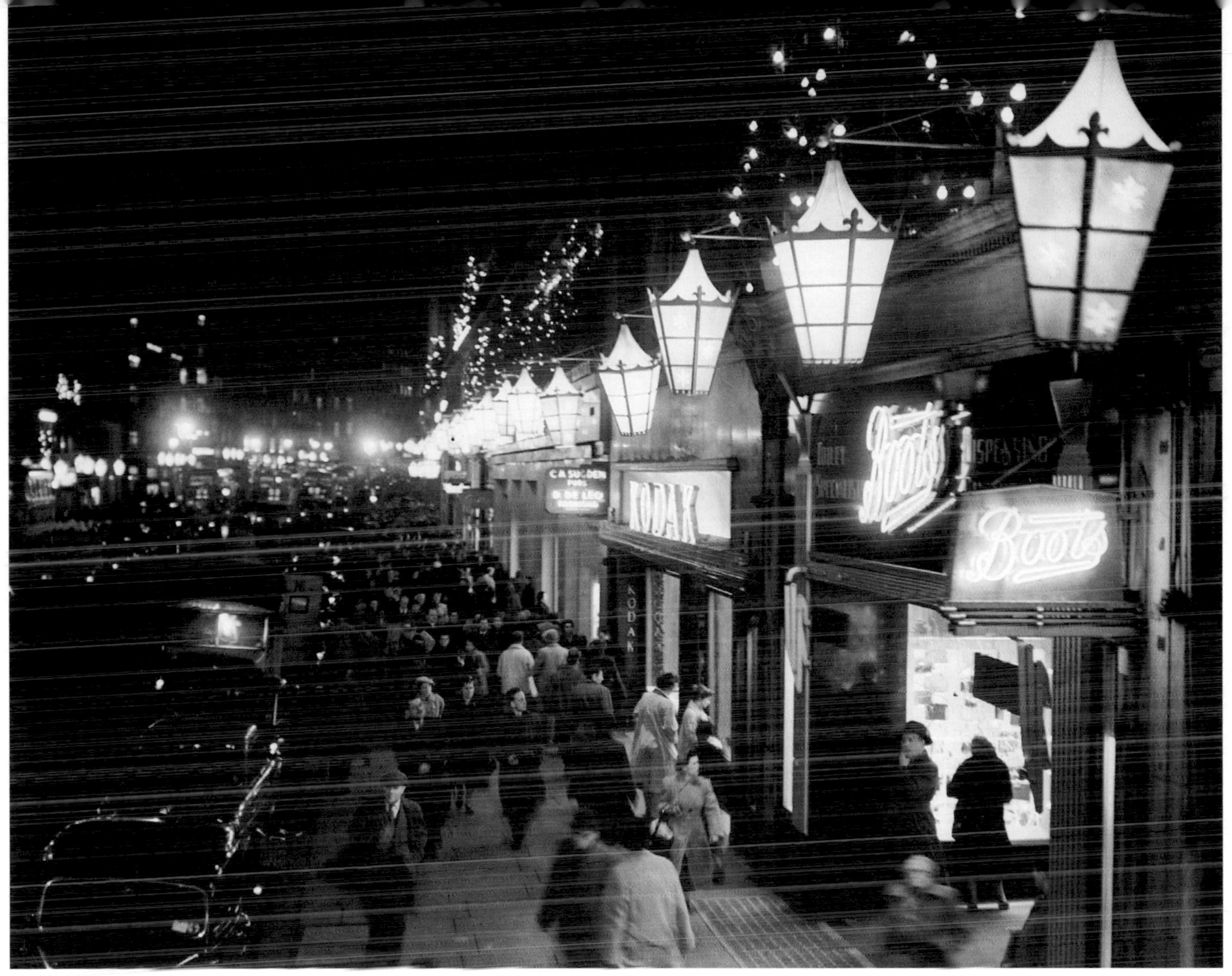

Regent Street, Christmas illuminations.
2nd December, 1954

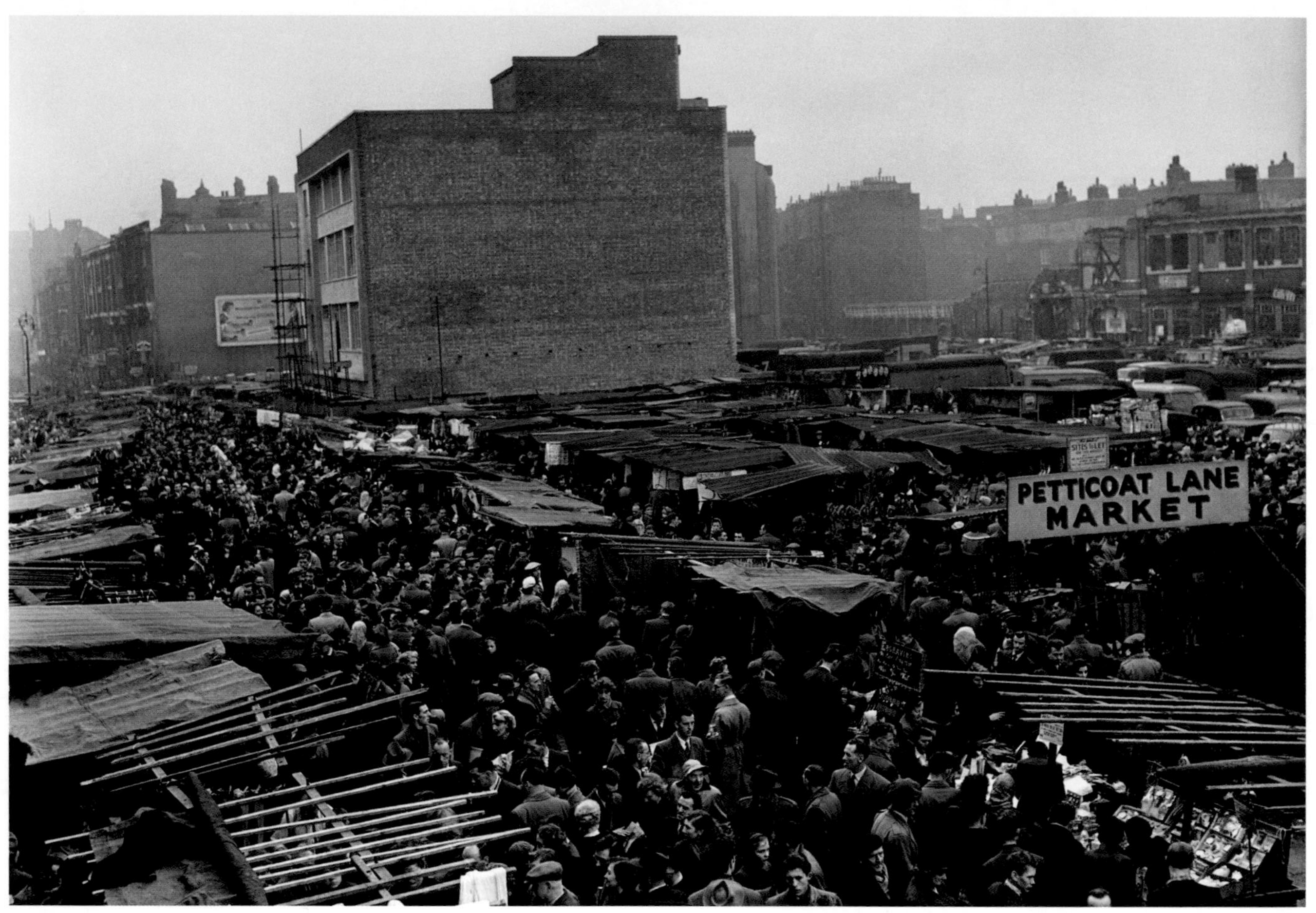

Christmas shopping at Petticoat Lane Market.
20th December, 1954

Facing page: Tower Bridge.
1955

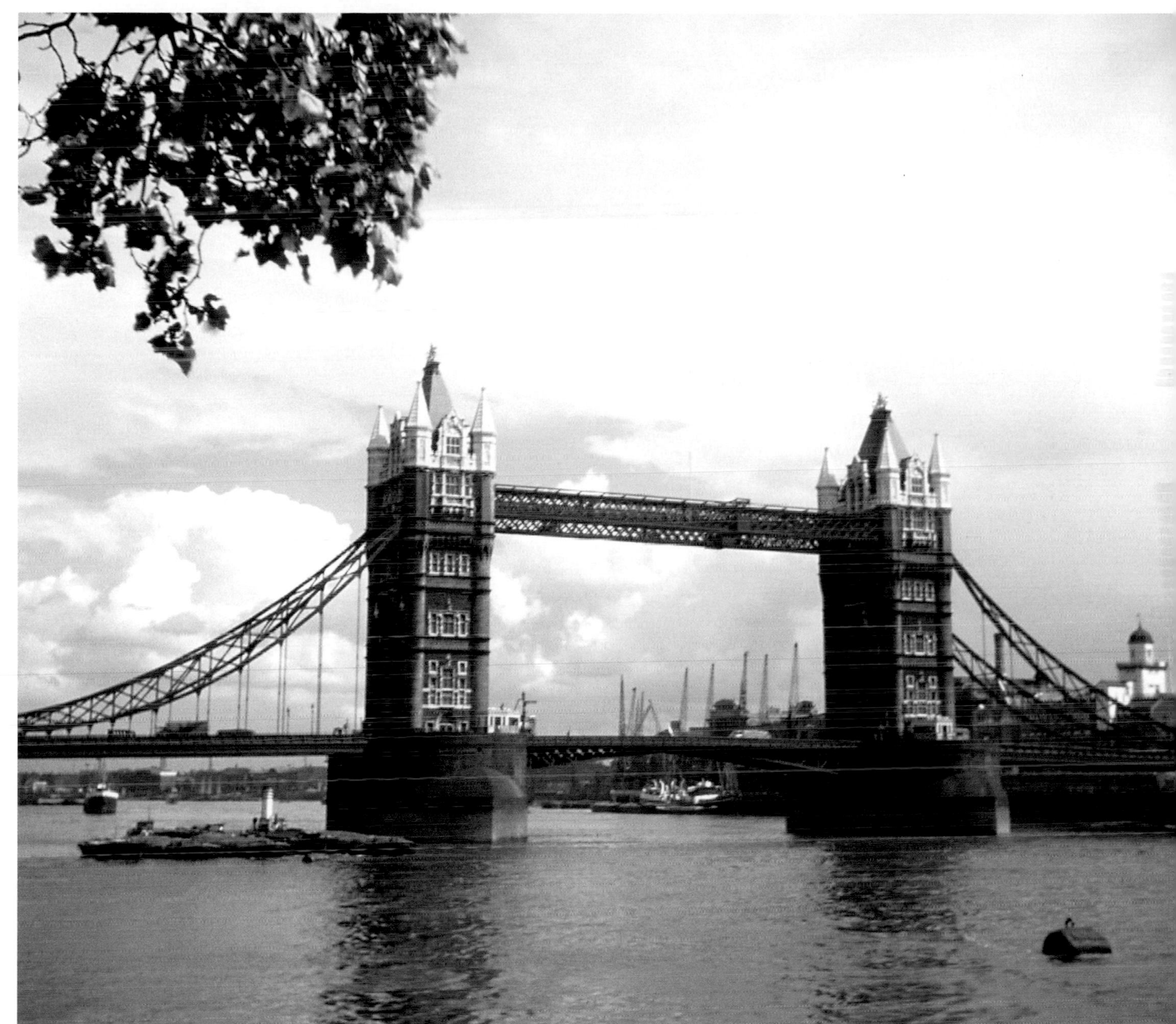

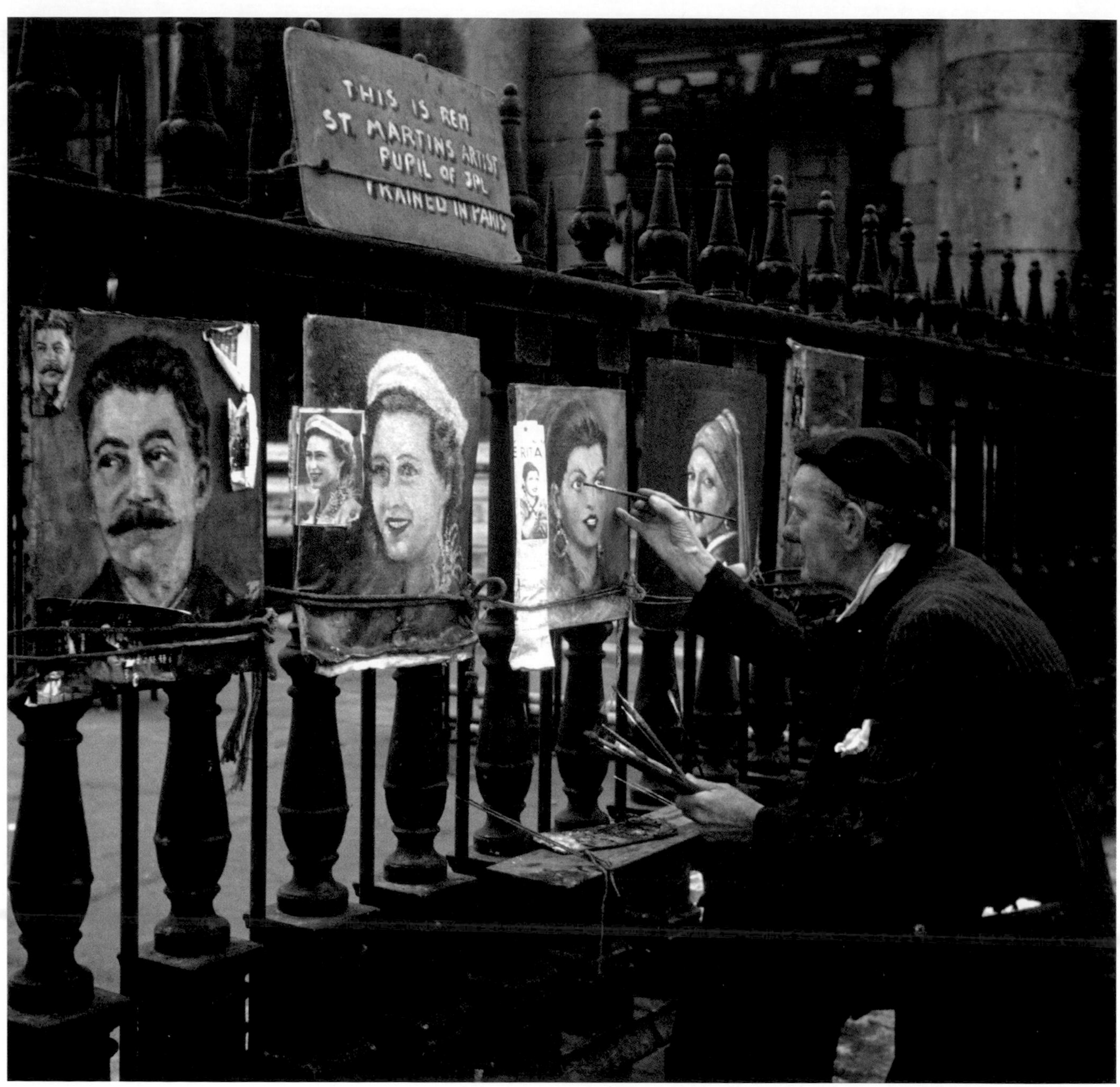
THIS IS REM
ST. MARTINS ARTIST
PUPIL OF 3PL
TRAINED IN PARIS

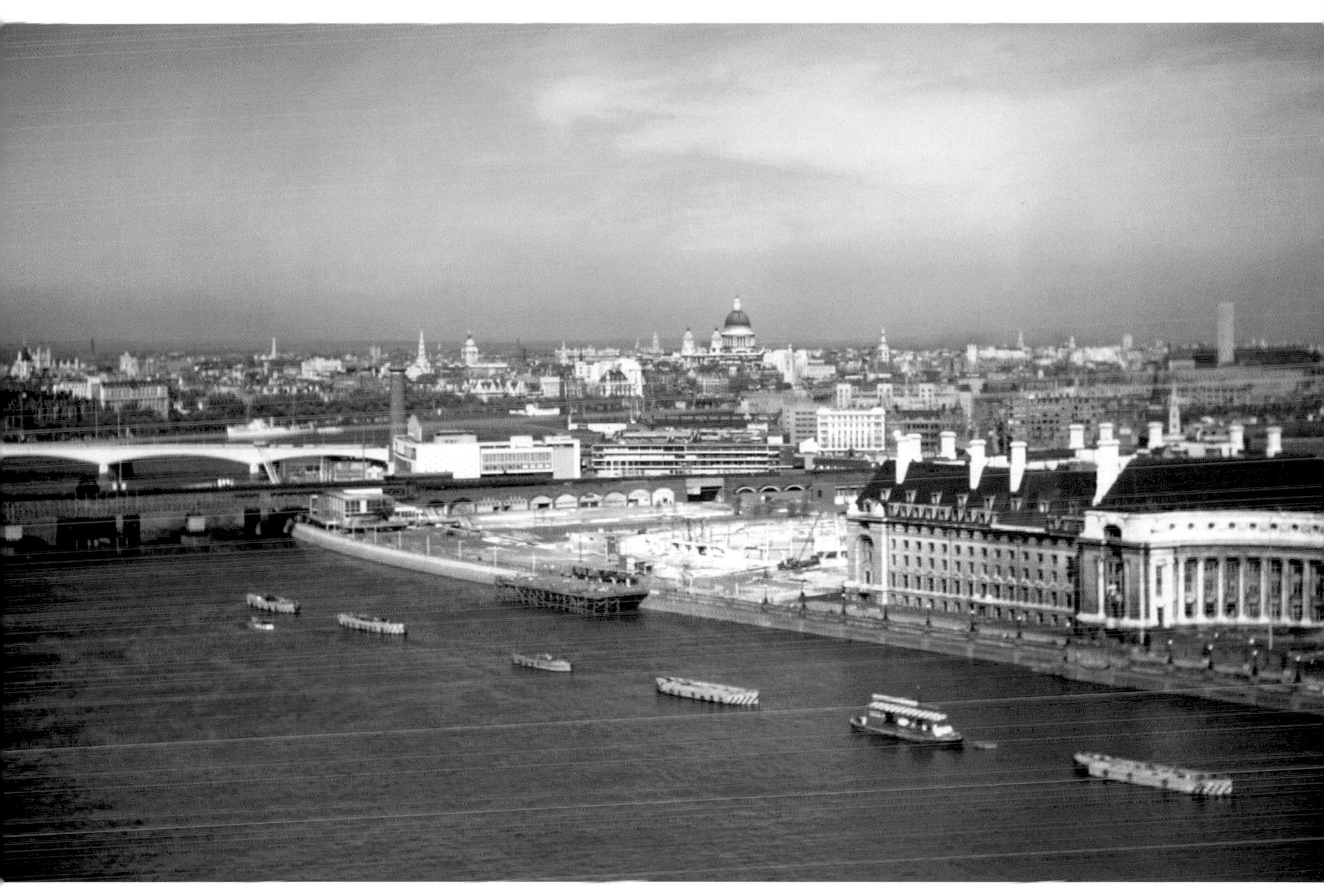

The River Thames and Festival of Britain site beside County Hall.
June, 1955

Facing page: A pavement artist at St Martin-in-the-Fields.
May, 1955

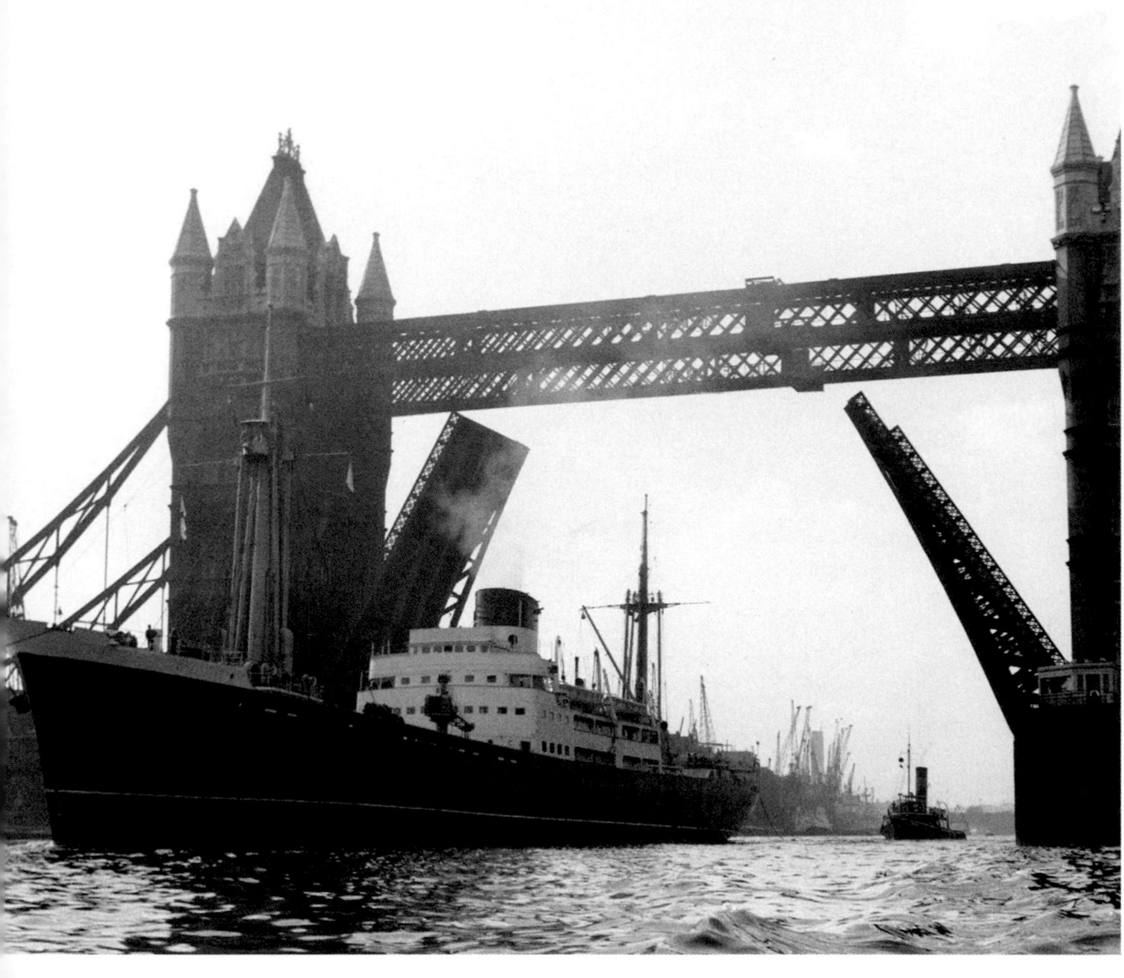

Tower Bridge with bascules raised.
5th February, 1957

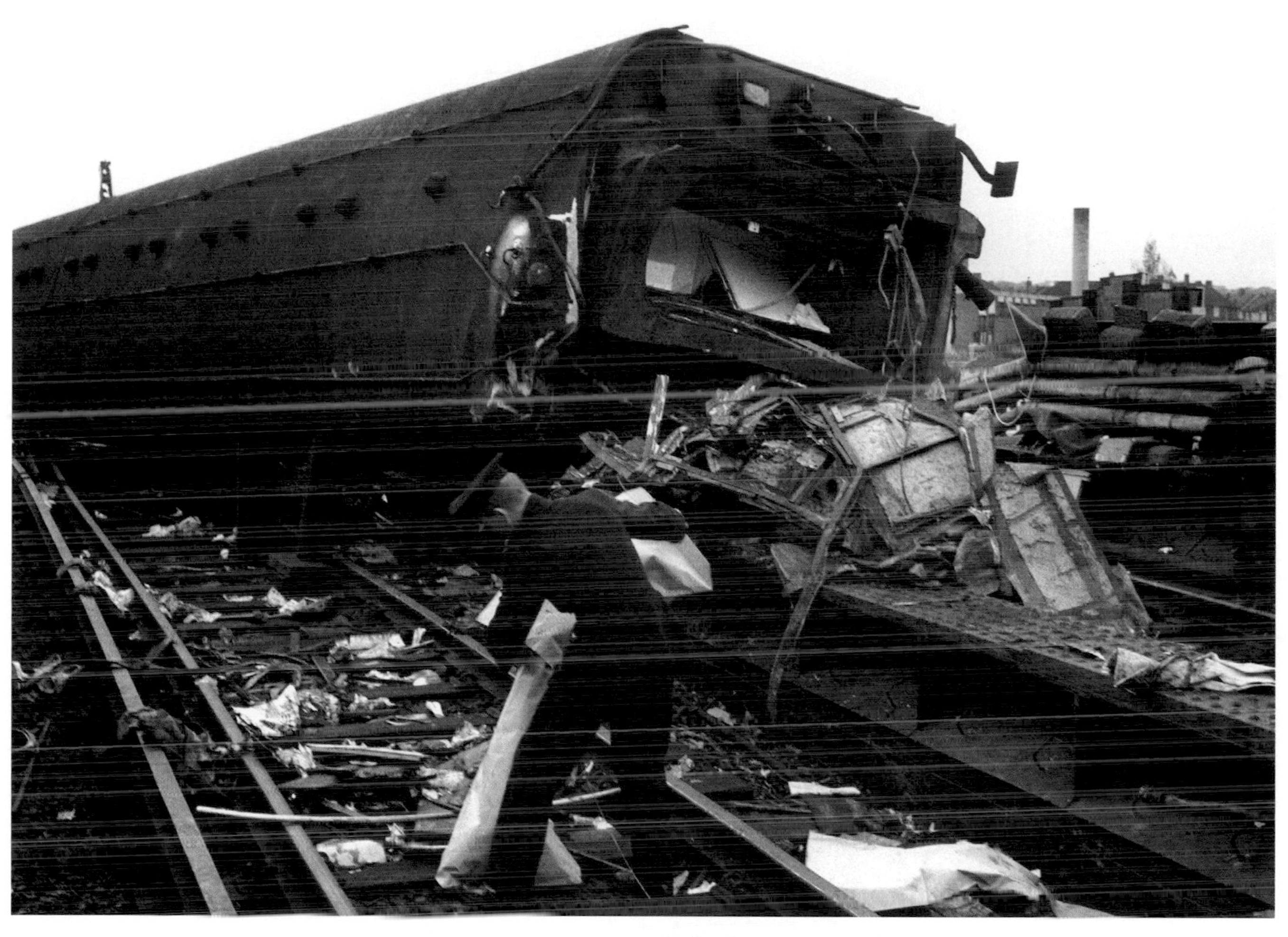

Gathering up personal belongings of passengers on the London-bound train derailed near Hither Green goods depot, killing 92 people.
6th December, 1957

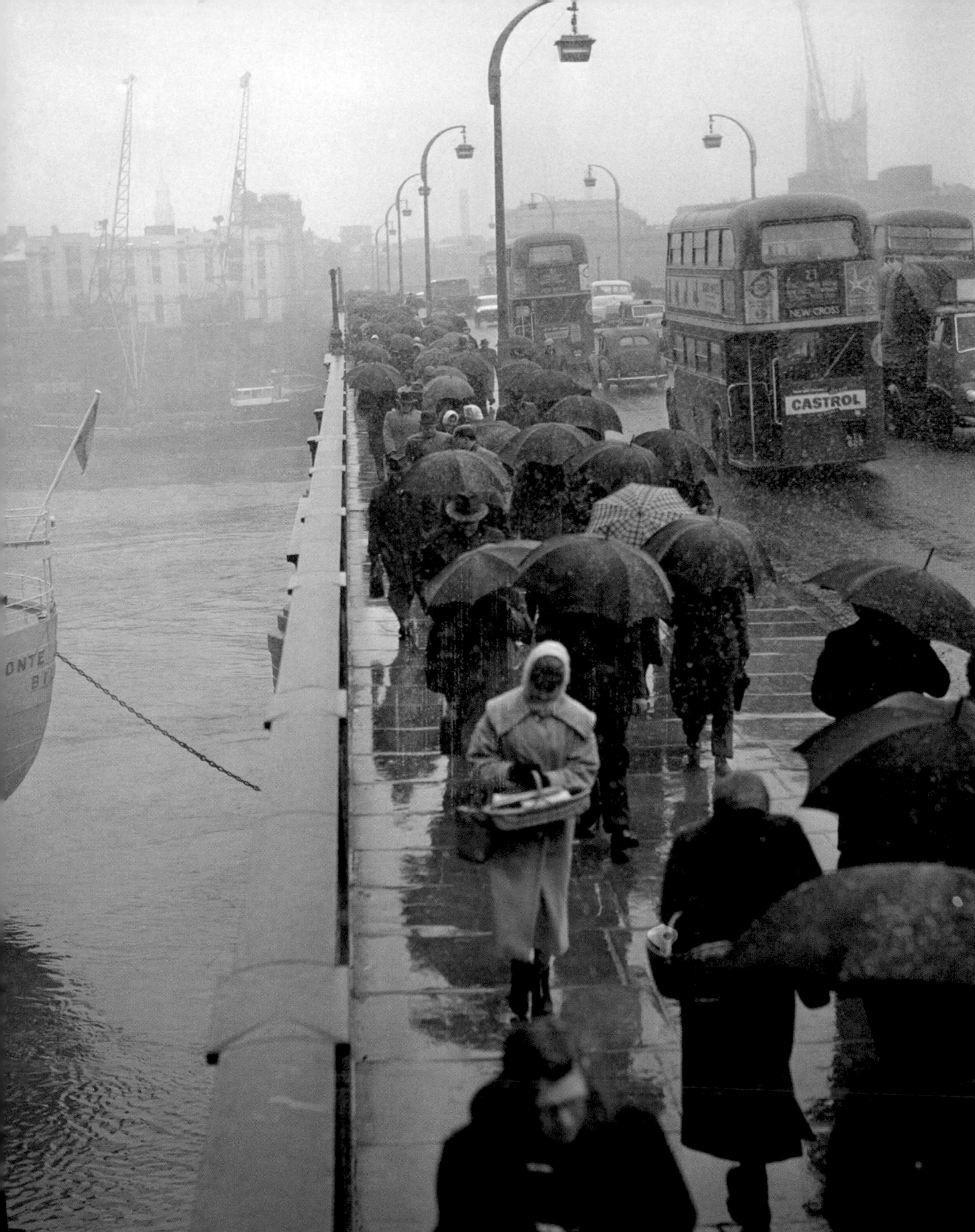

London Bridge.
25th February, 1958

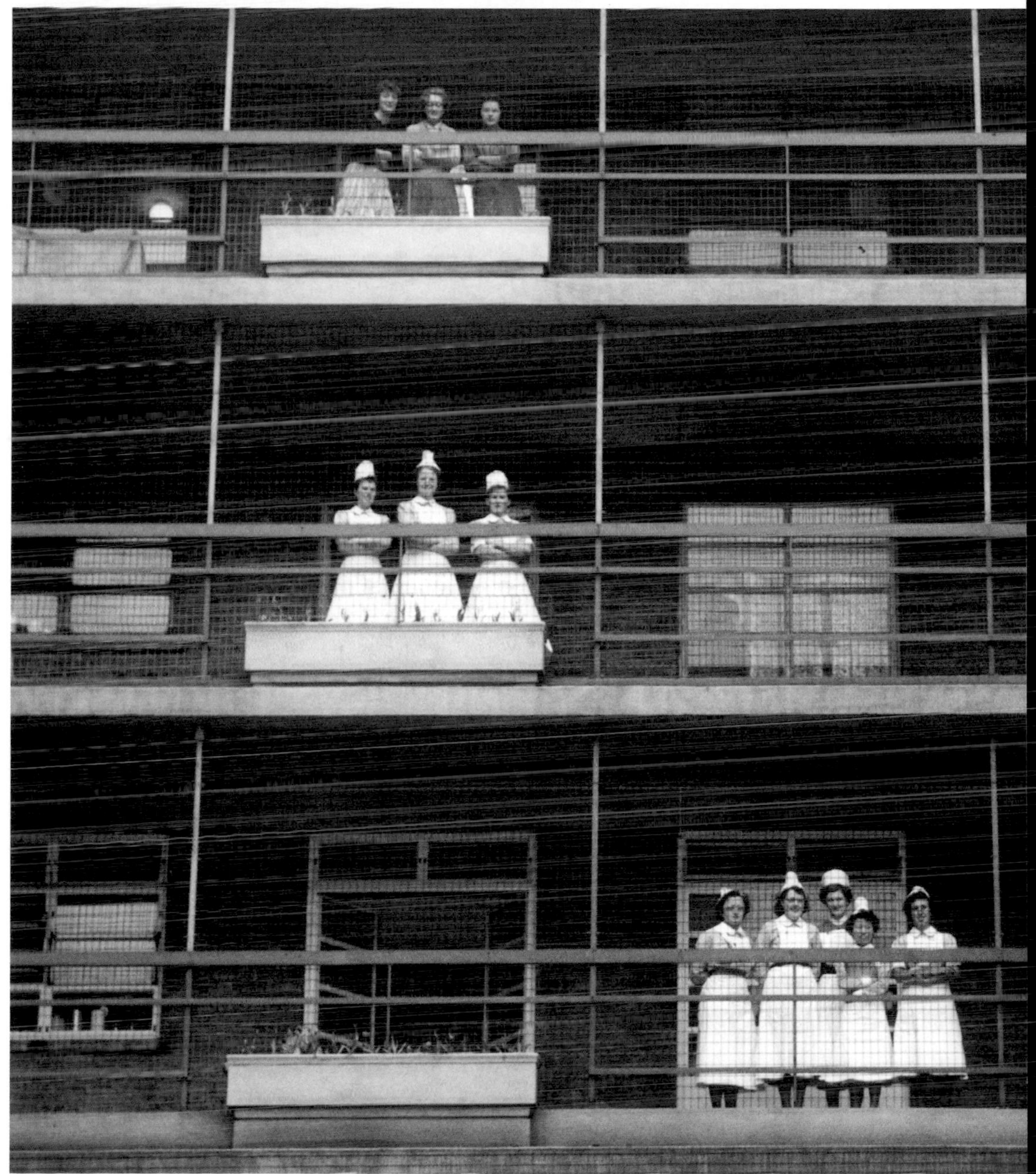

Nurses watch as Princess Anne leaves the Hospital for Sick Children, Great Ormond Street, after an operation to remove her tonsils and adenoids.
16th May, 1958

Facing page: All Soul's Church and Broadcasting House.
June, 1958

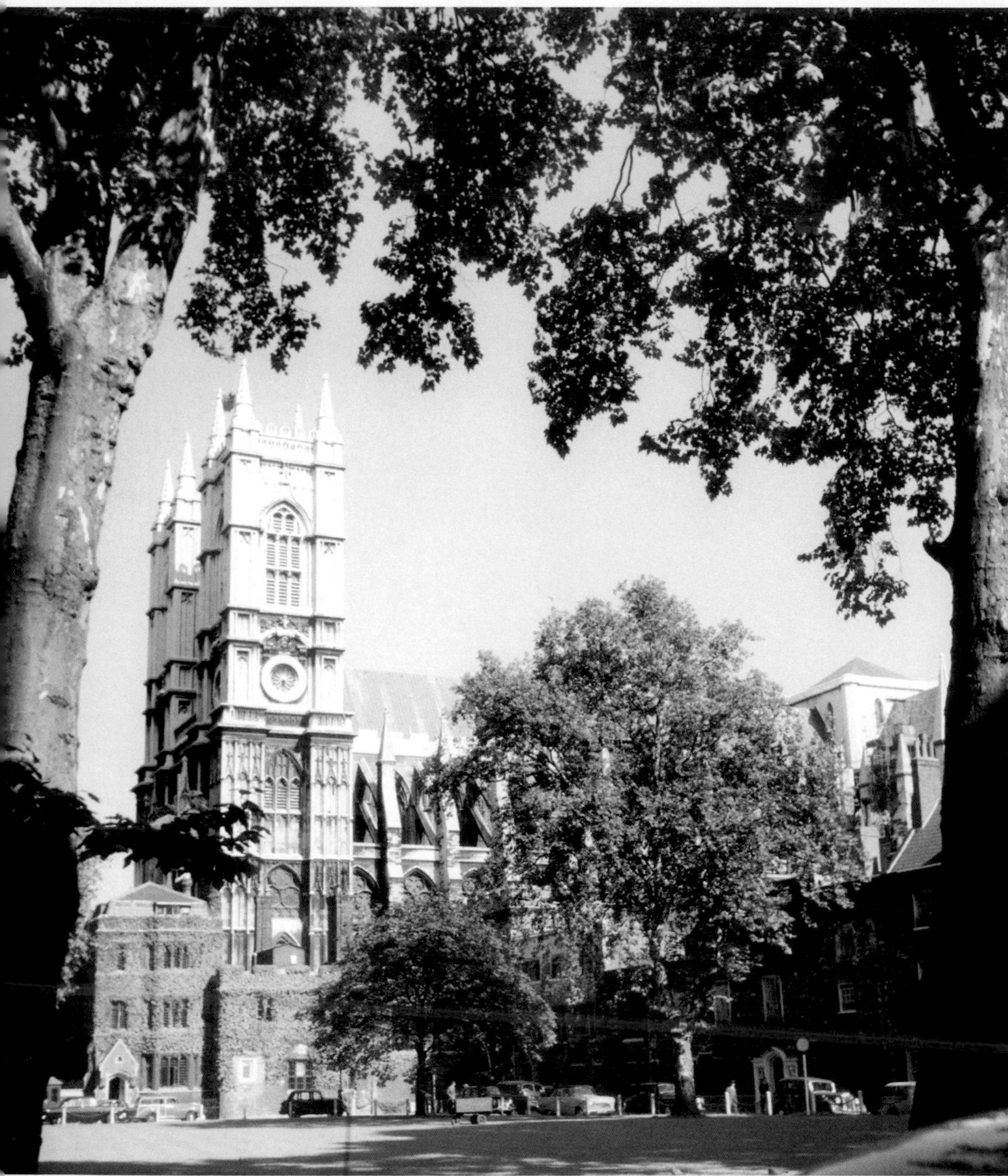

Westminster Abbey.
June, 1958

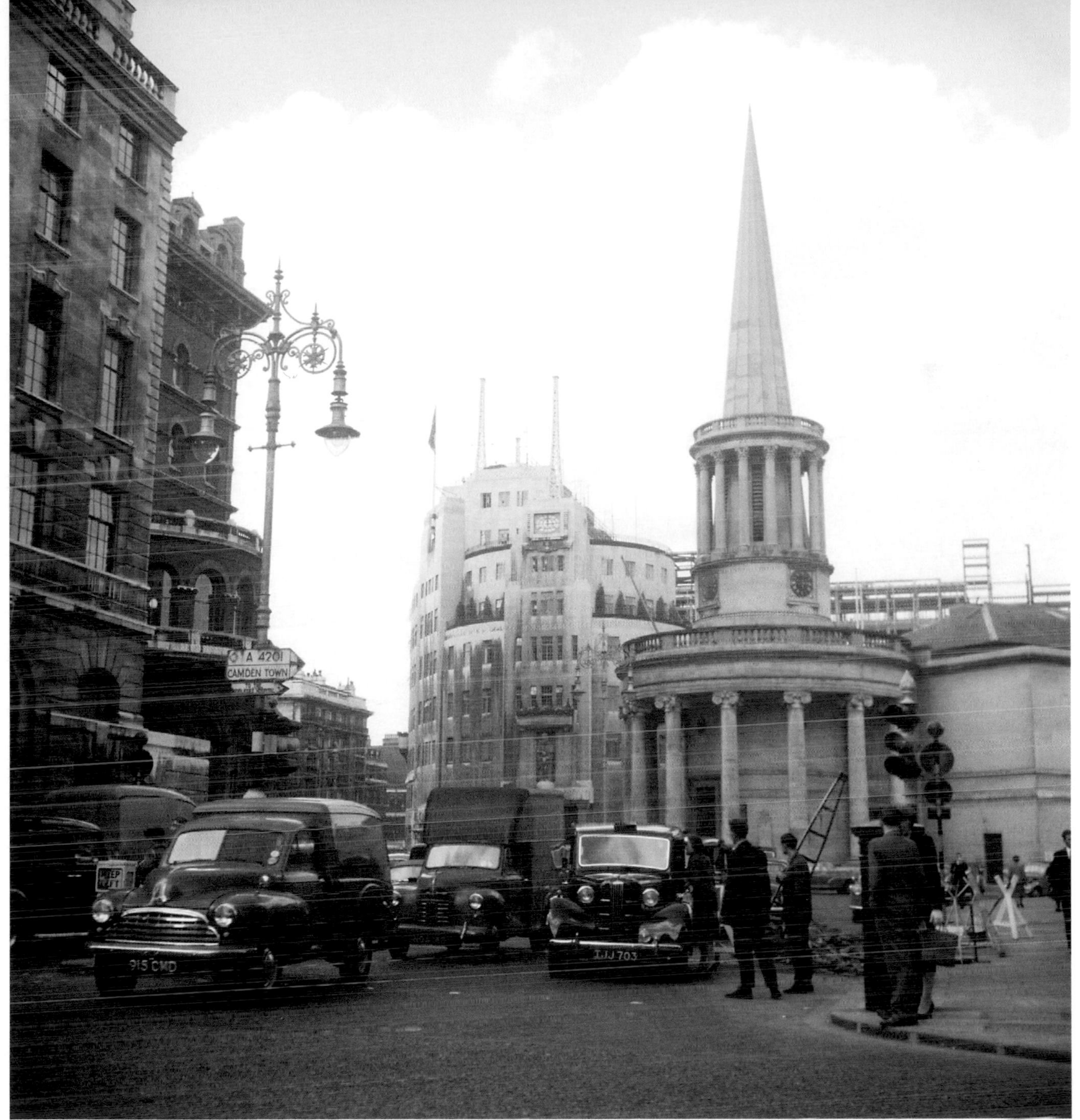
A 4201
CAMDEN TOWN
915 CMD
LJJ 703

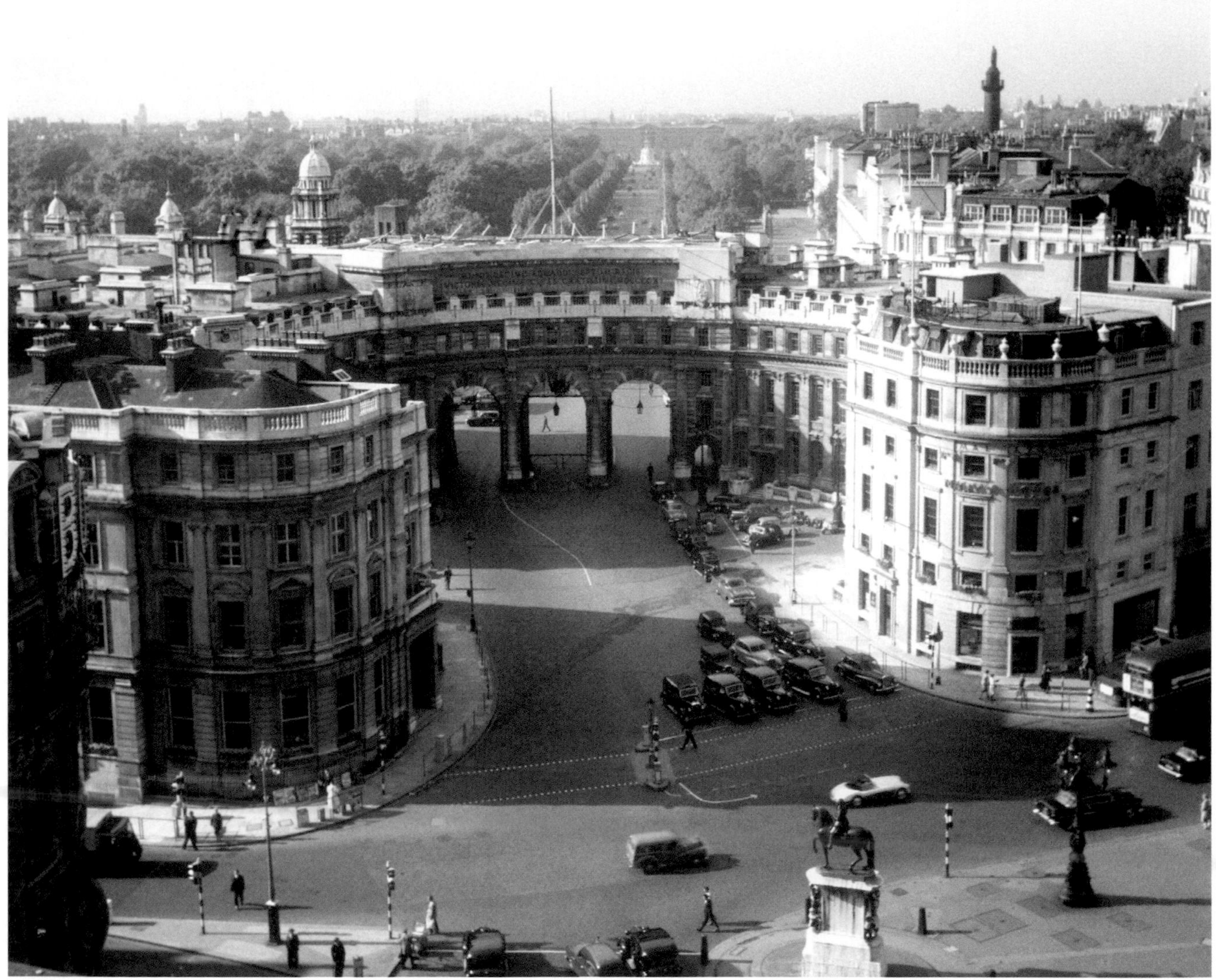

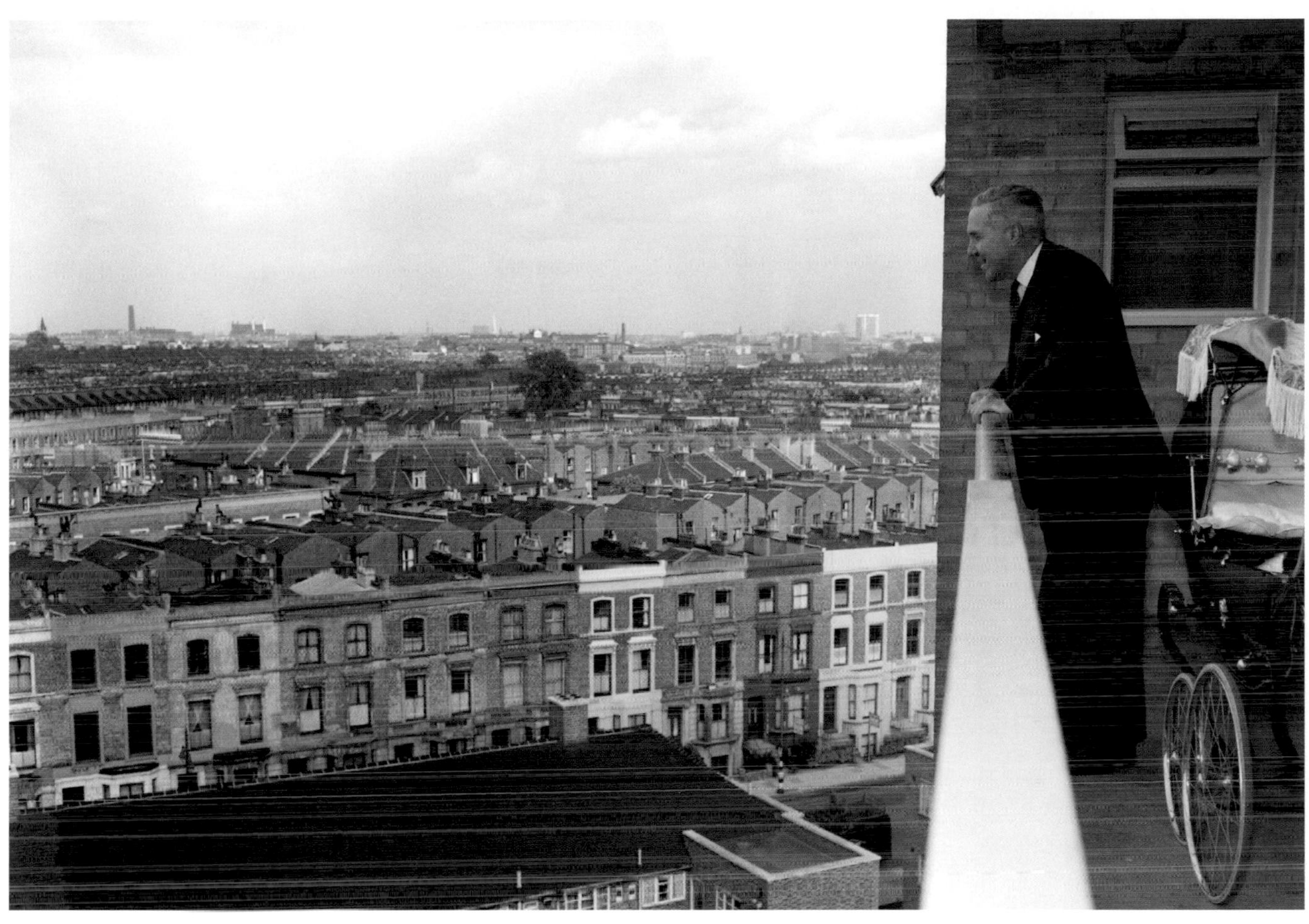

Housing Minister Henry Brooke on the 10th floor of a new block of flats in Treverton Street, Notting Hill, while inspecting rehousing and slum clearance schemes.
10th June, 1959

Facing page: Admiralty Arch and The Mall, seen from South Africa House.
June, 1959

Facing page: Victoria Station. A group of Indians were permitted to enter Britain following inquiries about their passports.
November, 1959

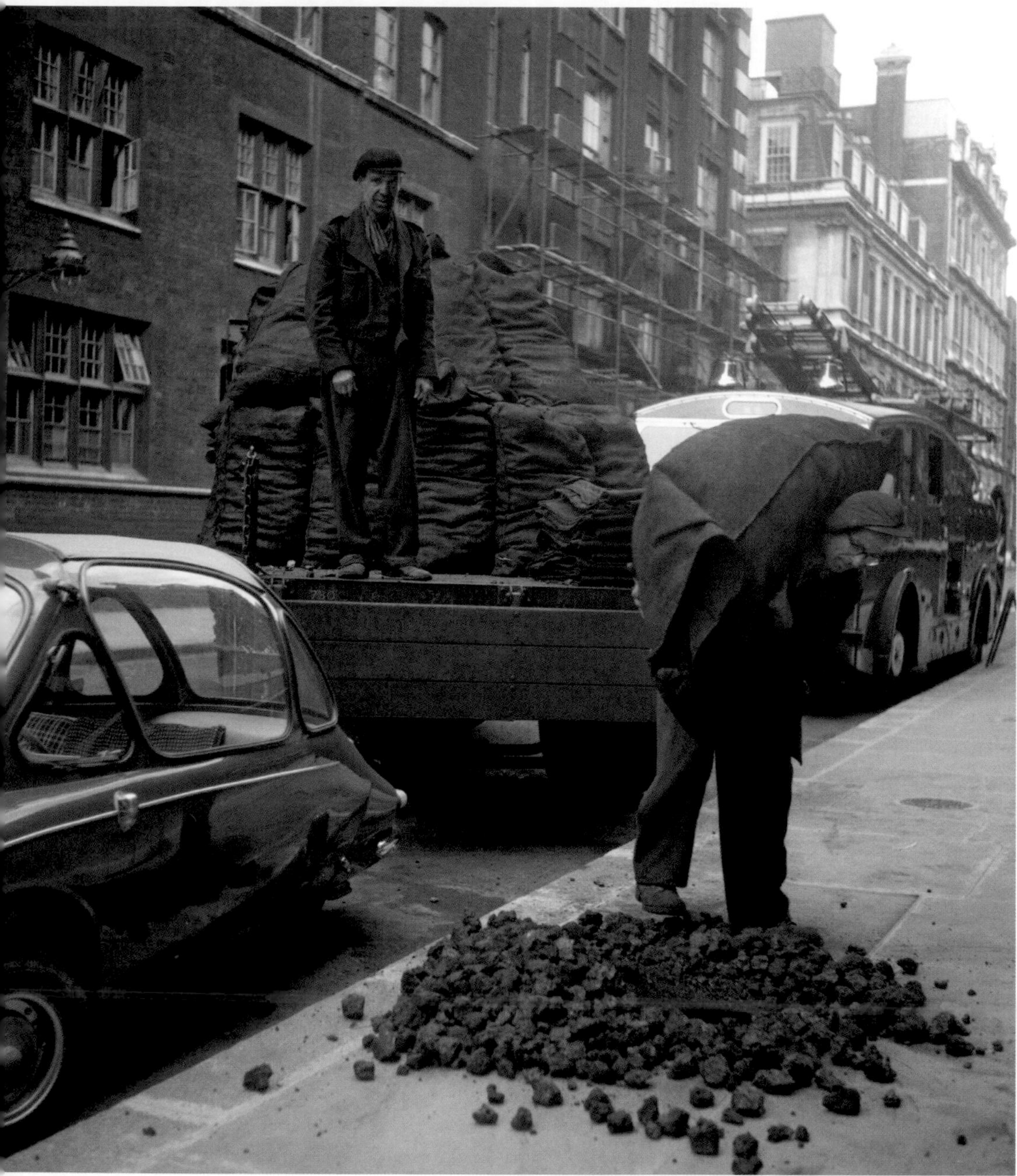

Coalmen deliver via a coalhole in a London street.
5th September, 1959

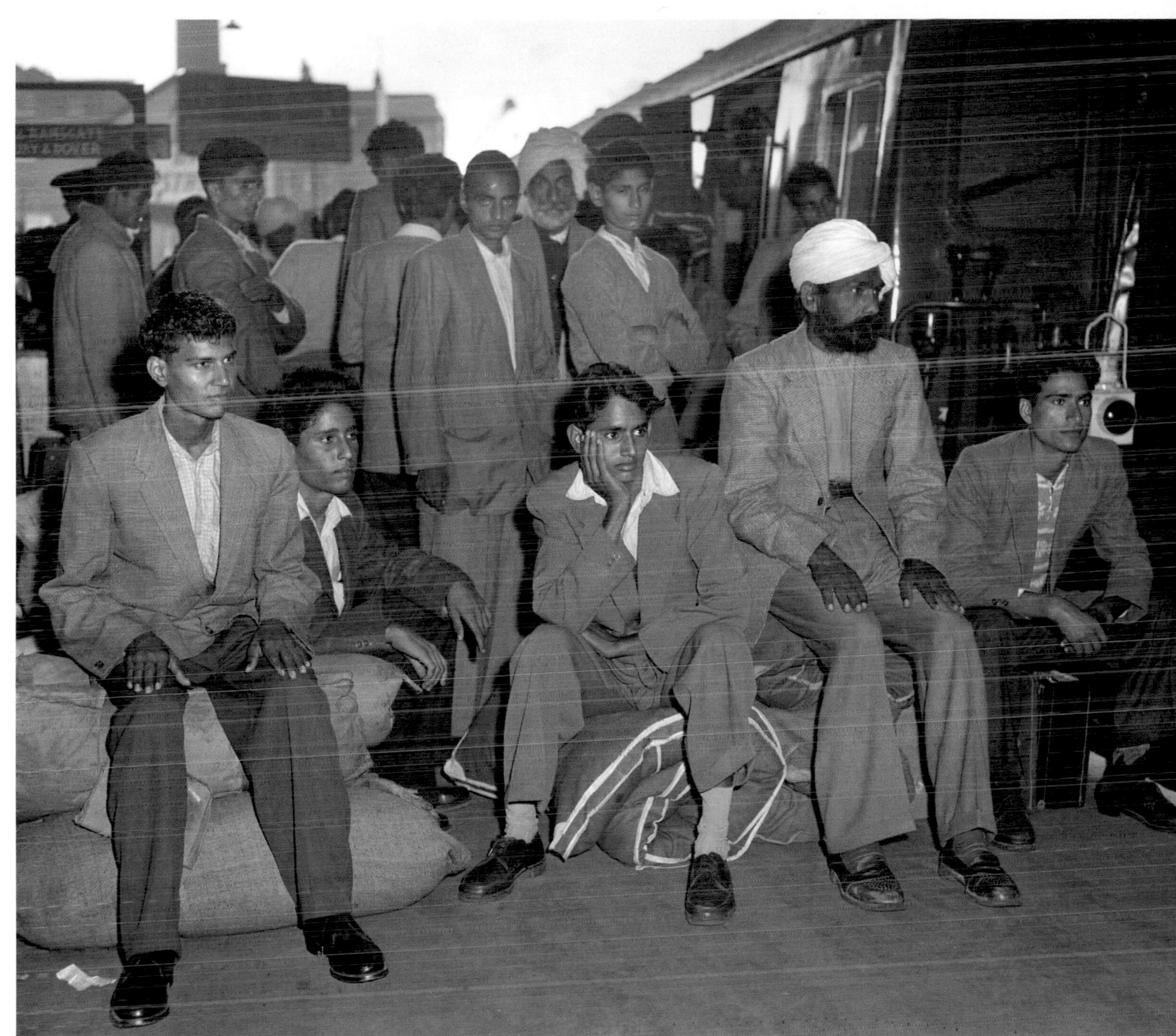

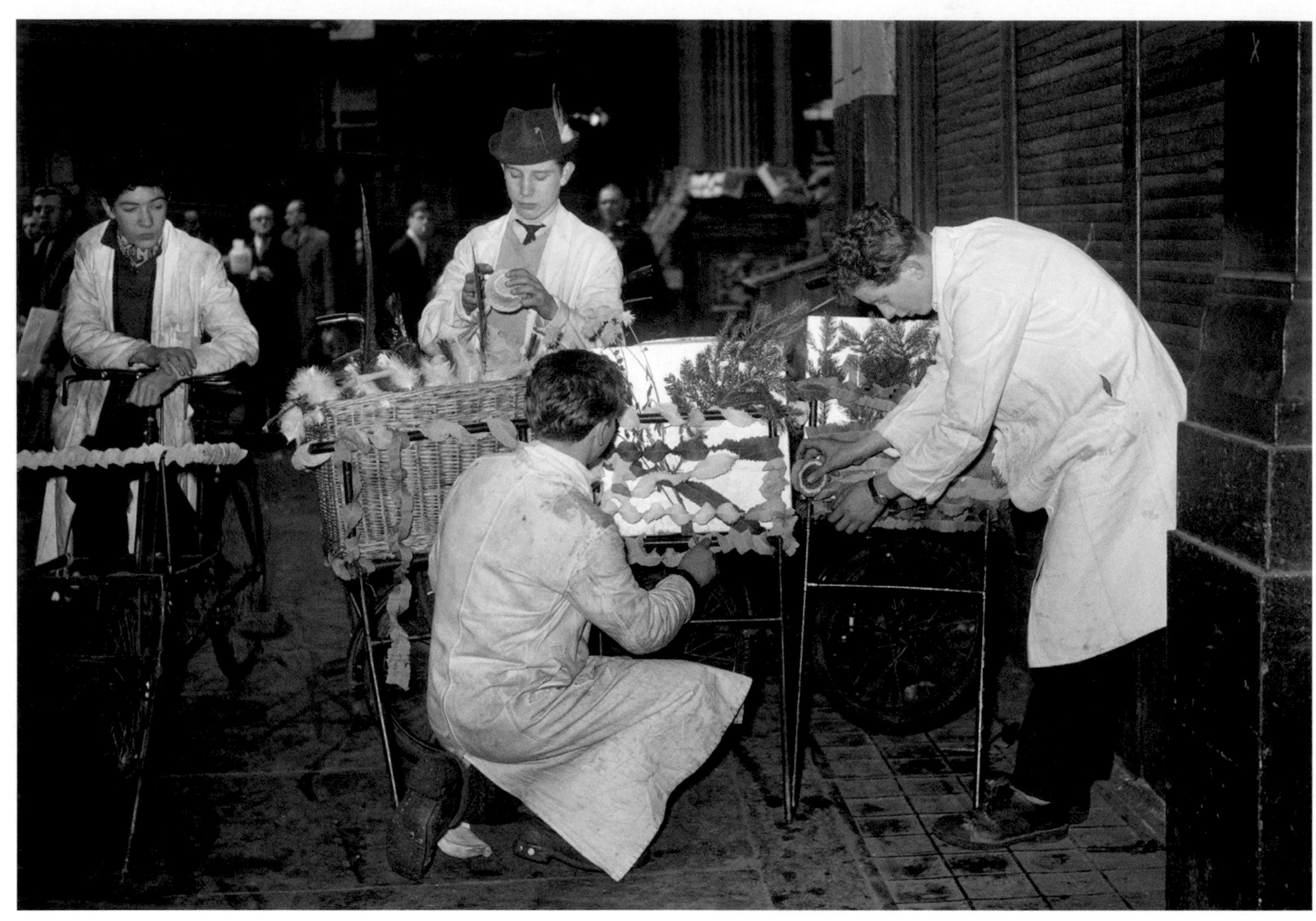

Butchers' boys decorate their delivery bicycles for Christmas.
22nd December, 1959

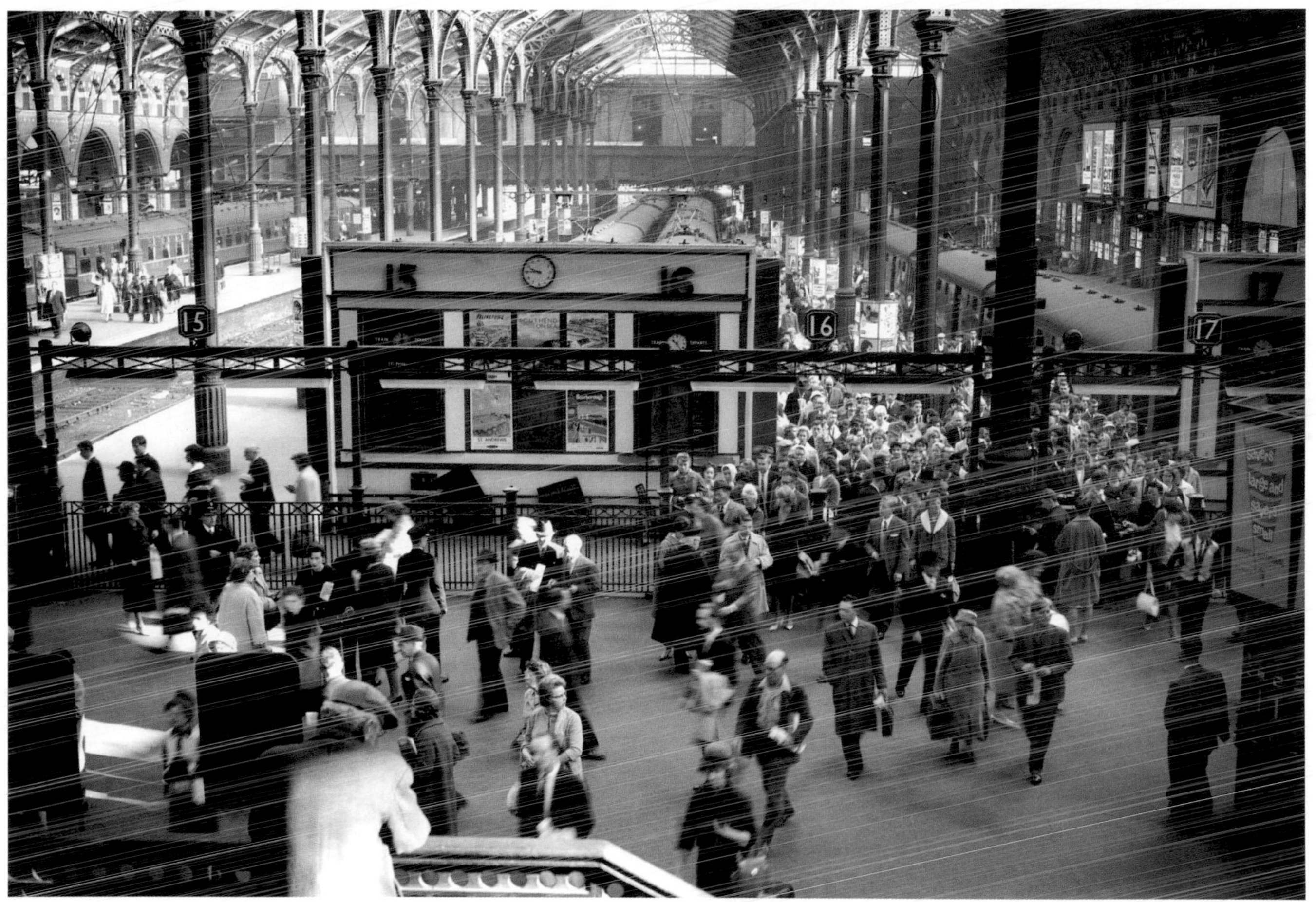

Victoria Station.
2nd October, 1962

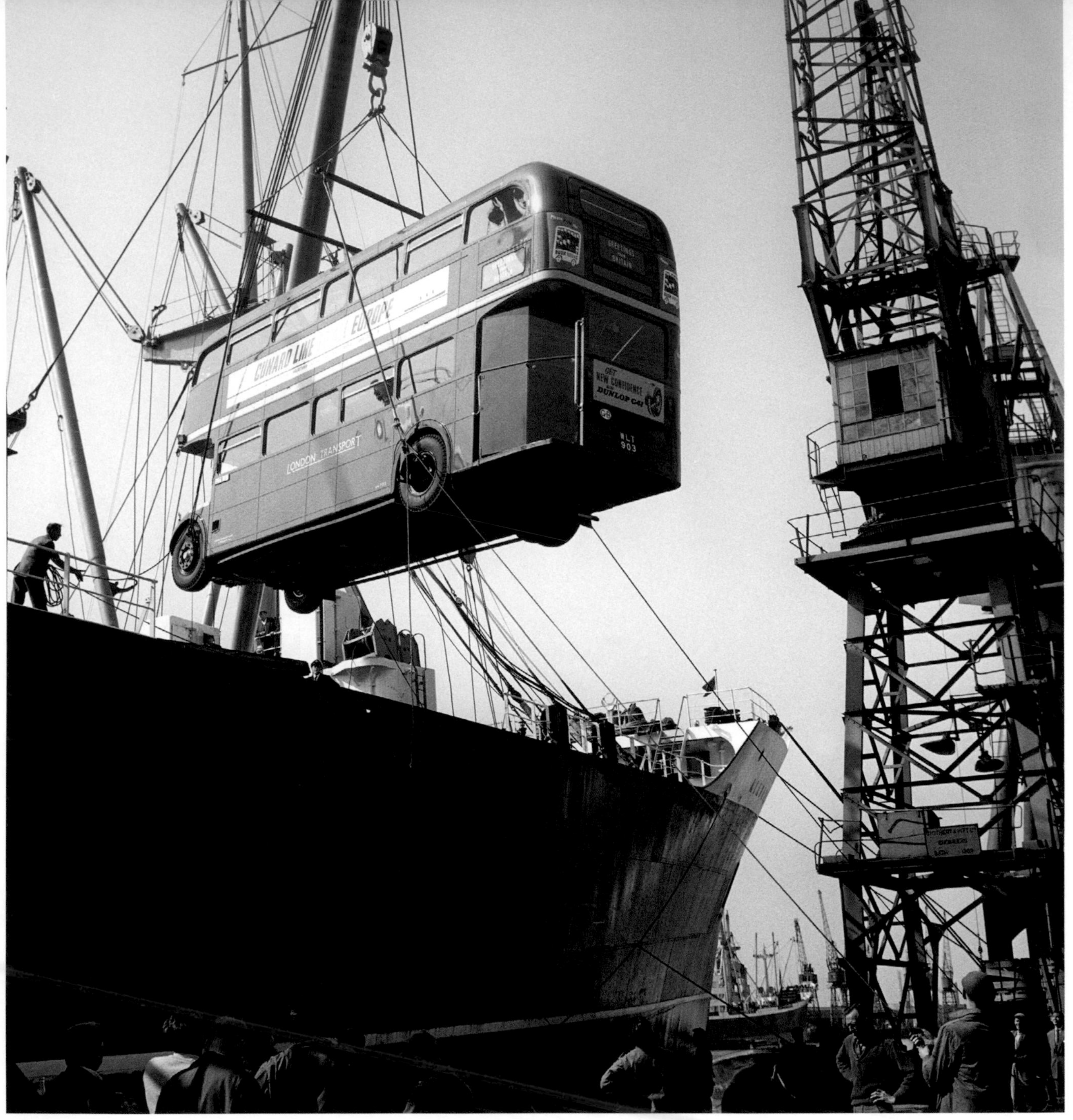
CUNARD LINE
EUROPE
LONDON TRANSPORT
WLT
903

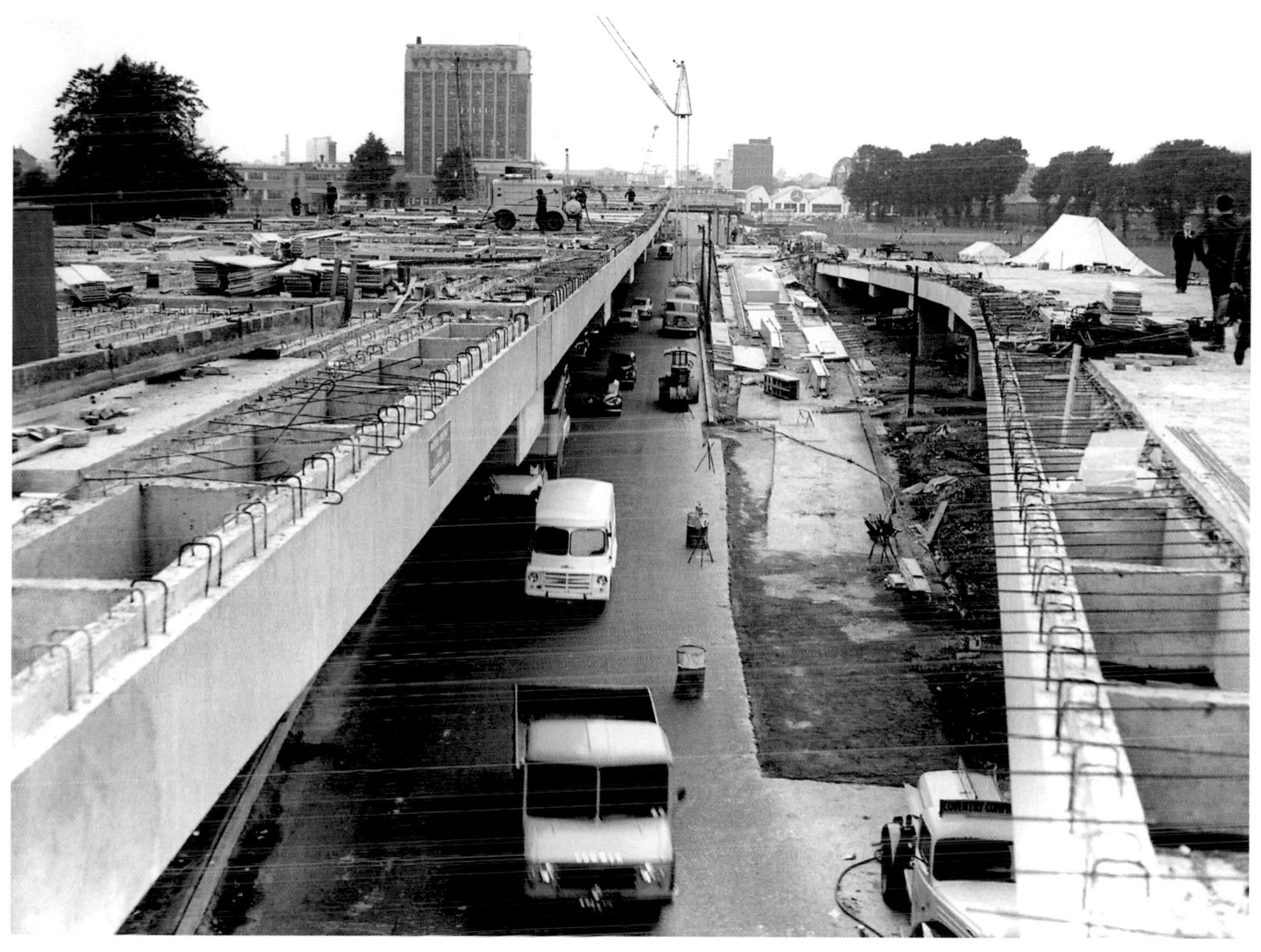

Junction 2 of the new M4 at Brentford.
4th October, 1963

Facing page: *RML 903*, one of London's latest and biggest double-decker *Routemaster* buses, is swung aboard the Cunard cargo liner *Alaunia* at King George V Dock, for a month's visit to Philadelphia's Exposition Britannia.
12th September, 1963

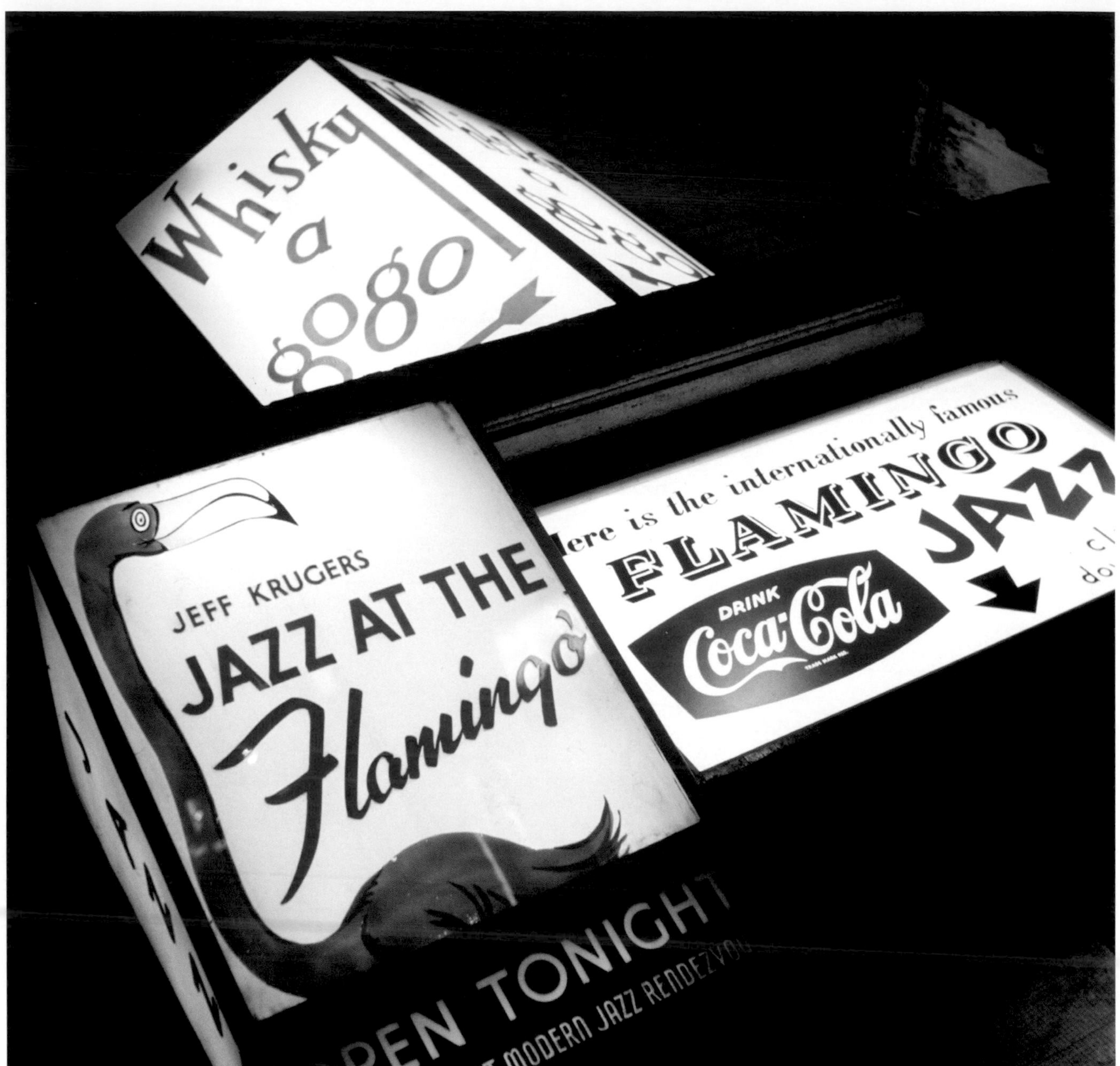
Whisky a gogo
JEFF KRUGERS
JAZZ AT THE
Flamingo
OPEN TONIGHT
MODERN JAZZ RENDEZVOU
ere is the internationally famous
FLAMINGO
DRINK
Coca-Cola
JAZZ

Facing page: Jazz at the *Flamingo* in Soho.
September, 1964

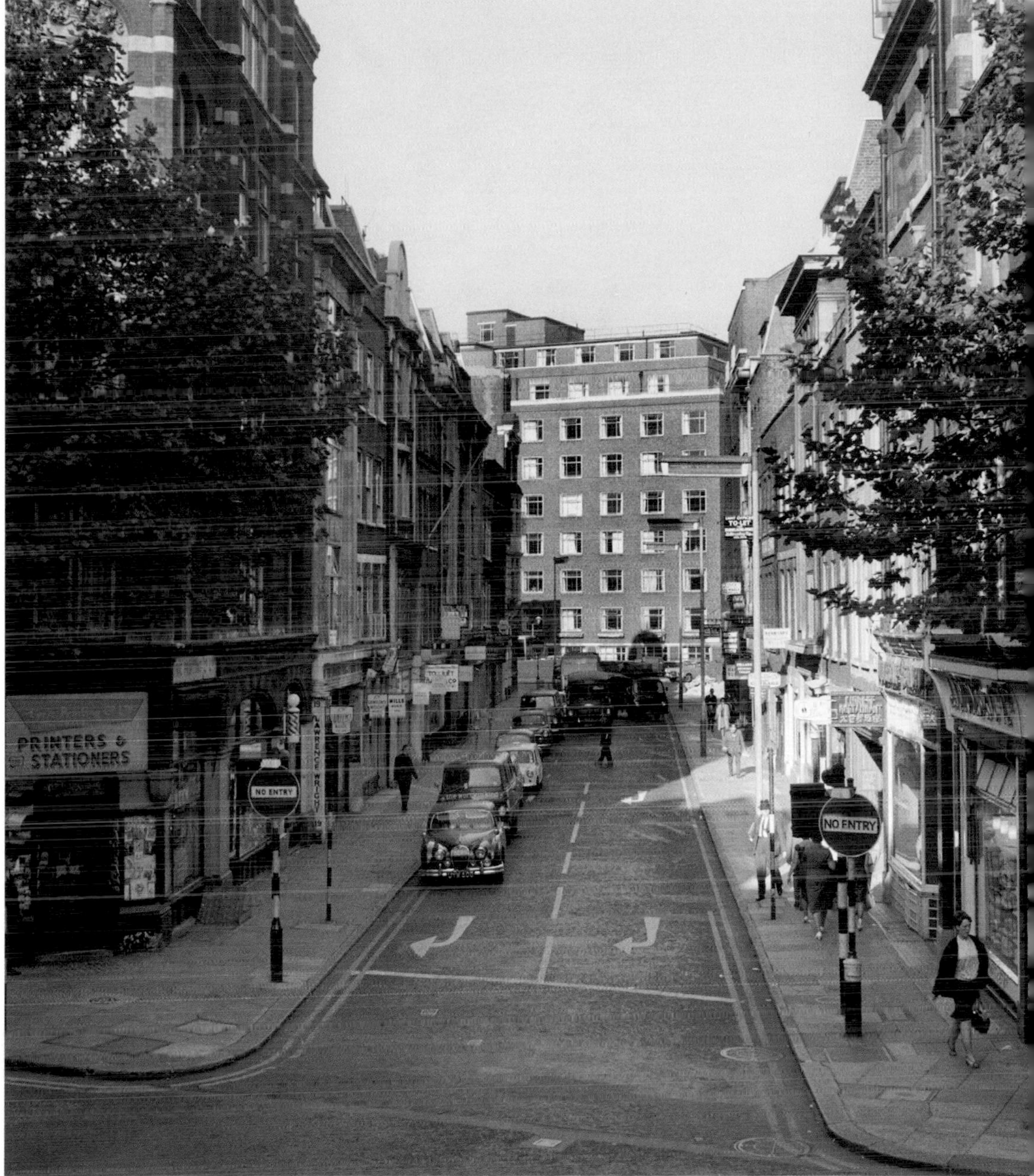

Denmark Street, home to many music publishers and an unofficial employment exchange for jobbing musicians since the 1920s.
September, 1964

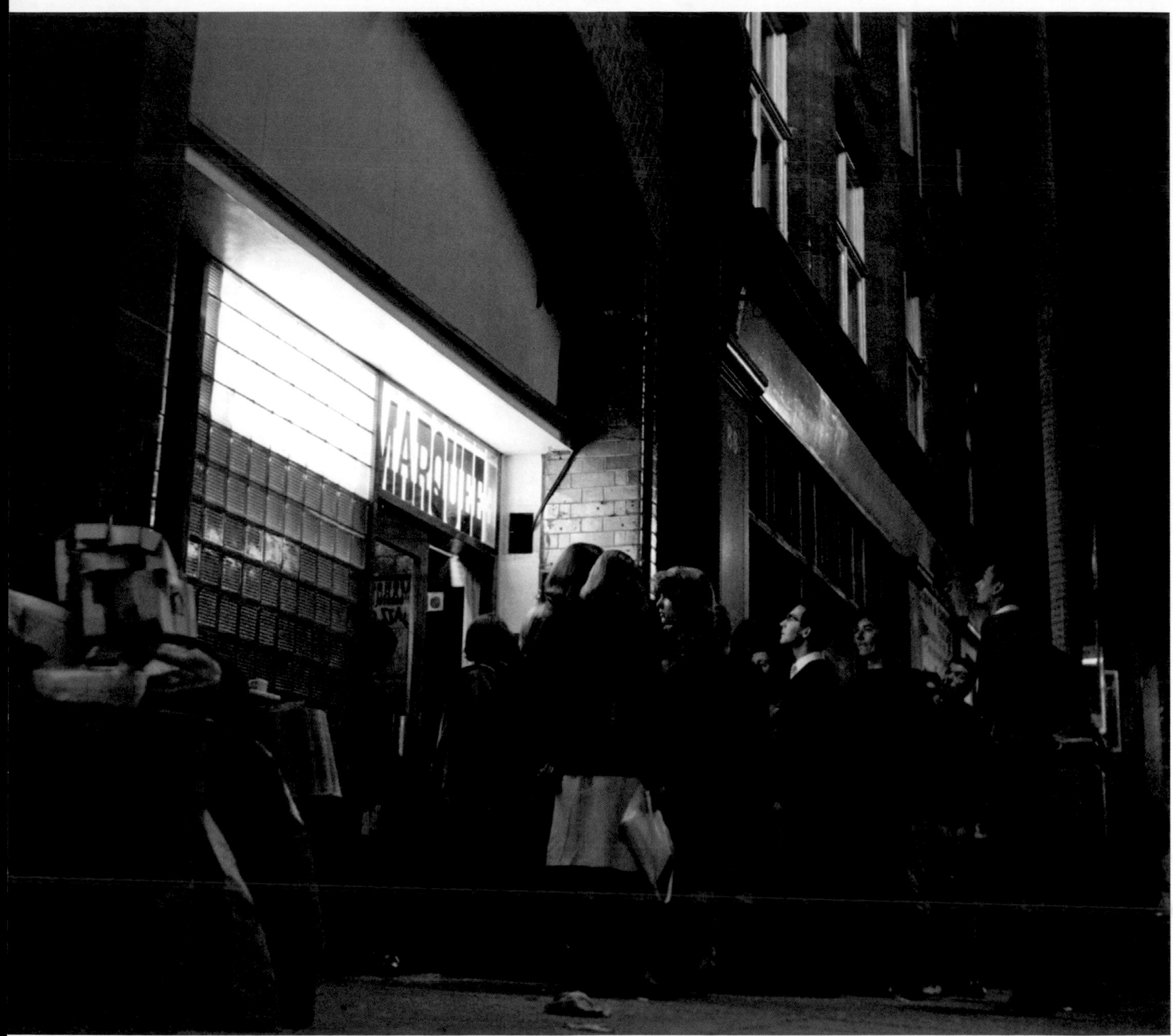
MARQUEE

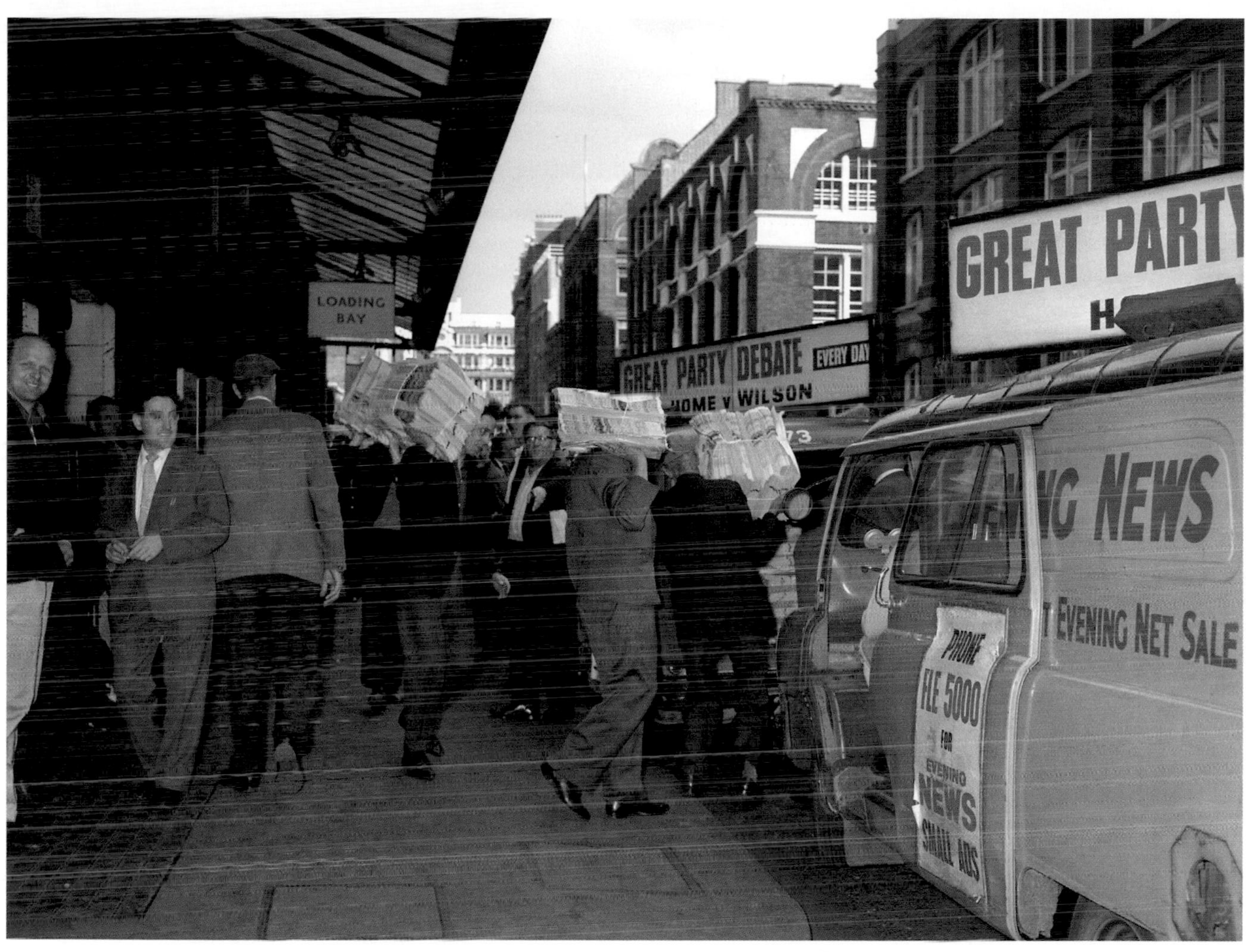

The London Evening News is loaded into delivery vans in Tudor Street.
September, 1964

In this month, groups playing at Soho's Marquee Club include The Moody Blues, The Yardbirds, Long John Baldry and Manfred Mann.
September, 1964

Facing page: Life on the Underground.
1965

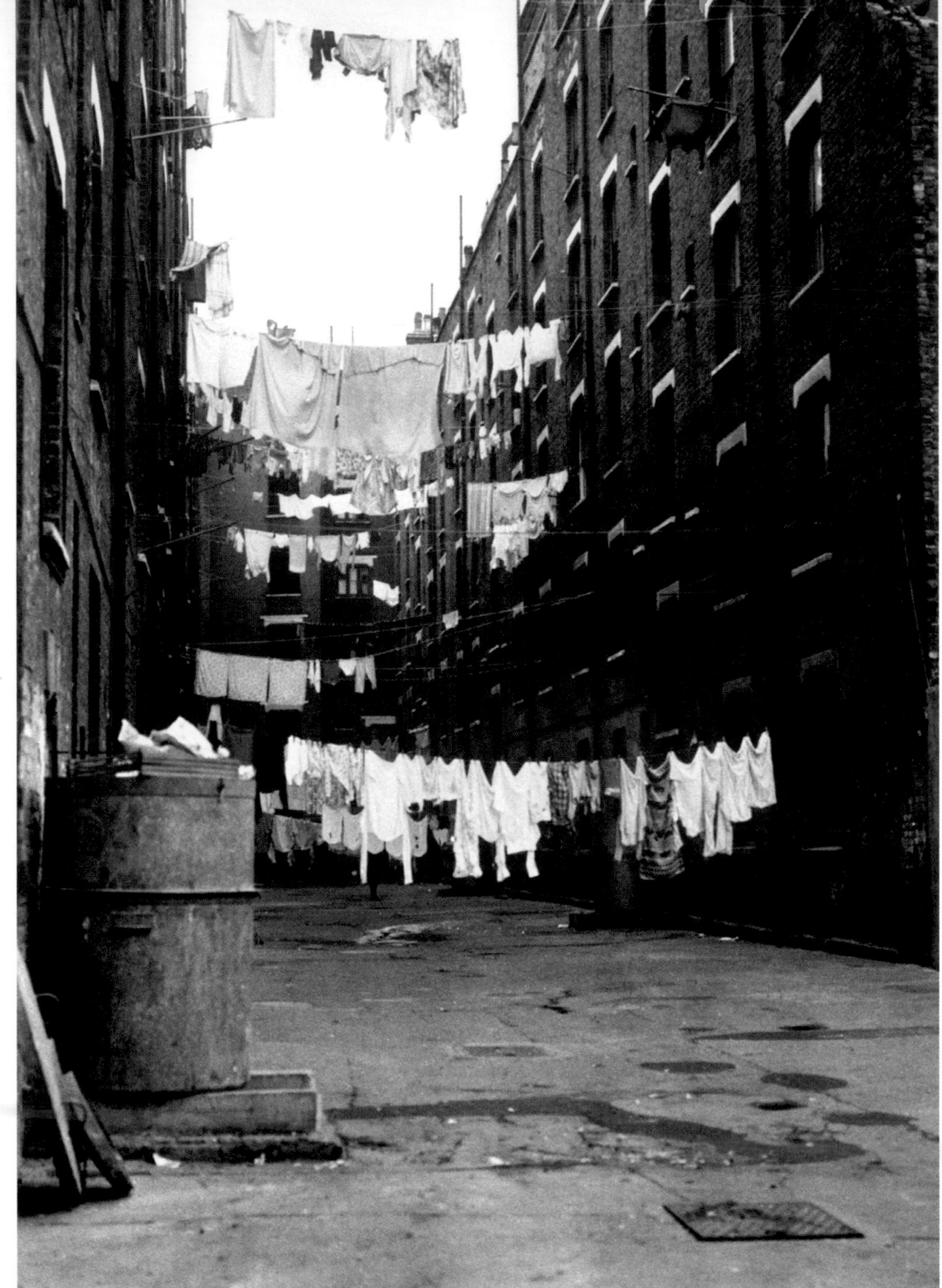

Slum tenements in Southwark.
1965

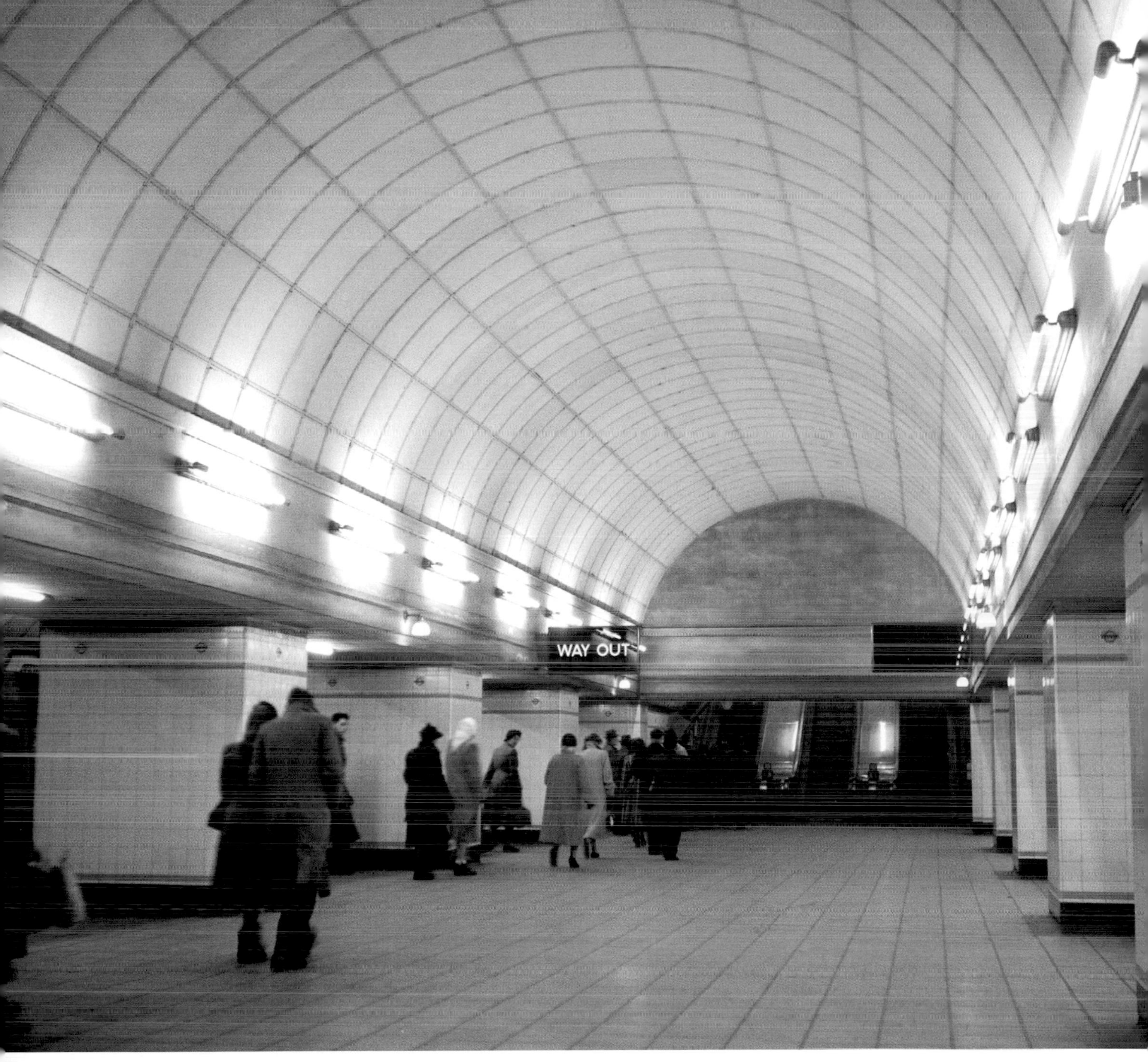
WAY OUT

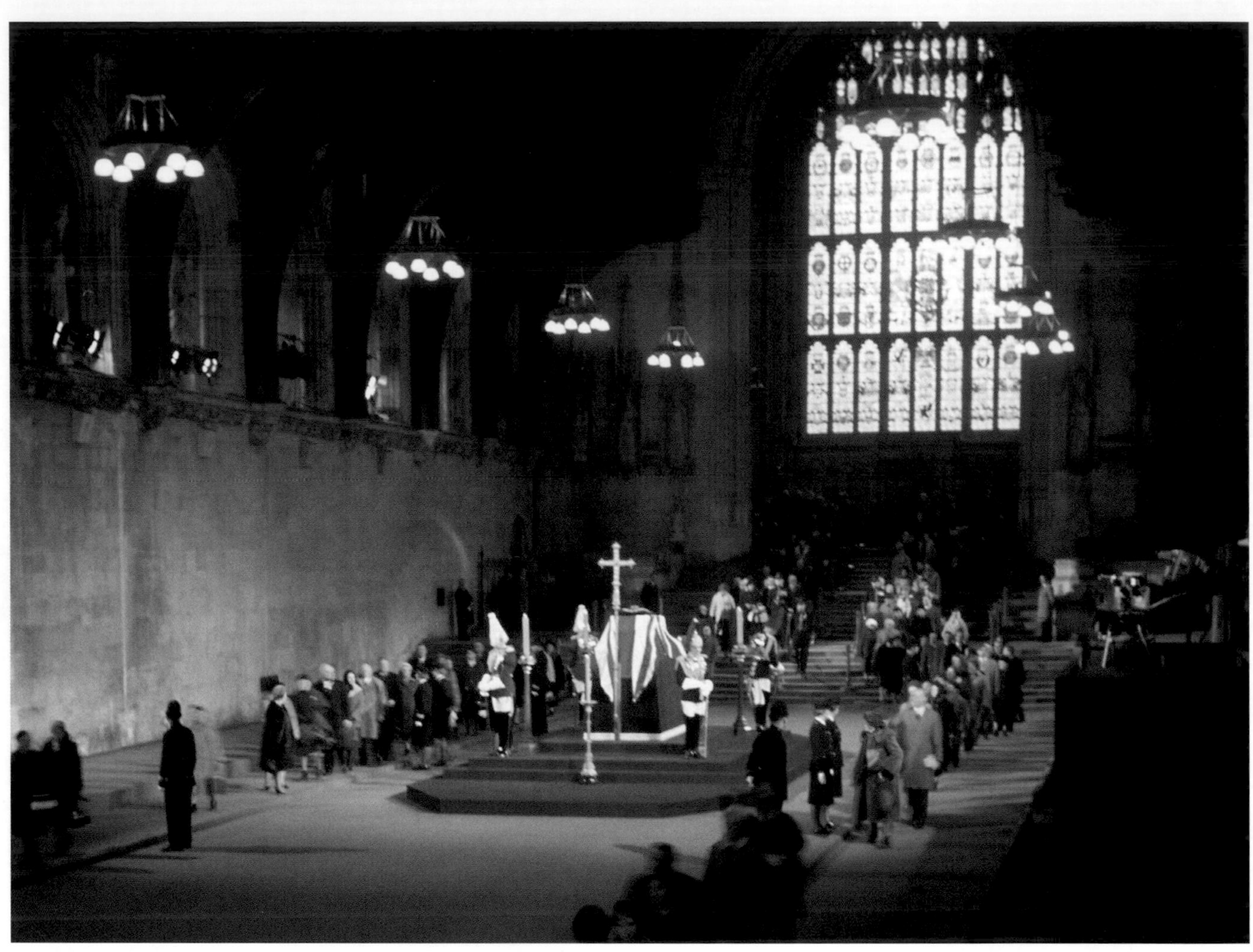

Officers of the Household Cavalry stand guard over the coffin of Sir Winston Churchill in Westminster Abbey.
27th January, 1965

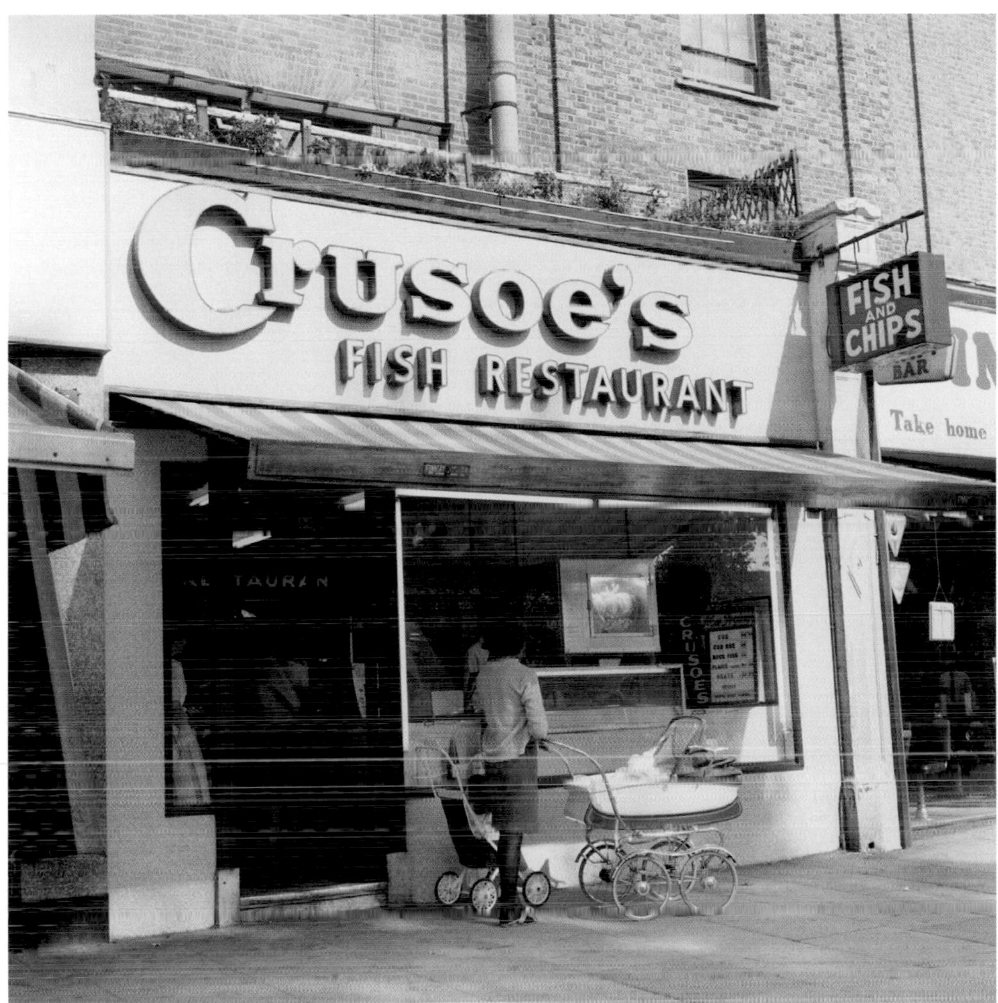

Fish and chips on the Uxbridge Road.
9th September, 1965

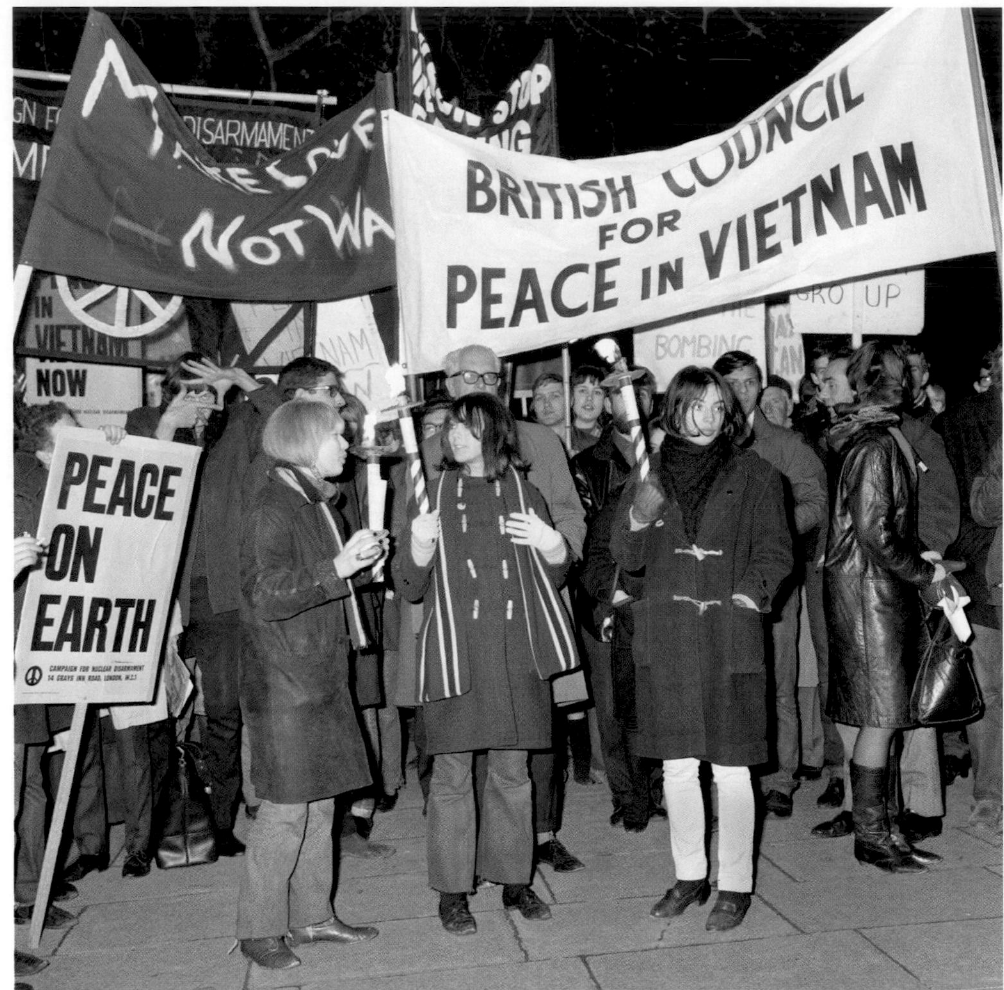

Marchers call on the US government to end the war in Vietnam. Subsequent demonstrations would be less peaceful.
27th November, 1965

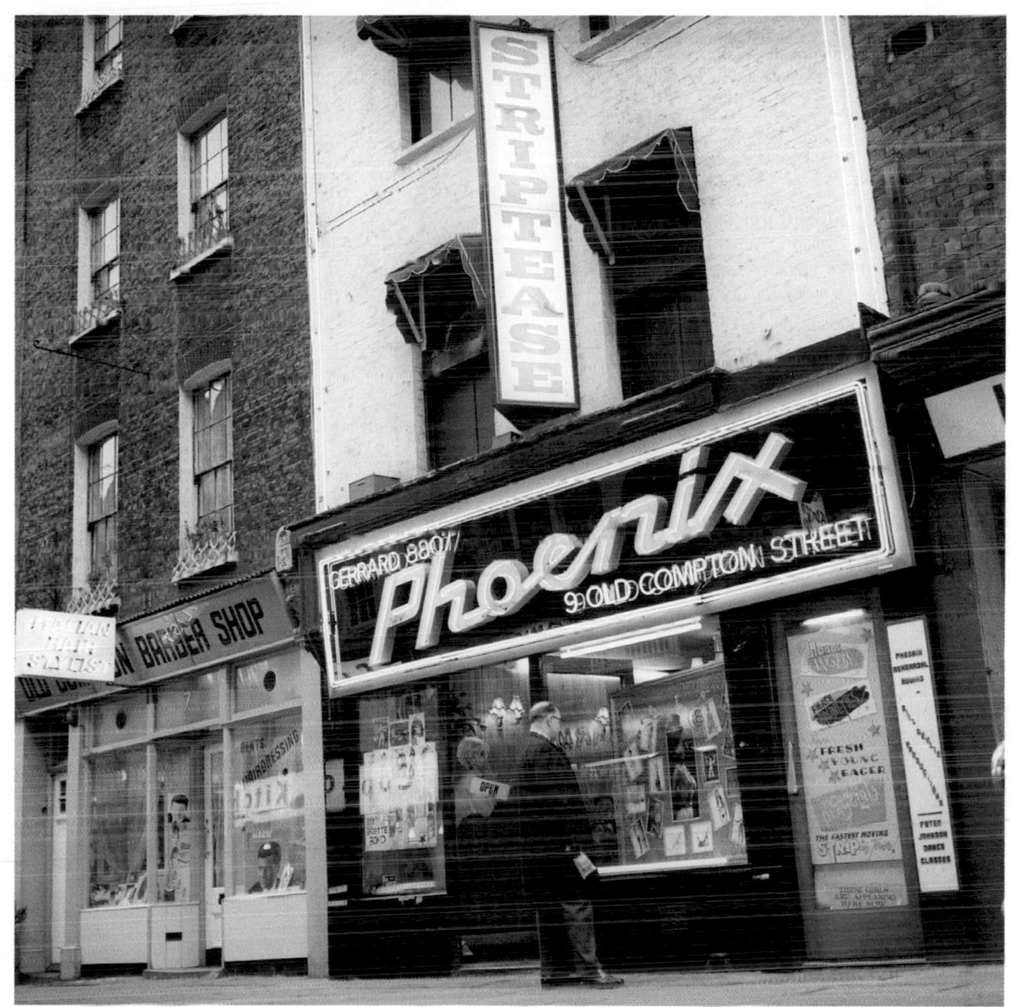

The *Phoenix* strip club in Old Compton Street.
15th March, 1966

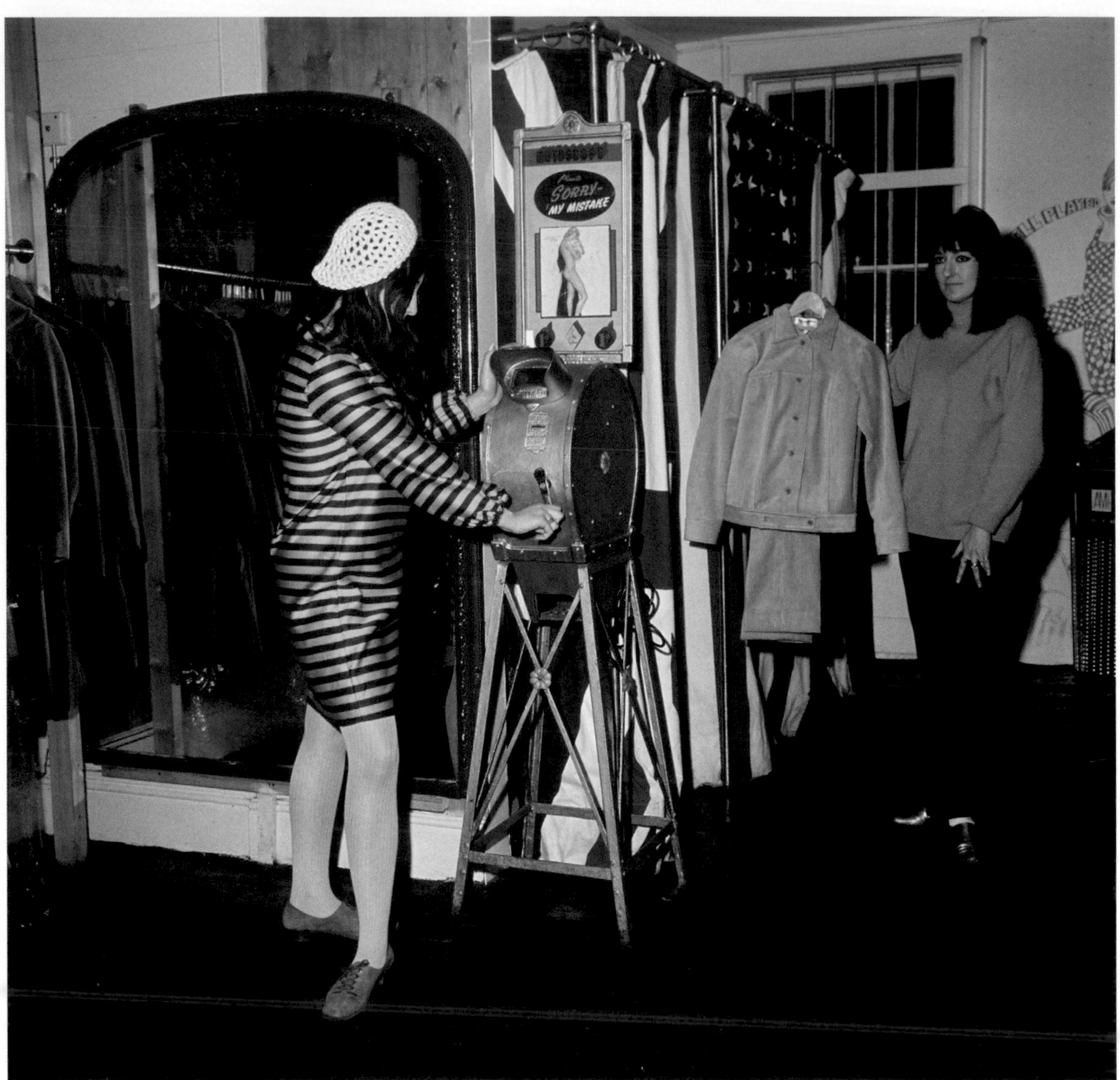
SORRY-
'MY MISTAKE

Facing page: Swinging London: Pauline Fordham's boutique in Ganton Street, off Carnaby Street.
April, 1966

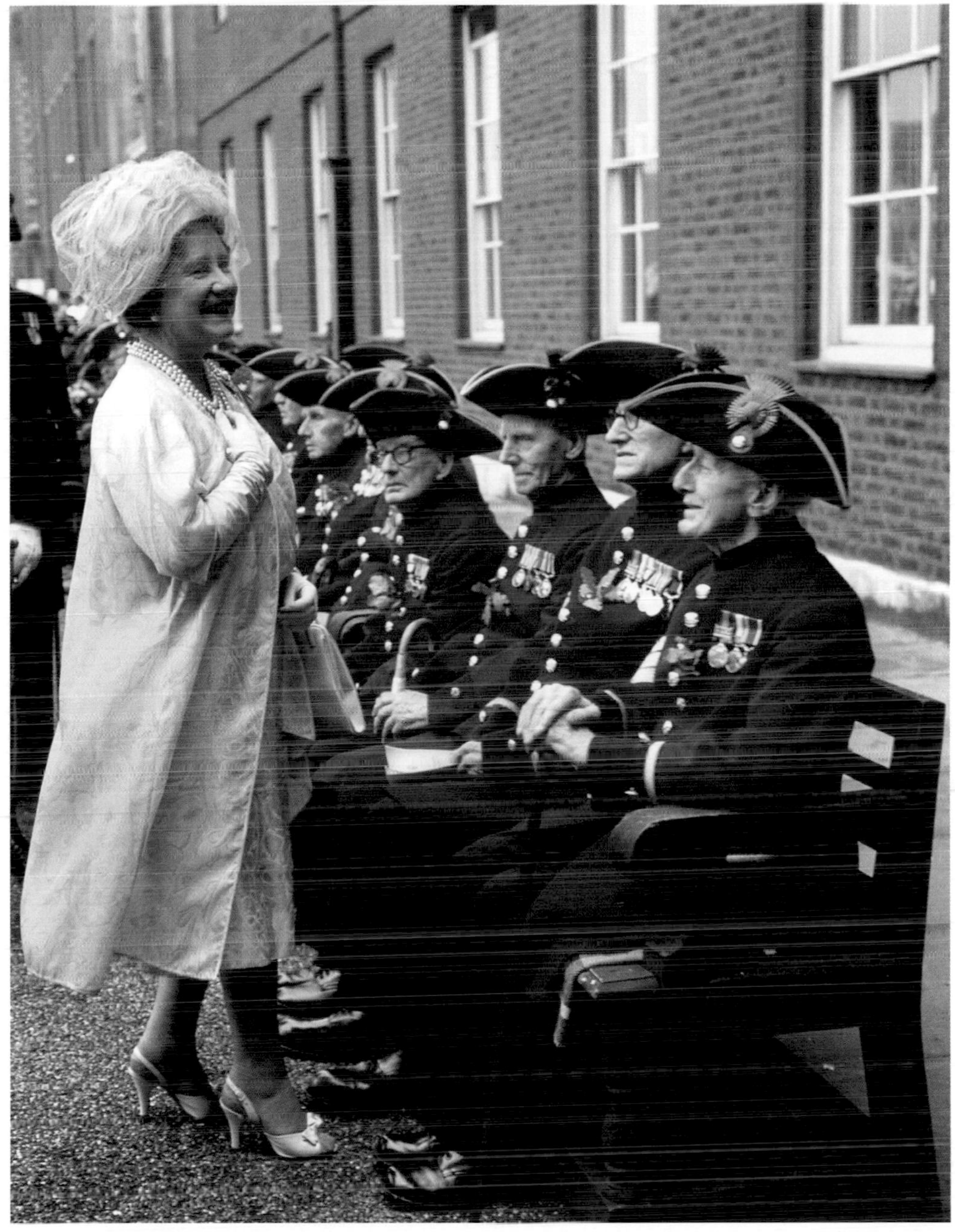

The Queen Mother talks to Boer War veterans among Chelsea pensioners at Founder's Day, Chelsea Hospital.
10th June, 1966

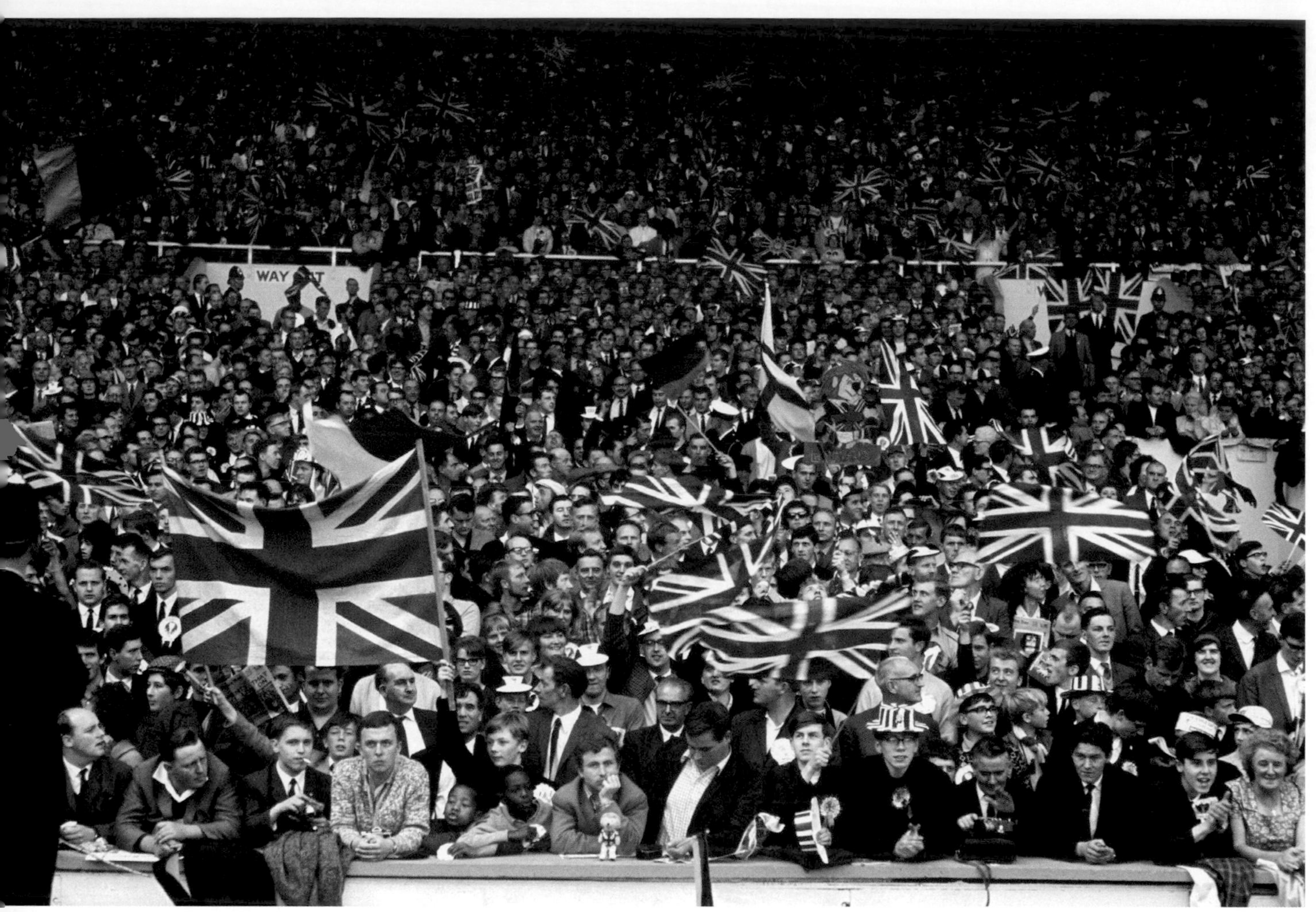

England fans struggle to control their excitement at the World Cup Final.
30th July, 1966

Facing page: Inside the new Elephant and Castle shopping centre. During the 1980s the building was painted shocking pink in an attempt to 'brighten it up'.
13th March, 1967

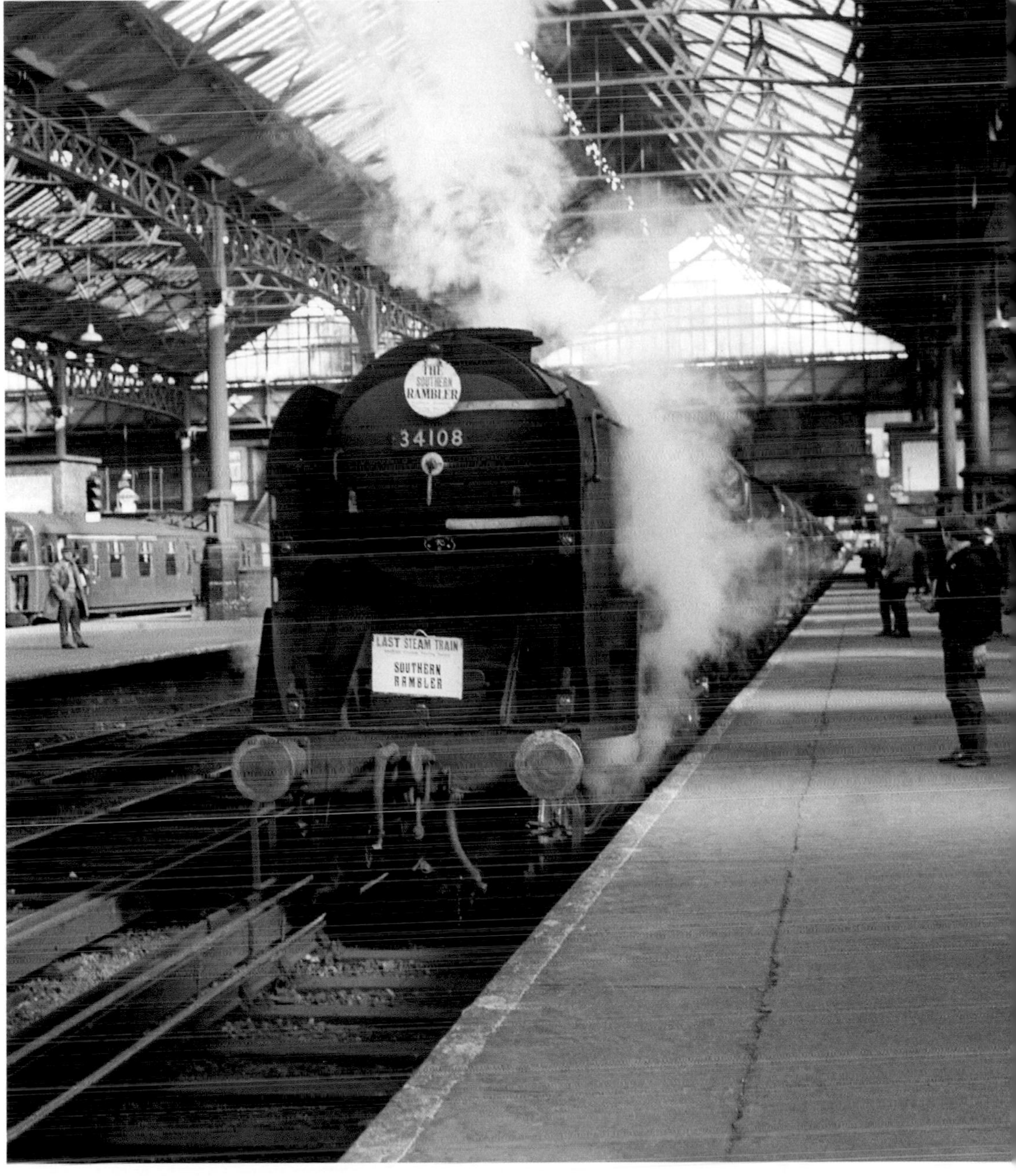

Wincanton, the last steam locomotive to leave Victoria Station for Brighton and Eastbourne.
19th March, 1967

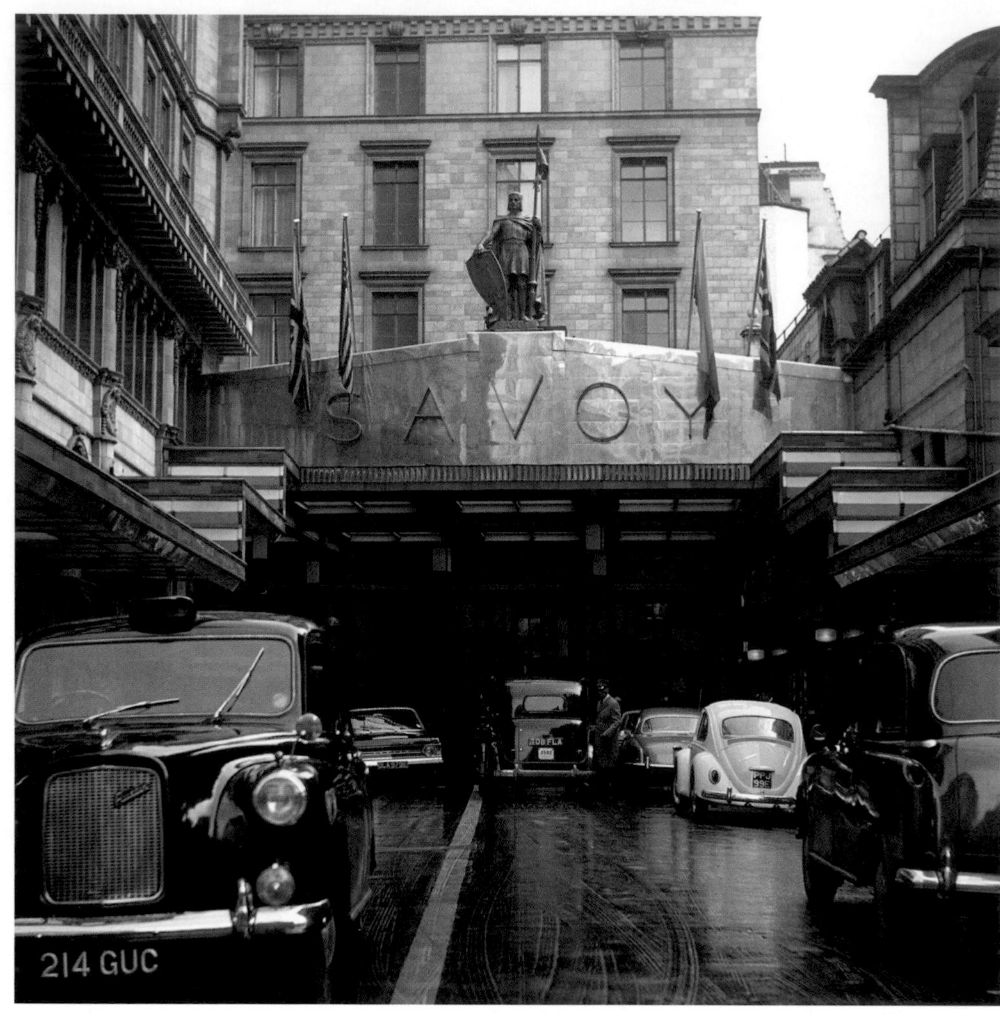

The Savoy Hotel.
22nd May, 1967

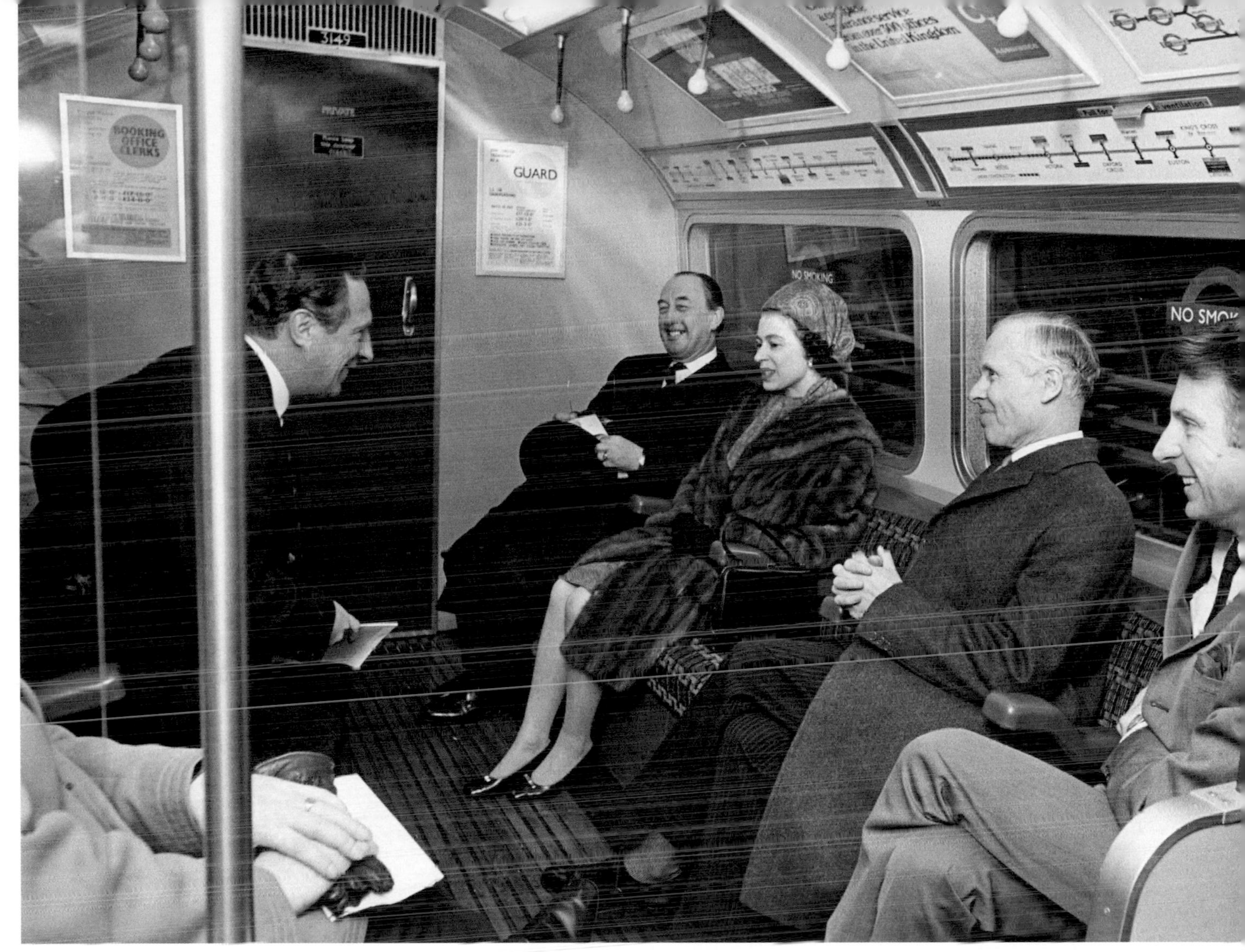

The Queen takes the tube to the opening ceremony for the new Victoria Line. It is the first time a reigning monarch has ridden on the Underground.
7th March, 1969

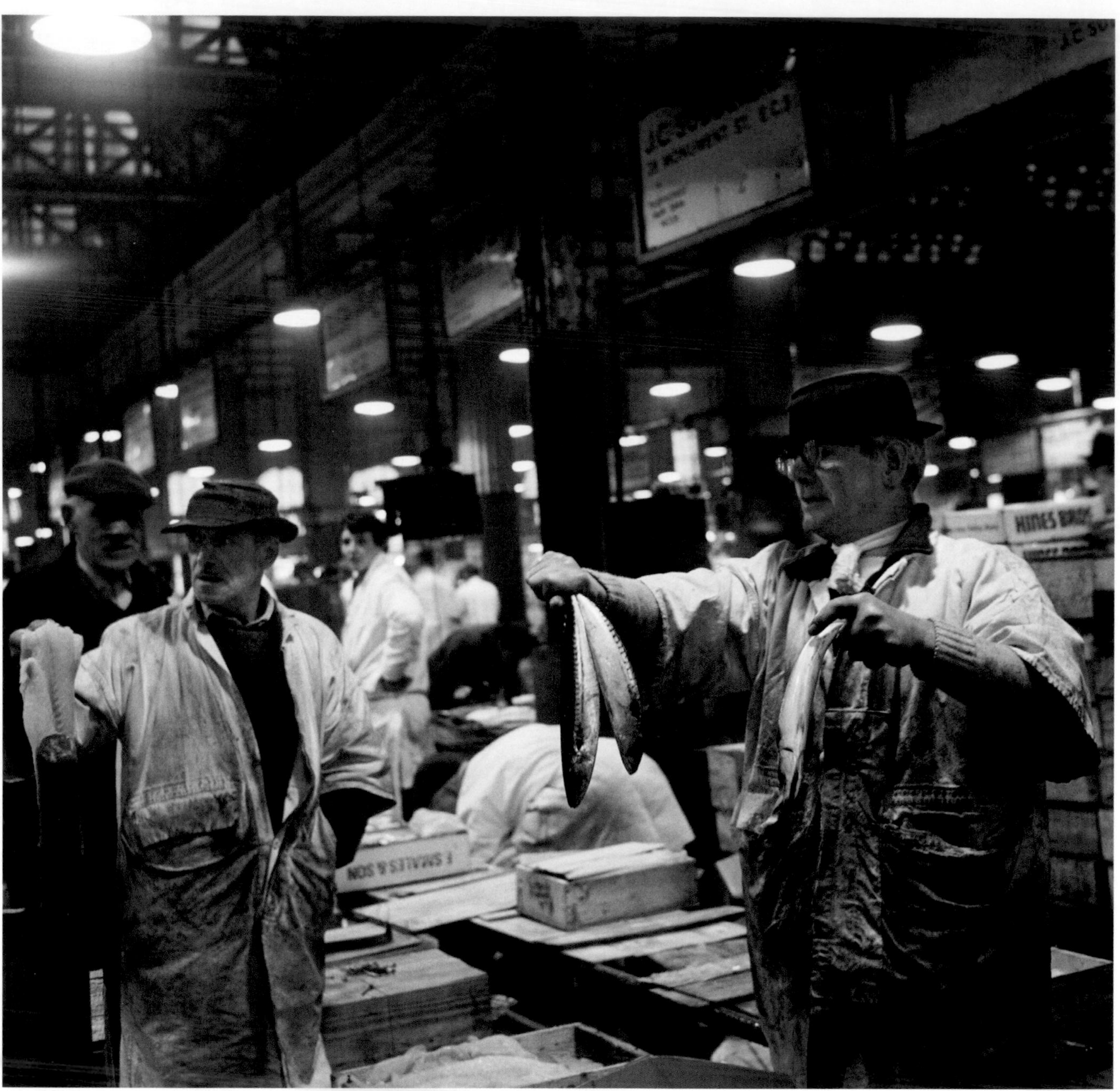
HINES BROS

Facing page: Billingsgate fish market.
8th December, 1969

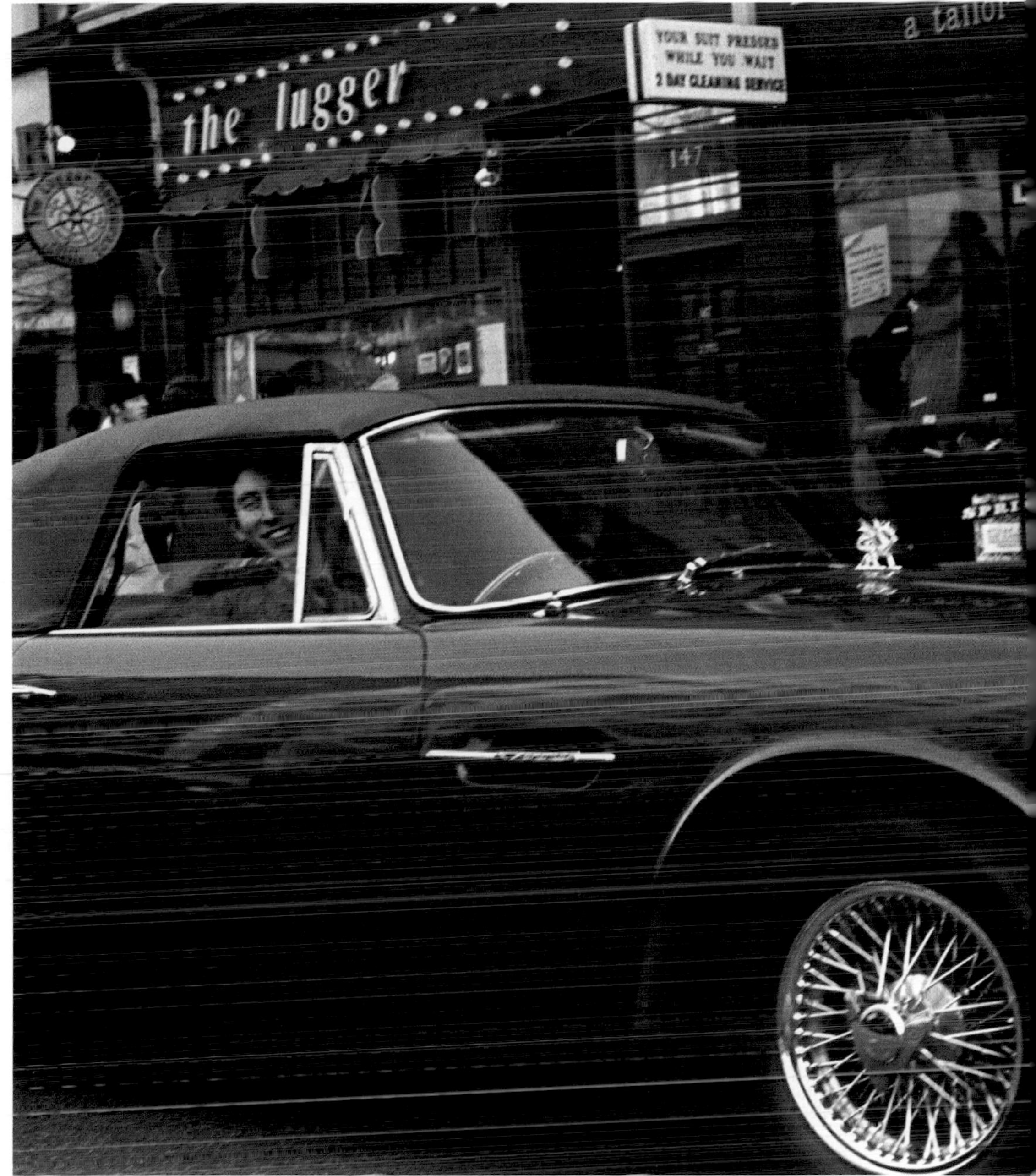

The Prince of Wales at the wheel of his Aston Martin *DB6* convertible, on the Strand after visiting the Press Association in Fleet Street.
4th February, 1971

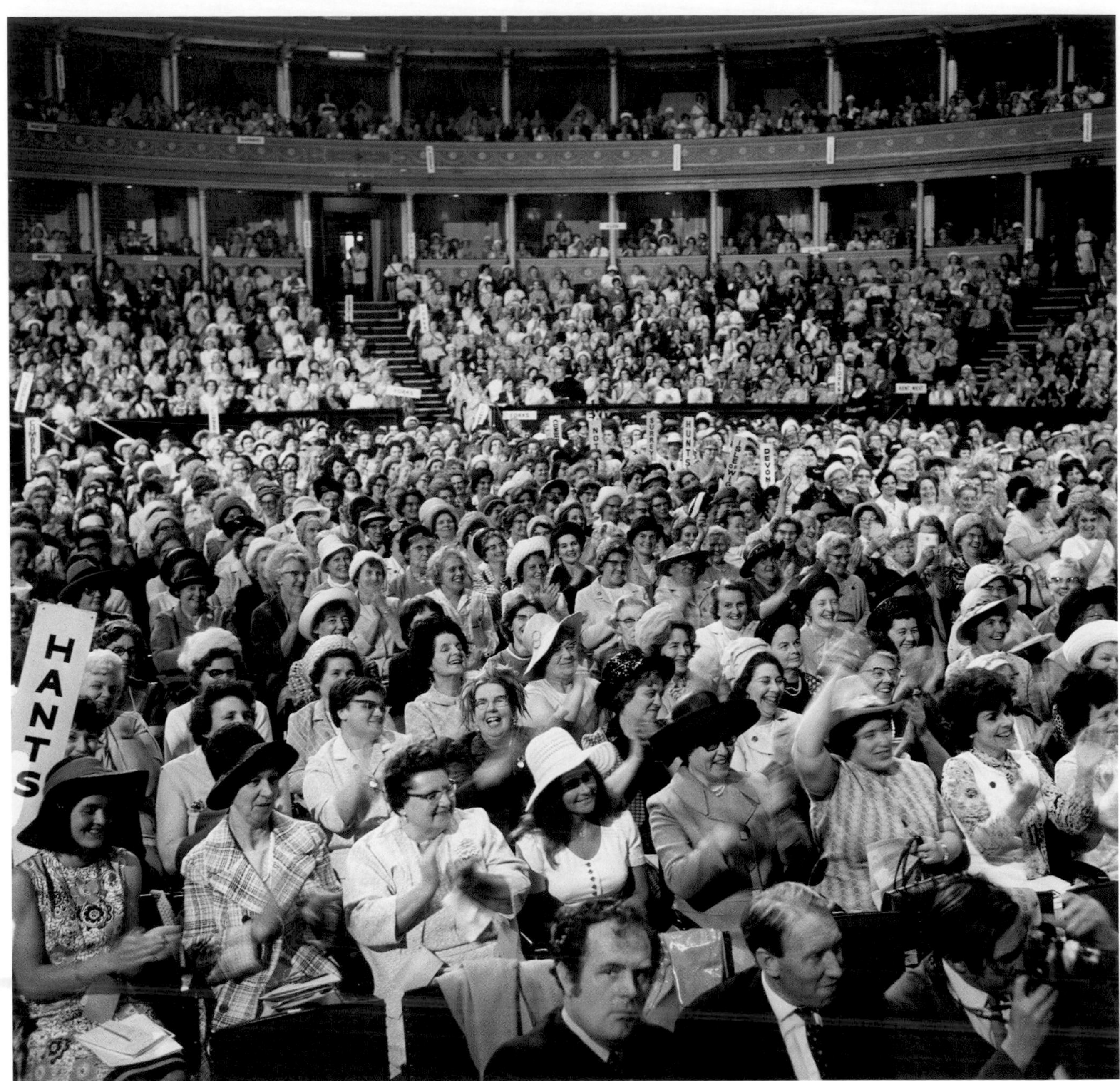
HANTS

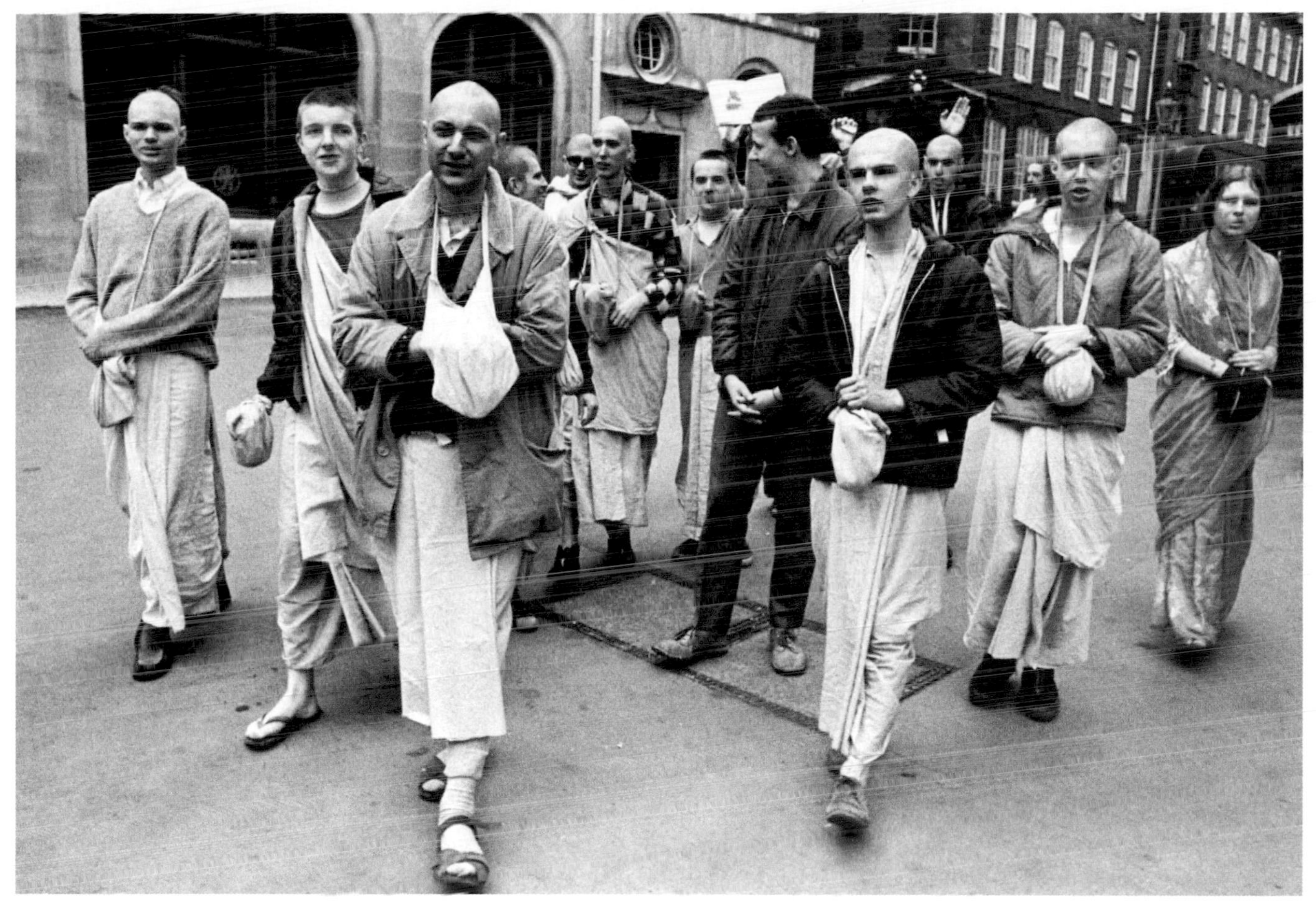

Devotees of Hare Krishna.
1971

Facing page: The 50th traditional Annual General Meeting of the National Federation of Women's Institutes, at the Royal Albert Hall.
8th June, 1971

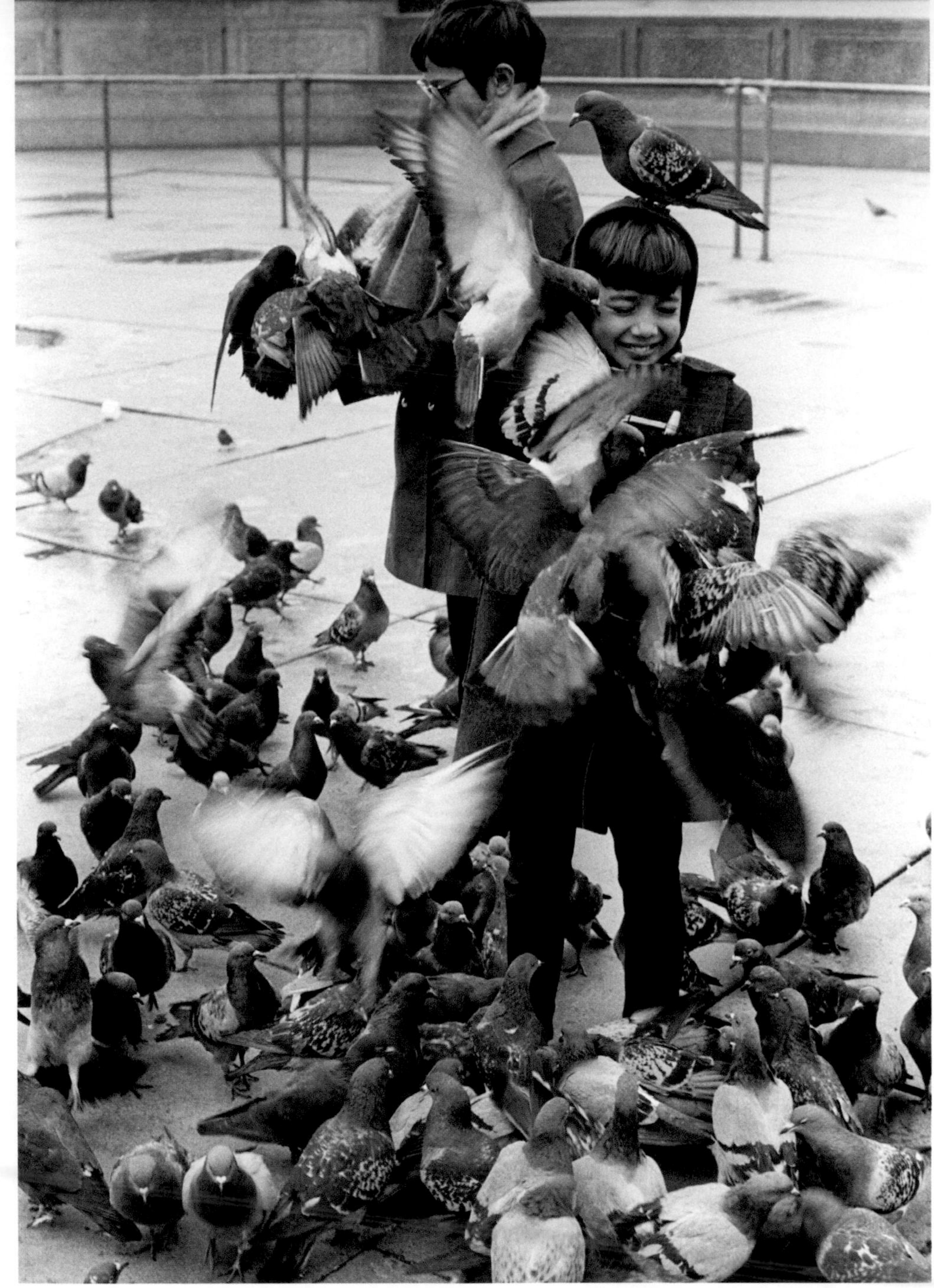

Feeding pigeons in Trafalgar Square.
1972

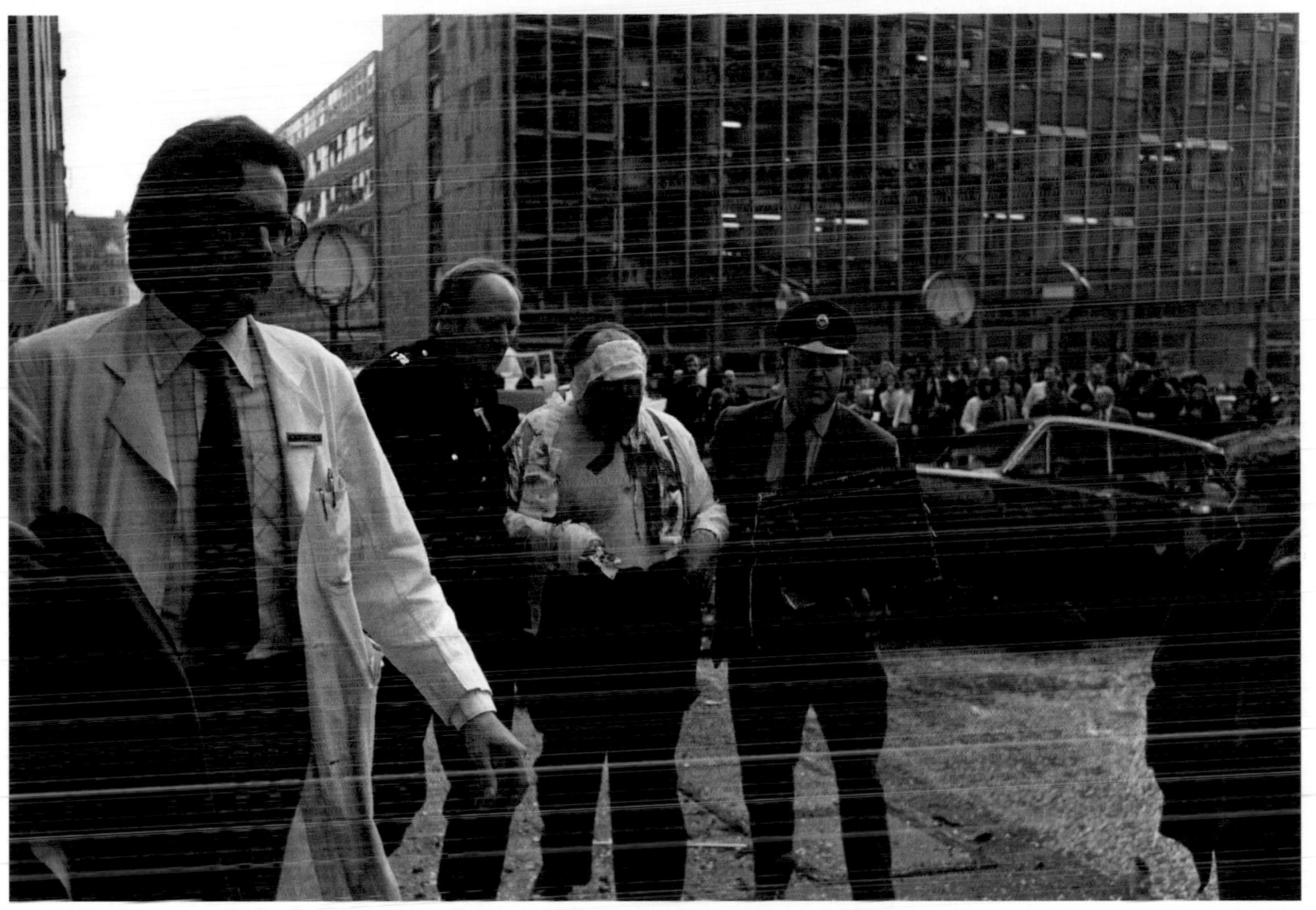

Barrister James Crespi, a casualty of an IRA car bomb attack at the Old Bailey. One of the terrorists convicted of the crime, Gerry Kelly, who received two life-sentences, went on to become law and order spokesman for Sinn Féin and a member of the Northern Irish Assembly.
8th March, 1973

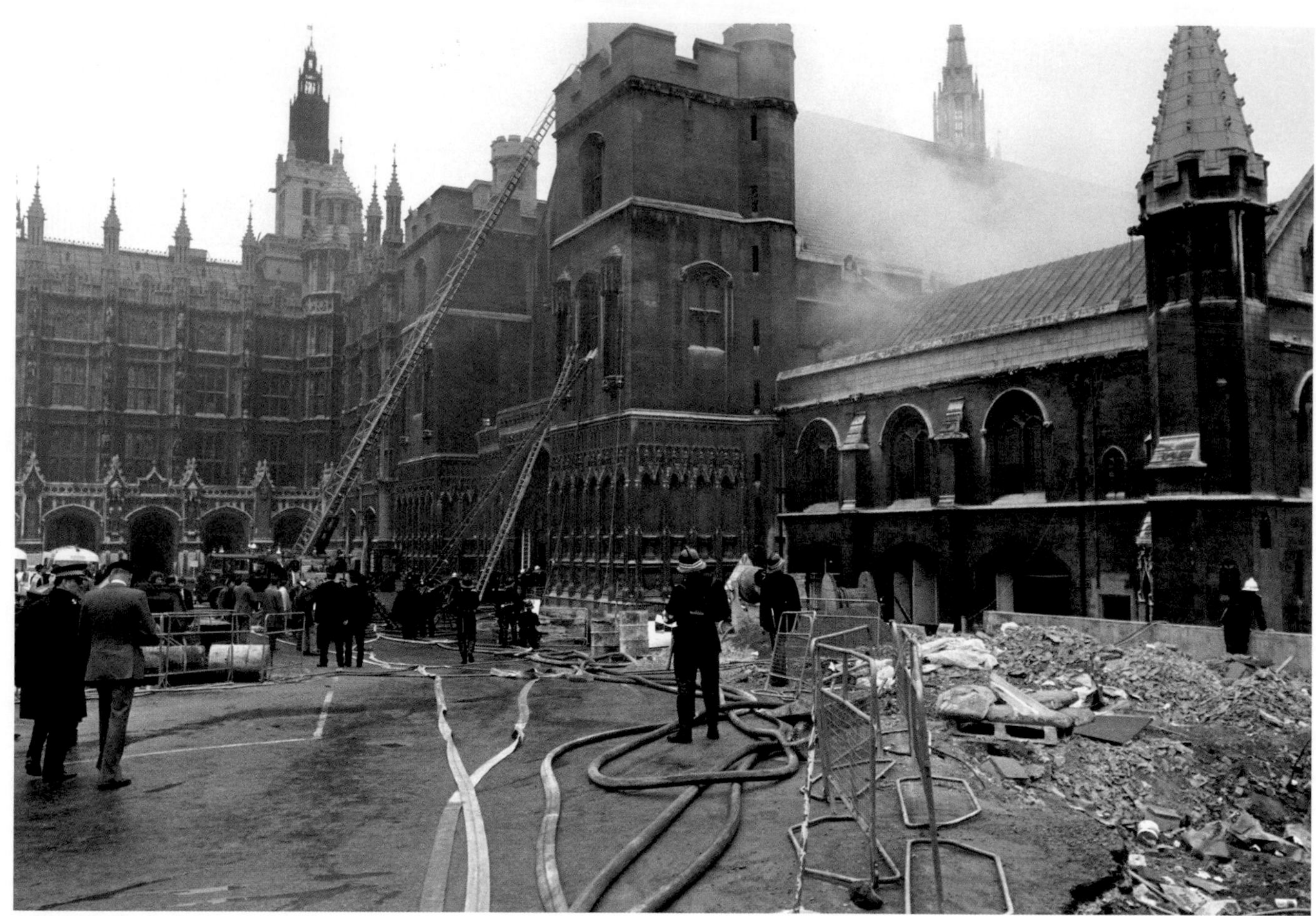

Firemen fight a blaze caused by an IRA bomb in the crypt chapel of the House of Commons.
17th June, 1974

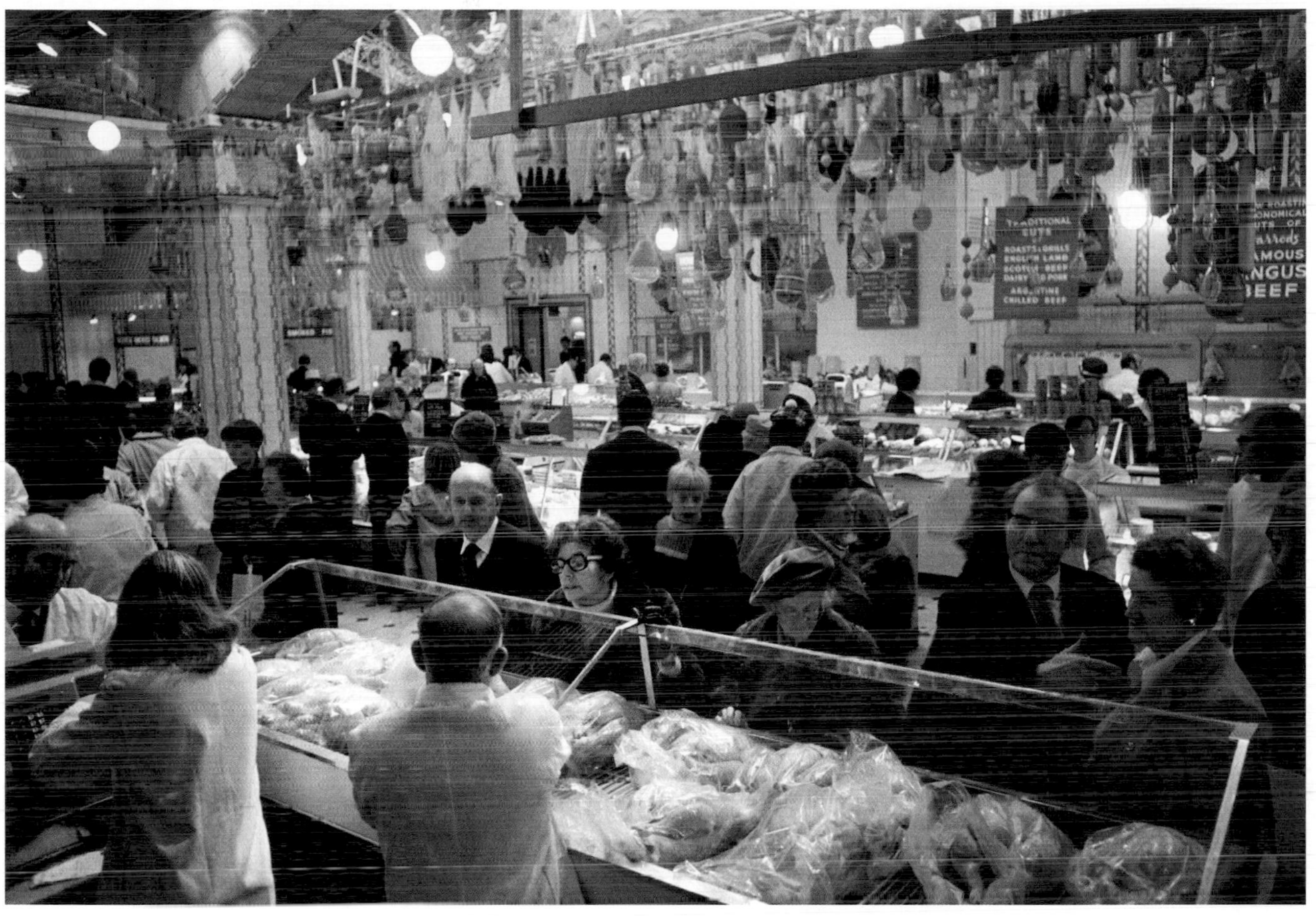

Christmas shoppers in the food hall at Harrods, as business returns to normal following a bomb blast on the second floor of the store in Knightsbridge.
23rd December, 1974

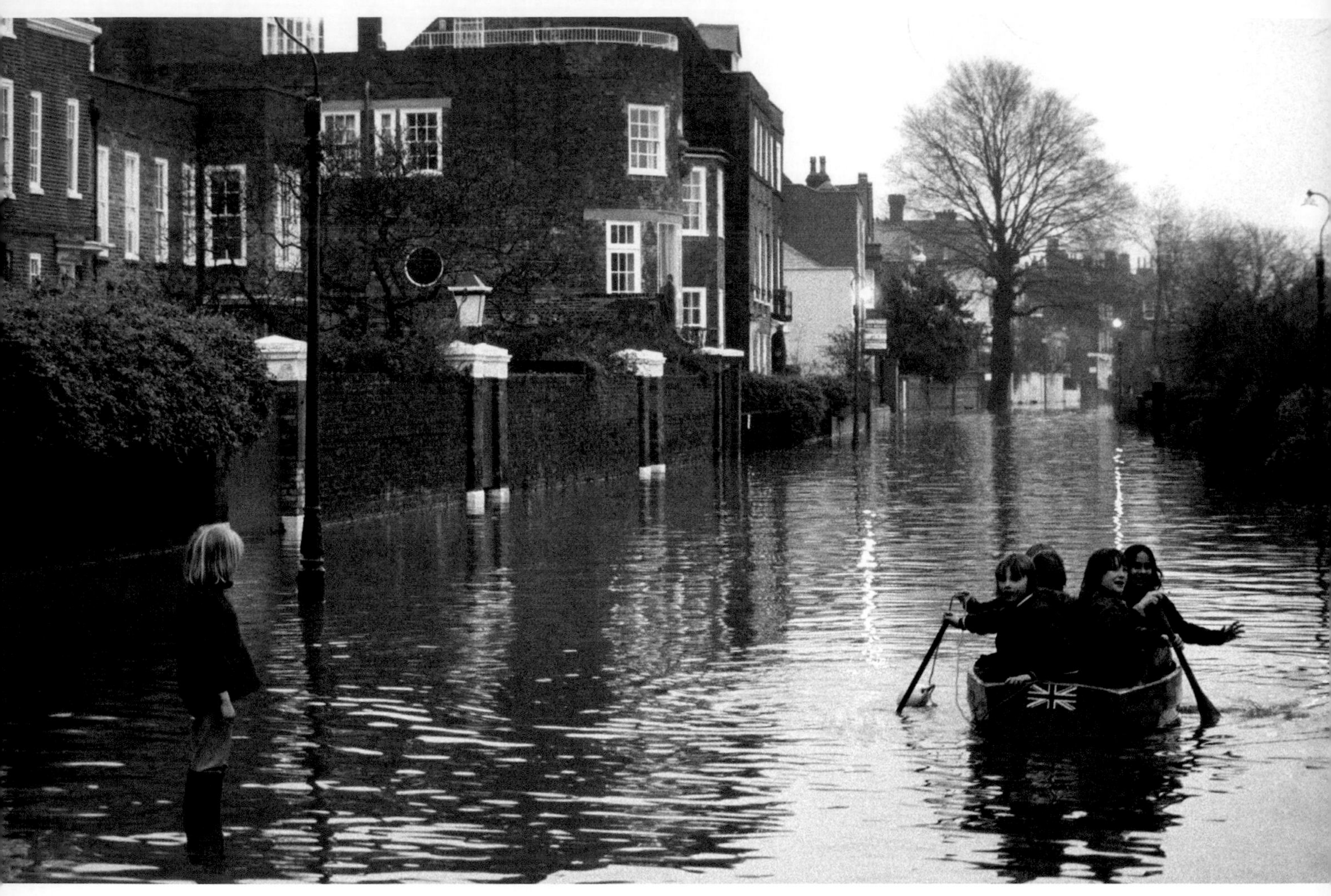

The Thames overflows its banks at Putney. An exceptional tide – over 25 feet at London Bridge – was further swollen by heavy rain upstream.
30th January, 1975

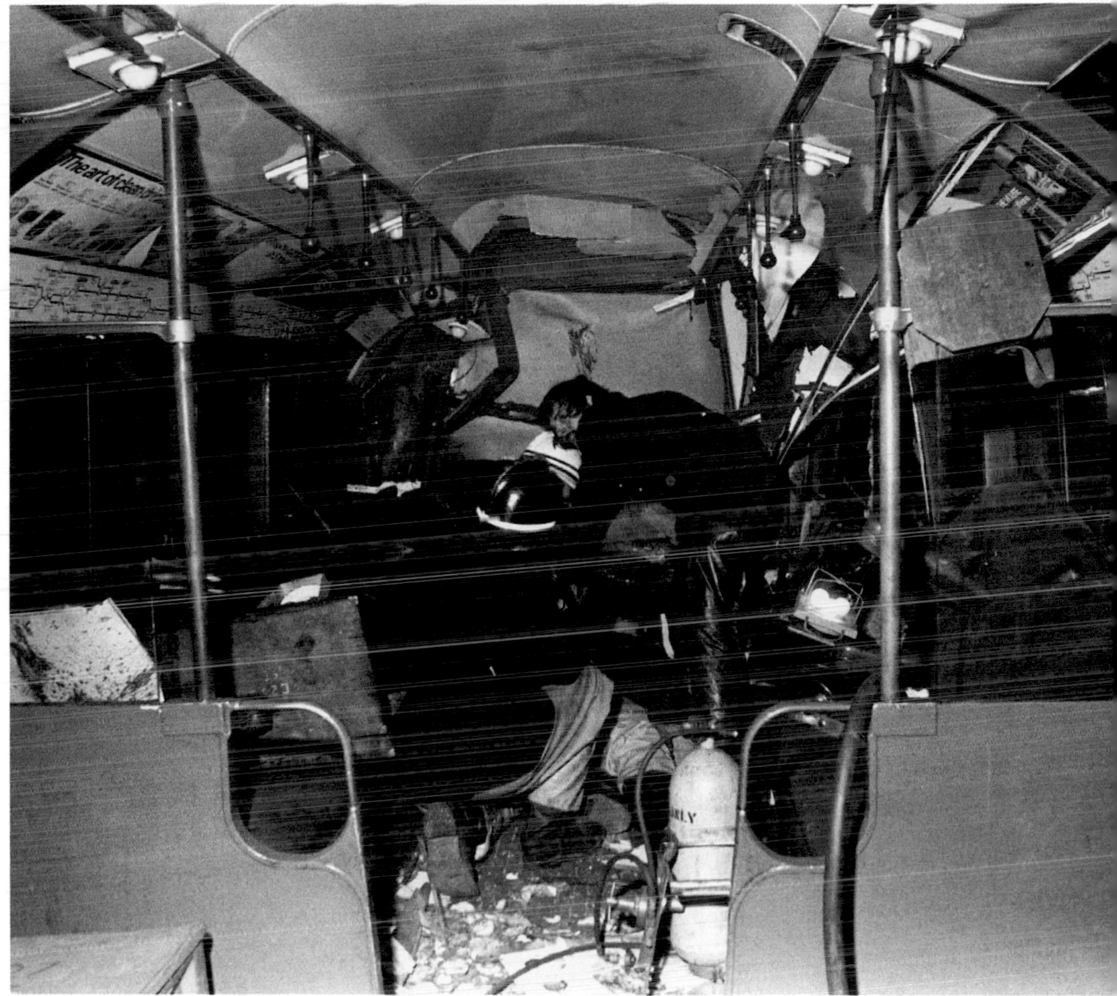

Fireman at work after 43 people were killed when a tube train overran the platform, crashed through buffers and into an end wall at Moorgate Station.
28th February, 1975

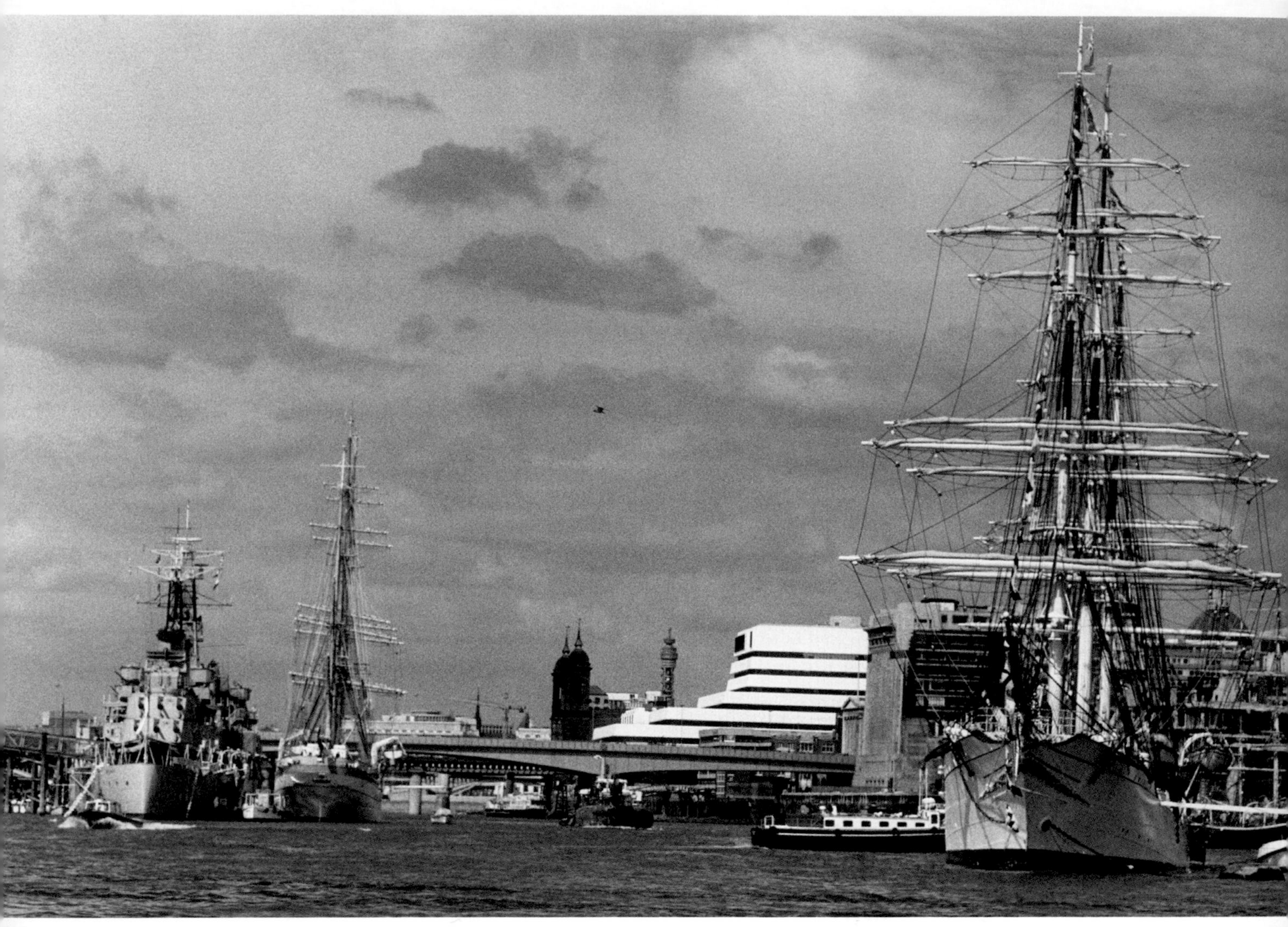

Sail training ships moored alongside *HMS Belfast* for the London Festival of Sail. The West German Navy's barque the *Gorch Fock* and the full-rigged Danish ship *Danmark*.
23rd August, 1975

The Balcombe Street Siege saw policemen in bulletproof vests and wielding guns on Britain's streets for the first time in such a public manner. The gang, four highly-trained IRA men who held a middle-aged couple hostage in their central London home, gave themselves up after a six-day stand-off when the SAS were called in with instructions to shoot to kill if they tried to escape.
8th December, 1975

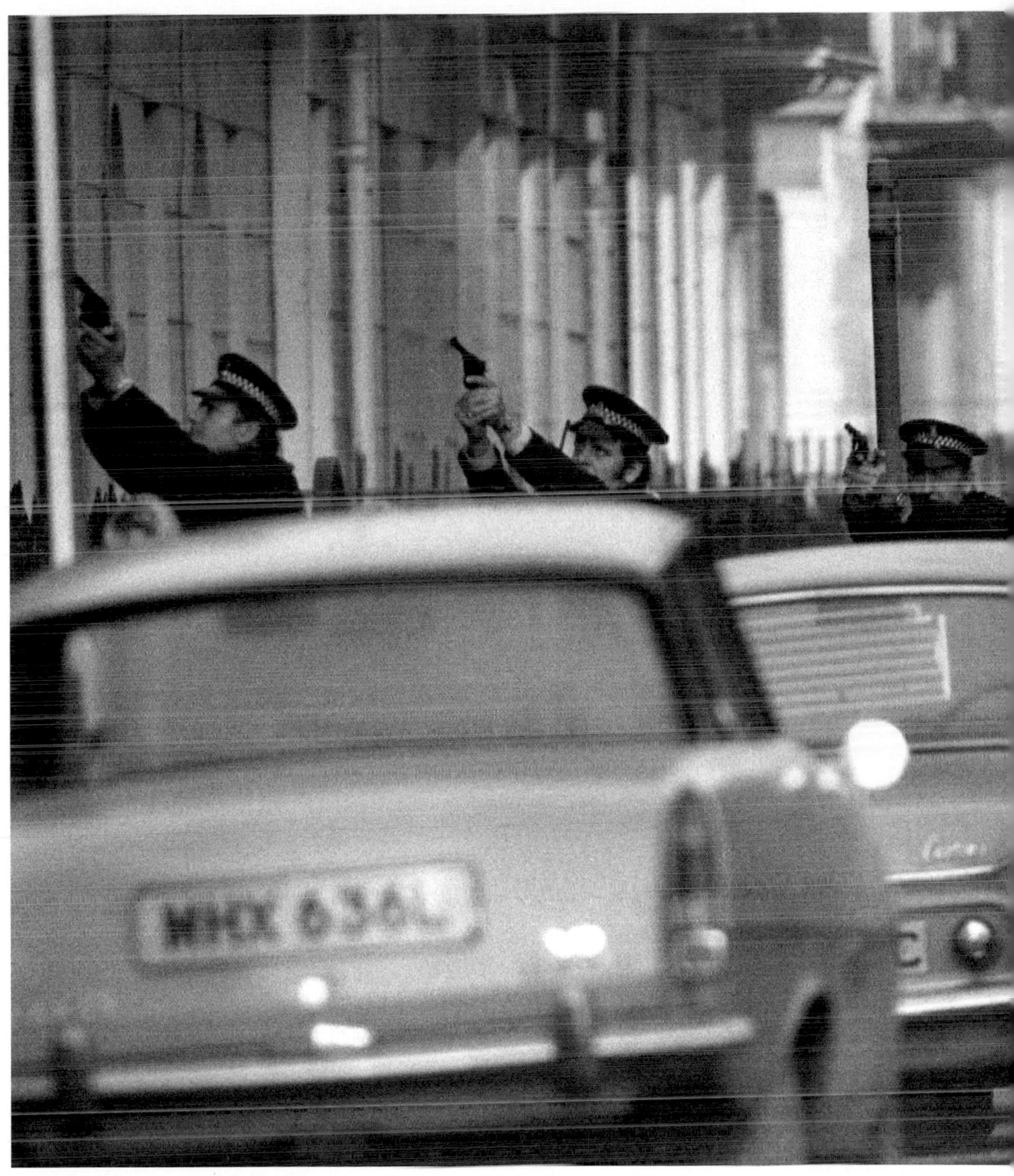

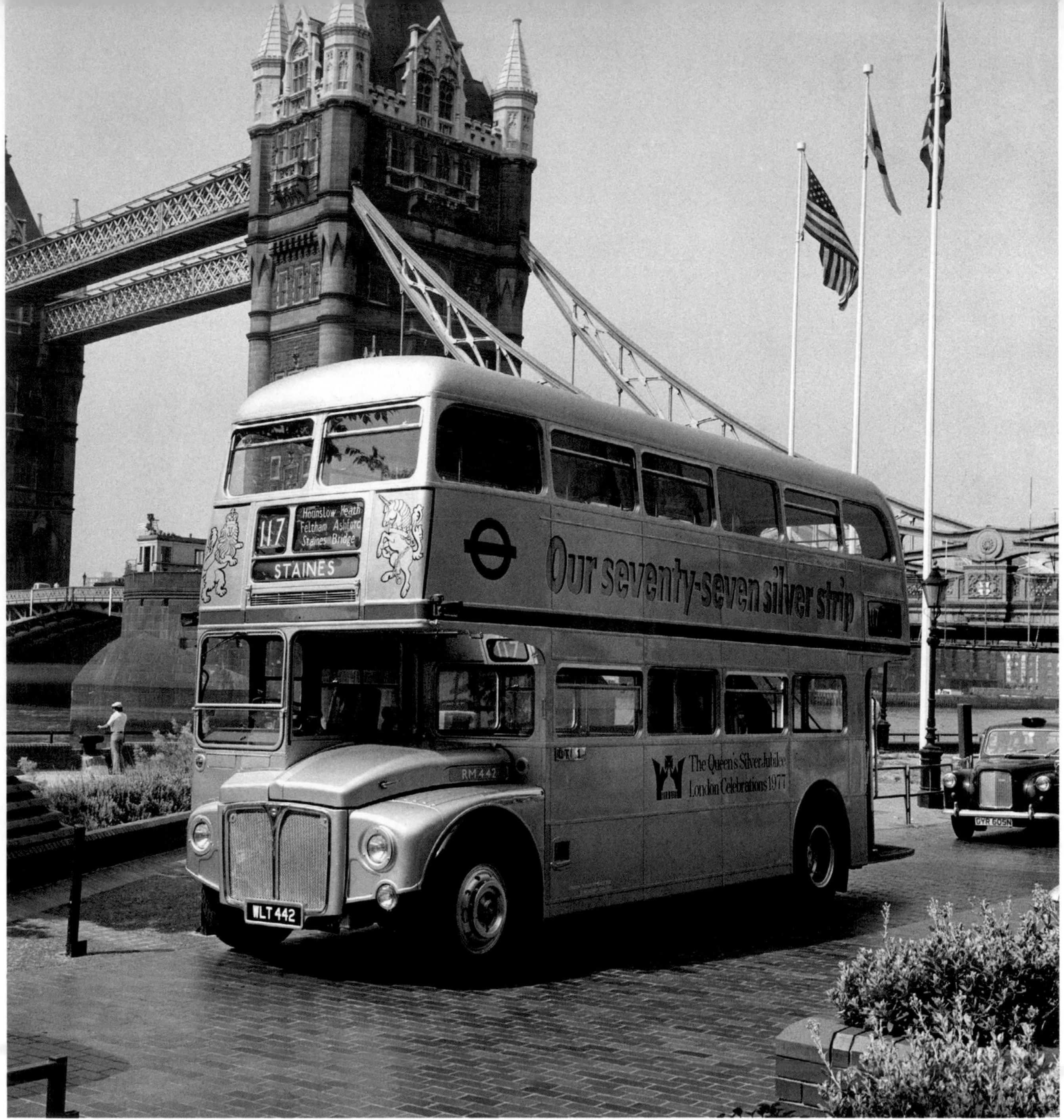
117
Hounslow Heath
Feltham Ashford
Staines Bridge
STAINES
Our seventy-seven silver strip
The Queen's Silver Jubilee
London Celebrations 1977
RM 442
WLT 442

Facing page: A prototype of the 25 silver buses destined for several busy London routes as a London Transport contribution to celebrations marking the Queen's Silver Jubilee.
6th July, 1976

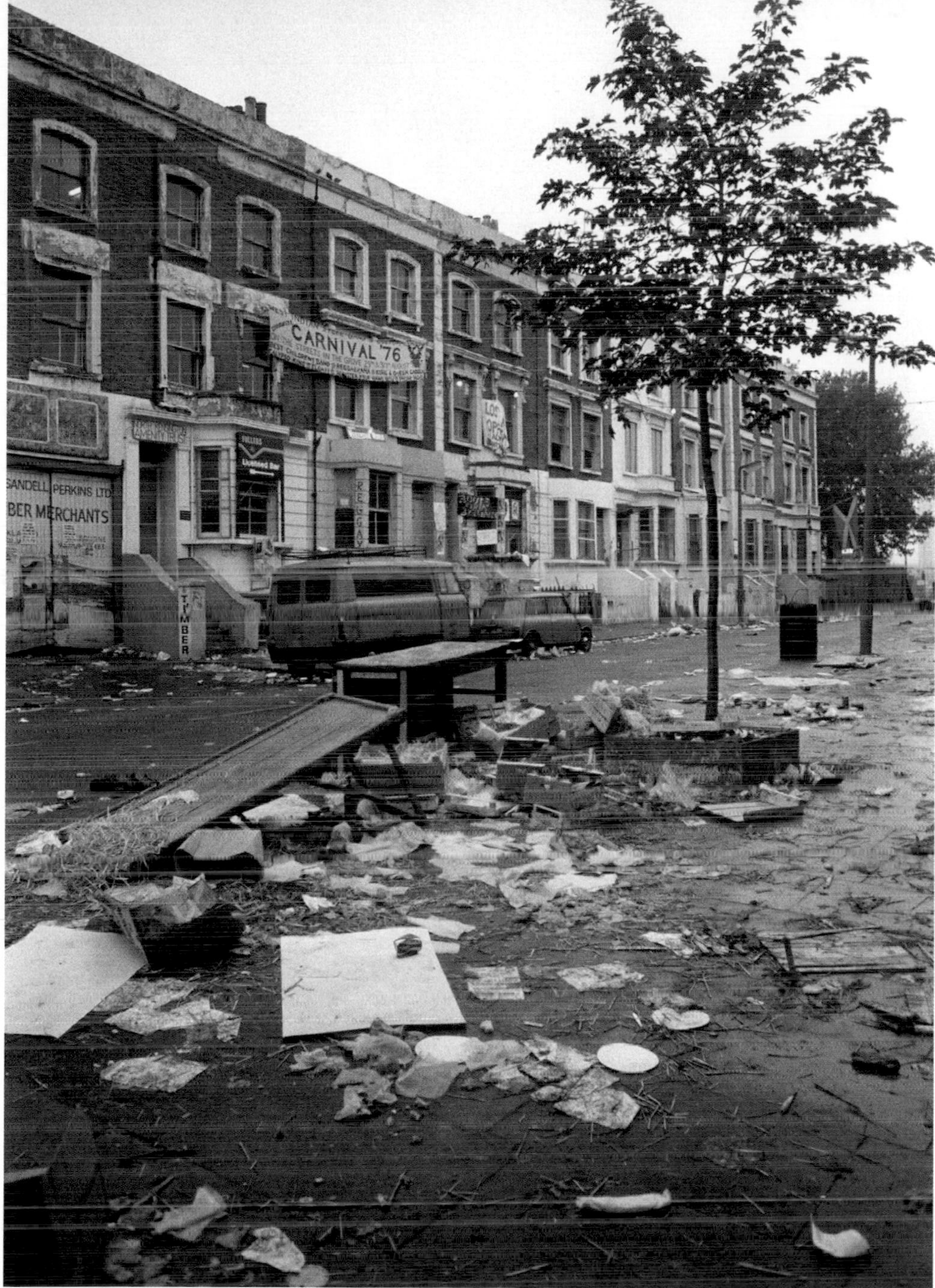

Rubbish strewn across Acklam Road, West London, following scenes of violence when the Notting Hill Carnival erupted in rioting.
31st August, 1976

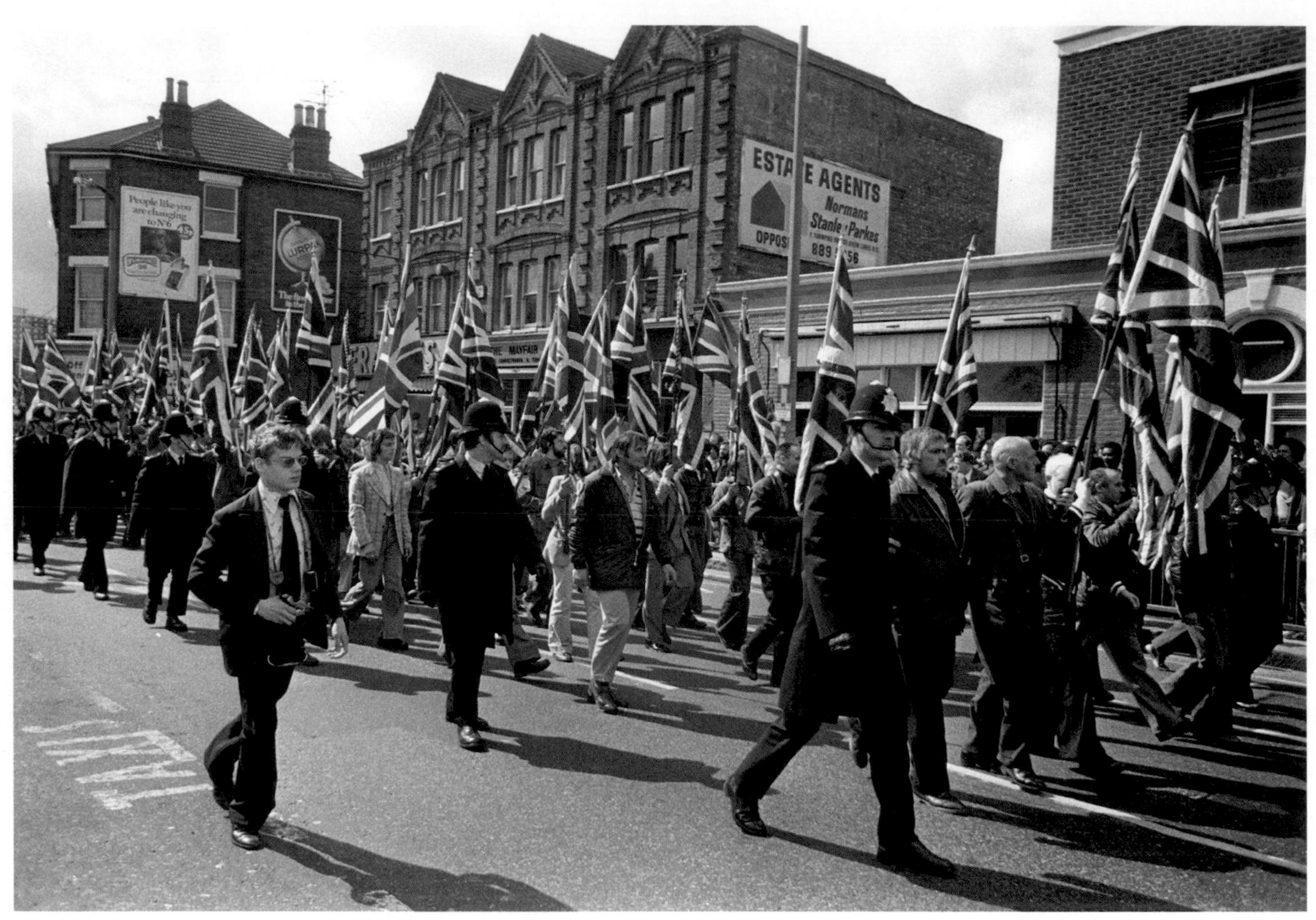

National Front supporters march through a largely immigrant area, a show of force in their campaign for the Greater London Council elections.
23rd April, 1977

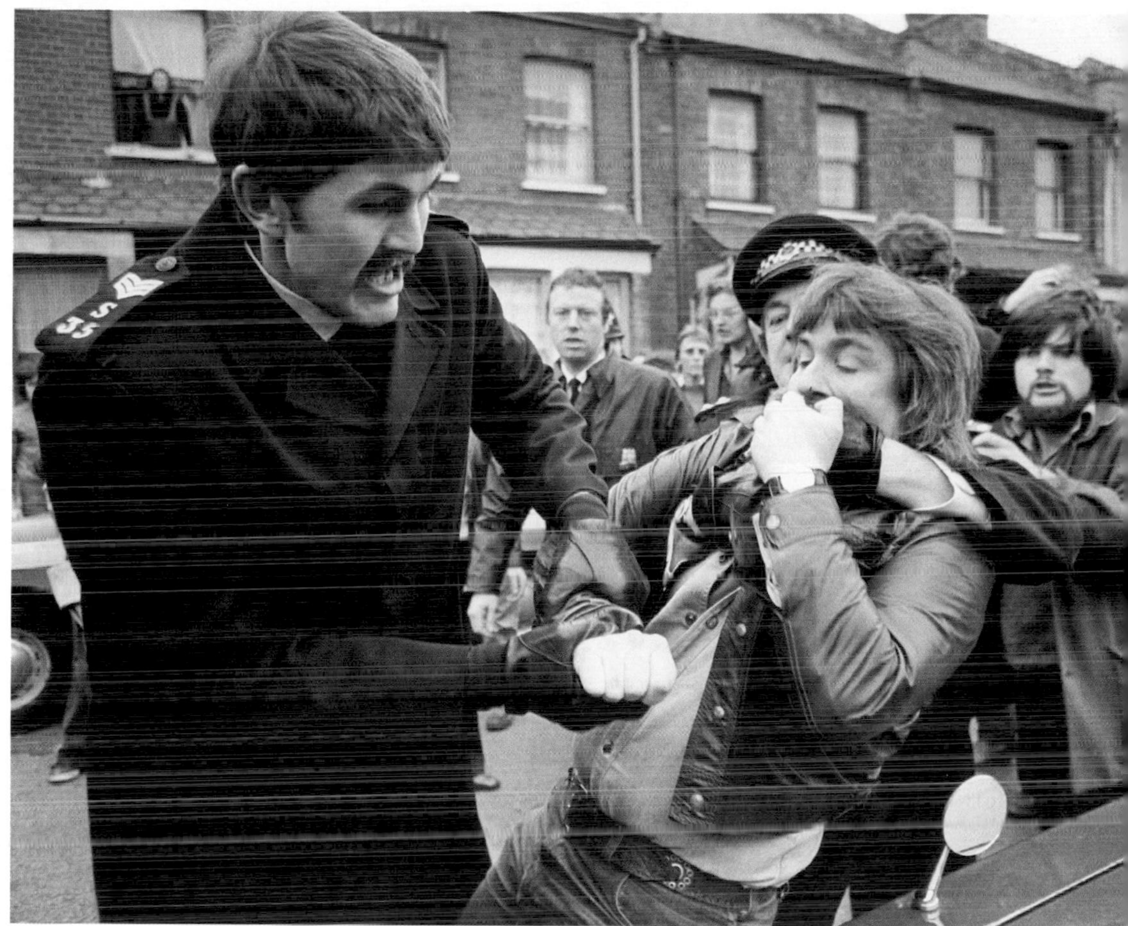

Police restraining pickets supporting an official strike by process workers outside the Grunwick film processing laboratories at Willesden.
23rd June, 1977

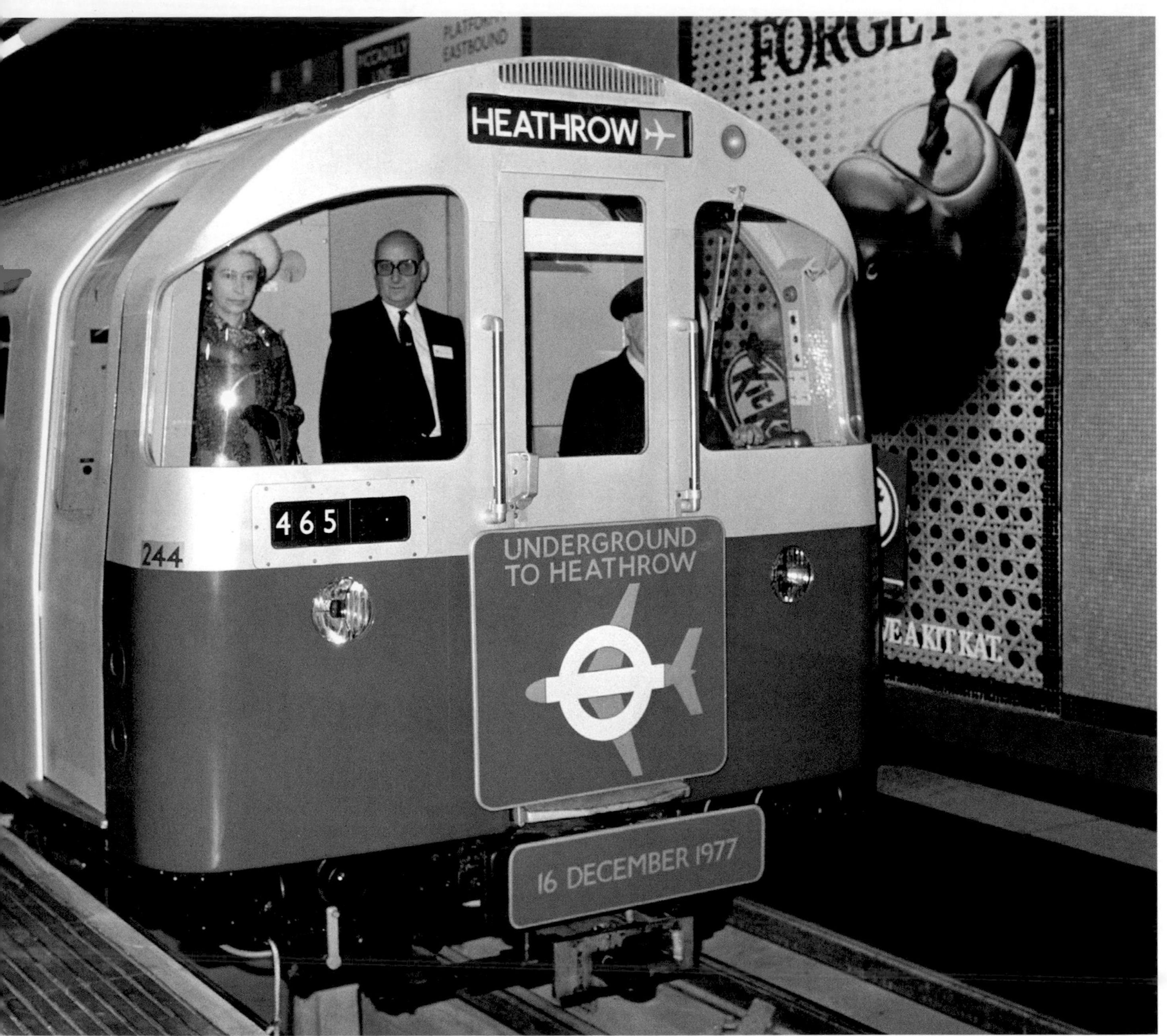
FORGET
HEATHROW
465
244
UNDERGROUND
TO HEATHROW
16 DECEMBER 1977
VE A KIT KAT.

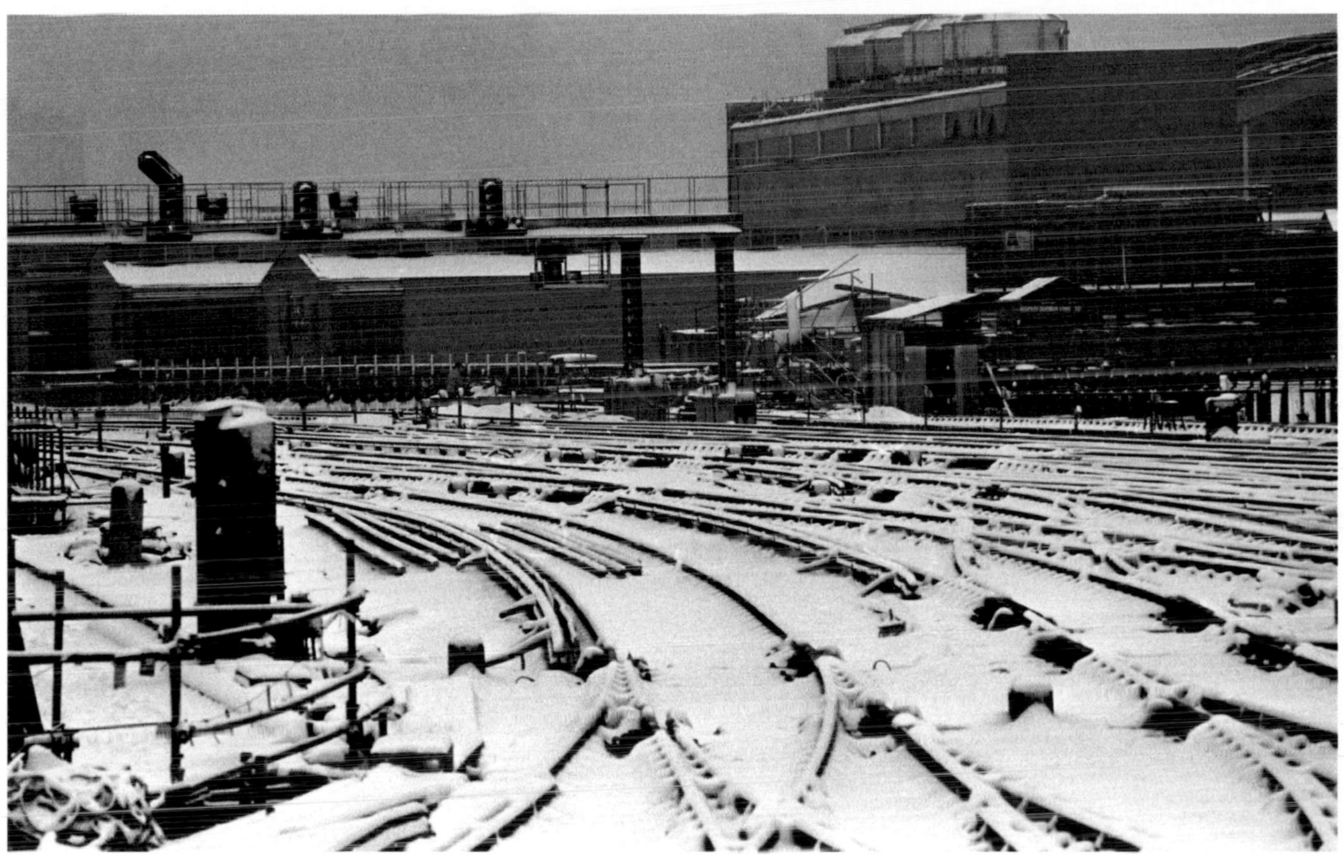

Rush hour at Cannon Street station and not a train in sight. A taste of the double misery faced by commuters struggling in to work, with a third one-day rail strike and arctic conditions caused by blizzards throughout southern Britain.
23rd January, 1979

Facing page: The Queen arrives at Heathrow Central station by tube, to open the £30m Piccadilly Line extension linking Heathrow Airport with the Underground.
16th December, 1977

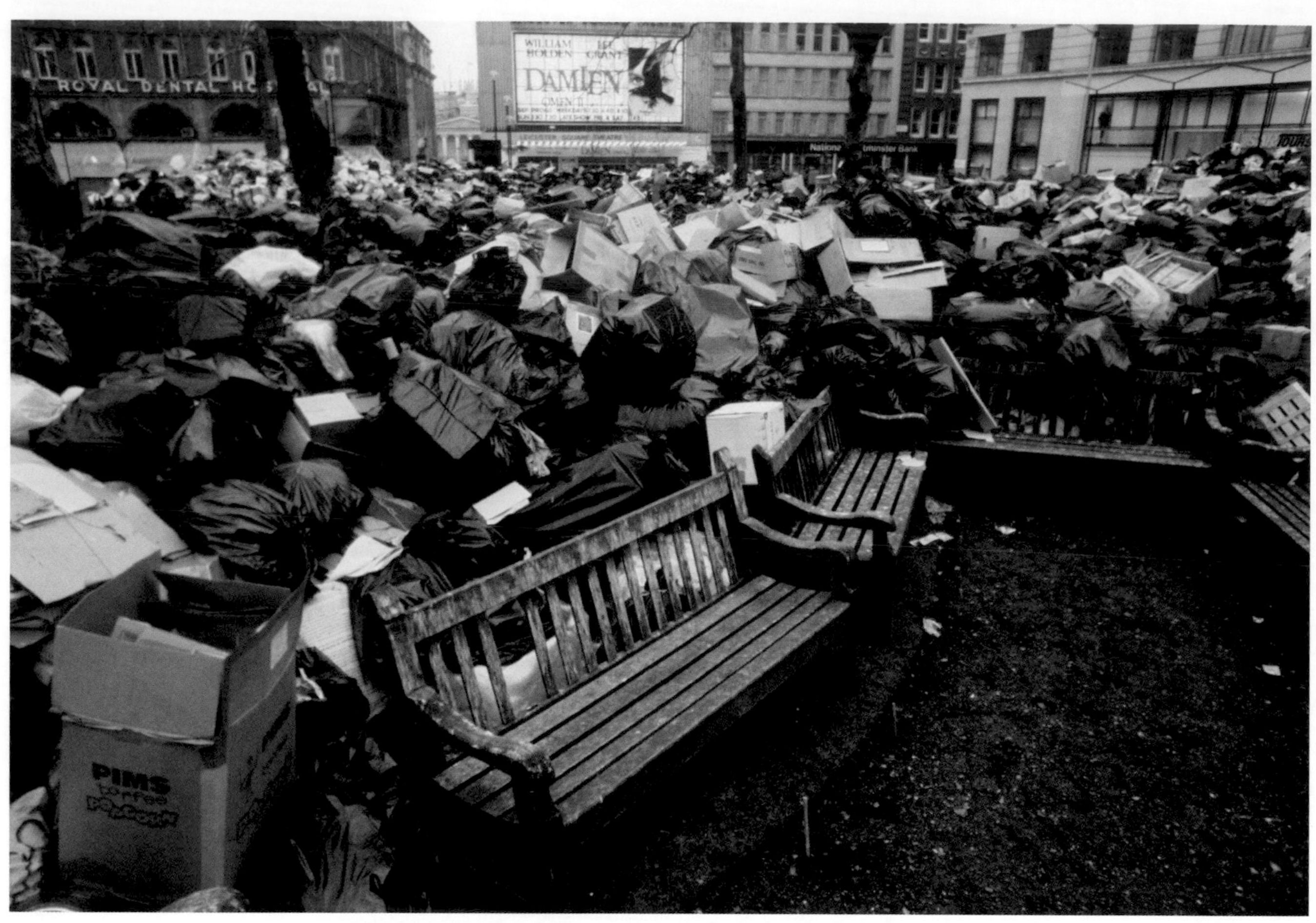

Mountains of rubbish dumped in Leicester Square. Rubbish remains uncollected during a strike by City of Westminster dustmen in support of a pay claim: part of a rash of industrial unrest known as *The Winter of Discontent*.

31st January, 1979

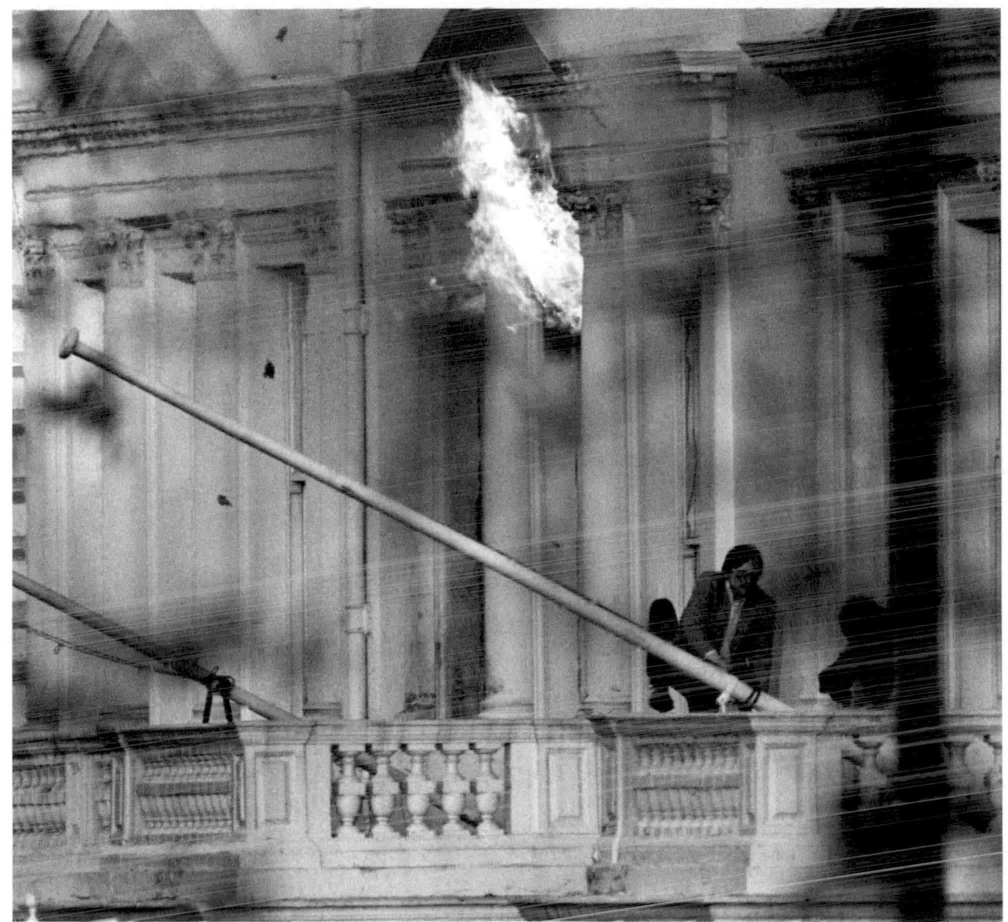

BBC sound recordist Sim Harris scrambles to safety as flames billow from the Iranian Embassy. The six-day siege at the building in Princes Gate ends when SAS commandos storm the building, rescuing 19 hostages.
5th May, 1980

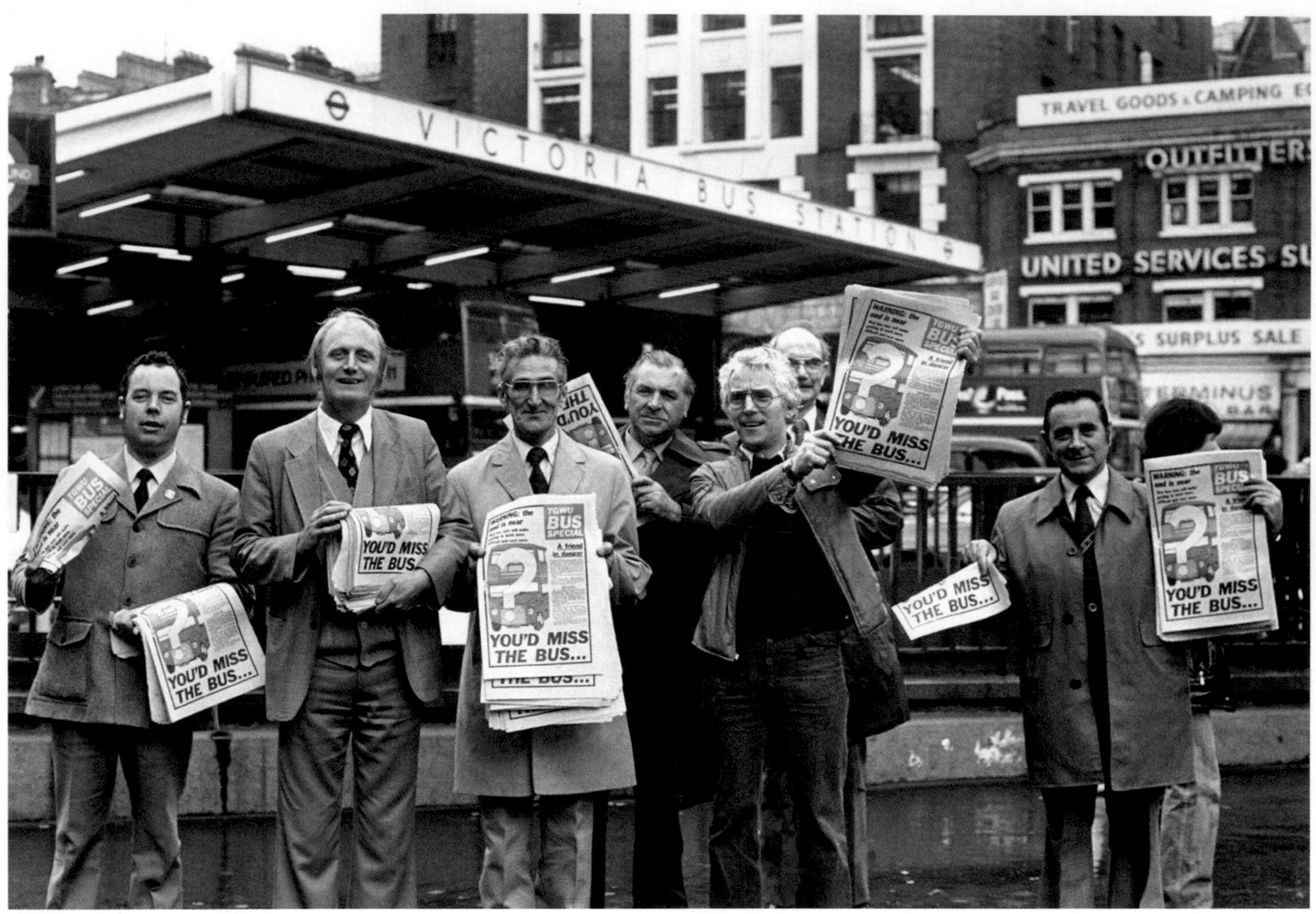

Transport and General Workers Union drivers and conductors at Victoria Station, handing out leaflets calling on commuters to fight the new Transport Act.
July, 1980

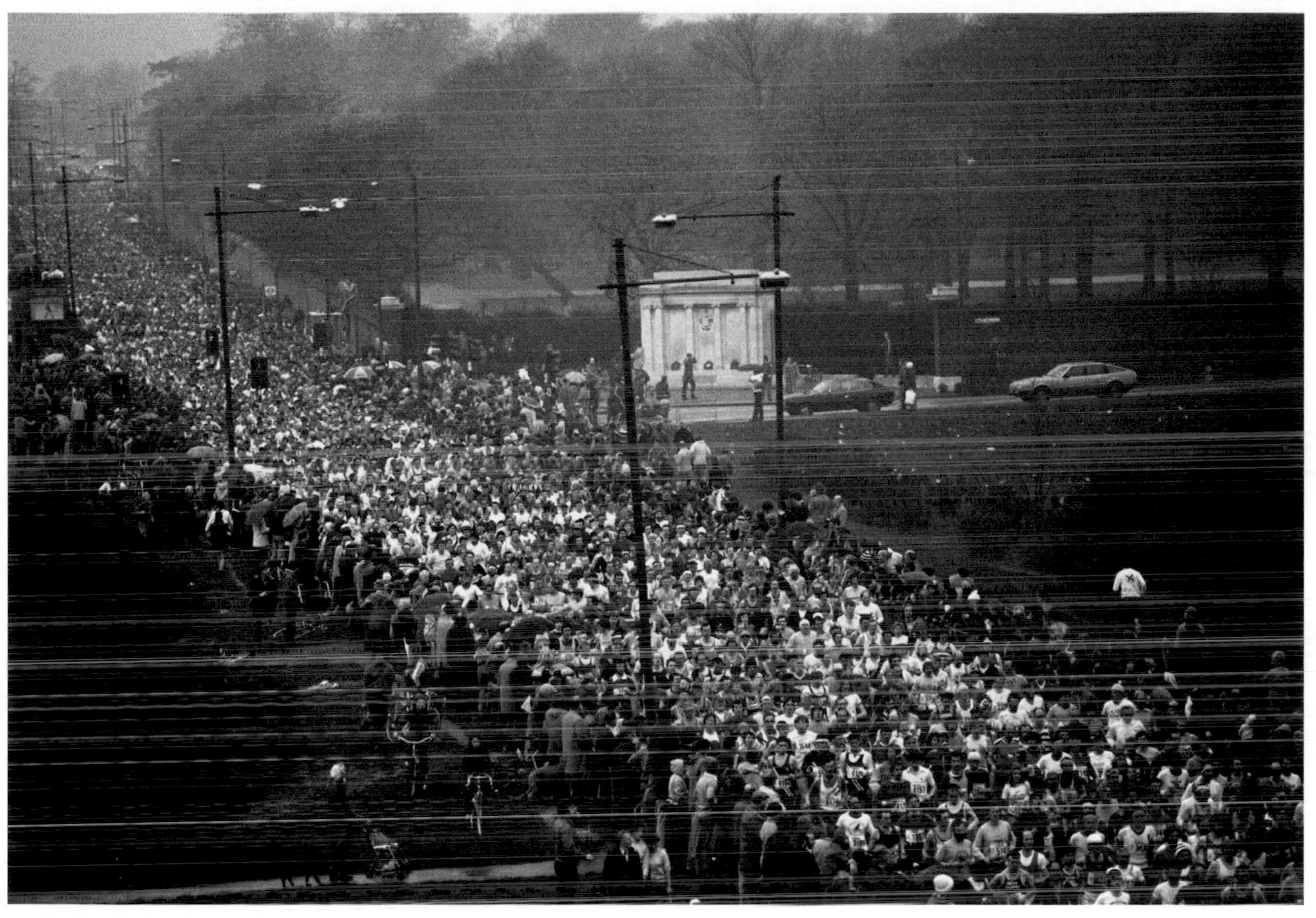

The start of the first London Marathon in Greenwich Park. Of the 6,747 entrants, 6,255 crossed the finish line on Constitution Hill.
29th March, 1981

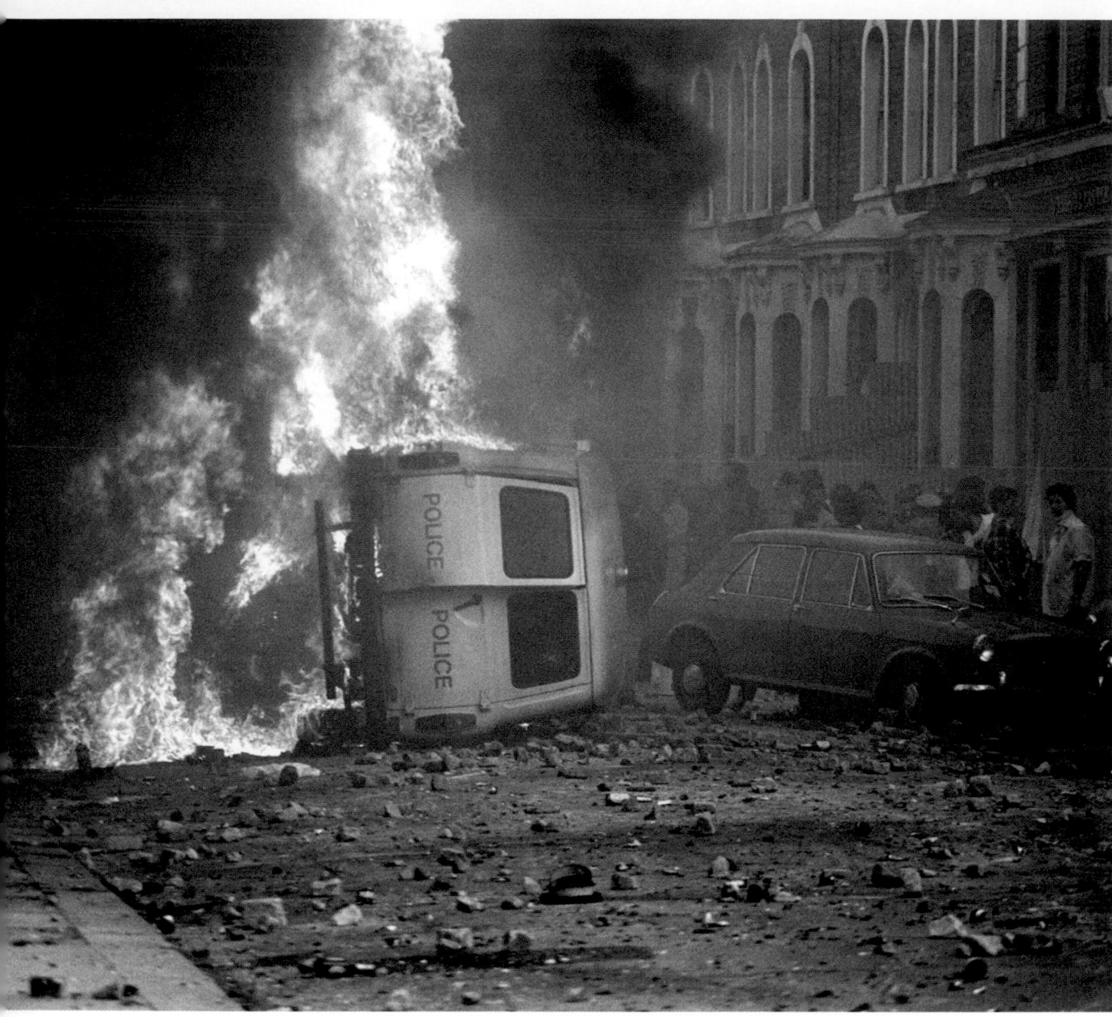

A police van on fire during a riot in Brixton. Clashes between police and rioters left 23 police officers injured.
11th April, 1981

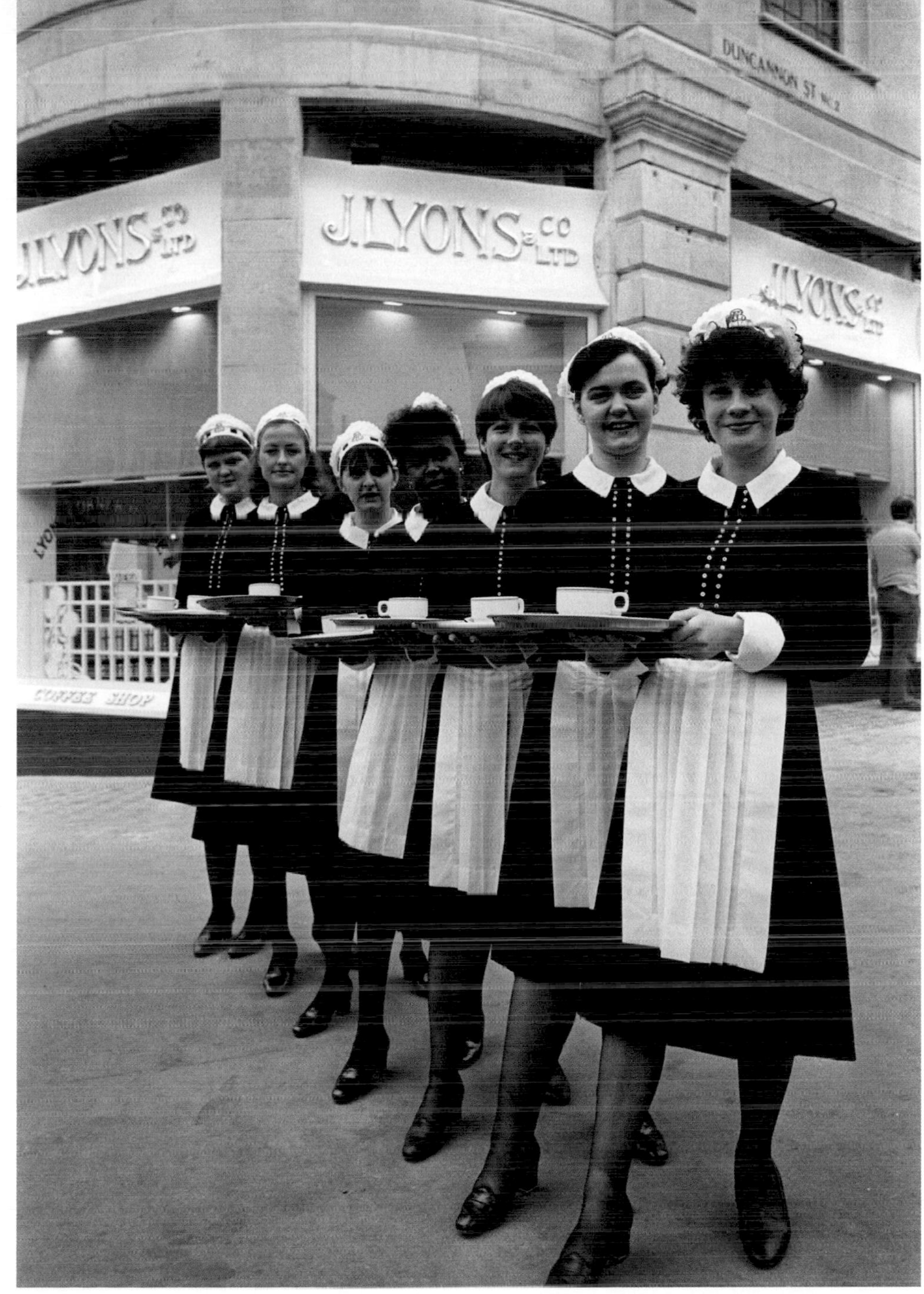

Waitresses rehearsing for the opening of an old-style Lyons Corner House restaurant in The Strand.
19th June, 1981

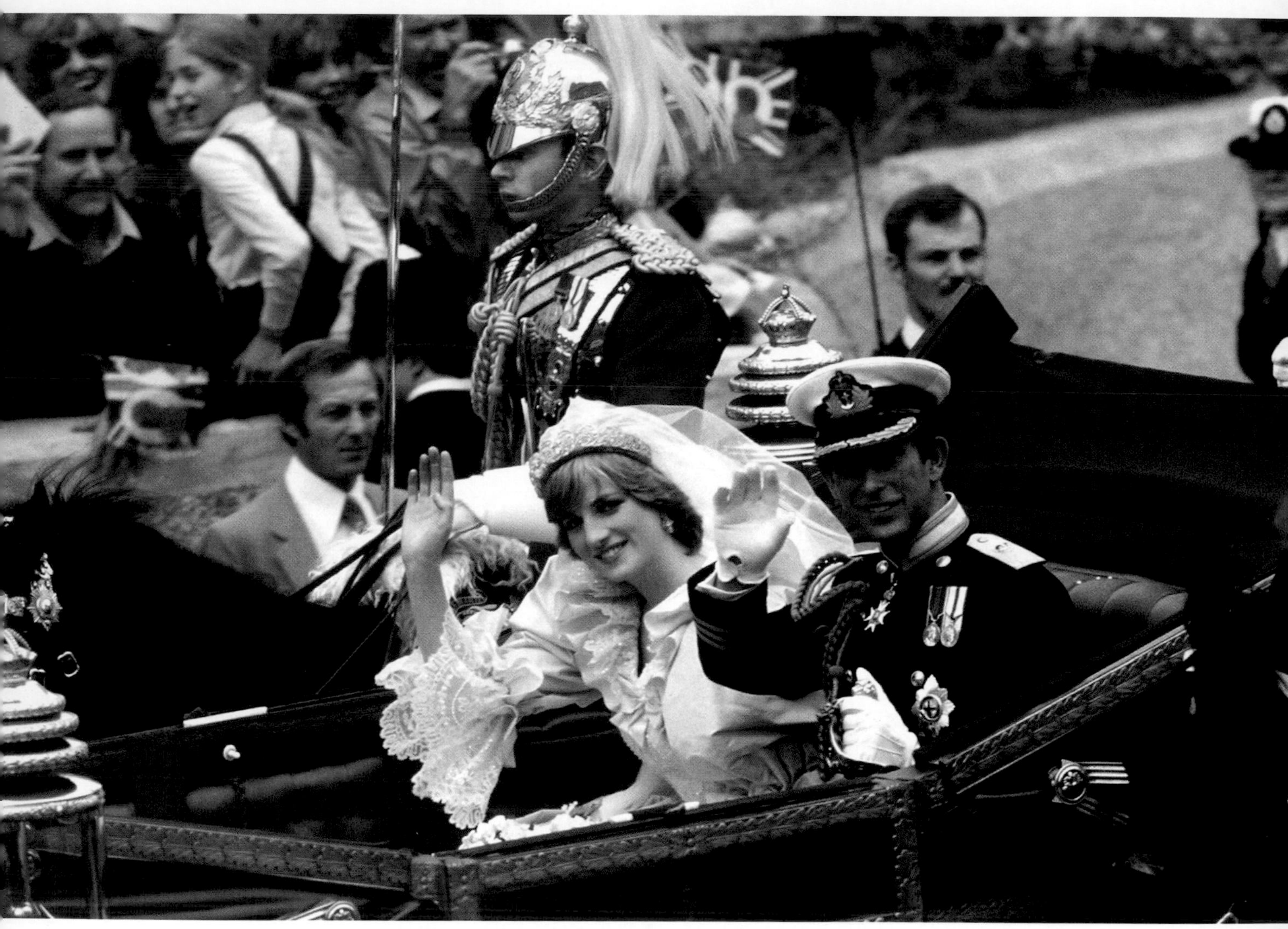

The Prince and Princess of Wales make their way to Buckingham Palace after their wedding ceremony at St Paul's Cathedral.
29th July, 1981

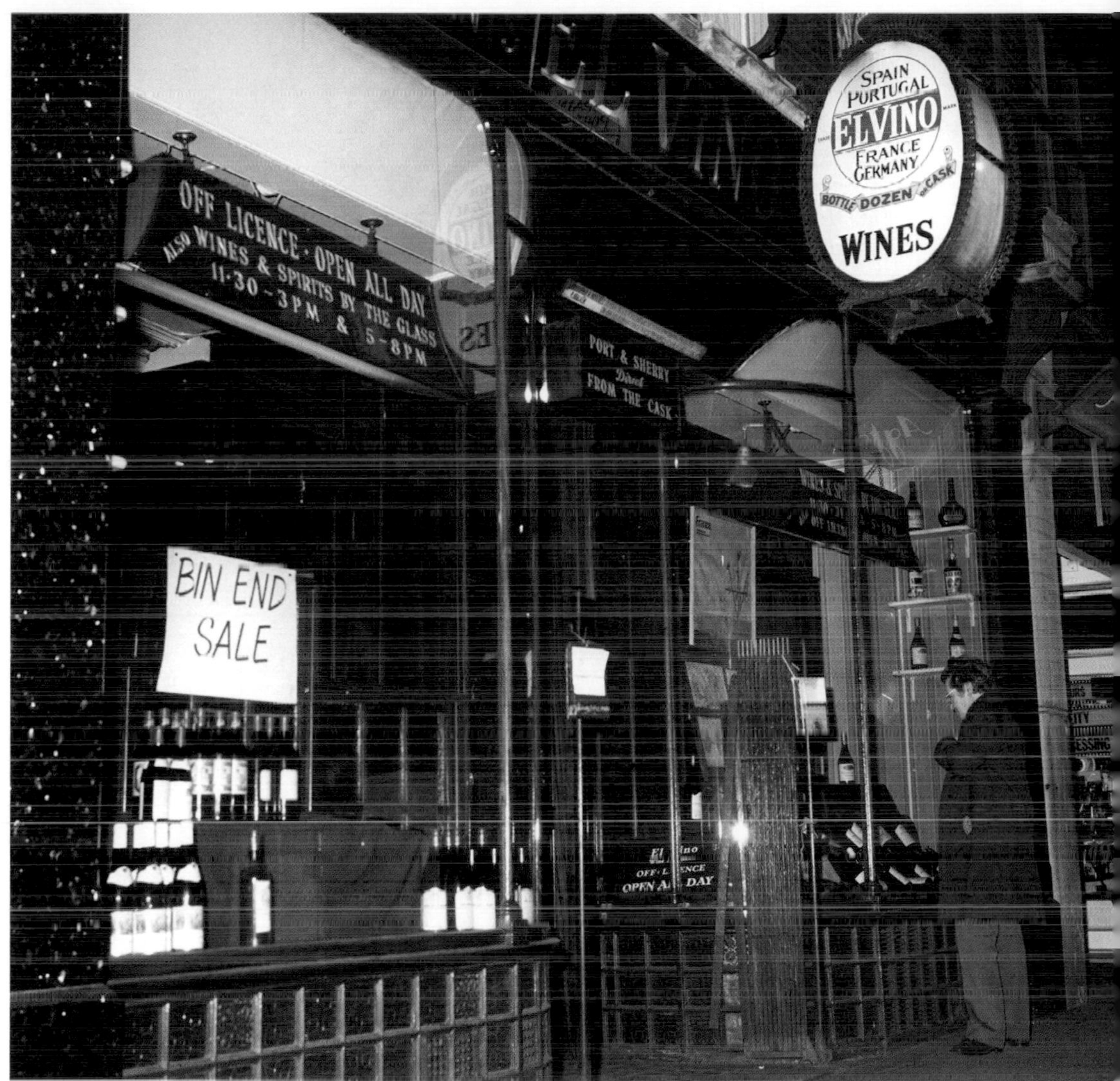

The *El Vino* wine bar and off licence in Fleet Street, an old haunt of news journalists. The last news agency left the area in 2005.
10th November, 1982

The remains of the Austin *1100* used in an IRA bomb attack which killed five people outside Harrods.
18th December, 1983

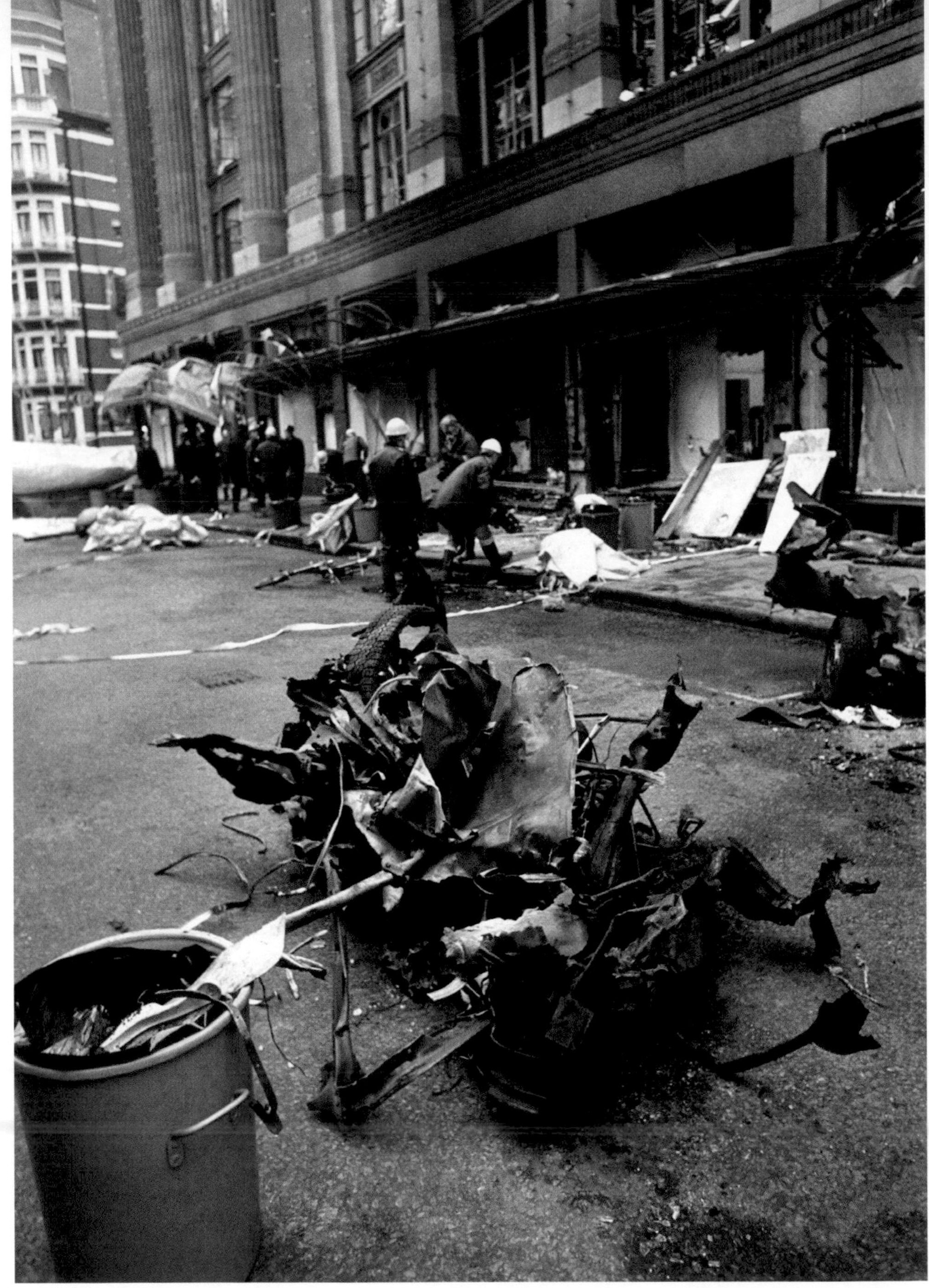

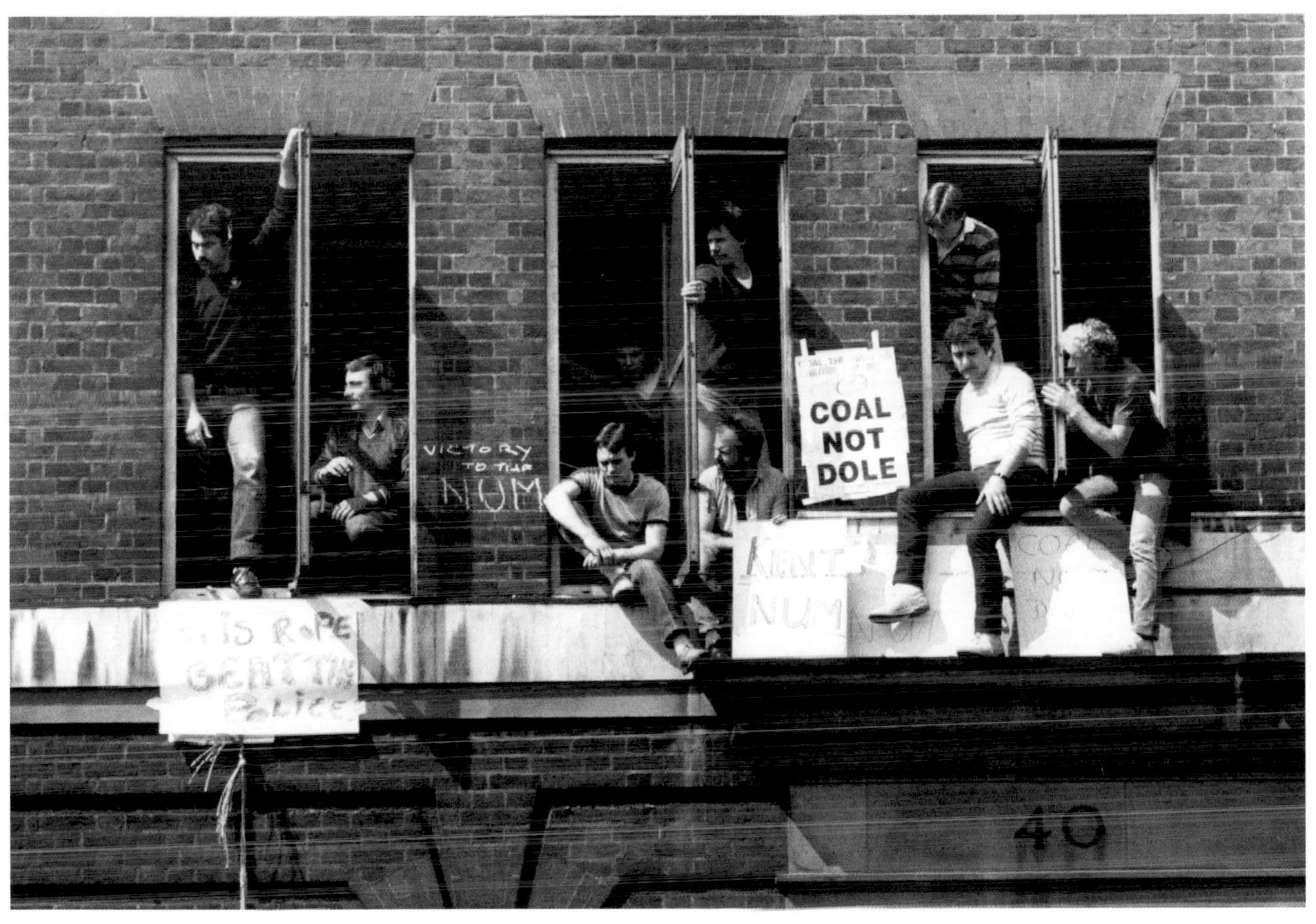

Miners occupy first floor offices of the National Coal Board in Hobart House, Grosvenor Place.
1984

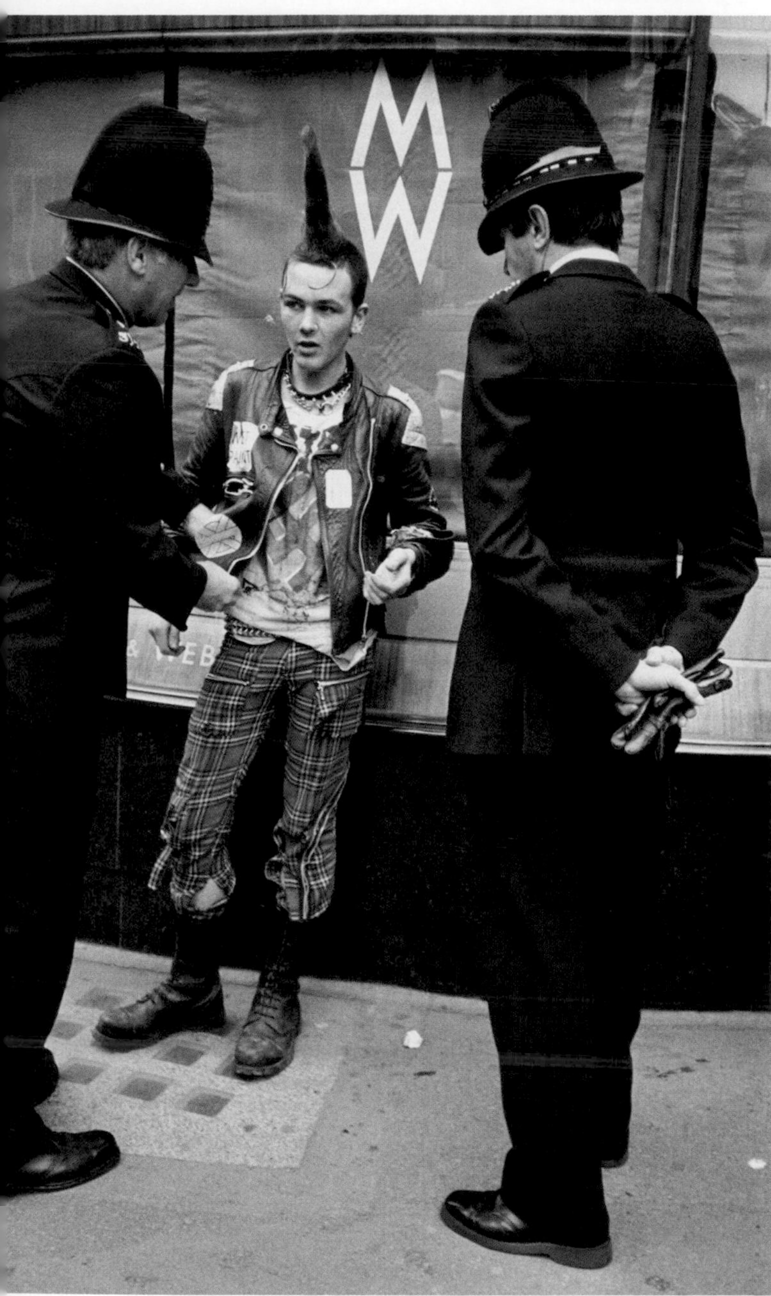

Policemen search a youth near the Stock Exchange during the second *Stop The City* protest.
27th September, 1984

The State Opening of Parliament.
6th November, 1984

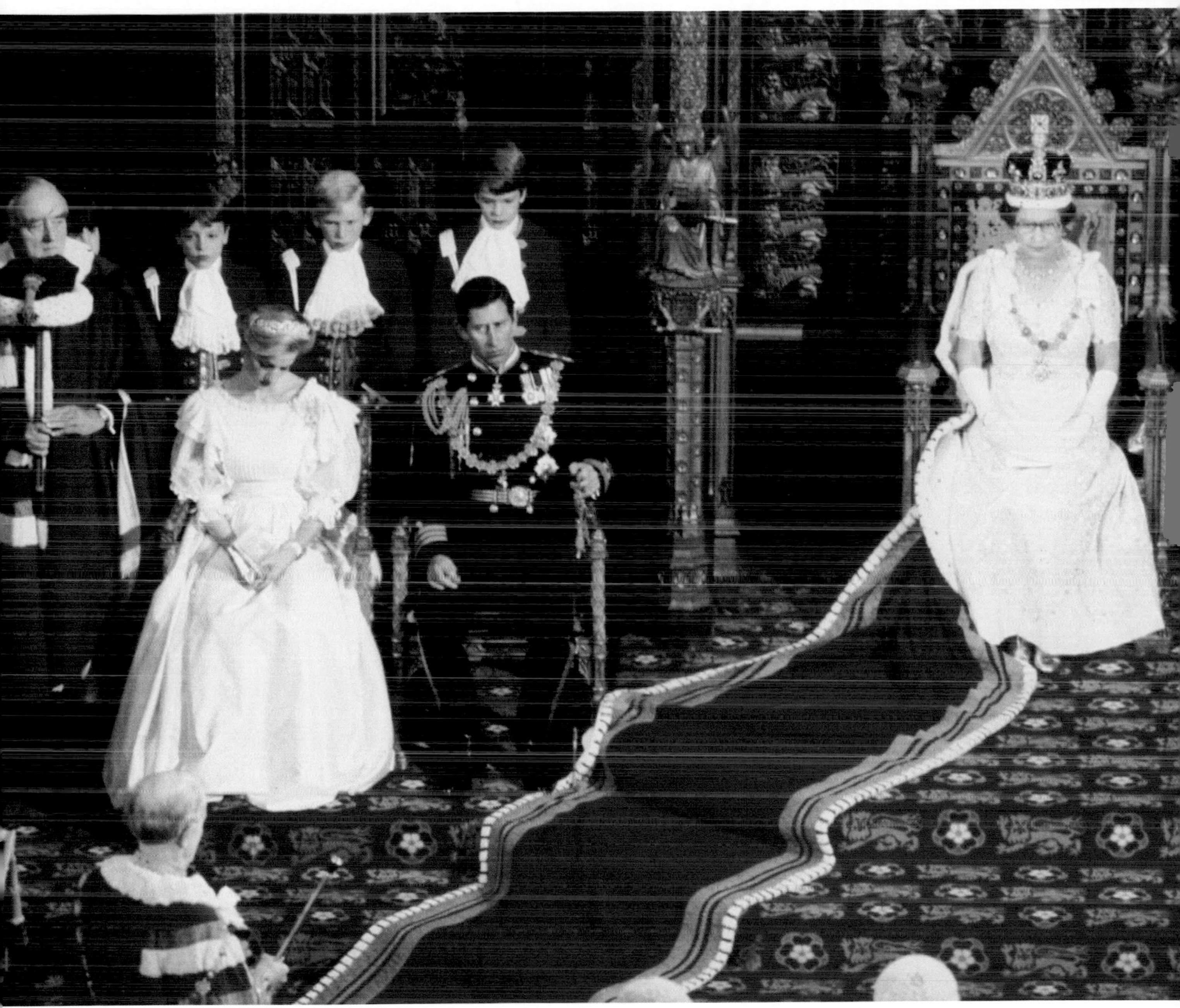

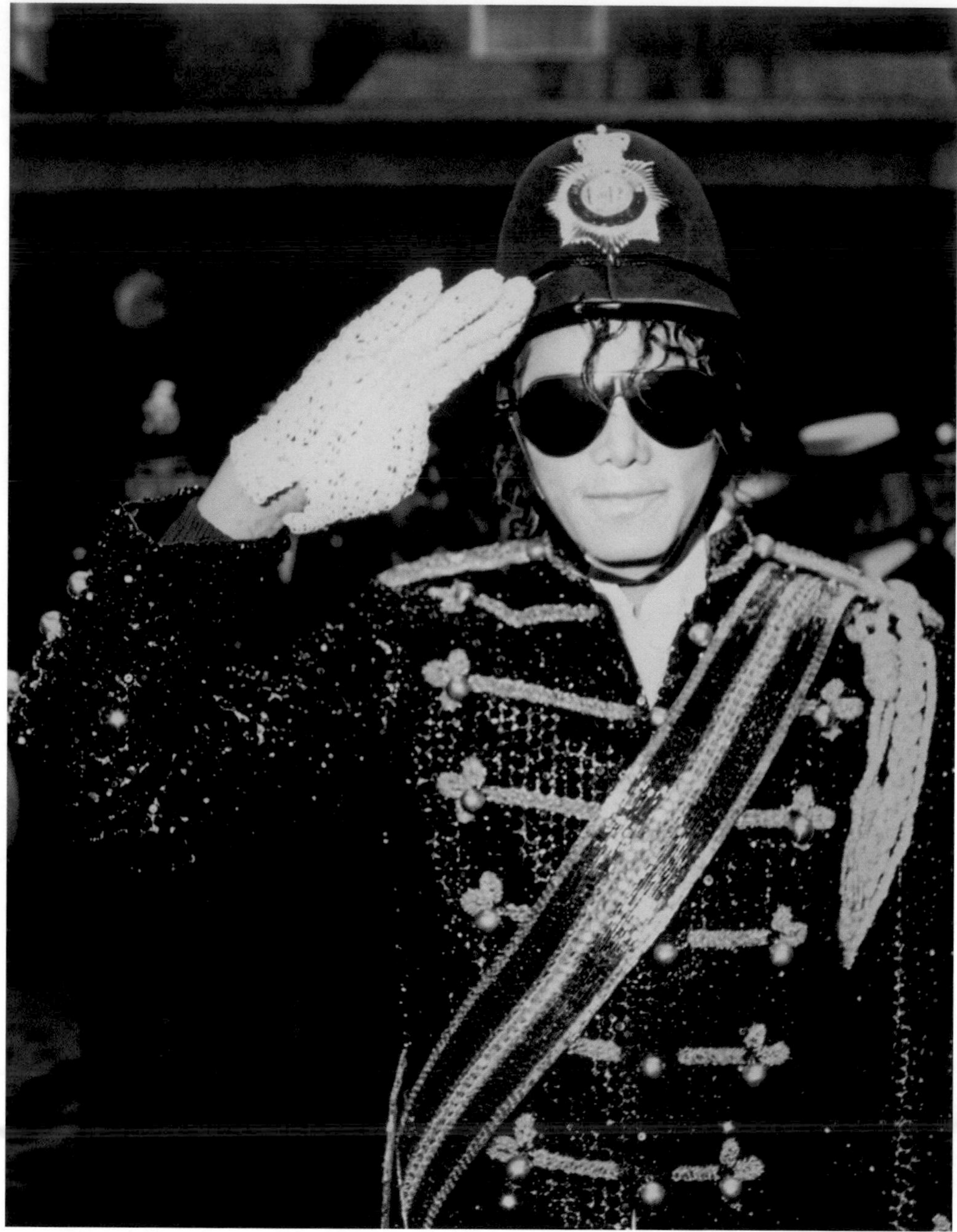

Michael Jackson at Marylebone Police Station, the base for the Metropolitan Police team responsible for his safety.
30th March, 1985

Greenpeace members climb the Harrods building to protest against the killing of animals for fur.
28th April, 1985

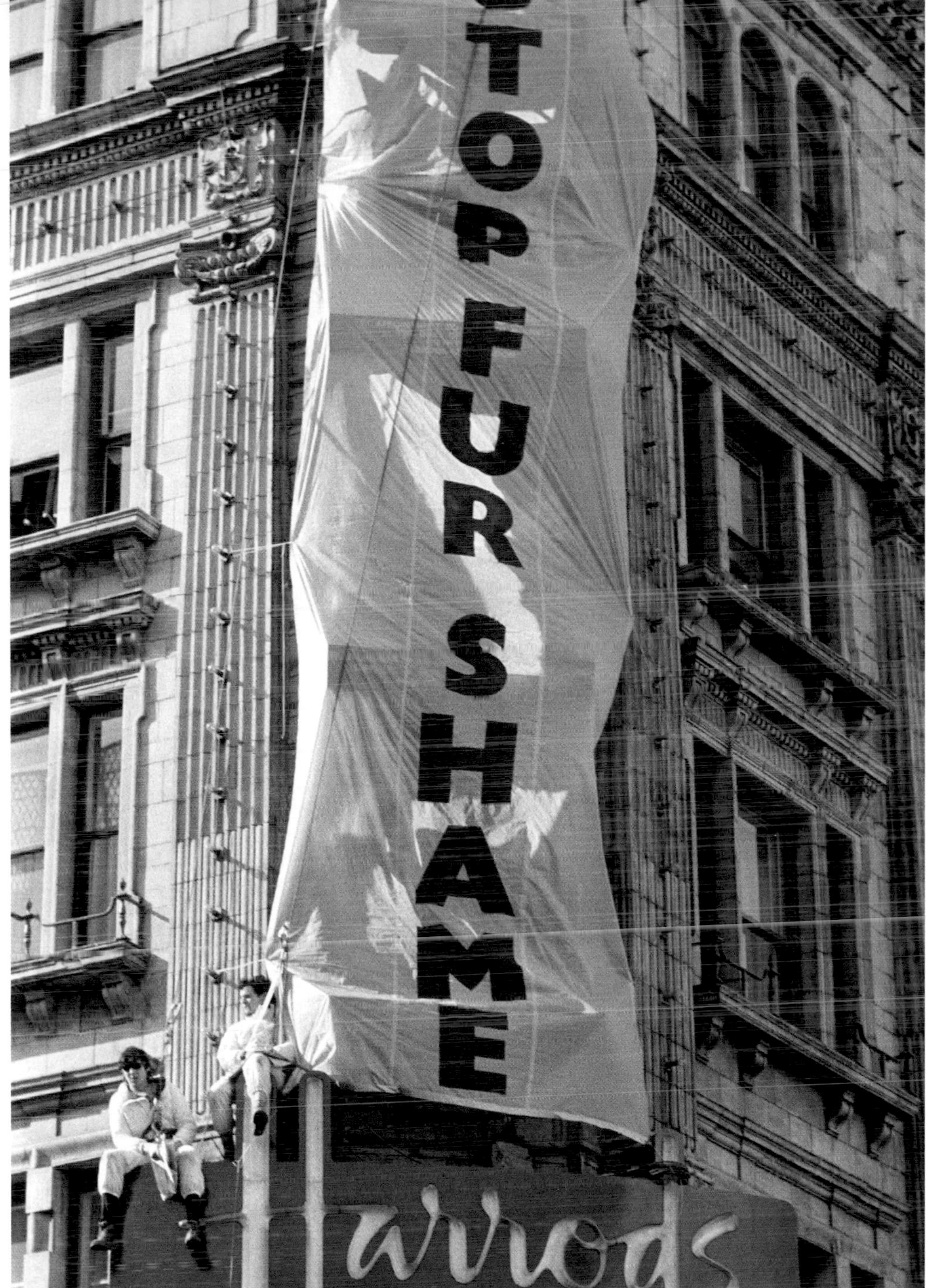

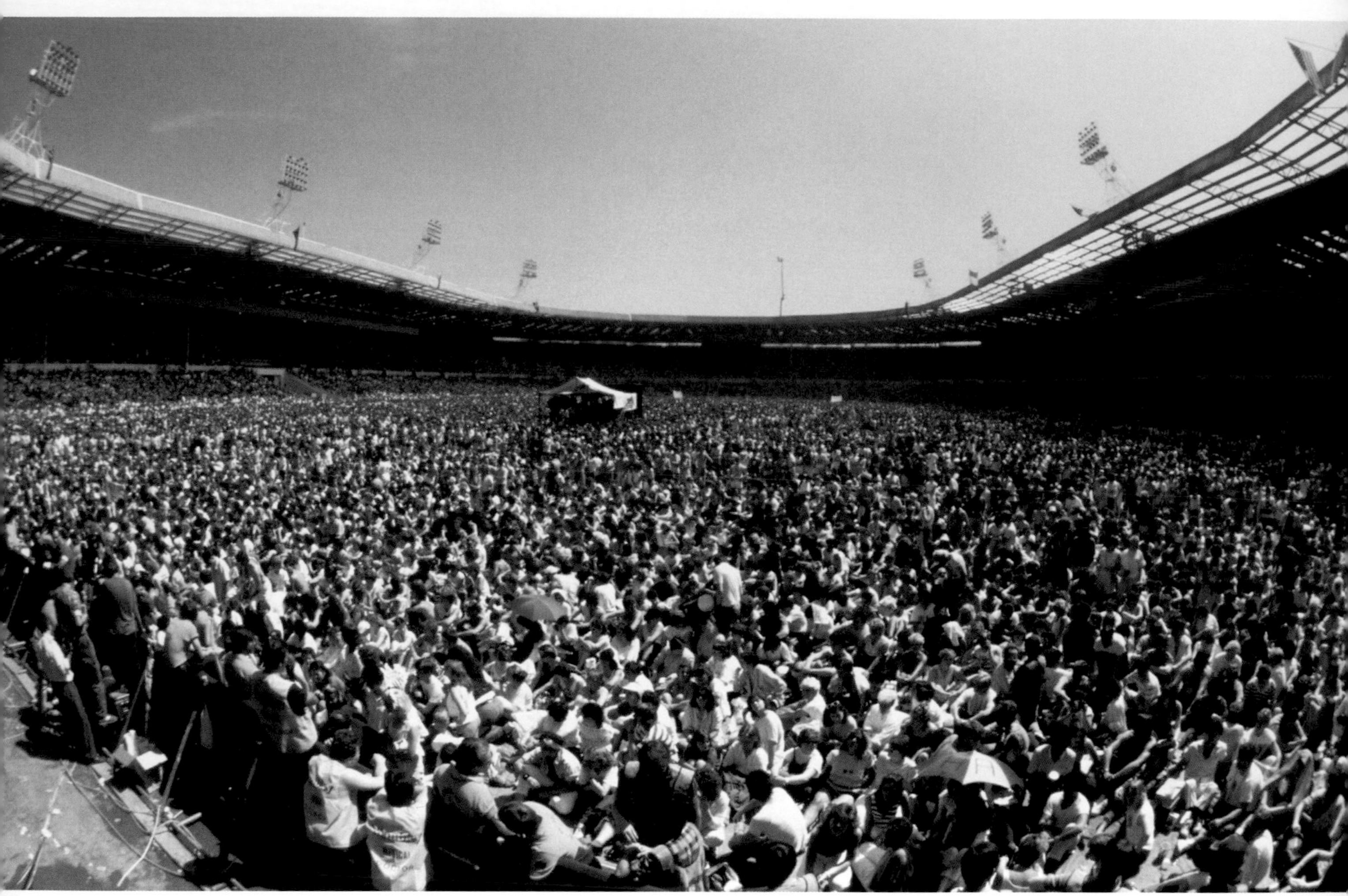

Wembley Stadium during
the *Live Aid* concert.
13th July, 1985

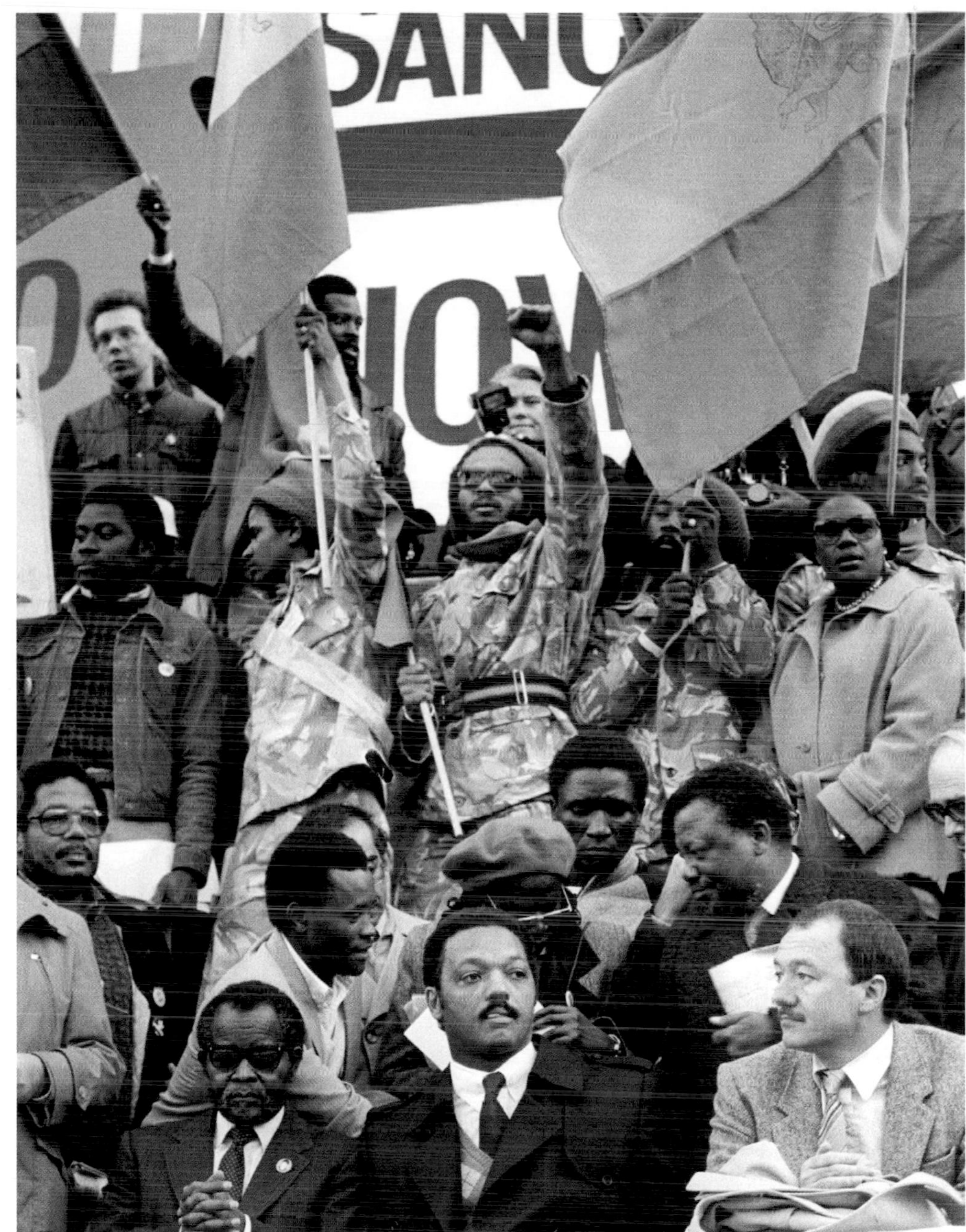

ANC President Oliver Tambo, US Democrat and civil rights campaigner Reverend Jesse Jackson and GLC leader Ken Livingstone, on the plinth of Nelson's Column in Trafalgar Square, during an anti-apartheid rally.
2nd November, 1985

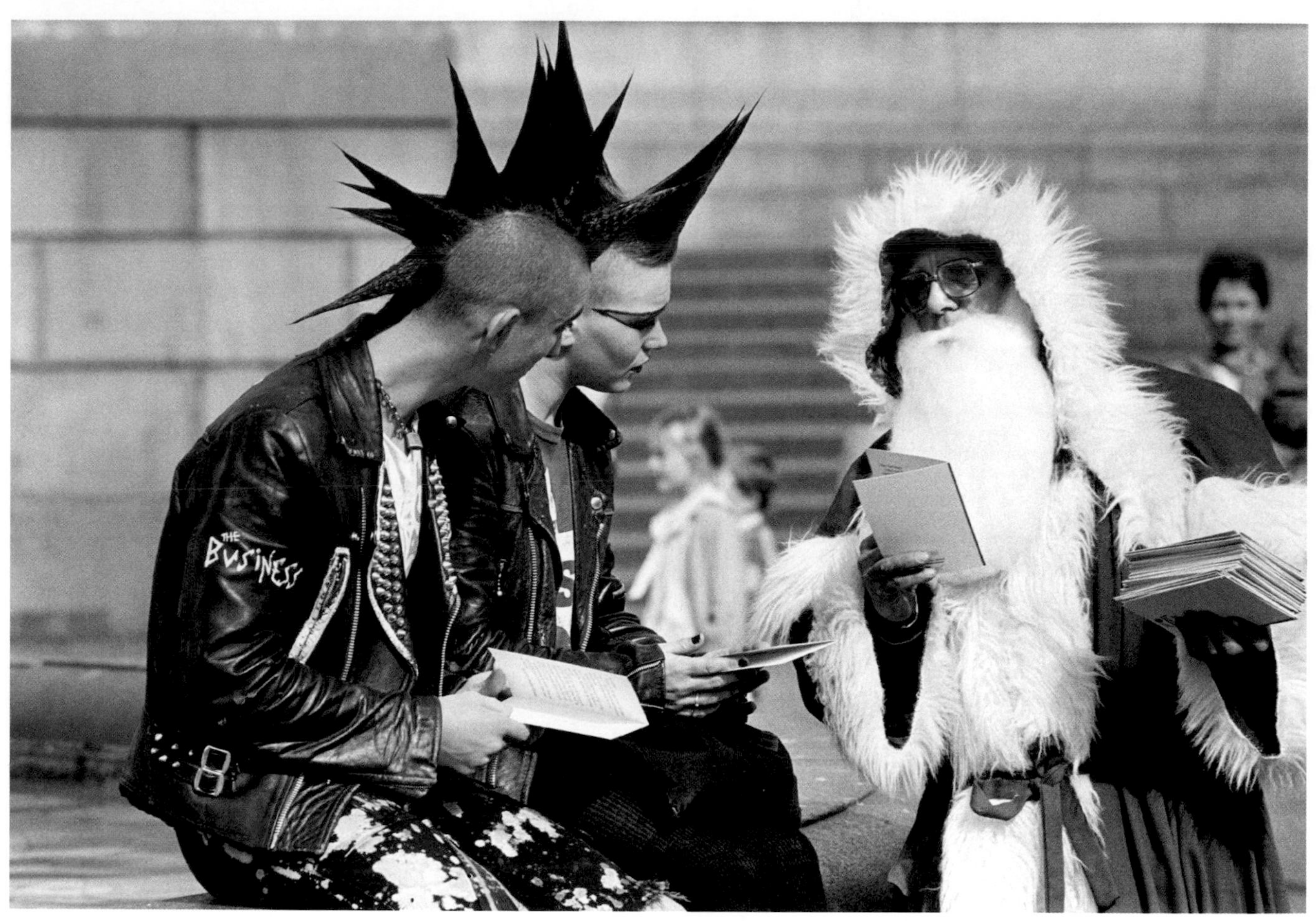

Santa Claus hands out early Christmas cards to punk rockers in Trafalgar Square to promote a charity campaign.
18th September, 1986

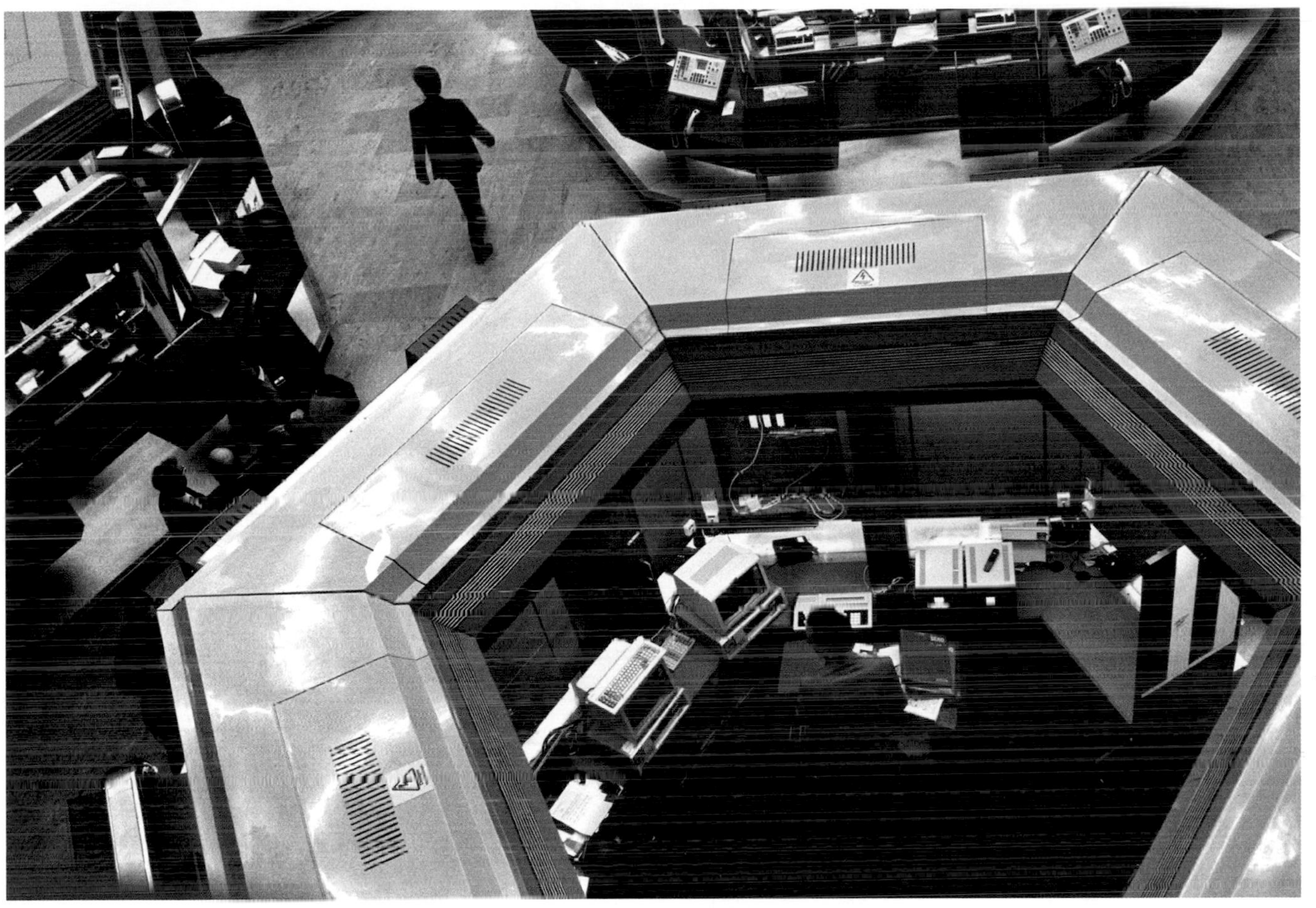

Dealing on the new high technology computer systems begins on the floor of the London Stock Exchange as the City's *Big Bang* shake-up takes off.
27th October, 1986

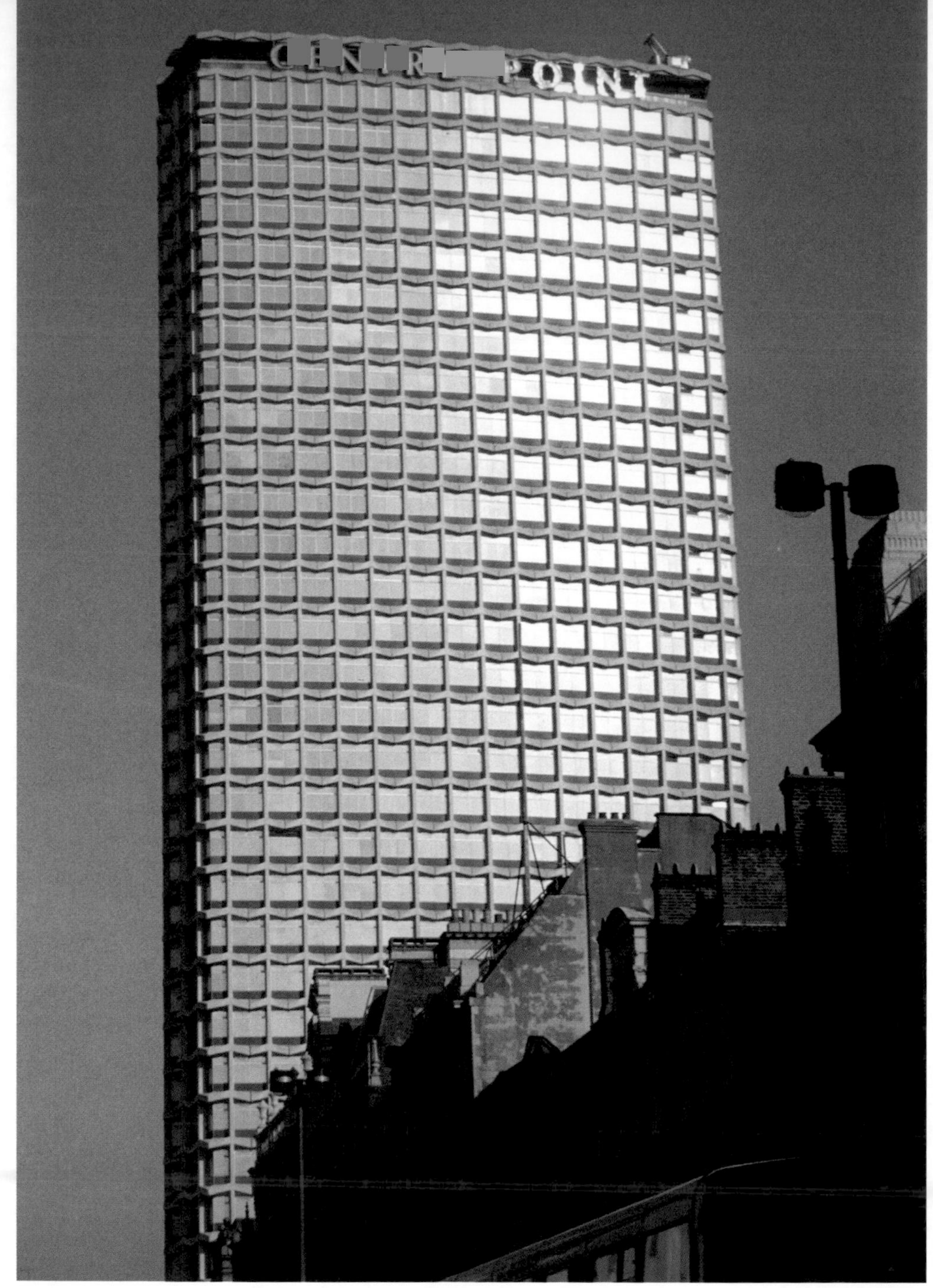

Centre Point.
March, 1990

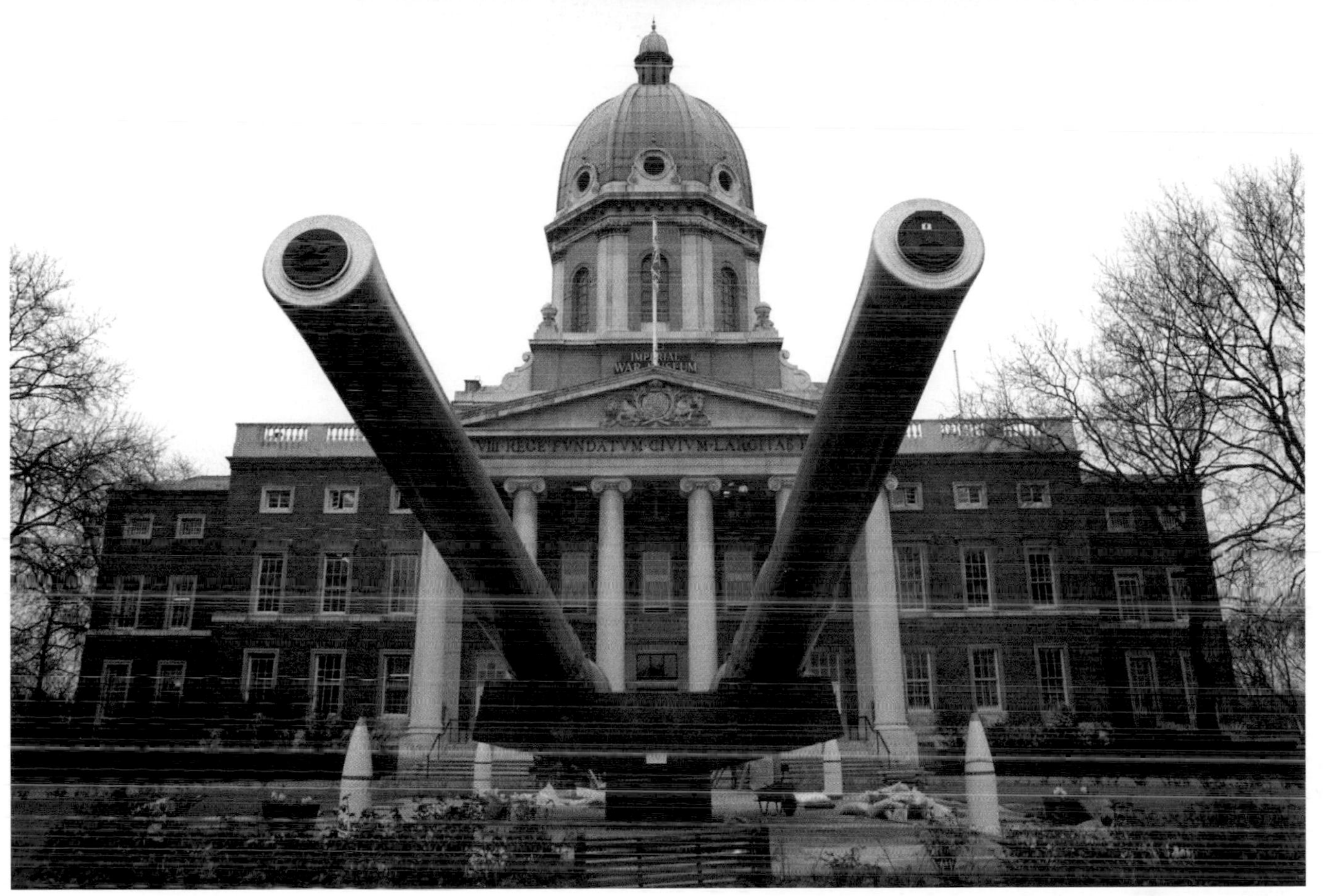

The Imperial War Museum.
March, 1990

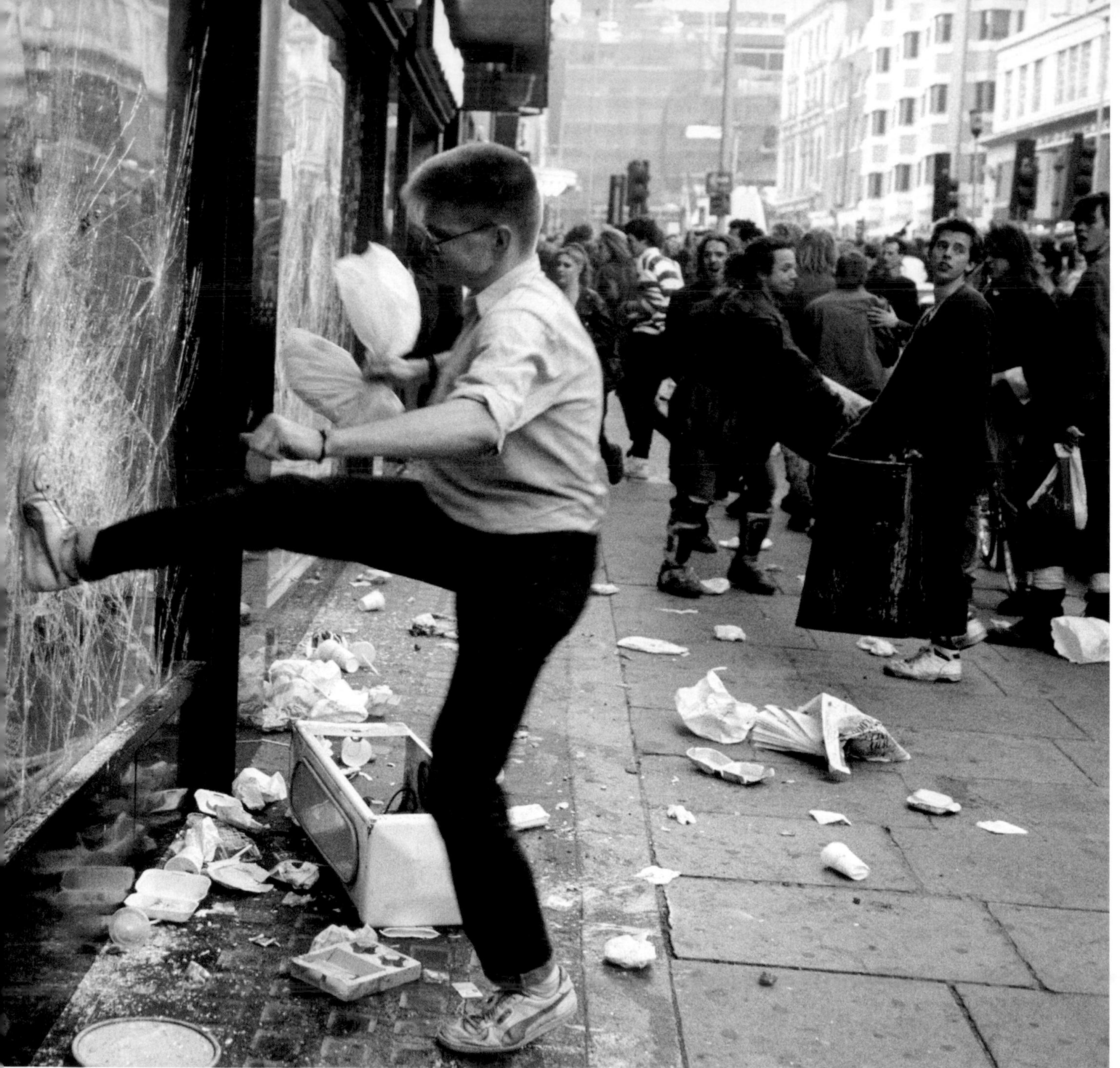

Facing page: A protester kicks the window of McDonalds in Lower Regent Street as poll tax demonstrations descend into rioting.
31st March, 1990

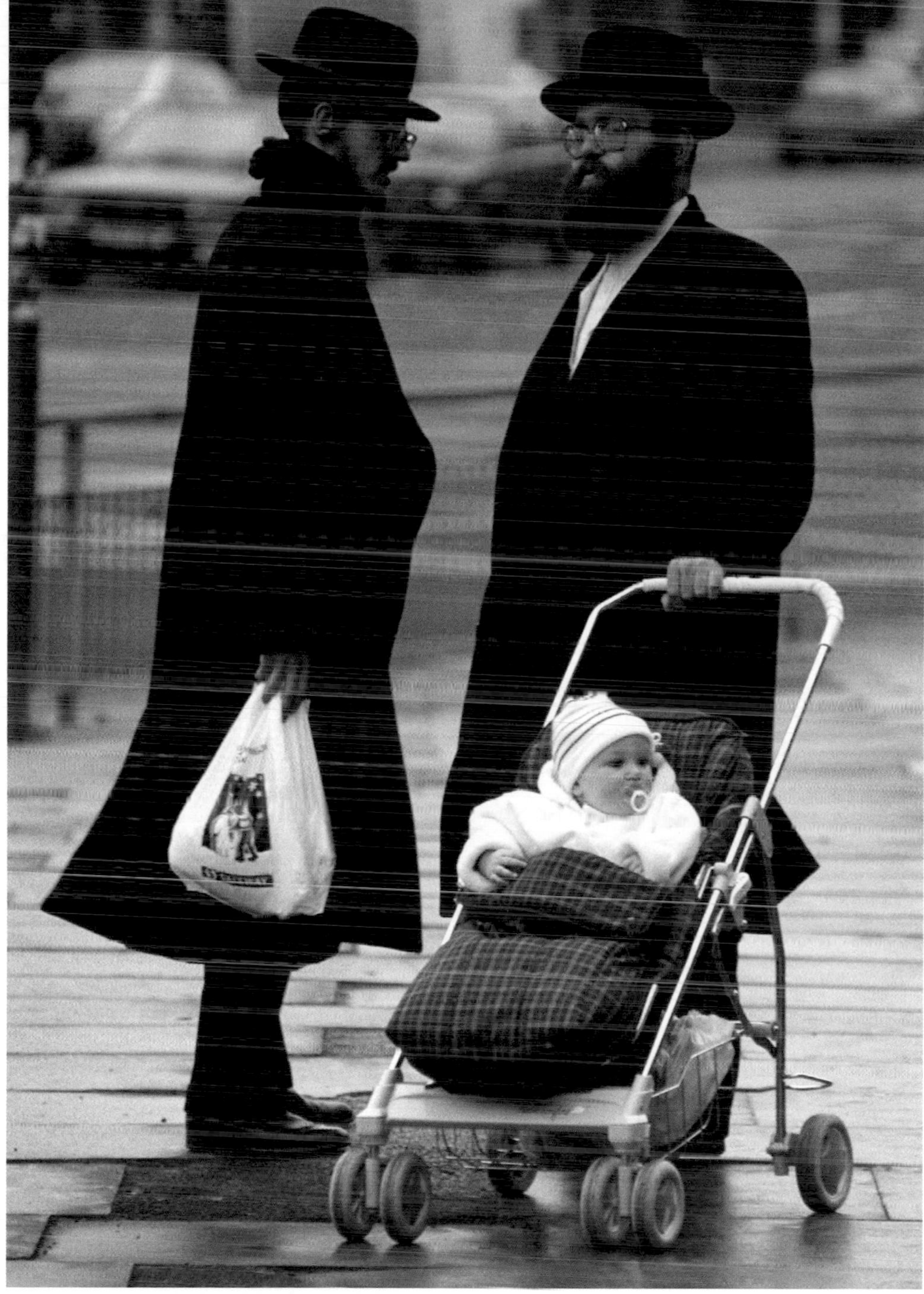

Members of the Hasidic Jewish community in Stamford Hill.
18th March, 1991

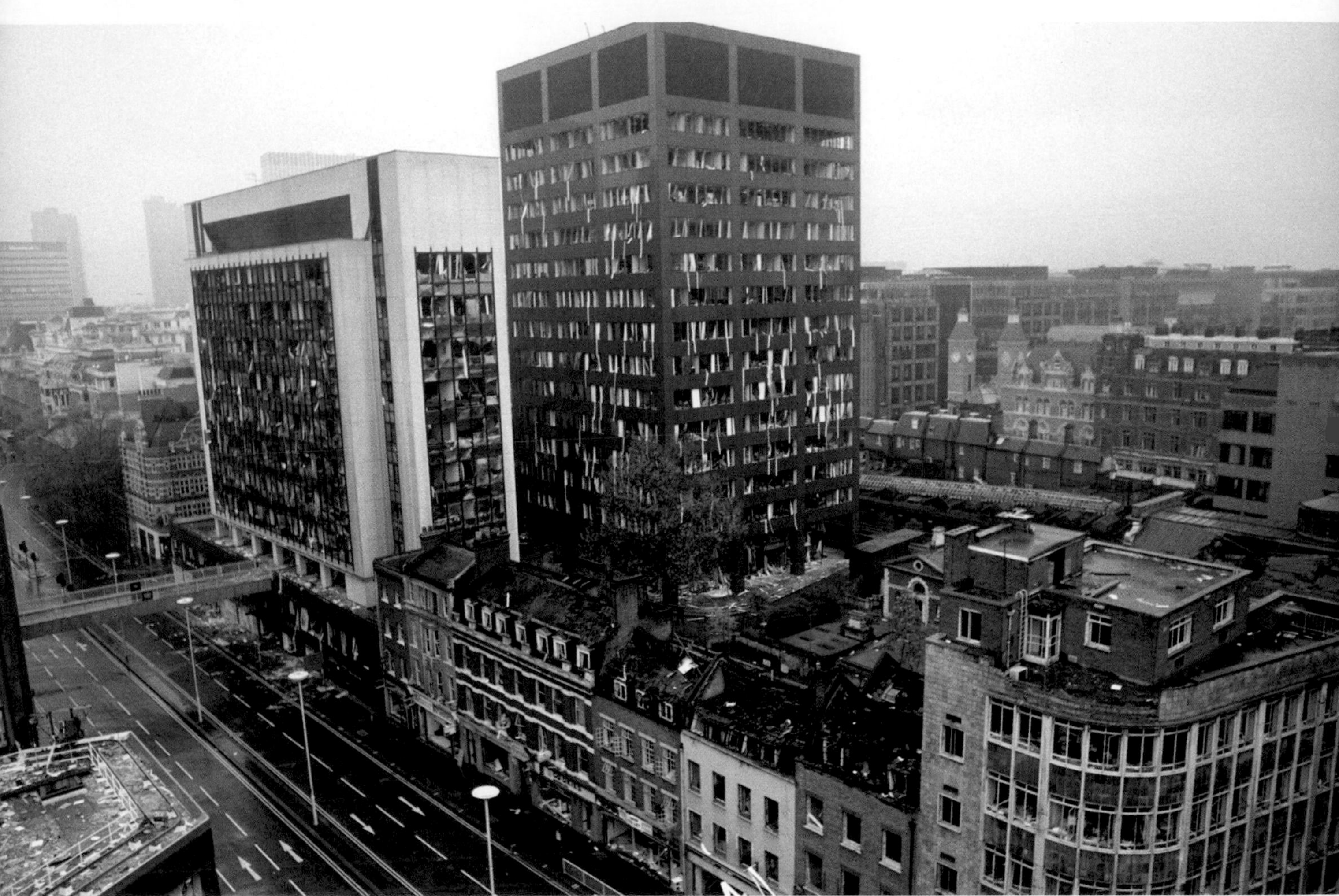

A massive IRA bomb outside the HSBC building killed one and injured more than 40 people.
26th April, 1993

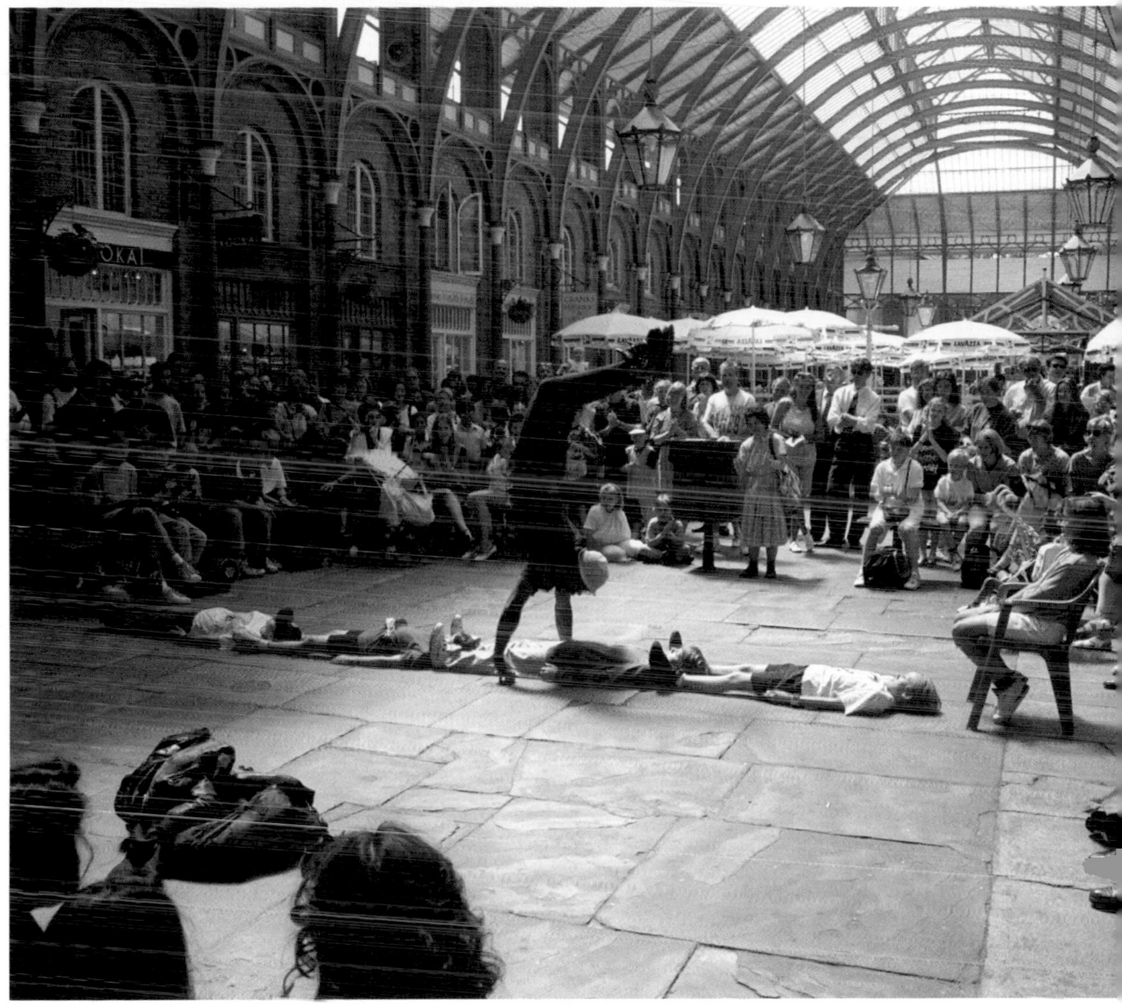

Covent Garden market has long since departed, leaving a space for shops and buskers.
8th July, 1993

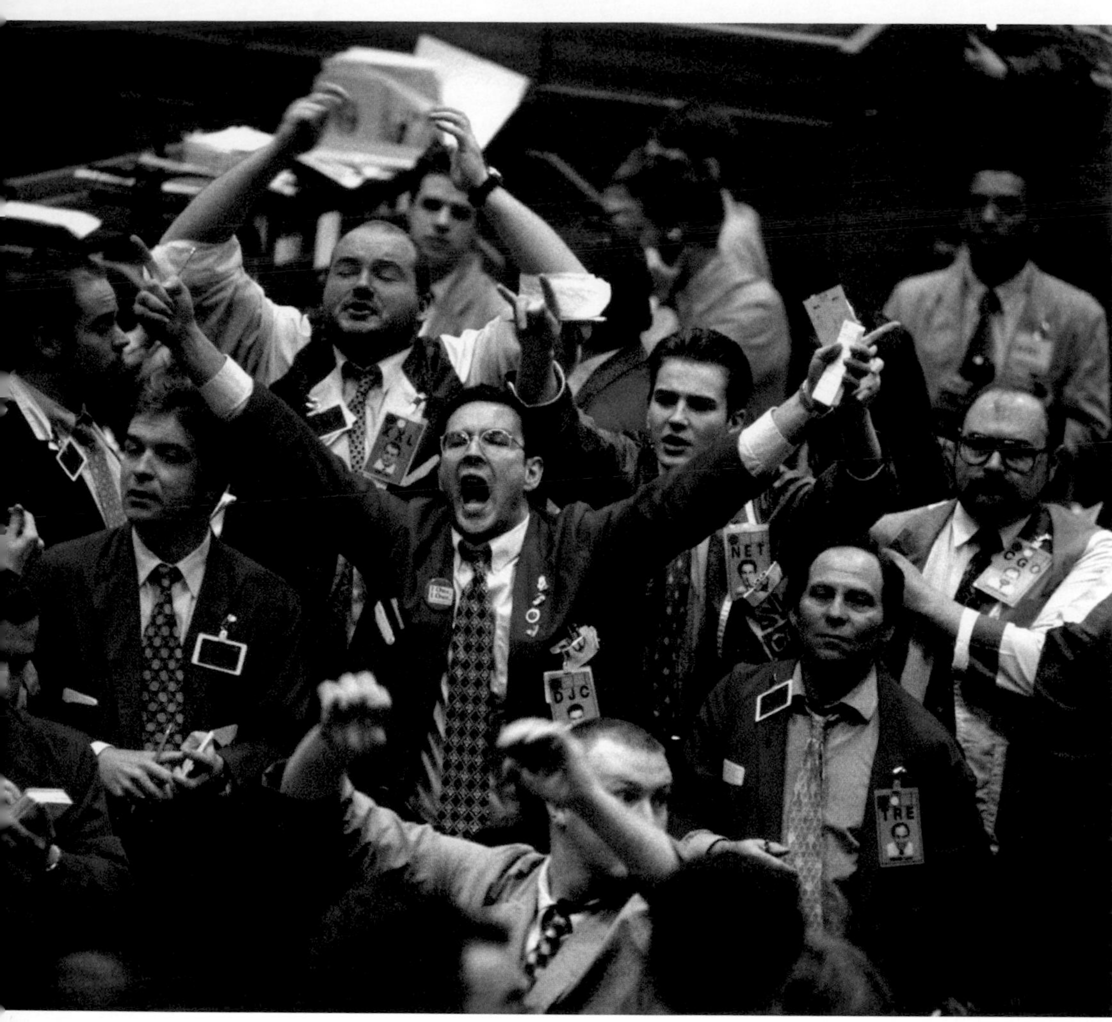

Frantic bidding on the floor of the LIFFE, after the Bank of England raises interest rates in a bid to cool the economy.
2nd February, 1995

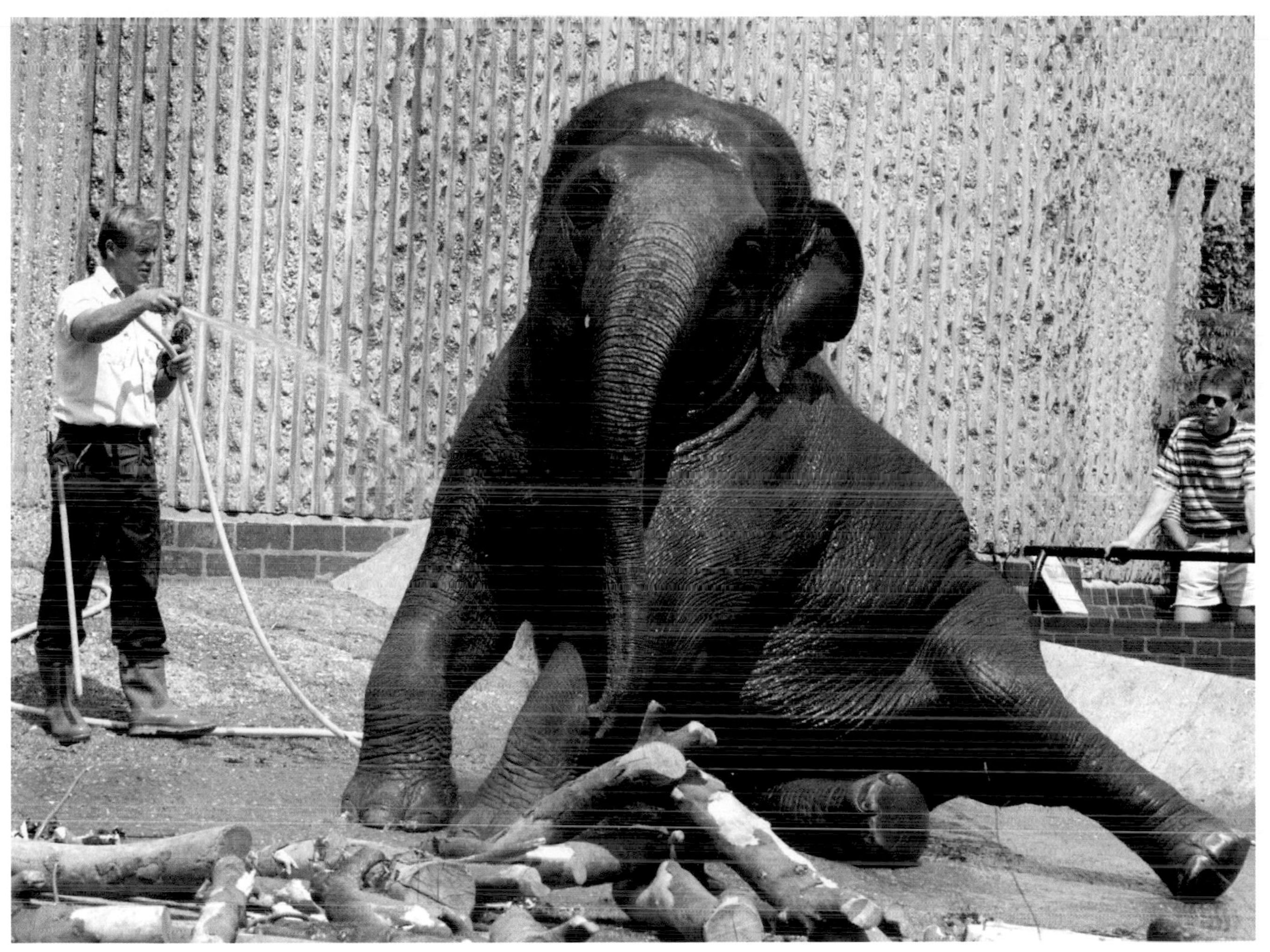

Hosing down London Zoo's elephants on the hottest day of the year.
1st August, 1995

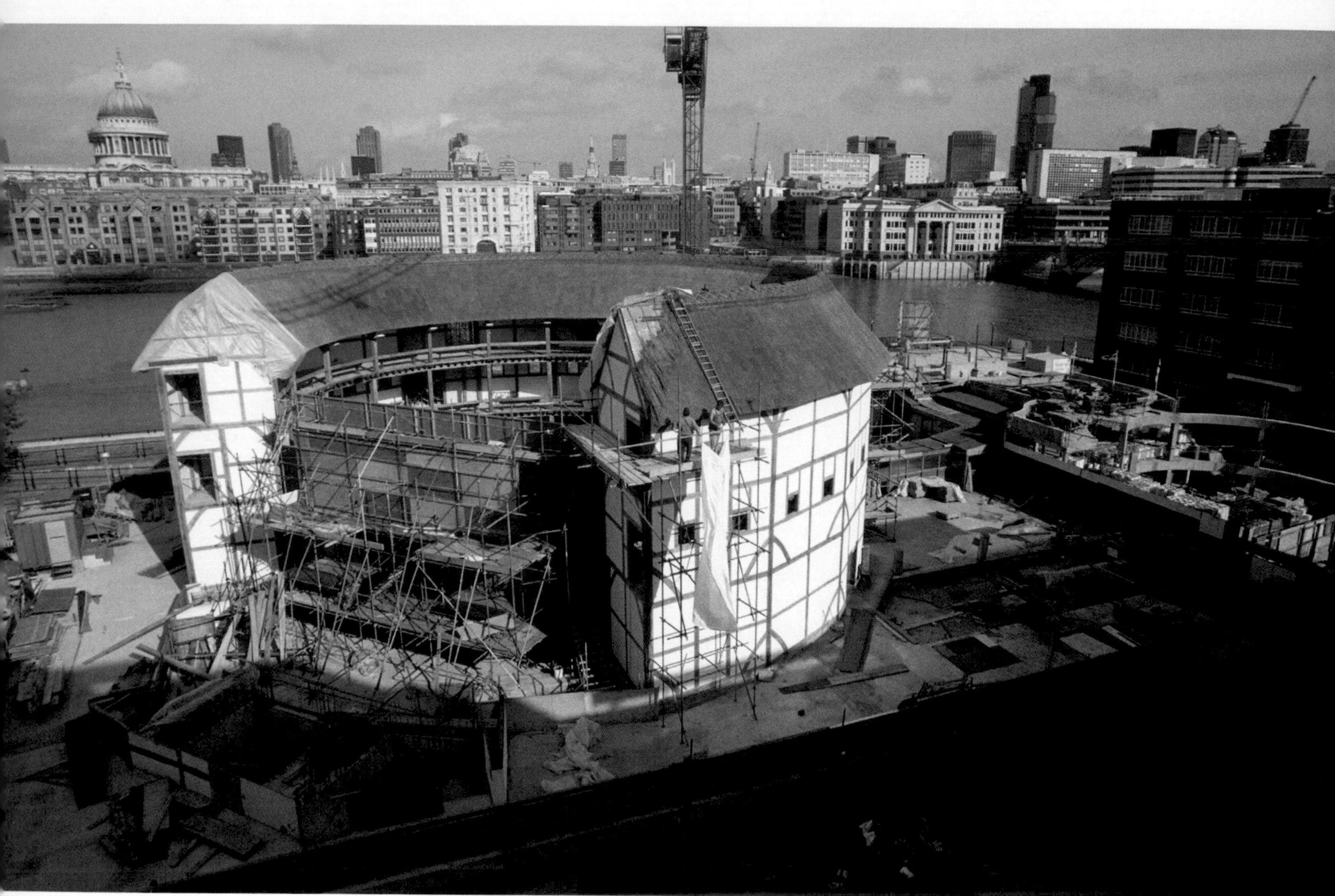

Work on the *Globe* theatre, on its original site on the South Bank.
16th October, 1995

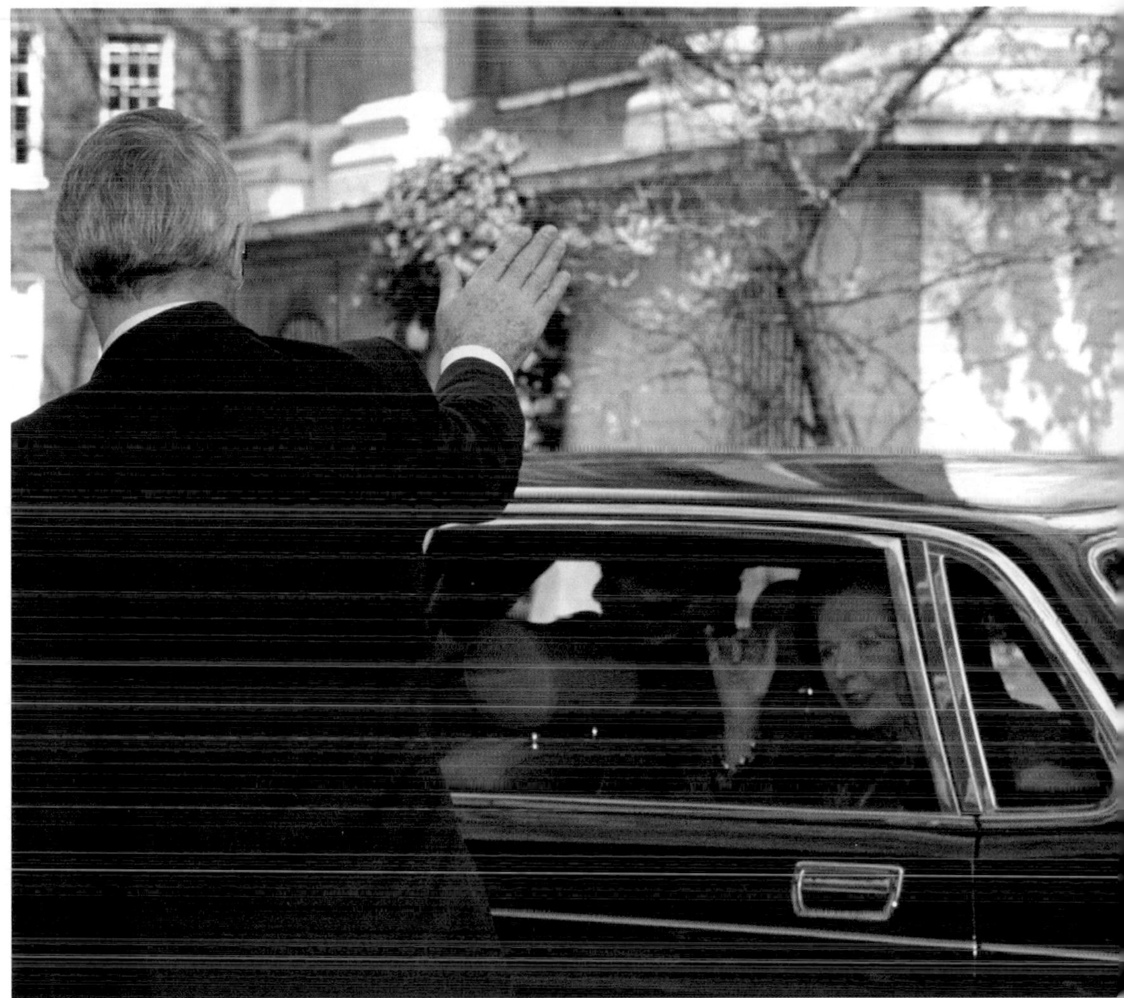

Prime Minister John Major waves goodbye to Baroness Thatcher as she leaves Conservative Central Office in London. Prospects for the following General Election looked bleak for the Tories.
6th April, 1997

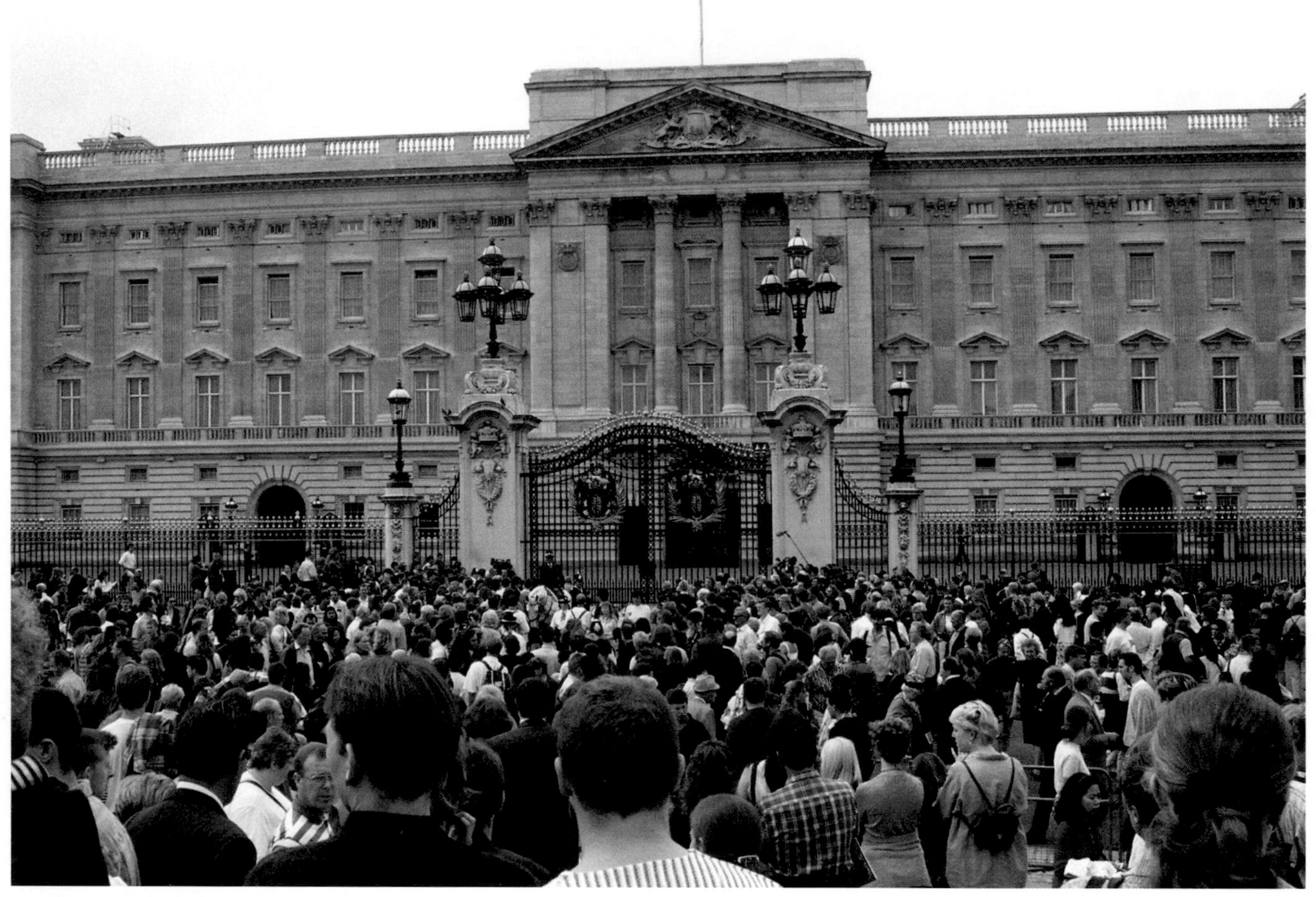

Crowds outside Buckingham Palace following the death of Diana, Princess of Wales.
31st August, 1997

Facing page: (L-R) The Earl Spencer, Princes William, Harry and The Prince of Wales, wait as the hearse carrying the coffin of Diana, Princess of Wales, prepares to leave Westminster Abbey.
6th September, 1997

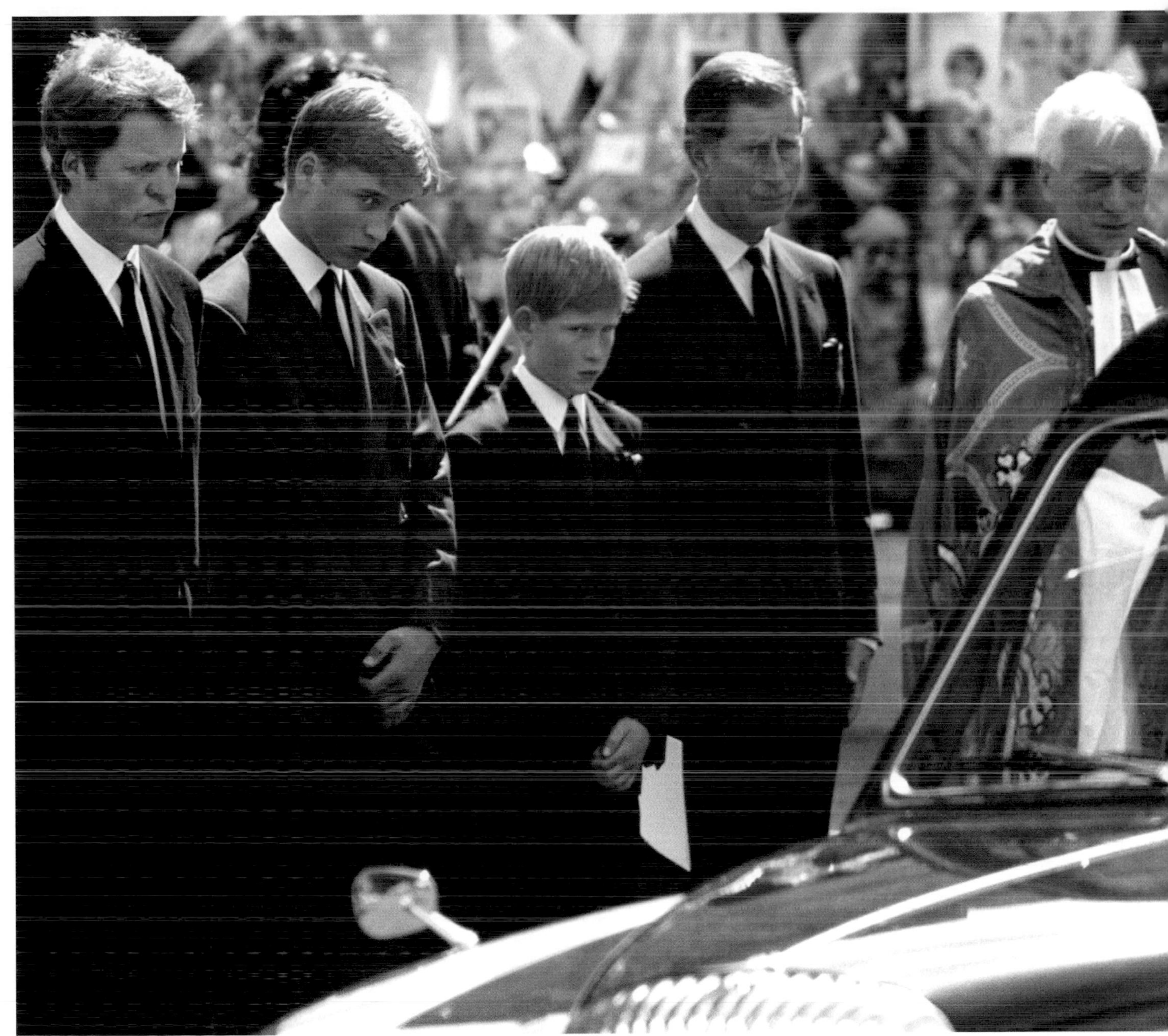

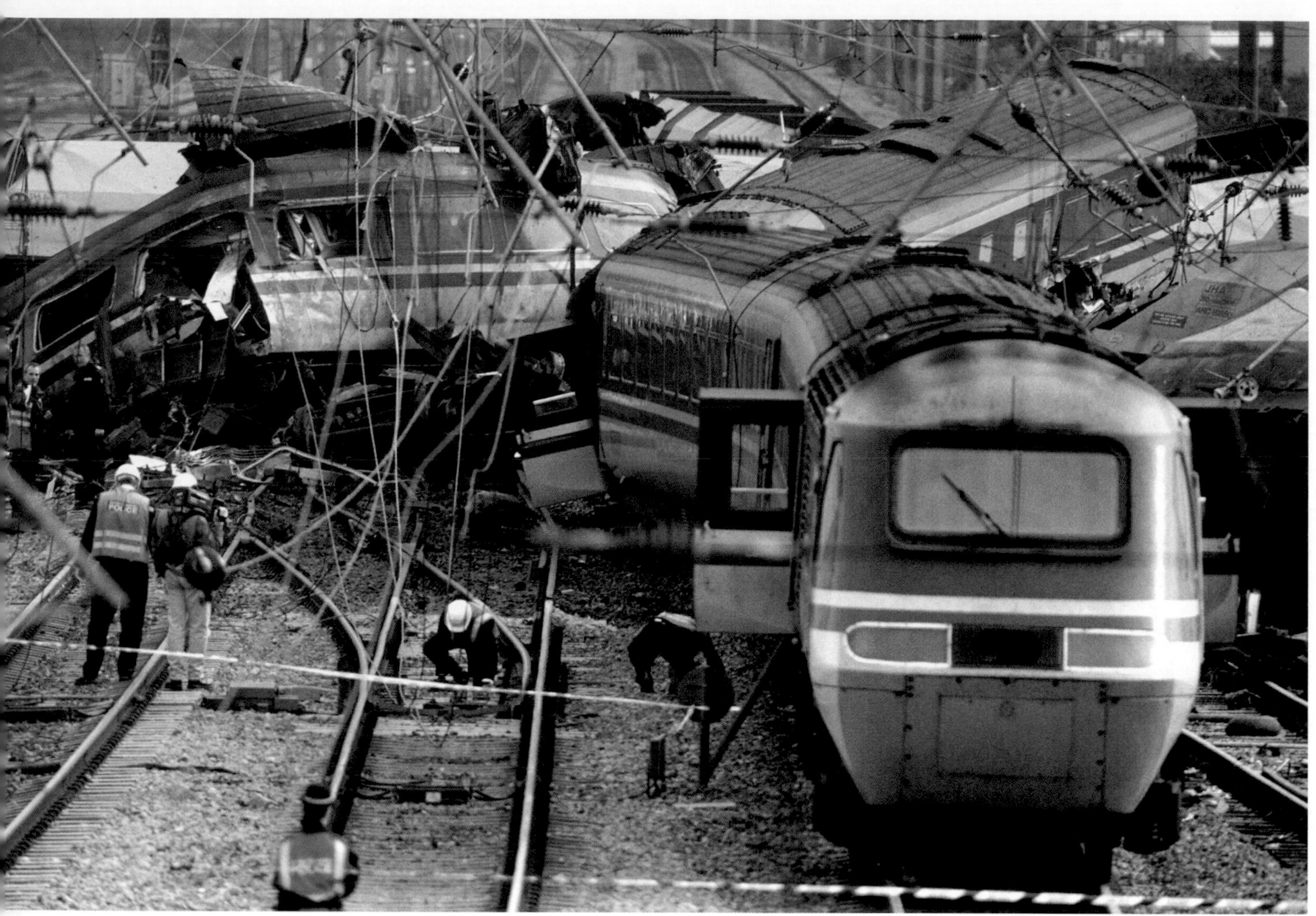

Clearing the site of the Southall rail crash after a Great Western express train ploughed into a goods train, leaving six dead and more than 160 injured.
20th September, 1997

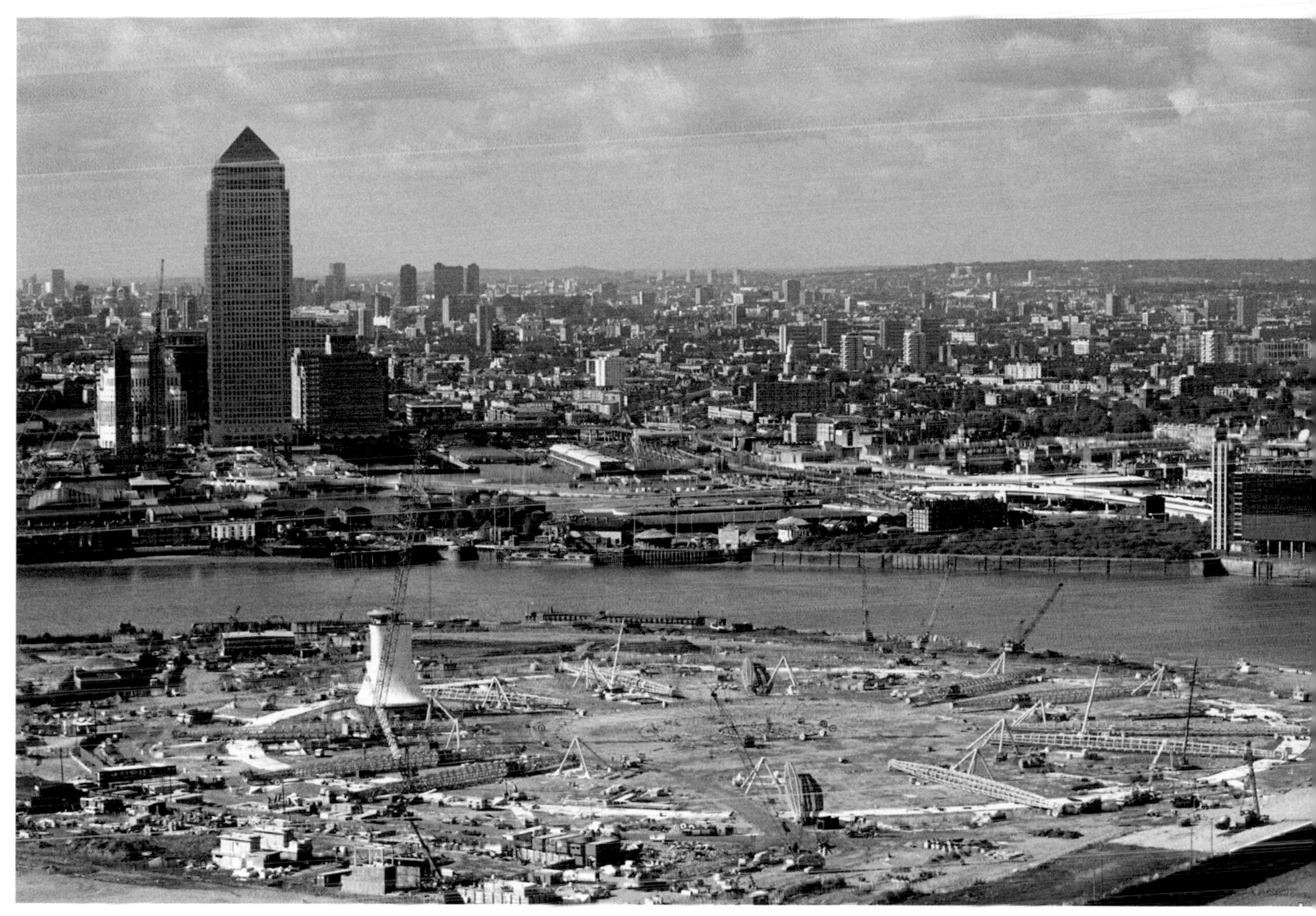

London's Docklands, as construction work begins on the Millennium Dome.
10th October, 1997

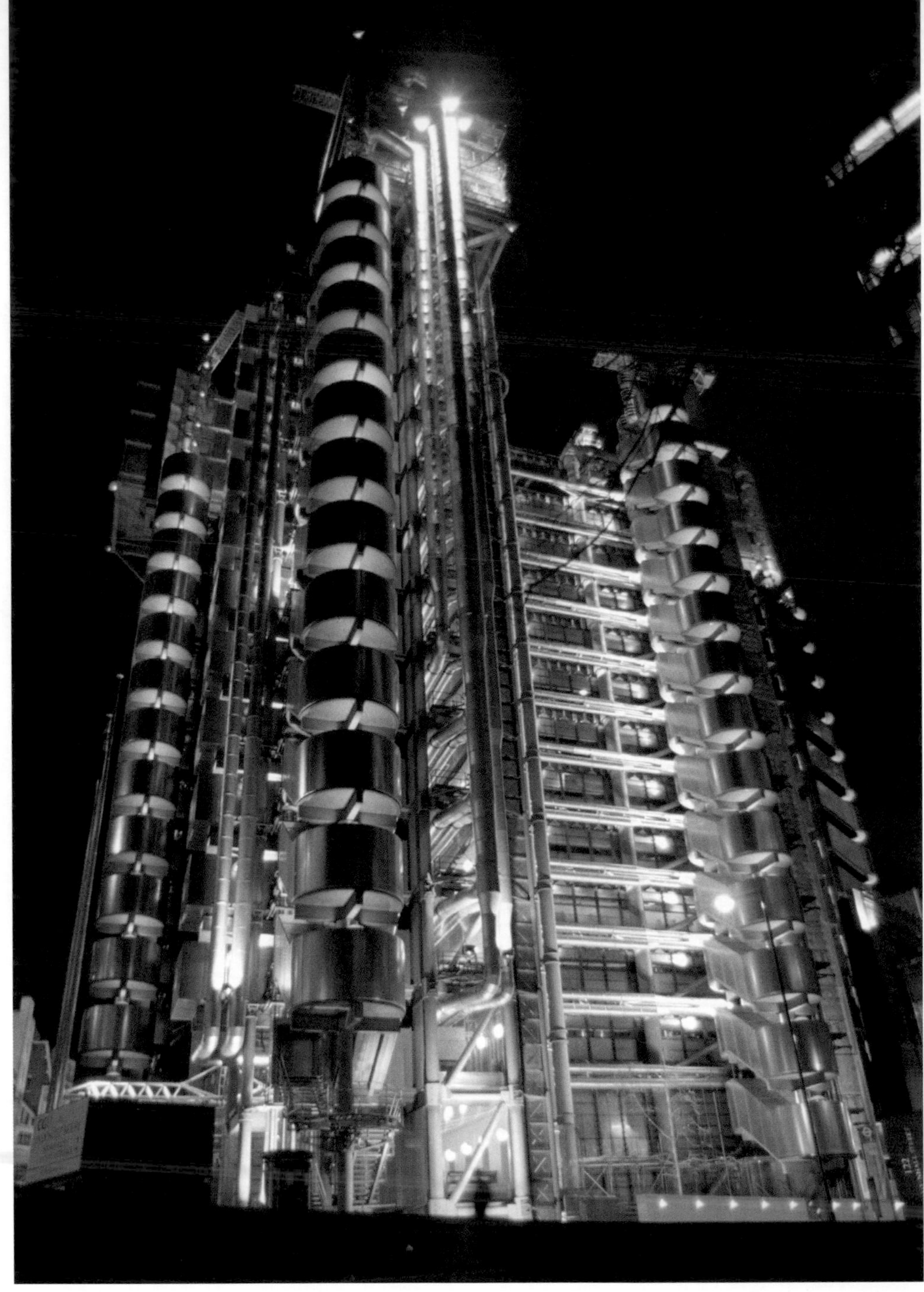

Richard Rogers' Lloyds Building in the City.
12th February, 1999

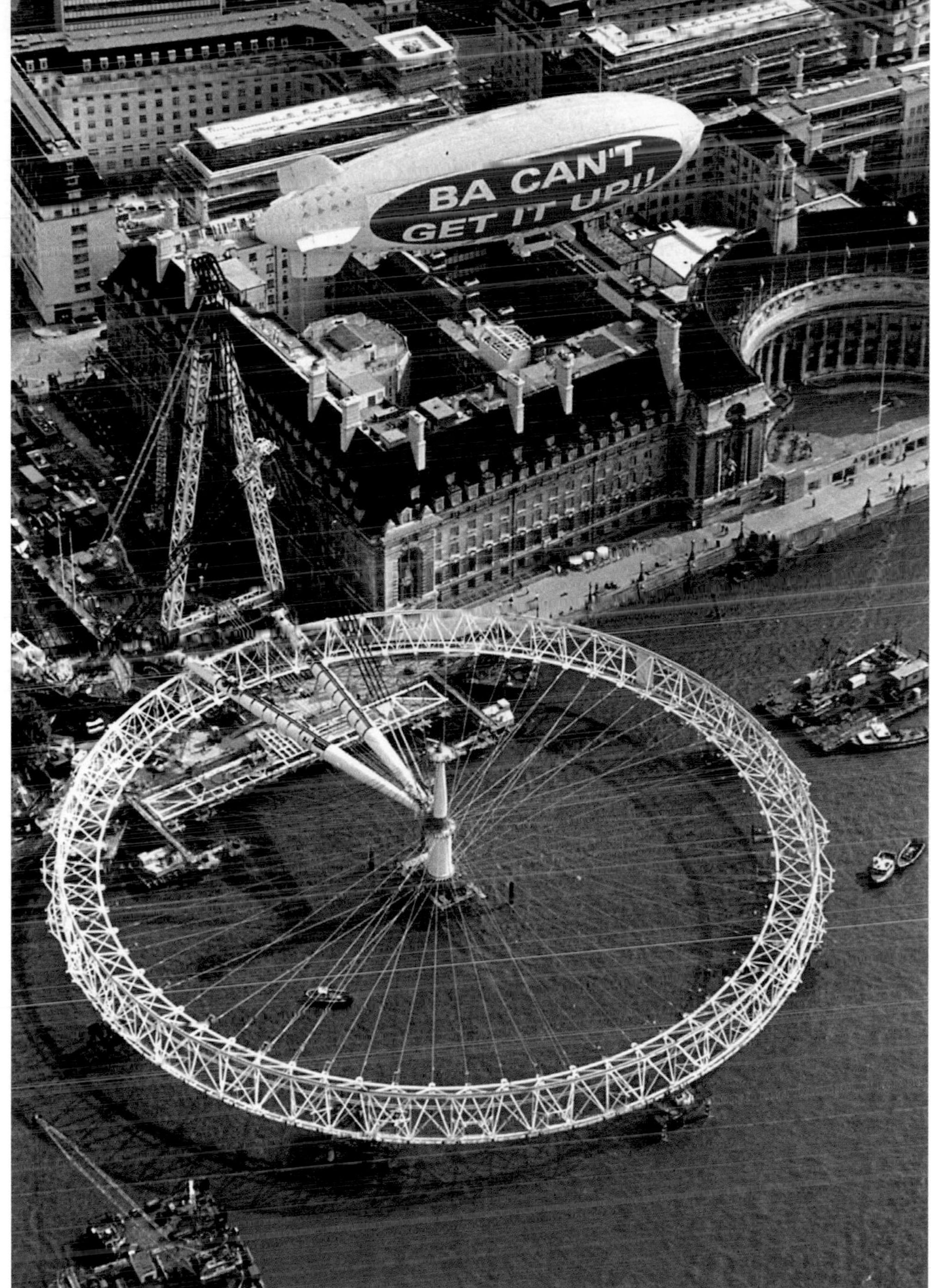

A Virgin light airship floats over the horizontal Millennium Wheel (the London Eye). The Wheel, sponsored by British Airways, was supposed to be lifted to its full height – three times taller than Tower Bridge – that month but when anchor clips holding its support cables started to buckle under the weight, the operation was aborted.
28th September, 1990

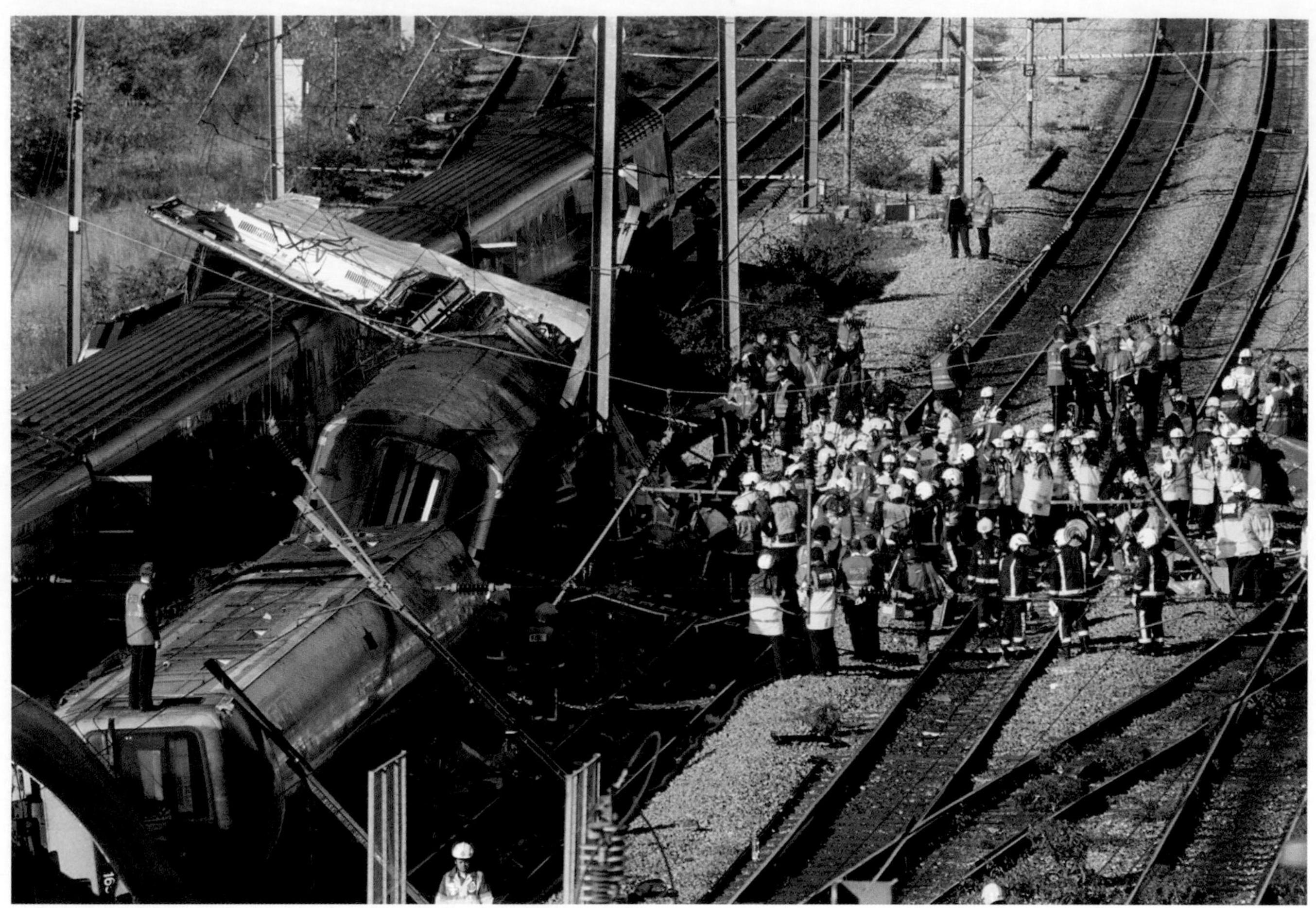

The Paddington rail crash; two mainline trains collided and caught fire in the morning rush hour outside Paddington Station. The disaster, which killed 31 people and injured over 500, was an echo of 1997's Southall crash which occurred close by on the same line.
5th October, 1999

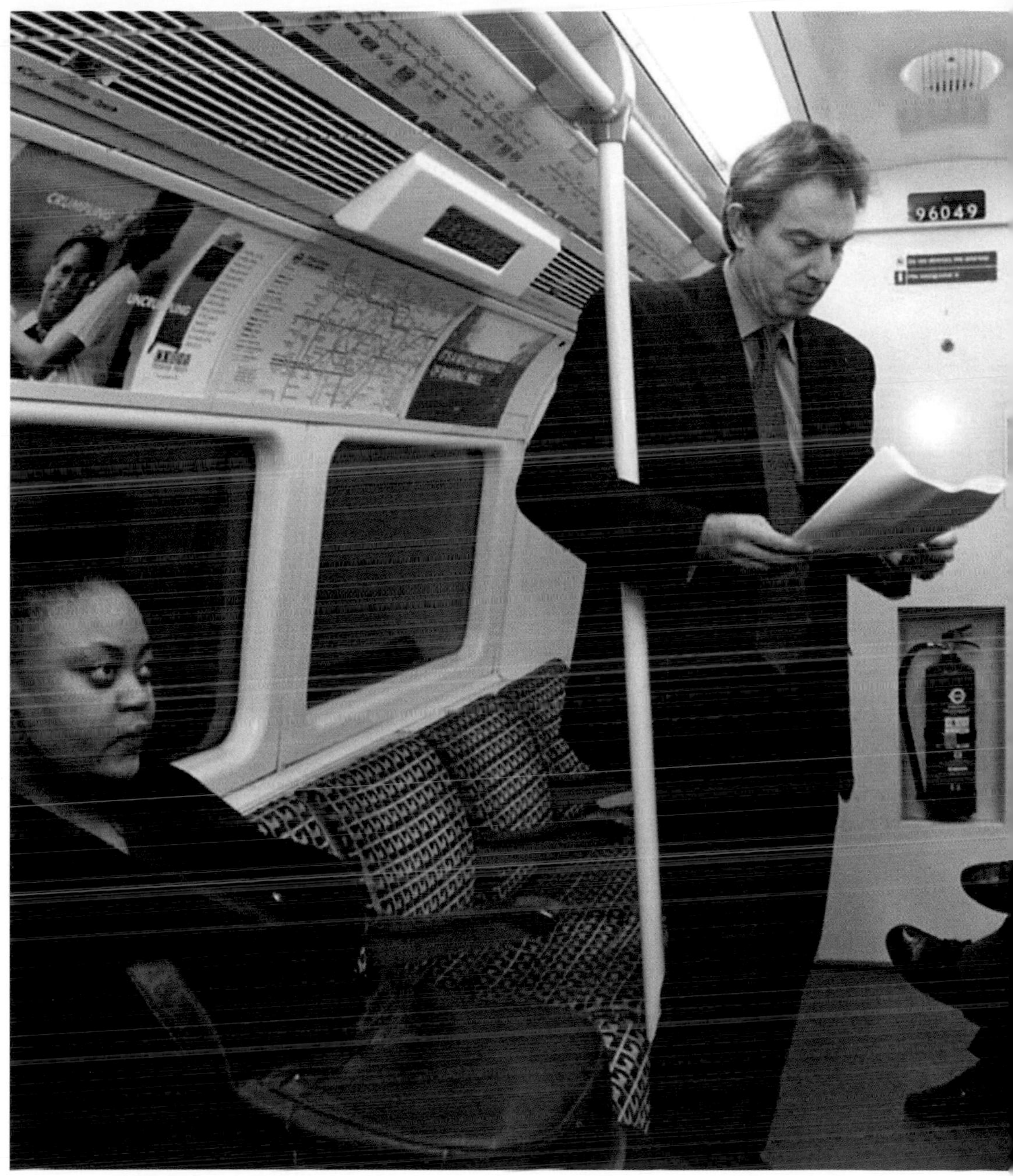

Prime Minister Tony Blair on the newly built Jubilee Line extension, on his way to the Millennium Dome.
14th December, 1999

Facing page: Abseilers clean one of the faces of Big Ben.
20th August, 2001

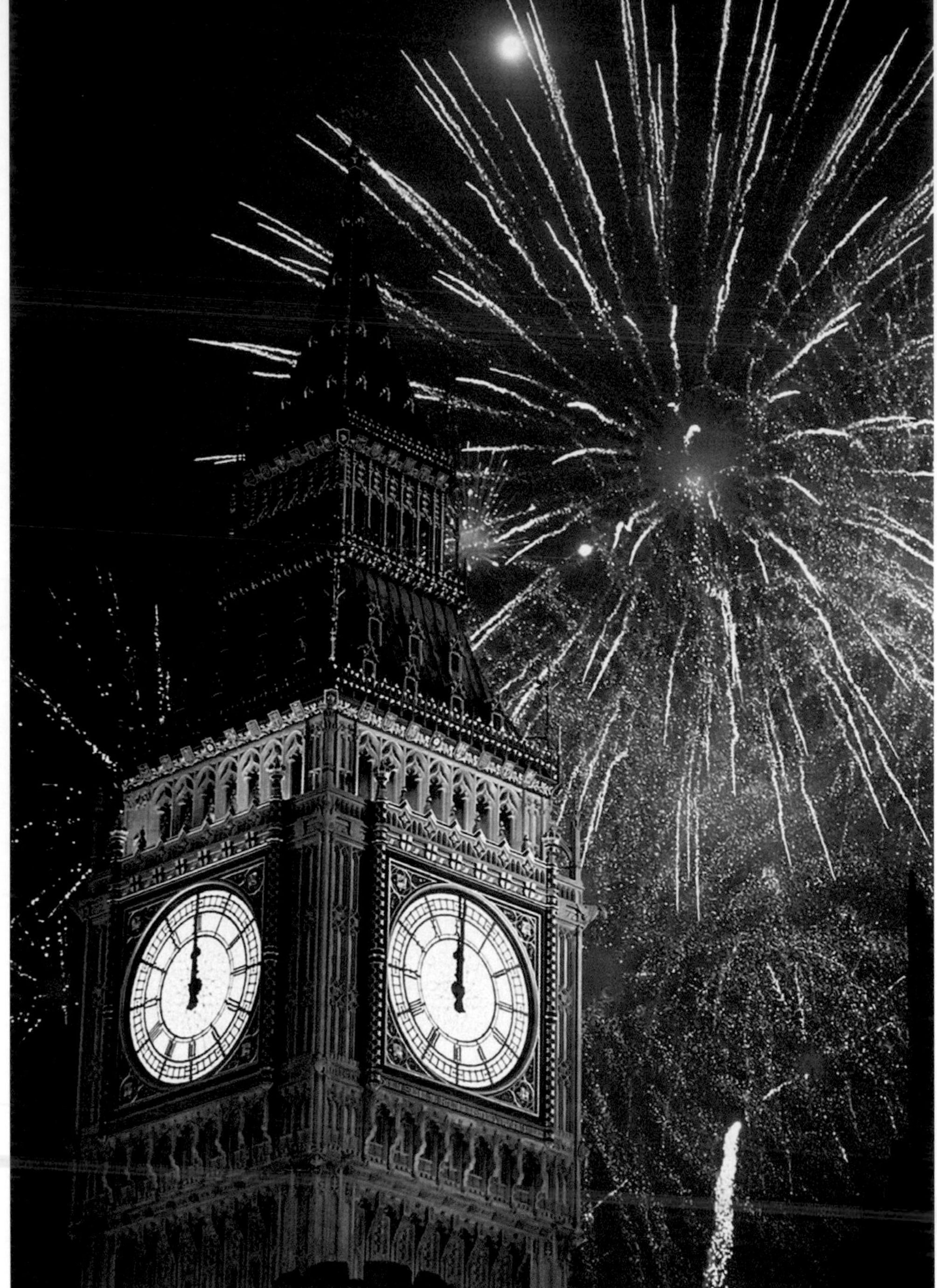

Fireworks usher in the new millennium.
1st January, 2000

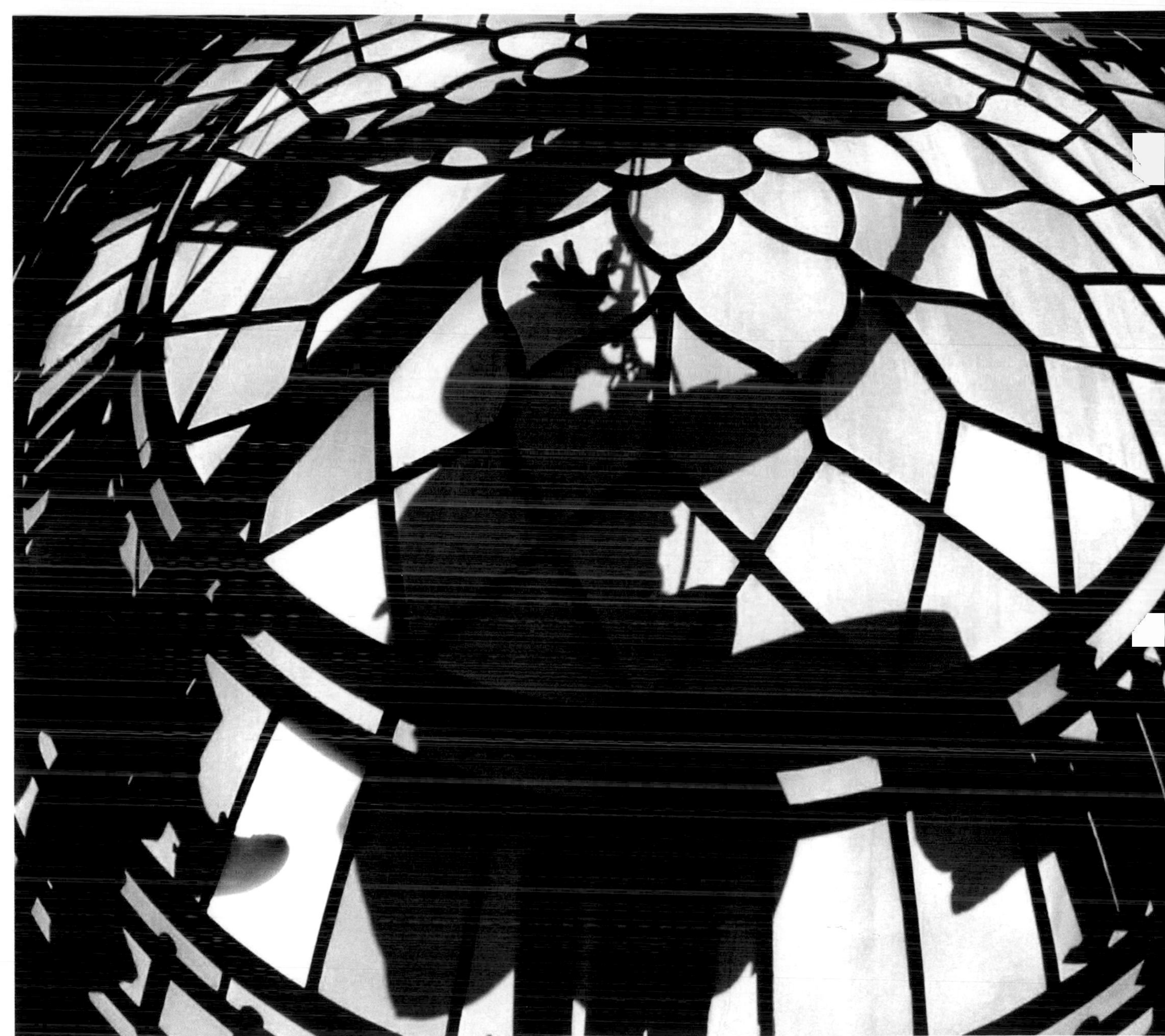

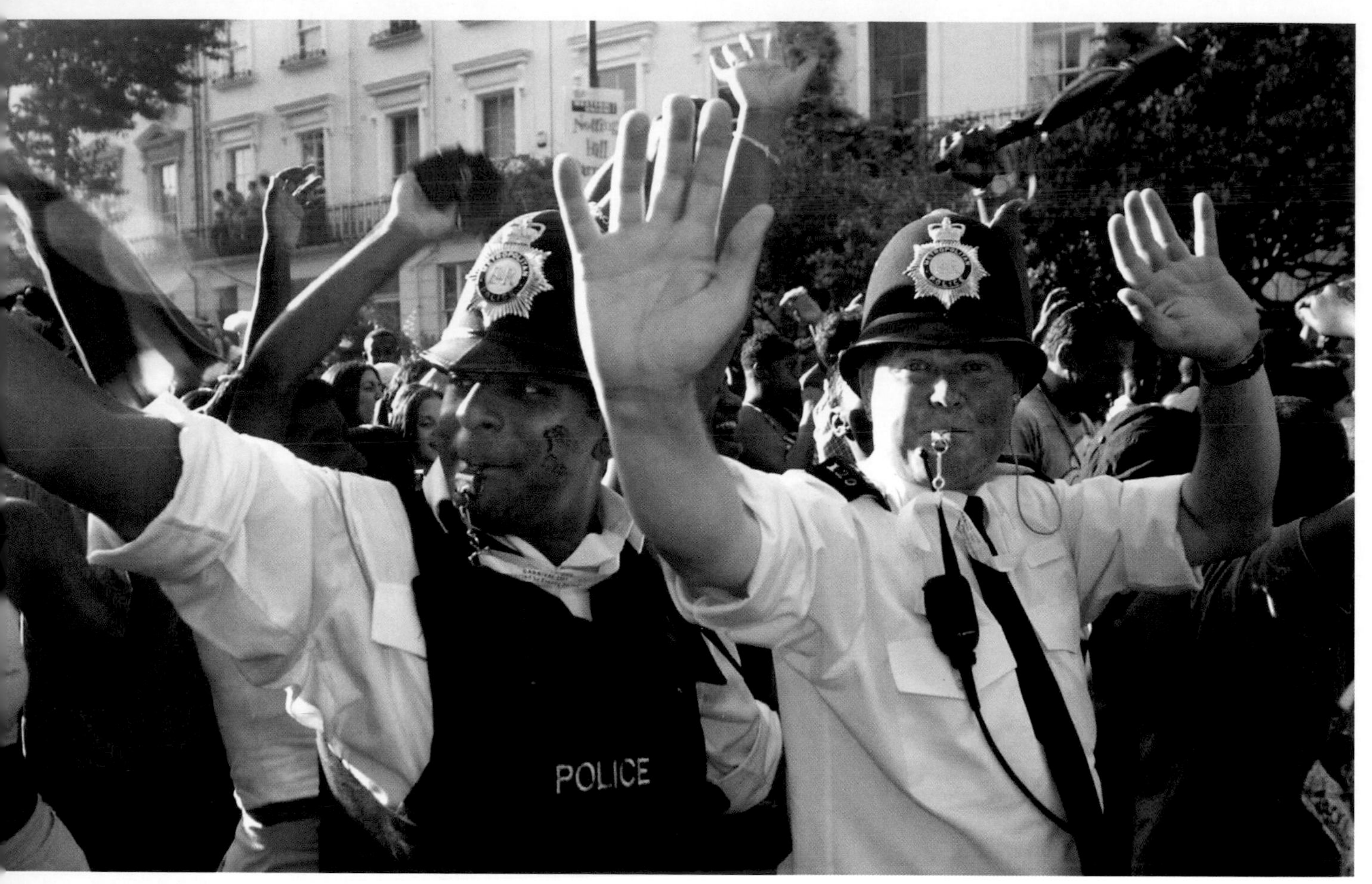

Policemen join in the fun at
the Notting Hill Carnival.
27th August, 2001

The Stock Exchange closes early after terrorist attacks destroy the World Trade Center in New York.
11th September, 2001

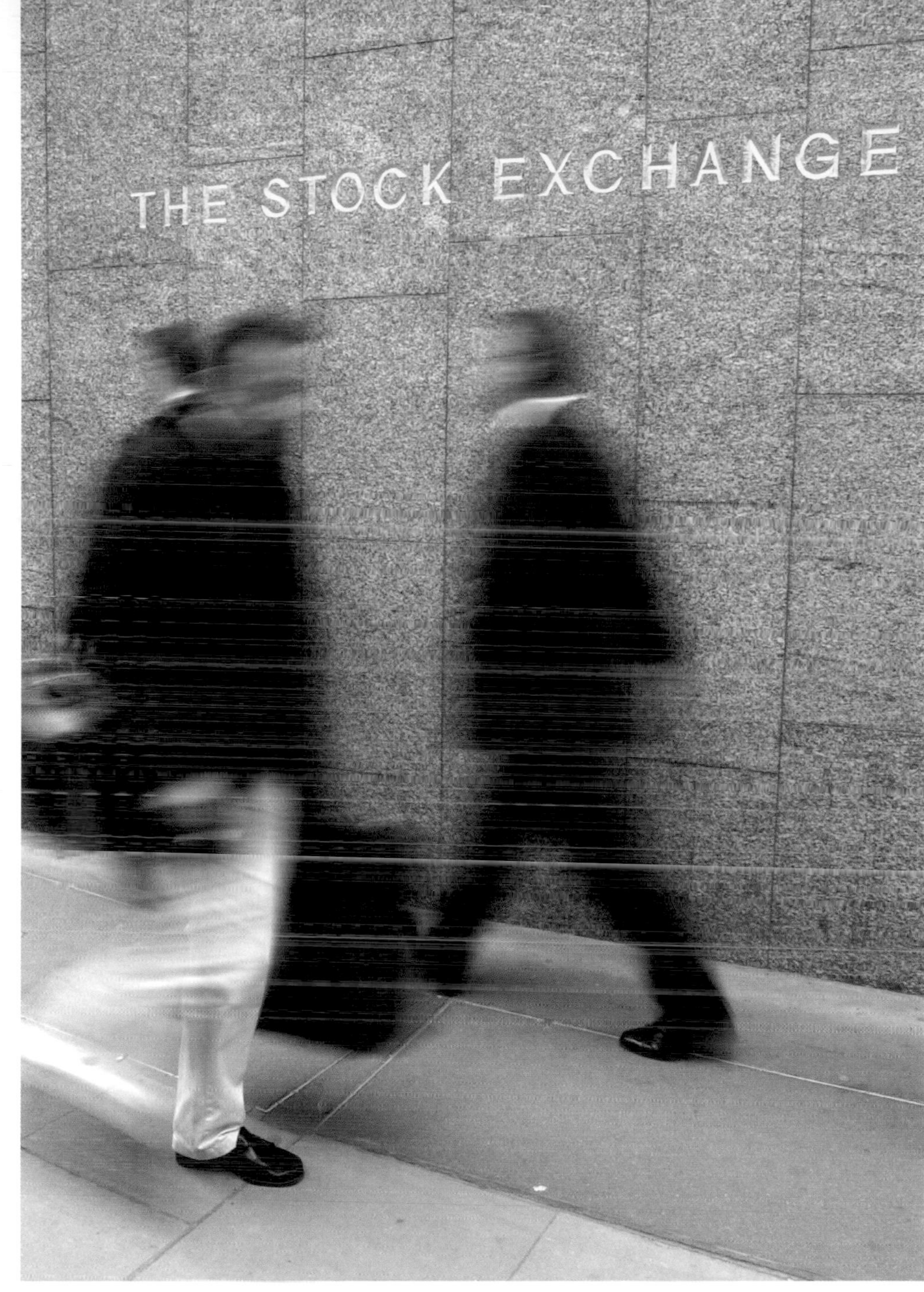

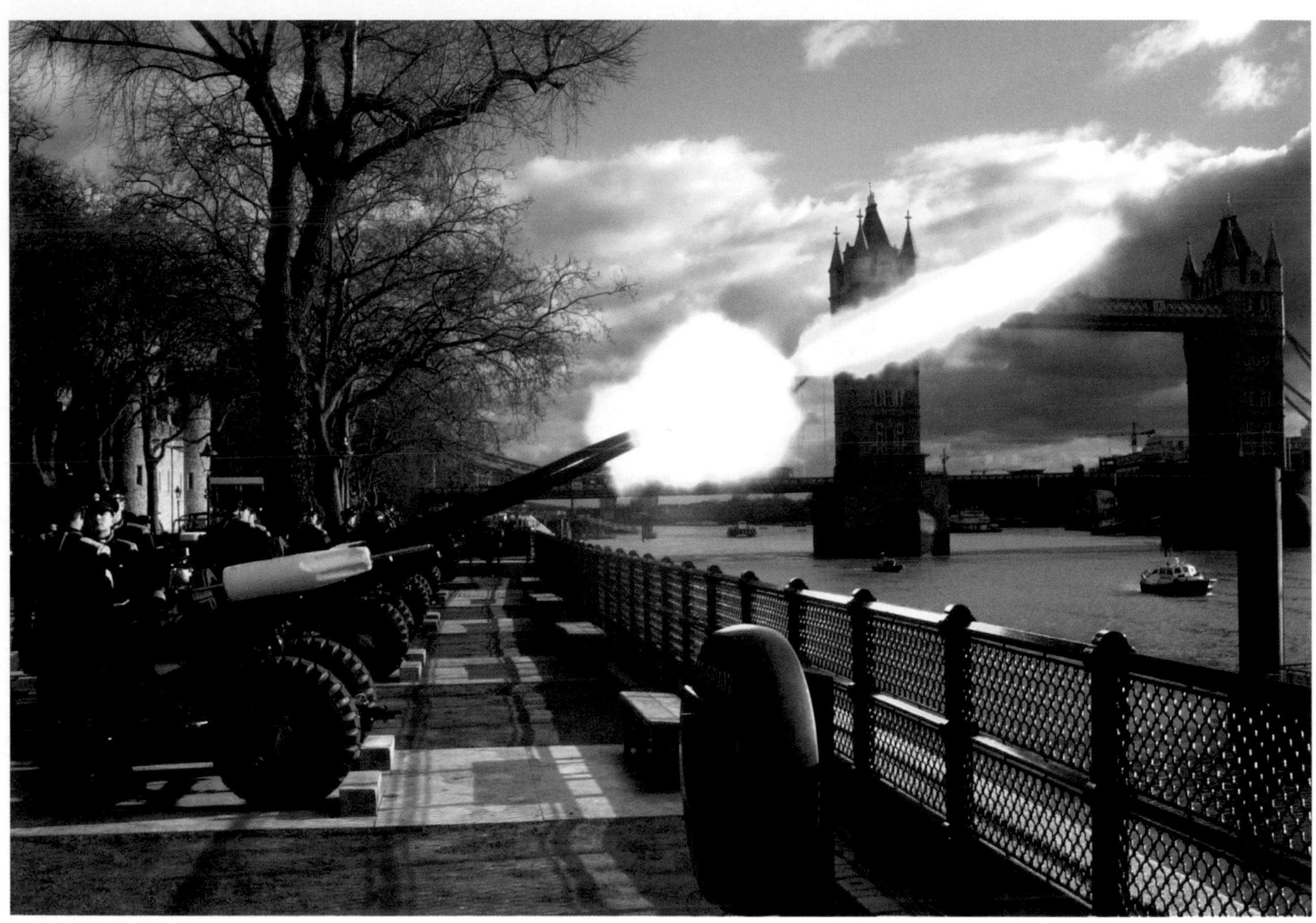

The Honourable Artillery Company marks the 50th anniversary of the Queen's accession to the throne, with a 62-gun salute at The Tower of London.
6th February, 2002

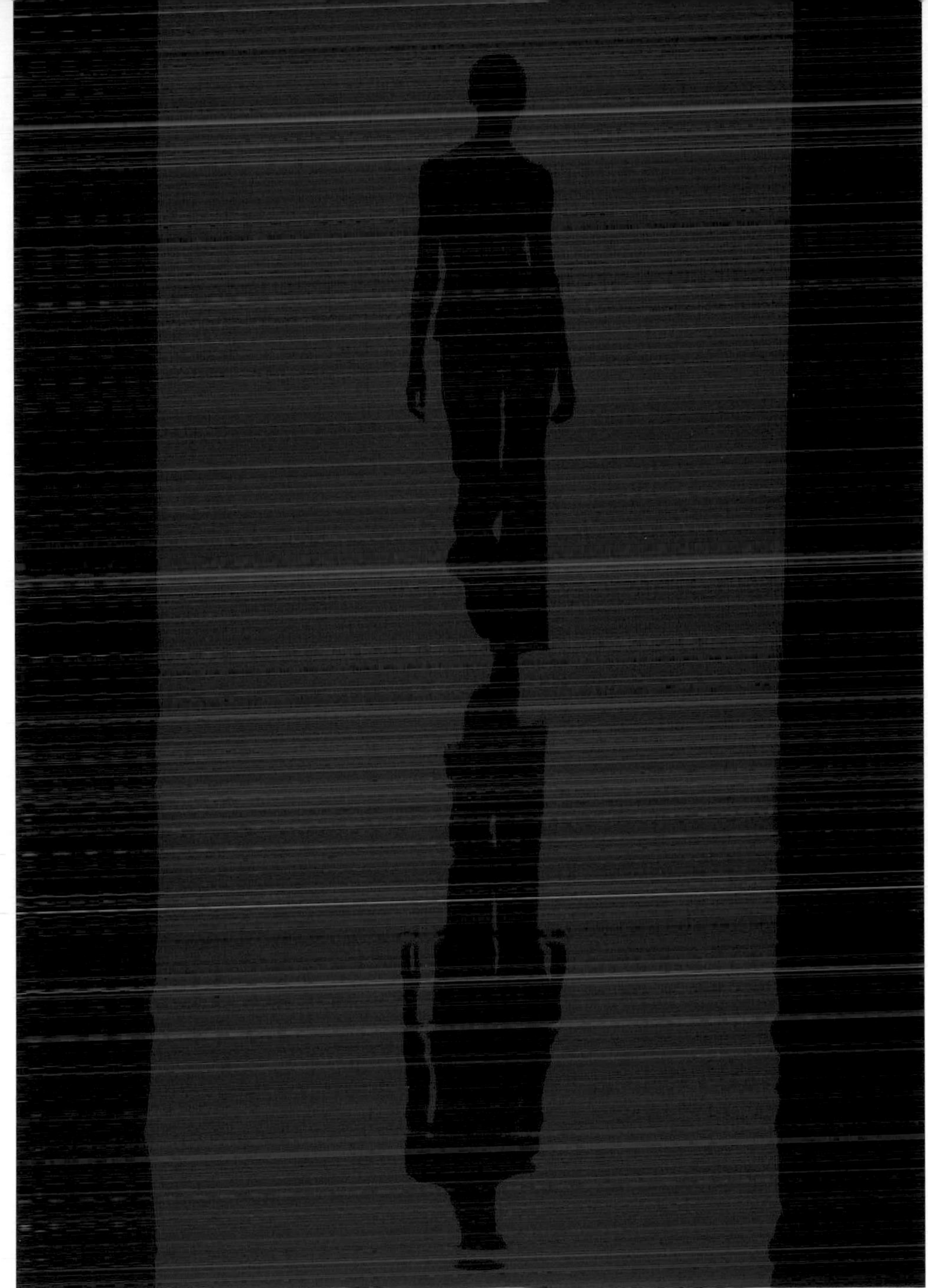

London Fashion Week, at Porchester Hall, Paddington.
20th February, 2002

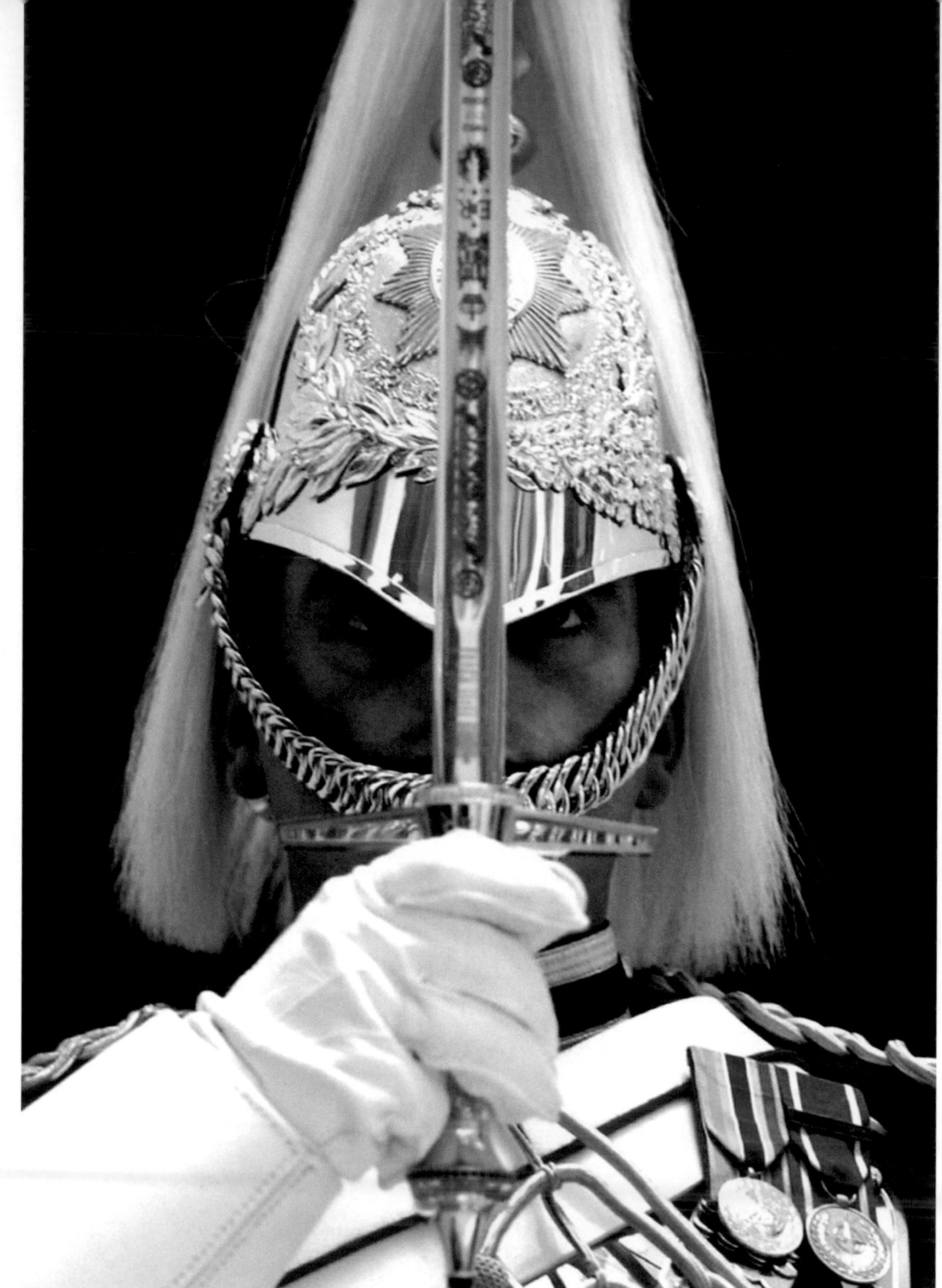

Lance Corporal of Horse, Nick Hunt, of the Life Guards from the Household Cavalry, with a commemorative sword, commissioned to celebrate the Queen's Golden Jubilee.
20th March, 2002

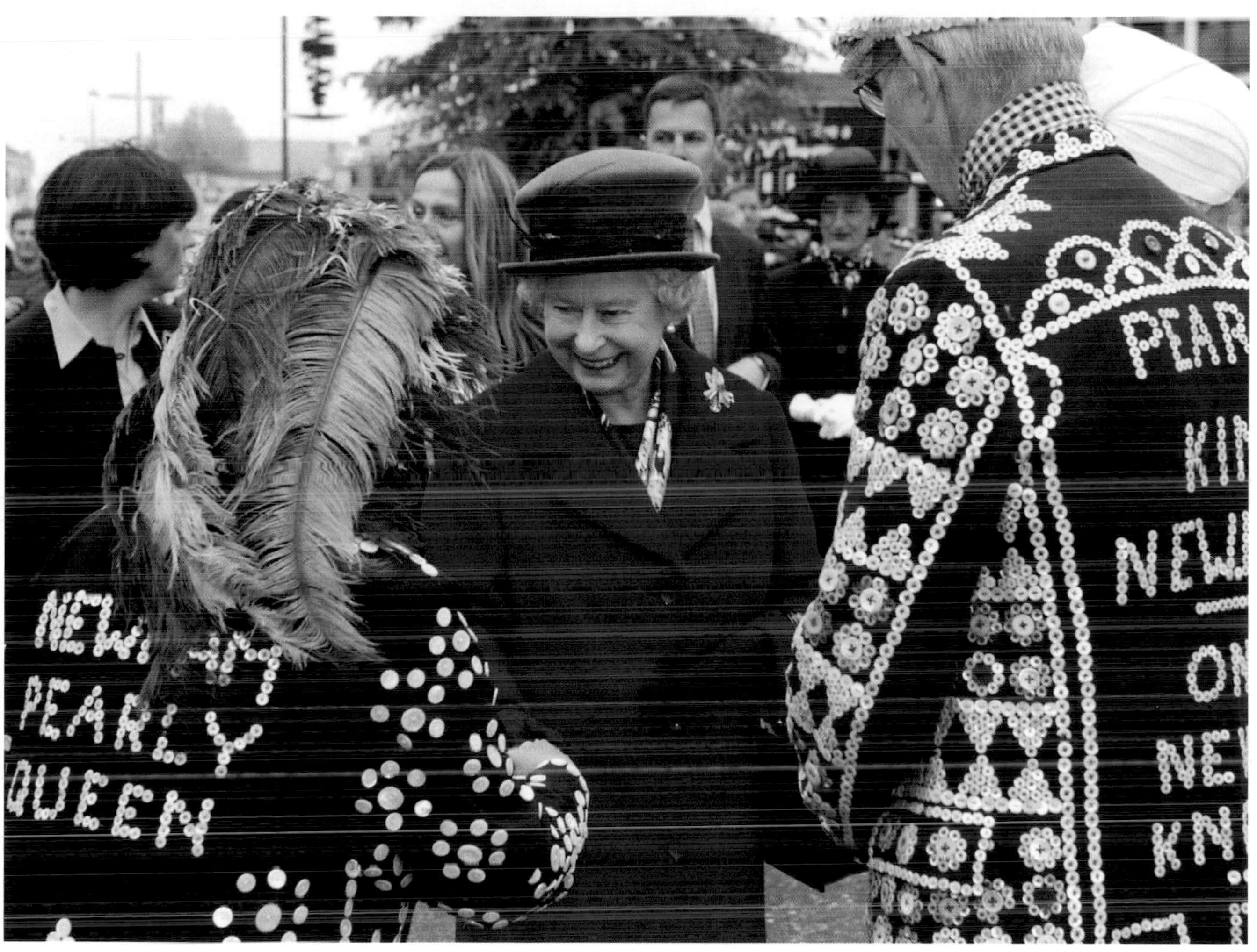

Queen Elizabeth II meets the pearly King and Queen of Newham during her Golden Jubilee tour of the UK.
9th May, 2002

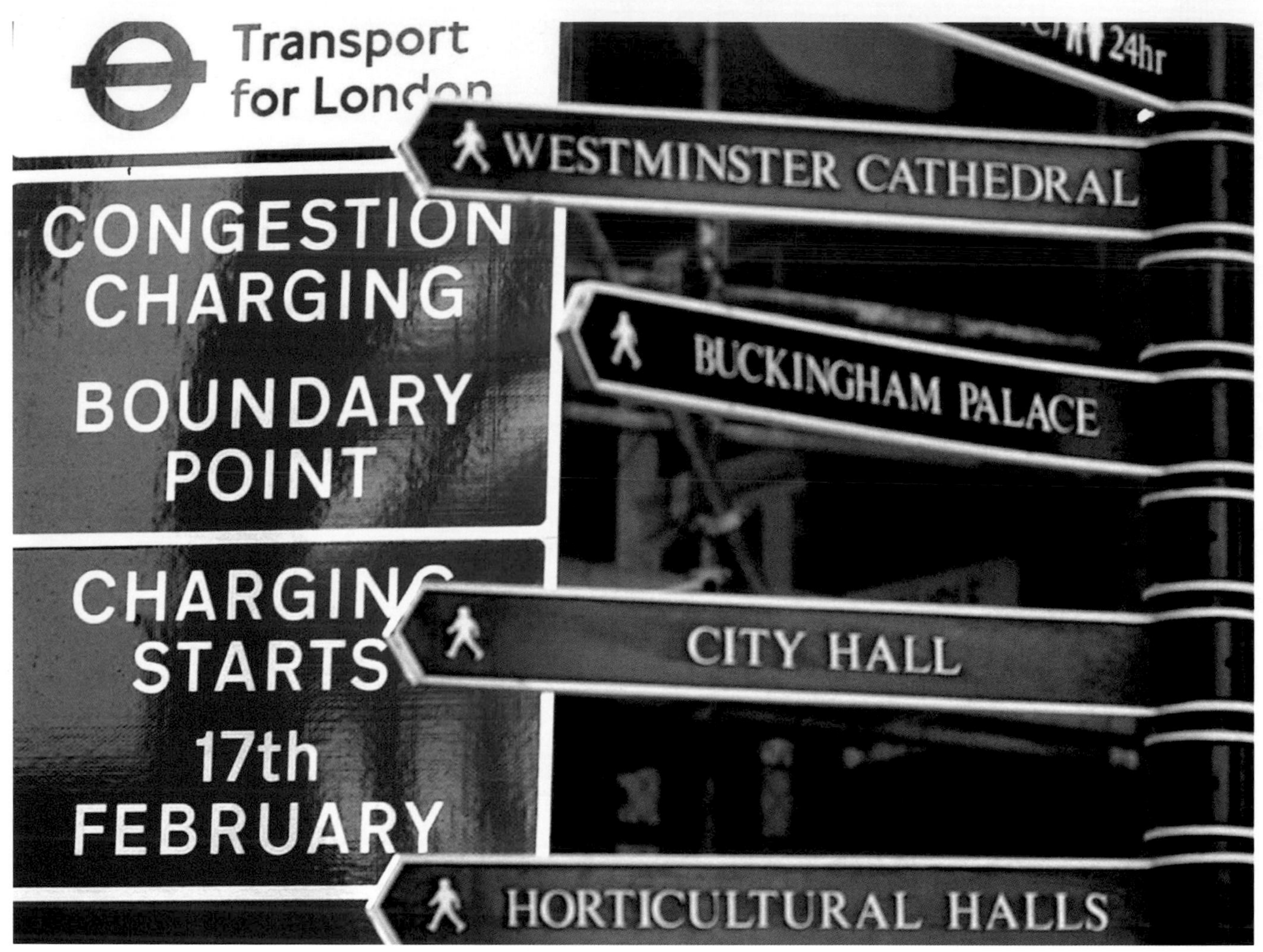

A sign on Victoria Street warns motorists of the London congestion charge.
5th February, 2003

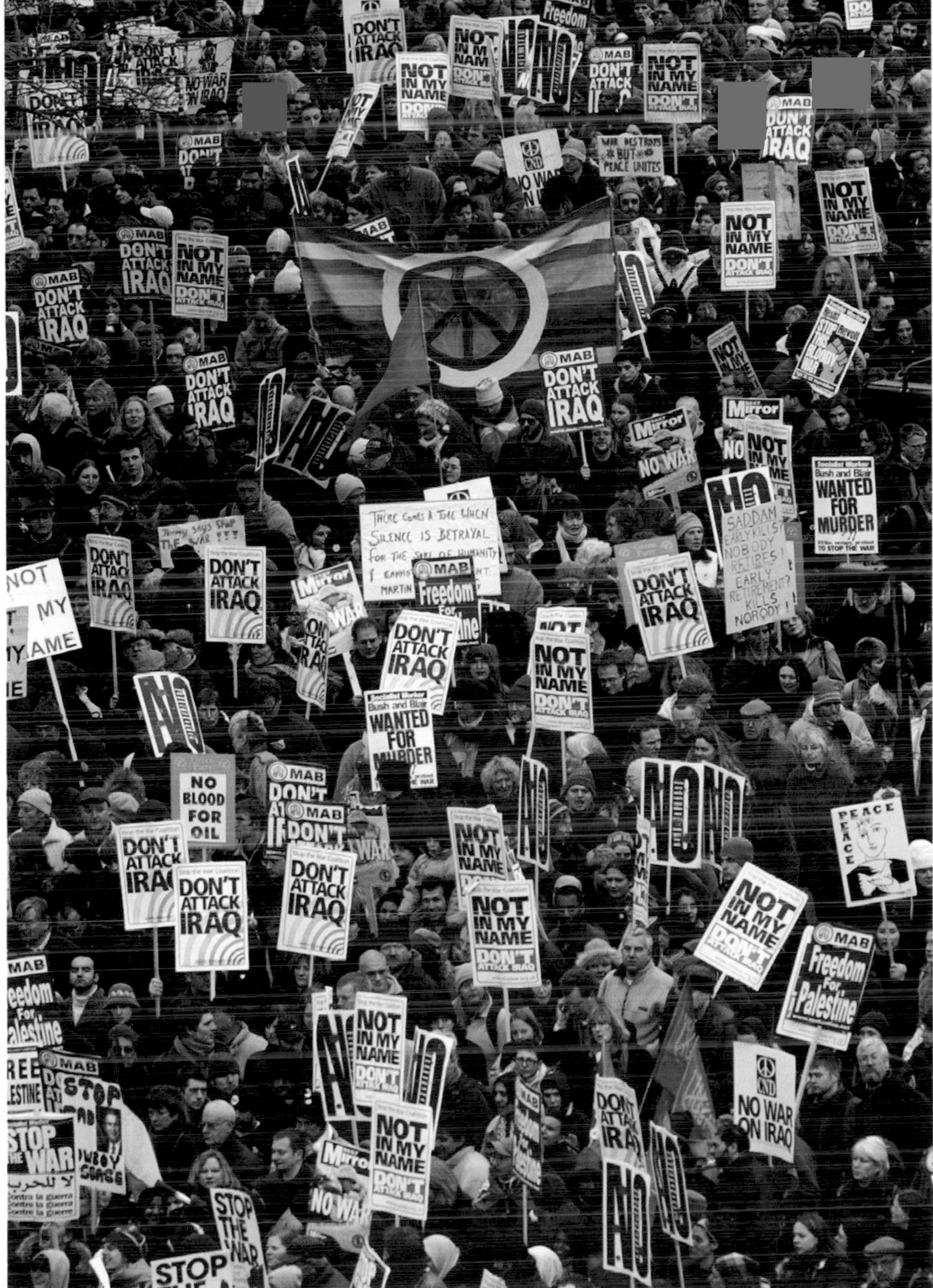

Anti war demonstrators head down Piccadilly in central London on their way to a rally in Hyde Park. Over a million people turned out to register their opposition.

15th February, 2003

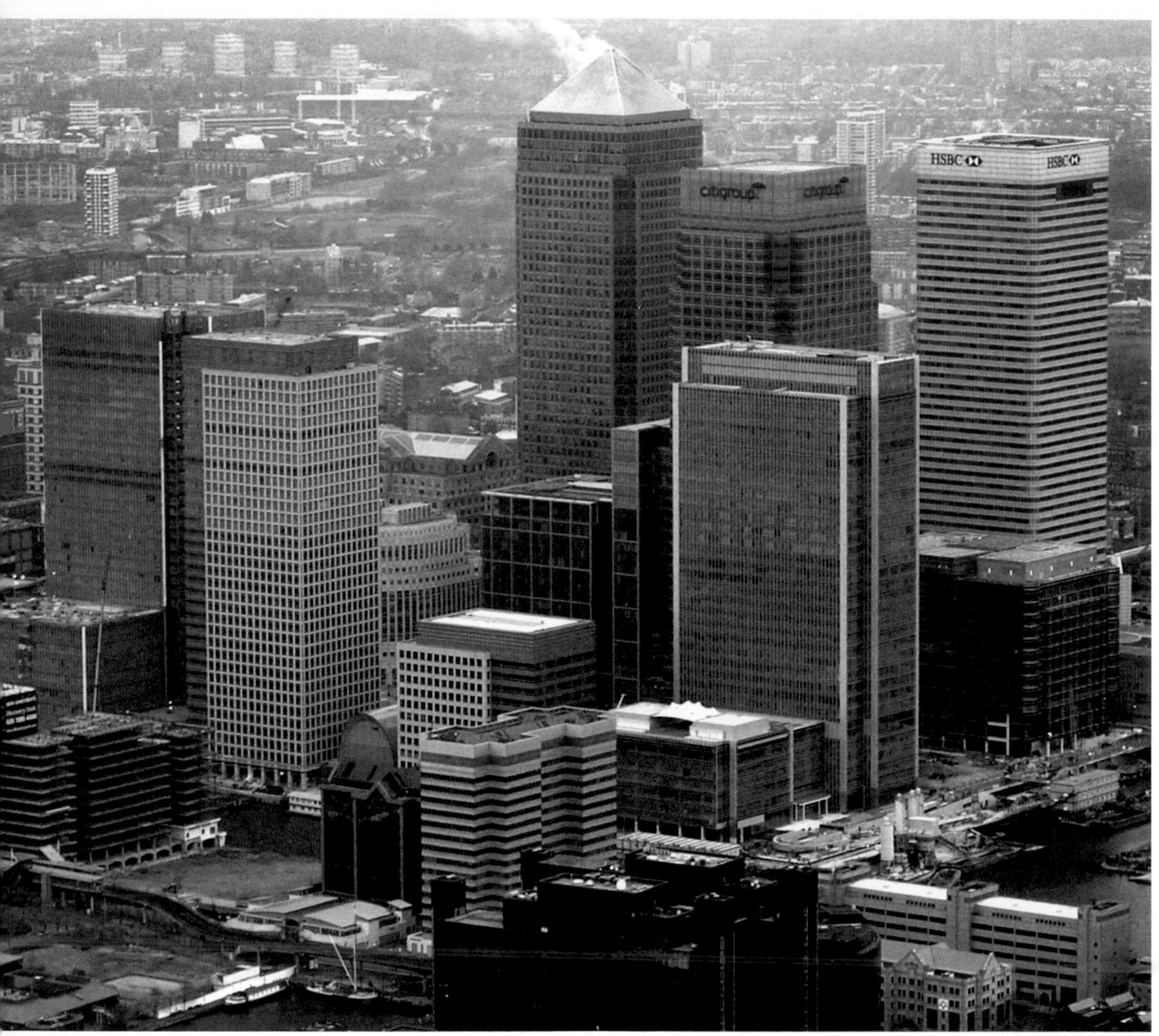
citigroup
citigroup
HSBC
HSBC

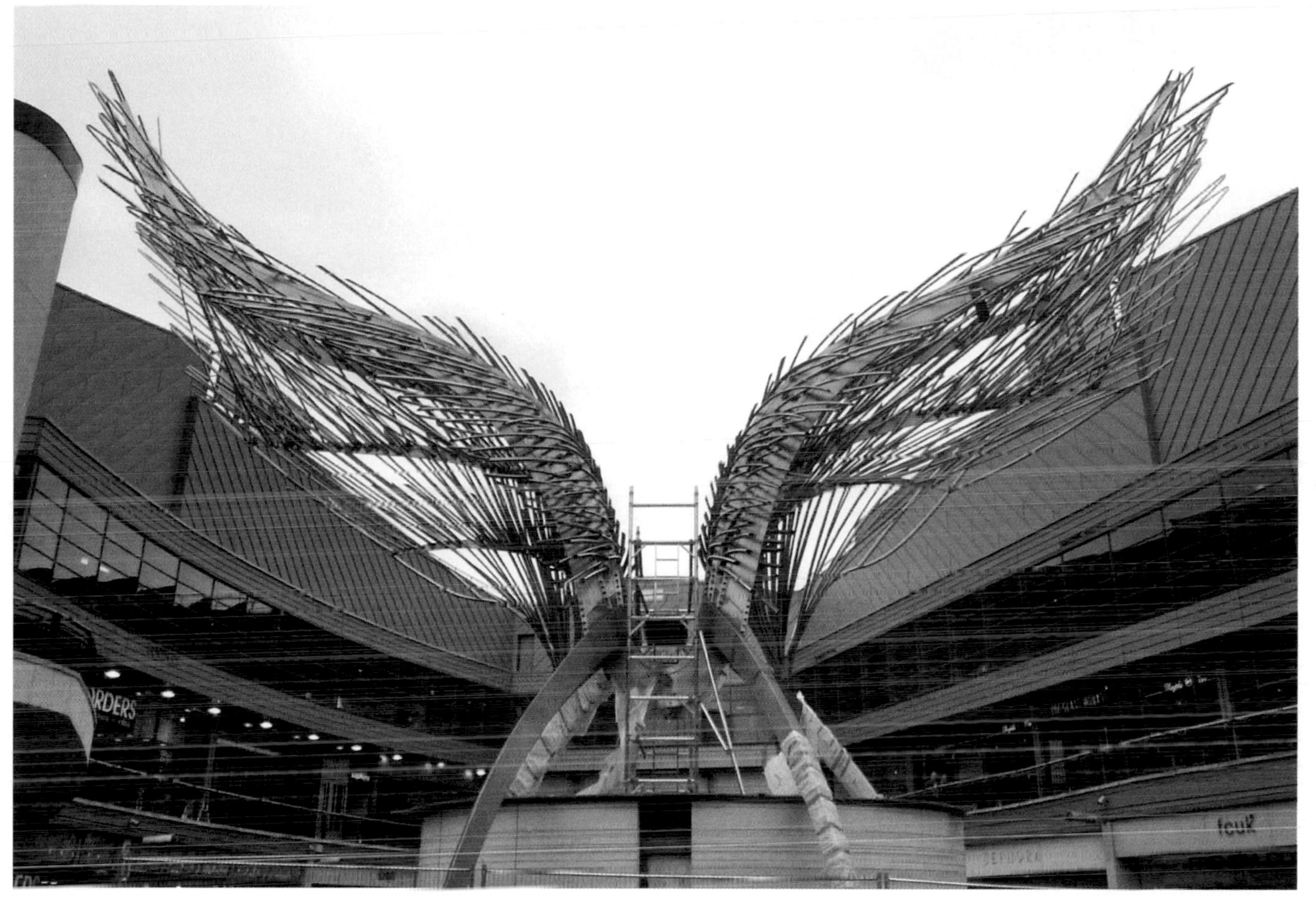

A model of the *Angel Wings* sculpture to be installed in the Angel Shopping Centre in Islington. It was designed by sculptor Wolfgang Buttress.
4th March, 2003

Facing page: Canary Wharf.
21st February, 2003

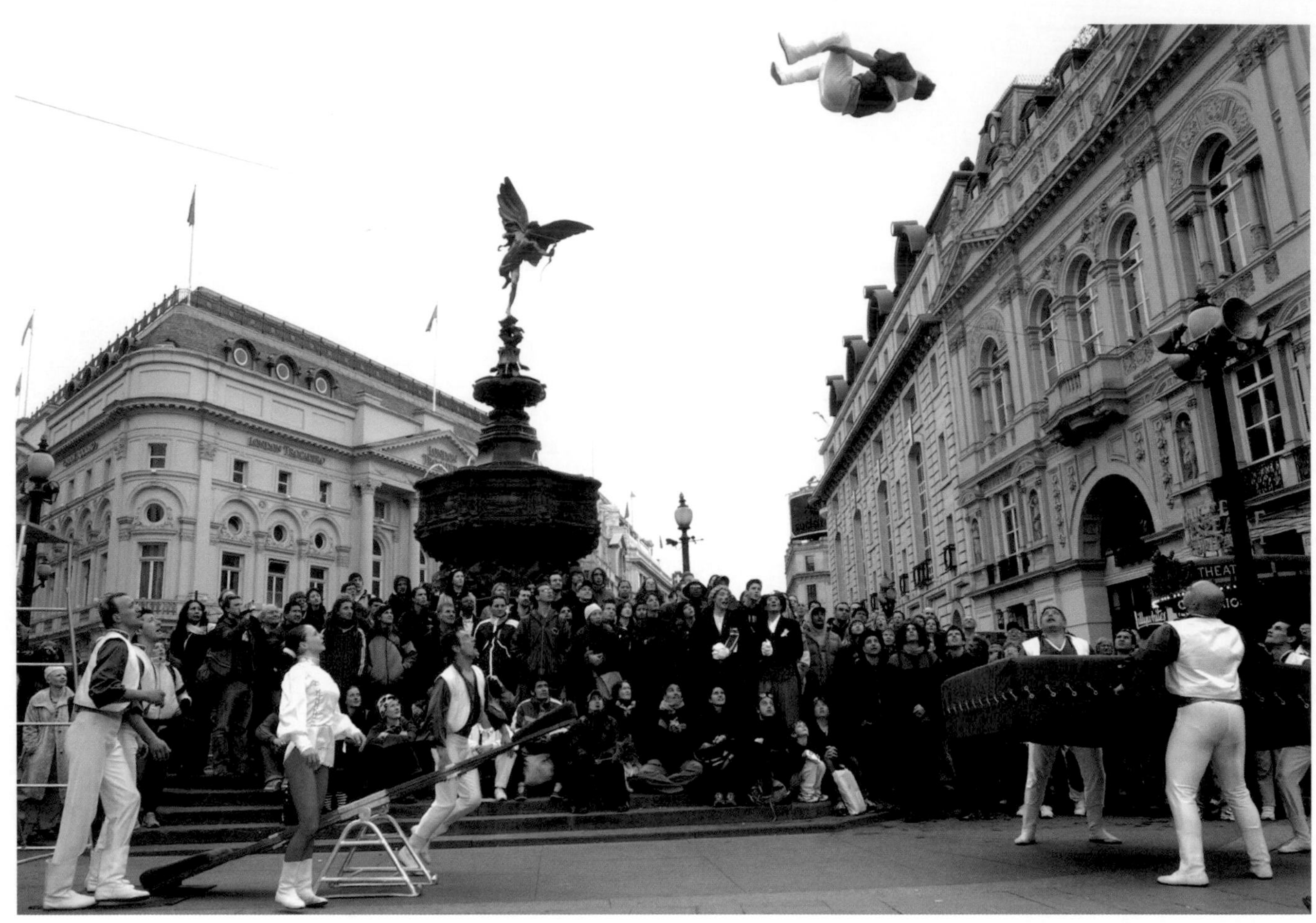

Acrobats from *Arnett & Paulo's Circus* perform in Piccadilly Circus to mark the first National Circus Day.
8th April, 2003

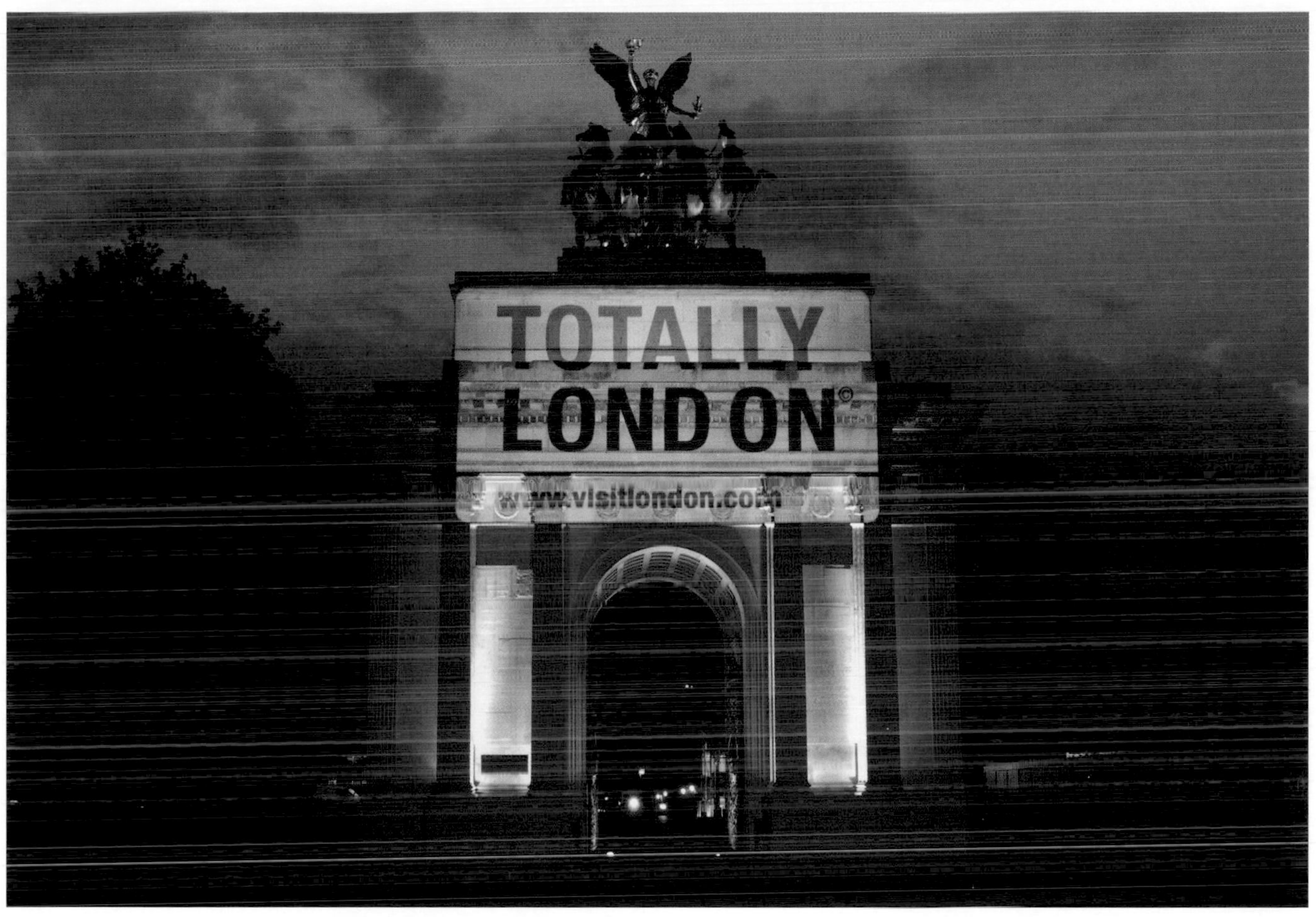

The Wellington Arch displays the *Totally London* logo to promote the capital as a tourist destination.
24th May, 2003

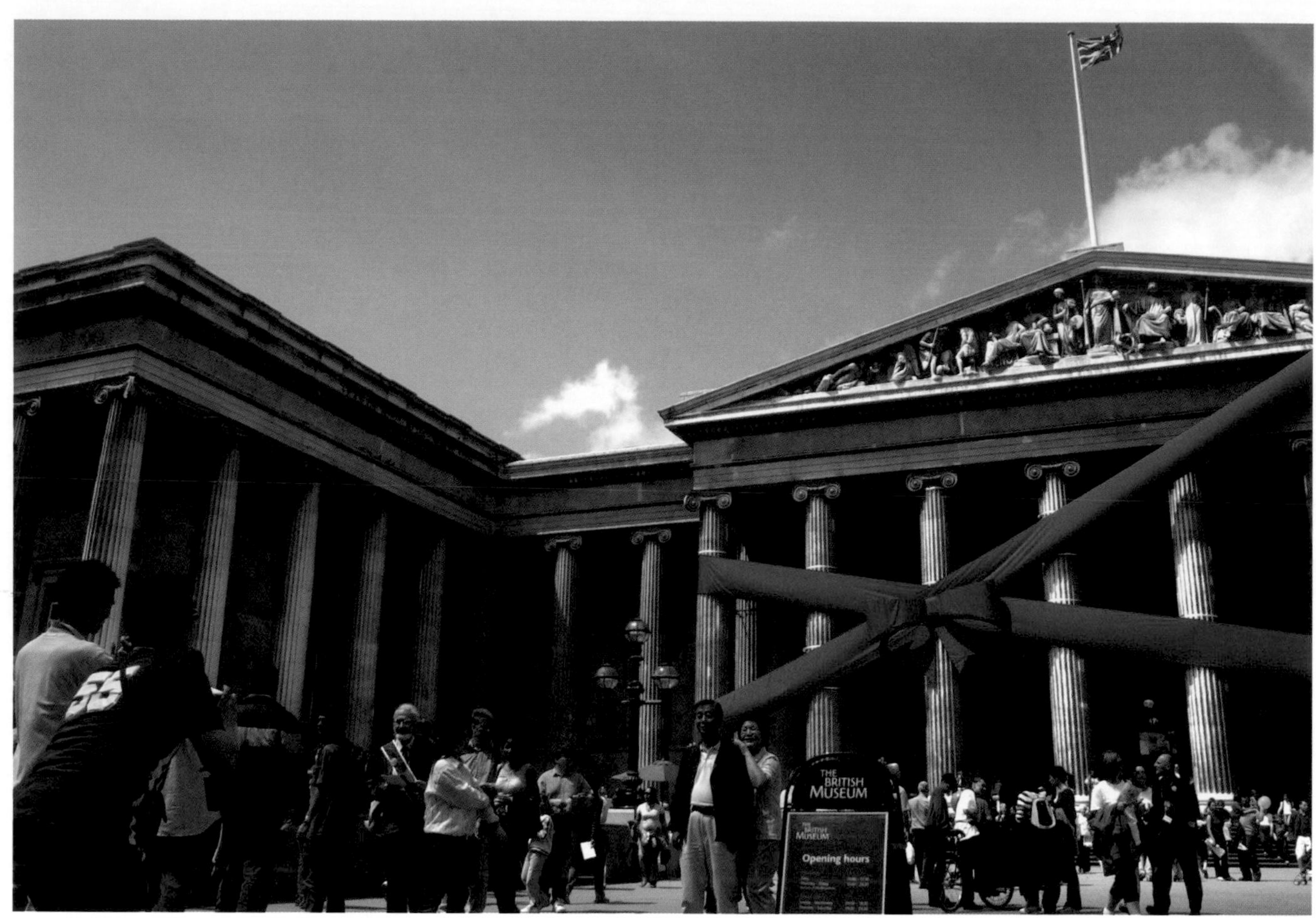

The British Museum's 250th anniversary celebrations.
7th June, 2003

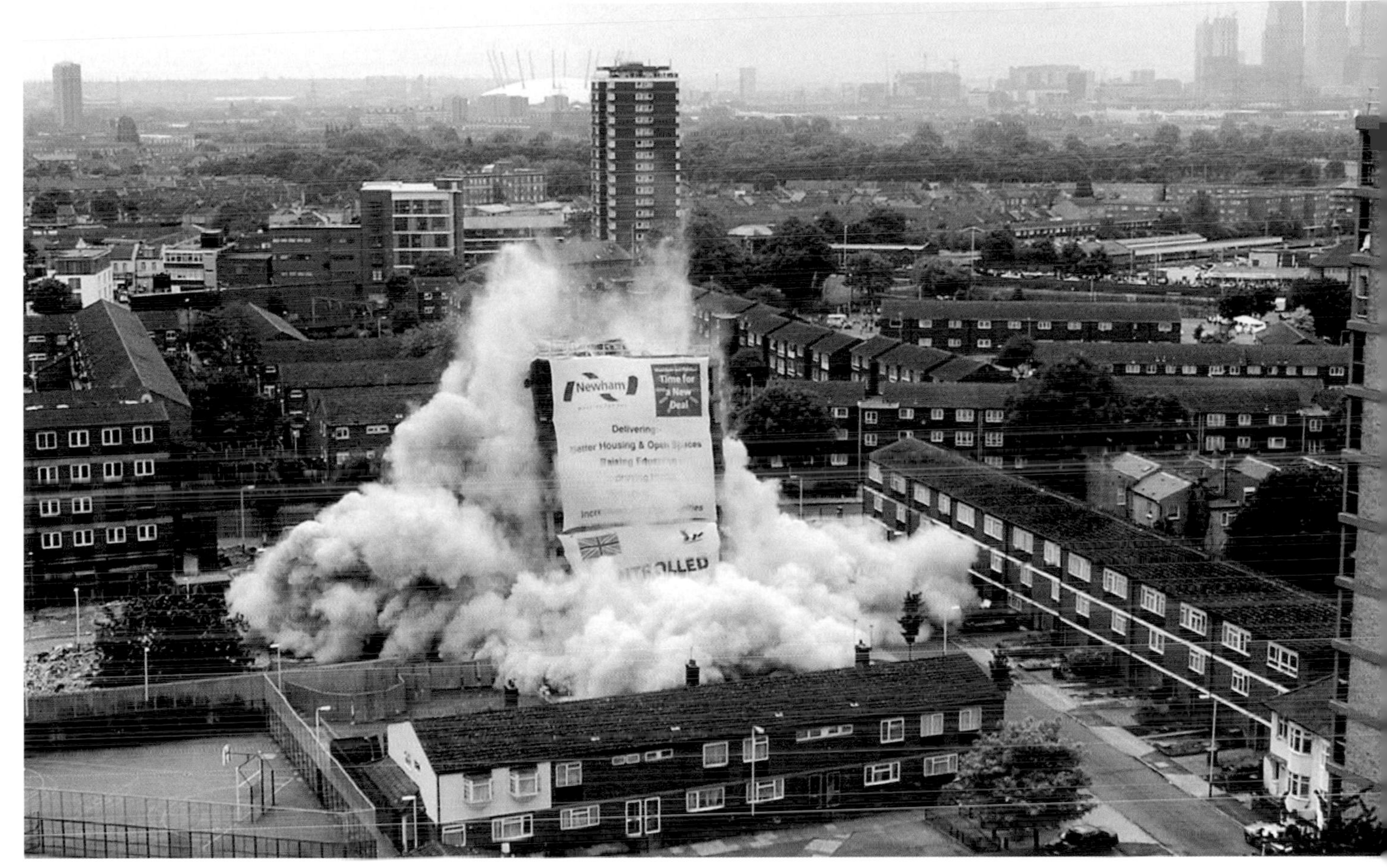

A tower block on the Brookes Estate in Plaistow is blown to the ground by controlled explosion. The demolition is part of a five-year regeneration project.
8th June, 2003

Olafur Eliasson's installation entitled *The Weather Project* in The Turbine Hall at the Tate Modern.
15 October, 2003

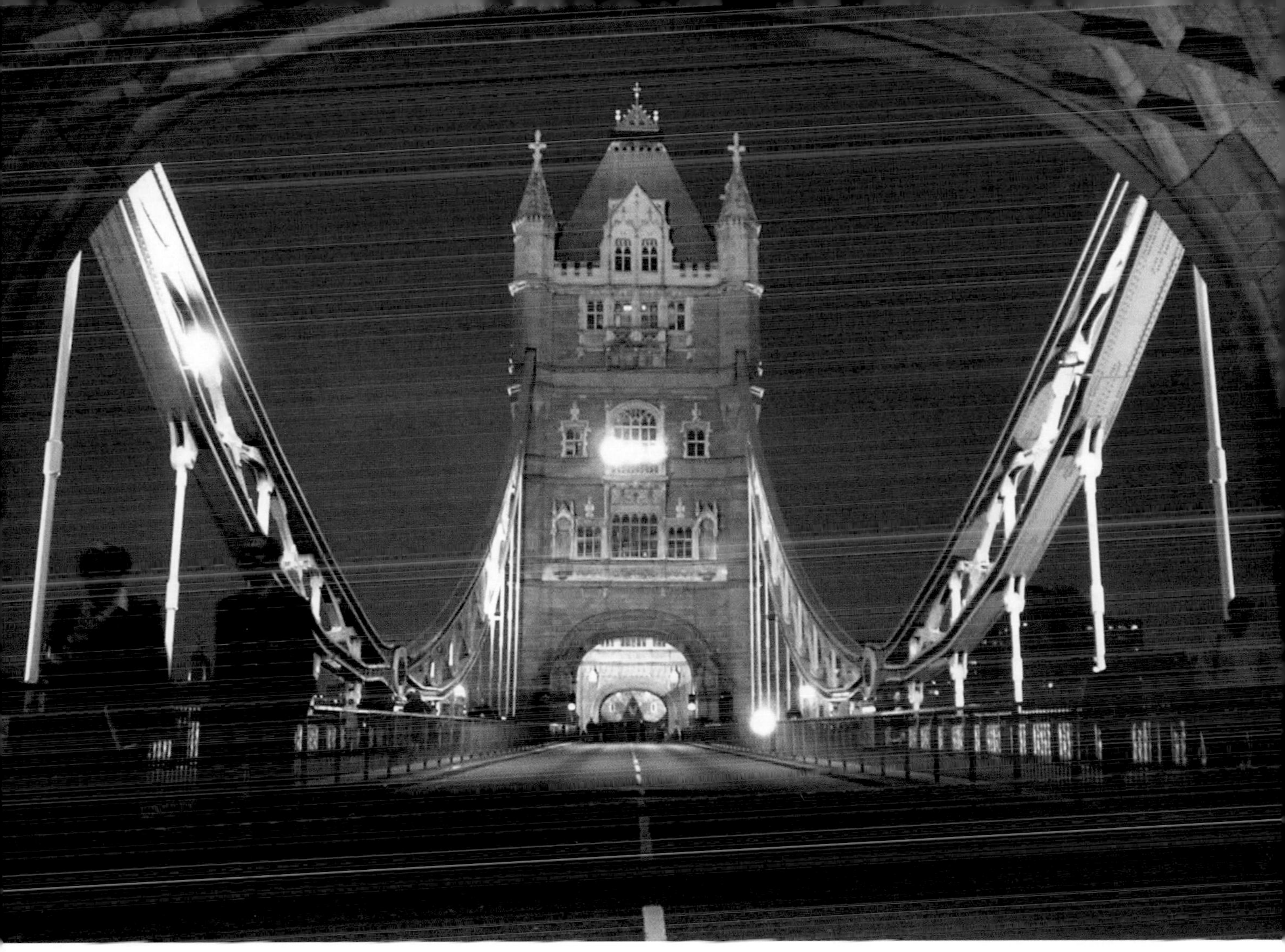

Tower Bridge is closed by a Fathers 4 Justice protestor, dressed as *Spiderman,* occupying a crane over the roadway.
4th November, 2003

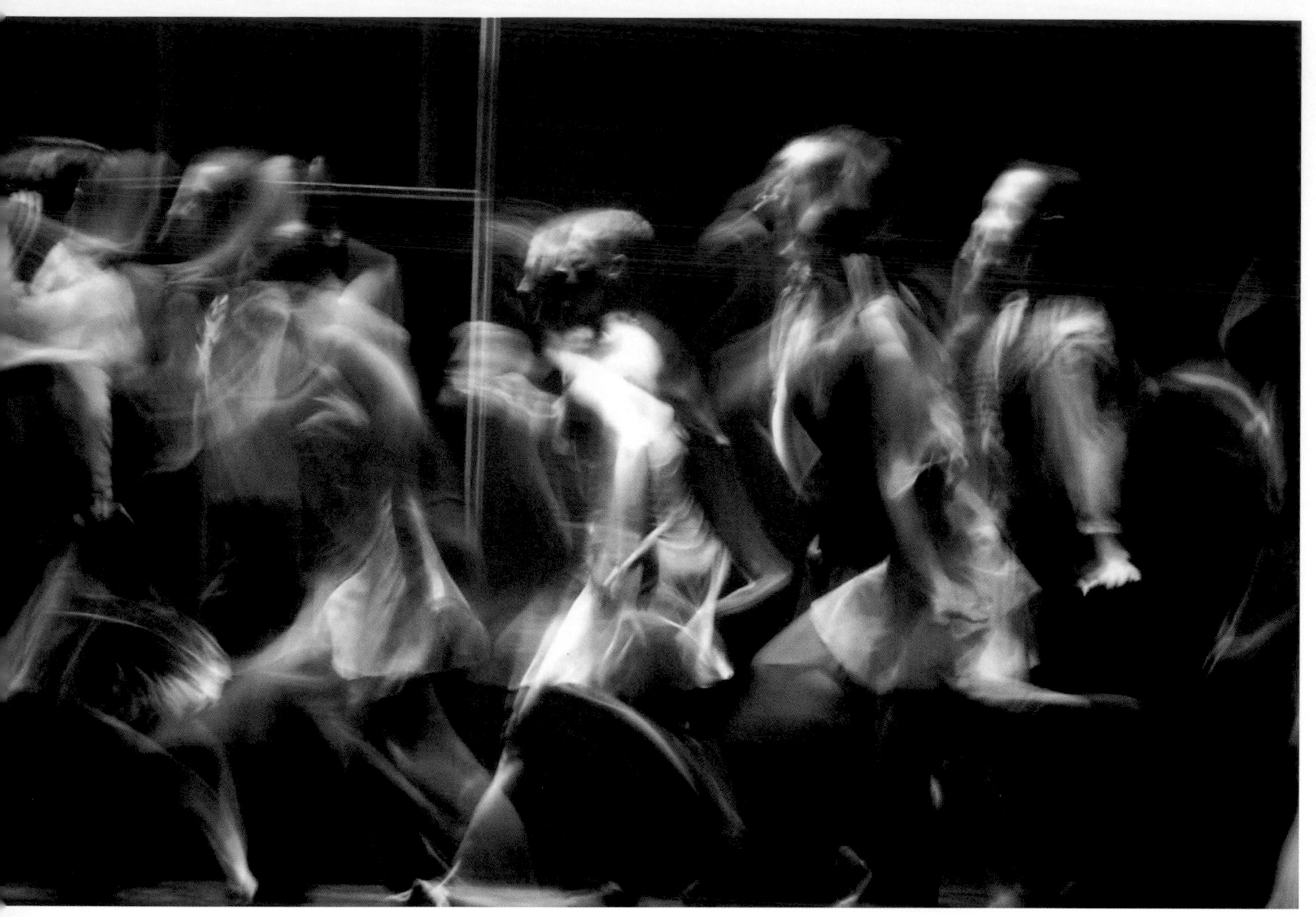

Dancers from the Rambert Dance Company rehearse at Sadler's Wells.
25th November, 2003

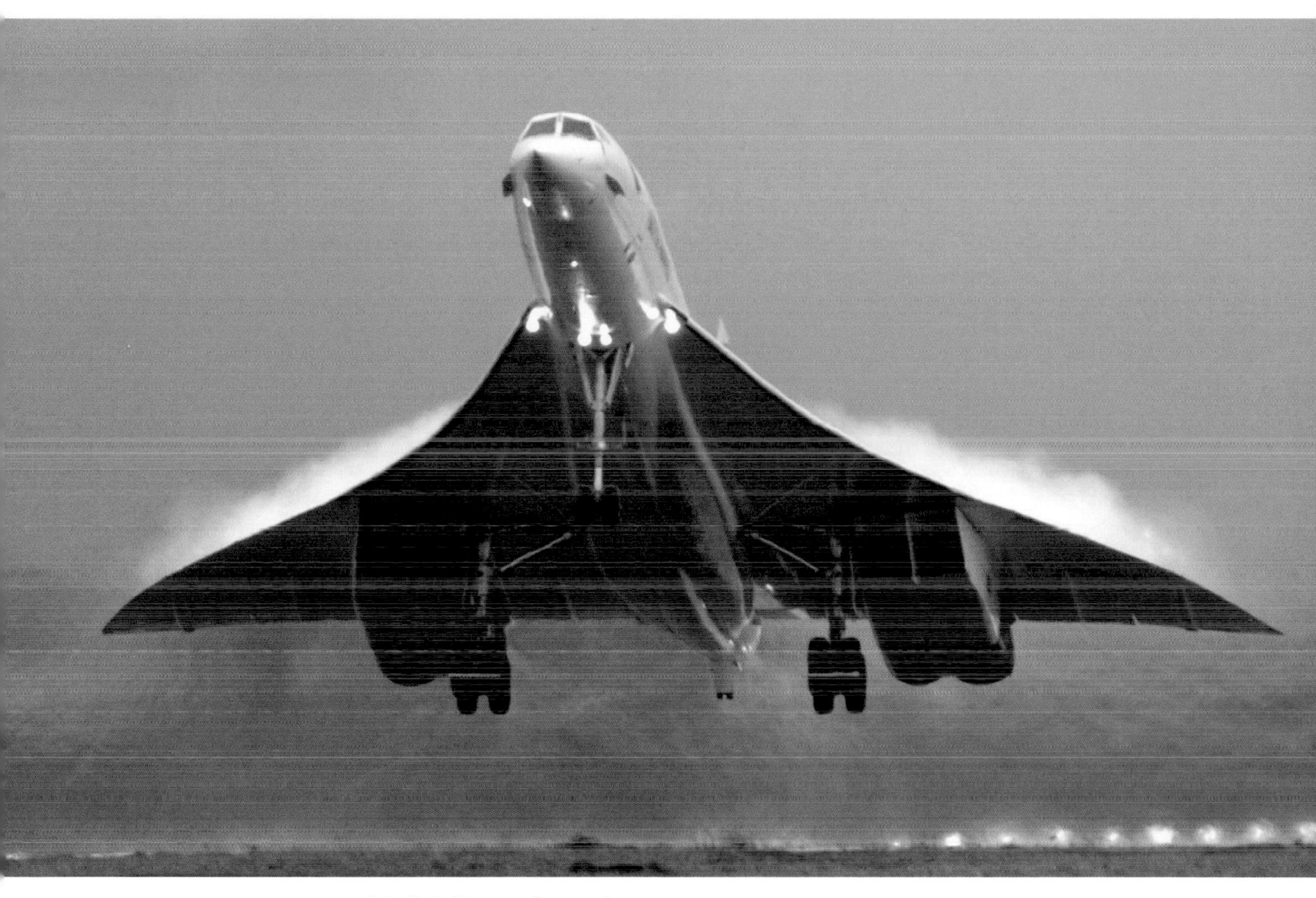

A British Airways *Concorde* takes off for the last time from Heathrow Airport.
26th November, 2003

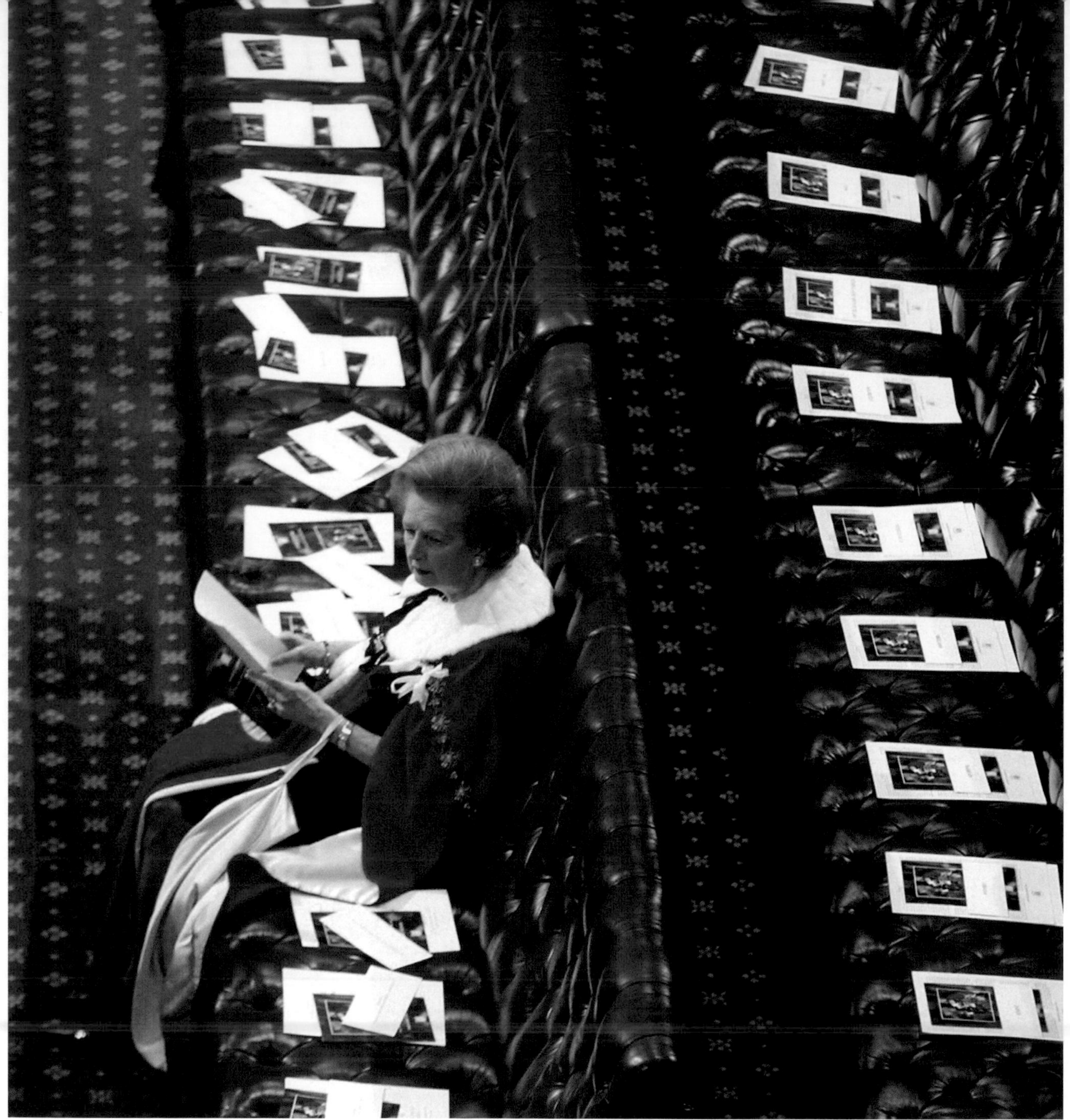

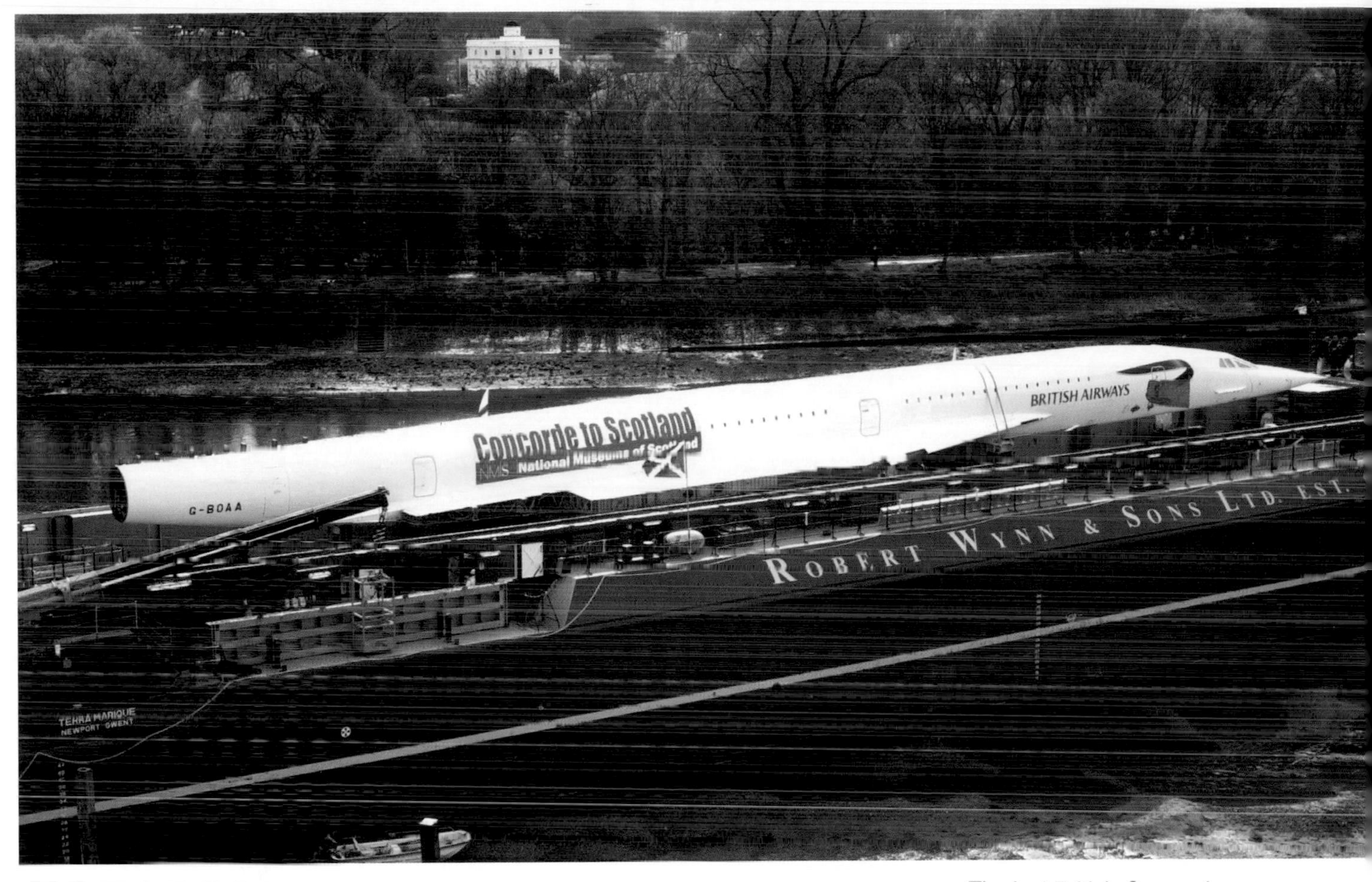

The last British *Concorde* begins its final journey, by barge from Isleworth to the Museum of Flight near Edinburgh.
4th April, 2004

Facing page: Former Prime Minister Baroness Thatcher arrives early for the State Opening of Parliament at the Palace of Westminster.
26th November, 2003

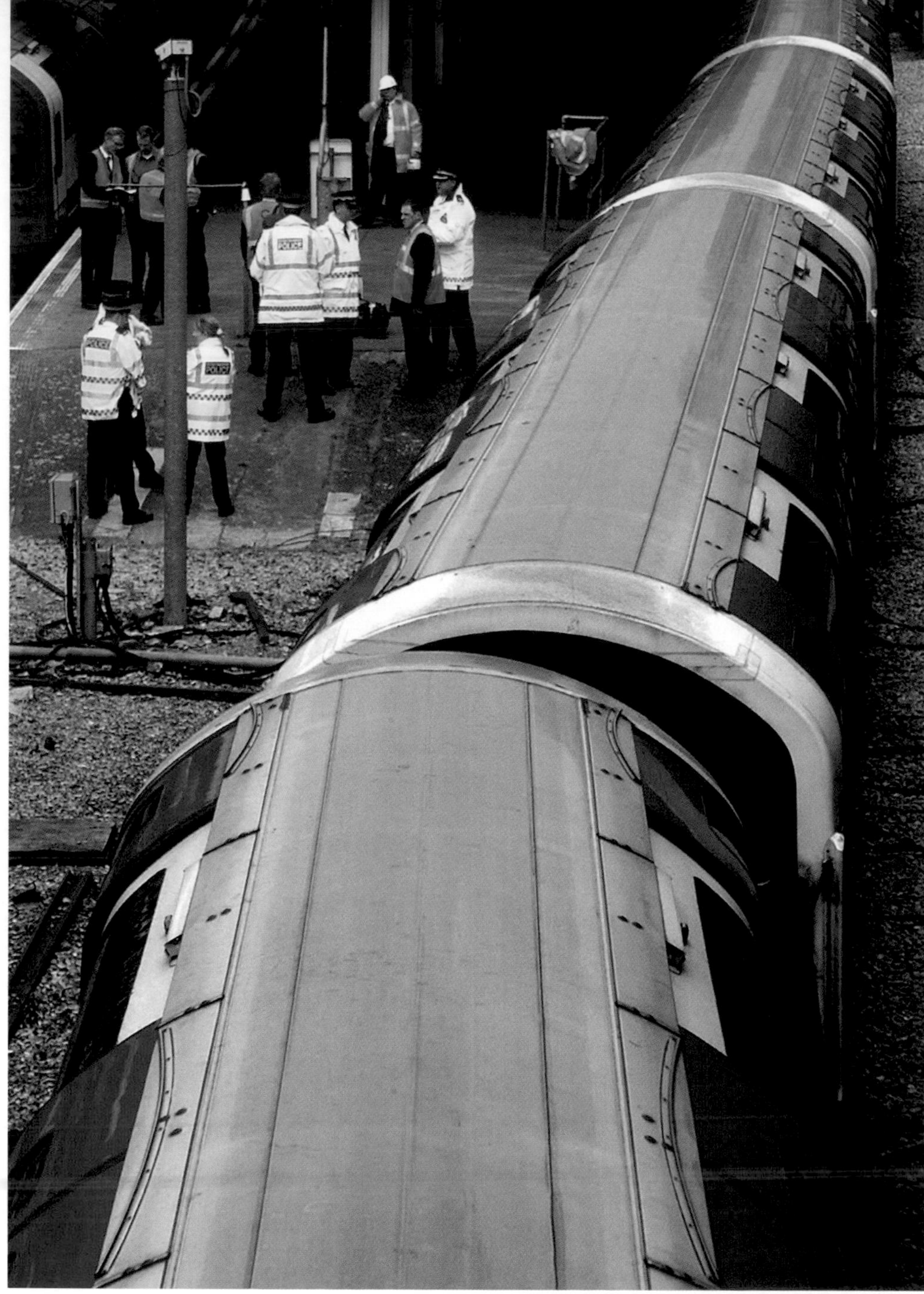

A derailed tube train at White City. None of the 150 passengers were hurt in the incident, which was the fourth derailment on the network in less than 16 months.
11th April, 2004

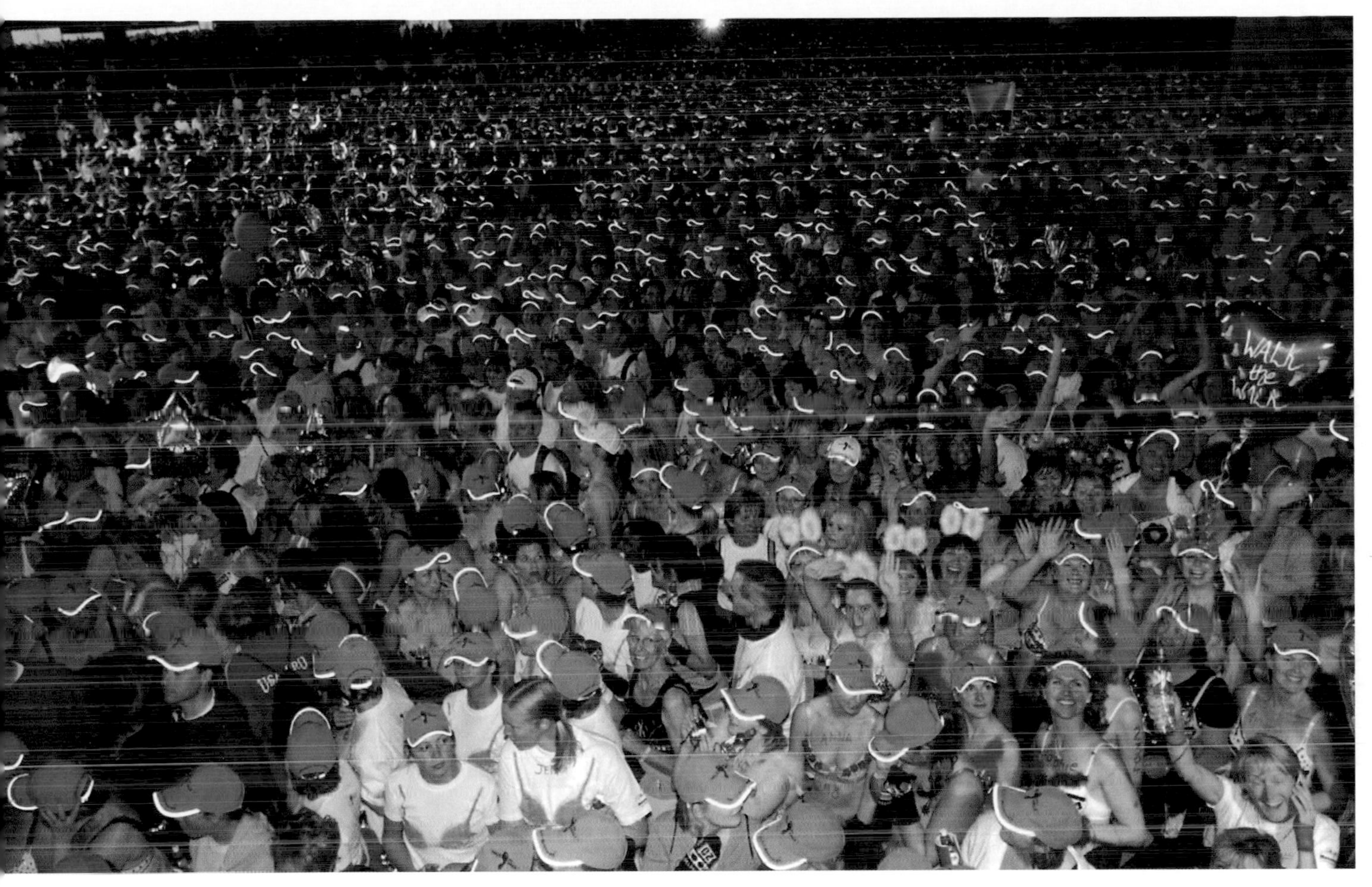

15,000 people take part in the *Moonwalk* night-time charity walk in aid of Breast Cancer Research, at Hyde Park.
16th May, 2004

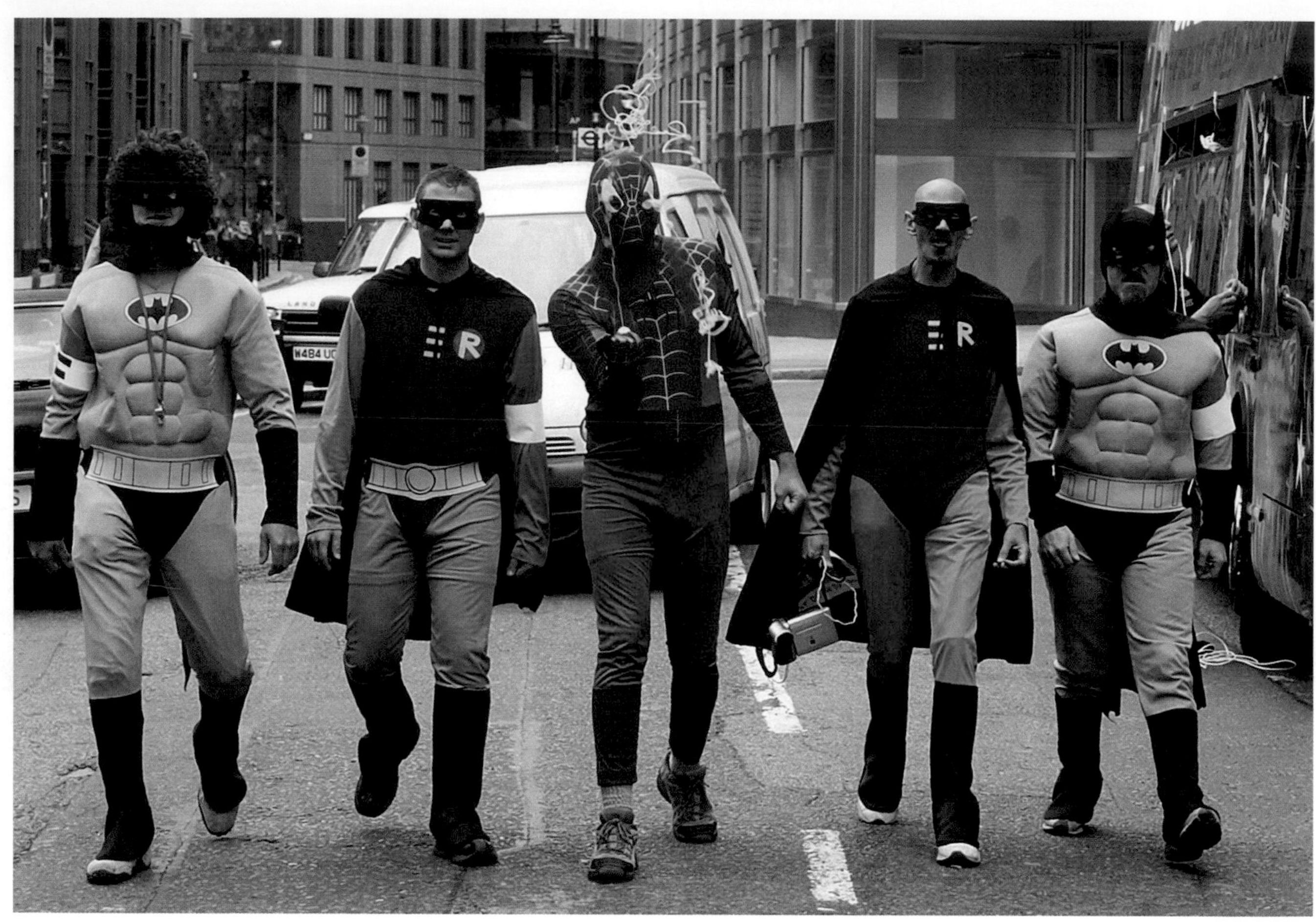

Members of Fathers 4 Justice
prepare for Father's Day.
18th June, 2004

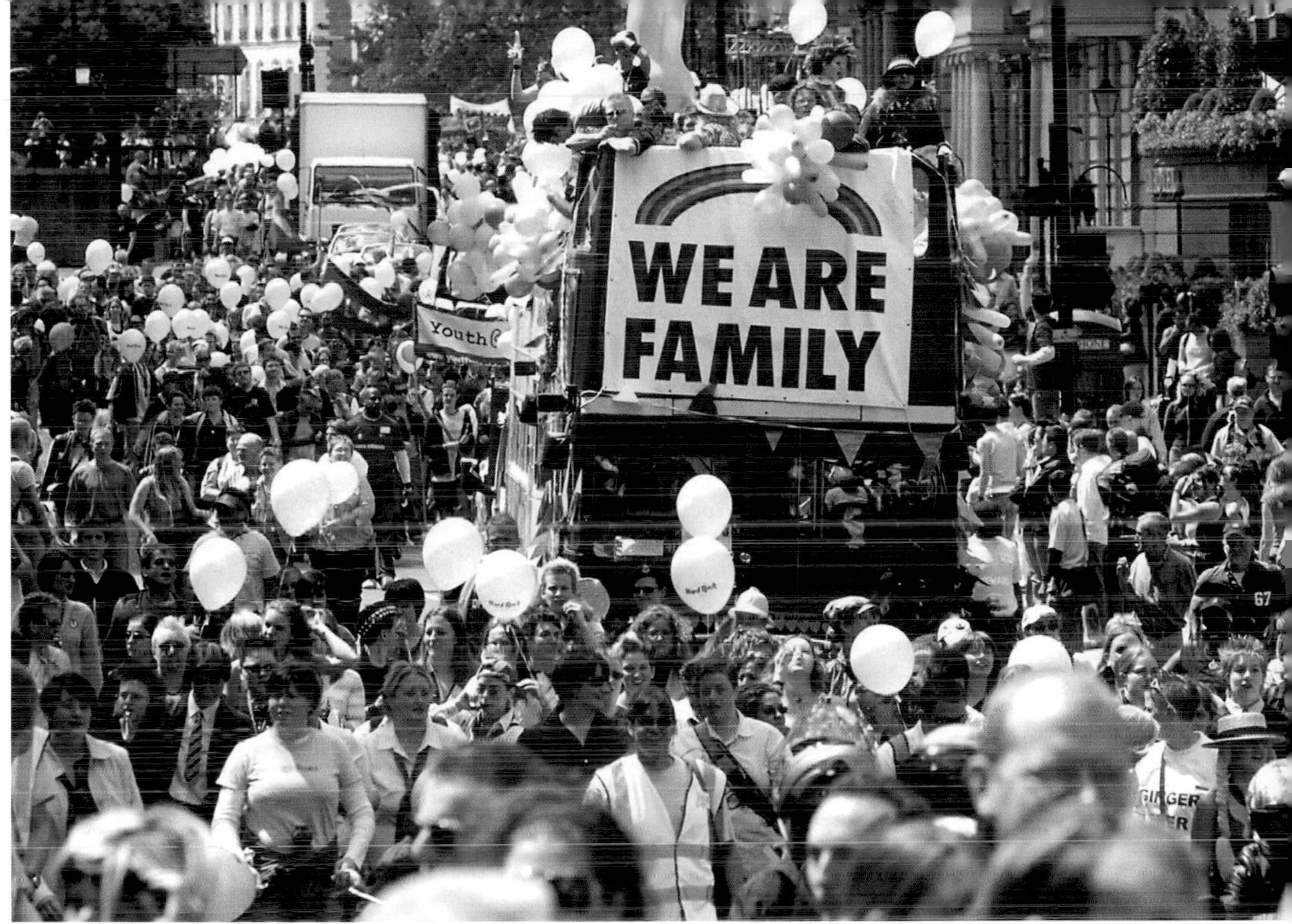

The Pride Parade travels through Piccadilly. The event is thought to be Europe's biggest gay festival.
3rd July, 2004

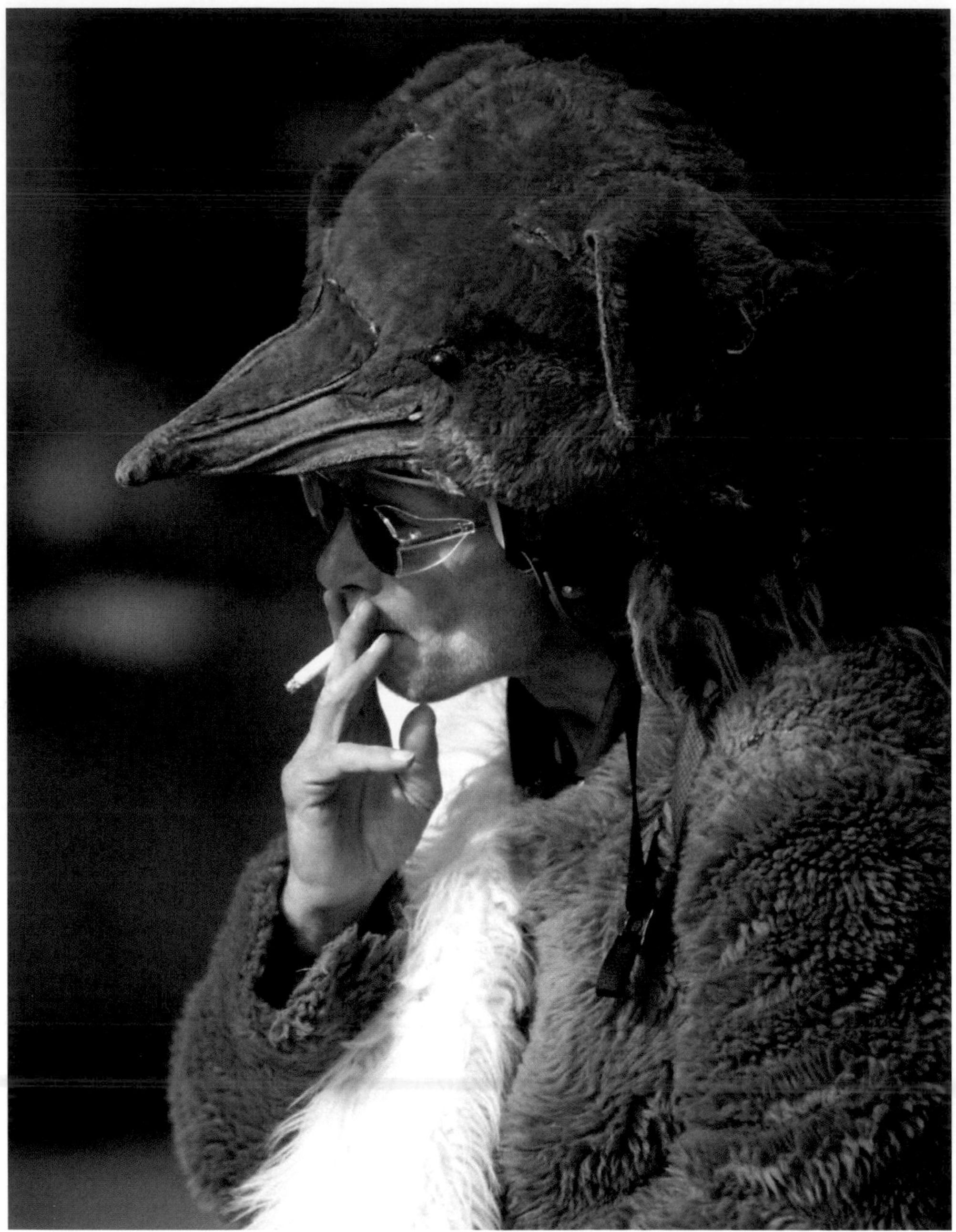

Facing page: A floral tribute at the National Service of Remembrance at the Cenotaph.
14th November, 2004

A pro-hunting demonstrator in Parliament Square.
15th September, 2004

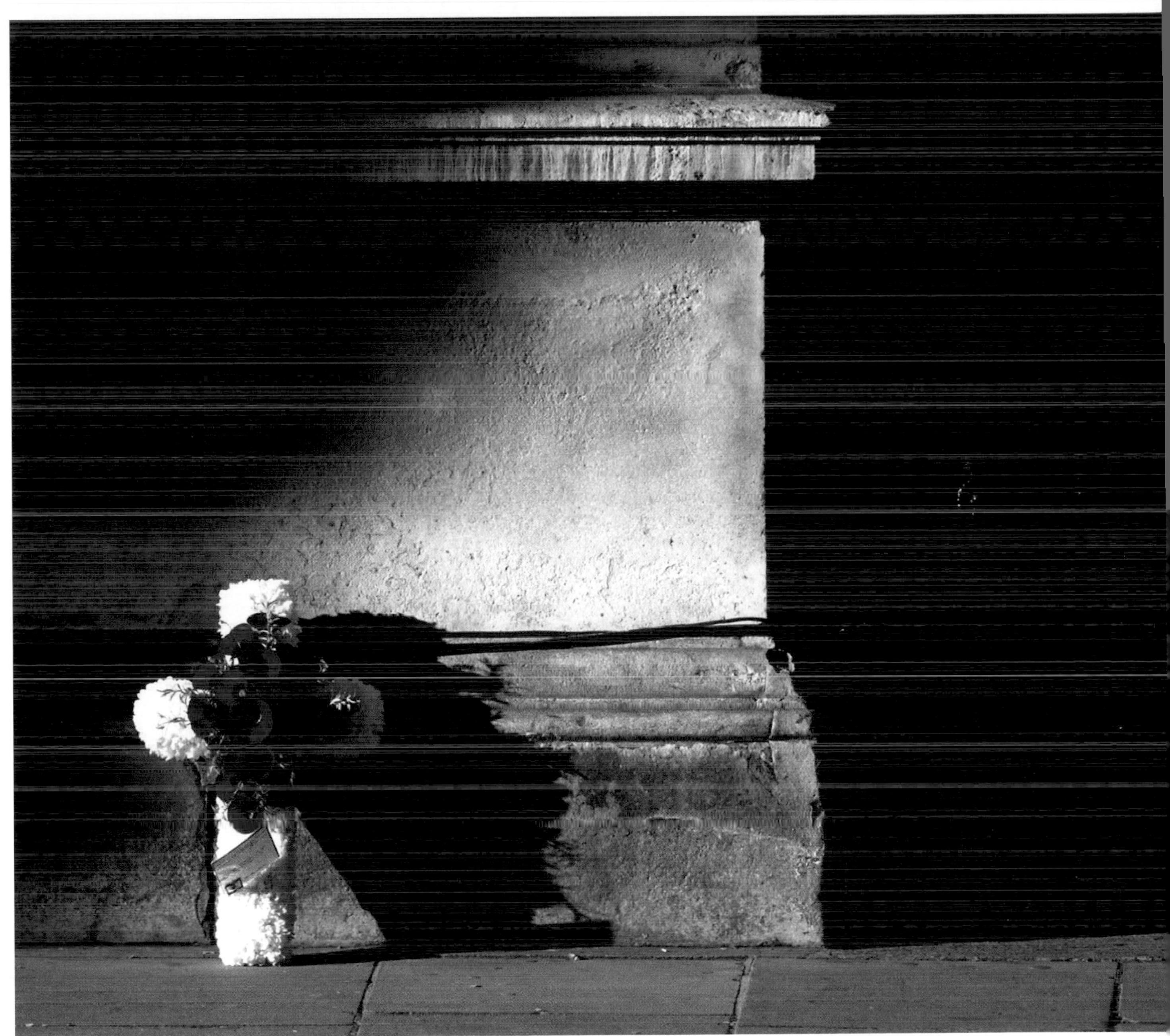

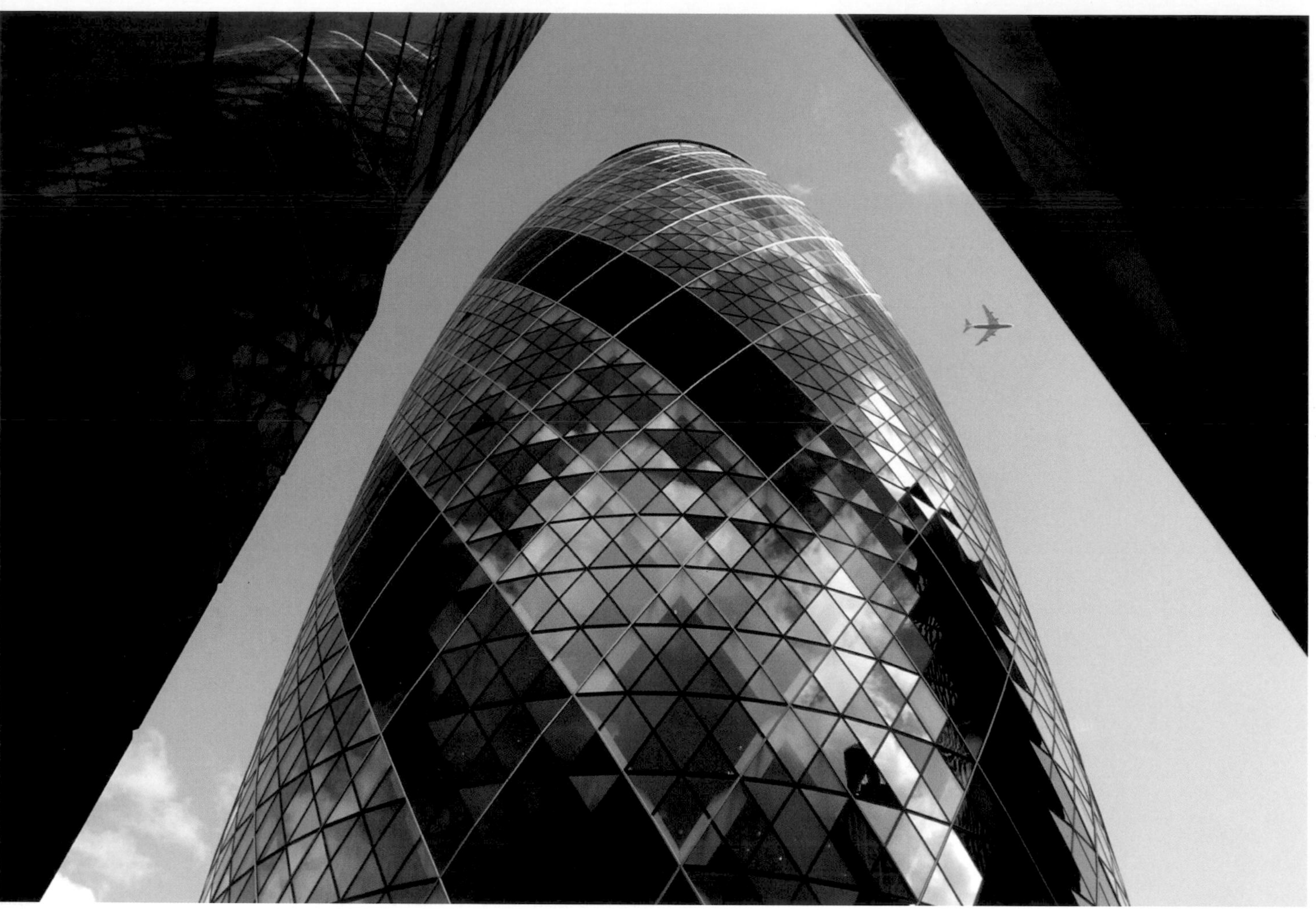

The Gherkin – more formally known as 30 St Mary Axe – built on the site of the old Baltic Exchange building, demolished after being structurally ruined by a terrorist bomb.
6th April, 2005

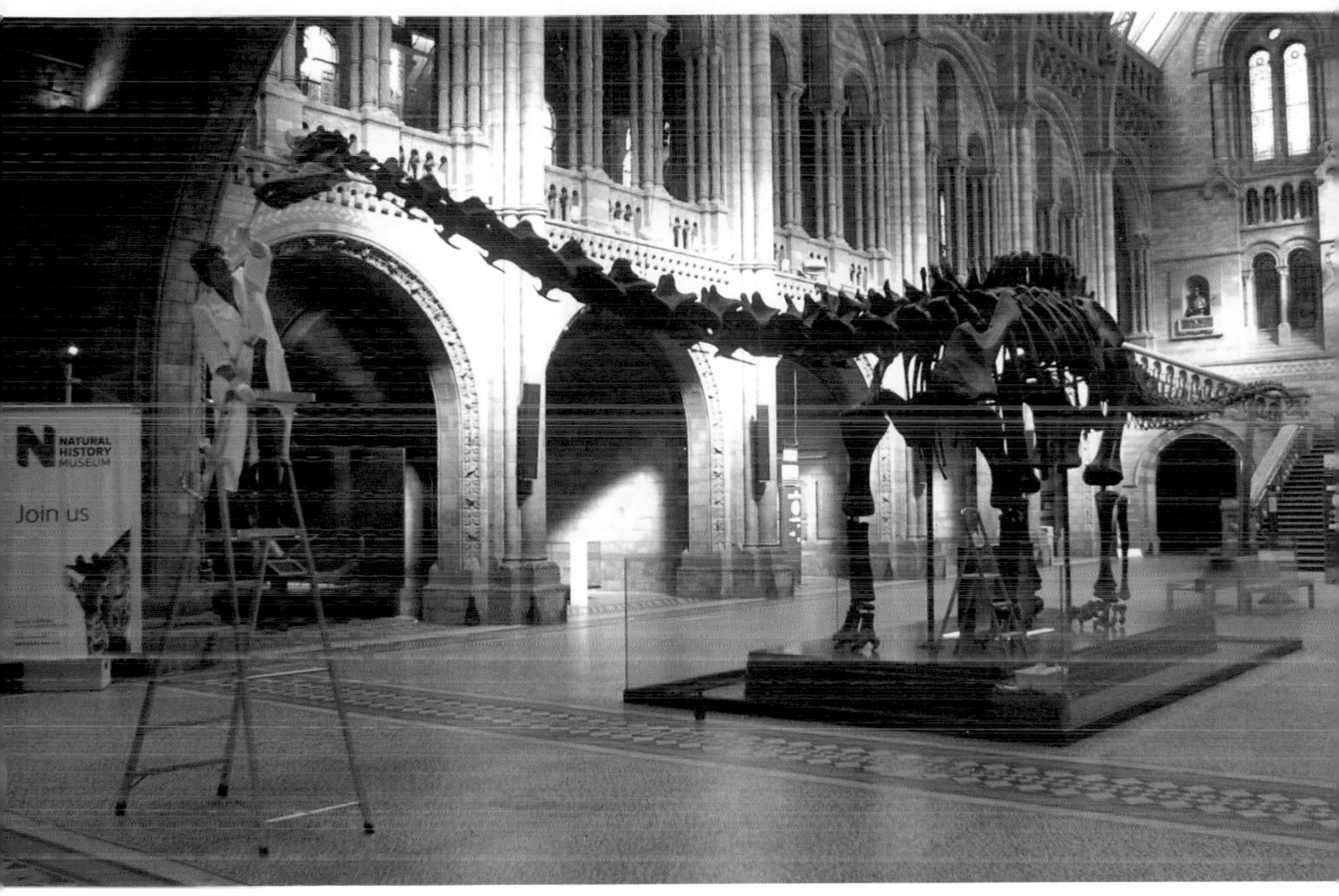

Museum conservator Lorraine Cornish cleaning the skeletal cast of *Dippy* the diplodocus for its 100th birthday in the Central Hall of the Natural History Museum, South Kensington.
11th May, 2005

Walking wounded leaving Edgware Road tube station to be treated at the London Hilton Metropole Hotel after explosions ripped through central London.
7th July, 2005

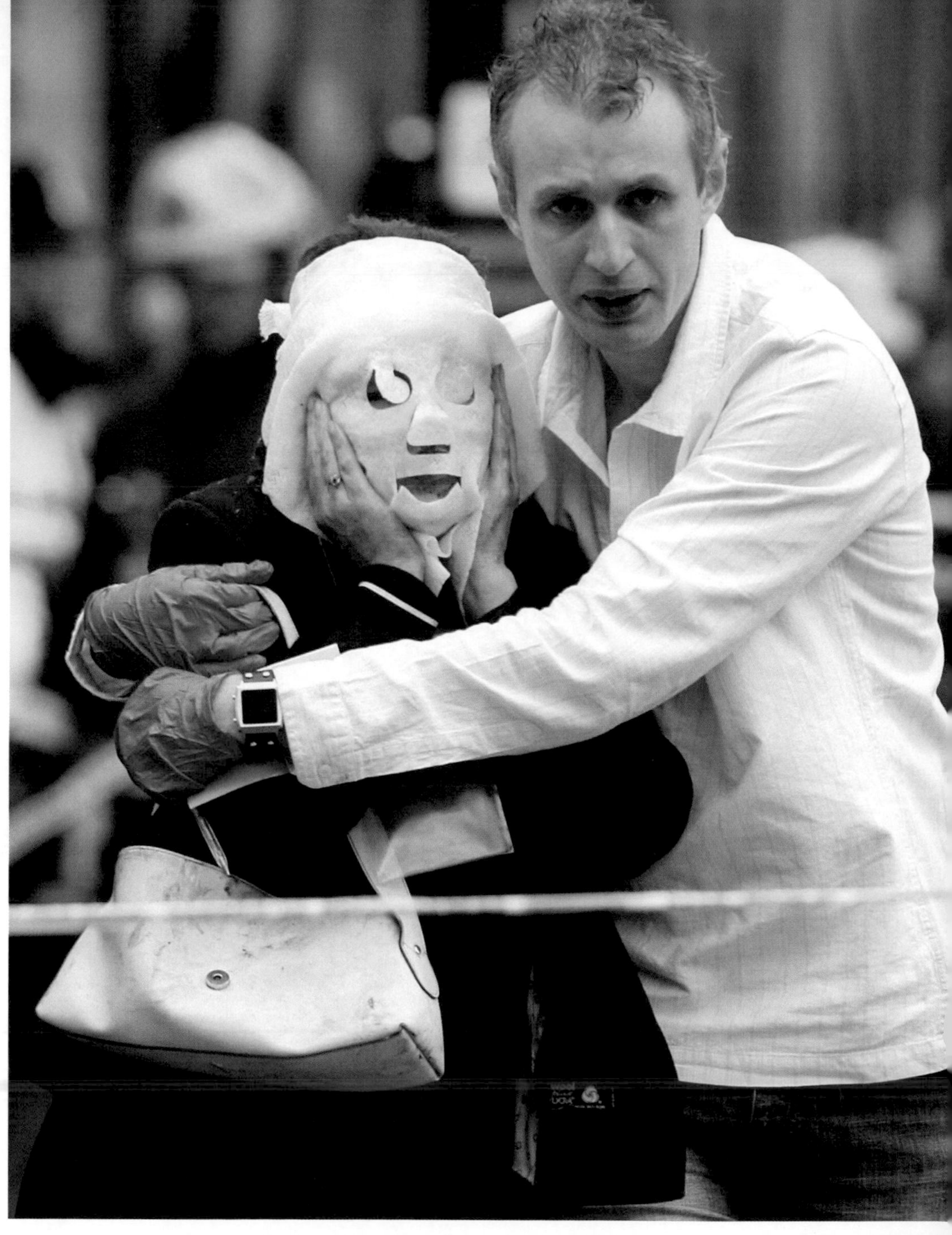

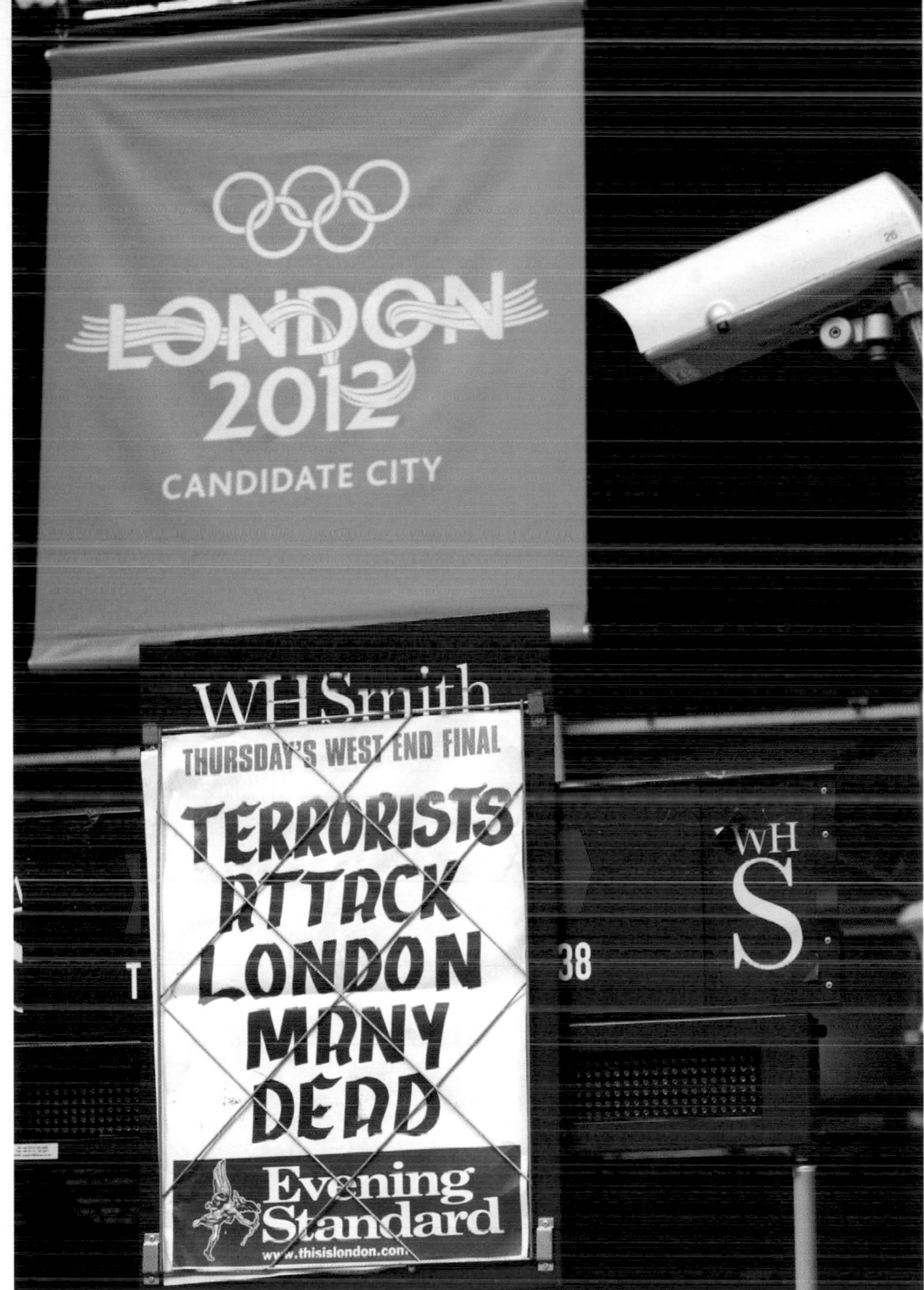

Suicide bombers struck as London prepared to celebrate being awarded the 2012 Olympics.
7th July, 2005

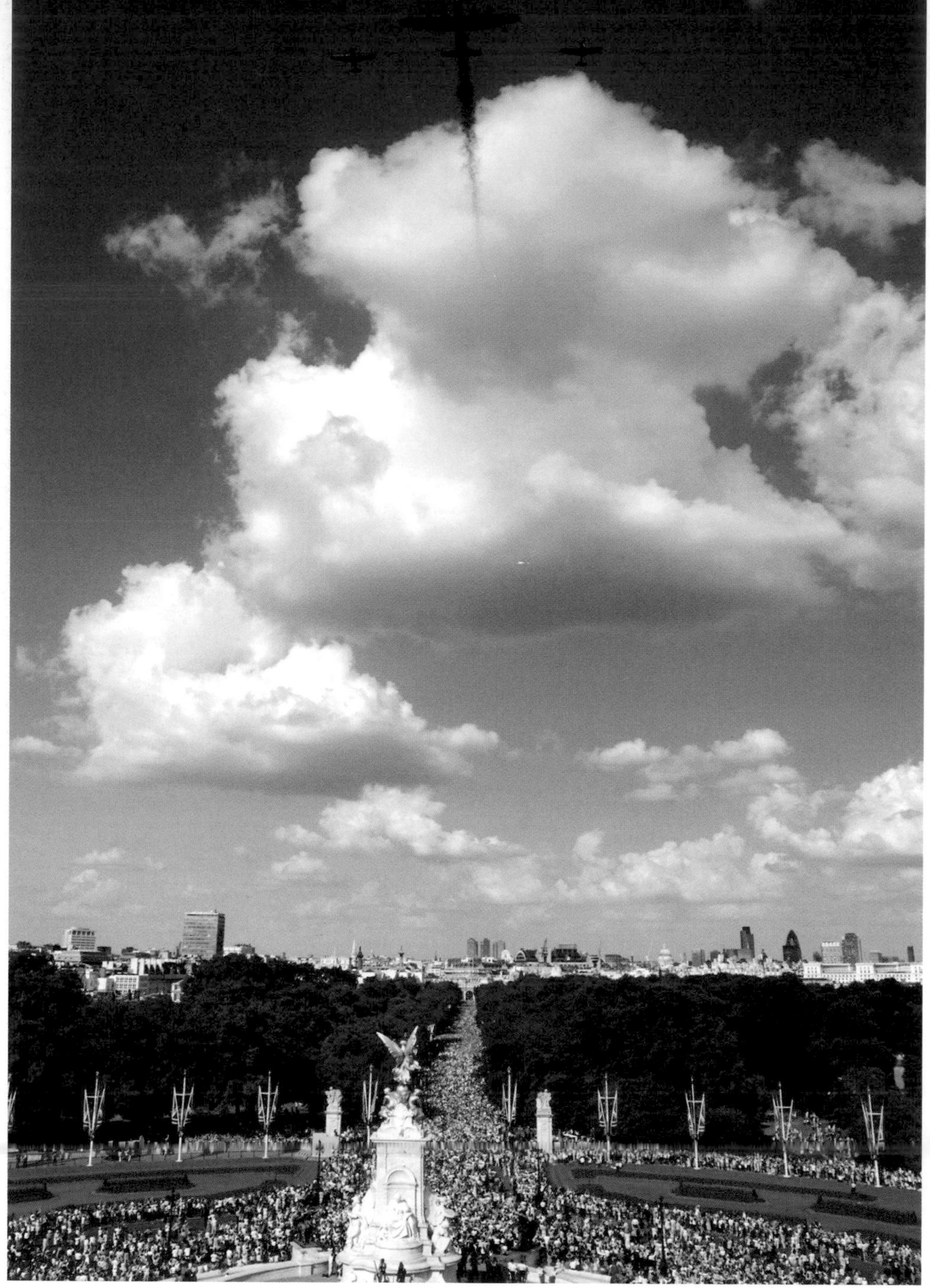

A *Lancaster* bomber from the RAF Battle of Britain Memorial Flight, flanked by a *Hurricane* and a *Spitfire*, drops one million poppies over The Mall as it flies over Buckingham Palace.
20th July, 2005

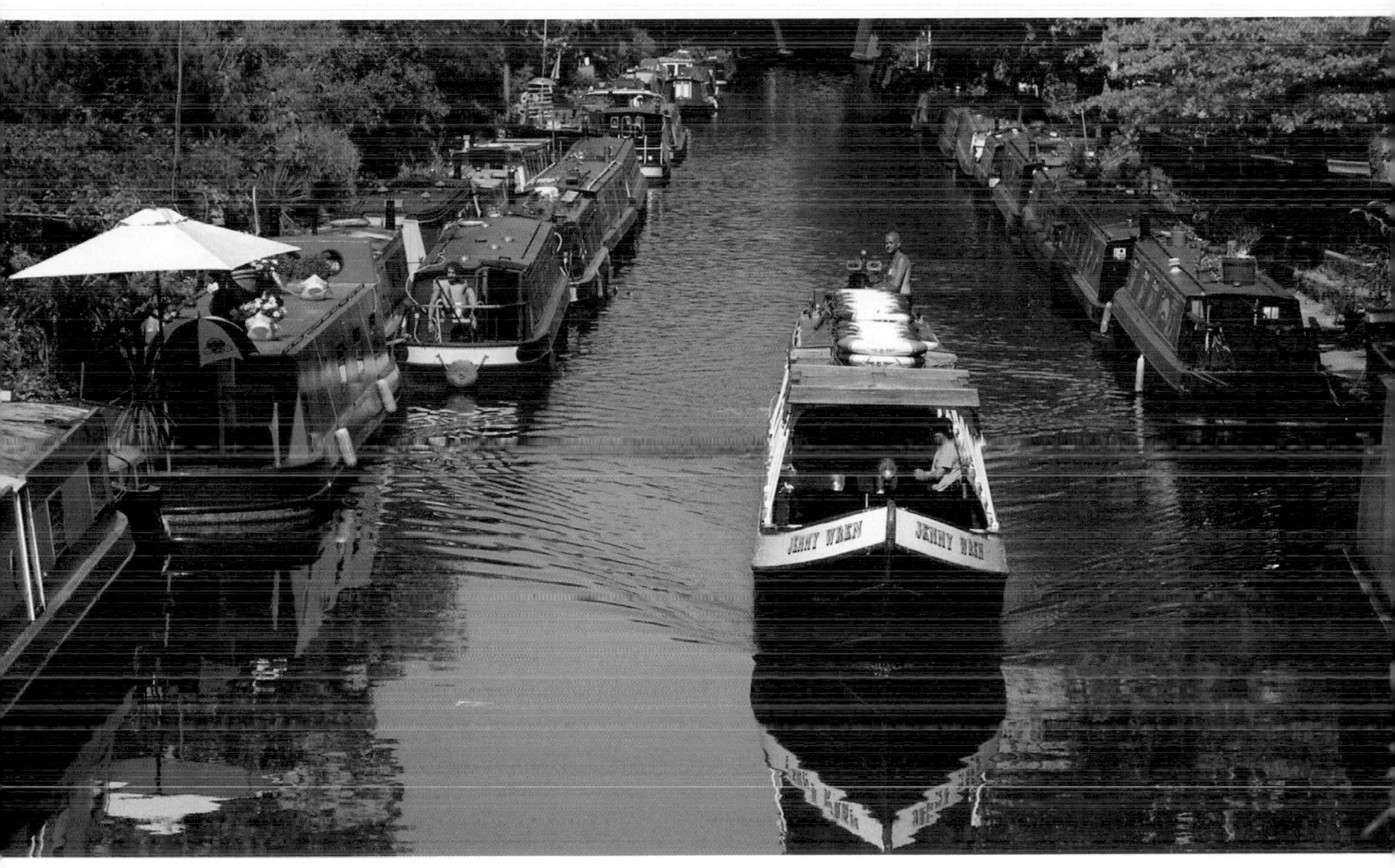

Canal boats in Little Venice,
Malda Vale.
17th July, 2006

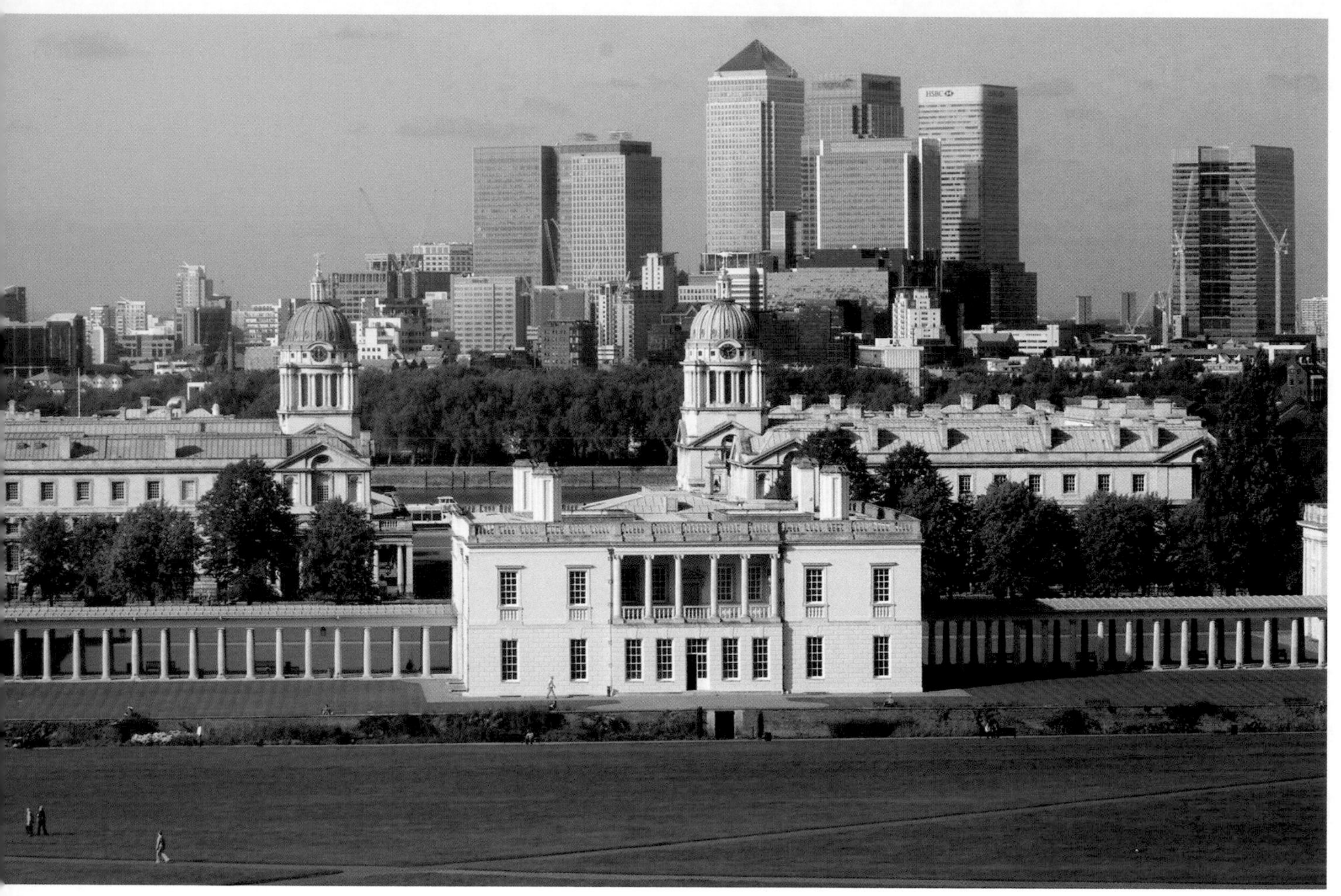

Canary Wharf and the National Maritime Museum, Greenwich.
12th October, 2006

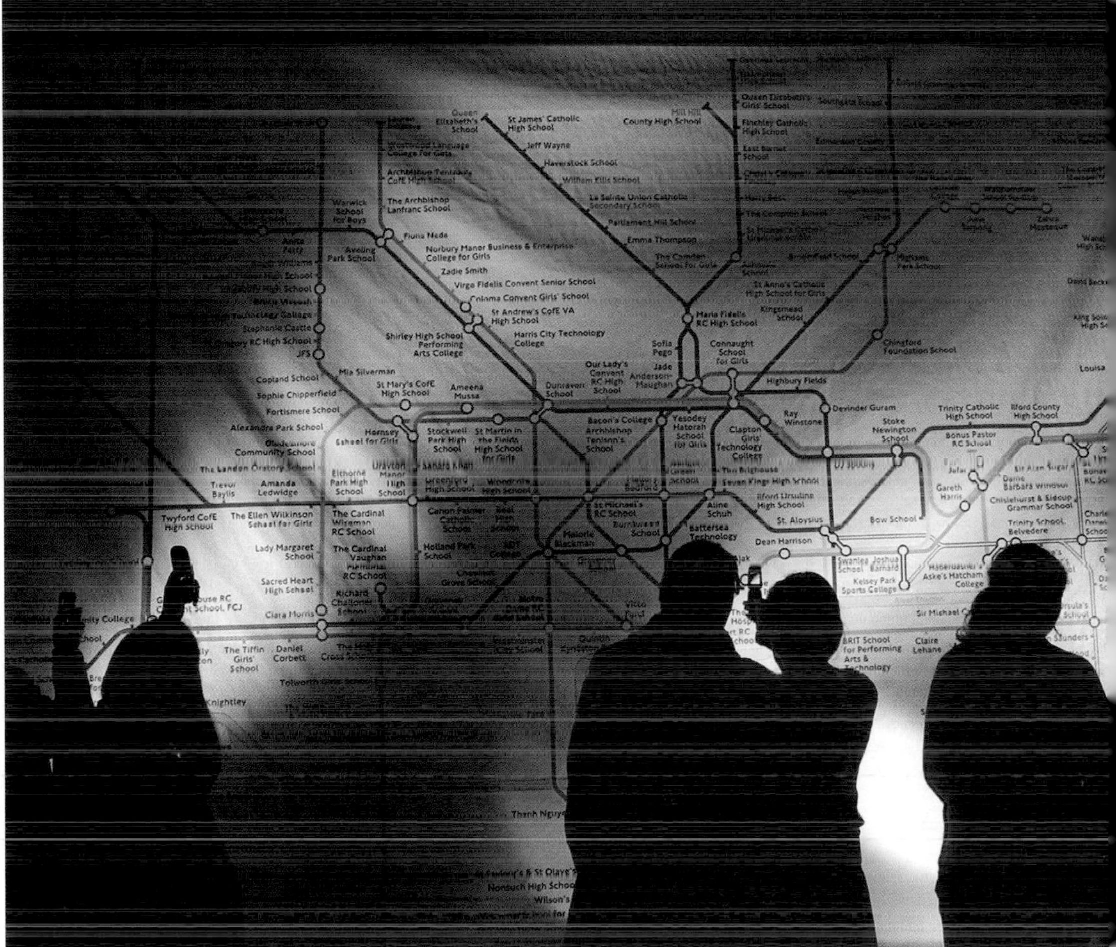

Pupils take photographs of a specially adapted London Underground map, produced to celebrate the success of the capital's schools and pupils.
11th January, 2007

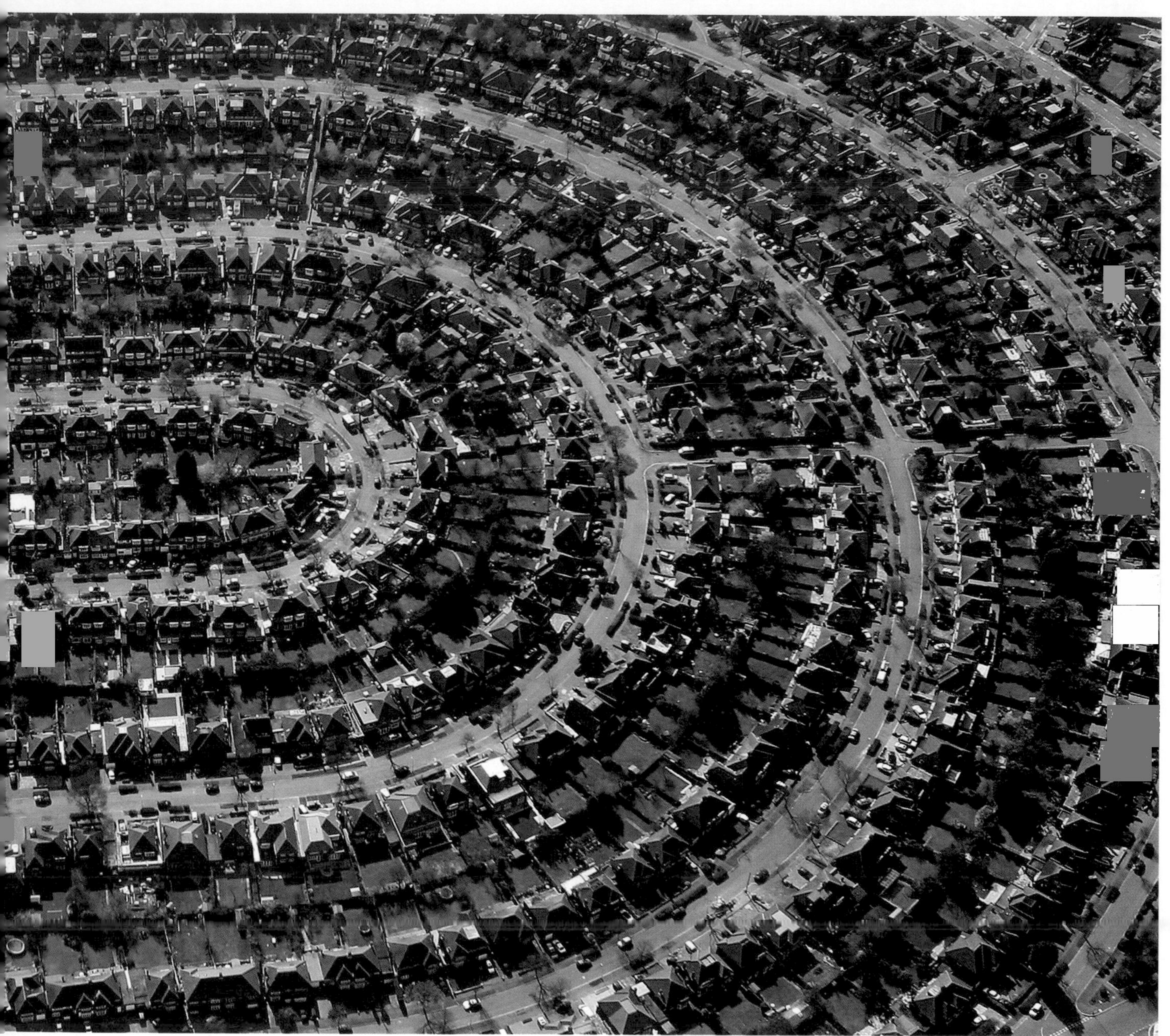

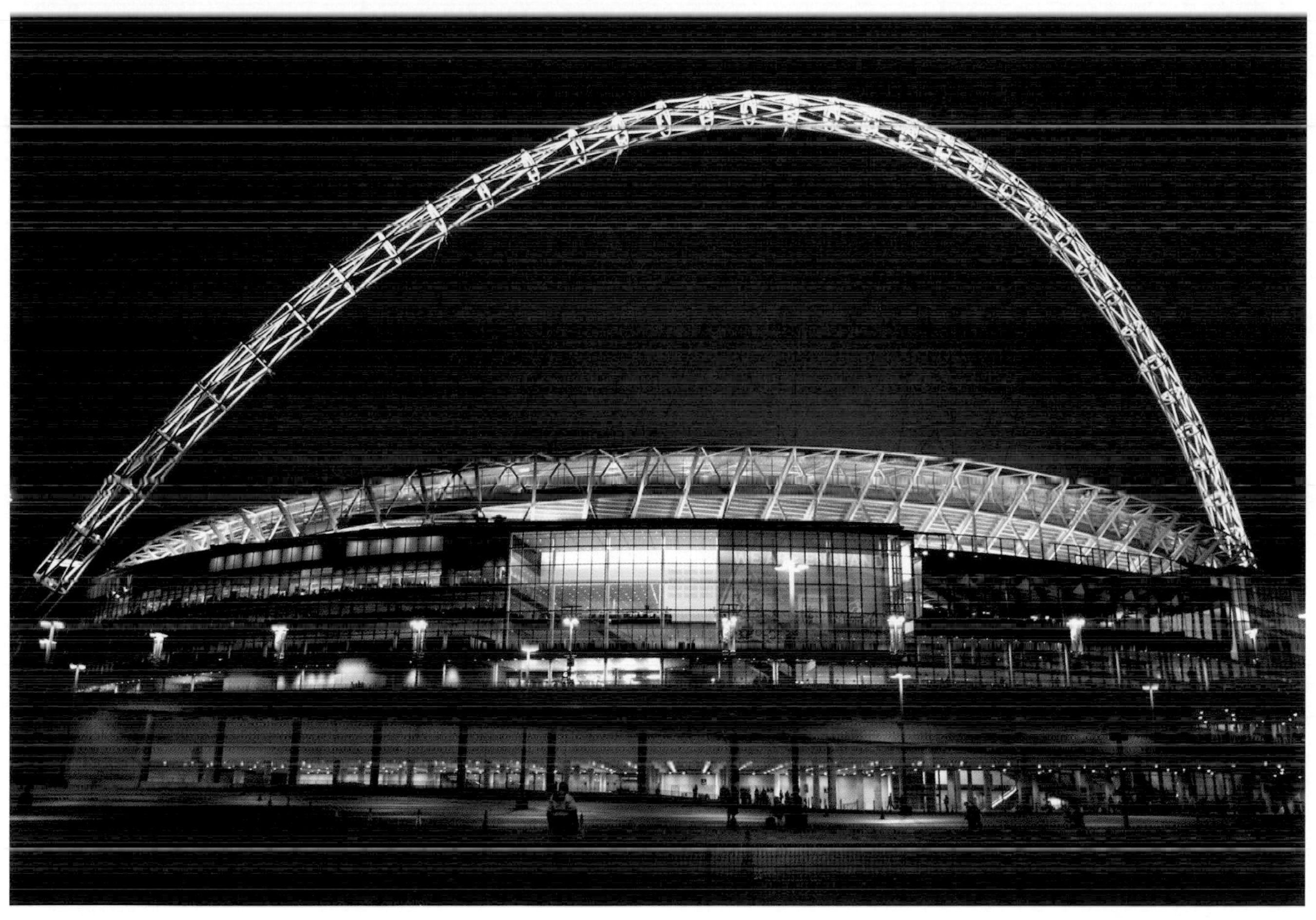

The new Wembley Stadium.
21st November, 2007

Facing page: Edgware
from the air.
11th March, 2007

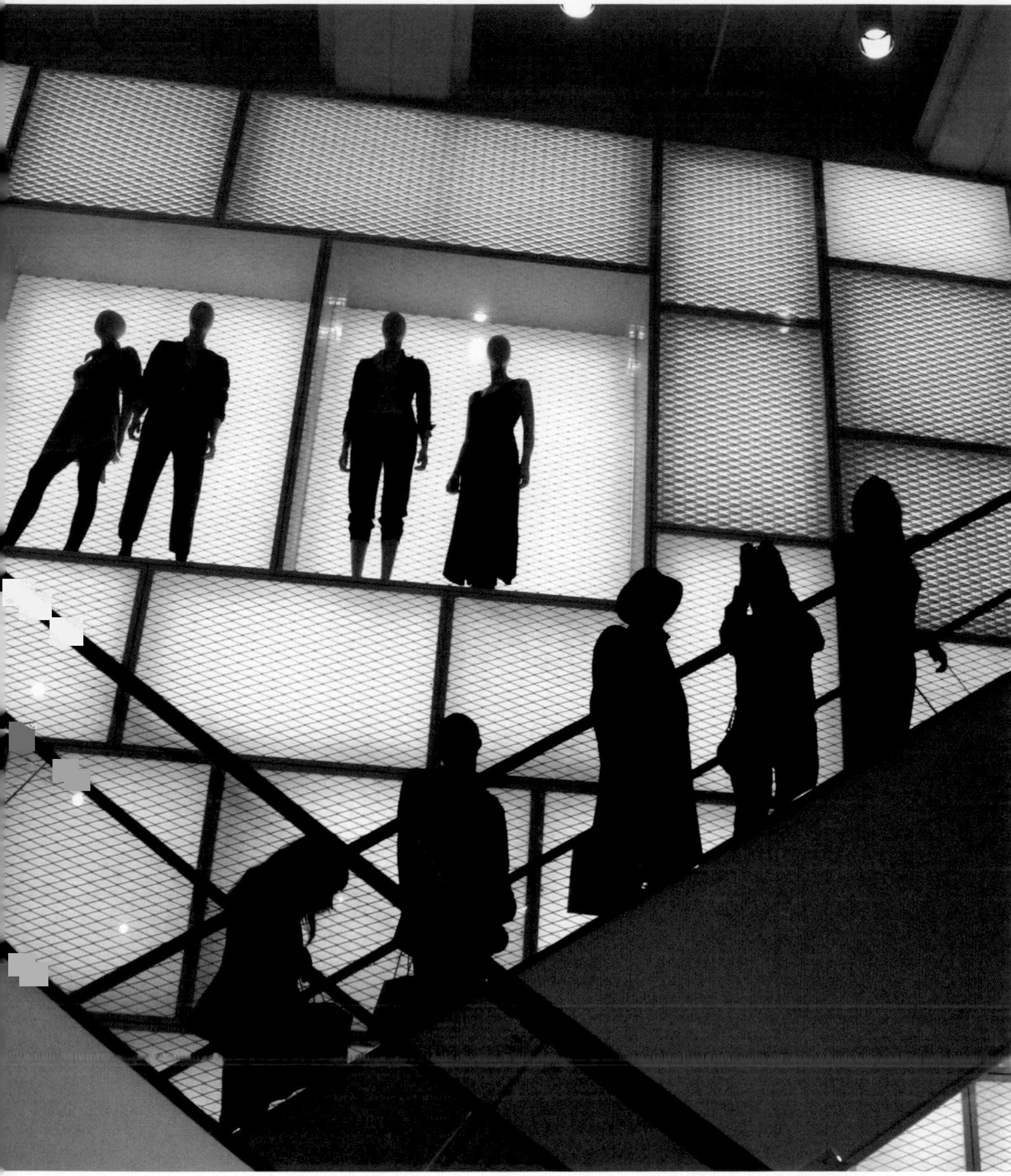

Customers inside the new H&M flagship store in Regent Street.
14th February, 2008

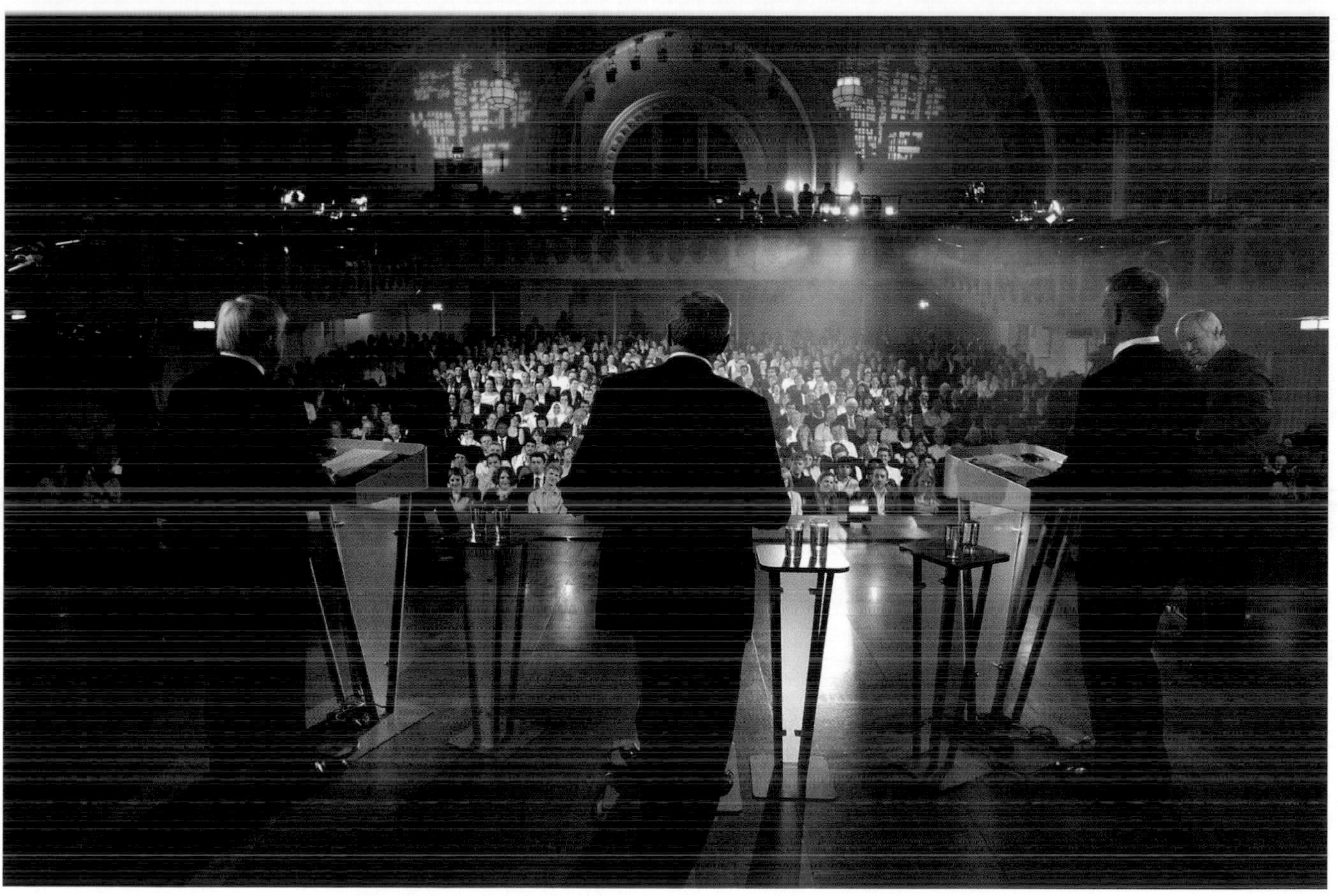

London Mayoral candidates Brian Paddick (R), Ken Livingstone (C), and Boris Johnson (L) take part in a Mayoral debate at Cadogan Hall in London. It was the final televised debate before London's Mayoral elections.
28th April, 2008

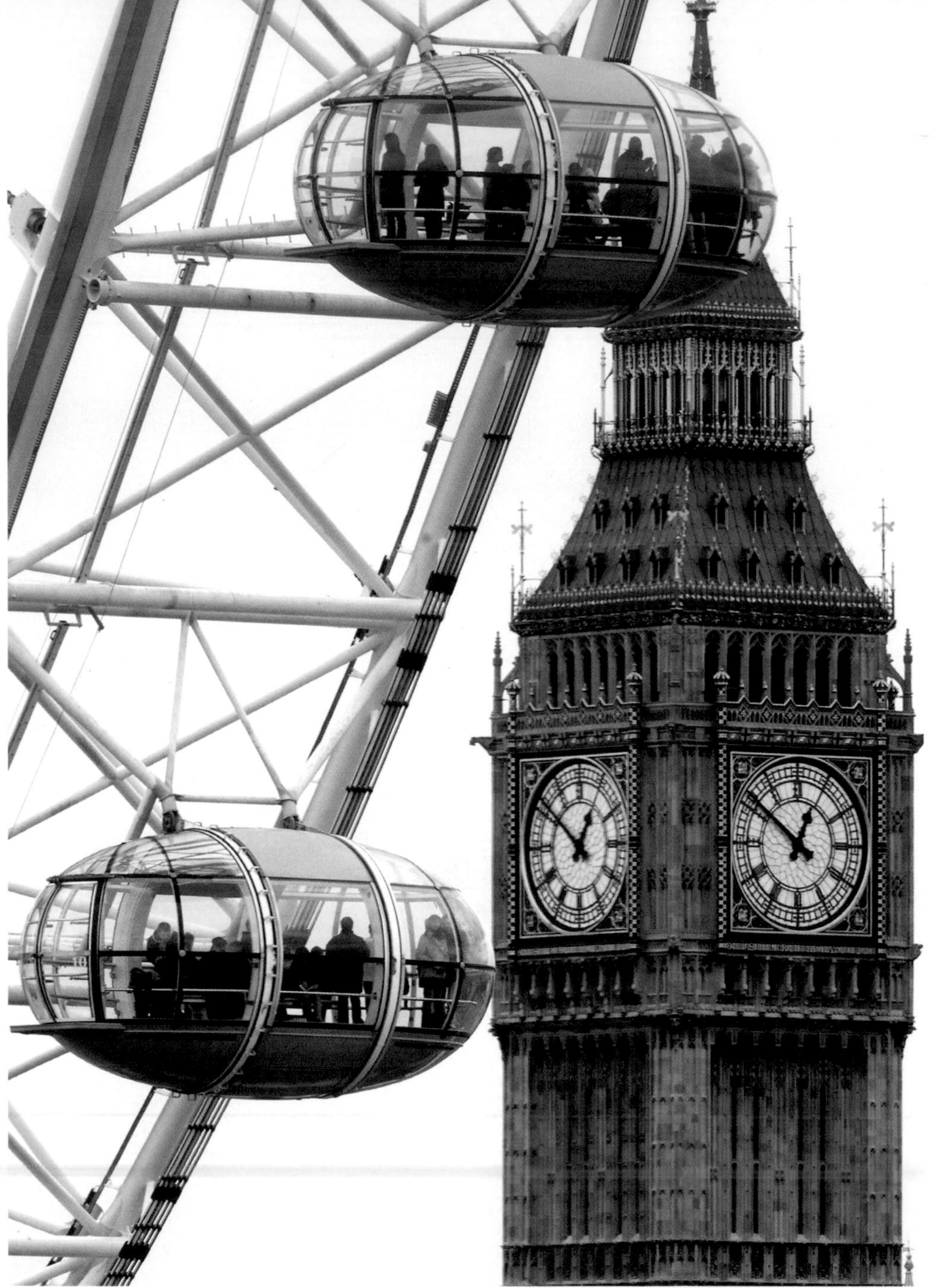

Thirty million people have visited the London Eye.
5th June, 2008

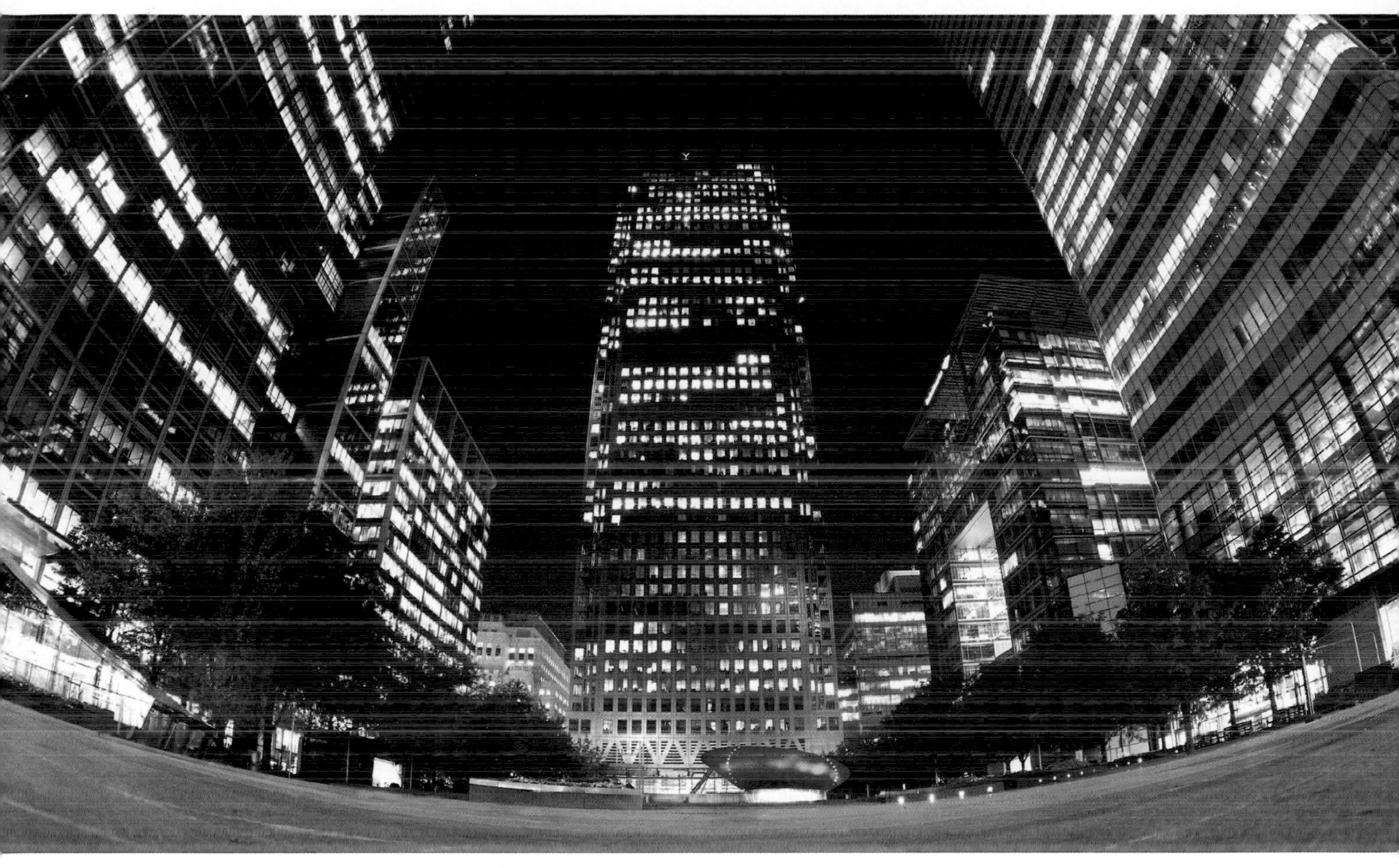

Canary Wharf by night.
28th September, 2008

The Publishers gratefully acknowledge Press Association Images, from whose extensive archive the photographs in this book have been selected. Personal copies of the photographs in this book, and many others, may be ordered online at www.prints.paphotos.com

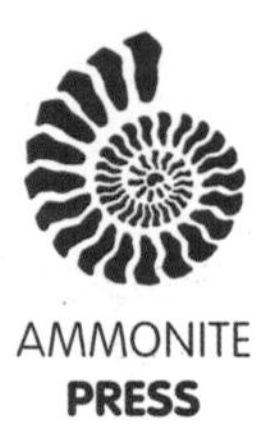

PRESS ASSOCIATION
Images

For more information, please contact:

Ammonite Press
AE Publications Ltd. 166 High Street, Lewes, East Sussex, BN7 1XU, United Kingdom
Tel: 01273 488005 Fax: 01273 402866
www.ammonitepress.com